Evaluating Outcomes

Evaluating Outcomes

EMPIRICAL TOOLS FOR EFFECTIVE PRACTICE

John D. Cone

American Psychological Association
Washington, DC

Published by
American Psychological Association
750 First Street, NE
Washington, DC 20002

Copies may be ordered from
APA Order Department
P.O. Box 92984
Washington, DC 20090-2984

In the U.K., Europe, Africa, and the Middle East, copies may be ordered from
American Psychological Association
3 Henrietta Street
Covent Garden, London
WC2E 8LU England

Typeset in New Baskerville and Futura by EPS Group Inc., Easton, MD

Printer: United Book Press, Baltimore, MD
Dust jacket designer: Naylor Design, Washington, DC
Technical/Production Editor: Amy J. Clarke

The opinions and statements published are the responsibility of the author, and such opinions and statements do not necessarily represent the policies of the American Psychological Association.

Library of Congress Cataloging-in-Publication Data
Cone, John D., 1942–
    Evaluating outcomes : empirical tools for effective practice / John D. Cone.—1st ed.
        p.   cm.
    Includes bibliographical references and indexes.
    ISBN 1-55798-723-8 (cb : acid-free paper).
    1. Psychology—Practice—Evaluation.   2. Psychotherapy—Practice—Evaluation.
    3. Clinical psychology—Practice—Evaluation.   I. Title.
    BF75.C66   2001
    616.89'14—dc21   00-040608

British Library Cataloguing-in-Publication Data
A CIP record is available from the British Library.

Printed in the United States of America
First Edition

Contents

Introduction

In the past, when students were in training to provide psychological services, they were rarely, if ever, asked to consider who would provide the funding for those services. Nor was it suggested that they might be asked to prove that their services were cost effective. With the advent of managed behavioral health care and competitive pressures brought on by the globalization of our economy, the situation has changed. Graduate students are eager to learn more about the health care and corporate environments in which they will be earning their livelihood. They want to know how to equip themselves to meet the challenges they will face in putting their hard-earned knowledge and skills into practice in the marketplace. One of the main challenges they will face is the increasing demand for accountability from third-party payers and consumers as to the effectiveness of the services they provide.

Evaluating Outcomes: Empirical Tools for Effective Practice is about helping psychologists and other behavioral health professionals to determine their effectiveness in a reliable way and to demonstrate that effectiveness to others. This book is written particularly for the graduate students who want to be prepared right from the beginning of their careers to collect and analyze the kind of data that will help shape the type of practice that they dream of having.

The goal of this book is to provide readers with realistic tools for evaluating their work. The tools are not specific to a particular type of practice. Examples come from a number of sources and include the evaluation of clinical, consulting, and educational practices as well as work with individuals, families, corporations, and agencies. It is expected that the principles of practice evaluation described here will be of general use to applied psychologists in a variety of pursuits.

Psychologists and those in related professions are inquisitive by training. They want to know why people, organizations, and systems behave the way they do. The science of psychology is devoted to discovering new facts about why we do what we do. Some psychologists are interested in advancing the science of behavior, but more are interested in learning about local matters. They want to know whether they really made a difference in their clinical work with a particular client or whether the teams they helped establish in a particular corporation resulted in a more efficient workforce. Simply put, psychologists want to know whether they are effective at what they do. The managed health care environment has added a significant layer of extrinsic motivation to proving one's effectiveness.

Graduate students in applied programs in psychology, marriage and family therapy, and social work as well as practicing professionals in a variety of related disciplines should find this book useful. Physical therapists, occupational therapists, speech and language professionals, chiropractors, organizational consultants and trainers, and anyone else providing behavior change services and wanting to show whether they make a difference will be interested in this book.

Evaluating Outcomes assumes a basic understanding of graduate-level statistics and research methodology. At the same time, the material is arranged to be accessible and friendly to users who have been away from those subjects for a while. For this audience, the book includes supplemental readings at the end of most chapters so readers can update their methodology skills to implement the activities the book describes.

The philosophical basis of the approach to outcomes evaluation advocated here is avowedly empirical. At the same time, it does not advocate a particular theoretical orientation to behavior change. Nor is one necessary. The principles and procedures described here are ecumenical with respect to theory. One can apply them whether holding a theoretical perspective that is psychodynamic, interpersonal, humanistic, cognitive, applied behavior analytic, systemic, or integrative.

This book is intended to be highly useful as a supplemental text in graduate research methods courses as well as a primary text in the growing number of graduate seminars in practice evaluation. The book is designed to present many of the major concepts included in any good text on research methods and serves to reinforce those ideas with practice examples. The principal difference is the care taken to present the concepts in the context of practice evaluation.[1] To this end, the book is filled with the kinds of examples practitioners routinely encounter.

A major aim of the book is to show students the artificiality of the separation between science and practice. Research methods will assume more importance and relevance to students in applied programs when they see that the concepts and approaches to studying human behavior are directly relevant to the practice of their profession. For example, formulating research questions and defining and measuring variables are essentially the same whether one is studying the etiology of a disorder or determining if an intervention is effective for a particular client. Mastery of the material contained in this book will position readers in the helping professions to improve their services continually and remain competitive in an increasingly challenging independent-practice environment. It will help those in community agencies make the most effective use of the often limited number of sessions they can offer the seemingly overwhelming number of clients who seek their services.

The Plan of the Book

As this introduction and subsequent chapters reveal, the focus of this book is decidedly practical. Chapter 1 describes in more detail the reasons for conducting outcomes evaluation and shows how the data collected in this process can help in making sound business and clinical decisions. Chapter 2 shows how to develop a design or model for one's practice. The design is built around one's life vision and the reasons one might start a practice in the first place. Chapter 3 elaborates on some of the parallels between practice evaluation and science touched on in chapter 1 and shows how to evaluate one's practice. It recommends an approach that closely parallels the research process, beginning with carefully worded evaluative questions.

Although most people think of direct services to clients when they think of evaluating practice outcomes, other important components (e.g., administration, staff training, community service) must function well if the direct services component is to be most effective. Chapter 4

---

[1] This book uses the terms *outcomes evaluation* and *practice evaluation* interchangeably. Both refer to determining the effectiveness of service.

describes those components and the needs of the multiple stakeholders who are concerned with service outcomes. Chapter 4 also presents an overview of the types of change clients are likely to go through over the course of interventions and the kinds of measures to use in documenting those changes. It also discusses the controversial topic of provider profiling and identifies the kinds of information health care managers are likely to accumulate on practitioners.

As most of us learned in courses on research design and methodology, we supplement good research questions with specific hypotheses. This practice is true of evaluation questions as well. Chapter 5 argues that good practitioners and evaluators conceptualize cases clearly, know specifically what is expected at the outset, and state those expectations in terms of directional relationships between specified variables that are examined in well-defined cases or samples of participants. Chapter 5 also illustrates the types of evaluation questions one is likely to ask.

No matter how skillfully we word them, we can test hypotheses and answer evaluation questions only if appropriate data are available. Chapter 6 details the kinds of data routinely collected in most practices. It includes information specific to evaluating the direct services component as well as the effectiveness of the business-related components of the practice. Patient and payer profiles, demographics for marketing purposes, and information about referral sources are important data to have current and readily available. Efficiently managing this information is critical to human services providers, just as it is to any business, so chapter 6 includes information on the mechanics of information management using computerized databases and less technological approaches.

Determining the quality of client services requires that measures be identified and carefully described, as discussed in chapter 7. High-quality evaluation includes integrity checks on the independent variable or procedure and uses more than one type of assessment method (e.g., interview, self-report, direct observation). Especially important in evaluating direct services are measures of the different types of change described in chapter 4. Those measures assess variables determined by theory to be relevant to accomplishing the client's ultimate goals.

Chapter 8 emphasizes the importance of carefully choosing an evaluative design; attention to internal validity is a minimum requirement. Whatever arrangement one uses, however, it is important that it include repeated measurement before treatment and at its termination, at a minimum. Ideally, it would include ongoing assessment of instrumental and intermediate goal attainment.

Chapter 9 describes how to plan an analysis that is appropriate to the evaluation question and the audience interested in the findings. An important consideration is the need for complicated statistics versus a relatively more straightforward visual presentation of the findings. For program evaluators in managed care organizations, for example, population statistics are important; their designs need to address the relevance of findings to an entire population served (or potentially served) by the organization. Small, statistically significant changes that might not reach clinical significance can be of considerable importance when multiplied over many lives. Conversely, independent service providers and those in small practices, like many new practitioners, will find single-case analyses of great value. Concerns with clinically significant change will play a greater role in those evaluations as will graphic displays of change in clients over time.

Multiple criteria exist for evaluating effectiveness. In addition to "normal" functioning, chapter 9 describes the criterion of effective performance, which has to do with altering behavior to a level that is sufficient to permit competent performance of other types (e.g., managing compulsive rituals well enough to permit arriving at work each day on time). Experienced practitioners who have accumulated significant amounts of data and have answered some of the basic questions related to the effectiveness of their services are likely to be interested in questions requiring the more advanced measurement, design, and analysis tools described in chapter 10.

Studying examples of others' evaluations is a good way to learn to evaluate one's own professional activities. Chapter 11 offers examples of psychologists' attempts to show the effectiveness of specific behavior change strategies and calls attention to the distinction between efficacy and effectiveness studies. The latter demonstrate whether procedures shown to be efficacious in tightly controlled, randomized clinical trials are effective when applied in the real world. The chapter includes examples of evaluations of treatments for chronic headaches, panic attacks, and depression as well as couples in distress and sex offenders. It also presents exemplary uses of single-case analyses.

The overarching concern of the outcome evaluator is to determine the effectiveness of services offered by a particular professional or group of professionals; the overarching concern of any practice, however, is the welfare of clients. Balancing these two priorities requires conducting practice evaluations in ways that uphold the highest ethical standards. Chapter 12 extensively discusses the ethics of practice evaluation. Ethical practice evaluators have the informed consent of participants and avoid harm, degradation, humiliation, and the release of potentially harmful information about those participants. The chapter highlights ethical concerns of special interest to the evaluator.

The last chapter of the book pleads with practice evaluators to give away the results of their findings. Chapter 13 assumes that practice evaluation, like science, is a cumulative endeavor, with each new effort standing on the shoulders of previous ones, answering more and more useful questions. To build this knowledge, one needs to subject one's evaluation work to scrutiny and commentary from others; this can take several forms, including informal presentations in and around the practice offices, formal presentations at professional meetings, articles in newsletters of professional organizations, and articles published in scholarly journals. Chapter 13 presents the advantages and disadvantages of different dissemination outlets and offers hints for using them successfully.

Conclusion

It is my hope that this book will encourage readers to make a lifetime commitment to assessing the quality of their services and creating a climate supportive of accountability in their work environments over the course of their career. Continually improving services—and seeing this improvement concretely through outcomes evaluation—is one important way to prevent burnout and to keep one's enthusiasm alive.

Acknowledgements

Looking back through the voluminous correspondence that has accompanied this project alerts me to two rather astonishing facts: (a) It has taken a long time to bring this book to completion, and (b) a lot of people have supported me along the way.

Two patient and persistent women are especially significant to this book's production: Peggy Schlegel and Jan Cone. As an acquisitions editor at APA Books, Peggy kept after me for years to write something —anything—that might inspire young psychologists to approach their work with care and scientific rigor. She was there to pore over very rough early drafts and to make major suggestions for reorganizing the entire enterprise. Jan, as spouse and soul mate for over 33 years and chair of our department for the past 7, has provided unqualified (well, nearly!) emotional and professional support for this and crazier undertakings. Writing a book is selfish work, in a sense, and Jan never complained about all those times when I was not available to shoulder a larger share of other responsibilities or just be there to relate.

Reviewers of an early proposal for this book took their task seriously and offered useful reactions. For their contributions, I thank Albert D. Farrell, William C. Follette, Richard G. Heimberg, and Gene Pekarik. Al Farrell teamed with an anonymous reviewer to provide major input on the initial draft of the entire book; for that I am extremely grateful, although I cannot say I was thrilled at all the extra work it involved at the time.

Several people read parts of the book and offered suggestions from their particular perspectives: Barbara D. Ingersoll, Charles Martinez, and Bonnie Van Fleet. To them and to the many students who reacted to draft versions as assigned readings in my classes, I say thanks for so generously giving your time and insights.

Finally, there are the foot soldiers who gave tirelessly and uncomplainingly (at least to me!) of their time and energy in the myriad production aspects of bringing this book to life. My research assistants, Sherry Casper-Beliveau and E. Kent McIntyre, logged many miles and expended much "sneaker power" in searching for and retrieving references from libraries all over San Diego. The staff of Walter Library at United States International University contributed significantly by providing books and journals from their own collection and in arranging interlibrary loans from others. Finally, there is Amy Clarke, APA Books production editor, who worked feverishly to get the book to the typesetter on time, burning up the Internet with dozens of queries to me. She has a particular talent for realizing when to take *no* for an answer; for that reasonableness I am thankful.

Before ending, I want to say thanks to Neil S. Jacobson, whose untimely death during the writing of this book deprived us all of a phenomenal talent. Neil was quick to answer emails when I had questions about his writing. But more important, he was a model for all whose jobs are helping others. He showed us that the humane way is to evaluate what we do and to commit to doing what we find is effective. I am not alone in thanking Neil for that.

Evaluating Outcomes

What Is Outcomes Evaluation?

E ffective, high-quality goods are the current standard in the global economy; the same is true for services. Competition in nearly every commercial sphere is the primary driving force behind this standard, and psychologists and other behavior-change specialists have not escaped the economic pressure. In this age of managed care, behavioral health practitioners are being forced to reconsider the way they practice and, at times, to reorganize the way they deliver services. For example, some formerly independent practitioners are banding together to work in health maintenance organizations (HMOs), preferred provider organizations (PPOs), or independent practice associations (Patterson & Berman, 1991). These organizations then contract with individuals or businesses to provide all the health care needed over a specific period of time. Obtaining such contracts requires the promise of high-quality, effective services delivered in an efficient (i.e., cost-effective) manner.

HMOs and PPOs make promises to potential clients about the services they provide. To do this, they must have confidence in the quality of their services and must know precisely how much it costs to provide them because the financial risk is borne entirely by the service practitioner group. It receives a certain amount of money (i.e., is "capitated") to provide certain services for a specific group of people (e.g., all employees of a company). To remain financially viable, it has to provide its services for the amount of its contract or less.

To illustrate these points, imagine that a group of psychologists and other service providers decide to form a PPO. They then contract with a large manufacturing company in their community to provide its em-

3

ployees all the mental health services (including alcohol and drug treatment) they might require in the coming year for $334 per employee. At 10.5 months into the contract, however, the PPO has spent all the money awarded it for the entire year because the actual costs per employee have turned out to be $376. In essence, the PPO members have to work the next month and a half for free. Because all the service providers in the group have personal financial obligations to meet, they have to take on additional paid responsibilities (e.g., psychological assessment in a prison system). The additional work results in a deterioration in services provided under the contract and increased complaints by the company's employees that they are not getting the quality of care they want. When the contract ends, the company selects a competing PPO because its quality ratings are higher.

Whether you are in independent practice or work for a larger entity, your success depends on avoiding troubling experiences such as these. To do so, you must know two things about the services you offer: (a) how effective they are and (b) how much they cost to provide. Obtaining this information is the primary purpose of outcomes or practice evaluation. Taken together, the two measures indicate the value of the services provided.

This book explains how to determine the effectiveness of your services. Knowing your effectiveness—more specifically, your cost effectiveness—allows you to bid on and obtain various contracts as well as to discharge your contractual obligations successfully. In addition, you learn how to plan and evaluate the effectiveness of a traditional fee-for-service practice.

The remainder of this chapter discusses the nature of outcomes evaluation. First, it builds a case for outcomes evaluation. Then it points out the artificiality of and attendant problems with the common distinction between research and practice in psychology and other human services. Although differences exist between pure scientific research and evaluation of practice, the two enterprises have much in common. Finally, the chapter deals with theoretical issues and the value of practitioners having a philosophy of science that governs their overall approach to providing services.

Why Learn About Outcomes Evaluation?

There are at least six good reasons for taking the time and trouble to evaluate the effectiveness of human services professionals:

1. to satisfy our intellectual curiosity
2. to provide economic and financial information
3. to improve practice efficiency
4. to maintain high ethical standards
5. to avoid errors in judgment
6. to obtain information not available in the published literature.

The following sections describe each reason in more detail.

Intellectual Curiosity

Why do most of us study human behavior in the first place? Most likely, the answer is that we are curious about why and under what circumstances certain behavior occurs and what we can do to change it. Educational programs in the science of human behavior rely on research findings that describe and promote understanding of human behavior. So that we can understand those findings, a substantial part of our formal training as service providers focuses on research methodology, including courses in research design, measurement, and statistics. We learn to be appropriately skeptical of claims unsupported by empirical data.

When we finish our graduate training, however, many of us put away our books on research methodology and busy ourselves with making a living in our profession. A survey of 3,343 members of the clinical division of the American Psychological Association (APA) between 1965 and 1969, for example, shows that 55% had not published anything. A scant 10% of the members had provided 56% of the published research (Pasework, Fitzgerald, Thornton, & Sawyer, 1973). To be sure, many of us occasionally read an article from the scientific literature and dust off our methodological skills enough to understand the essence of its findings. Our primary motivation for learning more about a particular behavioral phenomenon is likely to stem from concerns that arise in the course of our practice. An industrial–organizational psychologist, for example, might want to know whether group-based incentives are superior to individual bonuses for motivating sales in retail clerks. A clinical psychologist might want to know whether interpersonal psychotherapy (Klerman, Weissman, Rounsaville, & Chevron, 1984) is better than cognitive–behavior therapy (Beck, 1995; Beck, Rush, Shaw, & Emery, 1979) for treating people with depression. These and other types of questions of interest to practice evaluators are discussed in detail in chapter 5.

Applied research projects within a practice can satisfy your own curiosity and provide you with new knowledge that can lead to advances in the science of human behavior and the application of that science. Such research projects can motivate you and provide benefits in terms of showing what does or does not work. Moreover, sharing the results with other practitioners can have positive effects professionally, such as giving you a reputation as a practitioner who strives to stay in the forefront of developments. This positive "aura" can lead to more referrals and consultations.

Presenting applied research findings at professional meetings provides further beneficial exposure for your practice. Comments from audiences can lead to insights for improving the quality of services beyond what might become apparent as you conduct the research. Finally, interacting with other professionals concerned with similar issues can produce a network that continues sharing information long after the meetings have ended. Indeed, some experts see practice research networks in psychiatry and psychology as a way of facilitating the development and dissemination of effective interventions (Barlow, 1996). (See chapter 13 for an in-depth discussion of disseminating information from practice evaluations.)

Economic and Financial Information

As practitioners, we also seek answers to questions of effectiveness for economic reasons: We want to be effective organizational consultants, psychotherapists, or other service providers, so that people will continue using our services. In addition, by continually evaluating our practice, we are more likely to collect and manage information in ways that facilitate prompt reimbursement for services.

The changing health care environment increasingly requires data on the effectiveness of individual providers. Indeed, practitioners who join panels of managed care organizations (MCOs) can expect their effectiveness to be monitored routinely. The MCO may develop a profile of each practice, and it is likely to include the average number of sessions practitioners spend in the treatment of clients, their general effectiveness with clients, and the theoretical orientation they espouse.

In this environment, it is important for you to be able to provide evidence that the funds spent by the MCO for your services are worth it. Knowing the mechanics of practice evaluation therefore can give you a head start when you finish graduate school and enter practice. As

Hawkins, Mathews, and Hamdan (1999) noted, MCOs look for professionals whose effectiveness will make the MCO look good when it seeks to retain existing contracts or gain new ones. Maintaining a habit of continually evaluating your effectiveness will keep you organized and provide you with information to satisfy MCOs.

Maintaining the information necessary for practice evaluation has additional benefits, including the ability to obtain financing; respond to requests to provide services on a prepaid, contractual basis; and create advertising copy. The first, obtaining financing to expand the practice in some way, is likely to involve preparing a presentation to a loan officer or lending committee of a local bank. Having up-to-date information about critical aspects of the business, especially financial data, can make the difference in getting a loan and might affect the amount and terms the lender is willing to offer in a positive way. This information also can be of inestimable help in responding to requests for proposals to provide services (e.g., to an HMO or a large company). Finally, good data collection can help your marketing efforts. Anything showing effectiveness for clients who resemble an advertisement's target audience can have a positive effect (e.g., "98.2% of our Spanish-speaking clients rate their 'overall satisfaction' with our services as high"). A computer database can enable rapid sorting and retrieval of information for targeted advertising, which tailors ad messages to specific groups.

Practice Efficiency

Readily available data can help in the day-to-day operations as well as effectiveness of your practice. For instance, practice information systems can help you quickly retrieve information at the right moment. A busy practitioner often can forget important details about a particular client, such as the last time the client was seen, the name of the client's spouse or children, and whether information promised the client was ever provided. It can be of tremendous benefit for the service provider to have the client database running continuously on a desktop computer near the telephone. When a client calls or someone calls about the client, it is a simple matter to key in the first few letters of the client's name while exchanging pleasantries with the caller and have the client's entire record appear on the computer screen. This visual reminder of important information can cue you to ask questions about the client's children, whether the recently forwarded information was useful, and so on. Moreover, such systems can enable you to record matters requiring follow up and even provide automatic reminders.

Ethical Considerations

Ethical concerns can motivate practice evaluation efforts as well. Ethical issues are covered in depth in chapter 12, but some introductory comments are relevant here. As practitioners, we want to know whether our services are helpful. We would like to be able to say that a particular intervention results in a 100% improvement in quality of life, takes 12 weeks to implement, and costs $2,000. Likewise, we would like to be in a position to tell clients that another approach results in less improvement, takes longer, and costs more. We are unlikely to achieve this ideal, of course, but we can approach it if we begin to evaluate what we do on a consistent basis.

As for professional ethics, most organizations of human services professionals presently do not require their members to evaluate their effectiveness. For psychologists, however, the APA provides an opening for such a requirement in Standard 1.06 of its ethical principles. It states that "psychologists rely on scientifically and professionally derived knowledge when making scientific or professional judgments or when engaging in scholarly or professional endeavors" (APA, 1992, p. 1600).

Some judgments that psychologists and other service providers make involve whether to serve a particular client, what intervention makes the most sense, whether the intervention is working, and when to make changes to improve its effectiveness. In making these professional judgments, reliance on scientifically derived knowledge would seem to require the use of objective measures such as those described in chapter 6. A psychotherapist might initially justify his or her selection of a particular intervention by referring to literature showing its effectiveness. Continuing to use it with the client would depend on evidence that it is working, however. To illustrate, look at the progress of the psychotherapy client in Figure 1.1. Actual progress for the client is below predicted progress. What are the implications of such data? Should the therapist share them with the client? Should therapy continue unchanged in hopes of eventual improvement?

Providers of human services collect data and evaluate what they do so as not to fool themselves or anyone else into thinking that some change or improvement is occurring when it is not. If we did not collect the type of progress data depicted in Figure 1.1, how would we decide whether to continue serving a client? Psychologists have an ethical obligation to strive for effectiveness in the services they provide, and evaluating those services is a critical part of meeting this obligation.

Figure 1.1

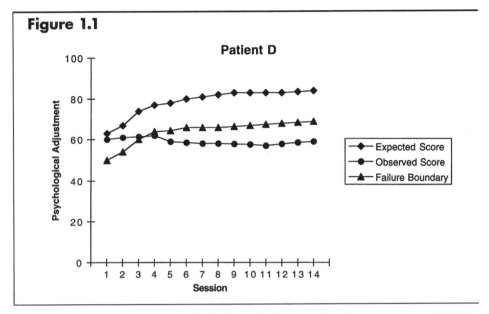

Change over sessions in an individual psychotherapy client (see Howard, 1996). The line of diamonds shows the client's expected rate of improvement over sessions, which is based on assessment of the patient prior to the start of treatment. The line of circles shows actual improvement over sessions and is based on periodic assessments by both therapist and client. The line of triangles shows a failure boundary, and represents the 25th percentile for scores for that client on the outcome measure being used. From *Patient Profiling: Quantifying Progress,* K. I. Howard, November 1996, seminar presented at the annual meeting of the Association for Advancement of Behavior Therapy, New York. Copyright 1991 by K. I. Howard. Reprinted with permission.

Errors in Judgment

Ethical practice is related to informed and appropriate decision making by the practitioner. Unfortunately, it is well established in psychology and other behavioral sciences that bias and distortion often accompany information processing and decision making. The conscientious, ethical, well-trained practitioner is aware of this problem and strives to control it, in part by being skeptical of each piece of information obtained about clients and the process of serving them. The literature extensively discusses pitfalls in clinical decision making (e.g., Bromley, 1986; Meehl, 1960; Schwartz, 1991; Turk & Salovey, 1988). We know, for example, that clinicians (and scientists, too, for that matter) tend to adopt a confirmatory approach to testing their understanding of a particular client. That is, they form early hypotheses about the client's problems and go about recruiting evidence to support those hypotheses.

Snyder and Swann (1978) showed this phenomenon to be true for nonclinicians as well. They gave female college students a list of questions and asked them which questions could help determine the personality characteristics of a person. Half the students were told to select questions that would test the hypothesis that the person was the "prototypic extrovert"; the rest were told to select questions from a list that would test whether the person was the "prototypic introvert." As anticipated, the women tended to select questions consistent with the "hypothesis" (extrovert vs. introvert) they were given. From the questions chosen, they planned an interview designed to confirm their a priori hypothesis. The obvious difficulty with such a tendency is that it can foreclose the search for additional information that might further understanding of a problem or lead to different explanations for it. Moreover, an hypothesis can be self-fulfilling. A second study by Snyder and Swann (1978) shows that interviewees actually behaved more like extroverts if they were interviewed and they knew they were being interviewed by someone testing the hypothesis that they were likely to be extroverted.

Many years ago, Shapiro (1961) warned clinicians of the traps of preconception. He advocated conducting small experiments to test hypotheses about clients before undertaking therapy with them (Shapiro, 1966). More recently, Turkat and Maisto (1985) advocated similar approaches.

Chapman and Chapman (1967, 1969) explored the impact of common stereotypes on clinical assessment activities. As they suspected, characteristics stereotypically associated with one another are said to covary even though no empirical support may exist for the association, a phenomenon they called *illusory correlation*. For example, a common superstition among psychologists is that people who elaborate the eyes of figures in draw-a-person tests are likely to reflect signs of paranoia. Although research does not support this relationship, clinicians continue to report it. Exhibit 1.1 describes the Chapmans' research.

Tversky and Kahneman (1974) interpreted the "illusory correlation" of the Chapmans in terms of the *availability heuristic,* the idea that people judge the probability of an event by how easy it is to imagine its occurrence. To illustrate, one might judge the likelihood of breast cancer in middle-aged women by thinking of acquaintances who have experienced it. Such an occurrence might be statistically more probable in one's acquaintances than in the population at large, leading to erroneous impressions of its likelihood. In the case of illusory correlation, the judgment of how often two events go together relates to the fre-

Exhibit 1.1

Associations Can Be More Illusory Than Real

Psychologists Loren and Jean Chapman (1967) asked undergraduate judges to consider information concerning hypothetical men with emotional problems. First, the judges viewed a drawing of a person, which one of the men presumably drew. With each drawing the judges were given two statements allegedly representing symptoms experienced by the man making the drawing (e.g., "the man who drew this [1] is suspicious of other people and [2] is worried about how manly he is").

The judges then pointed out features of the drawings they thought to be characteristic of men with that symptom. Thus, after being reminded that some pictures were drawn by men "worried about how manly they are," judges were asked to list corresponding features in the drawings of those men. As part of this study, previously the researchers had asked experienced clinicians to list characteristics most likely to appear in drawings by men reporting the same symptoms. The earlier findings allowed the researchers to compare the characteristics noted by the naive undergraduates and the clinicians.

The agreement was striking. For example, when "manliness" was a concern, 80% of the clinicians and 76% of the undergraduates reported features in the drawings dealing with muscularity, broad shoulders, and other manly features. Similarly, when "suspiciousness" was a concern, 91% of the clinicians and 58% of the undergraduates reported features dealing with atypical eyes. Because research consistently fails to find any systematic differences in drawings that stem from a person's emotional or psychological problems, the basis for correlations such as these is spurious or "illusory," as Chapman and Chapman (1967) termed it.

Similar findings emerged from another one of their studies (Chapman & Chapman, 1969) using the Rorschach Inkblot Test. Unlike the draw-a-person test, however, some validity exists for the theory that interpretation of the Rorschach signs indicates certain types of psychological difficulty. For example, research shows that some of the 20 Rorschach indicators originally offered by Wheeler (1949) as diagnostic of male homosexuality do, indeed, appear statistically more often in responses of gay males than in those of heterosexual males.

Using both valid and invalid Wheeler signs, Chapman and Chapman (1969) studied whether diagnosticians rely on valid indicators (vs. popular, stereotypical but invalid signs) when interpreting Rorschach protocols. They first determined the popularity of both valid and invalid signs by having 32 diagnosticians experienced in using the Rorschach list the content they had observed from men who actually had problems related to sexual orientation. Among the most frequently mentioned signs occurring in these lists were "human or animal anal content," "feminine clothing," and "male or female

continued

Exhibit 1.1, continued

genitalia." Only one of the signs obtained from the clinicians was among those previously shown to be valid, and only 2 of the 32 respondents mentioned it.

The Chapmans (1969) then determined the stereotypical popularity of the diagnosticians' signs by asking 34 undergraduates to rate the strength of the association between sexual orientation and the signs. An example of one of the items the undergraduates rated is as follows:

The tendency for "homosexuality" to call to mind "rectum" and "buttocks" is
a. Very strong.
b. Strong.
c. Moderate.
d. Slight.
e. Very slight.
f. No tendency at all.

"Rectum" and "buttocks" are not valid signs of homosexuality in Rorschach responses. (An example of a valid sign for homosexuality is seeing monsters in a card.) The Chapmans interspersed invalid and valid signs and presented them to the raters.

The mean associative ratings (between homosexuality and the signs) were consistently higher for the popular (most often mentioned) but invalid signs than for the unpopular but valid ones. Chapman and Chapman (1969) concluded that popular (i.e., stereotypical) associations have a powerful influence on the interpretations of psychodiagnosticians.

quency of their association in the general social–verbal community. In the case of paranoia, Chapman and Chapman (1969) showed that it is common to associate suspiciousness with features of the eyes. Thus, when a clinician encounters a symptom involving suspiciousness and is asked to indicate features that might occur in drawings made by people experiencing the symptom, such an association is more available than others are. Because of its greater availability, judges are likely to report this association even when it is absent from the stimuli they are viewing.

Other sources of bias include the personal experiences of the practitioner, theoretical predilections, particularly salient but unrepresentative characteristics of the client, and other therapists and variables in the intervention setting itself. The study of information processing and its associated errors is an area of lively research and controversy in psychology and cognitive science, and many philosophical as well as practical implications drive it. In a sense, it goes to the heart of the reasons for writing this book.

One might assume that some types of data (e.g., objective information resulting from the application of scientific reasoning) are better than others for making decisions relevant to the quality of human services. Unfortunately, although this assumption is appealing, it has not yet been empirically tested; until it has, we will not know the actual impact of such cognitive errors (Holt, 1988). For now, ethical practitioners need to be aware of these issues and avoid claims of effectiveness that stem from cognitive distortion, bias, and other information-processing phenomena.

Obtaining Information Unavailable in Published Research

A final set of reasons for engaging in vigorous practice evaluation efforts has to do with limits on what we can reasonably expect to extrapolate from the scientific literature. Although as practitioners, we often can get partial answers to our questions from published research, we often have to qualify them on the basis of similarities between our actual experience and the research contexts described in the literature.

Most research involves a *nomothetic* approach to knowledge discovery (Allport, 1962; Windelband, 1921), meaning that the researcher is interested in learning more about a particular variable as it correlates with other variables in groups of people. In the behavioral sciences, the ultimate purpose of such research is to produce general laws explaining human behavior. If nomothetic research uncovers a relationship that is true for most people most of the time under most circumstances, we consider the finding to be valuable. If our local circumstances match those of the published research, we can have some confidence that the research applies to our situation. A close match is unlikely, however.

To illustrate this point, consider the question of whether incentives for retail clerks should be based on teamwork or individual behavior. Our hypothetical client, California Lingerie Boutique is exploring the reorganization of its sales force into work groups, or teams. The company wants to know whether to change its compensation practices as well. If research exists on this issue, it is likely to involve sales forces in industries other than lingerie, companies of a different size, employees of different educational backgrounds, and locations in different regions of the country. We have to determine whether the client's situation is similar enough to those described in the research literature to warrant generalizing the findings, usually a difficult determination to make. Many of the descriptive details needed for effective comparison do not appear in the pages of journal articles. Moreover, published data generally are summarized in terms of means, ranges, and other statistics, and it is rare that data appear for individual companies. Without detailed information, it is a leap of faith to conclude with any confidence that the research findings apply to our client.

Leaps of faith, however, are common when translating research findings from nomothetic studies to local applications. Notwithstanding this practice, as human services professionals we are interested in *idiographic* analyses; we want to know about relationships among variables in an individual client or an individual practice of psychology, counseling, or social work. We generally want to explain the behavior of unique cases rather than develop laws that apply to most cases. Our prevailing view is of the individual case as a "self-contained universe with its own laws" (Shontz, 1965, p. 244).

Ashbaugh and Peck (1998) offer an evaluation of a procedure for dealing with multiple sleeping problems of a typically developing 2-year-old girl. Figure 1.2 illustrates how the child's disturbed sleep was eliminated over the course of the month of treatment. The data illustrate the usefulness of single-case experimental designs in practice evaluation. (This subject is covered in more detail in chapter 8.)

Unfortunately, graduate studies do not prepare us to establish laws in self-contained universes, so we finish our coursework with a fairly significant gap between what we read in the literature and what we need to know to understand a particular case. A major purpose of this book is to provide the tools for studying relationships idiographically, as in the examples presented in this section.

How Service Providers Make Decisions

What does it take to convince us that something is any good—that we should read a particular book, buy a specific product, or keep going to a particular doctor? Is it the charismatic exhortations of professional athletes, the advice of a trusted cleric, or a combination of logic and common sense? How do we make those decisions?

As practitioners, we make decisions throughout much of our professional day. We decide whether to accept someone as a client, how to assess that client's needs, what interventions make the most sense for

Figure 1.2

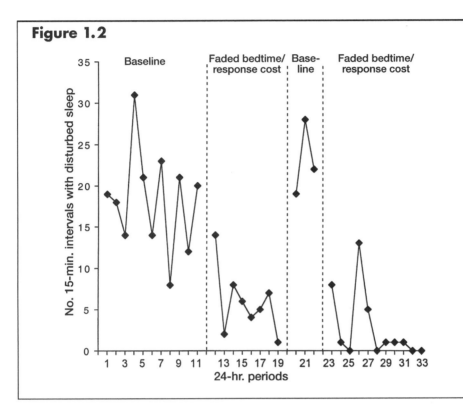

Intervals of disturbed sleep over 24-hr periods in a 2-year-old girl during baseline and faded bedtime–plus–response cost treatment phases. "Disturbed sleep" was defined as being awake at normal sleep times and sleeping during normal waking times. Data collection involved noting whether the child was awake or asleep every 15 minutes during the day; parents and preschool staff were trained in observing and noting this behavior. During the pretreatment, or baseline, period, the child typically fell asleep around 10:30 p.m. Treatment involved "fading" the bedtime by adding 30 minutes to the typical time and putting the child in bed at 11:00 p.m. The timing was adjusted depending on whether she fell asleep within 15 minutes of going to bed. If she did, 30 minutes was subtracted from her bedtime the next night. If she did not, 30 minutes was added to her bedtime the next night. The child was prevented from falling asleep before scheduled bedtimes by playing with her and was awakened at scheduled wake times. This routine continued until the goal of a 9:00 p.m. bedtime was reached. If the child did not fall asleep within 15 minutes of being placed in bed, she was played with for 30 minutes, a procedure Ashbaugh and Peck (1998) termed "response cost." This procedure was repeated if she still did not fall asleep within 15 minutes after being placed back in bed and continued until she did. Note that withdrawing the treatment for 3 days and then reinstating it was associated with respective increases and decreases in disturbed sleep. The study supports the effectiveness of the faded-bedtime and response-cost procedure for the child. From "Treatment of Sleep Problems in a Toddler: A Replication of the Faded Bedtime With Response Cost Procedure," R. Ashbaugh and S. M. Peck, 1998, *Journal of Applied Behavior Analysis, 31,* p. 129. Copyright 1998 by the *Journal of Applied Behavior Analysis.* Reprinted with permission.

the client, how to monitor the success of the interventions, and how to respond to progress data on an ongoing basis. Most of us follow a regular pattern in making these decisions. If we break our thinking into component steps, we can show it to be relatively systematic. For example, our first step usually is to pose a question, such as "What treatment will work best for this particular client?" On the basis of information from various sources (e.g., literature, formal training, professional experience, and advice of colleagues), we conclude that Treatment X is the intervention of choice. Using Treatment X, we then set about helping the client, and we observe to see whether the client is benefiting. If certain behavior or characteristics of the client change in expected ways, we say the treatment is beneficial.

In essence, our approach to decision making follows the pattern outlined in Exhibit 1.2. As seen in chapter 3, decision making in applied human services is not that different from decision making in science. Indeed, everyday decision making generally parallels the steps scientists take in discovering knowledge.

For example, consider a hypothetical situation in which you have decided to buy a new car. You have a certain amount of money you plan to spend. Let us suppose further that you have narrowed your choices to sedans. The next step in the process might involve asking "What is the best four-door sedan I can buy for $15,000?" To answer the question, you have to decide what "best" means. Best could mean "roomiest," "highest miles per gallon (MPG)," "fastest," "most dependable," "will make the best impression on my friends," and so on. After deciding the relative importance of your criteria, you apply them to available four-door sedans selling for $15,000 or less. To do so, you have to find out the extent to which each model meets each of your

---

Exhibit 1.2

Steps to Follow in Making a Decision

1. Ask a question.
2. Clarify the question, and specify criteria for answers.
3. Gather information (data) by consulting others (e.g., colleagues, literature).
4. Think about the data obtained from these consultations.
5. Assert an answer.
6. Act on the basis of that answer.
7. Determine whether the action was effective.

criteria, a process that resembles data gathering in research. Where do you go for the relevant data? What source can provide you with the best information on each of the criteria that you have articulated? Perhaps you choose *Consumer Reports* for information related to the mechanical criteria because it is an independent, highly respected source. For the "impression on friends" criterion, you could ask five friends.

Next, you weigh all the information you have gathered, a process similar to the scientist judging the significance of data collected in an experiment. Are the data compelling enough to make a decision? What model does your information suggest you should buy? You conclude that a Mercury Sable is the best car for you. In other words, you assert an answer to your original question. You then act on that answer (i.e., make the purchase) and proceed to evaluate the soundness of your purchase decision over the next several years of car ownership. It helps to appreciate how making everyday decisions resembles the research process because in our graduate studies, word can filter back from professionals in the trenches that research methodology and statistics are of no help to the practitioner in the "real world." As a result, students frequently resent and complain about having to take methodology courses. In addition, such courses take time away from learning how to provide services: How can we survive if we are not taught the skills we need to practice effectively? This is a reasonable question, which this book sets out to answer on the basis of two simple premises: (a) Our survival as professionals depends on learning and using systematic approaches to decision making, and (b) the research process exemplifies those approaches best.

Decision Making in the Human Services and in Science

Human services professionals and scientists are alike in that both make decisions in systematic ways. What this similarity primarily means is that we rely on information of a certain quality in reaching conclusions. It also means that we use information in particular ways to make decisions. Finally, it assumes that human problems have a cause.

It is unfortunate that in the human services professions, especially psychology, it has become popular to separate science from practice. Many graduate training programs in clinical psychology refer to themselves as "Boulder model" programs, meaning that they train students in "both" the scientific and applied aspects of the discipline. This unfortunate bifurcation of the field leads to people being referred to as "researchers" or "scientists" on the one hand, and as "clinicians" or "practitioners" on the other.

As noted in the preceding section, however, the formal process of inquiry characteristic of science pervades our work as human services providers as well; we therefore are not just practitioners or scientists, as McFall (1991, 1995) observed. Referring to clinical psychology, he noted that it is "defined by its fundamental commitment to a scientific epistemology" (McFall, 1995, p. 127). Indeed, we use the tools of science each time we attempt to solve a clinical problem. As Kazdin (1993) observed,

> psychologists have by training, common experience, and orientation a concern for the methodological tenets of scientific research. . . . The model required for clinical psychology is not necessarily special . . . the commitment to systematic assessment and evaluation . . . comes from entry into the field rather than from theoretical orientation, specialization area, and so on. (p. 39)

For the purposes of this book, evaluation is a type of research that involves determining value by applying scientific procedures involving empirical data. Thus, the careful appraisal or evaluation of one's practice activities involves the collection of objective observations and their treatment using reasoning that is logically valid. Although the process of outcomes evaluation and of basic scientific research is fundamentally the same, their goals are not necessarily comparable. The goal of science is to generate new knowledge that advances a field of inquiry. The goal of outcomes evaluation is to ascertain the effectiveness of an application of that scientific knowledge to a practical problem.

For example, consider recent discussions of whether psychotherapy works (Barlow, 1996; Hollon, 1996; Jacobson & Christensen, 1996; "Mental Health: Does Therapy Help," 1995; Seligman, 1995, 1996). It has become common to try to answer this question with two types of research: (a) efficacy studies and (b) effectiveness studies (Seligman, 1995; chapter 11 presents examples of both). Different questions form the basis for the two types of study (Howard, Moras, Brill, Martinovich, & Lutz, 1996). Efficacy studies determine whether a particular intervention works under relatively tightly controlled experimental conditions. The purpose of effectiveness studies is to determine whether a particular intervention works under actual practice conditions.

When determining whether to use a particular type of intervention, it is important to distinguish between evidence from efficacy and effectiveness studies. For example, some psychotropic medications appear to be quite effective under the tightly controlled conditions of efficacy studies. Their benefits in the context of less tightly controlled effectiveness studies have been considerably less impressive, however, partly because of low levels of patient compliance with taking the medication (e.g., data show Prozac to be 70% efficacious but only 25% effective; Howard, 1996). In a recent study, cocktails of various medications shown to be highly efficacious in suppressing HIV levels are apparently much less effective. In clinical trials, close to 74% of patients receiving highly active antiretroviral therapy (HAART, or "cocktail therapy") show undetectable levels of HIV 1 year later. Only 37% of patients participating in a less tightly controlled effectiveness study showed such improvements, however (Lucas, Chaisson, & Moore, 1999).

Whereas efficacy studies address whether a treatment works under tightly controlled conditions and effectiveness studies ask whether it works in the real world, a third question is also important: Does the treatment work with this particular patient? (Howard, Moras, et al., 1996). This last question about treatment quality most clearly relates to practice evaluation. Arguing a number of problems with efficacy research, Sperry, Brill, Howard, and Grissom (1996) proposed a systematic, quasinaturalistic, case-based approach involving (a) "the systematic use of objective data, (b) continuous assessment, (c) a model of problem stability, (d) diverse and heterogeneous samples of patients, and (e) clear evidence of an effect that can be measured" (p. 37).

Other observers (e.g., Fensterheim & Raw, 1996) have argued for the complete independence of research and practice and suggest that clinicians should not concern themselves with attempting to do research in their offices. Unfortunately, this argument appears to equate all research with basic research and does not address the issue of accountable practice. Effective practice, however, involves an approach to problem conceptualization and solution that parallels what happens in science; distinguishing between research and practice on this basis is illogical and misleading.

Philosophy of Science and Outcomes Evaluation

Two characteristics of science—careful observation and the application of the principles of logic to observations—are the basis for the self-correcting character that sets science apart from other ways of evaluating ideas. Careful observation occurs in the course of assessment and measurement. By careful ongoing observation and continual adjustment of procedure, empirical service providers use the same self-correcting tactics as scientists. In doing so, they build in continual improvement in quality, just as scientists continually find increasingly adequate explanations of the phenomena they study.

Although empiricism is the basic philosophical approach put forth in this book, it is not the only philosophy of science one could bring to practice evaluation (see Sechrest & Figueredo, 1993). For example, a person who sees research and practice as inherently incompatible might suggest that hermeneutics would be a more clinically relevant approach. Hermeneutic formulations rely on validation in terms of logical consistency and "metaphoric coherence" (Schacht, 1991, p. 1346). Such a philosophy is common among adherents of psychodynamic approaches to psychotherapy. Empirical formulations, in contrast, rely on validation in terms of the systematic collection of data to test hypotheses.

Another perspective is qualitative practice evaluation. This approach relies more on verbal descriptions than on numbers in characterizing phenomena, and it focuses more holistically on individuals and the context within which their behavior occurs. Rather than seeing the evaluator as a dispassionate, objective observer, qualitative approaches view the evaluator as enmeshed in the context of the evaluation and as having significant influence on it. Instead of formal, standardized psychometric instruments, qualitative analysis relies heavily (if not exclusively) on the evaluator as the principal measuring device. This brief characterization does not do full justice to qualitative approaches, and interested readers should consult the excellent descriptions of qualitative and quantitative strategies in Kazdin (1998) and Cook and Wittmann (1998).

One can organize an approach to case conceptualization and service delivery in terms of hermeneutic, logical positivist, functional contextualist (Biglan & Hayes, 1996), qualitative, or some other philosophy of science. The ultimate issue, however, is the stakeholders' view of the service. Sperry et al. (1996) identified six types of people as having a stake in the outcome of any treatment: (a) the patient, who receives the service; (b) the therapist, who provides the service; (c) the clients, who request the service (e.g., schools, parents); (d) the managers, who allocate treatment resources (e.g., officials of MCOs who determine the amount of service reimbursable for a particular condition); (e) the sponsors, who pay for the treatment (e.g., insurance companies, government agencies); and (f) the researchers, who have a scientific interest in the outcome of the treatment. Note that people are often more than one of these types. What the stakeholders are willing to accept as evidence of effectiveness may depend on their own worldviews. Thus, the happiest of circumstances in program evaluation might occur when the philosophies of the service provider and the other stakeholders match. Given the diversity of people with vested interests in services delivered today, however, such happy matches are rare. Chapter 4 describes in more detail the various stakeholders and outcome measures specific to each.

This book is not the place to argue the advantages of different philosophical approaches to science. It is useful to be aware of various viewpoints, to be sure, and of arguments concerning the limitations of strict empiricism (see Weimer, 1976). At the same time, a logical positivist, empirical worldview placed a man on the moon and has served us well in other respects (Kazdin, 1998). Empiricism is the dominant perspective in psychology and the behavioral sciences, generally, and it is the basis for the practice evaluation strategies advocated here. As Barlow (1996) observed, arguments about the adequacy of various approaches to science are not likely to influence policy makers in the health care industry or Congress; the "rules of evidence have been well worked out and rely on empirical demonstrations of relief of dysfunction or enhancement of functioning" (p. 1053).

Summary

The philosophical basis of the approach to practice evaluation advocated here is empirical. At the same time, this book does not advocate a particular theoretical orientation to behavior change, nor is one necessary. The principles and procedures described here are ecumenical with respect to theory: One can apply them whether one's theoretical perspective is psychodynamic, interpersonal, humanistic, cognitive, applied behavior analytic, or interbehavioral. Whatever philosophy of behavioral science a practitioner holds, he or she would benefit by becoming an empirical service provider.

2 Envisioning Your Practice

This chapter describes the foundation concepts for arranging a successful practice to provide the basis for a template for practice evaluation. Several writers recently have called attention to the value of having a model to guide evaluative efforts (Berman, Hurt, & Heiss, 1996; Howard, Moras, Brill, Martinovich, & Lutz, 1996). Models can help organize and guide our efforts; they also can serve a protective function. As seen in chapter 1, the activities of a practice generate many interesting evaluative questions. Although we might like to have answers to all of them, it is unrealistic to think that we ever will. How do we protect ourselves from pursuing questions that may seem interesting at the time but may not yield the highest payoff in terms of practice improvement? Models can guide us in selecting the best questions.

This chapter begins by discussing the scope of a practice. It then shows how the practitioner's life vision provides the foundation for practice evaluation. Next, it describes how personal value premises, mission statements, and goals derive from one's life vision and then outlines a process for developing measures to assess progress toward actualizing that vision. Similarly, the vision statements, mission, and goals for one's practice derive from one's personal visions. The chapter ends with a discussion of goal setting with clients.

The Scope of Your Practice

After obtaining your degree, you might find yourself working independently in a relatively circumscribed practice (e.g., you might see only individual psychotherapy clients who come to your office). Alternatively, you might specialize in geriatric cases and travel to your clients' homes. This singularity of focus appears to be diminishing as the managed care initiatives mentioned in chapter 1 bring about changes in service delivery practices. More and more health practitioners find it useful to diversify their professional activities. It is not unusual to find a psychologist, for example, who sees some private clients in his or her office, conducts several group therapy sessions at a community agency, teaches a course for a local university, and provides routine psychological evaluations for a residential facility serving people with disabilities.

In designing an evaluation plan or model, it is wise to consider all of your diverse professional activities as part of the practice, rather than segmenting your professional life into direct services, teaching, consulting, and so on. Segmentation gets unwieldy and makes it difficult to hold each activity accountable for its contribution to the big picture. To use an accountant's spreadsheet analogy, when we consider all aspects of a practice as part of the same activity, we easily can see how changes in one area affect the entire practice. Moreover, we also can see the effects of those changes on the "bottom line."

Whether segmented or not, the scope of one's practice relates directly to one's purpose for being in practice, which in turn relates to the values, goals, and vision one has for one's life. The sections that follow discuss vision statements, values, mission statements, and goals; having a clear conception of each area is important to shaping one's practice.

What Is Your Vision?

It is increasingly common in the corporate world to see vision statements and descriptions of a company's values and purpose displayed prominently in publications, on business cards, or on the walls of corporate headquarters. Kouzes and Posner (1995) defined vision in terms of images of the future that are ideal and unique. Their definition implies a standard of excellence or quality not yet achieved; it provokes us to get beyond what *is* to consider what might be. Two other aspects of Kouzes and Posner's definition are uniqueness and image. The first concept involves that which sets us apart or makes us different from others; the second involves a visual representation of what will happen when we actualize the vision. Typically, our image of the future is somewhat abstract. It becomes more concrete as we take steps toward making it a reality.

A good vision statement serves three functions: (a) It focuses attention and effort, (b) it directs activities, and (c) it motivates. Visions are important to businesses because they provide focus and clarity. Kouzes and Posner (1995) referred to organizational vision statements in terms of the magnetic north of a compass, noting that such statements serve to attract and guide the behavior of those having contact with them. Vision statements tell customers and employees alike just what the company stands for. Carefully composed, they contain easily identified values or messages of what a person or organization sees as important. When everyone who works for an organization knows its vision, it is easier for each person to stay focused. Employees can emphasize activities that are consistent with the vision while ignoring or avoiding those that are tangential.

The values embodied in the vision provide the basis for individual and organizational goals. Mission statements describe how goals are to be accomplished. Determining whether and how those goals are met is the essence of practice evaluation.

Personal Vision Statements

The approach to developing organizational visions parallels the development of our individual visions. Although our visions may not be in writing and posted on our office or bedroom walls, we each have some idea of where we want our life to be going. Often (perhaps most often) we define our vision vaguely and do not commit it to writing. (Until relatively recently, this has been true for businesses as well.) I have counseled hundreds of executives of major corporations, many of whom tell me about the hours they spend on vision committees, in visioning exercises, and on vision retreats to formulate lofty-sounding, important vision statements for their companies. It occurs to few of them that the logic applies to their personal lives as well. They know what their company strives to become—but what do they seek for themselves? As individuals, we can emulate vision-producing activities of the business world to our great personal benefit. These activities can be especially helpful in formulating effective ways of evaluating our professional activities.

An important feature of a vision statement is that it deals with how we want to be some time in the future, a concept that implies values.

For example, a vision to become the best parent we can be while growing spiritually and attaining financial independence implies that parenting effectiveness, spirituality, and financial independence are important. The mission statement stems directly from those values.

The design or arrangement of our life in ways consistent with our values constitutes our mission statement. It describes what we need to do on a day-to-day basis to accomplish our vision. A carefully worded mission statement leads to easily recognizable goals, such as "to arrange my professional life to permit lots of time with my children." Goals should be stated in terms of outcomes (e.g., "find a job requiring no more than 30 hours out of the house a week"); operationalized outcomes enable us to measure them. When we achieve measurable outcomes, we move closer to making our long-term vision a reality.

A student of mine once suggested a cake-baking metaphor to clarify the process. The picture of the cake provides the vision. The way we want the cake to look and taste implies certain values. The recipe provides the mission, or steps involved in realizing the vision. Making a shopping list of needed ingredients is a goal involved in achieving the mission of making the cake. Going to the store and buying them is another. Figure 2.1 outlines the process and its major elements.

This approach assumes that one begins with a vision and continues in a more or less linear sequence from that point. It is not necessary to follow this order slavishly, however. Some people prefer to list personal values first and fashion a vision afterward, as a composite of the values.

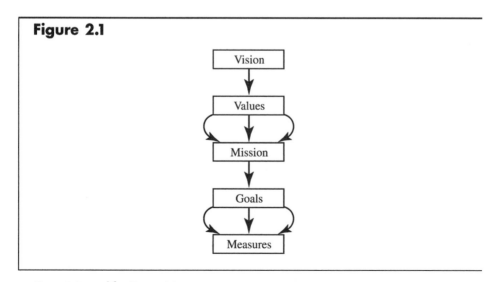

Figure 2.1

Organizing a life: From vision to measures.

However flexibly one treats the process, it is important to end up with all five of the major elements: vision, values, mission, goals, and measures.

Creating Personal Vision Statements

Most of us do not have well-articulated visions guiding our lives. If asked to produce one, we might have trouble knowing just where to begin. Kouzes and Posner (1995) suggested doing some of the activities in Exhibit 2.1 to help form a vision. Interested readers should consult their book for more detail.

Another useful approach to fashioning a vision is to make a list of our values or highest priorities. These can be traits (e.g., honesty and dependability) or they can be conditions or states of being (e.g., financial independence or optimal physical health). Once listed, they can be rephrased as action statements (e.g., be honest; attain financial independence). Then we can clarify them by writing a paragraph about each (Hobbs, 1983). Starting each sentence in the clarifying paragraph with a verb (e.g., be honest with myself and all around me) provides a set of goal statements for each priority or value. Finally, we can order the values from most to least important. Various values clarification exercises are available for this purpose (e.g., "If I could be known for only three things after I die, they would be X, Y, and Z"; see Morrisey, 1992).

Exhibit 2.1

Activities to Assist in Formulating a Vision

Recall "peak" experiences you have had in the past.
Decide what it is you want to accomplish and why.
Write a newspaper or magazine article about how you have made a difference.
Become a future thinker.
Act more on intuition.
Write a draft of your vision.
Identify and write down assumptions implied in your vision.
Test those assumptions.
Rehearse the vision by forming a visual image of what it will be like when realized and rehearsing this image over and over.

Note. This information is a compilation of suggestions from Kouzes and Posner (1987) and from my own work and time management workshops over the years.

A personal vision statement resulting from clarified values might look something like the following:

> *Personal Vision A*: To become the most loving spouse and parent I can be while proceeding toward optimum physical health and financial independence doing work that is intellectually challenging, socially supported, and helpful to humanity and that maintains the highest esteem of my colleagues.

Before you begin your own practice, it is a good idea to write a personal vision statement. Armed with an image of the future that is uniquely yours, you can set about the task of actualizing that vision. As you move forward, you can refer to the vision statement to ascertain whether your practice is in harmony with your values. To bring our professional activities more clearly under the control of our personal vision, it is helpful to identify some of the values implied in that vision. Exhibit 2.2 lists the eight values implied in Personal Vision A.

Characteristics of Good Vision Statements

Good vision statements are specific and indicate the priority of the values they reflect.

Specificity

Vision statements are brief, focused descriptions of some unique, ideal future state. For them to have the guiding, energizing functions often ascribed to them, their implications should be clear. The more carefully worded the vision, the clearer its implications will be. The process is similar to writing a good research question. Some questions are worded so vaguely as to be metaphysical (Kerlinger, 1986). For example, the question "Are group processes good for children?" is so vague that it

---

Exhibit 2.2

Values Implied in Personal Vision A

- Be a loving spouse.
- Be a loving parent.
- Have optimum physical health.
- Attain financial independence.
- Be intellectually challenged at work.
- Be socially supported.
- Be helpful to humanity.
- Be esteemed by colleagues.

cannot direct or control research efforts aimed to answer it in any consistent way. Any given approach is likely to be idiosyncratic because the variables implied in the question are so broad as to be interpretable in many different ways. What are "group processes," for example? What does "good for children" mean?

Priority

A good research question provides guidance to those seeking to study it. Similarly, a good vision statement provides guidance in terms of direction, focus, and motivation. For example, in Personal Vision A above, the value premises are clear and include "loving spouse," "loving parent," "optimum physical health," and so forth. Knowing what a person values means knowing what that person seeks to achieve. Moreover, good vision statements imply the relative priority of the different values. In Personal Vision A, it appears that marital and family values may be of higher priority than professional values, given the order in which the values appear. Consider the following vision:

> *Personal Vision B*: To attain and maintain optimum physical, spiritual, and social health doing work that is intellectually challenging, useful to humanity, and esteemed by my colleagues to have the most satisfying family life possible.

The value premises of this vision statement are much the same as those in Personal Vision A, but rearranging them shifts the focus of what is most important. An evident hierarchy exists among the different values: All other values exist to make a satisfying family life possible. When the relative priority of value premises is clear, the vision statement has a better chance of directing and focusing our efforts. Given the need to choose between several alternative activities at a particular moment, we know which one to choose to be consistent with our priorities. For example, according to Personal Vision B, we are not likely to choose a highly prestigious overseas assignment that separates us for a lengthy period from our school-aged children.

If personal vision statements have clear implications for values and the relative priorities among them, it is easier to align professional vision statements with them. Moreover, just as with research questions, the more explicit the variables implied in our vision, the better. That is, the easier it is to operationalize the value premises, the more effective the vision will be in directing, controlling, and motivating our actions. If our values are explicit and their relative priorities known, we can design our practice to support them. When personal and practice visions are in alignment, we use our resources more effectively than when they are not.

Personal Mission Statements

Whereas the vision statement reflects "an image of what we aspire to be or become" (Albrecht, 1994, p. 152), the mission statement describes how we are going to behave to achieve our vision. Ideally, we write a personal mission statement to provide the "recipe," or road map, for actualizing our personal vision. Within our personal mission should be activities that relate to professional and financial goals, some of which we can advance by establishing an independent practice. As we shall see, the steps involved in developing a personal mission statement are similar to those involved in developing mission statements for one's practice.

A good way to "rough out" a mission statement is to begin by identifying the values implied in one's personal vision as discussed above. An example of a personal mission statement emerging from such an analysis appears in Personal Mission A.

> *Personal Mission A*: My mission in life is to become the most loving spouse and parent I can while doing intellectually stimulating work that is helpful to society. I accomplish this mission by behaving consistently in ways that my spouse and my children value positively. I maintain a regular program of exercise, watch my diet, and obtain routine physical examinations. I save money regularly and have an organized approach to retirement. I interact frequently with a close group of friends, and my practice includes three other psychologists. Together we conduct applied research and present our results at professional conferences at which we receive feedback that improves our effectiveness in serving others.

A carefully composed mission statement can be an excellent guide to living. Because it reflects the values implied in our personal vision, following it allows us to make decisions consistent with this vision and assures coherence to our lives. For example, referring to our mission facilitates choosing between sleeping another hour in the morning or getting up and going running. Which alternative is consistent with maintaining a regular program of exercise? The mission statement makes it clear that exercise is the choice to make.

To assess progress toward accomplishing our goals, we must operationalize them, or make them more specific. An operational definition of something is essentially a definition of that thing in terms of the procedures we use to measure it. For example, earning enough income to be able to save and invest at a rate that accumulates a certain specified sum by a certain specified time is an operational definition of attaining financial independence. Attaining and maintaining optimum physical health can mean engaging in aerobic exercise for a minimum of three 30-minute sessions per week, keeping weight within 5% of recommended levels, and keeping cholesterol and triglycerides below critical levels. Measures of operationalized values are relatively easy to produce. For example, one can chart time spent exercising and weight levels on a weekly basis. Similarly, one can chart personal net worth on a quarterly or semi-annual basis.

Practice Vision Statements

Now that we have clarified our personal vision and composed a personal mission statement, we can move to a parallel process for our practice. Most of us work to live, rather than the other way around. We work in our practice to enable a particular life, a life described by our personal vision. To realize that vision, we want our professional activities to be in harmony with that vision. Compare the following two examples of practice vision statements:

Practice Vision A: We aspire to be known among Fortune 100 companies as the preeminent provider in the western United States and Pacific Rim countries of organizational consultation.

Practice Vision B: We aspire to be known in the professional community as the preeminent provider of organizational consultation to small and medium-sized manufacturing companies in the Chicago area.

Which of the two vision statements seems more aligned with Personal Vision A? Because Personal Vision A emphasizes family interaction, Practice Vision B seems more consistent with it because it limits the scope of practice activities to a smaller geographic area. Presumably this practice would entail less travel and thus provide more opportunity to be available for family activities. Now, consider the following vision statement:

Practice Vision C: I aspire to be known in the local medical community as the most immediately available low-cost provider of psychological services to low-income residents of Atlanta.

This practice vision might be consistent with some of the values identified in the personal vision and not with others. For example, it might be out of alignment with an interest in attaining financial independence, depending on the time frame identified for achieving this aspect of the personal vision. Given the emphasis on immediate availability, this statement also might be out of alignment with the family interaction value that the personal vision mentions.

Finally, consider the following practice vision statement:

Practice Vision D: We aspire to be known in the local behavioral health and medical communities as the best providers of empirically supported, time-limited treatment based on applied behavior analysis for private-paying adults seeking outpatient therapy for psychological problems.

Can you identify the value premises implied? Does your list look something like the following?

- Be the best providers.
- Treat psychological problems.
- Provide treatment that has empirical support.
- Provide treatment that is time limited.
- Use treatments grounded in applied behavior analysis.
- Provide therapy on an outpatient basis.
- Serve adults.
- Avoid third-party payment.

This practice vision statement is useful because it makes clear what is important to or valued by the practitioner. It states a theoretical orientation, identifies potential clients, mentions the types of service to be provided, includes the level of quality ("best") to be achieved, and refers to revenue arrangements. Defining these values clearly so that measures of them can be selected is a relatively easy task. The elaboration of values can occur in the practice's mission statement.

Practice Mission Statements

As with personal mission statements, a good way to begin drafting a practice mission statement is to identify the value premises implied in the practice vision. The next step is to clarify those values. We can define the eight values implied in Practice Vision D to various degrees of specificity. Again, it is a good idea to write a paragraph about what we think each value means. To illustrate, "treating psychological problems" suggests a rather wide span of practice. Imagine a person advertising that he or she "repairs all problems in and around the home." To be the "best" at this would no doubt require involving other specialists (e.g., plumbers, electricians, roofers, and landscape architects). To provide the "best" treatment for psychological problems would require a range of expertise unlikely to be present in a single practitioner. Thus, either the mission statement must narrow the range, or the practice must involve other psychologists.

Similarly, serving "adults" seems to narrow the scope, but adults span quite a range of ages. Are you likely to have the skills to cover the problems of young adults as well as senior citizens and be the "best" at it? Narrowing the age range to "working adults" or "young adults" would help, as would planning to involve experts in geriatric psychology in the practice. It is also helpful to have an explicitly stated theoretical position. In the example in Practice Vision D, basing services on applied behavior analysis means that the mission is likely to measure progress based on objective measures of what the person does rather than on verbal reports of change. Moreover, the practice is likely to analyze what is effective in producing the progress and develop explicit descriptions of its interventions. Such a theoretical position also implies concern with the size of improvements seen—they must be sufficient to be socially important—and the behavior changes must show generalization over time, place and, perhaps, to other forms of behavior (Baer, Wolf, & Risley, 1968). Finally, limiting services to those with empirical support, as in Practice Vision D, further defines the practice and facilitates writing a clear mission statement.

Whatever the theoretical basis implied in a practice vision, it is extremely important to include one because it can have significant bearing on the conduct of the services. For example, other people included in the practice, either as associates, partners, or subcontractors, can be selected with an eye toward theoretical consistency. In addition, interaction among participants in the practice can be more effective when everyone "speaks the same language" and conducts his or her professional activities accordingly. The clearer the mission, of course, the easier it is to communicate. Finally, if the practice primarily treats anxiety disorders in working adults using exposure-based treatment shown to be effective in peer-reviewed journals, it is distinguishable from practices that do something else. In being different, the practice advances the vision of "being known in the local behavioral health and medical communities" because it is easier to get recognition for uniqueness than for something that is indistinguishable from what others are doing.

An example of a mission statement emerging from a careful analysis of Practice Vision D appears in Practice Mission A.

> *Practice Mission A*: Our mission is to provide the best adult outpatient psychological services we can. We achieve this mission by producing outcomes collaboratively agreed upon with our clients using evidence-based, brief treatment approaches with a theoretical basis in applied behavior analysis. We analyze our effectiveness objectively and continually, and we strive to produce change in our clients that is socially meaningful and generalizable over time and setting. We accomplish our mission using staff specifically trained in and committed to applied behavior analysis, who maintain and improve their competence by individual programs of continuing education.

A well thought-out mission statement becomes the heart of the operations manual that guides the practice. By referring to the mission, we can select activities that are consistent with it in preference to those that are not. For example, if a new approach to treating anxiety disorders becomes available, participants in the practice can determine whether to obtain training in it on the basis of whether the approach has empirical support, is consistent with applied behavior analysis, is usable on an outpatient basis, is time-limited, and applies to adults.

Practice Goals

Articulating the mission statement reveals how the practice will achieve its vision. Practice achievements relate to accomplishing specific goals. Evaluating how well the practice performs involves measuring how well it achieves the goals implied in its mission statement. This section discusses outcomes of two basic types: (a) those for the practice as a whole, considering all of its components and (b) those more relevant to the direct services component of a practice.

Setting Practice Goals

Goals are assertions of a behavioral state of affairs that exists some time in the future. The first step in articulating practice goals is to identify values. Among the values implied in Practice Mission A are "being the best," "brief treatment," and "a continuously educated staff." Writing a paragraph to elaborate more precisely what those values mean is the next step to creating clearly stated goals. To illustrate, the value of being the best can mean any of the following:

- Continually obtain data on service quality from clients served.
- Have clients rate their satisfaction with various aspects of the service.
- Monitor progress toward client goals.
- Determine cost-effectiveness of primary services.
- Compare quality of services with that of major competitors.
- Be listed in *The Gray Book of Top 10 Behavioral Health Practitioner Groups* (fictitious book).

Maintaining staff competence can mean obtaining continuing education in new, empirically supported forms of therapy. Similarly, "providing time-limited treatment," can mean keeping running totals of the number of sessions for each client, graphing and posting the data for each therapist in the practice, and preparing dose–response curves (Howard, Kopta, Krause, & Orlinsky, 1986) showing the amount of improvement associated with amounts of service provided. Value-elaborating paragraphs are indispensable bridges to practice goals. When each sentence in the paragraph starts with a verb, it is a relatively straightforward matter to go from global vision and implied values to actionable goal statements.

You can set goals for your practice to be accomplished in various time periods (e.g., long-term, annual, or monthly). Long-term goals are those that take more than 1 year to attain. These and annual goals are probably most realistic at the practice level, although individual practitioners might want to have monthly or even shorter range goals that are related to the practice's long-term goals. Thus, a long-term goal related to being the best could be "to maintain a grand mean above 4.0 for outpatients on the Mental Health Corporations of America (MHCA) Client Satisfaction Survey" (MHCA, 1995). An annual goal to facilitate this long-term goal could be the following:

Achieve a mean of 4.0 or better on the dimensions of the MHCA survey related to physical environment and client–staff interaction by December 31 of this year.

A monthly goal related to the physical environment dimension of the annual goal could be the following:

To hire an interior decorator to suggest improvements to the physical layout and furnishings of the practice's offices by January 31 of this year.

Each practice should have goals in line with its vision and the values implied in this vision and elaborated in its mission statement. When the goals are explicit, it is relatively easy to establish measures of their attainment. For the quality goals discussed in the previous paragraph, the use of a nationally standardized customer satisfaction measure provides part of the data needed to monitor progress and is even part of the goal itself. Measures of actual change in client well-being, symptoms, and life functioning (e.g., Howard, Brill, Lueger, & O'Mahoney, 1995) can provide data relevant to the quality of outcomes therapy produces. By using measures of change with all clients, you can assess progress toward improving and maintaining quality of service more or less continuously. (See chapter 6 for more information on evaluation measures.) Note also that you can improve quality by empowering all participants in the practice to meet personally tailored performance goals that address issues of quality.

Setting Goals for Direct Services

Arguably, the most important activities of a practice are those related to providing services to clients. The effectiveness of those services can be measured in terms of whether we meet specific client goals. Rosen and Proctor (1981) differentiated among three levels of goals in assessing client progress in psychotherapy. *Ultimate goals* have to do with the reasons clients seek help in the first place. These goals are what the client wants to change as a result of our service. For example, the organizational client may want the cultures of two merged companies to blend into one with minimum disruption. The psychotherapy client may want to get rid of his depression, and the marital therapy clients may want less conflict over child-rearing practices and money. We can view these goals as service outcomes and measure them as changes in the client that occur outside the treatment context. Greenberg (1986) referred to these goals as "ultimate (or final) outcomes" (p. 4).

Rosen and Proctor's (1981) second category of goals, *instrumental goals*, reflects client changes thought to relate directly to accomplishing the ultimate goal. For example, reducing the frequency of negative automatic thoughts might correlate with improvements in depression—it is not synonymous with the ultimate goal of being rid of depression altogether, however. Similarly, improving the reflective listening skills of members of a marital dyad can be instrumental to reduced conflict over child rearing and money, but it is not synonymous with it. Whereas the client determines the ultimate goals, the therapist selects the instrumental goals. Instrumental goals are usually consistent with the therapist's theoretical understanding of the type of change needed.

Finally, Rosen and Proctor (1981) identified *intermediate goals* as activities related to the successful implementation of the intervention being considered. Thus, participating in role plays and modeling reflective listening skills in conjoint treatment sessions can represent intermediate goals for the marital therapy clients. Keeping daily records of dysfunctional thoughts (Beck, Rush, Shaw, & Emery, 1979) might be intermediate to reducing negative thoughts in the case of the psychotherapy client seeking help with depression.

One often hears a distinction between two types of goals for direct services: outcome and process. In Rosen and Proctor's (1981) terminology, outcomes correspond to ultimate goals, or changes in the client's presenting complaints external to the intervention itself. The activities we engage in to accomplish the ultimate goal relate to process goals; Rosen and Proctor's instrumental and intermediate goal categories both seem to be of the process type.

Summary

Practice evaluation starts with the vision we have for our life. Before we can evaluate our practice, however, we must first develop a well-articulated personal vision statement, which implies certain values. We clarify these values by writing a paragraph defining each value. These clarifying paragraphs help prioritize values and become the basis for a personal mission statement, which becomes the document that organizes our life. From there, we can develop long- and short-term goals. Operationalizing these goals provides us with measures to use in gauging our progress toward actualizing our vision.

A parallel process serves to organize our practice. The practice exists to meet the goals of its owners, and those goals, in turn, derive from the owner's personal vision statements. Thus, our practice vision statements reflect our personal vision and values. Writing paragraphs to elaborate those values helps focus the practice vision and provide a basis for the practice's mission statement. Carefully composed mission statements lead easily to the goals for the practice. These goals can have various time frames, but we usually state them in terms of a year or longer. Operationalizing our practice goals leads to relatively straightforward identification of goal and performance objectives for each participant in the practice. The time perspectives of an individual participant's goals and objectives are shorter than those for the practice as a whole.

The process that starts with articulating one's personal vision and leads to specifying the goals of one's professional activities is seamless. The presumption is that a well-integrated life is one in which the parts all fit together. When we organize our life—both our practice and our personal life—to realize the values implied in our personal vision, we are using time effectively and optimizing our mental health. The ultimate question is, To what extent do all our activities contribute to the realization of our personal vision? It is a good idea to take stock of such contributions from time to time. Are they continuing to yield the highest value in terms of actualizing our vision, or should we replace them with other activities likely to contribute more? Outcomes evaluation can help answer questions such as these.

Supplemental Reading

Howard, K. I., Kopta, S. M., Krause, M. S., & Orlinsky, D. E. (1986). The dose-effect relationship in psychotherapy. *American Psychologist, 41,* 159–164.

Kouzes, J. M., & Posner, B. Z. (1995). *The leadership challenge: How to keep getting extraordinary things done in organizations* (2nd ed.). San Francisco: Jossey-Bass.

Morrisey, G. L. (1992). *Creating your future.* San Francisco: Berrett-Koehler.

Quigley, J. V. (1993). *Vision: How leaders develop it, share it, and sustain it.* New York: McGraw-Hill.

Rosen, A., & Proctor, E. K. (1981). Distinctions between treatment outcomes and their implications for treatment evaluation. *Journal of Consulting and Clinical Psychology, 49,* 418–425.

3 The Practice Evaluation Cycle

In determining how well a practice is meeting one's personal goals, one can ask many questions. Indeed, evaluative questions are important enough to merit a separate chapter of their own (see chapter 5). For now, as a starting point for examining a general process to use in evaluating human services, we can content ourselves with several rather straightforward questions a practitioner might ask. You can immediately recognize parallels between this process and one that appears in many university courses on research methodology.

Typical Evaluation Questions

Human services providers typically ask questions such as the following:

- Are my clients happy with the services I provide?
- Is my approach to treating alcohol abuse effective with my particular clients?
- Should I spend $2,000 on a *Yellow Pages* ad?
- Would it make sense to open a second office in another part of town?
- Should we add an onsite follow-up component to the executive leadership training we do?
- Is the psychological therapy I provide helping clients with their depression? Is it as or more effective than medication they can receive from general practitioners or a psychiatrist?
- Is my practice helping me achieve my life's goals?

The questions vary somewhat in terms of specificity, and they focus on several different practice components. All practices involve a direct services component as well as administrative services, continuing education and training and, sometimes, community service. Each component has different goals. For example, opening a second office or spending $2,000 on advertising relates to the administrative services component, the "business" part of the practice, in which one makes decisions as to office location, advertising, fee schedules, billing practices, and professional liability insurance, among others. The need to make decisions in each component can lead to evaluation questions. Whether to spend $2,000 on a yellow pages ad, for example, is an easier decision if we have an answer to "What percentage of practice revenues over the past 2 years are directly attributable to yellow pages advertising?" It is also possible to ask questions of varying degrees of specificity about the effectiveness of each component. With respect to direct services, for example, we might ask a question related to the course of improvement over treatment sessions, such as "What is the relationship between the amount of treatment I provide and the gains that my clients make?"

The Evaluation Cycle

Evaluative questions are like research questions in that both initiate a cycle of activities that ends with further questions (see Figure 3.1). Consider the question "Is my practice effective?" As with research questions, there are good and bad ways of phrasing evaluative questions. Kerlinger (1986) observed that a good research question is one that is answerable (i.e., is not metaphysical). The same is true in practice evaluation. The question "Is my practice effective?" is much too vague to lead to useful information for improving services. What do we mean by practice? What do we mean by effective? A more useful question is, "What specific form of practice, applied to whom and resulting in what kind of changes, is considered effective?" By becoming more specific, we enhance the answerability of the question.

Just as social sciences research takes place to advance our knowledge of human behavior, practice evaluations occur to improve our understanding of human services. Scientific knowledge advances by establishing laws that in the aggregate constitute theories. Laws in science are nothing more than the relationships between observed phenomena. The phenomena are represented by variables. Thus, if a physicist finds

Figure 3.1

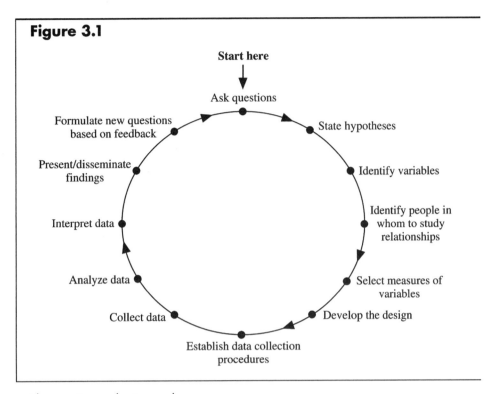

The practice evaluation cycle.

a relationship between the hardness of a substance and its solubility in hydrochloric acid, a law is "discovered." As another example, imagine a psychologist with an interest in how anxiety and complexity affect performance on cognitive tasks. He or she asks the following research question: "Does task complexity mediate the effect of anxiety on cognitive performance?" Answering this question involves studying the relationships among three variables: anxiety, task complexity, and cognitive performance. If the psychologist finds that there is a relationship between anxiety and performance but that it depends on task complexity, he or she is discovering a law (or laws) about human behavior. Similarly, a practitioner might wonder whether a relationship exists between the amount of treatment and improvement. It is reasonable to expect that gains in therapy do not continue in a linear fashion indefinitely. Indeed, at some point it is likely that gains will slow down or "level off." That is, after relatively rapid progress in the early stages of therapy, subsequent change comes more slowly. This is known in psychotherapy as the dose–response relationship (see Kadera, Lambert, & Andrews, 1996).

Hypotheses

The quality of an evaluative question rests in part on the ease with which it leads to testable hypotheses. Hypotheses are useful in basic research for several reasons. For one, doing research without them is like playing games of chance without first specifying the rules (Kerlinger, 1986): It is like rolling the dice first, seeing a *1* and a *3* and declaring the winning combination to be *4*. Unfortunately, rules constrain this kind of freedom. Hypotheses are a bit like rules: They are statements about relationships between variables.

As in scientific research, hypotheses guide practice evaluation efforts and assist in using resources efficiently. Good hypotheses follow directly from evaluative questions. Furthermore, well-worded hypotheses suggest the nature of the relationship under study, specify the direction of the relationship, mention the people in whom the relationship is to be studied, and carry implications for the evaluation design. For example, an hypothesis to answer the evaluative question "How much treatment does a client need before improvements begin to level off?" is "We achieve stable, clinically significant improvements in people with unipolar depression in eight or fewer sessions."

Operationalizing Variables

The more precise the variables specified in an hypothesis are, the easier they are to operationalize and measure. Consider fee arrangements: We might wonder whether billing practices relate to profitability. A formal evaluation question might be "Does time-of-service billing lead to more profitability of the practice than end-of-month billing?" An hypothesis following from this is: "Time-of-service billing leads to more net profit than end-of-month billing in a psychotherapy practice serving adult outpatients." The variables in this hypothesis are type of billing and profitability. It should be relatively easy to come up with measures of these variables. In contrast, the variables implied in the question "Do our substance abuse treatment services work?" are "substance abuse services" and "work"; they are so imprecise as to be unmeasurable. Hence we cannot answer the question.

Participants

It does us little good to have well-worded research questions involving well-chosen variables if we do not have the resources to carry out the evaluation plan. For instance, if the people we need to take part in the study are not available, or no design permits us to study the specific kind of relationship, then the question is not answerable. One of the advantages of practice evaluation over basic research is that it usually comes with built-in participants. In some cases, participants are all the clients of a practice, as when a practitioner attempts to find out how clients learned about his or her practice. Alternatively, they may be a subset of our clients, as in "Cognitive therapy is more effective than interpersonal therapy for adult clients diagnosed with major depression." In such situations it may be necessary to recruit from within the clients of a particular practice. For example, when outcome studies are the focus, volunteers must be obtained for various treatment and control groups.

In addition to clearly identified variables and participants, another important resource is the measures to use. The variables in the questions often can be operationalized in numerous ways, each of which has advantages and disadvantages. Should we use a self-report measure of anxiety, ratings by experienced clinicians, or self-observation? If we choose a self-report measure of anxiety, which one should we choose? Should we define task complexity in terms of the number of different steps involved in solving a problem or the number of alternative ways to reach solutions? Should our measure of cognitive performance be time to solution, quality of solution, novelty of solution, or some other characteristic?

Consider this question: "How many sessions of individual cognitive therapy are needed to produce stabilized, clinically significant improvement in adult clients with unipolar depression?" The variables involved are "amount of therapy" and "clinically significant improvement." One way to operationalize the first is in terms of the number of a certain type of individual therapy sessions a person receives. The simplest way to define clinically significant improvement is to consider a person to have improved when the score on a formal measure, such as the Beck Depression Inventory (BDI; Beck, Ward, Mendelsohn, Mock, & Erbaugh, 1961), moves from the clinical to the nonclinical, or "normal," range. Thus, a person with an initial score of 33 who drops to below 9 may be showing significant improvement in a clinical sense. The literature discusses other, more statistically sophisticated ways of defining "clinical significance" (e.g., Jacobson, Roberts, Berns, & McGlinchey, 1999; Lambert & Brown, 1996; Speer, 1992).

Design

The formal arrangements for collecting and using data to answer evaluation questions constitute the design of the study. Again, good evaluation questions make the design evident. For instance, the question "What is the relationship between distance traveled to reach the office and satisfaction with our services?" implies a straightforward relational design involving correlations between the variables of distance and satisfaction. Such designs are easy to develop. The example dealing with fee arrangements suggests an experimental design because it compares two ways of billing for their impact on profits: The type of billing (the independent variable) is hypothesized to lead to differences in profitability (the dependent variable). It is reasonable to imagine randomly assigning consecutive referrals to time-of-service or end-of-month billing arrangements and tracking the net revenues that they generate over some period of time.

Sometimes, however, for ethical and other reasons, we cannot rely on simple experimental designs. For example, suppose one has an interest in whether childhood sexual abuse leads to psychological maladjustment as an adult. We cannot manipulate the independent variable in this situation in order to demonstrate a causal relationship. Chapter 8 treats the subject of appropriate designs in more detail.

In many cases, the procedures for collecting data to test hypotheses are relatively straightforward. These are the best kind for busy practices. For example, most practices routinely track the number of sessions conducted with clients and the fees collected. Furthermore, service providers serious about assessing their effectiveness are likely to administer outcome measures, such as the BDI, on a regular basis. Other evaluation questions might present more challenging measurement issues, of course, but experience with evaluation develops skill at establishing and maintaining manageable systems, and modern technology makes the process highly efficient.

Analysis

After the data have been collected, the next step in the evaluative cycle is to analyze them. Analysis can take different levels of formality (see chapter 9). It is worth noting that optimal practice evaluation entails ongoing data analysis. One need not wait until the end and all data are available; indeed, when one collects data continually, the process can end when clear trends become evident. Often such trends are detectable visually, using graphs or charts. In addition, a variety of statistical analyses can confirm their presence. Thus, one does not always have to specify ending times for practice evaluation projects at the outset. We know we have enough data when we can confirm or reject the hypotheses. Then we can move on to interpreting the data and disseminating our findings.

Interpretation

Interpreting data involves deciding whether they confirm formal hypotheses. Working with individual clients in psychological treatment, we often entertain informal hypotheses, such as "If I use relaxation therapy and exposure plus response prevention, the problem will resolve itself." We apply the treatment over the course of some number of sessions and monitor its effectiveness. On a periodic basis we administer a formal outcome measure to confirm the client's progress. By examining scores on that measure, together with collateral information, we determine whether our original hypothesis is supported. Interpreting a variety of data in this way leads to conclusions concerning the effectiveness of our work with that client. It also alerts us to any shortcomings and to additional interventions the client may want to consider. Discussing these interpretations with the client is the first step in disseminating the results of our evaluation.

Dissemination

Sharing our findings is an extremely crucial aspect of the process (see chapter 13). Here it suffices to note that if the purpose of conducting evaluations is to learn how to run a practice effectively, logic requires us to communicate the results. When we do, others can react and give their own interpretations of the data. They can comment as well on aspects of the research design, including the measures and intervention approach. Reactions of professional colleagues can be especially useful in alerting practitioners to newer, better ways of doing things. Disseminating results widely throughout the professional community is important because people not intimately involved in the evaluation itself have the potential to be more objective.

Of course, it is extremely useful to discuss findings with our colleagues in the practice in order to hear their interpretations and reactions. Doing so permits us to refine our evaluation questions and undertake new studies. The result is a cumulative body of knowledge about the practice, with each study building on earlier ones. This process parallels the evolution of scientific knowledge. Research adds to the information we already have about certain phenomena and, in this sense, is cumulative. If we do not disseminate research outcomes to others, we limit the elaboration of scientific knowledge. Extensive formal mechanisms are therefore in place to communicate research findings. Thousands of professional journals and hundreds of professional conferences exist to provide forums for the exchange of scientific information.

The results of some practice evaluation efforts get disseminated through journals and professional conferences. When they do, it is because their purveyors want to influence fellow professionals. Other stakeholders may be the targets of dissemination as well, and the alert evaluator also considers tactics most likely to influence them.

Finally, it is worth considering that the person who talks about her or his work to others comes under their influence to some extent. That is, reactions to our descriptions shape our professional behavior in subtle ways. It is reasonable that the more talking (i.e., disseminating and sharing) practitioners do about their activities, the more likely their behavior is to change, presumably for the better. This is a good argument for group practices, in which multiple service providers work together and frequently discuss what they are doing with their clients. Informal dissemination such as this can have significant benefits for our professional effectiveness.

Applying the Practice Evaluation Cycle to Evaluating Direct Services

To illustrate the usefulness of the evaluation process diagrammed in Figure 3.1, let us consider typical examples one might face in providing psychological services. Dissatisfaction with the status quo leads clients to seek our help. A person might seek relief from anxiety or depression, a company might want help reducing high levels of employee turnover or, occasionally, a client might even seek help with preventing a future problem.

Ask Questions

The evaluation activities in Figure 3.1 start with a question. Notice that the client might ask, "How can I get over this depression?" or "How can we cut down on employee turnover?" The service provider and client collaborate to clarify the questions. Recall the earlier discussion of the difference between good and bad evaluative questions. Good ones involve definable relationships among measurable variables and lead to specific hypotheses. As described earlier in this chapter in their initial form, most questions clients ask are not adequate to drive our service delivery efforts, let alone any attempts to evaluate them.

State Hypotheses

Well-phrased evaluative questions lead easily to hypotheses. Again, the questions are an implicit part of service provision, not something unique to evaluation or research. The client's hypothesis is that receiving services will result in benefits. The practitioner's hypothesis is that by arranging for a particular type of intervention, the client's situation will improve (i.e., "treating this client with cognitive therapy will lead to reductions in depression"). Hypotheses related to direct services almost always involve causal relationships among variables, and the direction of the relationship is usually clear. Often, the service (independent variable) is seen as causing changes in some aspect of client functioning (dependent variable).

Identify Variables

To test an hypothesis, one must clarify the variables embedded in it. The process of defining the dependent variable involves collaboration between the client and the practitioner. For example, the organizational consultant may explore the concept of turnover with the client, providing information as to how the profession typically defines it. The client reacts to this definition and to suggestions the consultant makes for reducing turnover, and the two of them decide on a level of intervention satisfactory to the client. Similarly, the psychologist helps the client seeking to "get over depression" to clarify what that means. Definitions of independent variables are likely to come from the literature, although their implementation with individual clients involves a collaborative tailoring of the intervention to the client's situation. Treatment manuals (e.g., Beck, Rush, Shaw, & Emery, 1979) prescribe how cognitive therapy is conducted in general, for example, and practitioners modify the prescription to fit the particular client.

It is important to be clear about the independent variables in practice evaluations so as to know with confidence what leads to changes in clients' problems. To improve our practice, we must know exactly what was responsible for producing (or failing to produce) beneficial changes. Moreover, disseminating the results of our work to others, be they fellow psychologists at professional conferences or other stakeholders, such as third-party payers, requires precise description of procedures. In this way additional practitioners can evaluate them, providing important information as to their general usefulness.

Identify Participants

In practice evaluations the participants are usually evident. The service provider applies a procedure to a client. It is important to be clear about various characteristics of participants, however, and to document them as much as possible. Various attributes of the practitioner (e.g., age, gender, ethnicity, experience, formal education and credentials, theoretical orientation) and client (e.g., age, gender, ethnicity, marital status, education, problem severity) are worth tracking, especially if there is reason to think they might interact with the intervention and change its effectiveness.

Select Measures

Clarifying the variables involved in the evaluation is essential to selecting appropriate measures. Chapter 2 described Rosen and Proctor's (1981) three types of goals in the provision of psychological treatment: ultimate, instrumental, and intermediate. Ultimate goals are what the client wants to be different after receiving services, and instrumental goals are what the practitioner thinks must happen for that change to occur. To evaluate service effectiveness, one must have measures for the two types of goals.

The measures used for ultimate goals are likely to be different from those used for instrumental goals. They are typically more extensive, take more resources (e.g., time and expertise) to administer, and are constructed differently. To illustrate, one can assess the level of depression by self-report measures such as the BDI or the Center for Epidemiologic Studies–Depression Scale (Radloff, 1977), or a rating measure such as the Hamilton Rating Scale for Depression (HRSD; Hamilton, 1960). These measures vary in length, complexity, and administration time and generally are not appropriate to use as ongoing measures of treatment effectiveness. The HRSD requires a knowledgeable professional to interview the client, form an impression, and rate the extent to which depression is evident. The BDI is brief enough to use repeatedly over treatment sessions, but it is unsuitable for this because retesting alone tends to produce lower scores (Atkeson, Calhoun, Resick, & Ellis, 1982; Hammen, 1980; Sharpe & Gilbert, 1998). Moreover, measures of characteristics such as depression, anxiety, and self-esteem often are developed using psychometric procedures that favor stability or consistency. As such, they are not appropriately sensitive to change over short time intervals (Messick, 1983). Measures of ultimate goals are best to administer periodically, such as at the beginning of intervention, midway through it, at termination, and at follow up.

Measures of instrumental goals tend to be more specific and to focus on change in variables hypothesized to affect the ultimate goals. Self-observation of daily pleasurable activities might provide one measure of rewards improvement experienced by a client being treated in accord with Lewinsohn's reinforcement theory of depression (Lewinsohn & Hoberman, 1982). Similarly, self-observation of negative automatic thoughts or completion of the Daily Record of Dysfunctional Thoughts (DRDT; Beck et al., 1979) provide measures of distorted thinking relevant to Beck's cognitive therapy for treating depression. Measures of instrumental goals are administered repeatedly over the course of an intervention and are constructed to be sensitive to moment-by-moment change. They are essential to making ongoing adjustments in treatment to reflect the current status of the client. If progress is not sufficient, we can make appropriate changes, resulting in continual quality improvement (Maruish, 1994) and keeping the intervention on track. Moreover, the measures provide evaluative data as to the relevance of constructs that compose the interventionist's theory of change. If measures of ultimate goals show change in the absence of corresponding change in instrumental goals, the theory can be examined for possible revision. It is therefore helpful to select measures of ultimate goals to administer periodically as well as measures of instrumental goals to administer on an ongoing basis.

Scriven (1967) provided a distinction from another context that may be useful here: summative and formative assessment. Evaluation that we use continually and "to improve the course while it is still fluid" (p. 43) is *formative evaluation*, whereas evaluation that appraises the completed product is *summative*, according to Scriven. Monitoring the progress of therapy in the two examples above is formative assessment. The process of periodically evaluating the effects of psychological treatment —the ultimate goals—is summative assessment. The two forms of assessment are essential to effective program evaluation. They serve different purposes, though, and are constructed accordingly. Using summative measures in a formative context can understate effectiveness, just as using formative measures in a summative context can.

The selection of ultimate outcomes and instrumental goals, along with their associated measures, does not occur in a vacuum, to be sure, nor does it result from unquestioned acceptance of the changes the client wants. Effective human services involve the collaborative development of a case formulation. The provider and client work together to form an understanding of the changes sought, the variables represented in those changes, and the intervention most likely to bring about the changes. Extensive literature exists on the importance of careful case formulation (Bromley, 1986; Malatesta, 1995; Persons, 1991; Persons, Mooney, & Padesky, 1995; Schacht, 1991; Wilson, 1996). Although space does not permit detailed treatment of the subject here, it is worth observing that case formulation should be governed by a theory of behavior. The practitioner can discuss this theory with the client and use it to provide the conceptual context for identifying appropriate change targets and relevant measures.

Develop the Design

Once we know the variables involved in the intervention and have measures for them, we can proceed to deciding how to document the relationship between the variables. A simple, commonly used design involves assessing the client before and after treatment and examining changes in measures of the ultimate goals (i.e., summative measures). This approach is referred to as a single-case design with pretest and posttest measurement. The service provider should find the single-case designs illustrated in chapter 1 and chapter 8 to be helpful in demonstrating relationships between interventions and client change.

If a practitioner wishes to undertake large-scale practice evaluations, experimental designs, which involve the assignment of participants to experimental and control groups, can be useful. The research design depends on the nature of the relationship the hypothesis implies. The examples above suggest causal relationships, so experimental designs are most appropriate. Other hypotheses (e.g., "client self-disclosure is positively correlated with therapist self-disclosure") suggest relational designs because there is no clear assumption of causality.

Establish Data Collection Procedures

When the measures and design have been selected, it is a simple matter to determine data collection procedures. In the example involving a client with depression, the measure of the ultimate goal (e.g., the BDI) can be given before and after treatment, with ongoing monitoring of the instrumental goal using self-observation or diary methods (e.g., DRDT). Collecting data specific to instrumental goals is more challenging than data collection for ultimate goals: It requires greater frequency and is more labor intensive, and it relies more heavily on the client providing the data. Various clever tactics exist to facilitate ongoing measurement, including paging clients at random intervals to cue them to make observations (Csikszentmihalyi & Larson, 1987), outfitting clients with palmtop computers that beep to remind them (Shiffman, Hufford, Hickcox, Paty, Gnys, & Kassel, 1997), and having clients phone the practitioner's office and leave data on a voice-mail system. Whatever procedures are used, they are most successful when advance discussion takes place between the provider and the client. The importance of obtaining reliable, consistent information cannot be overstated, although it is something most clients do not appreciate when initially seeking services. Educating the client about the importance of data collection at the outset and showing how the data are used throughout service provision can be effective ways of gaining compliance with data collection procedures.

Collect Data

The intervention can begin at this point: The question is clear, testable hypotheses are available, variables are known, the client is described, measures of the variables are available, a design is at hand, and procedures for collecting the data are in place. This extensive preliminary work occurs before any significant intervention with the client. It sets the stage for effective service delivery in that it involves self-conscious consideration of precisely what the client wants to be different, how we know when differences occur, and how we go about collecting the information to tell us this.

Analyze Data

Although it appears as a distinct step in Figure 3.1, this step occurs concurrently with other activities. Data analysis is an ongoing process for the effective practitioner, even when formal, numerical data are not involved. The service provider obtains some type of information, however informal or subjective, on an ongoing basis from clients.

Data analysis involves organizing information so that it can be interpreted. Formal ways of doing this include generating statistics and creating graphic displays of the data and statistics (see chapter 9). Graphic displays can be useful because they show trends and patterns to which the practitioner can react and make appropriate adjustments. Even simple bar graphs can do a lot to show clients how much change has occurred (see Figure 3.2).

Interpret Data

Care must be taken in interpreting data from evaluation efforts. It is important to be sure that you understand the data fully before disseminating them to others. In Figure 3.2, the fact that the client's BDI score is still in the slightly depressed range is useful information and can help the client and practitioner plan relapse prevention strategies. In addition, it might lead the practitioner to recommend switching from individual to group treatment to bring the score down even further.

Disseminate Findings

When you are sure that you fully understand the implications of the data, share them with others. When discussing the findings with clients, it is important to put changes in perspective and provide answers to the clients' questions. For example, in response to the data in Figure 3.2, the client might ask "Does this mean I'm still depressed?" You should anticipate such questions and prepare effective responses.

Recall that telling others about your results is important in shaping more effective professional behavior. Interpreting the data for the client is the first step in dissemination, and the client's reaction will affect how you work with future clients. With the client's consent, show the results of your work to others in your practice and get their reactions. If you think there is something unique about the case or the way you handled it that might be of interest to other practitioners, present your findings to them. If the client consents, provide other stakeholders in the client's treatment with information about its effectiveness. Providing objective, comparative information such as that in Figure 3.2 to third-party payers can create favorable impressions that have benefits in terms of future referrals, more lenient session limits, and so on.

Figure 3.2

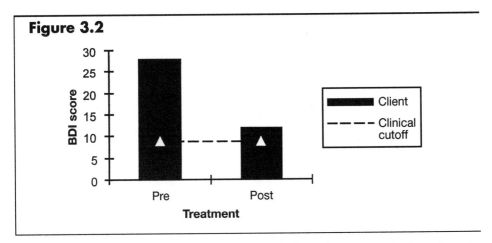

Change in depression for a client receiving psychological treatment. The bars show the Beck Depression Inventory (BDI) scores for a client being treated for depression. Before treatment, the client's score of 28 is substantially above the cutoff score that indicates clinically noteworthy levels of depression. The posttreatment score of 12 indicates considerable improvement.

Formulate New Questions

Reactions from those with whom you share your findings will provoke consideration of changes you can make in working with similar clients in the future. Colleagues in your practice might suggest changes in the therapeutic approach, such as combining your psychological treatment with pharmacotherapy. The managed care organization might tell you that your outcome is only average compared with that of other members of their panel. This information can motivate you to change your approach to increase its effectiveness. Changes based on others' reactions lead to new questions and position you to begin the evaluation cycle again.

Summary

Evaluative questions center on whether practice goals are being met. The type of question varies, depending on the maturity of the practice and on the stakeholders who see the outcome data. More advanced questions involve, for example, comparisons of the effectiveness of two or more treatment approaches. Discovering why a practice works can be important in retaining a competitive advantage because it allows service providers to retain effective treatment components while eliminating unnecessary ones, leading to reductions in overall costs.

The chapter draws parallels between the cycle of activities involved in scientific research and those relevant to service provision and its evaluation. The cyclical approach this chapter describes is essentially the same process most service providers use each time they take on a new client, although those steps are informal and rely on different terminology. The next time you provide services for an individual client, notice how closely you follow this cyclical process.

The process of effectively providing and evaluating services depends on adequately gathering and using information. Organizing the extensive data that are routinely available to practitioners is critical to using it successfully in evaluation activities, an area covered in the following chapter.

Supplemental Reading

Cormier, S., & Cormier, B. (1998). *Interviewing strategies for helpers: Fundamental skills and cognitive behavioral interventions* (4th ed.). Pacific Grove, CA: Brooks/Cole.

Kerlinger, F. N. (1986). *Foundations of behavioral research* (3rd ed.). New York: Holt, Rinehart & Winston.

Persons, J. B. (1991). Psychotherapy outcome studies do not accurately represent current models of psychotherapy: A proposed remedy. *American Psychologist, 46,* 99–106.

Wilson, G. T. (1996). Manual-based treatments: The clinical application of research findings. *Behaviour Research and Therapy, 34,* 295–314.

Types of Change in Human Services

The preceding chapters provided the theoretical and conceptual groundwork for examining the effectiveness of one's practice. This chapter begins to put meat on those conceptual bones. It starts with a review of the different components of a typical practice and narrows its focus to the direct practice component. After distinguishing between process and outcome variables, the discussion focuses on Howard's (Howard, Lueger, Maling, & Martinovich, 1993) phase model of change in human services. The chapter presents examples of measures associated with each of the three phases and emphasizes the importance of assessing effectiveness from multiple perspectives. Ways of appraising service use are becoming more important in the age of managed costs, and the chapter includes a brief discussion of such utilization measures. Finally, it introduces the controversial practice of provider profiling and gives examples of how third-party payers are building dossiers on providers that include data on effectiveness along with general characteristics of practices.

What Practice Components Should We Evaluate?

Evaluation begins with selecting one or more components of a practice to examine closely. As noted in chapter 3, direct services to clients are only one type of activity occurring in a practice. Even a small practice involves other components, including administrative activities, staff training or continuing education efforts, community service and, possibly research and development. Although most practitioners think first of direct services when approaching practice evaluation, each practice component requires assessment of its individual effectiveness. Much of the material in this chapter that focuses on evaluating the direct services component applies to other parts of the practice as well.

Process and Outcome Measures

The minimum elements of a satisfactory evaluation effort include measures of the process and the outcomes of service provision. *Process* refers to change occurring in the course of treatment that we believe relates to change in the problems precipitating services. Important changes occurring in clients outside of treatment also are process changes if they relate to changes in precipitating problems. Process change is necessary to achieve treatment outcomes. As described in chapter 2, Rosen and Proctor's (1981) concept of instrumental goals also is process related because such goals represent changes in the client during treatment that are required to accomplish the ultimate goals. Rosen and Proctor's concept of ultimate goals parallels the concept of treatment outcomes. These outcomes represent the change in the client's presenting complaint that occurs outside of treatment and represents the resolution of the reasons for undertaking treatment in the first place (*outcomes of service provision*).

Berman, Hurt, and Heiss (1996) defined an *optimal outcome* as "the least amount of treatment that produces the best result in the least restrictive setting, at the least cost to the patient, family, and community" (p. II.D.4). They identified three critical aspects of optimal outcomes: (a) clinical change, (b) satisfaction with the service received and the outcome produced, and (c) costs. Follette (1995) recommended identifying theoretically relevant variables that mediate the effects of treatment (i.e., mediating variables), which warrant attention along with the customary outcome variables. Follette's mediating variables seem much like the instrumental goals of Rosen and Proctor's (1981) analysis. Whereas Follette focused on the importance of mediating variables in evaluating the effectiveness of theory-driven treatment, Rosen and Proctor's conceptualization appears more generally applicable to theory- and non-theory-driven treatments alike.

Process and outcome measures are critical to any effort at continuous quality improvement. Focusing exclusively on outcomes tells us whether change has occurred, but it does not tell us why. Only by having objective data on process variables can we understand variation in outcomes and ultimately reduce that variation. With appropriate ongoing measurement in place, one can make changes in process that improve outcomes. The most comprehensive evaluations include objective and subjective measures of both process and outcome variables. At a minimum, practice evaluations include subjective measures of the satisfaction of the client and the practitioner along with objective measures of change in the client. Table 4.1 outlines the minimum elements of a practice evaluation. It is easy to see how complexity can rise rather rapidly as the number of stakeholders increases.

The model in Table 4.1 includes 24 different measures. Of course, every evaluation does not involve all the stakeholders shown in the table. At a minimum, the first two rows of the model would be included, requiring at least eight measures. The viability of the practice, however, can depend heavily on impressions of other stakeholders, such as payers and referral sources. Wonderful data of both process and outcome variety can come from the client and the practitioner, but if they do not impress the payer, implications for the practice can be negative.

Although the approach depicted in Table 4.1 is most relevant to evaluating the direct services component of a practice, one can evaluate other components using a similar framework. The stakeholders are likely to be different, but the need for both process and outcome variables is the same. For example, the administrative service component of a large practice is likely to have several personnel engaged in a variety of activities that support the overall mission of the practice, such as appointments management, filing, office management, bill payment, and human resources. Assessing the effectiveness of administrative services could include measures relating to each activity, but to keep the illustration simple, we focus on appointment management. Processes here include scheduling appointments, reminding clients of upcoming appointments, and notifying them of any changes. Objective measures of the processes include the percentage of clients receiving mailed or telephoned reminders, the time between initial office contact and the initial appointment, and the cost of providing reminders. Subjective process measures include client ratings of their satisfaction with the ease of making appointments and the cordiality of the staff in arranging them. Outcomes for the appointments management function of the administrative services component could include objective data on the percentage of clients keeping appointments and subjective ratings by the staff of their effectiveness in handling these functions.

Table 4.1

Minimal Elements to Include in Practice Evaluation

Stakeholder	Process variables		Outcome variables	
	Satisfaction	Clinical change	Satisfaction	Clinical change
Client	Client rates how long the wait was for services	Client records negative thoughts daily	Client rates how happy he or she is with benefits of intervention	Client completes an objective measure of depression
Practitioner	Practitioner rates effort client is putting into treatment	Practitioner monitors client's negative thoughts using objective measure over course of treatment	Practitioner rates own satisfaction with effects produced	Practitioner administers objective outcome measure to assess accomplishment of ultimate goal
Payer	Payer indicates satisfaction with the way in which services are being handled	Payer tracks changes in client's work attendance over course of treatment	Payer rates satisfaction with changes seen in client	Payer completes objective measure indicating changes in work functioning after treatment
Significant others	Spouse rates ease of accessing services	Spouse completes daily ratings on client's mood	Spouse rates overall satisfaction with changes in client after treatment	Spouse completes objective measure of changes in client relevant to the ultimate goal of treatment
Referral source–community	Referral sources rate how quickly calls are returned	Referral sources rate client's behavior periodically over the course of treatment	Referral sources rate their satisfaction with changes produced in client	Referral sources complete objective measure relevant to the ultimate goal of treatment
Researchers	Researchers rate ease of access to client's ongoing data	Researchers monitor client's physiological reactions to stimuli presented during treatment sessions	Researchers complete measure assessing practitioner's cooperation throughout the course of treatment	Researchers complete objective measure relevant to client's achievement of the ultimate goal of treatment

Note. The list of stakeholders in the table is representative and not meant to be exhaustive. The notes include examples of the types of measure one might use.

Because of its central importance, the remainder of the chapter focuses on measures of the direct services component of a practice. In doing so, we adopt Howard's (Howard et al., 1993) phase model of change (see also Sperry, Brill, Howard, & Grissom, 1996). Although the purpose of this model is to assess change in psychotherapy, it has clear implications for assessing other types of human services as well.

Howard's Phase Model of Change

Howard et al. (1993) studied the relationship between change in psychotherapy and the number of sessions provided through a meta-analysis of 15 studies involving more than 2,000 patients receiving a variety of types of therapy. Data from clinicians treating a variety of problems yielded the dose–response relationship presented in Figure 4.1. Howard, Moras, Brill, Martinovich, and Lutz (1996) reported that 48% to

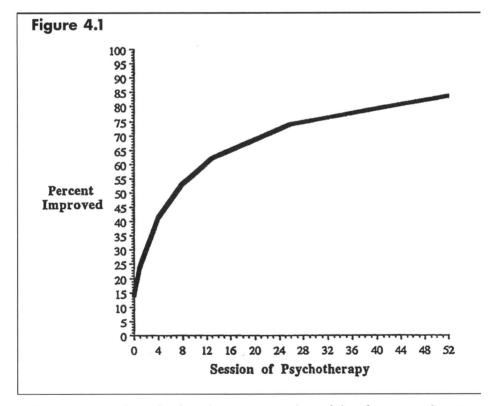

Dose–response relationship based on a meta-analysis of data from 15 studies. From *Treatment Outcomes in Psychotherapy and Psychiatric Interventions* (p. 42), by L. Sperry, P. L. Brill, K. I. Howard, and G. R. Grissom, 1996, New York: Brunner/Mazel. Copyright 1996 by Brunner/Mazel. Adapted with permission.

58% of patients can be expected to show measurable improvement after about eight sessions. The curve in Figure 4.1 accelerates negatively, indicating that most of the benefit occurs in the earlier part of therapy. More recently, Kadera, Lambert, and Andrews (1996) expanded on Howard's work, finding a somewhat slower rate of improvement.

From this dose–response relationship, Howard et al. (1993) conceptualized three phases to the change process in psychotherapy. In the *remoralization phase*, the client comes to treatment demoralized and feeling little hope for improvement. The task of the practitioner is to "remoralize" the client, give hope, and reestablish a sense of positive well-being. According to Sperry et al. (1996), remoralization can result from interventions of various types, including talking to someone, taking a vacation, or taking medication. The sense of distress abates relatively early in treatment and is sufficient for some clients to move on with their lives, requiring no further services. Other clients need additional intervention and move into what Howard et al. referred to as the *remediation phase*. Here the focus is on alleviating the client's symptoms that led to seeking therapy in the first place. Working with the client to achieve symptomatic relief can take 3 or 4 months of treatment, or about 16 sessions. For a substantial percentage of clients, this relief is sufficient for them to terminate services. Clients who see that the problems motivating their involvement in treatment have been with them consistently through their lives and interfere with attaining their goals move into a third phase, the *rehabilitation phase* of treatment. The focus then becomes the unlearning of old patterns and the learning of replacement patterns of behavior—new ways of responding to life's challenges. This process can take many more months (even years) of intervention, depending on the client, therapist, intervention, setting, and other variables.

Howard et al. (1993) reported that change in psychotherapy is an orderly process that moves through these stages sequentially; the same logic can be applied to services other than psychotherapy, such as physical therapists, speech and language clinicians, personal trainers, and dietitians. To illustrate, consider the large corporation seeking the services of an organizational consultant to deal with problems of low workforce productivity. The company may have tried a variety of approaches to dealing with the problem on its own and may now be experiencing some distress at its lack of success and its deteriorating financial condition. The corporate leadership might feel that the situation is acute and have real concern about the company's ability to remain in business. Phase I (remoralization) intervention efforts with the organization would be to reassure its leaders that the situation is not hopeless, that something can be done, and that the consultant has the skills and resources to help the company turn things around. Phase II (remediation) efforts follow the regained optimism with specific interventions aimed at increasing productivity in the short run. Employee incentive programs, improved training for frontline supervisors and managers, and small changes in organizational structure can be effective at this stage. Phase III (rehabilitation) interventions are likely to follow the successes of the earlier phases with more extensive organizational changes. Divesting itself of peripheral enterprises and refocusing on its core business, arranging capital expenditures for new plants and equipment, and shifting production to lower wage locations would be some long-term steps the company could take to respond more effectively to challenges of the contemporary marketplace.

To apply Howard's phase model in practice evaluation, it is useful to have measures appropriate to assessing the type of change specific to each phase. Thus, we might arrange to assess a client's general morale or sense of well-being (remoralization), the amount of symptomatic distress the client is experiencing (remediation), and finally, the client's functioning in everyday life (rehabilitation). Howard et al. (1995) assessed the quality of psychotherapeutic intervention by measuring change in all three phases, tapping well-being, symptoms, and current life functioning. Their outpatient-tracking assessment system called COMPASS tracks progress in treatment using client and therapist measures of each type of change. The following sections describe the COMPASS system in more detail.

Phase I Measures: Assessing Morale or General Well-Being

The COMPASS system assesses well-being using the four-item Subjective Well-Being Scale (Howard et al., 1995), which includes content related to stress, health and energy, psychological adjustment, and satisfaction with current life circumstances. Despite its brevity, the Subjective Well-Being Scale appears to be internally consistent ($\alpha = .79$) and stable over time ($r = .82$, 1-week interval). In addition, its scores converge with generally accepted measures of well-being, such as Watson and Tellegen's (1985) measure of negative affect ($r = -.70$), their measure of positive affect ($r = .51$), and Dupuy's (1977) General Well-Being Scale ($r = .79$).

Phase II Measures: Assessing Current Symptoms

Howard et al. (1995) also assessed client symptomatology using their 40-item Current Symptoms Scale, a self-report measure developed from an analysis of the signs and symptoms of six commonly occurring diagnoses listed in the *Diagnostic and Statistical Manual of Mental Disorders, Third Edition Revised* (American Psychiatric Association, 1987) along with symptoms of substance abuse. It provides a total score as well as subscale scores representing each of the seven diagnoses. Again, this scale shows good psychometric characteristics; internal consistency (α) ranges from .60 to .88 for the subscales and .94 for the total score. Stability over a 3- to 4-week period ranges from .65 to .83 for the subscales and is .85 for the total score. The Current Symptoms Scale has some concurrent validity as well; its total score correlates .91 with the total score of an abbreviated version of the Symptom Checklist–90 (SCL-90; Derogatis, 1983). In addition, its Depression subscale scores correlate .87 with the Beck Depression Inventory (Howard et al., 1995).

Phase III Measures: Assessing Current Life Functioning

The 24-item Current Life Functioning Scale assesses functioning in everyday life activities. It is a self-report measure in which the client indicates the extent to which emotional or psychological difficulties are interfering with performance in six major areas: family, health and grooming, intimate relationships, self-management, social relationships, and work–school–household activities. The internal consistency (α) of the total score on this measure is .93, with a temporal stability of .76 (3- to 4-week interval). Internal consistencies of the subscales range from .71 to .85, with temporal stabilities of between .42 and .79. Howard et al. (1995) did not report validity information for this measure. In the COMPASS system, an overall Mental Health Index (MHI) score results from summing the three self-report measures just described. The MHI is internally consistent ($\alpha = .87$) and temporally stable ($r = .82$; 3- to 4-week interval).

Other Outcome Measures

Howard et al.'s (1995) measures are not unique; indeed, hundreds of others exist. In reviewing outcome studies in psychotherapy alone, Froyd, Lambert, and Froyd (1996) identified 1,430 different measures. Among some of the more recent, widely used instruments are the OQ-45 (Ogles, Lambert, & Masters, 1996), the MOS 36-Item Short-Form Health Survey (SF-36; Ware & Sherbourne, 1992), the SCL-90 (Derogatis, 1983), and the BASIS-32 (Eisen, Grob, & Klein, 1986). Of these, the SF-36 is considered by some to be the "single best instrument" (Berman et al., 1996, p. II.D.9) for assessing outcomes in behavioral health care. Among its advantages are its psychometric soundness, its wide familiarity, its use in a number of health outcomes research efforts, and its availability in the public domain. In addition, the SF-36 covers eight different health-related areas, among which are limitations in physical and social activities as a result of health problems, pain, general mental health, limitations in usual role activities, and vitality. Examples of other measures are available in Fischer and Corcoran (1994); Goldman, Mitchell, and Egelson (1997); Ogles et al. (1996); Sederer and Dickey (1996); and Strupp, Horowitz, and Lambert (1997), and on the Internet at http://ericae.net/testcol.htm.

Multiple Evaluative Perspectives

As illustrated in Table 4.1, it is important to assess intervention effectiveness from the viewpoint of multiple stakeholders (Lambert, 1994), a difficult task with quality of life because of its inherently subjective nature. The more objective variables of psychological and physical symptoms as well as life functioning are easy to see from different perspectives, however. Howard et al. (1995) included measures in the COMPASS system to be completed by the clinician to complement the self-reports of the client. For example, the Global Assessment Scale (GAS; Endicott, Spitzer, Fleiss, & Cohen, 1976) provides an overall rating of the client's current functioning. Interrater reliabilities and temporal stabilities for these scores are adequate and correlate positively with greater rater experience and shorter time intervals, respectively (Howard et al., 1995).

In addition to the GAS, clinicians provide ratings of client functioning in each of the six life functions mentioned above. Summed ratings for all six areas are internally consistent (α = .86) and stable over time (r = .77; 2- to 3-week interval), even when different raters are used at the time points. Temporal stabilities for the subscale scores range from .58 to .70 over the same time interval. The sum of the six subscales' scores correlates with the GAS (r = .74), and separate subscale scores' correlations with the GAS range from .47 to .67. Neither Howard et al. (1995) nor Sperry et al. (1996) presented data pertaining to interrater reliabilities for the subscale scores.

Comparable with the MHI, which combines the client's self-report scores, the Clinical Assessment Index (CAI) combines clinician ratings to arrive at a composite score. The instrument includes a two-item rating of the clinician's impression of the client's subjective well-being along with the GAS rating and the sum of the ratings for the six areas of life functioning. It is not clear just how one combines the scores, but it is likely that one simply adds them together. The internal consistency of the CAI is .84; its temporal stability, .77 (2- to 3-week interval; different raters at Times 1 and 2).

Although not reported by Howard et al. (1995), it is likely that the client and therapist perspectives on these outcome measures are not in perfect correspondence. Ample evidence in the research literature on psychotherapy outcomes points to differences in assessment of therapy effectiveness that stem from the source of the information (Beutler & Hamblin, 1986; Eugster & Wampold, 1996; Lambert, 1994). Most studies to date have involved a limited number of perspectives, usually the client's and the therapist's. For example, when researchers use multiple outcome measures to assess change—some involving client self-report and others involving various types of input from therapists—factor analyses frequently result in a client and therapist factor (Beutler & Hamblin, 1986).

Unfortunately with few exceptions (e.g., Eugster & Wampold, 1996), much of the research on the convergence of different perspectives in evaluating treatment outcomes confounds the source of information and the assessment method. That is, client data usually come from self-reports, whereas therapist data come from informant reports or direct observation methods. When factor analyses show separate client and therapist factors, they are comparing self-report and informant-report factors. Is it the perspective or the method that causes the differences? Eugster and Wampold held method constant and found that rating evaluations of psychotherapy sessions by client and therapist were substantially unrelated. Future research would do well to compare sources while holding method of assessment constant. Meanwhile, the prudent practice evaluator would do well to include outcome measures from a variety of stakeholders.

Continuous Measurement

A hallmark of Howard's work is the repeated assessment of clinical outcomes over the course of treatment. Data are obtained using the measures of the COMPASS system at frequent intervals, usually every third session. This schedule permits ongoing tracking of therapy effectiveness and the use of data to alter the treatment if progress is not forthcoming.

The COMPASS system also permits clients to provide their impressions of the quality of the *therapeutic bond* on a regular basis over the course of treatment. The concept of therapeutic bond involves three components of the relationship between therapist and client: working alliance, empathic resonance, and mutual affirmation. Briefly, working alliance deals with the perceived effort put into the treatment by the therapist and the client. Empathic resonance involves the client's perception of the extent to which the therapist understands him or her. Mutual affirmation relates to the sense of openness, caring, and trust between the clinician and the client (Sperry et al., 1996). The 12-item Therapeutic Bond Scale (TBS) consists of four items tapping each of these three constructs. It is internally consistent ($\alpha = .88$) and modestly stable across three sessions ($r = .62$).

By using the MHI, the CAI, and the TBS repeatedly over the course of therapy, one can relate progress as assessed by the CAI and MHI to the quality of the therapeutic relationship as perceived by the client. One can argue positively for maintaining treatment when progress is continuous in terms of both MHI and CAI data and when TBS scores are satisfactory. Figure 4.2 illustrates progress in psychotherapy by a single woman in her 20s receiving psychotherapy. Note that steady progress is evident in MHI scores across the 11 therapy sessions. CAI scores also reflect progress, if not as consistently. The quality of the therapeutic

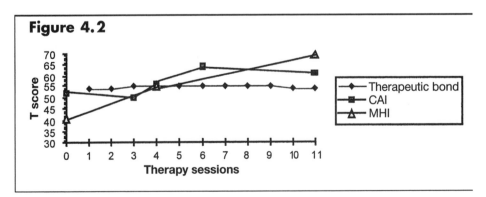

Figure 4.2

Continuous assessment of therapist and client views of therapy progress. CAI = Clinical Assessment Index; MHI = Mental Health Index. From *Treatment Outcomes in Psychotherapy and Psychiatric Interventions* (p. 86), by L. Sperry, P. L. Brill, K. I. Howard, and G. R. Grissom, 1996, New York: Brunner/Mazel. Copyright 1996 by Brunner/Mazel. Adapted with permission.

bond is slightly above average at the outset and remains that way throughout treatment. According to Howard et al. (1995; Sperry et al., 1996), a T score of 60 on the MHI represents normal functioning. The client in Figure 4.2 reaches this criterion by the 7th session.

When continuous progress is not forthcoming and TBS scores are not satisfactory, one can argue for changes in treatment. Figure 4.3 illustrates the steady deterioration of a client over the course of 24 sessions of psychotherapy, as documented by scores on the MHI and the CAI. Moreover, therapeutic bond ratings start below average and stay there. The therapist evidently was not aware of the ongoing data and therefore did not have the opportunity to adjust treatment accordingly.

If continuous progress monitoring is to have maximum therapeutic impact, therapists need to have access to it on a regular basis. Indeed, clinicians monitoring progress against instrumental goals over the course of treatment can fine-tune their intervention to maintain or accelerate that progress. In the example here, the therapist or other stakeholder (e.g., third-party payer) could take steps to alter treatment be-

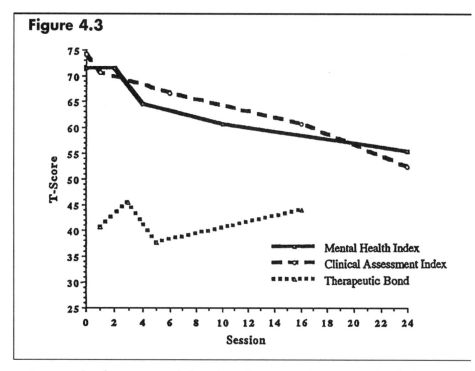

Figure 4.3

An example of a treatment failure. From *Treatment Outcomes in Psychotherapy and Psychiatric Interventions* (p. 89), by L. Sperry, P. L. Brill, K. I. Howard, and G. R. Grissom, 1996, New York: Brunner/Mazel. Copyright 1996 by Brunner/Mazel. Reprinted with permission.

fore completing 24 sessions. One obvious concern is the quality of the therapeutic bond—if it does not improve, the managed care organization (MCO) or other referral source can offer the client another therapist, with whom the relationship might be better.

These two rather uncomplicated examples illustrate the notion that intervention quality improves when relevant information is available to appropriate stakeholders. Note that the measures in the examples focus on outcome. As such, they do a good job of telling us whether the client is getting better. They are less informative with regard to why the client is changing, however. For optimal intervention quality, data as to what aspects of it are working (and not working) are critical. To get this kind of information, process measures are necessary.

For example, in the scenario in Table 4.1, the client is keeping daily records of negative thoughts; this record keeping documents a process variable (i.e., reduction of negative thoughts), which is a means toward achieving the ultimate goal of reduced depression, an outcome variable. Periodically readministering the depression measure (to examine the outcome variable) throughout therapy should reveal the impact of changes in negative thoughts (the process variable). If negative thoughts are decreasing without concomitant changes in depression, there is a lag in the relationship, another variable plays a role, or perhaps there is no relationship at all.

When the design of an intervention is theory driven, relevant instrumental or process goals become apparent (Follette, 1995). If the whole enterprise has a theoretical basis, so much the better, because the theory provides the variables to assess and monitor. More important yet, the theory suggests the nature of the relationship between the variables. For example, the theory might dictate that more of a particular treatment component leads to a particular outcome.

Assessment Versus Measurement

It is perhaps useful at this point to call attention to a difference between assessment and measurement in practice evaluation. Haring (1977) observed that assessment involves determining the status of a person, organization, or object at a particular moment in time; it is static, like a snapshot that freezes the object of the lens for a split second. In contrast, measurement involves repeatedly determining the status of a person, organization, or object as it changes over time; it is dynamic. When we administer a final outcome measure to evaluate the effect of an intervention, we are assessing that outcome. When we obtain data on measures repeatedly over the course of that intervention, we are measuring its progress. In terms of the material covered in this chapter, measurement involves the use of process measures; assessment, outcome measures.

Objectivity Versus Subjectivity in Practice Evaluation

One of the elements of the minimal practice evaluation depicted in Table 4.1 is satisfaction. Corporate America is very much concerned with customer relations and responding intelligently to customer behavior so as to increase the sales of products or services, as evidenced by the ubiquitous customer satisfaction surveys at auto shops, restaurants, and hotels. Indeed, customer satisfaction has become somewhat of an academic discipline in its own right, complete with its own professional journal (e.g., *Journal of Consumer Satisfaction, Dissatisfaction, and Complaining Behavior*).

Satisfaction measures also play an important role in assessing health care effectiveness, often eclipsing other ways of determining service benefits. Their inclusion in Table 4.1 alongside measures of clinical change emphasizes the fact that they assess an important aspect of effectiveness. Satisfaction is the client's subjective impression of "(a) the degree of change in ultimate or instrumental goals, (b) the treatment procedures, and (c) the therapist" (Foster & Mash, 1999, p. 314). There is danger, however, in the common assumption that satisfaction is an index of whether a product or service is any good or whether people will buy it. In psychotherapy, numerous factors contribute to satisfaction over and above the amount of change the client experiences, including the friendliness of the practitioner, the comfort of the service setting, the apparent expertise of the practitioner, access to the offices, and ease of making and changing appointments. None of these is equivalent to actual achievement of ultimate goals.

Although customer satisfaction measures are essential to a comprehensive evaluation of any service, problems can arise when one gives excessive weight to them relative to more objective measures of change. A recent *Newsweek* article emphasized the difference between satisfaction and other measures of the quality of services provided by health maintenance organizations (HMOs; Spragins, 1997). The article pointed to the fact that the members of an HMO really have no way to evaluate the adequacy of its services comprehensively. Referring to a

Massachusetts study of 17 HMOs, the story noted that some of the HMOs who were best at satisfying customers were among the worst on other measures of quality. At the same time, some of the best plans medically produced only mediocre satisfaction ratings. The article discussed the relationship between overall health of a service's members and their satisfaction with its services. It is the rare HMO that reports satisfaction by level of health. It would be informative to do so, however, given the generally known tendency of sicker patients, who use the services more, to rate them lower. It is not difficult to obtain high satisfaction ratings from customers who are essentially healthy and use HMO services infrequently.

Kidder and Judd (1986) provided an illuminating empirical example of how client or customer satisfaction measures can show positive outcomes when all objective criteria contradict them. They review the findings of a well-known study reported by McCord (1978). McCord looked at whether childhood intervention can prevent subsequent criminal behavior. In this study, Cabot, a physician in Boston, randomly assigned more than 500 boys ages 5 to 13 to treatment or control groups. For boys in the treatment group, counselors visited them and their families about twice a month to provide counseling and assistance in obtaining medical, social, and welfare services. In addition, tutoring, summer camps, psychiatric services, and other community programs were offered to boys in the treatment group. Cabot's study continued over a 5-year period beginning in 1939. McCord and her colleagues conducted a follow-up study of the boys some 30 years later. Through painstaking efforts the researchers were able to locate 95% of the study participants. Using a variety of measures, including court records, reports and statistics from psychiatric facilities and programs for alcoholism, and self-reports from the men themselves, McCord was unable to find differences between the two groups on many of the measures. When differences were found, they surprisingly were in the direction of worse outcomes for the treatment group. Of the more challenging boys, roughly one-third wound up with juvenile records regardless of whether they were in the treatment or the control group. Furthermore, men from the treatment group were more likely to commit multiple crimes than were men from the control group, suggesting that the treatment might actually have been harmful.

According to Kidder and Judd (1986), the single measure on which the treated men showed clearly favorable outcomes was their subjective evaluation of program effectiveness. When asked whether the program had been helpful to them, a substantial majority of the treated men said they thought it had been, and many of them provided anecdotal comments to support their opinions. Kidder and Judd pointed out that client satisfaction measures are minimally useful unless they are provided by informed clients, and they asked whether the treated men in McCord's evaluation of Cabot's experiment would have made such positive appraisals if they had known of the "subsequent criminal records, poor health, lower occupational standing, and earlier deaths of the treatment group?" (p. 419). The standard for using client satisfaction measures proposed by Kidder and Judd appears to restrict them to circumstances in which clients have additional information about service effectiveness besides whether it made them feel good.

Kidder and Judd (1986) pointed to other reasons to distrust satisfaction measures; among other research, they cite the findings that parents almost universally evaluate compensatory educational programs positively (e.g., McDill, McDill, & Sprehe, 1969). They also noted the findings of workers reporting satisfaction with their jobs, whereas other information indicates that dissatisfaction of the same workers is widespread (Gutek, 1978). Furthermore, people are likely to report high levels of personal satisfaction in situations in which they rate the general satisfaction of others as low. In other words, they see their experience as the exception.

An overlooked but potentially more serious problem associated with the use of such measures is that they actually can undermine service quality. To illustrate, suppose a novice psychotherapist sympathizes strongly with his or her "victim" client and spends inordinate time "supporting" that client in the client's view of his or her "awful" circumstances. It would not be surprising to find such a therapist rated higher on customer satisfaction measures than colleagues who spend less time sympathizing, more time pointing out how the client is responsible for part of the predicament, and suggesting homework and other extratherapy "work" for the client. Now, suppose empirical studies show that the less sympathetic approach is more effective. If an MCO relies excessively on satisfaction measures, it might approve more work for the "sympathetic" therapist, even though the less sympathetic one produces more lasting client change. The obvious result can be a lowering of the overall quality of services customers receive from the MCO.

In health care, customer satisfaction measures may receive more emphasis than is desirable. Perhaps this is because measures more directly related to service quality are just beginning to make their appearance. When data begin to circulate showing actual success rates of health care providers for various types of problems, satisfaction measures receive less emphasis. The ready availability of large amounts of information by way of the Internet hastens the arrival of data that allow comparison of service providers on standard measures of effectiveness. Meanwhile, satisfaction measures continue to have an important place in service evaluation. Indeed, some standardization is beginning to appear in their use as well.

Examples of satisfaction measures include those developed by the National Committee on Quality Assurance (Iglehart, 1996), the American Managed Behavioral Health Association, the National Alliance for Mental Illness, and MHCA. MHCA's Client Satisfaction Survey was developed from interviews with clients receiving behavioral health services at 10 different locations throughout the United States. Critical service incidents were identified in the interviews and became the basis for items in the measure. Subsequent factor analyses yielded three domains: personal therapy perceptions, impressions of the physical environment, and perceptions about the nature of interactions with staff. Each of the domains has a high degree of internal consistency, with αs ranging from .94 to .96, with an overall scale reliability of .98 (MHCA, 1995). Interactions with staff receive the highest ratings from clients, on average. Of the more than 3,000 surveys analyzed, the mean rating of satisfaction with staff interactions is 4.0 on a scale of 1 (poor) to 5 (excellent). Even the domain with the lowest ratings (physical environment) received a high mean (3.6). Clients completing the MHCA Client Satisfaction Survey also rate "the degree to which treatment helped" with their problem. It is interesting that the respondents' perceptions of benefit correlate highly and positively with their satisfaction with services. These subjective impressions do not correlate well with actual clinical change, however, a finding consistent with McCord's (1978) findings for predelinquent youth.

Lebow (1982) summarized research showing that satisfaction with behavioral health services relates to global judgments by clients of benefits derived; it does not relate as strongly to more specific judgments (e.g., whether communication between family members is better), however. Consistent with this finding is Attkisson and Zwick's (1982) report of a low correlation between client satisfaction and symptom improvement, with only 10% of the variance shared between them. Sperry et al. (1996) noted that another problem is that healthier clients at the outset of therapy report more improvement during treatment and higher levels of satisfaction at its end. In developing the COMPASS system, the authors also observed a statistically nonsignificant correlation between clinical improvement and client satisfaction, a finding that was true for clients completing treatment and those still receiving it.

In summary, subjective measures of clients' perceptions of services are an important element of comprehensive practice evaluation efforts. Satisfaction measures are likely to reveal whether the client will speak positively of the services to others and whether the client will return for services in the future. Furthermore, they are likely to correlate with the client's perceptions of change brought about by the service. It is unclear whether it makes sense to apply the strict standards implied by Kidder and Judd (1986)—that client satisfaction measures should be limited to situations in which the client is truly informed about service effectiveness—doing so seems unduly restrictive. Subjective and objective perceptions can inform comprehensive practice evaluation efforts because they often result from different environmental or service variables. Having information of both types continuously available can lead to optimum improvements in service quality.

Quality-of-Life Measures

Recent years have seen a shift in the focus of outcomes assessment in medicine from a relatively narrow concern with disease treatment and prevention to broader issues involving subjective assessments of the overall quality of life. Heroic medical and technological efforts can result in the maintenance of life, although the patient's perceived quality of life may not be high. With regard to behavioral health, it has become common to distinguish between services that are "medically necessary" and those that are needed to enhance the quality of life. MCOs and insurance companies are more apt to reimburse services meeting the medical necessity criterion, not those aimed primarily at improving quality of life. At the same time, there is increasing recognition that quality of life is just as important an outcome for evaluating health care services as are medical or psychological symptoms (Frisch, 1998).

The definition of what is medically necessary can vary. A common approach is to define it in terms of scores of particular diagnostic groups on measures of psychological health. As noted earlier, Sperry et al. (1996) used a T score of 60 on the MHI as a cutoff, with scores above that point being outside the medically necessary range. This decision stems from defining medical necessity as the point at which a person's score is more like that of a patient than that of a nonpatient. Kadera et al. (1996) warned of the hazards of relying on scores from a single instrument in reaching such decisions.

Frisch (1998) made a strong case for moving beyond lists of symptoms or objective measures of functioning and to measures specifically targeting quality of life. Although assessing this construct can be a daunting task (Gladis, Gosch, Dishuk, & Crits-Christoph, 1999; Phillips & Rosenblatt, 1992), specific measures now exist for this purpose (e.g., Ferrans & Powers, 1992; Frisch, Cornell, Villanueva, & Retzlaff, 1992; Keith & Schalock, 1992; Ruta, Garratt, Leng, Russell, & MacDonald, 1994). Discussing the definition of quality of life, Frisch suggested that it represents the extent to which one has achieved the "best possible way to live" (p. 19). If a person reports enjoying him- or herself, being happy, and doing things that make life worthwhile, that person is likely to have a high quality of life. Frisch characterized quality of life as an "inherently subjective, personal phenomenon" (p. 23) that is cognitively mediated and not equal to objective factors such as functional effectiveness or freedom from physical and psychological symptoms.

Three measures specific to quality of life that might be useful in practice evaluation include the Quality of Life Inventory (Frisch et al., 1992), the Satisfaction With Life Scale (SWLS; Pavot & Diener, 1993), and the Quality of Life Index (QLI; Ferrans & Powers, 1992). These range in comprehensiveness from the 5-item SWLS to the 64-item QLI. Overall scores are provided for each measure, and scores for four subscales (health, social/economic, psychological/spiritual, family) are available with the QLI as well. Limited validity data are available for these measures, although their favorable psychometric qualities provide a basis for more such evidence in the future.

Explicitly behavioral approaches to assessing happiness are evident in studies of people with severe disabilities (Favell, Realon, & Sutton, 1996; Green & Reid, 1996). Noting that such people often lack well-developed verbal ways of expressing satisfaction, Green and Reid developed and validated a direct observation measure of behavior "generally associated with subjective feelings of happiness" (p. 69). Observed responses included facial expressions such as smiling and vocalizations occurring while smiling, such as laughing or yelling. These responses were more frequent in the presence of preferred compared with nonpreferred stimuli and when engaging in certain "fun activities."

Because of the general relationships that exist between quality of life and such variables as physical illness (Anderson, Kiecolt-Glaser, &

Glaser, 1994), psychological problems (Baruffol, Gisle, & Corten, 1995), and health care expenditures (Ware, 1986), measures of quality of life are likely to become routine in assessing the effectiveness of health care services in the future. These measures can effectively supplement other subjective measures, such as those tapping satisfaction.

Utilization Measures

A more objective type of process variable is the so-called "utilization" measure, such as the number of sessions clients cancel, their promptness in arriving for sessions, and whether they remain for the entire course of treatment. Measures of this sort seem indirectly related to satisfaction and may serve as good supplements to satisfaction measures. It is unlikely that a satisfied client is habitually late, cancels numerous appointments, or drops out of treatment early. Ongoing monitoring of these variables might provide sensitive ways of detecting problems with service quality. Again, however, it is important to remember the independence of satisfaction measures and other objective data. As Gutek (1978) noted, in the work context, ratings of satisfaction correlate weakly with objective data on such variables as absenteeism and turnover. In the human services sector, it is likely that utilization measures will correlate modestly with satisfaction measures, if at all.

Calibrating Measures of Service Effectiveness

Practice evaluators face a substantial challenge developing measures that consumers can understand. When a merchant lowers the price of an article from $20 to $10, the meaning of the change is immediately apparent. When a program of therapy produces a decrease of 10 points on the State–Trait Anxiety Scale (Spielberger, 1983), the meaning of the change is not so immediately apparent. How does this translate into improved functioning or quality of life for the client? The improvement may not necessarily be noticeable.

Within psychology, Sechrest, McKnight, and McKnight (1996) recently observed that "few psychological measures of any kind are expressed in a metric that is intuitively or immediately meaningful" (p. 1065). They argue the need to calibrate measures so that we can interpret scores more easily. To illustrate, they ask, "How many points on the Eysenck Introversion–Extraversion Scale (Eysenck & Eysenck, 1963) are associated with each additional hour spent alone each day?" (p. 1067). Sechrest et al. suggested a number of ways to improve the meaningfulness of our measures. One is to interpret scores in terms of other phenomena that we understand better. For example, we might tell someone that the amount of radiation they would experience from a particular X-ray procedure is approximately the same as spending the weekend in Denver, CO, rather than Tucson, AZ. Another calibration method involves matching psychological or emotional states with physical quantities. This popular approach appears in song lyrics, such as "my love is taller than the tallest mountain." Thus, we clarify the meaning of one form of experience by representing it in terms of a different form of experience that is possibly more familiar.

Sechrest et al.'s (1996) argument for calibrating measures builds on the evaluative logic described earlier in this chapter. With their approach, we would interpret an instrument in terms of the amount of change necessary for third parties to be aware of it—for example, we would ask "By how much would we have to reduce depression before significant others in the client's life notice differences in the client's behavior?" As Sechrest et al. noted, this approach resembles the concept of social validity (i.e., to assess whether an intervention is socially valid, we determine both changes in the behavior of clients and the impact of this change on other people; Kazdin, 1977; Wolf, 1978). Note that clinical change, social validity, medical necessity, and quality of life can have complex interrelationships. It is possible for someone to show clinically significant change on a measure of psychiatric symptoms (Jacobson & Truax, 1991) and thus no longer meet the medical necessity criterion for HMO coverage. At the same time, significant others in the client's social environment might not notice a change, and the client might not experience improvement in quality of life. Sechrest et al. call attention to the independence of functional status and quality of life, as discussed above, further supporting the inclusion of both in comprehensive practice evaluation designs. Finally, the need for calibration clearly applies to subjective evaluation measures as well (e.g., what amount of change in clinical measures of psychiatric symptoms, speech fluency, range of motion, and so on is necessary for the client to report improvements in quality of life?).

In summary, the measures of behavior change typically used by providers of human services are not inherently meaningful. For them to be so requires calibrating their scores in terms of other variables that have greater face validity. Such activities enhance the interpretability of measures commonly used in practice evaluation, making them more useful for the various stakeholders involved. The type of calibration discussed here does not homogenize the data from the different perspectives, however, and their separate (and sometimes overlapping) meanings still need careful, independent consideration. Finally, although treated here wholly in practical terms, calibration can have implications for scientific undertakings as well. Future methodological research should explore those implications more fully.

Provider Profiling

Before leaving the discussion of the types of change that human services promote, it is worthwhile to focus briefly on an issue of some concern to practitioners in the managed care environment. As employers, insurance companies, and HMOs come to manage care more completely, they will subject it to forms of evaluation and accounting that are novel to practitioners. Service providers who are members of panels of professionals for various MCOs have to submit information about themselves and their practice on a regular basis. This chapter already has discussed the advantages for treatment effectiveness of ongoing monitoring of patient and therapist data. In addition to these data, however, clinicians must provide such demographic information as their age, gender, education, and years of experience. They also inform third parties of their theoretical orientation, special expertise, insurance coverage, and information about the number and characteristics of people working with them in their practice.

All of these data become part of the provider's profile. Together with information such as the types of problem or diagnosis the clinician usually treats, the number of sessions clients typically attend, objective and subjective measures of improvement, and service costs, the payer develops a profile or characterization of the practitioner. The purpose of profiling in this manner is to permit comparison across providers, treatment agencies, or other forms of service organization using objective data (Berman, Rosen, Hurt, & Kolarz, 1998). Payers can use any discrepancies to induce change, provide training, set reimbursement rates, retain or release practitioners from provider panels, and simply learn more about what is and is not effective. An example of an individual provider profile appears in Figure 4.4. Data of this type can be useful to practitioners, who previously labored in relative ignorance of how their own performance compared with that of others.

One could ask many questions about the information presented in Figure 4.4. Space does not permit treating them in detail here, but

Figure 4.4

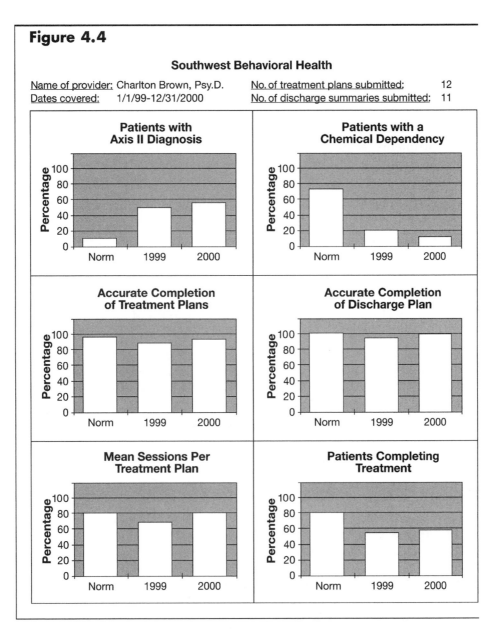

Southwest Behavioral Health

Name of provider: Charlton Brown, Psy.D.   No. of treatment plans submitted: 12
Dates covered: 1/1/99-12/31/2000   No. of discharge summaries submitted: 11

Hypothetical example of an individual provider profile from a health maintenance organization.

readers who are or become members of provider panels of managed health care companies can anticipate seeing these kinds of data eventually, and some general points are worth considering. Questions the astute practitioner might want answered include the following:

- If the company defines successful treatment in terms of achieving all intervention goals (as in this example), has there been any weighting to account for possible differences in goal difficulty across providers and patients? This is of central importance because relatively simple goals can be more easily accomplished.
- Has there been adequate consideration of the severity of the problems treated? For example, has there been any weighting to account for differences in diagnoses or initial functioning level of clients? We have good evidence that clients with greater severity of initial difficulty are more challenging to treat.
- How is goal accomplishment assessed, and are both patient and therapist perspectives considered?
- How are treatment completion and dropping out defined?
- Are data summaries based on sufficient numbers of clients to provide reliable estimates?
- How will the managed care company use the data in future dealings with me?
- What do the data imply about how I currently run my practice? Sperry et al. (1996) observed that knowing the relative effectiveness of different providers with the same and different types of client can improve the cost effectiveness of services. They provide a powerful illustration of how to do this in Table 4.2.

Table 4.2 presents hypothetical data from clients seeking psycho-

Table 4.2

Costs of Providing Psychotherapy to Clients of Differing Severity by Clinicians of Differing Levels of Effectiveness

	Cost of providing service			
	MHI change per session			
Initial MHI	0.50	2.00	4.00	6.00
70	$2,080	$520	$260	$173
50	$5,280	$1,320	$660	$440
30	$8,480	$2,120	$1,060	$707
10	$11,680	$2,920	$1,460	$973

Note. MHI = Mental Health Index score. From *Treatment Outcomes in Psychotherapy and Psychiatric Interventions* (p. 102), by L. Sperry, P. L. Brill, K. I. Howard, and G. R. Grissom, 1996, New York: Brunner/Mazel. Copyright 1996 by Brunner/Mazel. Adapted with permission.

logical treatment from clinicians with varying levels of proficiency. The data are from the MHI described earlier and are based on the assumption that a score of 83 is necessary to be in the normal range; the higher the score, the better the mental health. To understand the table, imagine a client who enters treatment with moderately good mental health, as reflected in an initial MHI of 70. If a clinician achieving up to a 6-point change in MHI score per session treats the client, it will take (83 − 70)/6 = 2.16 sessions to reach the normal range; at a cost of $80 per session, the total cost is $173.33. If a clinician of the same level of effectiveness treats a second client—someone with substantial initial difficulties who enters treatment with an MHI score of 30—services cost $707, at a cost of $80 per session ([83 − 30]/6 = 8.83 sessions).

Now imagine that the second client receives treatment from someone achieving only a half-point change in MHI score per session. To attain a score within the normal range with such a clinician will take 106 sessions, for a total cost of $8,480. It is apparent that profiling provider cost and effectiveness in this way can lead to more efficient allocation of behavioral health resources. Third-party payers are unlikely to refer clients to providers effecting such small increments of change. Of course, practitioners assume that their profile is reliable and results from at least minimal adherence to common principles of descriptive statistics. Note that the data for the provider profile in Figure 4.4 are from 11 clients. Suppose the practitioner worked with an especially difficult case that required an extraordinarily large number of sessions. With so few clients contributing to the profile, a distorted view of the practitioner's effectiveness could result. In other words, provider profiles must be based on sufficient data to ensure their reliability, and third-party payers must know how reliable the data are.

Because the ease of treating clients of different initial levels of severity varies, one must take account of those differences when evaluating clinicians. It is inappropriate to conclude that one particular clinician or agency is more cost effective than others if it specializes in treating people of higher levels of motivation and education and lower levels of initial problem severity, for example. Accounting for differences in types of clients involves statistical procedures collectively known as risk adjustment (Berman et al., 1998) or case-mix adjustment (Sperry et al., 1996). Research involving experimental comparisons generally ensures group equivalence by random assignment of people to groups after randomly selecting them from a larger population. Because random assignment is seldom possible in practice evaluation, case-mix adjustment is a statistical method for producing *approximate equivalence* (by weighting or adjusting patient groups to account for the different difficulty level of treating different types of clients; e.g., people with borderline personality disorder would be viewed as more difficult to treat than people with acrophobia and would thus be given more weight). Sperry et al. provided more description of the requirements for adjusting on the basis of differences in the types of cases that practitioners treat.

Before deciding that you want to look elsewhere for work that is less closely scrutinized, be assured that provider comparisons at the level of individual diagnosis are unlikely any time soon because reliable statistical analyses require a large number of clients (Howard, 1996). At best, we can expect comparisons across provider networks or panels at this level. Comparisons among individual practitioners are more likely to involve aggregations of clients across diagnoses, all of whom have been assessed using a common outcome measure such as the MHI. At a minimum, doing so allows comparisons grossly adjusted for case mix, as recommended by Berman (1998) and Sperry et al. (1996). Chapter 10 discusses analytic procedures for making such comparisons using hierarchical linear modeling.

Summary

This chapter describes an approach to measuring the types of change routinely produced in human services. It is important that objective measures of clinical change be supplemented with subjective quality-of-life indicators. This chapter calls attention to the value of ongoing progress monitoring or continuous measurement and distinguishes between assessment (i.e., static appraisals) and measurement (i.e., dynamic appraisals). It also points to the need to calibrate outcome measures and discusses the important concept of provider profiling. Keeping these issues in mind, let us turn to the kinds of questions practitioners are likely to ask about change.

Supplemental Reading

Follette, W. C. (1995). Correcting methodological weaknesses in the knowledge base used to derive practice standards. In S. C. Hayes, V. M. Follette, R. M. Dawes, &

K. E. Grady (Eds.), *Scientific standards of psychological practice: Issues and recommendations* (pp. 229–247). Reno, NV: Context Press.

Gladis, M. M., Gosch, E. A., Dishuk, N. M., & Crits-Christoph, P. (1999). Quality of life: Expanding the scope of clinical significance. *Journal of Consulting and Clinical Psychology, 67*, 320–331.

Howard, K. I., Lueger, R. J., Maling, M., & Martinovich, Z. (1993). A phase model of psychotherapy: Causal mediation of outcome. *Journal of Consulting and Clinical Psychology, 61*, 678–685.

Ogles, B. M., Lambert, M. J., & Masters, K. S. (1996). *Assessing outcome in clinical practice.* Boston: Allyn & Bacon.

Sperry, L., Brill, P. L., Howard, K., & Grissom, G. R. (1996). *Treatment outcomes in psychotherapy and psychiatric interventions.* New York: Brunner/Mazel.

Case Conceptualization and Evaluation Questions

Is your practice meeting its goals? This is the overriding question when assessing effectiveness. As chapter 2 makes clear, practice goals derive from the value premises implied in your and your partners' personal and practice vision statements and are specified in the mission statement of your practice. The most effective service providers have goals for each component of their practice; moreover, their goals span a variety of time periods into the future.

This chapter focuses on evaluation questions specific to the direct services component. It restricts itself to evaluating direct services goals extending a year or less into the future. The purpose of the chapter is to identify the types of questions routinely asked about the primary component of a practice and its services to consumers and to consider ways of framing those questions effectively. The chapter begins with a discussion of case conceptualization and how it leads to specific goals, then demonstrates how different types of goals lead to different evaluative questions. It ends by discussing how good questions involve specific variables and sets the stage for their operationalization, a topic chapter 7 pursues more fully.

Conceptualizing a Case

"The effective practice of psychotherapy requires a basis from which we can draw to account for the complexities, vagaries, and idiosyncrasies of human temperament, personality and behavior" (Davidson & Lazarus, 1995, p. 109). The "basis" referred to by Davidson and Lazarus is a theoretical position. A theoretical orientation provides important guidance in all aspects of our interactions with clients. It shows us what to observe, how to describe and interpret our observations, how to use them to develop effective treatments, and how to determine whether those treatments are effective.

Although it is helpful to have *some* systematic perspective, it is not necessary to subscribe to a *particular* theoretical point of view to undertake organized, effective practice evaluation. The pragmatic approach to service delivery, which selects tactics based on whatever makes sense to the practitioner at the time, is not likely to be viable in the long run, however, because it lacks a formal rationale. Although the effectiveness of services provided in such a context can be established, it is hard to see how specific information emerging from evaluations can produce improvements in such practices over time. Without a theoretical basis, the variables controlling the practitioner's behavior cannot be identified systematically, making it impossible to validate the controlling variables or modify them in ways that lead to practice improvements. The rest of the discussion in this chapter therefore assumes that the practitioner's decision making has a theoretical basis.

Identifying Client Problems

As Persons (1991) noted, the greatest challenge facing the service provider is identifying a problem and an approach to solving it that is most relevant to a particular client at a particular time. Most clinicians listen thoughtfully to the client's explanation of why services are being sought at the moment and attempt to frame the explanation in terms of problems to be solved. The practitioner listens to the client's description and asks him- or herself, "How can I be of help to this person? What are the real problems we need to resolve?"

Using the client's words to determine what the difficulties are, the clinician imposes some organization on the problem. This organization includes verbal filters that focus attention on some details and minimize attention to others. The overall organization the clinician imposes and the relative importance she or he gives to different aspects of the client's story stem from the theoretical orientation adopted by the practitioner. Theories of behavior vary in comprehensiveness: A particular clinician may subscribe to a rather grand theory or one that is relatively circumscribed. Having some theoretical perspective to guide clinical decisions is more important than how broad it is, however.

One may have a formal rationale for deciding how to help a client with particular problems and still not be guided by a formal theory of human behavior. The point of view a given practitioner takes can range from a highly idiosyncratic "theory" unique to the practitioner to a formally composed, carefully articulated theory that has appeared in published literature and has been subjected to extensive empirical verification. Along this continuum one can find treatment approaches that are relatively "canned" or prescribed and that merely require following a list of steps. For example, treatment manuals have been developed for dealing with depression (Beck, Rush, Shaw, & Emery, 1979), panic and agoraphobia (Barlow & Craske, 1989, 1994), obsessive–compulsive disorder (Riggs & Foa, 1993), and eating disorders (Fairburn, Marcus, & Wilson, 1993). Relatively inexperienced therapists can be trained to read and follow such manuals and to produce improvements in clients as a result (Wilson, 1996). Authors of such manuals base them on formal theory to various degrees. The most widely used manual for treating depression, for example, is based on Beck's (Beck et al., 1979) cognitive theory. Whether the user of the manual must adopt the author's theory to use it successfully is unclear. Some clinicians (e.g., Eifert, Schulte, Zvolensky, Lejuez, & Lau, 1997; O'Brien & Haynes, 1995; Persons, 1991; Persons & Silberschatz, 1998; Malatesta, 1995) have argued the importance of idiographic case formulations and the application of treatment manuals in a flexible way based on a thorough functional analysis. Others (e.g., Wilson, 1996, 1997) have pointed to the lack of support for clinical intuition and the relative superiority of actuarial approaches in assessment, arguing that the same finding is likely to apply in the treatment arena as well. Thus, close adherence to the guidelines set out in treatment manuals that have some empirical support is likely to lead to the most effective practice.

A variety of checklists (Bloom, Fischer, & Orme, 1995), flowcharts (Gottman & Leiblum, 1974), and even computer programs (Farrell, 1999a; Farrell & McCullough-Vaillant, 1996; Farrell, Camplair, & McCullough, 1987; Fowler, Finkelstein, Penk, Bell, & Itzig, 1987) can help identify client problems. These tools are particularly helpful in organizing information from clients at the outset because they offer a reminder of areas to explore and, often, a sequence useful in obtaining information efficiently and sensitively from the client. For example, Farrell et al. (1987) found that their computerized interview identified three times more problems than clinician-conducted interviews for 103 outpatients experiencing both types of interview.

Exhibit 5.1

Psychology Clinic Initial Appointment Checklist

Welcome to Centerville Psychology Associates. To help us prepare for your first appointment, please take a few moments to provide the following information. When you have completed this form, please mail it in the enclosed envelope. Thank you for your time.

Name: _____ Date: _____

Please check all current concerns:

___ Relationship with spouse	___ Relationship with children
___ Relationship with parents	___ Relationship with boss
___ Relationship with coworkers	___ Relationship with brothers/sisters
___ Relationship with friends	___ Angry
___ Nervous	___ Depressed/blue
___ Lack of energy	___ Interest in sex
___ Money matters	___ Eating problems
___ Job performance	___ School performance
___ Alcohol/chemical substances	___ Medical problems
___ Memory problems	___ Learning problems

Other (please specify): _____

It can be helpful for service providers to send some type of initial screening checklist to clients before their first appointment. Exhibit 5.1 shows a simple example from a clinical practice. Having the information provided on a checklist before the client comes to the first appointment can help the psychologist prepare to meet the client. Moreover, although the focus of the initial appointment is likely to be on the areas the client checks, the astute clinician probes some of the areas the client does not check as well; some clients are not comfortable acknowledging personal information on such forms. It is interesting in this regard that some clients actually provide more candid information when interviewed by a computer than by a live clinician (Erdman, Klein, & Greist, 1985).

Checklists such as these can be seen as general screening instruments. They initiate an assessment process that gets progressively more specific as the client works with the practitioner to clarify service goals. The practitioner's theoretical understanding of depression is likely to drive the assessment process. For example, a theory that depression is largely interpersonally determined (Klerman, Weissman, Rounsaville, & Chevron, 1984) is likely to lead to assessing the type, frequency, and quality of social interactions. Alternatively, a theory that relates depressive behavior to type and number of reinforcers (Lewinsohn & Hoberman, 1982) is apt to evaluate the frequency of pleasant events experienced by the client over some period of time. Finally, a theoretical explanation of depression as anger turned inward (Freud, 1917/1957) is likely to focus additional assessment attention on the quality of the client's early relationships, especially with regard to parents and other family members.

Thus, the initial screening of a range of potential concerns can be an essentially clerical process, mechanically undertaken, and with minimal theoretical guidance. Once general problem areas are identified, however, more narrowly focused assessment is needed.

Setting Client Goals

The practitioner's theoretical orientation is likely to play a central role in narrowing attention to more specific aspects of the client's initial concerns. The particular theoretical understanding of the client's issues dictates the variables that are relevant to the current case. To illustrate, imagine a provider who believes there is a link between depression and negative automatic thoughts, which in turn result from underlying cognitive schemata (e.g., Beck, 1983). The provider and client select the ultimate goal of eliminating the client's depression. Such a goal is likely regardless of the practitioner's theoretical orientation. The view that depression relates to negative automatic thoughts comes from a specific theory of depression, however, and leads to the formulation of instrumental goals that are relevant to that theory. Reducing the frequency of negative automatic thoughts thus becomes an instrumental goal of treatment.

Having formulated one or more hypotheses based on a particular theoretical understanding of depression (e.g., that reducing negative automatic thoughts is associated with lower depression; Beck, 1983), the practitioner selects interventions appropriate to the theory and evaluates their effectiveness in terms of achieving theory-relevant goals. That is, treatment reduces the client's level of depression (the ultimate goal) by achieving a reduction in dysfunctional beliefs (the instrumental goal). The instrumental goal is accomplished by achieving certain intermediate or process goals (Rosen & Proctor, 1981), such as consistent daily recording of negative automatic thoughts (Beck et al., 1979).

To illustrate the general applicability of this logic, consider a case of depression from another theoretical perspective. Conceptualizing depression from a psychodynamic point of view leads to the same ultimate goal of eliminating the client's depression. As in the previous example, the practitioner formulates a question and related hypotheses (e.g., "increasing the client's awareness of anger and its appropriateness is associated with lowering depression"). This hypothesis derives logically from the theory relating anger turned against oneself to the experience of depression. Different instrumental goals emerge, however, such as increasing the client's awareness of his or her anger (e.g., toward his or her unfaithful spouse) or teaching the client the relationship between repressed anger and feelings of depression. Intermediate goals consistent with this case formulation can include discussing the client's sadness and disappointment on learning of the spouse's affair. As in the earlier example, conceptualizing the case in this way leads to designing a treatment consistent with the theory.

The Role of Theory in Developing Basic Effectiveness Questions

The most important practice evaluation question relates to accomplishing ultimate client goals: Does the service provide what the client wants and expects? This is an important question, but it should serve mainly as a starting point for practice evaluation. A major difficulty with "Does it work?" questions is that they can be asked without reference to any theoretical orientation. When data provide an affirmative answer, the practitioner can keep doing what he or she is doing. When data provide a negative answer, however, what is the practitioner to do? Without a theoretical basis for guidance, it is hard to respond effectively to negative outcomes.

To illustrate the advantages of starting with a theoretical basis, suppose someone approaches you for help with anxiety. On interviewing the person, you learn that anxiety attacks occur quite often. The client says that he worries often about many things, feels "edgy," and has great difficulty concentrating. You and the client collaboratively establish a long-term or ultimate goal of reduced anxiety so that the client can experience more comfort in daily activities. Because he reports edginess and restlessness as well as some occurrence of increased heart rate, you decide to refer him to a physician for a medication evaluation and train him in progressive relaxation (Bernstein & Borkovec, 1973). You also formulate the following instrumental goals for the client: (a) to obtain a physician's evaluation for possible antianxiety medication within 2 weeks and (b) to learn progressive relaxation techniques by the end of six individual psychotherapy sessions.

After several months both instrumental goals are accomplished. The client reports only moderate reductions in general feelings of anxiety, however. What do you do next? If your decisions to this point have been largely opportunistic and pragmatically driven, the answer may not be obvious. Perhaps it makes sense to explore some past emotional issues of the client and see how they relate to current experiences of anxiety. Perhaps the client is thinking irrationally and unnecessarily upsetting himself. If so, you might decide to focus on identifying maladaptive thoughts and teaching the client to replace them with more rational ones.

How do you decide which course to follow if your decisions have had no theoretical basis up to this point? Armed with a well-developed theory of anxiety, the next step might be more apparent. To illustrate, suppose your view of the client's anxiety is that it is his way of reporting suboptimal effectiveness in a variety of everyday situations. When in certain situations, the client's behavior leads to outcomes other than those he hoped to obtain. For example, when interacting with strangers he averts his gaze, makes inane remarks, and shifts his weight from foot to foot. Afterward, he notices he is sweaty and feels that he did not make a good impression on the other person. Your "theory" of anxiety is that it represents a loosely knit collection of responses that clients experience as incompatible with what they really want to happen in common situations. Moreover, their responses tend to occur in a fairly regular sequence that begins with the client appraising the situation as one in which success is not likely. In other words, the client experiences fear of impending difficulty or possible failure. The fear takes the form of self-talk, such as "This is awful—I'm never any good at meeting people. I never have anything clever to say." Similar statements can follow, as can motor (e.g., shifting weight, averting gaze), and physiological (e.g., sweating, breathing rapidly) responses.

If you have a theoretical position such as this, you are likely to use it to provide theory-relevant assessment information early in your contact with the client. You evaluate the client's self-talk (cognitive behavior), motor, and physiological responses to determine which, if any, of these are deficient in the situations the client identifies as likely to lead to anxiety. You might discover from your assessment information that your initial therapeutic effort should focus on cognitive aspects of the client's repertoire because ineffective self-talk seems to start a chain of behavior that includes other negative self-talk as well as motor and physiological responses. Because all of these responses characterize suboptimal performance, it makes theoretical sense to interrupt the chain at its earliest link in order to forestall the remaining ineffective responses. You therefore begin therapy by focusing more specifically on the kinds of things the client says to himself in situations that he regards as fearful or problematic. You and the client work collaboratively to identify his maladaptive thoughts, challenge them, and replace them with more adaptive ones. You formulate instrumental goals that relate closely to the theoretical basis for the treatment, such as replacing maladaptive automatic thoughts with adaptive ones when encountering fearful situations. After you devote five sessions to accomplishing this goal, you administer an "automatic thoughts in fearful situations" questionnaire and find that the client has replaced 93% of his maladaptive thoughts. As a check on progress toward the ultimate goal of lower anxiety, you also administer the Beck Depression Inventory. Unfortunately, your client's general level of anxiety shows only slight improvement.

Imagine that your theory holds that the various components of "anxiety" are correlated but not causally related to one another. In other words, the client thinks maladaptive thoughts and avoids making eye contact, but he does not avoid eye contact because he thinks he is inadequate. You conclude that there has not been enough change in the client's repertoire to produce generally effective performance in fearful situations. He therefore continues to experience discomfort in those situations, to the point of avoiding as many of them as possible. Especially noteworthy is his heightened physiological reactivity, which appears to occur early in the chain, seemingly concurrent with the maladaptive automatic thoughts already a focus of treatment. You decide to teach the client effective physiological responses to the anxiety-producing situations. You establish an instrumental goal of "breathing normally when thinking about or actually approaching fearful circumstances." Your treatment sessions begin to address this behavior, and you record data on the client's physiological responses.

To summarize, working with clients collaboratively to identify problems does not require a formal theoretical orientation. A theory, however, does help determine which aspects of a problem to assess further and which interventions to use; when a particular approach does not achieve the ultimate goal, the theory tells us what to do next. Moreover, failures are instructive because they reveal potential shortcomings of a theory and lead to modifications. The process of continually testing propositions generated from our theoretical understanding leads to casting off or changing ineffective approaches while retaining and refining those that work, resulting in improvements in practice. Without the benefit of a theoretical basis, treatment failures provide little guidance. Furthermore, they cannot lead systematically to more effective treatment.

Evaluative questions related only to the reasons clients are seeking services (i.e., did they accomplish what they wanted the service to provide?) are important for immediate survival, to be sure. They are not as helpful for long-term survival, however, because they do not inform us about how to make continued improvements in our practice. Long-term survival questions are more likely to be theoretically driven. They are also likely to be of the "did it work as well as (or better than) another approach?" and "why did it work (or not work)?" variety. Identifying instrumental (i.e., theory-driven) goals and ultimate goals for each case sets the stage for asking questions about comparative effectiveness and the ingredients of that effectiveness.

Comparative Evaluation Questions

Basic effectiveness questions do not advance us beyond simply finding out whether our services work. Comparative questions ask how our services compare with others having the same purpose. Comparative questions are appropriate when we already know that the interventions we are comparing are effective and want to know whether one works better than the other does.

Comparative evaluations can be undertaken simultaneously with basic "does it work" evaluations; they merely require somewhat more complicated designs (see chapter 8). Because it can get so complicated, it is probably best to separate the two and address basic effectiveness first. Once we have solid evidence of the basic effectiveness of a service, we can compare it with another approach.

Comparative evaluation is important to carry out early in the treatment process. The approach or service in question should be compared with a simpler, less intrusive, less expensive, generally available alternative that has essentially comparable goals. For example, suppose we or someone else has demonstrated that both our services and a physician-prescribed exercise program are effective at treating depression. In this example, psychology services are compared with an exercise regimen (the generally available alternative).

The simpler, less intrusive, less expensive, generally available alternative can be viewed as a baseline standard or benchmark against which just about any service can be compared. For example, psychological treatment often is compared with interventions that merely listen or pay attention to a person's concerns, so-called attention-placebo conditions (Shapiro & Morris, 1978). A lawyer's services might be compared with outcomes available from merely reading a book, using computer software, consulting Web sites or paralegals, or using other less expensive sources of legal information. Tax-filing assistance from certified public accountants (CPAs) can be compared with that of enrolled agents (people trained in the tax codes but who have no formal preparation as CPAs). Additionally, it might be compared with reading a book on how to file one's taxes or using computer programs to complete a return.

When a service has been shown to work better than a simpler, less intrusive, less expensive, generally available alternative, we can compare it with "peer" services. Peer services are those of comparable complexity, intrusiveness, cost, and availability. Suppose as a tax preparation specialist you provide complete and accurate returns in a timely manner. Moreover, you do so more effectively than simpler, less intrusive, less expensive, generally available alternatives. Now you can be compared with your peers. How does your effectiveness stack up against theirs?

In the business world such questions involve comparing a company with its competition. Such comparisons can be most important to staying in business. Similarly, it is naive for practitioners to confine their evaluative efforts only to showing that their services work. If they do not do as well as their competition, they will eventually go out of business even if they are effective. For these reasons, it is critical to know how your effectiveness compares with the same or highly similar services provided by others. If you make such comparisons on an ongoing basis, you sow the seeds for continued improvement.

Effective-Ingredients Questions

To stay ahead of the competition requires providing more effective service than they do. To be more effective involves examining how you provide your service. In other words, you analyze the processes you use, asking "What makes us effective?" or "What are the critical ingredients in our services?" When you isolate and examine how the individual components of your service contribute to your therapeutic effectiveness, you increase your cost effectiveness. If you eliminate superfluous elements, cost effectiveness increases. If you redirect resources previously committed to the superfluities to the contributing components, your overall effectiveness improves. Asking "why" questions is akin to determining what chemical compounds in a particular medication are responsible for its effect. In psychotherapy research, *dismantling* or *decomposing* studies have to do with dissecting an intervention into its components and determining what contribution they make to the treatment's overall effectiveness.

To illustrate, a common tactic of many professionals is to offer free initial consultations. This would seem to be an important service, one that would contribute significantly to the success of the business by recruiting new clients. But is this merely an assumption? Is there any empirical support for the idea? The appropriate evaluation question becomes "Does the initial free consultation really contribute in significant ways?" More specifically, "Do clients who come for free consultations become long-term clients? Offering free consultations has a cost to the practice—could the time and effort spent in this activity be used in more profitable ways? Evaluating the free consultation component can answer this question.

Another aspect of the practice is its billing procedures. Assume that your approach is to bill clients monthly, charging no interest for unpaid balances over 30 days. Your accountant suggests that your collection rate (and thus your profitability) would improve if you request payment at the time you deliver the service. This concerns you, however, because clients may not have the money at that moment, and expecting time-of-service payment might drive them away. Your accountant responds that you could start accepting credit cards, which would permit clients to defer payment to the end of the month and allow you to collect your fee immediately. Of course, the bank charges a percentage of each transaction amount, so you would not receive your entire fee. The evaluation question then becomes "Does time-of-service payment result in greater profitability than billing at the end of each month?"

Questions about administrative matters such as these are not as interesting as those about service quality, however. If one provides psychological treatment for depression to adults on an outpatient basis, for example, there are many questions one can ask of that treatment. A critical one deals with the relationship between amount or "dose" of therapy and rate of improvement discussed in the previous chapter. If progress data are kept on an ongoing basis, it is easy to determine when the rate of improvement levels off. By keeping comparable data on numerous clients treated with the same approach, we can examine the regularity of this "leveling off." Suppose it is found to be consistent across clients, and suppose further that clients typically continue in treatment many sessions beyond the leveling-off point.

Continuing treatment produces additional improvement, but the rate of change is much reduced. What if we inform clients of this typical pattern—would they choose to continue in treatment? Would it make sense to alter the form treatment takes after the leveling-off point? For example, clients could receive treatment every other week or be placed in a group receiving similar treatment; as a result, total costs to the client would be lower. Revenue generated from continuing weekly individual treatment also would be lower, of course, but the effect on the revenue stream might be positive when evaluated over time. For example, group therapy can provide continuing improvements in the original symptoms and open up additional areas for the client to consider. Likewise, switching to every-other-week treatment could result in an increase in sessions per completed case because the immediate financial burden for individual clients is lower. The practitioner who is sensitive to client costs is likely to be rewarded, because the service sector continues to be increasingly customer driven. In summary, having the data to answer such questions as, "How much therapy is needed before improvements level off?" puts a practice at a competitive advantage because it can allow lower costs to the client, thereby maintaining their involvement in treatment and retaining or even enhancing the profitability of the practice.

Questions of the "why does it work?" variety also can be of the "would it work if I do it this way?" type. That is, one might keep the overall composition of the intervention the same while varying the order of the ingredients or their proportions. In other words, one might alter certain parameters of the treatment.

A relevant illustration comes from the author's own work with parents of children with developmental disabilities. Caretaker burden can be eased for such parents if their child learns to perform certain activities of daily living independently. Thus, it is common to show parents how to teach their children elementary self-help skills, such as feeding or dressing themselves. It also is common to show such parents how to manage problem behavior when it occurs. Recently, the functions of problem behavior have been shown to include communication (e.g., Carr et al., 1994). That is, a child with little or no speech might throw a temper tantrum to get someone's attention or to get out of doing something unpleasant. It is logical to expect that a child more able to do things independently will have less need to ask for help from parents. This hypothesis forms the basis for showing parents how to teach self-help skills to their child and ways of handling problem behavior.

A question arises as to how to sequence these two components of a parent training program, however. That is, would it be more effective to show parents how to handle problem behavior first, or to teach their children to be more independent with self-help tasks? Note that the question is not whether parent training works, nor is it whether parent training works better than some alternative (e.g., parent counseling or play therapy). Furthermore, the question does not address whether parents should be shown how to teach self-help skills and how to manage difficult behavior. The assumption is that these questions have already been explored. We know that parent training works, that it works as well as or better than common alternatives, and that it is important to include content related to both self-help skills and difficult behavior in parent training programs (e.g., Baker & Brightman, 1997).

The issue, therefore, is the most effective order of the ingredients in parent training. A relevant hypothesis is, "Training parents to develop self-help skills first results in greater posttreatment reductions in children's problem behavior than training parents to handle problem behavior first." The variables implied in this hypothesis are children's problem behavior and the order of training components. Thus, problem behavior and order of training components are dependent and independent variables, respectively. (Incidentally, our hypothesis was not supported. We found that parents receiving training in handling difficult behavior first actually reported more improvement in their child's problem behavior than parents receiving instruction in teaching self-help skills first; Cone, Sweitzer, Casper-Beliveau, Rausch, & Sousa, 1995).

In summary, practice evaluation questions range from whether an intervention works to why a certain treatment is effective. Beyond "whether" questions, more advanced evaluation is guided by theory. Improvements in practices result more consistently from theory-driven evaluation because results are more easily interpreted and their implications for practice changes are more clearly understood.

Evaluative Questions Related to Other Practice Components

This chapter focuses on the direct services aspects of a practice, but its logic applies to other practice components as well, albeit with minor qualifications. It is unlikely, for example, that questions about the efficacy of support components of a practice are informed by formal theory. In areas outside of direct client services, the questions most often revolve around whether a component is accomplishing the goals set for it. We are not likely to focus much attention on whether it accomplishes goals better than some other practice or to ask what makes it effective.

To illustrate, consider evaluation of the community service component of a practice. A goal of this component is to have each employee participate in at least one civic organization on an ongoing basis. At the end of some period of time (say, a year), the practice gathers data on such participation and notes the appropriate percentage. If the goal of 100% participation is reached, success is acknowledged and new goals are developed in community service. If less than 100% participation has occurred but the proportion reflects a considerable increase over previous years, the goal may be retained and progress evaluated over future time periods. It would be unusual for the practice to ask more sophisticated evaluative questions about this component, however. For example, it would not evaluate how its participation in civic organizations compared with that of other practices. Nor would it be all that interested in the comparative effectiveness of its tactics for obtaining staff participation. Such questions are likely to be restricted to the direct services component.

Up to now the emphasis has been on evaluative questions and hypotheses stated a priori and examined in a rather formal way. The typical practitioner collects much data in the course of everyday work, however, and may wonder whether they can be used to improve effectiveness. For instance, it is routine practice to collect demographic data on nearly every client. Can this information be examined for potential relationships with practice variables? Suppose you examine the relationship between satisfaction ratings and such personal characteristics as age, gender, and years of education. All you need to do is calculate the correlation between satisfaction and each of these variables at periodic intervals (see chapters 6–9). What if you find a positive correlation between satisfaction and years of education? What if you find a negative correlation between satisfaction and distance traveled to the office?

Does this constitute practice evaluation? The answers may be *yes* and *no*. In the sense that you are motivated to improve your services and you therefore "snoop" the data to see what turns up, you are conducting a form of practice evaluation, albeit a rather low form. We might refer to this activity as describing rather than actually evaluating a practice.

As another example, suppose you worked for a large managed care organization (MCO) responsible for all health services for several hundred thousand people. In the interest of cost-effective care, the company wants to be able to predict usage levels for several of its services, including psychotherapy for symptoms of depression. Assuming that an average of 8.3 therapy sessions is enough to enable clients to return to generally satisfied, productive lives, the cost to the company of providing this health benefit can be determined relatively easily. One or two additional pieces of information are needed before usage levels can be calculated, however. One is the percentage of people covered by the company who can be expected to need such services in a given period of time. Another is the variables that relate to seeking psychological treatment for depression. If we assume psychotherapy is relatively expensive as well as intrusive, we might want to minimize its use. An evaluative question worth pursuing might be, "What individual characteristics in our population of clients are related to seeking psychological treatment for depression?"

Before conducting the evaluation it is useful to consult the literature to see what is known to relate to depression already. Suppose there is literature showing a negative association between exercise level and depressive symptoms. Suppose additional literature shows positive relationships between dietary fat intake, smoking, alcohol use, and depression. As an evaluator, you would frame hypotheses that include these relationships and design a study to test them. One such hypothesis might be that people in the MCO's client population who exercise regularly experience fewer symptoms of depression than those who do not. Another hypothesis might be that people in the MCO's client population who smoke, have high levels of dietary fat intake, and consume significant amounts of alcohol use are more likely to experience symptoms of depression than those who do not. We can test these hypotheses using data from the archives of the MCO because the company periodically surveys its client population and stores the data in a large database.

If the analyses support our hypotheses, the MCO can benefit. For example, if exercise relates negatively to depressive symptoms in the client population, the company can implement preventive health education programs that focus on increasing exercise levels or offer memberships in neighborhood fitness clubs at a reduced rate. These actions can be healthy to its own bottom line if the costs are more than offset by lower utilization of expensive therapy services. Similarly, preventive programs aimed at improving eating habits, moderating alcohol use, and eliminating smoking might prove to be cost effective.

Time or other resources do not always permit the formulation of specific evaluative hypotheses in advance. Nonetheless, one might run correlational analyses involving large numbers of variables for which one collects data routinely. This form of practice evaluation can lead to benefits. Relationships "discovered" in analyzing the data can be explored further in more sophisticated ways, leading to prospective evaluative efforts. To illustrate, if one finds that decreases in client satisfaction are associated with increased travel time to get to the service provider's office, one might look for other variables implicated in the relationship. Is distance traveled related to degree of involvement in the intervention? Are there higher cancellation, no-show, reschedule, and early-termination rates in people living beyond a certain distance? Based on the findings, there may be value in altering the manner in which services are provided. Clients living beyond a certain radius might be invited to receive services at a satellite office closer to their home, or actual home visits for clients living long distances might be instituted. The impact of the service changes would be evaluated in a formal way, of course.

This type of evaluation thus can reveal interesting relationships worthy of further study. For example, the benefits of providing more accessible (i.e., closer) services can be examined by first posing the following hypothesis: "Clients living more than 10 miles from the office participate more successfully in services they receive at home than those they receive in the office." The hypothesis suggests a causal relationship between service location and participation. Experimental designs using randomized assignment to experimental and control groups then can be pursued. People living more than 10 miles from the practice office can be randomly offered in-home services; the progress of clients who continue to receive services in the office can be compared with that of clients who receive services at home. However, whether this is helpful for all diagnoses or just for depression is another question to evaluate.

It is important to remember that individual practitioners do not have to shoulder the entire burden for service evaluation alone. Many researchers report their evaluation findings in reputable, peer-reviewed journals, particularly for interventions based on formal theoretical positions for which active scholarly interest and empirical research are ongoing. Ideas for critical service components come from the formal literature describing the outcomes of such research. Astute practitioners stay abreast of this literature and incorporate elements into their services that seem to have empirical support. At the same time, such practitioners monitor the effectiveness of elements borrowed from nomothetic research as they are inserted into everyday, idiographic practice. It might be that the differences between the research context and the practitioner's application are such that the research findings fail to generalize. By accepting published results skeptically, incorporating promising ones into practice, and evaluating their effectiveness in the local application, the practitioner can maintain the highest level of efficiency. Such an approach is likely to lead to more effective practice than merely accepting published findings uncritically and using them with clients without monitoring whether they work.

Summary

This chapter describes how to frame good evaluative questions. Focusing on the direct services component of a practice, it describes the importance of conceptualizing a case from the advantage of a theoretical perspective. Evaluating service effectiveness takes the form of answers to three types of evaluative question: (a) Does it work? (b) Does it work better than other ways of solving the problem? and (c) Why does it work? The first of these is critical to short-term survival of a practice and can be asked completely atheoretically. However, answers to the second and third questions are critical to long-term survival and are most useful if they have a theoretical basis.

Using databases to look for relationships that can have significant implications for service delivery can be particularly worthwhile in large health care organizations, such as MCOs. Relationships discovered in such studies can be explored further in formal evaluations of the hypothesis-driven variety. The next chapter addresses how to organize the kinds of data routinely collected in human services practices efficiently to answer research questions.

Supplemental Reading

Farrell, A. D. (1999a). Evaluation of the computerized assessment system for psychotherapy evaluation and research (CASPER) as a measure of treatment effectiveness in an outpatient training clinic. *Psychological Assessment, 11,* 345–358.

Paul, G. L. (1969). Behavior modification research: Design and tactics. In C. Franks
(Ed.), *Behavior therapy: Appraisal and status* (pp. 29–62). New York: McGraw-Hill.

Getting and Managing Information in Outcomes Evaluation

he practice that is guided by a vision, mission statement, and associated goals is one that is positioned nicely to collect data appropriate for evaluating itself. The vision and mission statements imply certain value premises, which, in turn, lead to goals. Thus, the place to start in describing one's practice is with its goals. Information relevant to the goals needs to be identified, collected, and analyzed, and it should control our behavior. That is, we should adjust the way we run our practice on the basis of what the data tell us.

As with any business, a wealth of data is available for the human services practitioner. The operators of the most effective practices know which data are the most relevant to continued improvement and how to set up systems to collect and represent those data in the most efficient ways. Client data, such as demographic characteristics and service utilization rates, are routinely available. Data specific to practices include the number of clients seen, types of service provided, hours and days of service, geographic location, office characteristics, response time to client calls, promotional activities, costs of doing business, and gross monetary receipts. Perhaps the most important information for a practice, as for any business, is the combination of the last two items, wherein costs are subtracted from receipts to determine net profit.

Domains of Practice Variables

Practice evaluation, like science, involves examining relationships between and among variables. The variables involved in providing human

Figure 6.1

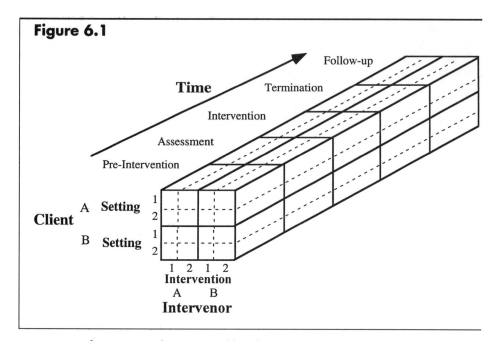

Domains of practice evaluation variables showing the interaction of client, intervenor, setting, and intervention over time. Only two levels (A, B; 1, 2) are shown for the client, setting, intervenor, and intervention variables to keep the diagram simple. More than two levels can easily be incorporated for each of these variables, however.

services can be classified in terms of a limited number of domains (Kiesler, 1971; Krasner, 1962; Levinson, 1962; Paul, 1969). Borrowing from Kiesler and Levinson, the analysis in this chapter focuses on five principal domains: client characteristics, intervenor (therapist) characteristics, setting, intervention, and time. Figure 6.1 diagrams the interaction among those domains.

Client Variables

Important client characteristics include demographic variables, such as gender, age, marital status, education level, income level, and socioeconomic status. When an organization is the client, noteworthy variables include the type of business; the organization's culture; the size, age, experience, education levels, diversity, and degree of unionization of its work force; geographic locations of its offices; organizational structure; and financial condition of the business.

Information related to the client's presenting concerns also is a valuable consideration in practice evaluation. These variables include the severity of the concern, its duration, previous attempts to deal with it, and the apparent effects the concerns are having on the general level of client functioning. An additional set of variables, important for individual clients, includes overall adjustment as well as current life functioning in specific areas such as physical health (including fitness and nutrition), work (or school or household), family, intimate relationships, psychological health, and finances. Finally, certain stable, personal–social characteristics of the individual client are important in practice evaluation. Those characteristics include personality traits (e.g., agreeableness, extraversion, and anxiety) as well as variables directly affecting treatment effectiveness, such as motivation to participate, verbal fluency, and intellectual functioning. In all cases, data on the motivation of the client to change and on the client's preparation to participate actively in the intervention are gathered.

Intervenor Variables

This domain includes characteristics of the practice itself and its service providers. Practice variables include the administrative, educational, and community service components of the practice. Within the administrative realm, for example, billing, advertising, facilities maintenance, and human resources are important sources of information. Payroll data and vacation schedules, as well as routine scheduling activities, involve administration. Billing of clients, insurance companies, or other responsible parties is an administrative function as well.

Intervenor (therapist) variables fall into subdivisions similar to those for clients. These include stable personal–social characteristics, such as gender, age, marital status, education level, and socioeconomic status. In addition, information concerning the therapist's theoretical orientation, educational background, licenses and certifications, memberships in professional organizations, and preparation in and experience with the specific intervention can be useful. Current life functioning of the therapist, including general functioning as well as adjustment in specific areas (e.g., physical health, physical fitness, psychological health), also can be a source of relevant information related to practice effectiveness.

Setting Variables

The context of the intervention can vary considerably. Provision of human services often takes place in an office setting, for instance. It also can occur in clinics, at homes and schools, in the community, and at places of work. It is reasonable to expect that services delivered as close to the point of performance as possible will be more effective than those provided in spatially remote locations, such as professional offices. Of course, this is an empirical question for any practice evaluator.

Intervention Variables

Variables in the intervention domain include factors such as whether treatment is delivered face-to-face or through some remote means (e.g., the Internet); whether treatment is individual or group based; whether homework or extrasession work is required; whether ongoing monitoring is involved; the total number, frequency, length, and cost of intervention sessions; the degree of active participation required of the client; and use of role playing and other modalities.

Temporal Variables

Providing services takes time. Data on clients are obtained at relatively discrete points in the service provision time frame. As suggested in Figure 6.1, convenient temporal demarcations include preintervention, assessment, intervention, termination, and follow up. Helpful practice evaluation information can come from carefully considering interactions involving clients at each of those points. Preintervention data can include when the client first learned of the practice, the time interval between initial contact and first appointment, and the number of times the first appointment had to be rescheduled. Temporal issues surrounding assessment include when assessment actually occurred (e.g., as part of the initial contact or prior to starting the intervention), how much time was specifically devoted to assessment, and how much time elapsed between assessment and intervention. Time factors related to the intervention include total time from start to finish, intercontact (intersession) intervals, lengths of each contact or session, and promptness of client and intervenor. At termination, temporal issues include the amount of time between any of the previous periods (e.g., assessment) and termination, the period of time over which the "termination phase" lasted, and the amount of time devoted to termination. Finally, the time from termination to follow up, the time spent in follow-up sessions, and the spacing of follow-up sessions are some of the temporal concerns related to this phase of service delivery.

Routine Data Collection

Each of the five domains of variables is the source of much valuable information as to how a practice operates. Before this information can be useful, however, variables from the domains must be operationalized (a topic covered in chapter 7). These operations result in data of various types.

Types of Data

To be of the most use in practice evaluation, data must be of the right type, routinely available, and skillfully presented. All data can be placed in one of four categories: nominal, ordinal, interval, and ratio.

Nominal Data

Nominal data involve assigning numbers for the purpose of identifying or "naming" something. Examples include numbers on football jerseys, telephone numbers and street addresses, and diagnoses (e.g., major depression or borderline personality disorder). Assigning people to categories involves nominal measurement, and examples in human services practice are plentiful. "No-shows" is a category familiar to all practitioners, as are type of admission (e.g., voluntary or court ordered), marital status, gender, ethnicity, insurance coverage, and treatment success. Sometimes called *categorical measurement*, nominal measurement assigns people or information to categories on the basis of some qualitative rather than quantitative difference between them (Ray, 1993). An evaluative question involving nominal data is "Are men or women more satisfied with the service provided?" The variables being related are gender and satisfaction, the first of which is nominal. "Are we more effective in treating anxiety disorders than major depression?" would be another evaluative question relying partially on nominal measurement for its answer.

Ordinal Data

Some practice data can be placed along a continuum or ordered in some way. For example, clients can be ordered according to the date they initiated contact with the practice. Similarly, referral sources might be ordered in terms of the number of referrals they provide each year. With ordinal measurement, a continuum is assumed to underlie the data. Everyday examples of ordinal measurement are plentiful. We hear of the most popular prime time television show of the week, the rankings of baseball teams, students' standing in their graduating class, and so on. For example, high school guidance counselors might make more referrals than pediatricians or ministers; the three sources could be ranked first, second, and third. We can then say that the guidance counselors are relatively more productive than the other sources. It is not possible to say how much more, because nothing is implied about the size of the differences between consecutive positions on the continuum, nor can we subject the numbers assigned to the various ranks to routine mathematical manipulations.

Consider another example of the use of ordinal data in managing a practice. In a large practice it might be the case that promotional mailings are used from time to time. A cost-effective way to address such mailings might be to send them to every third or fourth address in a city directory. Moreover, it might be useful to vary the density of the mailing according to the probability that a client will come from a particular neighborhood. The practice can sort the addresses of its current and former clients by ZIP code and arrange the ZIP codes on a continuum from most to least common. Mailings can be sent to every address in the most common ZIP code (i.e., the one in which the greatest number of clients live), to every other address in the second most prevalent ZIP code, and so on.

Few mathematical operations apply to ordinal data, but we can use some statistics with them, provided that the order of the ranked objects is not affected. For example, central tendency can be represented by the median, and the association or correlation between ranks can be indexed by Spearman's rank correlation coefficient (Hays, 1963) or by gamma (Goodman & Kruskal, 1954). Thus, if we are interested in the effectiveness of our strategy for mailing promotional materials proportionately to different ZIP codes, we can assess the association between neighborhoods ranked by density of mailings and the number of clients calling the practice for the first time after receiving the mailing. A high correlation would support our strategy.

Ranking items in terms of an underlying dimension allows us to use the transitive relation (Frankfort-Nachmias & Nachmias, 1992): For example, ZIP code 92117 is more productive than ZIP code 92143, which, in turn, is more productive than ZIP code 92113. Similar comparisons of larger than, faster than, taller than, and so on involve the > relation. Ordered items are in a transitive relation to one another such that if $A > B$, and $B > C$, $A > C$. Again, all we know is the relative position of the items in some hierarchy or on some dimension.

Interval Data

If it is possible to know the exact difference between the items and if that difference is constant, we are dealing with interval measurement. Examples of variables indexed using interval measurement are common in the behavioral sciences and include intelligence (IQ), standardized test scores, grade point average (GPA), and depression. With interval measurement it is possible both to order people or objects along a dimension, preserving the > relation, and to know by how much one position in the rank differs from the other.

Unlike nominal and ordinal forms of measurement, interval measurement requires a unit of measurement. Thus, with thermometers we speak of degrees Fahrenheit or centigrade; with GPA we speak of points on a continuum from 0 to 4.0 or 5.0. If there is a unit of measurement, an interval scale exists. Consecutive positions on an interval scale are equally distant. Thus, if Mary's score on the Hamilton Rating Scale for Depression (Hamilton, 1960) is 23, George's is 20, and Sam's is 17, not only does Mary have a higher depression score than George, her score exceeds George's by as much as George's score exceeds Sam's. Mathematical operations can be performed with interval data. For example, we can add a set of values, divide the sum by the number of values added, and obtain a mean. All the statistical concepts familiar to behavioral scientists can be applied to interval data (Frankfort-Nachmias & Nachmias, 1992).

Ratio Data

Interval data exist along a single quantitative dimension, as do ordinal data, and equal intervals separate them. When we also have the fortunate circumstance in which an absolute zero point can be defined, we are at the highest level of measurement, which involves ratio data. Many of the variables of interest to human services practitioners have absolute zero points. For example, specific behavior (e.g., appointments kept, words spoken, steps taken), physical characteristics (e.g., weight, length) and physiological responses (e.g., heart rate, galvanic skin response, muscle tension) can be measured at points starting with their total absence. The number of referrals from different sources is a ratio measurement because zero referrals can be defined.

All mathematical and statistical operations can be used with ratio scales. Indeed, one of their major advantages is that they can be subjected to more operations than other forms of measurement. For example, although a person with an IQ of 120 has a much higher score than someone with an IQ of 60, it is not possible to say that the first person is twice as smart or has twice the intelligence as the second because there is no natural zero point for intelligence. In contrast, it is possible to say that a person who kept 10 of 20 appointments on time was twice as prompt as someone who kept 5 of 20 on time and that a person keeping all 20 such appointments on time is twice as prompt as the first person. With ratio scales, equal ratios represent equal amounts of the commodity, object, or behavior being measured. Someone keeping 5 of 10 appointments on time is just as prompt as someone keeping 10 of 20. Likewise, a person paying $5,000 tax on an income of $20,000 is being taxed at the same rate as someone paying $20,000 tax on an income of $80,000.

Because of the greater mathematical and statistical treatments available for ratio scales, it is preferable to choose variables that can be measured on them whenever possible. More powerful statistical tests generally can be used with ratio data. Thus, if there is a choice between scale types, using higher forms (e.g., interval or ratio) will likely be associated with a more powerful evaluation design than using a lower form (e.g., ordinal). To illustrate, it often is useful to keep track of the ages of clients, their education levels, and their income levels. A common tactic is to use categories for such variables (e.g., Category 1 = 0–6 years, Category 2 = 7–12 years, Category 3 = 13–19 years, and so on). Thus, clients ages 6, 17, and 24 would be assigned to age categories 1, 3, and 4. Or, an item on a client information form dealing with income might ask clients to place their income in one of several categories (e.g., $10,000–$25,000, $25,001–$50,000). This practice is unwise because it involves converting ratio data to ordinal data (at best) or nominal data (at worst), with attendant loss of important information. This limits the kinds of analyses we can perform on them. Converting the categorical income data into interval data by assigning them to categories allows us to perform some statistical calculations, such as correlating income level with other variables of interest (e.g., probability of keeping appointments; adherence with treatment recommendations), but to retain maximum flexibility in terms of subsequent analyses, we should retain the ratio scale underlying such variables in the first place. Therefore, rather than asking clients to check age categories which are then converted to ordinal or interval data, it is better to ask them to give their actual years of age or their date of birth, from which age can be determined at a later time.

Cohen (1983) warned of the perils of converting data of a higher form of measurement (e.g., interval) to those of a lower form (e.g., categorical or ordinal). The greatest danger is the loss of information. Whether practice evaluation data are of the nominal, ordinal, interval, or ratio form, they must be readily available, routinely collected, efficiently analyzed, and presented to relevant audiences if they are to have maximum impact.

Sources of Information

As suggested by the diversity of information types just described, data used in practice evaluations come from a number of areas, depending on the component being evaluated. For the direct services component, client domain data come from clients directly as well as from other sources about the client, including referral sources and the client's significant others. Official archives can be an additional source of data about clients. Although rarely used by independent practitioners, police records, hospital records, and patient records from inpatient behavioral health facilities are commonly used in research on intervention effectiveness (Webb, Campbell, Schwartz, Sechrest, & Grove, 1981).

Practitioners serving large corporate clients can get important information from formal news services, such as Reuters or Standard & Poor's. They also can obtain detailed financial information from the Securities and Exchange Commission for companies that are publicly traded. Insurance companies and managed care organizations (MCOs) contracting with the practice can provide statistics concerning utilization and effectiveness of direct services.

Data for evaluating other practice components can come from sources as diverse as records kept routinely in the practice offices (e.g., billing, salary, and expense records) and the responses of participants to evaluative questionnaires administered at community education seminars. Clients can be asked how they initially heard about the practice as a way of monitoring the benefits of various types of advertising or referral development activities.

Ways to Obtain Information

Many options are available for obtaining client information. Clients can provide data directly in response to questions asked of them in person, over the telephone (e.g., Lawrence, Heyman, & O'Leary, 1995), or through written questionnaires. As described in chapter 5, they also can respond to questions administered by a computer terminal in the practitioner's office (e.g., Erdman, Klein, & Greist, 1985; Farrell & McCullough-Vaillant, 1996; Fowler, Finkelstein, Penk, Bell, & Itzig, 1987) or to questionnaires they download from the practitioner's Web site. In addition, clients can record data on a moment-by-moment basis using small, palm-top computers provided by the practitioner (e.g., Newman, Kenardy, Herman, & Taylor, 1997; Shiffman et al., 1997). Clients can call in and leave critical information on the provider's voice-mail system. This reporting can be done on a one-time or ongoing (e.g., daily or weekly) basis.

When significant others are the information source, they can be telephoned, asked directly in interview contexts, or asked indirectly through computer terminals in providers' offices (e.g., parents can describe their child to a psychologist by responding to behavior checklist items that appear on a computer monitor). Questionnaires also can be mailed to significant others, who complete and return them to the practitioner, as is often done with the 360° feedback approaches frequently used in business contexts (Timmreck & Bracken, 1997) and with teachers to obtain information about children.

Finally, trained collaborators of the practitioner can make direct observations of client behavior. For example, clerks in the waiting room can note the general demeanor of a client, whether the client interacts with others, engages in nervous habits, or talks to himself or herself. Clients receiving assertiveness training can be called and asked to comply with a series of progressively more demanding requests as a way of assessing their ability to refuse them. The provider also obtains information from direct observations of the client in sessions. Some of this information is formalized and monitored over time, as when a psychologist tracks the number of positive self-referent statements uttered by clients in treatment for depression or the number of delusional statements by clients with schizophrenia.

Managing Practice Information

To be useful in practice evaluation, information obtained about the client, the practice, the provider, and the intervention must be managed effectively. Managing information involves four major activities: organizing and storing it, updating it, evaluating it, and analyzing it.

Organizing and Storing Information

When it comes to keeping track of data, the practice evaluator has a more difficult task than the researcher does. Researchers formulate a relatively circumscribed research question and then obtain data specific to it. Practitioners, however, collect extensive amounts of data in advance of formulating evaluation questions. Their challenge is to arrange the data so that they can be used to answer questions as they occur. Practitioners also must organize their data to serve multiple purposes, including ongoing functions of the practice and answering evaluative questions. In addition, even though large amounts of information are collected on a continual basis, still more might be needed to answer specific questions as they are eventually formulated. A particular evaluation project might require data over and above those normally collected. It needs information not foreseen when the routine data for the practice were identified and mechanisms set up to collect and manage them.

Fortunately, technology is available today to assist practitioners in organizing and storing information. Its judicious use also makes it relatively easy to handle the other activities involved in data management (i.e., updating it, evaluating its quality, and analyzing it). Powerful database software now provides for the efficient entry, storage, organization, and retrieval of large amounts of information. Practitioners have a choice of a number of powerful computer programs that manage large amounts of information in efficient ways. Software ranges from stand-alone programs used for a variety of data management purposes (e.g., maintaining addresses, scheduling, indexing library holdings, and organizing forms and information from insurance companies and MCOs) to programs designed specifically to handle data for particular types of service providers.

Clement (1999) described his own database and the types of information he routinely collects to evaluate the effectiveness of his psychological practice. Much of the data he mentions are items included in the discussion above. Identifying and demographic information on the client take up a major portion of the entries; it includes name, age, date of birth, gender, race, ethnicity, address, telephone numbers, fax number, referring person, diagnoses, dates of initial and final sessions, treatment format (individual, group, family, couple, other) and treatment type. In addition, a 5-point rating of general outcome made by Clement is included, as is an estimate of the effect of the service, using a modification of the effect size estimate described in chapter 9.

In my own practice, I have found it useful to keep extensive amounts of information in databases such as Clement's. In addition to some of the items in his system, I enter progress notes and scores from assessment instruments commonly used with clients. Because I often make contracts with clients for one or both of us to do something by a certain time, I also include a "check back" field to prompt me to get back to the client and discuss how our respective contract-related tasks are progressing. The database allows me to input reminders so that it can generate a report of client-related tasks for each day (e.g., sending the title of a book, calling to check their homework progress, calling to get insurance information, or sending a birthday card).

Computerized databases are of two major types: flat file and relational. *Flat-file* databases are "simple" databases because all the information is contained in a single file (Cobb & Romfo, 1991). An example of such an approach would be the paper version of a card catalog in a public library. Information about the library's holdings is contained in the catalog, and managing that information involves looking through and physically sorting the cards in different ways, such as all books having to do with gardening, or all magazines dealing with sports and published after 1995. A difficulty with flat-file approaches is that they either have to be inordinately large to have enough information to be maximally useful or they have to be used in conjunction with several other databases. Although computers can manage large data sets, large databases can be cumbersome because they may require the practitioner to plow through dozens of types of information every time the system is accessed just to get to the data needed at the moment. Moreover, multiple users of the system might not need to have access to all the information. Suppose the practitioner preferred to keep progress notes separate from other information about the client, yet have them automated and readily accessible. With a flat file, this would not be possible, and all information on a client would be available in a single location.

Relational databases are more flexible than flat-file types because they permit the development and relating of any number of separate files containing different data. The files are related or linked by information they have in common, such as the client's name or social security number. It is typical to have a master file and several smaller, special-purpose files that are related to it. The master file is usually more comprehensive and contains more information on the client, such as demographic data, diagnostic information, and financial data. Related special-purpose files might contain recommended treatments for particular diagnoses, progress notes, goal statements for clients receiving specific types of treatment, assessment instruments for different diagnoses, bibliographic information arranged by diagnosis, or types of homework or extrasession activities useful for people with different types of problem.

Information in databases is entered in fields defined for each variable or information type. For example, a client's first name would be entered in the "first name" field, the date of birth in the "DOB" field, and so on. Each database file is made up of a finite number of data fields. Usually, fields are of specific types (e.g., numeric fields require numeric information, and date fields require dates entered in a specific format).

Databases can be programmed to manipulate the data in the fields to provide a wide variety of helpful information. For example, when working with children it is helpful to keep track of their ages. The computer can be instructed to calculate children's ages from their birth dates automatically every time a file is opened. Another example would be a field labeled "days since seen." Entries in this field would result from the computer automatically calculating the number of days between the date in the "last visit" field and the current date. This can be especially helpful in tracking clients' appointments or follow-up sessions.

Some programs can generate averages and other aggregate data from the information in the database. To illustrate, I routinely administer the Eyberg Child Behavior Inventory (ECBI; Eyberg & Ross, 1978) to children when they initially are seen in my practice. The mean for all children served is automatically updated and immediately available when I enter the score from each new administration. When I want to see whether children with particular types of problems or of particular demographic categories have different ECBI scores, it is a simple matter to sort on the appropriate field (e.g., gender), and find the mean score for boys and girls.

For service providers uninterested in designing their own database systems, commercially available practice-management software is a useful alternative. Several systems have been around for some years and have evolved to become quite comprehensive and sophisticated. These tend to be relational databases that are organized around a central file of basic client information, sometimes called a "face sheet" or "intake form." Additional, related files include some of those mentioned above, such as files for progress notes, billing, scheduling, medication history, managed care authorizations, capitation management, reports, diagnoses, and progress–outcomes documentation. The inclusion of libraries (files) of commonly used insurance forms, assessment instruments, diagnostic systems, and bibliographic items can be exceptionally helpful and time saving. Examples of comprehensive practice management systems for psychologists are advertised routinely in professional publications, such as the American Psychological Association's *Monitor on Psychology*.

Keeping Information Current

As suggested in the previous section, database software programs can facilitate updating practice information. Keeping information current is especially important in practice management and evaluation, and periodic inventories or audits are useful as checks on the success of such efforts. Follow-up contacts with clients can be difficult, for example, if locator information (telephone, address) is out of date.

Evaluating Information Quality

It is of little use to accumulate extensive statistics on the operation of a practice if the information from which those statistics are calculated is of poor quality. Indeed, the task of conducting an evaluation in the first place can be made exceptionally difficult if data are incomplete, inaccurate, unreadable, or out of date.

Objective checklists to assess data quality can be extremely helpful and are becoming popular with auditors overseeing the quality of services reimbursed by MCOs. For example, one system that a large MCO uses to monitor behavioral health services contains 55 items rated on 4-point scales. Areas evaluated include whether the content and format of the client records are uniformly organized, the adequacy of any rationale for ongoing appointment scheduling, whether the treatment plan follows logically from data, the expected number of visits, and the criteria for discharge. Additional items cover the legibility of record entries, whether they are typed, and whether client noncompliance and follow up are documented.

Clement (1996) recommended evaluating the record keeping of individual practitioners and revealed surprise at the "variability in the quantity and quality of information" (p. 152) he found on auditing 644 of his own case records. Shulman (1998) described a records checklist developed in his practice to prepare for a National Committee on Quality Assurance review. The checklist uses 24 items scored on a yes–no basis, including whether all entries are dated, whether relevant medical conditions are listed, and whether documentation exists as to past and present substance use. For example, one item reads as follows:

> Progress notes describe patient strengths and limitations in achieving treatment plan goals and objectives.
>
> _____ Yes _____ No _____ N/A.

Completeness and readability of the entries in practice records are important evaluative criteria; the accuracy of the information is also critical. For example, a survey checklist item that asks whether "allergies and adverse reactions are clearly documented" might show that the documentation has occurred, but whether the information is correct would require checking with an independent source, making accuracy a much more difficult attribute to evaluate. Nonetheless, future audit teams will no doubt want to know something about accuracy and eventually will develop effective ways of assessing it.

Analyzing Information

Well-organized, updated, and accurate data are of value only when analyzed and put to some use. The types of analysis a practice evaluator wants to perform depend on the reasons why the practice is being evaluated in the first place. The most important reason is to determine whether the practice's goals are being realized, because accomplishing goals moves the practice further toward realizing its vision (see chapter 2). For example, suppose one practice goal is "to achieve a mean of 4.0 or better on the dimensions of the Mental Health Corporations of America survey (MHCA, 1995) related to physical environment and client-staff interaction." If clients are routinely given the MHCA survey at the conclusion of services and their responses are entered in the practice's database, periodic summaries of their impressions can be prepared. Some database programs include powerful graphing programs that permit charts and graphs of various types to be produced relatively easily.

How frequently should practice data be analyzed? The answer depends on the nature of the variable being monitored. If the variable is something that changes slowly (e.g., ages of clients served, types of problems presented by clients), relatively infrequent analysis is appropriate, perhaps no more often than annually. Other variables (e.g., satisfaction with services, success of interventions) are likely to be less stable; for them, more frequent analysis is warranted. It is useful to remember that keeping the variables continually in focus enhances realization of practice goals. Being the "best" provider of a service involves meeting or exceeding client expectations a high percentage of the time. A large practice might want to summarize client satisfaction at least monthly in order to achieve this goal; if the service is failing to maintain high levels of satisfaction, it can take steps to improve matters right away.

Actual client progress should be monitored frequently throughout the course of service provision. This monitoring should focus on variables that mediate or are instrumental to the changes ultimately sought by the client. For example, weekly improvements in the range of motion in an arm can be charted for a patient undergoing physical therapy. Ongoing data analysis can be facilitated through the use of spreadsheet or database programs readily available to practitioners.

To illustrate the process of continuous progress monitoring, consider a psychologist who is treating a 32-year-old female client for major depression. Before the start of each therapy session, the psychologist brings up the client's file on her computer screen and reviews the previous progress note and any objective data being kept. As a measure of the client's general affect, the psychologist keeps track of the number of positive self-referent statements the client makes during the first 15 minutes of each session. When the session ends, the therapist enters the total in a spreadsheet and updates her progress notes at the same time. Figure 6.2 presents an example of what the spreadsheet might look like.

As the data for each session are entered in the spreadsheet, the graph is automatically updated. The psychologist can readily see whether her measure of affect is showing the kind of change anticipated and alter her intervention accordingly. Relatively little time is involved in using direct-observation data to monitor service quality in this way. Moreover, summary statistics for the client, payers, and other stakeholders can be produced periodically and at the conclusion of service. More complex graphs can be produced to show the effects of different types of intervention using time-series methodology (see chapter 8). Carr and Burkholder (1998) described how to use a popular spreadsheet program to create these graphs.

Using Practice Information

Data that have been managed well and that are organized, updated, accurate, and easily analyzed are available for a variety of uses. The following list describes the most important of those uses:

- Selecting interventions
- Monitoring client progress
- Evaluating the practice
- Assisting one's memory
- Informing and advertising
- Contributing to the discipline of outcomes evaluation
- Obtaining reimbursement.

Motivating Others to Provide Practice Information

Handling information efficiently assumes that it is available to be handled. Obtaining the data to manage can present challenges of its own, however. The most important source of information is the client, whether that is an individual or an entity such as a corporation or public agency. Getting facts and figures from clients takes skill and persistence. It is a good idea to obtain as much descriptive information (demographic, biographic) as possible even before services begin, because this is usually a time of maximum motivation and cooperation. Care must be taken to avoid overburdening the client, however, as it can jeopardize the ongoing provision of data. Indeed, it is a good idea to limit data

Figure 6.2

Session	1	2	3	4	5	6	7	8	9	10
Positive self-refs	0	1	3	3	1	2	0			

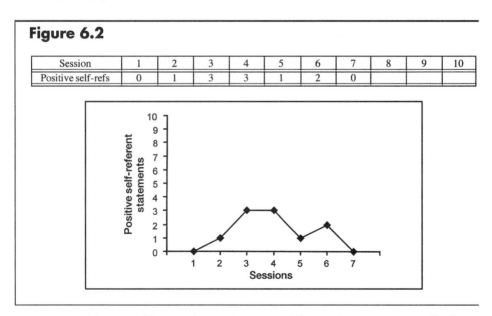

An excerpt of a spreadsheet and a graph generated from it showing positive self-referent statements over time.

collection demands on clients to information that is essential to providing effective services. "Need to know" information takes precedence over "nice to know" information; any requests for the latter should not jeopardize the former.

For each fact or figure needed to evaluate a practice, it is useful to consider alternative ways of obtaining it. This is true in basic research as well: Multiple converging data sources provide stronger evidence than a single source. Sometimes significant others can produce information to supplement that provided by the client. Proxy information may be able to substitute for the real data when it is not available or likely to be of questionable quality (e.g., using a person's occupation or address to represent income level).

Clients are more likely to produce necessary information when it is made clear to them how it will be used in providing services. They also are more likely to be motivated if they are involved in the choice of information and information source in the first place. When they see a clear connection between the data they are being asked to provide and the outcomes they are seeking from the service, they are more apt to bring in information on a regular basis. This connection can be strengthened when the practitioner begins each session with attention to the data asked of the client. It is beneficial to examine the data carefully, comment on it, and use the opportunity to inquire of any difficulties the client might have encountered in providing it. For example, if using the Daily Record of Dysfunctional Thoughts (Beck, Rush, Shaw, & Emery, 1979), the therapist and client can review the client's self-monitoring of strong emotions and the automatic thoughts they evoke. The client can then learn to challenge these thoughts and replace them with more rational ones. Clients also are more likely to comply with data provision requirements if they commit themselves in writing ahead of time (Levy, 1977). The client should be praised or otherwise rewarded for bringing the information (Nelson, 1981). Returning deposits contingent on bringing in data can be useful in some cases (Best & Steffy, 1971); reducing fees in return for data is another way of motivating reliable data provision, according to Mahoney (1977). Mahoney also described a series of progressively more compelling procedures designed to generate compliance with data collection requests, ending with making professional services contingent on the production of data. He argued that he has an ethical obligation to provide the best services possible; because the best services are based on data, he cannot provide them without the information. Therefore, it makes sense to terminate services in the few cases in which the "threat" of termination does not result in the appearance of data.

Other information collection procedures can be considered if clients are inconsistent in providing data. They can be given dated postcards and asked to mail one each day with the day's information on it. They can be encouraged to call and leave a message on the provider's voice mail at an agreed-on interval or to tape record the data and bring the tape in for the provider to analyze.

The most critical consideration in motivating consistent data provision is the actual use of the data. Using data frequently and publicly to make important decisions communicates their significance to everyone involved. The practitioner might consider creating a *culture of evidence*, in which data are usually consulted before decisions are made. Paraphrasing from the movie *Jerry McGuire*, practitioners can ask continually of themselves and others "Show me the data." Decisions as small as buying a new chair for the waiting area or as large as selling the practice to an MCO can be based on information showing how the decision advances the goals of the practice and the personal visions of its owners.

Summary

This chapter focuses on data: getting it, managing it, using it, and motivating others to provide it. Readily accessible data help select effective interventions, monitor client progress, assist the therapist's recall of important information, advertise the practice, contribute new knowledge to the discipline and profession, and obtain reimbursement for services from third parties. Of the uses for practice data reviewed in this chapter, the most important is evaluating the effectiveness of the practice itself. Creating a culture of evidence, in which all important decisions in a practice are controlled by objective data that relate to the goals of the practice, moves the organization closer to realizing its mission.

The next chapter discusses how to operationalize the variables from the five domains depicted in Figure 6.1. Once the practitioner has appropriate measures of relevant variables, data can be collected and a culture of evidence developed.

Supplemental Reading

American Psychological Association Practice Directorate. (1996a). *Managing your practice finances.* Washington, DC: Author.

American Psychological Association Practice Directorate. (1996b). *Organizing your practice through automation.* Washington, DC: Author.

Clement, P. W. (1999). *Outcomes and incomes: How to evaluate, improve, and market your psychotherapy practice by measuring outcomes.* New York: Guilford Press.

Kiesler, D. J. (1969). A Grid model for theory and research in the psychotherapies. In L. D. Eron & R. Callahan (Eds.), *The relationship of theory to practice in psychotherapy* (pp. 115–145). Chicago: Aldine.

Yenney, S. L., & American Psychological Association Practice Directorate. (1994). *Business strategies for a caring profession.* Washington, DC: Author.

Measurement Tools for Evaluating Outcomes

This is the first of three chapters that together provide the basic tools necessary for competent practice evaluation. This chapter deals with how to obtain the data you need to answer the evaluative questions discussed in chapter 5; chapter 8 presents the tools involved in arranging these data into evaluative designs, and chapter 9 discusses the statistical tools you need to determine whether your answers are reliable.

This chapter describes the importance of specifying the variables implied in your evaluation question as precisely as possible. It discusses the advantages of categorizing human behavior into cognitive, motor, and physiological responses and reviews the major approaches to assessment and their relative usefulness. The chapter also elaborates on criteria for evaluating the adequacy of different measures; it notes the advantages of using existing measures when possible and offers sources for obtaining such measures.

Operationalizing Variables

The preceding chapters have posed interesting questions to be asked in practice evaluations, emphasized the importance of phrasing the questions properly, and highlighted the relative ease of deriving well-worded hypotheses from properly stated questions. To establish the existence of the relationships implied in both evaluative questions and their associated hypotheses, the variables involved in the relationships must be operationalized. In other words, the variables must be measured in some way.

Consider the psychologist who wants to know whether panic attacks in clients are reduced as a result of the services offered. The evaluation question might be "Are panic attacks in clients less frequent because of the services we offer?" This question includes two variables: panic attacks and psychological services. The way the question is phrased makes it clear that panic attacks are considered the dependent variable. They are expected to relate causally to psychological services, the independent variable. Relevant hypotheses are easy to specify: "People receiving psychological therapy from us show decreases in the frequency of panic attacks." Testing the hypothesis is a simple matter of observing whether there is a relationship between the independent and dependent variables. But how do we make those observations? This chapter is devoted to that subject.

Dependent Variables

How do we define "panic attacks?" How do we define "decreases in frequency?" The answer, of course, is operationally. We compose definitions precise enough that anyone reading them knows exactly what we mean. The easiest way to obtain this level of precision is to describe the operations used to assess some characteristic of interest. Operational definitions differ from conceptual definitions in that the latter typically describe variables in terms of a theory or network of relationships involving the variable of interest as well as other relevant variables. Within Beck's cognitive theory of anxiety and panic, for instance, people experiencing panic are likely to misinterpret normal physiological reactions as "catastrophic." The definitions of both panic and catastrophizing can be found in Beck's writings (e.g., Beck, 1988), which are the source for the conceptual definitions of the terms.

Getting from a conceptual definition of panic to a measure of it can be challenging, however, in part because numerous ways exist of assessing any construct. As with other psychological characteristics, anxiety is an abstract, hypothetical concept that is not measurable directly. We must infer it from data produced by certain measuring instruments or operations. The operations must be carefully selected to represent the construct in terms of the larger theory of which it is a part. Terms in a conceptual definition of a construct, however, are subject to interpretation. Thus, merely understanding the definition and attempting to assess the construct based on that understanding might lead to different operations. The result is that different ways of assessing a construct tend to correlate less than perfectly.

For this reason, one encounters operational definitions such as "intelligence is what intelligence tests measure" or "intelligence is what is measured by the Kaufman Assessment Battery for Children" (Kaufman & Kaufman, 1983). By restricting the definition of a variable to the operations involved in assessing it, we promote clear communication. If someone else wants to know what is meant by intelligence, it is simple enough to examine the measure and note the types of behavior it assesses. The same is true for other psychological variables. To know what is meant by anxiety, one can examine the content of assessment devices with "anxiety" in their titles. However, just because something is named the same as something else does not mean it *is* the same. In psychology, this logic error is known as the *jingle fallacy* (Kelley, 1927). Different measures of anxiety come from different theoretical understandings of anxiety; because they derive from different conceptual definitions, it is not surprising when they correlate less than perfectly.

Limiting definitions to operational ones is not a common practice in the behavioral sciences, despite its obvious advantages, nor is it common in the physical sciences. Here it is less problematic to deviate from strict operationalism, however. In the physical sciences, concepts are defined according to measures that are relatively absolute (Johnston & Pennypacker, 1993). When weight is reported in kilograms, for example, general agreement exists as to what this means—because a kilogram is defined in terms of some physical quality that is measurable.

In psychology and other behavioral sciences, it is uncommon to use physical qualities to provide *absolute* (i.e., fixed, unvarying) references for measures. Indeed, instead of defining its subject matter in terms that are absolute, psychology defines its major concepts in terms of variation in scores on measures of the concepts. For example, when a person is said to have a high level of intelligence, it means that he or she achieved a score on a test of intelligence that is higher than most people on whom the test was standardized. Thus, the person's level of intelligence is determined by variation in scores of the original standardization sample. The same score can mean different things in reference to different standardization samples or norms. To illustrate, a raw score of 65 on a measure with a mean of 60 and a standard deviation of 5.0 means something different from the same 65 on a measure with a mean of 60 and a standard deviation of 2.5. In the second case, the person is more unusual because there is less variation in scores; he or she is said to have more of whatever is being measured.

Even though the practice is relatively uncommon, it is possible to use measures of behavioral characteristics that rely on units that are absolute and unvarying. A practitioner who tracks depression in terms of frequency of positive self-referent statements is using such a measure. The frequency of the statements is established as a ratio of the number uttered to the period of time over which they are assessed. A person making positive self-referent statements at a rate of 2 per minute is doing so at twice the frequency of someone uttering them at 1 per minute. This type of measurement means the same thing to anyone considering it and does not change from one measurement context to the next. Other temporal (and therefore relatively absolute) units used with behavior are *latency*, the time between the occurrence of an event and a behavior thought to be associated with it, and *duration*, the length of time a behavior lasts.

Returning to the evaluation question posed at the beginning of this section, the psychologist can define "panic attacks" in terms of movement of some part or all of the body through space in time, as occurs when a person avoids or approaches a frightening situation. Thus, the time it takes clients to cover a certain fixed distance (e.g., from their car to a certain store in a mall) can be an aspect of what is meant by panic attack. Further examples include statements such as "I'll lose control and pass out," increased heart rate, and rapid breathing. Each measurement approach can operationalize panic attacks or an aspect of them. Combining these leads to comprehensive assessment.

Independent Variables

We are halfway home when we have satisfactory measures of the dependent variable. Now let us look at the independent variable. What do we mean by psychological therapy? How do we operationalize it? Just as different measures with the same name do not necessarily tap the same dependent variable, different interventions with the same name may not actually involve the same therapeutic activities. *Uniformity myths* (Kiesler, 1971) are common in studies evaluating treatment outcomes; that is, it is often assumed there is a certain consistency among services all referred to using the same label. In the present example, the error lies in assuming that all psychological therapy is the same. Other examples include research questions such as "Does psychotherapy work?" "Does special education work?" and "Is chiropractic effective?" All involve the assumption that these interventions are uniform or consistent in their application. In reality, psychological therapy is not a homogeneous entity, and neither is special education.

To answer practice evaluation questions of the "Does it work?" variety most effectively, one needs to specify in some detail just what the practice involves. What does the practitioner mean by psychological therapy? The techniques used and their frequency, out-of-office practice, data keeping, qualifications of staff providing therapy, length of sessions, sequence of activities within sessions, time spent on each activity, and the physical context of the therapy are some of the treatment attributes the practitioner could describe. In medicine and psychology it is becoming common for treatments to be operationalized in terms of manuals that specify what is to be done in rather precise detail (see Wilson, 1996). Thus, one can define "interpersonal psychotherapy" by referring to the manual describing it (see Klerman, Weissman, Rounsaville, & Chevron, 1984). This practice makes possible a more precise comparison of treatments in randomized controlled trial research.

Although the practitioner is not likely to have the resources to develop treatment manuals for the various types of intervention provided, it is probably a good idea to base interventions on the empirically supported procedures described in such manuals as closely as possible. Often, developers of the treatment write the manuals. Who knows better than they do how to implement it? If the practitioner deviates from the manual, careful notes can be kept. This permits outcomes to be attributed as precisely as possible to the treatment that is actually delivered. This careful noting of what is done with each client puts the therapist in the best position to know what works and what does not and to replicate the former. A good practice is to establish a baseline of effectiveness for a particular procedure over repeated uses while following the manual as closely as possible. Then creative deviation can be examined while carefully documenting any changes in approach. In this way the treatment can be reproduced if it is shown to be effective.

Demographic Variables

Measuring the variables involved in practice evaluation can be a daunting task. It is critical to the success of the effort, however, and warrants our utmost attention. Continuous practice improvement requires decisions based on adequate information, or data, which should come from objective measures of one's dependent and independent variables. Even the most seemingly straightforward characteristics demand some thought if they are to be measured well. To illustrate, practitioners who want to know the demographic characteristics of their clientele face immediate decisions involving measure selection. They must develop a way of collecting the information from clients, for example. Most often this involves developing a form of some type, such as that provided in Exhibit 7.1.

The items on an information form should be carefully considered. Recall that it takes time for the client to complete and time for you to transfer the data to a database or some other repository. Respect the time it takes, and be sure to include only items of likely relevance. A good way to determine what information to obtain can come from looking at the forms used in practices similar to yours. Discuss the form with those practitioners, and ask about each item and how it has been helpful. (See Yenney and the American Psychological Association Practice Directorate, 1994, for examples of useful forms.)

In addition to the specific types of information you ask of the client, consider how you ask for it as well. For example, the client's age can be an important piece of information. Note that in Exhibit 7.1 this information is obtained by asking for the client's date of birth. Why not simply ask the client to write in his or her age? One reason has to do with precision. Computerized databases easily convert dates into numbers that can be used in various calculations. If clients merely indicate their age at the time they complete the form, it can be cumbersome to figure out how old they are some months or years in the future. Furthermore, using the date of birth allows a computer to provide more precise age information (in years and months, for example); this ability might not be critical in most practices, but it is certainly important to pediatricians, child psychologists, and others working with young children.

The point is to consider the format of your data carefully. The item in Exhibit 7.1 dealing with education illustrates an excellent way to obtain precise information. One could ask the client to provide information on education in terms of the highest level completed (e.g., grade school, junior high school, high school or GED, community college, bachelors degree, graduate degree), but this approach is clearly less precise. To check "graduate degree," does one have to have completed it or merely worked on it? What if someone dropped out halfway through the 11th grade? Does he or she check "high school" or "junior high school"?

In addition, asking for the actual number of years of education completed provides a ratio measure. As described earlier, because such data represent the highest form of measurement, they can be subjected

Exhibit 7.1

Sample Basic Information Form for an Independent Practice

Please Tell Us About Yourself

Our promise: The information on this form is not shared with anyone without your permission. We do not sell or otherwise make available your name, or even acknowledge to anyone that you are a client, without your consent.

Name: _____   Today's date: _____   Date of birth: _____

Address: _____   _____   ____ _____
           Street   City   State   Zip

Phone: (_____) _____   (_____) _____
              Daytime   Evening

Gender: _____ female   _____ male

Ethnicity: _____ African American _____ Hispanic _____ White _____ Asian

_____ Native American   _____ Other: _____

Significant relationships: ___single ___married ___separated ___divorced ___widowed

_____ in long-term committed relationship   _____ number of children

People living with you (please place number in relevant blanks, e.g., 0, 1, 2):

_____ children   _____ parents   _____ brother(s)   _____ sister(s)

_____ other: _____

Years of education you have completed: 1 2 3 4 5 6 7 8 9 10 11 12 13 14 15 16 17 18 >18
                                                          (circle one)

Occupation: _____   Currently working? ___ yes   ___ no

Employer: _____   Payment method: ___ cash ___ check ___ credit card

Insurance: _____   Please include your policy or account number: _____
              Insurance company

Approximate net annual income from all sources:

___ <$15,000 ___ $15,000–$25,000 ___$25,000–$35,000 ___ $35,000–$45,000

___ $45,000–$55,000 ___ $55,000–$65,000 ___ $65,000–$75,000 ___ >$75,000

Please tell us how we can be of service to you: _____

_____

to mathematical operations and treated with the most powerful forms of statistical analysis. Asking someone to provide categorical data results in the loss of potentially valuable information. Although the number of clients of a particular level of educational attainment can be useful for a practice, converting the categorical data to another format (e.g., assigning a "1" to grade school, a "2" to junior high) facilitates converting the information to other variables. Asking clients for the years of education completed requires no such conversion and permits us to distinguish finer gradations along the educational continuum.

Finally, lest there appear to be some inconsistency, take a look at the "net annual income" item in Exhibit 7.1. What about the fact that this item seems categorical? Why not ask the client to write in the actual net income received during the previous year? Indeed, doing so would be preferable from a purely measurement perspective. However, some types of information are more sensitive than others, and clients occasionally are more comfortable providing data in one form than in another. Thus, indicating a range of income rather than a precise amount of income can lead to greater compliance in providing the data. Even then information is withheld by a significant number of people, as a recent experience of the author shows: Of parents attending a workshop on interventions for children with autism, only 67% completed the portion of a basic information sheet asking them to check which of eight income ranges represented their total annual family income.

The information depicted in Exhibit 7.1 includes the basic demographic characteristics most likely to be obtained by typical practices. Individual practices may want to include items of specific interest not provided here.

Other Client Characteristics

The discussion of demographic characteristics of clients highlights the need to consider how information is to be used when setting up data collection systems. It points out the advantages of developing absolute measures. Some client characteristics, such as intelligence (described above), interpersonal effectiveness, dependability, and work-team orientation as well as level of anxiety and depressive tendencies, however, cannot be assessed in terms of absolute, standardized units. These are considered to be dispositional constructs or traits (see Allport, 1937) that develop early and are relatively enduring over the life span. Traits cannot be measured directly; their existence is inferred from differences observed in individual behavior. As Johnston and Pennypacker (1993) pointed out, such characteristics are defined in terms of variability in such differences rather than in terms of units that are standard and absolute.

The adequacy of trait measures depends entirely on the differences they reveal both when assessing a variety of people one time and one person numerous times. Are the differences consistently detectable? Are they stable over time? Are they apparent in a variety of settings? Are they detectable using more than one method of assessment? Do the differences relate to differences on measures of other characteristics? The behavioral sciences deal with these questions under the heading of concepts such as reliability, validity, generalizability theory, and item response characteristics (Nunnally & Bernstein, 1994; Pedhazur & Schmelkin, 1991). These concepts are discussed below. First, however, let us take a closer look at the nature of the client characteristics we are likely to find interesting in practice evaluation.

Again using evaluation of the effectiveness of services for panic attacks as our example, we can take several avenues to determine whether psychological therapy has helped the client. An easy approach would be to ask the client whether he or she is experiencing improvement, a method that is similar to asking students how much they feel they have learned at the end of a course. Certainly this is important information, but it is not the same as determining whether students actually did learn anything from a course. The effective practice evaluator is aware of the distinction between changes in *target behavior*, which is the focus of the intervention, and changes in *target-related behavior* (e.g., beliefs about whether the target has changed). In our example, the psychologist targeted motor aspects of panic attacks and initiated a program of therapy designed to improve motor as well as other forms of behavior. For the psychologist to document improvement, some measures are needed that assess changes in actual motor behavior. It is of some interest that the client believes that gross motor functioning has improved, but this is different from determining whether it actually has.

It also might be important for the clinician to know how the client feels about the services provided. How satisfied is the client? What about more generalized psychological changes the client is experiencing— does he or she feel less apprehensive about going outside the house independently or notice less physiological reactivity (e.g., accelerated heart rate, respiration)?

These questions relate to client characteristics that involve different types of behavior. Voluntary motor behavior requiring large muscles is one general category of responses (see Cone, 1978; Lang, 1971). As the questions about apprehensiveness and physiological responding suggest, other categories of responses include cognitive and physiological behavior.

How the anxious client feels about the services can be understood as verbal behavior or subvocal speech (things the client says to himself or herself). This type of behavior is private in that only the client knows how he or she truly feels about the service (indeed, whether there are any feelings at all). These private, *cognitive* behaviors, which include thoughts of the "I feel X; I think Y; and I want Z" variety, are among the most important and most difficult to assess. An example of cognitive behavior is reflected in the following item from a scale to assess depression: "I feel blue when I think about having to work for the next 30 years." Another example, from a measure of client satisfaction, could be "I feel the therapist really understood the issues as I do."

Cognitive behavior is important for psychologists to assess because it is likely to relate to other behavior of great relevance to the general functioning of the client. Unlike motor behavior, feelings (such as satisfaction, depression, and optimism) are in the private speech, or cognitive behavior, of the client, and only he or she can experience them directly. What others *can* observe is the client's report of that cognitive behavior, which can include thoughts, wishes, and other events in addition to feelings.

Finally, the psychologist can assess *physiological* behavior to determine generalized service benefits. Such activities as cardiopulmonary functioning, heart rate, muscle tension, galvanic skin response, respiration, and endurance can be an important component of a comprehensive client evaluation. The activities of the smooth muscles and glands are controlled by the autonomic (involuntary) portion of the nervous system and can be considered as small behaviors that can be observed with appropriate instrumentation. Their observability makes them different from cognitive behavior and more like the motor behavior described above.

The private nature of cognitive behavior sets it apart from motor and physiological behavior, at least in terms of how to go about assessing it. Some theorists (e.g., Skinner, 1945, 1953) have argued that no fundamental difference exists in private and public responses in terms of the laws of behavior needed to explain them. That is, cognitive, motor, and physiological responding all can be understood in terms of the same science of behavior, even though only the last two can be subjected to verification by independent observers.

It has become common in psychology to sort behavior into cognitive, motor, and physiological categories (Zinbarg, 1998). Although these groupings are admittedly somewhat arbitrary, they help focus our attention on just what is changing in clients as a result of our services. As practitioners we are trained to be skeptical about what clients say, wanting to see with our own eyes the changes they have made. Clients report success or the diligent completion of homework assignments for a variety of reasons; their statements might reflect what is "really" happening, and they might reflect other "realities" as well, such as what the client hoped would happen, but really did not.

The wise practitioner observes multiple types of client responding when evaluating the effects of services. He or she places the greatest emphasis on behavior that is directly related to the ultimate goal of the service, that is, the reason the client sought help in the first place. To illustrate, consider the client who consults a psychologist because she feels depressed all the time. The psychologist and client collaboratively set a goal that involves feeling happier, more energetic, and more optimistic. To clarify precisely how they know when the goal is reached, they spend some time operationalizing "happier," "more energetic," and "more optimistic." On a conceptual level, each component of treatment outcome involves a theoretical construct. What is happiness? Energy? Optimism? The defining work of the clinician and client focuses on each construct, ultimately determining the behaviors comprising them. For example, the client says she feels happy when she is in a committed relationship, when she does something socially at least twice per week, when she maintains her weight below a certain level, and when she participates in aerobic exercise at least three times per week. Of course, other things might contribute to the client's happiness, such as being completely debt free, having a nice house in the country, and so on. She is realistic, however, and decides that therapy will be successful if she achieves the components of happiness just listed.

Note that the client's goals can be sorted according to whether they involve motor, cognitive, or physiological behavior. "Doing something socially," involves activity of the large muscles assumed to be under the control of voluntary portions of the central nervous system and therefore involves motor behavior. Participating in aerobic exercise also involves motor behavior. Maintaining weight at a certain level involves motor behavior, primarily, in that weight is the index of food eaten, calories burned through exercise, and so on. Being in a committed relationship is the most complex component of the client's happiness and would be the most challenging to operationalize. For efficiency, most clinicians would take the client's word on this one. In doing so, the behavior relied upon is verbal (i.e., motor), and the referent is likely to be cognitive. That is, the client uses verbal (motor) behavior to report her feelings (cognitive) about the relationship.

A similar analysis can be undertaken for the energy and optimism constructs. Organizing aspects of the client's constructs in terms of cognitive, motor, and physiological types of behavior helps evaluate the impact of services. Imagine a situation in which a client reports no improvement in feelings of happiness after long treatment focusing on depression. If the clinician focuses solely on the cognitive component of the happiness construct, he or she does not have information about other components, such as doing something socially on a regular basis, being in a committed relationship, or maintaining body weight at certain levels. What if data on these components were inconsistent with the cognitive reactions of the client? What if the client were doing social things regularly, maintaining her weight at a desirable level, and still reporting feeling unhappy?

Perhaps the happiness construct has not been satisfactorily operationalized; other aspects may need to be included, such as the quality of the relationship the client has with her parents. Being aware of and measuring the multiple aspects of the client's constructs provides useful information to gauge how effective the services are for any particular client. Deciding the type of client behavior to use to establish outcomes is part of the task of developing measures in practice evaluation. It is also necessary to decide how that behavior is to be assessed. A number of possibilities exist with respect to assessment method, as shown in the next section.

Methods of Assessment

Techniques for assessing human behavior can be sorted in various ways, with greater or less specificity. This book focuses on five methods, which range from interviews to direct observation. Between interviews and direct-observation methods are self-reports, rating by others, and self-monitoring. Extensive bodies of literature deal with the usefulness of these methods and with the advantages and disadvantages of each. Interested readers are referred to basic texts in measurement for more comprehensive treatments (e.g., Aiken, 1996; Cronbach, 1970; Kaplan & Saccuzzo, 1997; Pedhazur & Schmelkin, 1991). The following sections briefly describe each method and present examples of their usefulness.

Interviews

The most common method of assessing human behavior involves asking about it. Interview techniques can range from asking specific questions of an interviewee to holding what appears to be an informal discussion. *Structured* interviews, which are of the first type, usually follow a specific sequence of questions; in this sense, they are standardized. There is likely to be a high level of consistency in the way the interview is conducted from one person to the next. *Unstructured* interviews, which can resemble informal discussions, tend to be less standardized. The interviewer is less constrained to follow a particular sequence and is correspondingly freer to follow interesting leads as they come up in the process.

Interviews can be extremely useful in practice evaluation and are nearly always the starting point for evaluation, whether explicitly recognized as such or not. The practitioner meets the client for the first time, either in person or over the telephone or some other medium, and begins asking questions (i.e., interviewing) to determine the type of help wanted and whether that help can be provided. In initial interviews of this type, it is generally a good idea to begin with open-ended questions and progress to more closed-end questions. The idea is to establish a relationship with the potential client and to obtain enough information in a limited period of time to determine whether services can be helpful to the person. If services are initiated, subsequent interviews can help zero in on the nature of the concerns for which the client is seeking help. Interviews can serve a broad mapping function, identifying major areas of concern that can be probed more deeply with specific assessment procedures. Interviews are probably best suited for this exploratory function.

In addition to their initial mapping function, interviews also are useful in following up with clients who have finished treatment. The careful practitioner wants to know not only the immediate benefits of the services provided but also whether the benefits have any lasting value. It is common to conduct follow-up interviews to find out whether improvements have been maintained. This is often done over the telephone, and the job of doing it sometimes falls to a professional marketing or survey company hired by the practice. Outsourcing evaluation activities is common in the business world but less frequent among small human services practices. An advantage is that this approach offers increased objectivity; clients interviewed by someone other than the practitioner can feel freer to state opinions.

Interviews can be conducted face-to-face or over the telephone. Each has advantages and disadvantages, and space does not permit in-depth treatment of them here. Beed and Stimson (1985), Bradburn and Sudman (1982), Cannell and Kahn (1985), and Gorden (1975) provided excellent reviews on the subject. The approach used depends on the purpose of the assessment; diagnostic interviews, for example, are common in psychology and the helping professions (Hersen & Turner, 1994), and exit interviews are common in the business world.

In addition, interviews can be distinguished in terms of structure, as mentioned above. With the advent of the American Psychiatric Association's *Diagnostic and Statistical Manual of Mental Disorders* (1952), an upsurge of interest occurred in the use of diagnostic structured interviews. Structured interviews have been developed to diagnose alcohol problems, neurological impairments, mood disorders, sexual dysfunction, schizophrenia, and eating disorders, among other disorders. The best known example of a structured interview related to the *DSM* is the Structured Clinical Interview for the *DSM-III-R* (3rd ed. rev.; Spitzer, Williams, Gibbon, & First, 1992), a well-developed process that includes ways to handle ambiguous responses from interviewees. Structured interviews such as these tend to have better psychological characteristics than unstructured ones. Although interviews certainly can achieve the levels of psychometric adequacy characteristic of other methods (Ulrich & Trumbo, 1965), their strength is in the breadth of information they provide rather than in the precision with which they provide it. Thus, they are less likely to be used on an ongoing basis to monitor the effectiveness of service.

Practitioners can benefit from exploring compouter-assisted interviewing, which is a flexible way of obtaining information to determine the type of assistance a client needs; it also can produce data on an ongoing basis to help evaluate service effectiveness. The computerized assessment system for psychotherapy evaluation and research (CASPER; Farrell & McCullough-Vaillant, 1996), for example, provides a broad range of intake data, including client functioning in a number of areas of living, specific presenting concerns and their severity, and the extent to which the client wishes to work on them in therapy. CASPER can be used at intake, to monitor progress, and at termination and follow up. At intake, clients respond to 122 interview questions, which appear on a computer screen, by pressing keys on a keyboard. The questions cover 18 content areas (e.g., health and physical symptoms, mood, leisure time, self-concept); 62 target problems are linked to the questions. When specific problems are identified, clients then are asked to rate the duration and severity of each problem as well as the extent to which the client wants it to be the focus of treatment. Over the course of treatment, clients rate their progress, entering data directly into a computer or completing paper-and-pencil forms. The therapist also rates the client's progress, and the client rates the therapist in terms of how interested, concerned, and sincere the client experiences the therapist to be. The ongoing interview can take as little as 3–10 minutes to administer.

Computerized interviews are the ultimate in structure and have several advantages. Questions are standardized, meaning that they are always asked in the same way, thereby reducing differences among interviewers. The same questions, and all of them, are asked each time and of each client, overcoming interviewer forgetfulness or selectivity biases (i.e., the tendency of interviewers to select or focus on issues that are of particular interest to them and ignore ones that others might emphasize). In addition, results of the interview can be easily quantified.

It is noteworthy that concerns about clients finding computer-administered interviews cold and mechanical have not been supported. Farrell and McCullough-Vaillant (1996) and Erdman, Klein, and Greist (1985) both reported data showing positive client responses to this approach. Indeed, Farrell and McCullough-Vaillant cited research showing that some clients prefer computer-administered questions and, under some circumstances, provide more candid responses. The potential for further developments in this area is considerable.

The Internet makes daily monitoring of client progress possible through service providers' Web pages. A provider could design a Web site that allows clients to enter a private section of the site specifically devoted to them and enter data, whereupon a computer program charts the information for the therapist, who analyzes and interprets it. At any point during treatment, either the client or the therapist can access the information to determine progress, and "circuit breakers" built into the system can automatically alert a therapist when problems exceed preset levels.

Self-Reports

When a standard list of questions is presented in closed-end form in a highly structured interview, the approach essentially becomes self-report methodology. A self-report scale can be viewed as a limited set of descriptive statements relevant to a single characteristic or behavior on which people are thought to differ. The descriptive statements or items are restricted to the concept being assessed, whether it be a personality trait such as agreeableness, or a disposition to behave in certain ways under certain circumstances, such as thoughts of suicide. Examples of items that might appear in a self-report scale on sociability are "My ideal way to spend free time is alone with a book," or "I enjoy meeting new people." A collection of statements like these comprise a scale. Response alternatives usually take the form either of binary options (e.g., yes–no, true–false), or a range of how often the respondent experiences the feeling or behavior being assessed (e.g., always/sometimes/never).

Once a limited set of descriptive statements is available and response alternatives have been chosen, the next step is to determine how to assign values to the responses so that a score can be derived. With binary formats, a 1 is usually assigned to the alternative that indicates an increased propensity for the characteristic a person possesses (e.g., if he or she marked "true" in response to "I enjoy meeting new people," a point would be added to the respondent's score on a test of sociability. If the scale consisted of 20 items, scores could range from 0 to 20; with more than two alternatives (e.g., always/sometimes/never), numerical values are assigned to each (e.g., 2, 1, 0); scores on a 20-item scale with such an assignment could range from 0 to 40).

Self-reports have the advantage of greater structure than interviews and thus can provide potentially more satisfactory measurement. Questionnaire items are standardized and presented in the same way to each respondent, and limiting response alternatives leads to easy scoring and a high likelihood of agreement between scorers. Thus, these methods are often referred to as *objective techniques*, in contrast to methods using stimuli that are less specific (e.g., inkblots), referred to as *unstructured or projective techniques* (Kaplan & Saccuzzo, 1997).

A major concern with interviews and self-report methods is the potential influence of self-presentation bias. It is well documented that respondents answer questions so as to portray themselves in certain ways (Edwards, 1957, 1990; Paulhus, 1984). Entire texts have been written about the subject (e.g., Rogers, 1997). It is not realistic to expect someone to be completely objective when describing himself or herself. Objectivity is even less likely with certain people, such as children or those with psychiatric disabilities. For this reason, information is often sought from third parties.

Rating-by-Others

Rating-by-others assessment (sometimes referred to as "informant reports") improves on the objectivity of interviews and self-reports by obtaining information about the client from an independent source. A common example is the use of parents or teachers to complete rating scales or checklists such as the Conners Parent and Teacher Rating Scales (Conners, 1990) or the Child Behavior Checklist (Achenbach, 1991). In the latter, a parent or teacher responds to items such as "talks too much" or "attacks people" by marking 3-point scales indicating the item's applicability to the child. Third-party ratings have been used extensively in psychology to provide information on a variety of attributes, including depression (Hamilton, 1960), social skills (Wallander, Conger, & Conger, 1985), liking of one's peers (Coie, Dodge, & Coppotelli, 1982), and self-control in children (Kendall & Wilcox, 1979). They have been used extensively outside psychology as well, including in the rating of White House staff (Pedhazur & Schmelkin, 1991), the rating of professors by students (Greenwald, 1997), and the rating of civil servants dating back to uses by the Chinese more than 4,000 years ago (DuBois, 1970). Perhaps because, like self-reports, rating-by-others measures are easy to develop, their use has proliferated. Unfortunately, as is true of self-reports, many such measures have been reported with insufficient information as to their scientific adequacy.

Although using an independent source to provide information about a person may appear to enhance objectivity on its face, important limits exist concerning the extent to which the information about the person being rated (i.e., the ratee) is unbiased. As with self-report instruments, third-party ratings reflect the perceptions of the person completing them rather than purely objective features of the phenomenon being assessed. One cannot be sure exactly how much of the score provided on the rating scale is the result of the phenomenon itself and how much is the result of other events that have biased or colored the rating. Perhaps the best that can be said is that third-party ratings provide the rater's impression of some aspects of the ratee. In doing so, they provide potentially useful assessment information about the rater as well as the ratee. Indeed, rating procedures have been used explicitly for this purpose (Fiedler, 1967; Kelly, 1955). Because individual raters may have idiosyncratic biases, it is a good idea to combine ratings from multiple raters, when possible, and use the average as the score for the ratee. This practice is common in the use of peer ratings, and leads to enhancements in both reliability and validity (Epstein & O'Brien, 1985).

Self-Monitoring

Assessment through self-monitoring (sometimes referred to as "self-observation") involves asking a person to observe his or her own behavior and make a record of its occurrence. Self-monitoring has been used to assess smoking (Shiffman et al., 1997), food intake (Wadden et al., 1997), exercise (Perri, Martin, Leermakers, Sears, & Notelovitz, 1997), anxiety and panic (Newman, Kenardy, Herman, & Taylor, 1997), and daily activities of adolescents (Larson, 1989). The approach also has a long history in organizational psychology and business, wherein time-use logs are kept to determine effectiveness of time management. Self-monitoring involves two distinct behaviors: (a) sensing or noticing a behavior and (b) making a record of its occurrence.

Usually, fairly specific behaviors are the target of self-monitoring, their definition coming from mutual discussions involving the therapist and client. Clients are instructed to record occurrences on small notecards or in small spiral notebooks carried with them throughout the day. In some cases, handheld computers have been used for data entry (Taylor, Fried, & Kenardy, 1990; Shiffman et al., 1997). Clients typically are asked to record every occurrence of a behavior along with details about the context in which the behavior occurs (e.g., the urge to smoke, the intensity of the urge, location, other people present, and the activity at the time). Occasionally, clients are prompted to record their behavior at random times during the day (Larson, 1989). The prompt may be internally generated from a device the client carries, such as a palm-top computer (Newman et al., 1997), or remotely (e.g., through a pager; Larson, 1989).

Self-monitoring is used in treatment for two purposes: (a) to provide assessment data about specific behavior and (b) as a type of intervention designed to alter behavior (Korotitsch & Nelson-Gray, 1999). The procedure is highly reactive, which gives it its usefulness as a form of treatment. Noticing and recording behavior are likely to change the behavior. For instance, daily frequency of Dexedrine ingestion decreased from 11.3 to 0 tablets per day when a 21-year-old female recorded time, setting, type, and amount of drug used (Hay, Hay, & Angle, 1977). Mean time spent smoking each cigarette dropped significantly when college students monitored actual smoking or urges to smoke (McFall, 1970).

The reactivity of self-monitoring makes it useful as an intervention but problematic as an assessment method. In its latter capacity, it is important to know the quality of the data produced. How accurately can people notice and record aspects of their own behavior? Accuracy of self-monitoring is the extent to which data provided by the self-monitor agree with those obtained from an independent source. Verification is important in determining whether accuracy is actually being documented. If the criterion for accuracy is merely that the observations match those of another person simultaneously observing the self-monitor, *agreement* is the more appropriate term because neither person may be accurately recording what is occurring. As Nelson (1977) noted, "only when there is a more direct measure of 'truth,' or of the target behavior, is observer accuracy assessed" (p. 231). She pointed to data from Fixsen, Phillips, and Wolf (1972) showing that boys' reporting on the cleanliness of their bedrooms agrees more with their peers (76% agreement) than with adults (50% agreement).

Obviously, the boys are responding to something other than or in addition to the actual cleanliness of the rooms; it could be that they have different standards of cleanliness. Unfortunately, relatively few studies have been published on the accuracy of self-monitoring. Studies of agreement have shown highly variable results, with agreement ranging from 98% for pill taking (Azrin & Powell, 1969) to zero for verbal dysfluencies during group discussions (Hayes & Cavior, 1977). It is likely that studies of accuracy would produce similarly variable results.

Given the uncertain accuracy of self-monitoring, the wise practice evaluator includes corroborating sources of information to determine practice effectiveness. In addition, steps can be taken to enhance accuracy, such as obtaining data periodically from corroborating sources (e.g., roommates, peers, spouses). This would occur after informing clients of this possibility and obtaining their consent. Another type of collaboration involves tracking products of behavior (e.g., worksheets completed, pounds gained or lost, blood alcohol levels).

Direct Observation

A source of some of the highest quality assessment data can be direct observation by others. Noting that assessment involves rules and procedures for assigning numbers to human performance, Barrios (1993) defined *direct observation* as "rules and operations for gathering information on objective client behavior through the use of human observers" (p. 141). This definition does not distinguish between direct observation and self-monitoring. Indeed, the principal difference is that the observer of the behavior is someone other than the subject. Kent and Foster (1977) used a camera metaphor to characterize direct observation. The ideal is for the camera to capture a specific behavior at the moment of its occurrence and preserve a high-resolution record of the occurrence for future use. Much has been written about the method, and excellent reviews are available (Barrios, 1993; Hartmann & Wood, 1990; Weick, 1985). Only a brief discussion is possible here.

At one level, all assessment can be viewed as direct observation. Interviews involve talking with a person, asking questions, and observing responses to the questions as well as other aspects of the person. Self-reports similarly involve observations of peoples' responses to standard sets of descriptive statements. Rating-by-others methods ask people familiar with the person in question to report their impressions, presumably based on direct observations over some period of time. What differentiates self-observation and direct observation from the other methods of assessment is that the data come straight from viewing the behavior itself rather than indirectly from verbal accounts of the behavior.

Observers can record different properties of behavior; choosing which properties to observe is one of several important decisions developers of direct-observation systems must make (Johnston & Pennypacker, 1993). They must decide whether frequency, duration, latency, magnitude, or some combination of these is the characteristic of interest and design the system accordingly. For example, if a physical therapist is evaluating the effectiveness of a set of exercises for strengthening the right arm of a client, direct observation is likely to be a primary method of assessment. She is likely to observe the number of repetitions (frequency) with which the client lifts a dumbbell of a certain weight (magnitude).

Another important decision to make in using direct observation is the form the record of the observations will take. In the early stages of evaluation, it might not be exactly clear just what behavior should be observed and recorded. Suppose, for example, you were asked as an organizational consultant to assist in changing the climate of a corporation from one that is relatively formal and hierarchical to one that is more entrepreneurial, less formal, and more horizontal in structure. To get some idea of important aspects of employee behavior to observe, you might visit the company on several occasions as a passive observer, making extensive notes of things you see. This is a form of direct observation known as *narrative recording* because the data are in the form of a narrative description. Sometimes the narratives are written, and sometimes they are spoken into a tape recorder for later transcription. After observing for some time and analyzing the narrative data, the observer focuses on certain specific behaviors. If every occurrence of the behaviors can be noted, *event records* can be kept, which provide complete records of the behaviors or events of interest.

When many different behaviors are to be assessed, event records are unsuitable, and *interval recording* is more commonly used. In interval recording, the time of observation is broken into smaller segments and observations are recorded in these. Instead of observing for an hour, for example, observations can take place over sixty 1-minute intervals. Observers note responses occurring in the first minute then move on to the second, the third, and so on. Segmenting the larger time period in this way makes it easier to compare observations from several observers to establish interobserver agreement, a form of reliability, which is discussed further below.

Observing many different behaviors is facilitated when coding sheets are constructed in such a way that each of the intervals is numbered and includes a symbol or an abbreviation for the different behaviors. The symbol is then marked if the response is observed to occur in the interval. If the symbol is marked each time a behavior occurs, *frequency-within-interval* recording is being used. In contrast, *whole-interval* recording requires the behavior to last the entire interval to be recorded, whereas *partial-interval* recording notes whether the behavior occurs at all anywhere in the interval. In both whole- and partial-interval recording, only one entry is made per interval, no matter how many times the behavior occurs. Exhibit 7.2 presents an example of a partial interval recording system.

Exhibit 7.2

Intervals From the Staff–Pupil Interaction Recording System

		1	2	3			1	2	3
Interval 1		AS	RT	VS	Interval 2		~~AS~~	RT	VS
		AT	NR	VG			~~AT~~	NR	VG
		RD	WR	TR			~~RD~~	~~WR~~	TR
		GS	IN	MR			GS	IN	MR
		PP	IR	GA			PP	IR	~~GA~~
		MO	SA	EL			MO	SA	EL
				TO					TO

The exhibit depicts a system designed to record observations of teachers working with children with developmental disabilities (Cone, Nyberg, & Watson, 1983). A teacher is observed for certain prompting behaviors, abbreviations for which are listed in column 1 (e.g., AS = "attention signal"). The child is then observed for responses to the teacher's prompt (column 2), and the teacher is observed for subsequent responses to the child (column 3). In the second interval, the teacher was observed to use an attention signal (AS, "Jimmy, _____") to get the child's attention (AT), and follow with a response direction (RD, "touch the blue circle"). The child made a wrong response (WR), and the teacher responded by giving the correct answer (GA).

When many different behaviors are being observed for many different people, an interval recording system known as *momentary time sampling* can be useful. With it, the observer acts much like a camera, taking a snapshot at a specific moment in time. Any of the predetermined behaviors occurring at that moment are noted. For example, a timer can randomly remind a classroom teacher to observe which of his 25 students are attending to the task and which are not (Kubany & Slodgett, 1973). Similarly, a recreation therapist at a convalescent center can be signaled to record which patients are engaged in different activities at a particular moment. Usually the signal occurs at the end of every 10-second (5, 15, etc.) interval.

Data from direct-observation coding systems are scored like other assessment methods. The data often are presented as graphs or charts showing change over time. When event-recording or frequency-within-interval systems are used, the number of responses per time period generally is charted. When other forms of interval recording are used, data are usually charted in terms of the percentage of intervals in which the behavior was observed. As the example in Figure 7.1 shows, such data can demonstrate the impact of interventions that are systematically introduced, withdrawn, or otherwise altered at different points across time. (See chapter 8 for more information on using charts to analyze treatment effectiveness.)

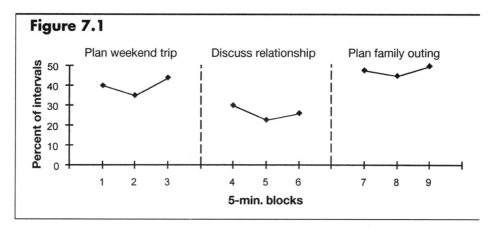

Figure 7.1

Variation in husband's engagement across discussion topics. The figure shows how observation-based data can be used to show the impact of interventions that are systematically introduced, withdrawn, or otherwise altered at different points across time. In this fictitious example, the percentage of intervals in which the husband is actively engaged in the discussion varies systematically with the issue being discussed, with the interventions in this case being the different discussion topics.

As with self-monitoring, *reactivity*—the principle that people being observed are likely to alter their behavior in certain ways if they are aware of the observations—is an important consideration when using direct-observation methods. Participant reactivity allows direct observation (as well as self-monitoring) to be used as an intervention procedure in its own right. For example, consider the messages that accompany telephone calls to some companies. The caller is informed that "this call may be recorded for quality-control purposes." It is likely that employees who know they are being recorded behave differently than they would if the company did not tape the calls.

Unfortunately, the beneficial reactive effects of direct observation for intervention purposes are a problem for using such data for assessment. Research has addressed whether reactivity occurs, the circumstances under which it is most likely, and ways in which it can be minimized (Foster & Cone, 1986; Haynes & Horn, 1982). It appears that reactivity is not an inevitable by-product of the use of observational assessment. Foster and Cone reported that observer presence affected only 34% of the behaviors assessed in a survey of 19 studies specifically addressing reactivity. Nonetheless, the potential impact of observers should not be overlooked when planning this type of assessment.

Reactivity is not unique to observational assessment, of course. All the methods discussed in this section have some effect on the behavior they are used to assess. Self-presentation bias in interviews and self-reports is just one example. The alert practice evaluator is aware of these influences and qualifies data interpretations accordingly.

The Directness Continuum

The five assessment methods can be ordered on a continuum representing the extent to which they involve observations of the behavior of interest at the time and place of its natural occurrence (Cone, 1977). Interview, self-report, and rating-by-other measures obtain information about behavior by *asking* about it. They involve no observation of the behavior itself; these methods therefore are described as *indirect*. Self-monitoring and direct observation, in contrast, obtain information about behavior by *looking* at that specific behavior; they therefore are considered *direct* methods. This difference highlights the fact that the topography, or form of the response, actually observed with indirect methods is different from that of the behavior of principal interest because it is a report of the behavior, not the behavior itself.

In addition, indirect methods obtain information at times other than the actual occurrence of the behavior. Although indirect data collection usually occurs retrospectively, or after the fact, it can take place prospectively as well (i.e., a person might be asked to predict what he or she will do at some time in the future). Direct methods, in contrast, involve observing the behavior at the precise moment of its occurrence; there is no temporal separation between the occurrence and the assessment of the behavior. Finally, indirect methods obtain information in locations different from those in which the behavior of interest normally occurs. Typically, questions are asked about the behavior in office or clinical settings. Direct methods usually involve observing the behavior in its natural context or environment, although they can be used effectively in office and clinic settings as well, just as indirect methods can be administered in the natural environment.

In summary, assessment methods can be ordered along a directness continuum consisting of three aspects: (a) topographical, (b) temporal, and (c) spatial. When topographical, temporal, and spatial differences between the behavior actually assessed and the behavior of interest are minimal, direct assessment is involved. When they are maximal, indirect methods are involved.

The concept of directness resembles the funnel analogy described by Hawkins (1979). In the early stages of information gathering, at the mouth of the funnel, the astute assessor uses relatively broad, imprecise methods, such as interviews. Noteworthy issues are identified in this stage and receive more focused assessment with somewhat more precise instruments at an intermediate stage (i.e., the funnel narrows). Self-reports and rating-by-other measures can be used at this point. Finally, specific behavior identified by the earlier methods is observed directly, using self-monitoring or direct observation. These high-quality methods are repeatedly used to evaluate the efficacy of interventions and are therefore part of the narrow, unchanging neck of the funnel.

Comprehensive assessment in practice evaluation takes advantage of multiple levels of information specificity. Relatively inexpensive information about a wide variety of issues is obtained first, using indirect methods (e.g., interviews) that produce much data. Quality can be compromised for quantity at this point. Once specific behaviors have been identified for intervention, however, the high-quality data provided by relatively expensive direct methods is required.

Evaluating Assessment Instruments

To use information from assessment instruments to evaluate a practice, the information must be of high quality. The best data are accurate, reliable, and valid.

Accuracy

Data are said to be accurate when they represent objective, topographic, and quantitative features of the behavior of interest. Accurate data come from instruments whose scores measure the phenomenon being assessed and not something else. An example would be information about how clerks in a retail establishment handle customer complaints. Suppose a clerk's semiannual performance appraisal is based partly on data showing the percentage of complaints he handled in a courteous manner over the preceding 6 months. Data for such an important purpose as this would come, ideally, from the most direct methods of assessment. For this reason, ratings by the supervisor might be less desirable than direct observations, given the likelihood that the supervisor's rating data could be influenced by many factors (e.g., how well the supervisor likes the person, how the person dresses). In other words, accuracy of the direct-observation data is likely to be higher than that of rating-by-other data.

With behavior, there can be more or less agreement that it did or did not occur. This is not the case with traits, which by their very nature are hypothetical; no consensus exists for how to define traits such as agreeableness and dependability. There can be agreement that a clerk greeted a customer courteously but not that the clerk is courteous. Accuracy applies to data about what a person does and is not relevant when describing what a person is like.

To establish the accuracy of an assessment device requires two components: (a) an incontrovertible index of the behavior, or "reality," and (b) rules and procedures for using the device. An instrument can have the limits of its accuracy determined in calibrating conditions much the way instruments in the physical sciences are calibrated. For example, before a microscope is used, the biologist knows the power and resolution of the scope and whether it is sufficiently accurate to reveal the existence of a substance if it is actually present. A direct-observation measure of the behaviors comprising courteous handling of complaints can be calibrated by comparing data it produces with scripted interchanges written to contain the behaviors at certain frequencies. Scripts are written so that they include a predetermined number of courteous responses to fictitious complaints. In other words, we know in advance what is real because of the way we construct the scripts. If our direct observation measure is used to score actors performing the script, it produces frequencies of behaviors that agree with the frequencies built into the script. The method's mean accuracy for detecting each component behavior is determined. Standard deviations around the means can serve as accuracy limits, or confidence intervals can be established. These accuracy limits then can be used to determine whether the instrument is appropriate for the purpose intended.

If the calibrating information is to be used to assert the accuracy of the data obtained in subsequent applications of the instrument, the data must be acquired in ways that match the calibrating conditions as closely as possible. In other words, users who wish to generalize the accuracy information to their own circumstances must use the measure in accord with the procedures for its use. The accuracy limits determined in the calibrating conditions can be used to set confidence intervals within which users can be assured that their scores are reasonably accurate.

Reliability

Another criterion is that an assessment instrument produce information reliably. Data are said to be reliable when they come from independent sources and they agree with one another. A commonly used synonym for reliability is consistency; a reliable instrument is one that consistently produces the same score when "brought into repeated contact with the same state of nature" (Johnston & Pennypacker, 1993, p. 138). If that "state of nature," or the phenomenon of interest, is wholly responsible for the score, the instrument is said to be accurate as above. Scores can be consistent and not be wholly determined by the phenomenon of interest, however. To illustrate, two adolescent boys might agree that they saw Bruce Springsteen walking down the other side of a street. Springsteen might not be within a thousand miles of the boys, yet both of them thought they saw him. Their observations thus meet the definition of reliability because their independent observations agree with one another. In this case, however, neither of the observations is accurate.

Classical measurement theory treats reliability as the absence of error. Error is considered to be random; its presence therefore sets limits on the magnitude of correlations involving scores. Traditional psychometrics recognizes several ways of looking at the consistency of data produced by assessment devices (DeVellis, 1991) and the extent to which they are free of error.

Scorer Reliability

The most fundamental type of consistency is scorer reliability, a concept that refers to the extent to which data produced by different users of an instrument agree with one another. Scorer reliability is fundamental because its absence compromises further study of both reliability and validity. Measures that produce inconsistent scores cannot be said to relate either to themselves (i.e., are not reliable) or to scores from instruments representing other variables (i.e., are not valid).

Each of the five assessment methods discussed above can be examined for scorer reliability. Although scores rarely result from interviews, certain structured interviews often lead to classifications of one sort or another. For example, the Anxiety Disorders Interview Schedule–Revised (DiNardo et al., 1986), a semistructured interview administered by experienced clinicians, has good scorer reliability, with kappa (κ) coefficients (Cohen, 1960) as high as .91 (Barlow, 1988).

When self-reports are used, interscorer reliability more often is assumed than actually documented. The assumption appears to be that scoring is so straightforward that there is no need to check its consistency. It is easy for scorers to become complacent and commit careless errors, however, and even relatively uncomplicated scoring procedures should be checked for consistency.

Rating-by-other measures are commonly examined for interrater reliability before being made available commercially. If you produce such a measure to evaluate some aspect of your practice, it is a good idea to check this dimension as well. For example, the Parent/Family Involvement Index (Cone, DeLawyer, & Wolfe, 1985) was developed to assess parents' participation in education programs for their child with disabilities. Teachers rate the parents on their involvement in 12 different areas, including volunteering in the classroom, disseminating information, and participating in fundraising activities. Scores are provided for each area, resulting in an involvement profile. In developing the index we asked teachers and aides to complete the measure independently for the same sets of parents. Interrater agreement was found by comparing the teacher and aide responses to each item across a sample of parents for each area. The resulting percentage agreements ranged from 85% (Classroom Volunteering subscale) to 99% (Involvement in Advocacy Groups subscale).

Direct-observation coding systems routinely address scorer reliability. Interobserver agreement is usually obtained by having two or more trained people make observations of the same behavior or events at the same time but independently. The two sets of data are then compared using appropriate statistics, such as percentage agreement, correlation coefficients, or kappa. Dozens of interobserver agreement indices have been reported in the literature, and interested readers are referred to extensive reviews describing them (Berk, 1979; Cordes, 1994; Kelly, 1977).

To illustrate the process of calculating agreement, consider two observers watching an assembly-line worker in a manufacturing facility to see whether the worker inspects the tightness of a circuit board after soldering it onto the motherboards of computers being produced. After an hour of watching, the two observers compare their data to determine agreement. A first step in this process might involve setting up a 2 × 2 matrix such as that in Table 7.1. The entries in the table represent the number of times each observer saw the worker check the tightness (the target behavior) of the circuit board after soldering it into a motherboard. The worker soldered a total of 25 circuit boards (A + B + C +

Table 7.1

Two-Way Table for Comparing Data

| | Observer 1 | |
| | Occurrence of target behavior | Nonoccurrence of target behavior |
Observer 2		
Occurrence of target behavior	[a]16	[c]2
Nonoccurrence of target behavior	[b]3	[d]4

Note. The entries in Cells A–D represent the number of times observers recorded or did not record an occurrence of the behavior.

D). The data can be examined for interobserver agreement in a number of ways. Some commonly used approaches are presented in Table 7.2. It is obvious that the value representing interobserver agreement differs considerably depending on the procedure used, largely because the various formulae have different ways of controlling for agreement merely resulting from chance. *Overall* percentage agreement does not include such a control and therefore tends to produce overly high levels of agreement. Chance agreement inflates this measure to the extent that occurrences and nonoccurrences of the behavior are considerably different, as in the present example. Whether we look at Observer 1's or 2's counts, we get a large difference between occurrences (18 and 19, respectively) and nonoccurrences (6 and 7, respectively). When the behavior is substantially more likely to occur than not (as in the present example), a conservative way of controlling for spuriously high values is to calculate agreement based on occurrence of the behavior only. When behavior is substantially less likely to occur than not, the conservative approach is to calculate agreement based on nonoccurrence of the behavior only. Kappa is an increasingly common interobserver agreement measure that statistically controls for chance. Although it requires a bit more effort to calculate, it is preferable to simple percentage agreement measures.

The astute reader notes that self-observation has been skipped in discussions of scorer reliability to this point. When the observer and observed are one and the same, there is technically no "second opinion" to permit scorer reliability to be calculated. For practical purposes, however, having another person observe and record the same responses

Table 7.2

Popular Ways of Calculating Interobserver Agreement

Approach	Formula
Overall agreement (agreement that it did or did not happen)	$\dfrac{A + D}{A + B + C + D}$
	$= \dfrac{16 + 4}{16 + 3 + 2 + 4}$
	$= .80$
Occurrence agreement (agreement that it did happen)	$\dfrac{A}{A + B + C}$
	$= \dfrac{16}{16 + 3 + 2}$
	$= .76$
Nonoccurrence agreement (agreement that it did not happen)	$\dfrac{D}{B + C + D}$
	$= \dfrac{4}{3 + 2 + 4}$
	$= .44$
Kappa (κ)	

$$= \frac{\left[A - \dfrac{(A + B)(A + C)}{A + B + C + D}\right] + \left[D - \dfrac{(B + D)(C + D)}{A + B + C + D}\right]}{\left[A - \dfrac{(A + B)(A + C)}{A + B + C + D}\right] + B + C + \left[D - \dfrac{(B + D)(C + D)}{A + B + C + D}\right]}$$

$$= \frac{\left[16 - \dfrac{(16 + 3)(16 + 2)}{16 + 3 + 2 + 4}\right] + \left[4 - \dfrac{(3 + 4)(2 + 4)}{16 + 3 + 2 + 4}\right]}{\left[16 - \dfrac{(16 + 3)(16 + 2)}{16 + 3 + 2 + 4}\right] + 3 + 2 + \left[4 - \dfrac{(3 + 4)(2 + 4)}{16 + 3 + 2 + 4}\right]}$$

$$= .45$$

Note. The data are analyzed for interobserver agreement using four approaches. Letters A–D refer to the cells in Table 7.1.

being self-observed often is an effective way to determine scorer reliability. An example would be having a roommate record cigarettes smoked or food eaten at the same time a client is self-recording. The client might have been informed of the possibility of such checking but not of the specific day and time checks actually would occur. Such an approach has the dual benefit of providing an estimate of the quality of the self-monitored data and motivating the client to record accurately.

Internal Consistency

Once scorer reliability is known, other forms of consistency can be examined. For example, if a person gets a score of 10 on a self-report scale of 20 items, numerous combinations of items could have produced the score. If a measure is internally consistent, however, all ways of obtaining a particular score are equivalent. The items within the measure are interchangeable indicators of the same underlying trait or latent variable. Indeed, the items are viewed as being the effects of the trait (Bollen & Lennox, 1991). Various ways of determining internal consistency exist, including split-half, Kuder–Richardson formulae, and Cronbach's coefficient alpha (Nunnally & Bernstein, 1994). The last is the most frequently used measure. Alpha is calculated according to the following formula:

$$\alpha = \left(\frac{k}{k-1} \right) \left(\frac{S^2 - \Sigma S^2 i}{S^2} \right),$$

where α = the reliability estimate; k = the number of items in the measure; S^2 = the total score variance; and $\Sigma S^2 i$ = the sum of the variances of the individual items. Although it can be computationally cumbersome to calculate the variance for each item, computer software packages for statistical analyses frequently include alpha as a subroutine, making the process relatively painless.

Temporal Stability

In addition to being unidimensional, or homogeneous, measures of traits are expected to show stability over time. Temporal stability (test–retest reliability) is an especially important characteristic of such measures because traits are assumed to develop early in one's life and to be relatively unchanging thereafter. The issue here is the extent to which scores obtained at one point in time provide the same information as those obtained at a later time. It is typical to examine stability by administering a measure to the same group of people at two different times and correlating their scores. The appropriate time interval depends on the purposes for which the scores are intended.

Suppose, for example, that a measure is used to predict whether clients will respond positively to a particular type of intervention. After the clients are assessed, the intervention begins and some time later the clients' responsiveness is determined. Correlating scores on the predictor with scores on the measure of responsiveness establishes the effectiveness of the first test in predicting the outcome. For the test to predict responsiveness, however, it must be stable over the time period required for the intervention to be applied. If it takes 5 weeks for the intervention to be applied, the retest interval for the stability analysis should be at least 5 weeks. If scores on the test are not stable over this time period, they are unlikely to enter into relationships with the responsiveness measure.

Temporal stability has been investigated for many trait variables in psychology and education. Generally speaking, stability has been found (Mischel, 1968). It is higher for some types of variables than others, however, with academic achievement and intellectual variables being among the most stable, and attitudes being the least (Kelly, 1955). Test–retest reliability is of particular importance in practice evaluation because of the frequent use of pre- and posttests to determine whether and how much change was produced. The use of the same measure in this way can work against the unwary evaluator, however: People often try to respond consistently when presented the same stimuli and may strive to remember their previous answers in order to duplicate them (Nunnally & Bernstein, 1994). This tendency can result in spuriously high temporal stability and render the measure insensitive to changes that really have occurred.

Alternate-Form Reliability

Alternate-form reliability offers a solution to the problem of temporal stability. For evaluations of the type just described, it is preferable to use two different forms of the same measure. One can be administered before services are provided, and the other after they are completed. Alternate forms are produced by starting with a large pool of items related to the characteristic being assessed. Typically, the items are randomly arranged in two or more sets, resulting in the alternate forms. The items are then keyed (i.e., assigned a value of 1 to indicate presence or 0 to indicate absence of the characteristic), so that a scoring key is available for each form. The different forms are then administered to a large number of people, scores on the forms are correlated, and the resulting values provide coefficients of equivalence (alternate-form reliability). Note that the administration of the forms must occur simultaneously, which is best achieved by the random assignment of items to a single large test, administering it, and scoring it using two different keys, as described above. Some researchers have suggested that alternate-form reliability be used in place of temporal stability because of the problems mentioned earlier (e.g., Nunnally & Bernstein, 1994). Temporal stability thus can be estimated by correlating scores on two forms of a test administered over some time interval. Differences in correlations obtained between the forms administered in a single setting and when separated by some time interval can provide information about the extent to which variation in the trait contributes to unreliability of the measure.

Generalizability Theory

The existence of different types of reliability led Cronbach, Gleser, Nanda, and Rajaratnam (1972) to propose that scores belong to different universes of generalizability. Using analysis of variance techniques, variance attributable to different facets (factors) in a *generalizability (G)* study allows the evaluation of different types of reliability. For example, scorer reliability can be viewed as generalizability within a universe of all possible scorers. To demonstrate this perspective, multiple scorers would assess the same group of people. A significant effect for the scorer facet in a subsequent analysis of variance might indicate that the scorers are not all scoring alike. The data depend, in this instance, on who does the scoring. This is tantamount to finding low interscorer reliability in the traditional sense.

Similarly, internal consistency can be viewed as generalizability within a universe of all possible item content. Conceptually, items are selected at random from a pool of content relevant to a particular variable or construct. If a G study fails to find a significant effect for the item facet, internal consistency exists, and there is generalizability within the universe of all possible items. Put another way, obtained scores do not depend on the particular items responded to in the measure; they are essentially interchangeable.

Similar logic applies to alternate-form reliability and temporal stability. A universe exists of all possible forms of a test and times that it can be administered. If different forms and times produce comparable information, the data do not depend on which were used. The G study facets for form and time are not statistically significant. Generalizability theory can be extended to incorporate convergent validity (discussed later in this chapter) as well. One can conceive of a universe of all possible methods to assess a variable. If the data from several randomly selected methods from this universe agree with one another, there is generalizability within the method universe. The results do not depend on the method used.

The beauty of generalizability theory rests in its comprehensiveness and its ability to incorporate seemingly diverse concepts under one conceptual and analytic umbrella. Unfortunately, its adoption has been slow (Aiken, 1996). Although it appears to be gaining greater popularity, it is limited by its requirement of large numbers of subjects or data points. More detailed information can be found in Suen and Ary's (1989) readable description of generalizability theory and the statistics involved in its application.

Validity

Assessment instruments may be accurate and reliable, but are they useful? Do their scores relate to scores on other measures in theoretically meaningful ways? Can we predict anything about people based on their scores on the instruments? Practical and theoretical uses of assessment devices relate to the validity of inferences we can make from their scores. Kane (1992) suggested that the validation process is actually the pursuit of evidence to support various arguments we want to make. If we wish to argue that a measure of work team orientation is a good predictor of employee effectiveness in a particular company, we must have empirical support (i.e., validity evidence) for our argument. Elsewhere (Cone, 1995), I suggested two phases for organizing validity studies: (a) representational validation and (b) elaborative validation.

Representational Validation

Representational validation involves gathering evidence that the measure really assesses what it is supposed to assess. Does it tap the behavior or construct as intended by its developer? If behavior is being assessed, this form of validation is synonymous with accuracy. An accurate measure, by definition, is one for which the scores are determined by the phenomenon being assessed, not something else. When a latent trait or hypothetical construct is the subject matter, representational validation provides evidence that that trait or construct determines the test scores.

Representational validation involves three major steps: (a) examining the content of a measure, (b) showing that scores on the measure correlate with scores on other measures designed to assess the same

---

Exhibit 7.3

Organizing Validity Evidence for Assessment Instruments

Phase	Type of Evidence
I. Representational validation	Content validity Discriminant validity Convergent validity
II. Elaborative validation	Criterion-related validity Construct validity

---

thing, and (c) showing that scores on the measure do not correlate with scores on other measures designed to assess different things. Traditionally, these three steps have been referred to as *content, convergent,* and *discriminant* validity, respectively. Exhibit 7.3 presents the customary types of validity evidence in terms of representational and elaborative phases.

If a test appears to represent a universe of content relevant to the phenomenon under study, the measure is said to have content validity. Content validity is of particular interest when behavior is the subject matter of the assessment. For example, when assessing the gross motor skills of a person with physical disabilities, it is important that the test include content broadly reflective of large muscle activity. Thus, "stands unsupported for at least 5 minutes" appears to be appropriate content; "closes fingers around a small object placed in the palm of the hand" is not appropriate because it represents fine motor behavior. Academic achievement measures rely heavily on content validity to support their usefulness. A test of math achievement for third graders must be broadly representative of the types of math problems normally taught in the third grade. The test construction process usually can ensure content validity in a case such as this: If material for the test is taken explicitly from texts of third-grade math, the test has a high level of content validity. Although no single quantitative score represents the degree or amount of content validity, Haynes, Richard, and Kubany (1995) reminded us that content validation includes structural issues, such as the format of the items, the response alternatives permitted, instructions, and scoring procedures. Haynes et al. (1995) recommended having experts examine various elements of an instrument and quantifying their judgments using rating scales. Lawshe (1975) and, more recently, Nunnally and Bernstein (1994) made similar suggestions.

Representational validation is further enhanced by showing that data from a given measure correlate with those from alternative ways of assessing the same phenomenon. For instance, self-reports of cigarettes smoked are a more cost-effective way of gathering information about a client's smoking habits than following the client around and observing smoking directly. Confidence that the self-report instrument represents smoking accurately is increased when its scores correlate with scores on direct-observation measures. If latent traits are the subject matter, however, alternative methods of assessing them must provide information to support the argument that something really is underlying scores on the test in question. Suppose we contend that a person obtaining a high score on a measure dealing with apprehension when talking to groups is experiencing speech anxiety. Before assuming that our measure truly represents speech anxiety, we must show correspondence between its scores and some other ways of assessing that construct. If we are able to do this, we can argue that high scores on our test represent speech anxiety. Traditionally, correspondence between alternative ways of assessing something has been referred to as *convergent validity* (Campbell & Fiske, 1959). The logic is that scores on different measures converge to provide a comparable picture of the person being assessed, at least with respect to one particular construct.

Showing that scores do not correlate with those from measures of distinctly different phenomena also enhances representational validity. In the example just given, speech anxiety is different from depression, so scores on measures of the two variables would not be expected to correlate. In personality assessment research, this concept is referred to as *discriminant validity* (Campbell, 1960; Campbell & Fiske, 1959). Campbell observed that certain pervasive constructs exist from which new measures should be distinguished before they are taken seriously. For example, everyone has a certain self-presentational bias when responding to items in assessment instruments; people can be ordered on a continuum representing the extent to which they represent themselves in socially favorable or unfavorable ways. This social desirability variable (Edwards, 1957, 1990) is so pervasive that new measures should be compared with it and shown to be distinct. If, for example, a high negative correlation exists between scores on a self-report measure of speech anxiety and scores on a measure of social desirability, the former may not be a good representative of its underlying construct. Do low scores on speech anxiety truly reflect its absence, or do they represent a tendency to deny socially undesirable things about one's self? The measures' scores may be reflecting two different variables, making it difficult to interpret them clearly.

To summarize, representational validation is a necessary first step in examining the usefulness of measures that have already met certain accuracy and reliability criteria. Examining the content of the instrument and whether it enters into relationships with other measures designed to assess the same thing shows whether scores on an instrument do an adequate job of reflecting a behavior or trait. Finally, the distinctiveness of the measure is supported by evidence that it does not enter into relationships with variables from which it is supposed to be different.

Elaborative Validation

When we are confident that a measure represents a phenomenon adequately, we can proceed to elaborating its usefulness, or elaborative validation. Traditionally, this form of validity has been referred to as *construct validity* (Cronbach & Meehl, 1955); a measure with good construct validity supports both the validity of the theory underlying the construct being assessed as well as the validity of the measure itself. In this phase of the validation effort, relationships between scores on the instrument and various theoretical and practical criteria are examined. Theoretical criteria include constructs stipulated to be related to the construct underlying the measure at issue. To illustrate, extraversion is a variable that might be included in a theory relating it to friendliness, confidence, and physical attractiveness. For simplicity, let us assume that positive relationships are expected among all of these constructs. Measures are developed for each construct and administered to a large number of people. The theoretical usefulness of our extraversion measure is supported if we find the anticipated correlations. In this way, elaborative validation is extended.

Practical criteria are virtually unlimited. They include correlations between a test and already existing measures, correlations between scores on a test and ratings by others, and correlations with behavior in natural or contrived (i.e., experimental) settings. In addition, criteria for membership in different groups or diagnostic categories can be examined relative to scores on a test. The test is said to be useful to the extent that it differentiates the groups in expected ways. To illustrate, imagine you have developed a measure of satisfaction in committed relationships. Your measure is of potential value because it is more generally applicable than existing measures, which are limited to marital satisfaction. Its usefulness can be established by showing that it correlates with existing measures of couple satisfaction, such as the Dyadic Adjustment Scale (Spanier & Filsinger, 1983). Furthermore, its scores can be correlated with ratings of apparent partner satisfaction made by skilled therapists following interviews. In addition, an experimental situation can be arranged in which the partners work to solve a problem that can be resolved only if both contribute information known only to them. Finally, scores on the measure can be examined to determine their ability to distinguish between couples independently known to be satisfied or dissatisfied.

When practical as opposed to theoretical criteria are used, it is customary to refer to the process as *criterion-related validity*. In the past, it was common to distinguish criteria on the basis of time and refer to *concurrent validity*, on the one hand, and *predictive validity* on the other. If data are available on the criterion at the same time the test is taken, immediate correlations can be obtained. For example, imagine an insurance company is going to administer a test to select salespeople. Existing salespeople can be administered the test and their scores correlated with their sales volumes. Strong correlations (i.e., statistically significant) elaborate the usefulness of the test for this purpose and establish its concurrent validity. Alternatively, the test might be administered to applicants for insurance sales jobs and not used in the selection process. Salespeople would be hired using the customary process, and their sales volumes monitored over time. After a suitable period, sales volumes could be correlated with scores on the test taken at the applicant stage. Strong correlations support the predictive validity of the test because test scores were obtained in advance of data on sales volumes.

In pursuing evidence of criterion-related validity, it is important to consider the symmetry of both the predictor and the criterion. Evidence of reliability and representational validity is needed for the criterion measure, just as it is for the predictor. Moreover, *criterion contamination* has to be avoided. To illustrate this last point, consider that ratings by trained therapists are to be used to validate scores on the hypothetical measure of relationship quality in committed couples. The therapists cannot be apprised of the couples' score on the measure before interviewing and rating them because advance knowledge of the scores might contaminate or bias the ratings in some way. Most likely the therapists would be influenced to provide ratings consistent with the data from the measure, thus spuriously inflating the resulting correlation.

Finally, temporal considerations must be taken into account. If there is a time lapse between obtaining data on the predictor and the criterion, the predictor must be shown to produce temporally stable scores over a comparable period of time. Suppose it takes 5 months to obtain enough sales data to establish an insurance salesperson's volume. To validate scores on a measure to select salespeople using sales as a criterion, the scores must be stable over at least a 5-month period. If the scores are not, failure to find a correlation between them and sales volume is difficult to interpret. It cannot be known whether the predictor is insufficiently reliable, the design of the study was flawed in some way, or there is simply no relationship. If reliability problems can be ruled out, attention can be limited to the other two possibilities.

Summary

This chapter has described the first of three sets of tools needed for competent practice evaluation. In some ways measurement tools are the most important. Interviews, self-reports, rating by others, self-monitoring, and direct-observation methods can be ordered on a continuum representing the extent to which they provide data on the phenomenon of interest at the time and place of its natural occurrence. The quality of those data is established based on their accuracy, reliability, and validity.

When one aspect of practice is assessed adequately, it can be related to other aspects, thereby advancing knowledge about practice effectiveness. To be sure, designing ways of looking at relationships among different aspects of a practice is important, as is determining whether observed relationships are significant; these topics are covered in the next two chapters. Unless the independent and dependent variables of a practice are described in accurate, reliable, and valid ways, however, evaluation design and analysis is meaningless. The next chapter examines tools for arranging information from assessment tools in order to answer research questions.

Supplemental Reading

Cone, J. D. (Sec. Ed.). (1999a). Clinical assessment applications of self-monitoring: [Special section]. *Psychological Assessment, 11,* 411–497.

Cone, J. D. (1999b). Observational assessment: Measure development and research issues. In P. C. Kendall, J. N. Butcher, & G. N. Holmbeck (Eds.), *Handbook of research methods in clinical psychology* (2nd ed., pp. 183–223). New York: Wiley.

Foster, S. L., & Cone, J. D. (1995). Validity issues in clinical assessment. *Psychological Assessment, 7,* 248–260.

Nunnally, N. C., & Bernstein, I. H. (1994). *Psychometric theory* (3rd ed.). New York: McGraw-Hill.

8 Design Tools for Evaluating Outcomes

Now that we have good measures for the important variables of a practice, we can use them to answer evaluation questions like those asked in chapter 5. It is not enough to have accurate and reliable measures, however. We must arrange our observations and the data from our measures so that consistent relationships among variables can be identified. These arrangements are the essence of research designs (Kazdin, 1998). Developing a design to answer a particular question is much like the work of the artist who arranges paints of different colors to produce a pleasing portrait. The artist can produce virtually unlimited arrangements, some of which result in more appealing pictures than others do. Likewise, this chapter describes how evaluators can arrange their data in pleasing ways, based on the assumption that designs that are well suited to answering specific evaluation questions are more pleasing than designs less well suited.

The chapter first discusses how to match the design to the purpose of the evaluation. Next, it covers the three basic approaches to evaluation, including the advantages and disadvantages of each. After an exploration of quasi-experimental designs, the chapter ends with a discussion of single-case experimentation.

Select a Design to Match the Evaluation Purpose

Before addressing specific research strategies, it is useful to focus on the importance of choosing a design that is appropriate for the evaluation question being posed. If your question does not concern relationships between variables, your design falls into the descriptive (also called enumerative) category. For example, you might want to know the demographic characteristics of all clients served over the past 5 years. This question can be answered by tallying such variables as age, gender, and occupation and summarizing each one in terms of an appropriate statistic (e.g., mean or median).

If your question extends beyond description to relationships among variables, you would use relational or experimental strategies. For example, suppose you want to know whether a relationship exists between age and the type of problem presented by clients seeking your services. Your hypothesis might be that older clients are more likely to be concerned about somatic issues, whereas younger ones are more concerned with relationship issues. You would select a relational design to answer this question, arranging your data to show any associations or correlations between age and probability of each type of concern.

Finally, consider the following question: Does assigning homework result in greater client satisfaction and more effective service? You would select an experimental design to answer this question. This is evident from the way the question is worded: You are asking whether homework results in greater satisfaction and effectiveness, not merely whether it relates to it. Questions implying causal relationships between variables require experimental designs for their answers.

Thus, there is an intimate relationship between the evaluation question asked and the type of design most suited to answering it. As stated in previous chapters, well-phrased questions imply the nature of the design that is needed. "What is the overall level of satisfaction with our services?" is the type of question likely to be answered in a descriptive design. "What is the relationship between . . . ?" leads one to expect a relational design. "What is the effect of . . . ?" suggests an experimental design.

Descriptive Approaches

A great deal of practice evaluation is descriptive. Indeed, it might be fair to conclude that most practice evaluation is of this type. A common example involves surveying clients to determine their satisfaction with a particular service. Typically, data from this form of evaluation are presented in terms of percentages of clients or customers reporting "much," or "complete" satisfaction.

Survey research has a long history in the behavioral sciences. Examples appear in the mass media nearly every day (e.g., "fifty-two percent of Americans think the president is doing a good job"). Polling the voting or consuming public is big business, and large organizations exist specifically to conduct such surveys. Surveys are used in different ways, and it can be helpful to distinguish between so-called status surveys and scientific surveys (Kerlinger, 1986). *Status* surveys document what exists at the moment. An example involves tallying all the demographic characteristics of clients served in a practice. Polls of the electorate to determine satisfaction with politicians are another type of status survey. *Scientific* surveys, sometimes referred to as *analytic* surveys (Rosenthal & Rosnow, 1984), study relationships between and among variables. They usually are conducted according to specific sampling guidelines for the purpose of generalizing to a larger population. For example, suppose a large managed care organization (MCO) in New York City conducts a survey asking about many variables related to the perceived quality of care and reports data on the relationship between race and satisfaction, such as those presented Table 8.1. Lower satisfaction among African Americans than among White Americans substantiates a relationship between the two variables.

The purpose of scientific or analytic surveys is to obtain generalizable information about relationships between variables of particular interest. The MCO is concerned with the relationship between satisfaction and race for all the recipients of its services, not just those living in New York; to generalize the findings from the New York study to MCO participants in other parts of the country requires adherence to

Table 8.1

Hypothetical Data Showing the Relationship Between Race and Satisfaction

	Low satisfaction (%)	High satisfaction (%)
African American	72	28
White American	38	62

Note. Based on services for members of a large managed care organization.

rules for selecting samples. Findings may be generalized to the entire population served by the company if the samples used are representative of these populations. Ideally, the MCO would survey participants from all over the United States because it is unlikely that samples drawn exclusively from New York City residents are sufficiently representative.

Representativeness relies strongly on random selection. If samples are drawn in such a way that every member of the larger population has an equal probability of being selected, they can be said to be drawn randomly. This is an obvious limitation of a survey using only residents of one city, whereas samples drawn randomly at least start out being representative of the populations from which they have been selected. Whether they remain representative throughout the data collection process is another story.

It is common for some loss of participants to occur during the course of any study; this loss is referred to as *attrition*. If attrition is differential, meaning that participants with certain characteristics drop out more frequently than others, the representativeness of the sample is compromised. Using the example above, suppose that participants were paid for their time. Suppose further that 10% of the participants of both races dropped out of the study. If those remaining were more in need of the income from participating, it is likely that their socio-economic standing differed from those who dropped out, an example of differential attrition.

Differential attrition compromises the representativeness of the samples and limits the extent to which findings can be generalized to the population of interest. If the remaining participants represent lower income Americans, it may be that the findings about race and satisfaction can only be generalized to that group. To determine whether attrition limits the generalizability of the findings, the extent to which differential attrition has occurred must be examined (e.g., one can compare the incomes of the remaining and departed participants). If the incomes are essentially the same, differential attrition has not occurred —at least with respect to the income variable. Unfortunately, the great likelihood that the remaining and departed people differ in other ways not thought of makes any attrition problematic. For this reason, researchers and practice evaluators go to great lengths to ensure high levels of both initial and continued participation.

Procedures for sampling and ensuring the representativeness of samples can be quite detailed, and space does not permit their elaboration here. A word of caution is warranted concerning the common practice of soliciting volunteers for research and practice evaluation projects, however: Evidence shows systematic differences between people who step forward on their own and those who do not. For example, Rosenthal and Rosnow (1975) found study volunteers to be more intelligent than nonvolunteers. Volunteers also were likely to be more sociable, better educated, of higher social class, and motivated by the approval of others. In addition, they found that volunteers tended more often to be female, Jewish, unconventional, arousal seeking, and nonauthoritarian.

Rosenthal and Rosnow (1975) pointed to the implications of such differences for interpreting the results of studies relying exclusively on volunteers. How safe are we in generalizing findings from such studies to the population at large? As one important example, they cite the well-known Kinsey surveys of the 1940s and 1950s (Kinsey, Pomeroy, Martin, & Gebhard, 1953), which documented the sexual behavior of Americans (Rosenthal & Rosnow, 1984). Kinsey et al. used thousands of volunteer participants. Given the characteristics of volunteers just mentioned, is there a slight possibility the sexual behavior of "typical Americans" might have been overestimated? Much more can be said about sampling and the precautions necessary to produce samples representative of larger populations. See Kerlinger (1986) for a readable treatment. Other good resources include Pedhazur and Schmelkin (1991) and Cochran (1977).

Two other concepts relevant to this discussion are probability and nonprobability sampling on the one hand, and sampling error on the other. When we survey students in our classes, or people in our office, or the next 30 clients coming through our door, we are engaging in nonprobability sampling (also called "convenience sampling"). More deliberate surveying of groups for whom researchers have predetermined criteria (e.g., the same percentage of male and female students in our sample as occurs in the general student population), sometimes called "quota sampling" (Kerlinger, 1986), is another type of nonprobability sampling. The essential characteristic of this approach to obtaining participants is that it is nonrandom, limiting the generalizability of our findings to larger populations.

Probability sampling uses the concept of randomization to enhance representativeness. As mentioned, the essence of this approach is the preservation of the requirement that every person in the population being generalized to has an equal probability of being chosen. Examples of probability sampling include stratified random sampling and cluster sampling. In *stratified random sampling*, characteristics or strata of the larger population (e.g., race, gender, age, income, and geographic locale) are identified. Percentages of the population belonging in each strata are then calculated. For example, 24% of the population might be over age 70. Samples then are drawn in such a way as to preserve these percentages. That is, 24% of the sample contains people over age 70. Statistics (e.g., mean percentage) are calculated separately for each stratum and weighted when combined to determine the value for the larger population. In *cluster sampling*, categories and subcategories are developed and then sampled. Thus, all states might be identified. From within each state a random sample of counties would be selected. Within these, community mental health centers would be selected at random, and finally specific social workers within those centers would be surveyed.

Randomness gives probability sampling more scientific credibility than nonprobability sampling, largely because sampling error can be established in the first case, but not in the second. In other words, the validity of generalizations to larger populations cannot be determined with nonprobability samples (Pedhazur & Schmelkin, 1991). When reporting results, researchers often note that a survey has a "sampling error" of a certain percentage (e.g., ±3%). What they are referring to is the standard deviation of the means of successive samples drawn from the larger population; this value is referred to as the *standard error of the mean*, and it can be estimated as long as the samples have been drawn randomly.

Before leaving the topic of surveys and descriptive types of practice evaluation, let us revisit the distinction between probability sampling and nonprobability (i.e., convenience) sampling. Although we may be more likely to use convenience samples in practice evaluation, we might not need to limit ourselves in this way. If we have a large practice, for example, or have served a large number of people over a significant period of time, it can be impractical to survey them all. We can conduct a probability sampling of our clients if we think of all the people served as constituting the entire population to which we wish to generalize our findings. We need merely organize our selection process so that every one of our clients has an equal probability of being chosen. If we do this, we can calculate our sampling error, just as we can in scientific sampling.

Finally, a word should be said about the value of status surveys in practice evaluation. Although it is somewhat interesting to know the percentage of clients "moderately" or "very satisfied" with a service, the immediate question becomes "Relative to what?" What if 85% of the clients responded in this range? On the surface this result might be satisfying (remembering that there is some sampling error and associated confidence interval). Suppose, however, you learned that surveys of client satisfaction typically find that about 85% of respondents fall in this range regardless of type of service or level of service quality? Would 85% still be as satisfying?

Descriptions of the characteristics of clients served can be of great value to practitioners. This information can provide the basis for targeted marketing efforts, for example, or development of a business plan. Unfortunately, although this type of information can be useful, it is not very interesting. With just a small amount of additional effort, however, even more useful and interesting information can be produced from such surveys by showing relationships between variables.

As illustrated above, associations between characteristics can be explored rather easily. When relationships among variables are pursued in practice evaluation, the cumulative benefits to the practice can be substantial. As a simple illustration, suppose we substitute age for race in the example presented earlier (see Table 8.1). Is there an association between age and satisfaction with services? Presenting satisfaction and age in a table permits an easy answer to this question (Table 8.2). Although it is apparent that most clients are moderately or very satisfied with the service received, an interesting relationship exists between satisfaction and age. If we examine the data in the last column of the table, it appears that the most satisfied clients are between ages 26 and 50. When the data are converted to graphic form (Figure 8.1), the relationship becomes even more apparent.

The astute practitioner uses the observed relationship between age and satisfaction to improve services. The finding leads to further investigation to determine why the youngest and oldest clients are less satisfied. It might be discovered that staff are not trained specifically to serve older or younger clients, for example. Inservice or continuing education goals targeted toward appropriate staff training could be developed. Alternatively, additional staff with relevant expertise might be hired. Asking an evaluation question involving a relationship can lead to practice improvements that are not obvious from questions that merely look at the status of practice variables.

Table 8.2

Percentage Relationship Between Client Age and Satisfaction With Service

Age	(1) Very unsatisfied	(2) Moderately unsatisfied	(3) Slightly unsatisfied	(4) Slightly satisfied	(5) Moderately satisfied	(6) Very satisfied	Columns 5 + 6
<18	8	12	14	16	45	5	50
18–25	2	6	7	15	50	20	70
26–35	1	3	5	6	60	25	85
36–50	1	4	4	6	55	30	85
51–65	6	5	14	15	47	13	60
>65	9	12	20	14	35	10	45

Figure 8.1

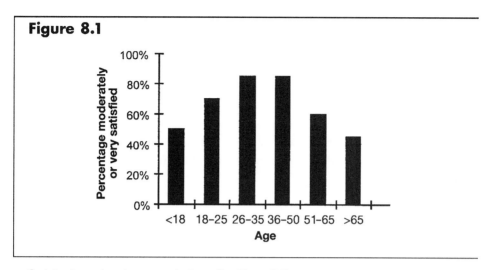

Satisfaction related to age of client. See Table 8.2 for data points.

A major strength in the use of descriptive methods for practice evaluation is that they are minimally intrusive. They can be carried out in the course of the daily operation of the practice. The data are routinely collected anyway, and they can be put to evaluative service without high levels of statistical sophistication and analytic resources. Descriptive methods also provide an important foundation or database on which to conduct more informative evaluations. For example, if we show that satisfaction with services varies among clients or that clients coming from one part of town present different psychological problems from those living in other areas, we eventually want to know why. Descriptive evaluative strategies are not equipped to answer "why" questions. To enhance our understanding of these apparent relationships, we need to use evaluative designs that document their existence and strength.

Relational Approaches

The primary reason for using descriptive approaches is to characterize a practice in terms of variables (see Figure 6.1). As we have just seen, however, descriptive approaches can be used to explore relationships between variables as well. The purpose of practice evaluation is to improve services, however; the most effective evaluation designs best accomplish that purpose. An approach specifically aimed at showing relationships, and thus able to do so more powerfully than descriptive tactics, is the *relational* strategy. With relational tactics, we can uncover myriad correlations between variables in our practices. Simple, zero-order correlations between different practice characteristics can lead to improvements in service quality such as those suggested by the relationship between age and satisfaction reported above. Multivariate procedures combining correlations between multiple characteristics can be an even more powerful way of analyzing relational data.

Essential Features

As mentioned earlier in this book, relationships among practice variables can be of two major types: associative or causal. At times, our interest merely concerns the extent to which events are associated, or occur together in time, such as when client satisfaction varies with age. On other occasions, we may be interested in the causes of behavior but cannot manipulate events that we presume to be causal. In both cases we must use relational designs to examine relationships.

As an example of an associative relationship, a psychologist might examine the frequency with which certain types of emotional disorders occur more often in girls than boys. The psychologist is interested in the relationship between gender and type of emotional difficulty because it facilitates understanding of the kinds of psychological services more likely to be needed by boys on the one hand, and girls on the other. The psychologist does not assume that gender causes particular types of psychological problems; there is no implication that the variables are related in a causal way. Relational analyses enhance our understanding of the relationships in such circumstances, and we explore them by documenting concomitant variation in the variables being examined. The two principal ways of doing this involve between- and within-case variation.

Between-Case Relational Approaches

The most common way to determine whether phenomena are associated is to assess them in multiple participants. Continuing with an interest in age and satisfaction, we would obtain age and satisfaction data from each client or from a sample of clients and correlate the variables. Assuming that the sample was randomly drawn, the correlation would provide an estimate of the degree of association between the two variables in some larger population. The best way to explore relationships between *status* variables (i.e., characteristics that do not change readily, such as age, IQ, and gender) or between them and more *dynamic* variables (i.e., characteristics that can change, e.g., anxiety, depression, or friendliness) is with between-case approaches. Within-domain (e.g., client, intervenor; see Figure 6.1) relationships can be examined this way, with many examples available from research in the behavioral sciences.

Practice evaluation offers many instances when within-domain relationships would be important to document. To illustrate, comorbidity is frequent in clients seeking help for various psychological dysfunctions (e.g., clients with drinking problems often have other difficulties). Knowing commonly occurring comorbid conditions can alert the practitioner to look for these and plan interventions appropriately. Likewise, simply describing relationships between variables within the client domain (see Figure 6.1) in the routine course of practice evaluation can uncover comorbidities that might not have been reported in the literature or are unique to the particular practice. Forewarned in this way, the practitioner can improve service quality.

Within-Case Relational Approaches

In the examples just given, the variation needed to produce the correlation came from differences between people at a particular point in time. It also is possible to obtain the necessary variation by assessing two or more characteristics in the same person over several occasions. For instance, a psychologist might be interested in the extent to which participation in activities outside the home is related to a client's reports of depressive feelings. The psychologist asks the client to keep track of the number of activities engaged in each day and to provide daily ratings of the level of depressive feelings. The client does so over the course of several weeks. The psychologist then correlates the number of activities with the ratings of depressive feelings. The magnitude of the correlation informs the psychologist in ways that can lead to the design of optimally effective interventions. For example, a positive correlation might result in the psychologist prescribing more activities for the client. The lack of a correlation might lead the psychologist to try other approaches with this particular person.

The psychologist might try a variant of the strategy just described before turning elsewhere, however. Suppose the beneficial effect of engaging in activities was delayed? What if improvements in mood were not noticed until the next day? (Delayed benefits of client behavior are probably more common than realized and should be examined more frequently.) Using the same example, a simple way to do this analysis would be to correlate the number of activities occurring on Day 1, 2, 3, and so on with depression ratings on Days 1 + 1, 2 + 1, 3 + 1, and so on. In other words, instead of computing correlations between variables occurring roughly at the same time, the correlations are computed between variables that occur at different (but sequential) times, an approach known as *cross-lagged* relational analysis.

Cross-lagged approaches have been reported in the literature as a way of studying causal relationships between variables that are not systematically manipulated (Nunnally & Bernstein, 1994). The logic is that correlations can be obtained between variables A and B at two different occasions. If the correlation between A at Time 1 and B at Time 2 is higher than that between B at Time 1 and A at Time 2, the assumption is that A causes B.

In the illustration involving depression and activity level above, a client rates depression and records the number of pleasant activities engaged in daily. To test whether these activities are negatively correlated with depression, one calculates a correlation between these two variables over the number of days. A correlation may be found to be −.45. The negative relationship does not tell whether the activity led to lower depression or vice versa. If we lag our entries by 1 day for one of the variables, we can recompute our correlation. This makes sense if we consider that participating in activities leads to a more positive mood; this might be most noticeable 1 day later. Thus, we enter activity counts into our data matrix for Days 1, 2, 3 through Day n. We offset or lag our entries for depression for 1 day, pairing Day 1 activity with Day 2 depression, Day 2 activity with Day 3 depression, and so forth. Suppose when we calculate a correlation for these Lag 1 data we find a value of −.60. Because depression data follow (lag) activity data by 1 day, it is hard to argue that depression leads to lower activity. To complete the analysis, we cross over to enter depression first, followed by activity offset (lagged) by 1 day. We calculate another correlation, pairing Day 1 depression with Day 2 activity, Day 2 depression with Day 3 activity, and so forth. Suppose the resulting correlation is −.30. Because the correlation is higher when activity data precede depression data in the analysis, we can conclude that a "causal" relationship exists; that is, the increases in pleasant activities lead to decreases in depression.

Significant conceptual and methodological challenges exist to this approach to determining causality (see Rogosa, 1980), and it is not pursued further here. The purpose of this analysis is not to establish causality but rather to explore the possibility of delayed relationships between some form of intervention and client behavior. By offsetting the second variable for systematically increasing time lags, one can uncover such delayed associations.

Relationships Between Multiple Concurrent Variables

The discussion of correlational strategies has proceeded to this point largely with examples of zero-order correlations. Most practice environments are more complex than the examples presented so far suggest, however, and they require strategies that permit a number of variables to be correlated at the same time. Procedures for this type of analysis are described in texts on multivariate statistics and are beyond the scope of this book.

Returning to the relationship between age and satisfaction, suppose the practitioner's main interest is in predicting client satisfaction. Assuming that a satisfied client is a returning client, good reasons exist for knowing which practice variables are the most highly correlated with satisfaction. To illustrate, suppose that in addition to age, variables involving the service provider (i.e., the intervenor), the intervention, and the setting were examined (see Figure 6.1). Suppose the practitioner wanted to test the theory that ecological relevance (i.e., the degree to which the context, time of service, intervenor, and intervention match the situation in which the client wants to be more effective) is related to client satisfaction. Variable domains (i.e., groups of related variables) that pertain to the theory include setting, time, intervention, and intervenor domains. More specifically, in the setting domain, ecological relevance is maximized when the service is carried out in the context in which the client wants to be more effective (i.e., home, work, school); this can be referred to as the *point of performance* (Barkley, 1998). In the temporal domain, the more quickly the service is delivered, the closer it occurs to the time when the client is concerned about it, thus further maximizing ecological relevance. Interventions can vary in terms of how directly relevant they are to the concerns of the client. In coaching executives, for example, the practitioner can take a systems perspective, designing interventions to change system variables and behavior characteristic of the executive. A more specific alternative would involve focusing directly on the executive, changing behavior to enhance the executive's performance in the context or system as it is presently constituted. Whereas system-level interventions can have more long-term payoff, their benefit can sometimes be a hard sell to the individual who sees more immediate relevance in approaches focused directly on her or him. Finally, intervenors can vary in apparent relevance. Suppose the practice is a large one, composed of multiple, diverse professionals who can deliver services. The practice owner wants to test the hypothesis that clients are more satisfied when people most similar to them in terms of demographic characteristics (e.g., age, gender, race, and education level) provide services.

To evaluate the practitioner's theory of ecological relevance, the following hypothesis is advanced: Client satisfaction is positively related to the ecological relevance of the services provided. Client satisfaction, the dependent variable, can be operationalized in a number of ways, as illustrated in chapter 7. Ecological relevance is composed of temporal, setting, intervenor, and intervention variables. The practitioner might choose one variable from each of the four domains (e.g., for the temporal domain, "time from initial contact to initiation of intervention" as the measure). To test the hypothesis, multivariate statistical procedures would be used to establish a mathematical formula describing the hypothesized relationship between satisfaction and ecological relevance of services. One approach would be to complete a multiple regression analysis incorporating all four of the service variables and satisfaction. To the extent that each of the four is correlated with satisfaction and not at all or only moderately with the other three, the result of the analysis would be a multiple regression equation of the form

$$Y' = a + by_{1.234}X_1 + by_{2.134}X_2 + by_{3.124}X_3 + by_{4.123}X_4,$$

where Y' is predicted satisfaction, a is the intercept, and the bs are beta weights usually known as "partial regression coefficients" (Pedhazur & Schmelkin, 1991, p. 417). Time, setting, intervenor, and intervention variables are represented as X_1, X_2, X_3, and X_4, respectively. The transcripts for each of the beta weights in the formula are designed to show that as each variable is correlated with satisfaction, the other variables are held constant or partialled out. Thus, when time is being correlated with, or "regressed," on satisfaction, setting, intervenor, and intervention, Variables 2, 3, and 4, respectively, are partialled out of the calculation. The general logic is to find the optimum weights to assign each variable so that satisfaction is predicted most accurately. To the extent that such weights are discovered, the hypothesis of a positive relationship between satisfaction and ecological relevance is supported.

Astute practice evaluators would want to know the relative contributions of each of the four variables to satisfaction. Knowing this can lead to changes in the practice to maximize satisfaction in the future. Determining the relative contributions of variables in multiple regression analysis can be a complex undertaking, especially when the independent variables are correlated, as is commonly the case in descriptive evaluations. Fortunately, sophisticated statistical treatments and associated software programs are available to facilitate the process (see chapter 10). For a more thorough treatment, interested readers should consult the well-written presentation of these concepts by Pedhazur and Schmelkin (1991).

In the example above, the practitioner had a theory of ecological relevance that guided the hypothesis suggesting the nature of the relationship and the choice of variables. Not all practitioners have a theoretical model guiding their activities, yet it is possible for them to conduct meaningful practice evaluations. Indeed, there is a lively ongoing debate among behavioral scientists as to the value of using highly formal, theory-driven, deductive approaches to science versus simpler, less formal, inductive approaches (see Johnston & Pennypacker, 1993). Strong arguments can be made for the dangers of preconception when providing services to others (Shapiro, 1961). Practitioners must work to keep preconceived ideas from limiting the scope of their observations and analyses; unfortunately, deductive theorizing can have such a limiting effect.

Wahler and Fox (1980) provided empirical support for a more inductive approach to the search for relevant treatment variables in their study of oppositional and aggressive children and their parents. Rather than hypothesize an "oppositional" response class in advance and limiting their observation of child behavior to supposed members of such a class, they took a more naturalistic tactic. During baseline observations of the children's behavior, they recorded a variety of child responses, including opposition, complaints, social interaction with adults, social interaction with children, toy play, and attending to a person or object. They also obtained daily reports from the parents of their child's problem behavior. What they observed was a consistent negative correlation between the frequency of the child's solitary toy play and parents' reports of problem behavior. This observation led to designing an intervention for the children that involved increasing the time spent in solitary play. The result was to reduce their oppositional responding and to increase their play with toys. Incidentally, the authors took precautions to make sure that the negative relationship between solitary toy play and problem behavior was not an artifact of having less time in which to behave problematically.

Relational evaluation strategies can uncover ways to improve services. Whether improvements occur faster when variable selection is determined by a formal theory underlying the practice or by more naturalistic, inductive approaches of the kind exemplified by Wahler and Fox (1980) cannot be answered. More important is that practitioners adopt a general strategy with which they are comfortable and examine relationships among practice variables on a continual basis. Over time, consistencies in relationships lead to the formulation of a theory of the practice inductively or modifications in a deductive theory that might have guided the practice from the outset.

Relational Approaches

As with descriptive strategies, relational methods of practice evaluation are minimally intrusive. They can be conducted in the routine operation of the practice and do not require special arrangements or control of variables in ways that might affect the provision of services. Relational approaches may be the best strategy to take when exploring associations between variables that cannot be manipulated systematically; many client characteristics fall into this category, including so-called organismic variables such as age, gender, race, family background, and physical condition. In addition, given the high degree of complexity involved in providing real services to real clients, relational strategies may be the only ones comprehensive enough to represent the relationships between variables, especially if multivariate statistical approaches are used.

Relational designs, however, are limited to exploring associative relationships between practice variables, rather than causal ones. For example, when a negative correlation is found between activities and depressive feelings reported by a client, as in the example above, the precise nature of the relationship cannot be known. Despite arguments of proponents of cross-lagged analysis, we do not know whether the client is less depressed because of engaging in the activities or whether he or she is participating in more activities because of feeling less depressed. A clear understanding of the direction of causal relations can come from experimental designs.

Experimental Approaches

Most human beings are, by nature, experimentalists. We try certain things to see what happens. In the more formal experiments of the natural sciences, conditions can be created that are equivalent in all respects. The "experimental" agent, or independent variable, then can be added to one condition and not to others and the differences in the dependent variables noted. In the behavioral sciences, precisely equivalent conditions cannot be created because we do not have control of all the relevant variables. Thus, we resort to random assignment: We assign participants randomly to one condition or another with the expectation that the process will produce equivalent groups. The independent variable is then delivered to one or more of the groups and not to others, and the differences evaluated. If such differences are reliable and cannot be attributed to anything other than the variable specifically manipulated, that variable is said to be the cause of the differences. In other words, a causal relationship has been established.

In practice evaluation, just as in science, we are often interested in causal relationships. Because it is extremely difficult to control all the variables that might change concurrently with the independent variable, it is challenging to conduct experiments in the practice evaluation context. With some practice and careful preparation, however, it is possible.

Essential Characteristics

The most important single consideration in successful experimentation is control: It is essential that we create or control events such that the independent variable is present in some conditions and not in others. In addition, it is essential that we control the independent variable so that it is delivered consistently and at predetermined levels of strength. Furthermore, we must have some way of evaluating the magnitude of any differences noted after applying the independent variable. The differences must be large enough to be reliable or statistically significant. Finally, we want some assurance that the differences produced under carefully controlled conditions in our experiment have relevance in other contexts (i.e., are generalizable to larger populations). In evaluations of the effectiveness of various forms of psychotherapy, for example, a distinction has arisen between a treatment's effectiveness and its efficacy (Seligman, 1995). When participants are randomly assigned to carefully controlled conditions, an *efficacy* study is being conducted. When participants are free to choose the treatment they receive and few, if any, controls exist over the specific nature of the treatment, conditions are more comparable with those in the real world, and an *effectiveness* study is being conducted (Hollon, 1996). Thus, a procedure might be shown to be efficacious but not effective and vice versa. Let us look closer at the "essential" ingredients of the experimental approach.

Experimental Control

The sine qua non of the experimental method is the ability to manipulate the independent variable. If it is applied in such a way that it can be said, unequivocally, to cause changes in the dependent variable, optimal experimental control has been exerted. If there is any ambiguity in interpreting the effects of the independent variable, experimental errors exist. These vary in seriousness from relatively minor discrepancies between what is concluded and what legitimately can be concluded from the results of a study to such serious discrepancies that the error is said to be *lethal* (Underwood, 1957). When lethal errors exist, an unambiguous relationship between the independent and dependent variables has not been shown, and the causal agency of the former cannot be asserted. In conducting experiments, the main goal is to control events precisely enough that the effects of the independent variable can be assessed. The most common way of controlling extraneous variables is through randomization. Random assignment can ensure equality of conditions prior to exposure to the independent variable. This procedure is particularly effective when the groups are large. Effective randomization results in groups that are statistically equivalent; they cannot be assumed to be equal in all possible ways, however. Randomization merely provides a strong probability that the groups are equal (Kerlinger, 1986). Another way of controlling extraneous variables is to hold a suspect variable constant. Using the above example, limiting the experiment to clients within a certain education range could control for the effects of education. Randomly assigning clients in that range to experimental and control groups would result in group equivalence on the education variable.

Another approach is to match participants on suspect variables before randomly assigning them to the experimental or control groups. This approach involves some difficulties, one of which is the complexity of matching when multiple variables are involved. Another concern is the requirement for a correlation between the matching and dependent variables (Kerlinger, 1986). Without a correlation, matching is not helpful and can lead to the impression of greater group equivalence than really exists.

Other forms of control facilitate analysis of the results of experiments. In addition to controlling exposure to the independent variable, the experimenter strives to minimize the effects of other variables. These variables are correlated with the dependent variable but are not the focus of the study being conducted; their presence is a nuisance in that it complicates the interpretation of the independent variable's effects; factors of this type are referred to as *extraneous variables*. Their existence is lethal when they vary concomitantly with the independent variable; in such cases, the experimenter cannot say that changes in the dependent variable result solely from changes in the independent variable. In other words, the effects of the independent variable are said to be *confounded* with the uncontrolled extraneous variable. For example, suppose education level is related to the speed with which reductions in stress typically are achieved. In evaluating the effectiveness of a therapy to reduce stress, clients are randomly assigned to an experimental group that receives the therapy and a control group that does not. If randomization results in group equivalence with respect to education, it can be ruled out as a confounding contributor to any changes that are produced. A final means of controlling potentially confounding variables can be achieved by building them into the design of the study. That is, the suspect variable can be made an independent variable along with the original one, and both can be manipulated. The separate and joint effects of the two variables can then be explored in a factorial design, about which more is said in a later section.

So far, this chapter has emphasized controlling variables that are systematically related to the dependent variable. Unsystematic or random variance (also known as "error variance") also must be controlled if an experiment is to reveal causal relationships. Error variance inflates differences between people within comparison groups and makes it more difficult to establish differences between the groups. A prime source of error is the method of measuring the dependent variable. If error is present, the measure is unreliable (see chapter 7). Intuitively, it makes sense that scores that vary unsystematically and randomly cannot be related to other variables, including independent ones. The careful investigator uses maximally reliable measures for this reason. Other randomly occurring events (e.g., participant fatigue, noisy conditions, and unscheduled interruptions) must be controlled as well, so as to maximize the effect of the independent variable.

Internal Validity

A study that uses the controls described so far is likely to lead to conclusions or assertions of relationships between the independent and dependent variables that are correct or appropriate. The validity of such assertions is supported to the extent that alternative explanations for changes in the dependent variable have been minimized. When they have been minimized, the study is said to have internal validity. Internal validity is thus the most important characteristic of experimental designs. If the effects of the independent variable can be interpreted unambiguously, the study is internally valid, and lethal errors have been avoided.

Threats to Internal Validity

Various reasons for qualifying the effects of independent variables have been noted in the literature on research design. These qualifications are considered threats to internal validity and have been described in detail by Cook and Campbell (1979). A brief mention is made of them here. In evaluation designs of the pretest–treatment–posttest variety, numerous events are occurring in the lives of participants at the same time as their involvement in treatment. The longer the pretest–posttest interval, the greater the likelihood that such variables can interfere with the study and cloud the interpretation of experimental results. Such variables are referred to as *history effects*; they can make it difficult to show the effect of the independent variable when they affect all participants in a study. For example, suppose a treatment for depression is evaluated in a study involving random assignment of depressed clients to experimental or control groups.

Suppose further that over the course of the 12-week treatment the weather changes from rainy and gloomy days to mostly sunny, clear ones. The depression levels of both groups might improve to the point where it is difficult for the dependent measure to show differences between them. This would be especially likely if both groups are showing scores close to the lowest possible on the measure. If they are, scores have no more room to move. History effects reduce the power of a design in cases like this. When they affect study groups differently, they can be lethal. Using the same example, suppose that the people in the experimental group began to be treated differently by friends and family members who knew they were in treatment—what if their reactions and not the treatment itself benefited the depressed clients the most? The total confounding of the reactions with the independent variable or treatment would make it difficult to isolate the effects of the independent variable. Reactions of family and friends constitute another history variable.

Gradual changes that take place in participants over the course of a study are called *maturation effects*. Examples of such changes are becoming older, wiser, bored, hungry, or tired. Again, when these factors affect all participants similarly, the sensitivity of the experiment is compromised. Imagine a study to increase creativity in which the experimental group spends time playing novel games while the control group is kept busy with a dull task such as marking out every *e* in *The New York Times*. At the end of the study, all participants are tested on some measure of creativity, and no differences are found between the groups. One possibility to consider is that even though the novel games increased creativity, both groups were so tired after participating that neither scored high on the creativity test. As with history effects, maturation can be lethal when it affects groups differently. Suppose, in the above example, the "e"-canceling task produces profound levels of boredom in the control participants. When subsequently tested, they do poorly relative to the experimental participants not because they are less creative but because they are too bored to attend effectively to the items in the creativity test.

Testing effects also can interfere with straightforward interpretations of the outcomes of experiments. It is likely that pretesting participants alters them in certain ways. Suppose the people being tested make an effort to be consistent, so when presented with the test again at the posttest, they try to remember their earlier responses. The effect of such an effort would be to minimize differences produced by any experimental variable. As another example, suppose the effect of the pretest was to sensitize the participants in certain ways. For instance, items in a test of eating routines for people about to undergo a weight-loss program might alert them to some ineffective ways of relating to food. Changes in body weight for experimental and control participants may show equally significant reductions. Again, the lethality of testing effects, as with history and maturation, depends on its differential impact on experimental and control participants.

Imagine an evaluation in which depressed people are administered the Automatic Thoughts Questionnaire (Hollon & Kendall, 1980) before and after cognitive–behavior therapy or participation in a wait-list control group. Suppose the pretest alerts the participants to the fact that their ways of thinking about things might contribute to their depression. Being "prewarned" by the pretest, participants receiving the treatment respond better to it than they would have without the prior sensitization. Moreover, on the posttest the treated participants show lower levels of depression than untreated participants do. In this case, pretesting and treatment have interacted to produce improvement that cannot be attributed to the treatment alone. Whether the treatment would work as well without the prior sensitization cannot be answered in a two-group design such as this.

Other changes that can affect the internal validity of an evaluation involve *instrumentation effects*. For example, suppose an evaluation involves directly observing the proficiency of teachers' one-on-one instruction before and after a training in certain teaching techniques. Observers of the teachers might become more proficient with the direct-observation coding system over the course of the study and more accurate in detecting correct and incorrect teaching sequences. Assume at the outset that observers give teachers the benefit of the doubt when they are unsure whether the observed sequence is correct. Over time, however, such "gifts" decrease as the observers become more adept at discriminating correct interactions. Comparing baseline observations with later observations might produce distorted results because of changes in the stringency of the observers' coding criteria. In other words, the systematic changes in instrumentation thwart clear interpretations of the impact of the independent variable (i.e., the training).

Finally, consider the change that can result from selecting participants who score at the extremes on measures of the dependent variable. A well-known tendency exists for successive measurements to show scores closer to the mean of a distribution. This regression toward the mean, or *statistical regression*, is a common threat to internal validity, especially when participants with high or low scores are initially selected for a study. This phenomenon has been known for some time for physical characteristics, such as height. Children of tall parents tend to be shorter, on the average, than their parents (Pedhazur & Schmelkin, 1991). Likewise, students who perform well on midterm exams in college courses tend to do less well on the final. Moreover the reverse is true (Pedhazur & Schmelkin, 1991). For example, simply reassessing people with high scores on the Beck Depression Inventory (Beck et al., 1961) results in lower scores whether they receive treatment during the interim or not (see Atkeson, Calhoun, Resick, & Ellis, 1982; Hammen, 1980; Sharpe & Gilbert, 1998).

In a detailed discussion of regression toward the mean, Pedhazur and Schmelkin (1991) called attention to the important work of Kahneman and Tversky (1973) involving flight instructors. It seems that the instructors felt that rewarding student pilots actually led to worse performance, whereas punishment improved it. The instructors' conclusion came from observing that whenever a student was rewarded for completing a smooth landing, the next one was invariably not as good; when admonished for a poor landing, however, the next one was invariably better. This variation in landing proficiency can be explained in terms of regression toward the mean. Failing to recognize the phenomenon can lead people to agree with the pilots' view that reinforcement does not work. Because of the ubiquity of the regression phenomenon, careful evaluators design studies to minimize its impact on internal validity.

Additional threats to internal validity include selection of participants and their assignment to groups; mortality, or participants' dropping out of a study; diffusion of treatments; and compensatory rivalry. Readers interested in information on these concerns would do well to consult the detailed treatment in Cook and Campbell (1979).

External Validity

Exercising enough control to permit clear determination of the effects of the independent variable is necessary to avoid lethal research errors and achieve internal validity. As it happens, exerting the control necessary to avoid such errors can lead to laboratory conditions that are sterile and unlike those of the "messy" real world. When the laboratory results are representative and the findings can be generalized to other contexts, we say the study has *external validity*. The specific participants (clients), experimenters (intervenors), levels of the independent variable (intervention), settings, and time that are studied are all values selected from larger populations. Externally valid designs permit generalizing beyond these values to the populations.

Similarly, in practice evaluation, an important form of external validity involves generalizing results to clients not included in the study itself. This process can be done with confidence only when a truly random selection procedure has been used to obtain study participants from among the entire client pool of a given practice. Other forms of external validity relevant to practice evaluation concern the level of the independent variable. For example, a particular type of psychotherapy might be studied over a period of twelve 50-minute sessions. In practice, psychotherapy requires various numbers of sessions, depending on the client. Is it as effective if clients are seen only eight times? What happens if the therapy extends to more sessions? If the variations do not matter, the independent variable can be said to generalize across numbers of sessions, and the study shows this type of external validity. We can say that treatment effectiveness does not depend on the number of sessions. Similarly, if the practice includes multiple professionals, there might be interest in the extent to which results obtained with the practitioners participating in the study are generalizable to those who did not participate.

Evaluations can be designed to maximize external validity, just as they are set up to ensure internal validity. Again, however, space permits only a rather cursory treatment of ways to enhance external validity; readers seeking more complete discussions of the issues should consult Bracht and Glass (1968), Cook and Campbell (1979), or Bernstein, Bohrnstedt, and Borgatta (1975).

Threats to External Validity

Treatment-by-attribute interactions can threaten external validity in that the intervention must be qualified by a characteristic (attribute) of the participants. *Attribute* is a general term referring to client variables such as age, gender, severity of presenting complaint, intelligence, and personality traits. An evaluation set up to permit generalization across attributes varies them systematically in the design and notes whether they interact with the intervention. If they do interact, the effect of the intervention must be qualified by (i.e., take into account) the attribute. For example, a treatment to reduce verbal aggression works for men but not for women. If no interaction is found, the results are not dependent on the particular attributes studied, and external validity is heightened. For example, an intervention can be applied to a group of clients with high levels of a presenting concern and to another group with only moderate levels. If the treatment is equally effective for both groups, there is no attribute-by-treatment interaction, and external validity has been demonstrated.

Treatment-by-setting interactions are another important threat to external validity, primarily because interventions often are carried out in settings of convenience, such as practitioners' offices. A treatment that works in the office environment might not work as well in the natural environment, be it home, school, or workplace. Evaluations can be designed to vary settings systematically and observe whether effects of the independent variable differ across them. If so, a treatment-by-setting interaction exists, and the interpretation of the independent variable must be qualified accordingly.

Another threat to external validity is *multiple-treatments interference*, which involves changes in participants resulting not from the use of a single treatment by itself but from its use in combination with others. In practice settings it is not uncommon for clients to receive several types of intervention at the same time. Occasionally this is under the control of the practitioner, but more often it results from the client seeking help from multiple independent sources, such as friends, family members, or colleagues. When several interventions occur concurrently, they can interact to produce changes; the effects would not be the same if the intervention being studied were applied by itself. A special type of multiple-treatments interference occurs when interventions are applied in a sequence. When those applied early in the sequence affect the strength of those applied later, they are said to have generated *crossover effects* (Pedhazur & Schmelkin, 1991).

Evaluations involving pretest–posttest comparisons face additional threats to external validity known as *pretest sensitization* and *posttest sensitization*. Recall that pretest sensitization means that assessing a person before an intervention is applied can communicate information that facilitates (or detracts from) the effectiveness of the intervention. In the case of posttest sensitization, the act of assessing the participant at the conclusion of an intervention might facilitate its impact. Imagine an evaluation in which a group of clients is exposed to an intervention but not assessed at its conclusion. Now imagine a second group that receives the intervention and is then assessed. Suppose delayed effects exist that are activated by the content of the posttest itself. If both groups are followed and observed for treatment benefits and the second group is found to be more improved than the first, the conclusion is that the use of the posttest interacted with the treatment to produce a combined effect greater than the treatment alone, thereby limiting the external validity of the evaluation.

Lest the reader believe that external validity is essential to a useful practice evaluation, a disclaimer is in order. In defending external *in-validity*, Mook (1983) noted that at times an experimenter has no interest in nor obligation to show that results can be generalized beyond the bounds of a carefully controlled (and, therefore, highly artificial) laboratory environment. The benefits of "unreal world" laboratory studies lie in the enhanced understanding they provide of phenomena, an understanding that "comes from theory or the analysis of mechanism" (Mook, 1983, p. 386). This understanding requires no generalizations to the external world. Of course, Mook also pointed out that we sometimes do want to predict real-life behavior, as in practice evaluations; in these situations, external validity is quite important. Failure to realize that these instances constitute but a small part of the entire universe of research activities, however, can lead to overvaluing the concept of external validity.

Ecology of Experimental Studies

In addition to threats to internal and external validity, other sources of extraneous variation can cloud the interpretation of experimental outcomes. An important source of such variation comes from inconsistencies in the way the practitioner implements the intervention.

More and more often in applied psychology and in medicine, evidence-based procedures are becoming the interventions of choice. These are usually accompanied by treatment manuals describing their implementation in great detail (e.g., Barlow & Craske, 1989, 1994; Beck, Rush, Shaw, & Emery, 1979; Blanchard et al., 1985; Fairburn, Marcus, & Wilson, 1993). Practitioners' training is based on the manual, thereby affording a measure of consistency over their implementation. Problems arise, however, when the practitioner improvises and diverges from the manual or script. When this happens, the integrity of the treatment can be compromised; that is, treatment is implemented in unique ways not described in the manual. In those cases, any effects of the intervention are actually those of an idiosyncratic use of it. Unless the practitioner takes careful notes and records them in an "exception log" (i.e., a list of deviations from the procedure outlined in the manual), there is no way to know the precise nature of the intervention that has produced the results. When multiple practitioners are involved in a study evaluating the effects of a particular intervention, it is imperative that they are controlled closely by written instructions so that everyone implements the same treatment. When they do, "treatment integrity" (Yeaton & Sechrest, 1981) is preserved. If the practitioners are allowed to improvise, they essentially introduce uncontrolled variation that lowers the power of the study to show whether the intervention is effective.

Of course, it is not possible for an evaluator to specify every aspect of the interaction with the client and standardize it across practitioners and clients. Because some variations in procedure cannot be anticipated, it is important to control whatever is known in advance (e.g., treatment can be described in detail in treatment manuals, and therapists can be trained in the manuals' use). In addition, standard ways of responding to specific situations can be determined before the study starts. For example, the researcher can anticipate the types of questions clients might ask, produce standard ways of answering them in advance, and train therapists to give those answers.

Another accepted way of increasing treatment integrity is to record treatment implementation using audio- or videotaping procedures. Later, the tapes are reviewed and the consistency with which the intervention is implemented is assessed. Simply knowing that their work might be reviewed is likely to enhance the extent to which interventionists "keep to the script," if data from intermittent checks on observers are any indication. For example, Romanczyk, Kent, and Diament (1973) found that more behavior was recorded when observers knew their work was being monitored than when they were unaware that the checks were occurring. (Reactivity of assessment procedures is discussed in chapter 7.)

If recording the sessions is not feasible, interviews or questionnaires can be administered to clients after treatment to get their descriptions of how the intervention was conducted. These procedures can have their own problems, however. At best, they represent the client's perception and do not map the intervention precisely (Kazdin, 1998).

Another source of unwanted variance in experimental investigations can be expectations entertained by the therapist (i.e., *expectancy effects*). If the experimenter anticipates a certain outcome, it can be more likely to occur, a phenomenon referred to as the *self-fulfilling prophecy* (Rosenthal, 1966, 1976), which likely stems from the experimenter behaving in a manner that increases the likelihood of the expected outcome (Rosnow & Rosenthal, 1999). In evaluating different intervention approaches in applied settings, expectancy effects can be particularly troublesome when all the approaches are carried out by the same practitioners. So-called *allegiance effects* can occur if the practitioner is positively disposed to a particular approach and shows more effort, care, and enthusiasm in the course of that approach. As an example of allegiance effects, Kazdin (1980) pointed to the evaluation of the relative effectiveness of three different forms of therapy, all implemented by the founder and energetic proponent of one of the three (i.e., Ellis, 1957). The difficulty, as Kazdin noted, is the strong possibility of therapist-by-treatment interaction, thereby threatening the external validity of the evaluation. In the example given, the results were perfectly predictable from the theoretical orientation of the investigator. Unfortunately, this problem is not avoided by having different therapists administer the different treatments. Unless they are equally proficient with all treatments, equally enthusiastic about their effectiveness, and randomly assigned to implement them, it is likely that any differences in treatment are confounded with differences in therapists. When a small number of therapists is available, they are almost certain to differ in ways that can interact with the treatment, even if randomly assigned.

Rosenthal and Rosnow (1984) suggested that one way to handle this type of expectation bias is to build it into the study as an independent variable in its own right. Some therapists can be given the expectation that a particular type of treatment will have certain effects, whereas other therapists are not. If the results favor therapists with the expectation, bias is likely. An even stronger design would involve giving some therapists negative expectations; some, positive ones; and some, no expectations. If the treatment is effective even when therapists are led to believe that it will not be, the results are rather convincing. Moreover, if no differences exist between groups, it is unlikely that expectancy effects are operating.

In pharmaceutical research, *blind* or *double-blind* designs are used to control for expectancy effects. In the first, the patients' expectations are controlled by administering either the experimental drug or a placebo and not telling the patient which drug they received. In the second, procedures are used that prevent both the patient and the therapist from knowing whether the drug is the active one or an inert placebo. When different interventions require therapists to perform in different ways, however, it is nearly impossible to keep therapists blind as to which one they are implementing at a particular time.

Orne (1962) warned that aspects of an experimental situation can tip off participants in certain ways. An obvious example occurs in practice when a client is given a pretest with a high degree of face validity (see chapter 4) for the intervention about to be administered. To illustrate, a measure of organizational climate (e.g., Denison & Mishra, 1995) might be used in a company to assess its culture prior to an intervention designed to alter it in certain ways. Imagine the goal is to move the company away from its current top-down, authoritarian culture to one that is more participatory and bottom up. After intensive organizational consultation over a period of several months, the test is readministered. Employees know consultation is occurring and what the consultants are hoping to show. It would not be surprising to find that they respond in ways consistent with these "demands" on the posttest. If they do, the posttest mean score supports the effectiveness of the effort to change the corporate climate. Whether the climate really has changed or merely appears to have changed cannot be determined because of the possibility that the responses of the employees were biased.

A related difficulty involves changes in participants that result simply from the special attention given them during the study. Formally identified in the 1930s, the *Hawthorne effect* took its name from research conducted in the Hawthorne plant of the Western Electric Company in Cicero, Illinois. The productivity of workers assembling and inspecting small parts was examined to determine the effects of lighting and other changes in working conditions (Parsons, 1974; Roethlisberger, 1977). Oddly, worker productivity increased in unexpected circumstances, such as when light levels were systematically decreased. Differences were attributed to the special attention given the workers rather than the specific environmental variables originally expected to produce them. Although explanations of these changes have varied (Shaughnessy & Zechmeister, 1990), the findings alerted researchers to the possibility of unintended or nonspecific effects affecting the results. To control these effects, researchers can give one group all the attention given experimental participants but not the specific experimental treatment itself. This is a form of nonspecific treatment referred to as an "attention-placebo condition."

The Hawthorne effect is akin to the nonspecific effects (e.g., special attention) that can interfere with straightforward interpretations of the results of treatment outcome studies from psychology and related fields. To take a simple example, when a practitioner seeks to evaluate whether a new form of therapy works, a common experimental approach involves randomly assigning participants to an experimental group, which gets the new treatment, and a control group, which does not. Differences in the expected direction are assumed to be the result of the novel treatment. The Hawthorne effect raises the possibility of another interpretation, however: The treated participants may show improvement just because of the special attention inherent in the provision of treatment itself. In other words, the new treatment might produce improvement, but no more so than existing approaches providing similar levels of special attention to participants.

The fact that inert chemical substances (i.e., placebos) can be associated with substantial change in physical as well as psychological characteristics has long been appreciated (Shapiro & Morris, 1978). In *Persuasion and Healing*, Frank (1961) pointed to the positive impact that faith or expectancy can have on the healing process. If belief in the effects of a drug can produce positive outcomes even when a drug is not actually taken, it is no surprise that belief in the effects of other forms of treatment can influence their effects as well. Indeed, findings to this effect have led to the common practice of including attention-placebo control groups in treatment outcome studies (e.g., Last, Hansen, & Franco, 1998). Such groups are expected to show a level of change midway between that shown by the experimental group and completely untreated control group. Protecting against or accounting for change produced by factors other than the specific independent variable is one of the concerns of the experimental designs discussed in the next section.

Between-Case Experimental Designs

Evaluative designs are selected to answer particular evaluative questions. As mentioned in chapter 5, for the practitioner these are typically as follows:

- Does an intervention work?
- Does it work better than alternatives?
- Why does it work?

Between-case designs are appropriate for all three types of questions, although designs of different levels of complexity are required for each type of question.

Two-Group Designs

When pursuing "Does it work?" questions, simple between-case designs of the two-group, true-experiment type can be used, as described earlier in this chapter. These experiments involve arrangements in which two equal groups are created, the independent variable (intervention) is applied to one of them, and the effects of the application on the dependent variable are assessed. Essential to the successful use of two-group, true experimental designs is the creation and maintaining of equivalent groups, usually through the random assignment of participants to the groups. Assuming the groups can be kept intact until the independent variable has been applied, they can be evaluated on the dependent variable and mean differences noted. Those differences can be subjected to analysis to determine their reliability (or significance) usually by statistical tests. If the difference is found to be reliable (i.e., statistically significant), it is reasonable to conclude that the difference results from the independent variable.

Before celebrating such a finding, however, it is important to be clear just what it tells us. In evaluating, for example, a new form of intervention, a reliable difference in favor of the experimental group supports the existence of a gross causal relationship between the independent and dependent variables. The intervention is likely to be a complex amalgam of general and unique ingredients, and all we can say is that this combination of factors produces an effect. As the preceding material pointed out, there are likely to be nonspecific factors inherent in the intervention that contribute to the differences we find. In other words, simply focusing attention on the participants, meeting with them multiple times, discussing problems, and conveying the expectation of change can be part of the reason the intervention works. These are ingredients common to most behavior change interventions, however, and are well established as effective change producers. To have confidence that a particular intervention is something unique, it is necessary to go beyond a simple, two-group true experiment.

In experimental psychology it is common for the experiment itself to take place in a relatively short period of time. The exposure of the experimental participants to the independent variable can even occur in a single setting. When behavioral change interventions are evaluated in applied contexts, however, it is likely that the application of the independent variable will take place over extended periods of time. The longer it takes to apply the independent variable completely, the more likely participants will drop out of the study. As noted earlier, the internal validity of the study is destroyed when participants drop out of groups differentially.

This problem can become especially acute in practice evaluation efforts examining the impact of direct services. Suppose one is evaluating a treatment for anxiety. Anxious clients might be randomly assigned to treatment and wait-list control groups; the latter provides a delayed-treatment condition in which people are essentially on a waiting list. They get treated after the study is finished, and their service as untreated controls is over. It would not be surprising for anxious people in the control condition to be on the lookout for alternative forms of treatment more readily available, nor would it be surprising if the control group members most likely to seek alternatives and to defect when they find one are those experiencing the highest levels of anxiety. If differential attrition of this sort occurs, the remaining control participants generally are less anxious and appear to have improved on their own. At the same time, differences between them and the treated participants are reduced, making it look as though the intervention is less effective than it is. Even if wait-list control participants remain available to receive treatment when the study ends, they are unlikely to be wholly untreated at that time because of the high probability that they will undergo informal types of treatment during the wait (e.g., talking with friends, meeting with clergy, or changing their lives in ways that result in lowered anxiety).

Three-Group Designs

To determine whether the treatment contributes anything unique, the question becomes whether it works better than existing approaches. For questions such as these, simple between-case designs of the two-group, true-experiment type are not sufficient. These questions are asked after we know the intervention works, at least in the gross way demonstrable in true experiments. In the example above, the evaluator might now want to know whether the impact of the intervention is greater than the result of nonspecific factors generally available in most forms of treatment. A third group therefore might be added to the two-group, true experiment. This *attention-placebo* group receives the attention, meetings with a therapist, and expectations of improvement. Deliberately missing is the ingredient specifically designed to reduce anxiety. Participants are randomly assigned to the three groups: (a) experimental, (b) attention-placebo control, and (c) wait-list control. Post-treatment differences like those illustrated in Figure 8.2 support the conclusion that both the treatment and attention-placebo groups received some benefit; each treated group shows lower mean anxiety after treatment than the untreated (wait-list) control group. Whether those

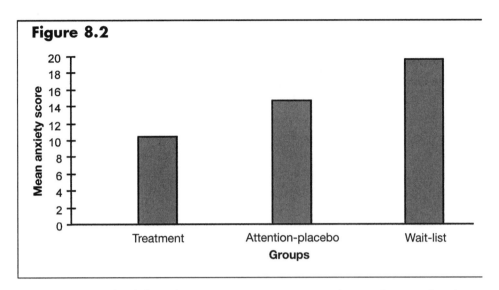

Figure 8.2

Mean anxiety score

Groups

Treatment   Attention-placebo   Wait-list

Posttest anxiety levels for a three-group true experiment. Both treated groups show lower mean anxiety after treatment than do the untreated (wait-list) controls.

differences are significant still needs to be evaluated, a topic discussed in the next chapter.

Suppose the data turned out like those in Figure 8.3 instead. Again, treatment seems to have worked. The benefits of the treatment do not appear to exceed those produced by factors generally available in most forms of therapy, however, because the treatment and attention-placebo groups show essentially equivalent levels of anxiety following intervention. Useful variations on the designs discussed thus far include assessing participants before as well as after intervention. Adding preintervention assessment information to the above example might produce results like those shown in Figure 8.4.

Several advantages to adding pretest information are apparent from the figure. For one, we can see whether the treatment really produces any change. In addition, the inclusion of two control groups helps clarify the nature of this change: By showing that no change occurred in the absence of treatment (i.e., among the wait-list group), it is evident that both treatment and attention-placebo groups improved. Differences between groups in a posttest-only design are assumed to reflect change, but it is possible that the groups were different from the start. Randomization may not always produce equivalent groups, especially when small numbers are involved. The addition of pretest data verifies the initial equivalence of the groups and permits the amount of change to be documented.

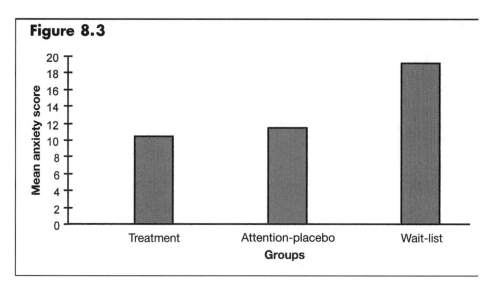

Posttest anxiety levels for a three-group true experiment. The benefits of the treatment do not appear to exceed those produced by factors generally occurring in most forms of therapy.

In the interest of economy, it might be tempting to omit the wait-list control group in the above example. After all, the pretest and post-test differences in the remaining groups document the change. What if the changes were the result of factors other than the treatments themselves, though (e.g., they merely reflected regression of extreme scores to the mean)? Including untreated controls enhances the internal validity of the evaluation by controlling for a number of additional threats to validity, such as history, maturation, testing, and instrumentation.

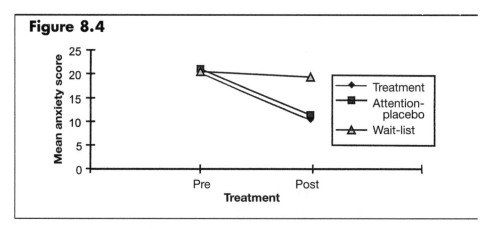

Comparison of pretest and posttest anxiety levels. Both treatment and attention-placebo groups improved, as evidenced by the lack of change in the wait-list control group.

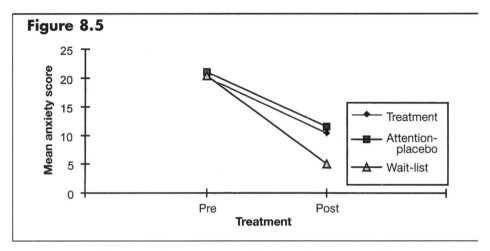

Figure 8.5

Comparison of pretest and posttest anxiety levels. Both treatment and attention-placebo groups have higher anxiety than if they had not been treated at all, and the wait-list control group shows more improvement than the two groups receiving treatment.

Another advantage of untreated control groups is worth noting. With behavior change interventions such as those of psychologists, physical therapists, speech therapists, and other professionals, it is important to show avoidance of harm. What if both treatment and attention-placebo procedures in the above example left participants with higher anxiety than if they had not been treated at all? Figure 8.5 shows this possibility. In it, the wait-list control group improves more than the two groups actually receiving treatment.

It is not always necessary to include untreated and nonspecific-treatment (or attention-placebo) groups in experimental practice evaluations designed to answer comparative questions. Some treatments have been shown repeatedly to work better than no treatment at all. In these cases, demonstrations of this effectiveness would be superfluous (see Jacobson et al., 1989). Furthermore, when comparative questions are pursued with treatments known to produce more change than nonspecific treatments, additional demonstrations of their effectiveness probably are not needed, either. The data from earlier evaluations can be drawn on to provide benchmarks against which to assess the results of the current evaluation. To illustrate, consider the data presented in Figure 8.6, which indicate that exposing anxious clients to the source of their concerns in the real world is more effective than exposing them to such concerns by asking them to imagine them. This interpretation relies heavily on the assumption that earlier work has established the relative superiority of the exposure treatments to untreated and non-

Figure 8.6

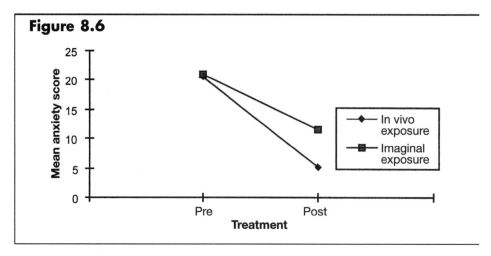

Comparison of pretest and posttest anxiety treated with imaginal versus in vivo exposure. Exposing anxious clients to the source of their concerns in the real world appears to be more effective than exposing them to such concerns by asking them to imagine them. This interpretation assumes that earlier work has established the relative superiority of the exposure treatments to untreated and non-specific-treatment controls.

specific-treatment controls. Indeed, it is wise to pursue an evaluative design like that in Figure 8.6 only after this information is available.

Of course, it is possible to provide data on this issue in a single study by comparing different treatments with each other as well as with no-treatment and attention-placebo treatment baselines (Figure 8.7). If resources permit, this design is a superior choice because of the amount and clarity of the information it provides. Because no differences are apparent on the pretest, it is immediately clear that the randomization process worked to equate the groups at the outset.

The beauty of a design like that shown in Figure 8.7 is that it simultaneously can provide answers to "Does it work?" and "How does it compare?" Even more complex designs can be created that also answer "Why does it work?" For example, suppose in the previous illustration the practitioner wanted to know why in vivo exposure seems to work. As practiced, the procedure involves going with clients to settings containing anxiety-eliciting elements and guiding them in gradual exposure to those elements. It is cumbersome to leave the office to do this, and the practitioner wonders whether anxious clients can be instructed to do this on their own; perhaps the therapist need not be present at all. Can clients expose themselves in gradual ways to frightening stimuli in the real world? The question becomes whether the

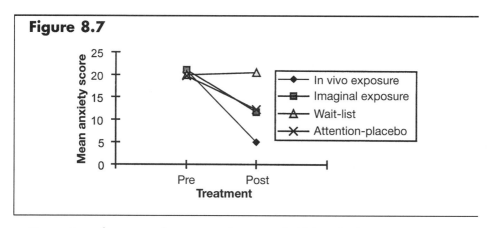

Figure 8.7

Comparison of pretest and posttest anxiety treated with imaginal versus in vivo exposure in a design including no-treatment and attention-placebo baselines. Because no differences are apparent on the pretest, it is clear that the randomization process worked to equate the groups at the outset.

presence of the therapist is necessary for in vivo exposure procedures to work. Another question might involve the need for gradual exposure to the anxiety-eliciting stimulus. This process can take time because it requires repeatedly presenting the client with approximations to the total fear-producing situation. The practitioner might wonder whether the gradual-exposure component of the approach is necessary.

Answers to both questions are possible through a carefully designed study. There are, in effect, two independent variables: (a) guidance and (b) type of exposure. Each has two levels: (a) self- versus therapist guidance and (b) gradual versus immediate exposure. The resulting design is referred to as a *2 × 2 factorial*, with participants randomly assigned to four groups (Table 8.3). The hypothetical data in Figure 8.8 show that the groups given therapist-guided exposure had

Table 8.3

A 2 × 2 Factorial Design for Treating Anxiety

	Exposure	
Guidance	Gradual	Immediate
Self	6.5	7.3
Therapist	4.2	4.6

Note. Values represent mean posttreatment anxiety scores.

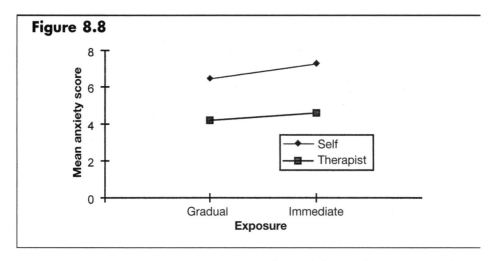

Figure 8.8

Posttreatment mean anxiety scores in a 2 × 2 factorial design. There appears to be no effect for the exposure variable, indicating that it is as effective to expose clients to feared stimuli immediately as it is to expose them in a more gradual fashion.

lower scores than those given self-guided exposure, regardless of whether exposure was gradual or immediate. In fact, there appears to be no effect for the exposure variable, indicating that it is as effective to expose clients to feared stimuli immediately as to expose them in a more gradual fashion.

A slightly different outcome is shown in Table 8.4. Here the same two independent variables are manipulated to determine their effects on anxiety, but this time, the results have to be qualified. As before, there appears to be an effect for the guidance variable, with therapist-guided exposure being more effective, in general, than self-guided exposure. However, exposure appears to depend on the speed with which it occurs. As the data in Figure 8.9 make clear, self- and therapist-guided forms of exposure have equivalent effects when exposure is gradual. Therapist-guided exposure is more effective, however, when exposure to the anxiety-eliciting stimulus is immediate. With such interactions, the results of one independent variable have to be qualified in terms of the other. The interaction depicted in Figure 8.9 indicates that the worst outcome occurs when self-guided exposure is combined with immediate exposure.

Multifactorial designs permit answering more specific questions than the multigroup, nonfactorial designs described earlier. For this reason, they are especially suited for probing the reasons why a given treatment appears to work. In the above example, the data indicate that

Table 8.4

A 2 × 2 Factorial Design Showing an Interaction in Treating Anxiety

	Exposure speed	
Guidance	Gradual	Immediate
Self	6.5	11.3
Therapist	5.8	5.2

Note. Values represent mean posttreatment anxiety scores.

the therapist is not needed to guide the client as long as the exposure to feared stimuli is gradual. Knowing this, the practitioner can treat anxious clients more successfully than others who have not done similar evaluations, thus staying competitive in the provision of behavioral health services.

Even though a substantial number of participants are needed, a factorial design requires fewer participants than would individual evaluations designed to answer the same questions. Imagine, for example, that we want to have 20 participants in each condition of an evaluation testing the effectiveness of self- versus therapist-guided exposure and that we want to have a similar number in each condition of a separate evaluation testing the effectiveness of immediate versus graduated exposure. Each evaluation requires 40 participants, for a total of 80 between the two of them. Examine the distribution of participants in Table 8.5. The total number of 40 is half the number needed to accomplish the same comparisons in separate, nonfactorial studies. Thus, factorial studies actually require fewer participants to test the same hypotheses.

A second potential difficulty with multifactorial studies of the type described above is that they require multiple interventionists, ideally trained in all treatments and then randomly assigned to one of them. There would need to be at least two interventionists per treatment in order to rule out therapist-by-treatment confounds. In the example above, at least eight therapists would be needed, two to work with half of the participants in each of the four treatment groups. For optimal results, the therapists would have to be of comparable experience, competence, and optimism with regard to the effectiveness of the treatments they are assigned to implement. Clearly, this scope is likely to be beyond the reach of most practices.

Figure 8.9

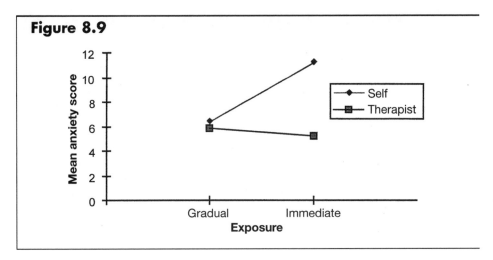

Posttreatment mean anxiety scores for the four groups in a 2 × 2 factorial design. Here, self- and therapist-guided forms of exposure have equivalent effects when exposure is gradual, but therapist-guided exposure is more effective when exposure to the anxiety-eliciting stimulus is immediate.

Finally, and perhaps most important, optimum control over threats to validity requires that all conditions of the study be implemented concurrently. Thus, all participants are recruited, randomly assigned to groups, pretested, treated, and posttested at essentially the same times. The logistics of managing such a feat would tax even the largest and best-run practice. Readers interested in more elaborate research designs are referred to chapter 10 and to Cook and Campbell (1979), Kirk (1982), and Winer, Michels, and Brown (1991) for more extensive treatments.

Advantages and Disadvantages

In practice evaluation, as in science, the goal is to study the impact of some variables on others so that we can achieve optimum understanding. Understanding our practice requires us to know whether what we do really has the effect on our clients we think it has. The only way to know this with a high level of confidence is to use highly controlled experimental designs. A well-conducted evaluation permits unequivocal conclusions about the relationships between independent and dependent variables. Experimental evaluations allow us to discard ineffective practices more rapidly than evaluations that cannot delineate causal connections between our work and changes in clients, thereby increasing the overall quality of the services we provide more rapidly as well.

Table 8.5

A 2 × 2 Factorial Design Showing the Number of Participants Needed for 20 to be Exposed to Each Level of Each Independent Variable

	Exposure speed	
Guidance	Gradual	Immediate
Self	10	10
Therapist	10	10

At the same time, well-conducted experimental evaluations are difficult to accomplish. Maintaining control is challenging enough in laboratory contexts, where high levels of control are possible; it is even more challenging in the "noisy" context of the typical practice. Merely standardizing the approach we take across a number of clients randomly assigned to the same intervention can be taxing. Clients are all different, and our training teaches us the importance of these differences. Clients form their own impressions of the most suitable approach for them and resist assignment to one they do not view as promising. It is difficult to adhere to standard protocols in the face of nonstandard clients, and the temptation to make adjustments is great.

In addition, ethical requirements can create difficulties. Even assigning participants randomly to conditions can be difficult because of the ethical requirement of informed consent. The need for untreated control participants further complicates the use of experimental approaches, again because of the ethics of withholding treatment (see chapter 12). Even when ethical issues are surmounted, differential attrition can ruin the equivalence of groups that were comparable after random assignment. In addition, seriously impaired clients are likely to want help immediately. They might drop out of untreated or wait-list control groups part way through an evaluation. Again, ethical practices prevent us from interfering with their decision to drop out if that is what they want to do.

Additionally, some variables simply do not yield to the systematic manipulation required by experimental evaluation designs. Those variables often are from the client domain and include prior experiences such as parental divorce, abuse, marital history, and accidents. None of these can be varied concurrently with variables from therapist, intervention, setting, or temporal domains in order to examine their individual and interactive impact on client functioning.

Finally, as noted with multigroup factorial studies above, it is a challenge to conduct evaluations that require all participants to be involved concurrently. Large numbers of clients with the same problem rarely present themselves at the same time. Moreover, assessing and treating a substantial number of people at the same time can be an extremely complex undertaking. For all of these reasons, it is likely that the savvy practitioner will explore alternatives to true experimental evaluation designs.

Quasi-Experimental Approaches

When independent variables of interest cannot be manipulated systematically, practice evaluators can resort to the relational design strategies described earlier. Alternatively, they can proceed as though control is possible and a true experiment can be conducted.

Retrospective Designs

Perusal of professional literature (and the popular press) turns up frequent instances of research in which manipulation of the independent variable is not under the control of the evaluator. Researchers attempt to study topics such as the effects of early childhood trauma on the psychological adjustment of young adults or the effects of divorce on behavior problems in children. Although the titles of such studies might include "the effect of ____," suggesting experimental studies, it would be unlikely to find true experimental research on the effects of independent variables such as early childhood trauma, divorce, and drug dependence on various dependent variables. Researchers cannot manipulate independent variables of this type.

Nonetheless, the principal aim of a study may be to determine the effects of some treatment, even if a true experiment cannot be conducted. A *quasi-experimental* study includes all the characteristics of an experiment except for the equivalence of groups prior to the introduction of the independent variable. An example might be the comparison of two different second-grade classes to determine whether a new way of teaching spelling is effective. One class receives the new approach, whereas the other continues to learn spelling using existing approaches.

Because children are not assigned randomly to the new and existing approaches, other differences between them may exist in addition to the type of spelling instruction their teacher uses. One obvious confound in such a study is the teachers themselves. Such a design is not a true experiment because of the potential effects of confounding variables over which the evaluator has no control.

Pedhazur and Schmelkin (1991), noting incomplete consensus among researchers concerning the term *quasi-experimental*, suggested the term *nonexperimental* to refer to studies such as these, in which there is no application of a treatment by the investigator. According to Pedhazur and Schmelkin, the principal aim of such studies is to explain differences between groups on some variables. They restricted using *quasi-experimental* to research arrangements in which treatments are applied but random assignment of participants to conditions is lacking.

Numerous reasons exist for nonrandom assignment, including ethical concerns, the fact that an intervention occurred before the evaluator was involved, political considerations (e.g., placing new educational programs within certain congressional districts), and self-selection (e.g., more seriously disturbed clients tend to seek treatment). Whatever the reasons, the result is to introduce the likely possibility of confounding, thereby compromising the internal validity of the evaluation and obscuring the interpretation of the effects of the independent variable.

Nonetheless, there are times when quasi-experimental or nonexperimental designs are preferable to no study at all. That is, instead of concluding that too many difficulties are associated with the interpretation of such studies, the prudent evaluator can proceed with caution, qualify results appropriately, and seek corroboration of findings with better controlled designs in the future.

Quasi-experimental and nonexperimental designs can be set up in several ways to maximize the quality of the data they produce. For example, suppose a practitioner had an interest in the impact of childhood physical abuse on children's academic performance. If he or she compared children known to have been abused with comparably aged children known not to have been abused, the results might reflect other differences between the children because they would not have been equal in all respects prior to experiencing abuse. It is especially important to equate groups on factors thought to be correlated with the dependent variable. For example, abused and nonabused children might differ in terms of their parents' income or marital status.

Prospective Designs

Although we cannot study child abuse in true experimental designs, it is important that researchers learn as much as possible about its impact as well as about the impact of similar independent variables. Consequently, research focusing on child abuse per se rather than on understanding differences between children exposed to it might be of interest. A study in which children are enrolled prior to experiencing abuse has the potential for yielding higher quality information than one in which children are enrolled after experiencing abuse. A *prospective study* on the topic would recruit a large pool of children at birth, assess them and their parents on relevant variables, and follow them longitudinally. After a number of years, some of the children will have been abused; they constitute the experimental group and are compared with the children in the sample who have not experienced abuse. Because data collection began before applying the independent variable, the groups' characteristics prior to the introduction of the independent variable are known and can be compared.

This type of study can help identify predictor variables for abuse; differences between the groups can be targeted as potential precursors and their predictive validity examined in subsequent studies. Likewise, characteristics thought to be the result of the independent variable can be ruled out if they were present in both groups prior to the manipulation of that variable. Finally, the effects of the independent variable can be pinpointed more precisely by comparing children exposed to it with a matched group of children selected from among those in the sample not experiencing abuse. Matching would occur on as many as possible of the variables known or suspected to be related to the dependent variable. Although such matching could take place in retrospective and prospective studies, the latter results in greater confidence in the groups' equivalence on the factors prior to experiencing abuse. Matching in this way can help rule out confounding variables often associated with abuse and increase confidence that postabuse differences in children result from the abuse itself.

Prospective studies of this type are expensive and must be carried out over significant periods of time. They can, therefore, be difficult to conduct. They can be useful in practice evaluations, however, because of the routine collection of information on clients over time. Family pediatricians are in an excellent position to conduct prospective analyses because of the large amounts of data they collect on children seen repeatedly over a number of years. Any practice having multiple contacts with clients can use prospective evaluation designs. It is best when such evaluations are informed by theory and use it to determine the variables to assess in advance. This is not required, however, and useful information can result from retrospective comparisons of data collected prior to an intervention.

A straightforward example of a study without a guiding theory involves analyzing the impact of a change in office location on subsequent revenues and client satisfaction. Pre- and postmove revenue can be compared easily enough, as can satisfaction data. A more informative evaluation can supplement this rather gross one, however, by examining additional data collected prior to relocating the practice. Imagine the change was associated with a net loss in revenues. Imagine further that a certain number of clients stopped using the service. Because of the practice's routine data collection, it is possible to compare the characteristics of the clients who stopped using its services with those of continuing clients. Suppose it is found that discontinuing clients tend to be older and tend to live farther from the new practice location. More analysis reveals an interaction between age and distance such that older clients living furthest away are the most likely to quit using the services. Because a significant number of clients are in this category, relocation of the practice has resulted in a revenue shortfall.

Further probing through telephone interviews or mailed surveys reveals a fear on the part of these clients to drive the complex and busy routes necessitated by the new location. The practice considers countering these concerns by mailing bus routes and schedules to each client and arranging other forms of transportation. The quasi-experimental design of this evaluation compared two groups of clients to determine the impact of changing office location. Because data had been collected prospectively on all practice clients, it was possible to determine not only the broad impact of the independent variable but also its effects on different clients.

More often than not, true experimental designs cannot be used in practice evaluations. Nonetheless, true experiments can produce such high-quality data that they deserve serious consideration before resorting to other arrangements. Because the alternatives do not involve random assignment and complete control over exposure to the independent variable, they also are of the nonexperimental or quasi-experimental variety. A special class of such designs that is particularly useful in practice evaluation is known as "time-series methodology" (Hayes, Barlow, & Nelson-Gray, 1999).

Single-Case Experiments

When we obtain data on some variable at regular intervals, we can order the data on a temporal continuum. The result is a time series. Requiring as few as two data points, a time series might be as simple as a pretest–posttest design in which one client (or a group of clients) is assessed before and after treatment. More commonly, time-series methodology involves numerous observations of one or a group of clients over time.

A type of time-series methodology that involves systematically manipulating some form of intervention so as to determine its effects is known as *single-case experimentation.* The essential components of single-case experimental designs include a client, some form of intervention, objective measures of at least one aspect of the client, and repeated administration of the measure over periods of time, during which the intervention is absent or present. Single-case experimental designs can be distinguished from case study designs, which have a long history in practice evaluation. Case studies are done for descriptive purposes and lack the systematic variation in the independent variable necessary to evaluate a treatment's effects. Case studies might or might not involve objective measurement.

Single-case experiments go beyond description and the study of covariation in behaviors over time, however. To illustrate, consider the hypothetical data presented in Figure 8.10; technically, the series was interrupted after Day 7, and it would be imprudent to conclude that the reduction in smoking depicted in the figure is a result of the intervention. Numerous other factors might have contributed. The design depicted in Figure 8.10, however, allows for control of some of the threats to internal validity discussed earlier. For example, repeated assessment controls for testing effects and instrumentation changes as well as for maturation. In addition, regression to the mean and selection effects are controlled, as is differential attrition. The design does not control for the effects of fortuitous events that could have occurred between the two phases, however. This confounding factor can make it difficult to be certain that the observed changes resulted from self-observation. What if the client had attended a lecture on health-related perils of smoking between the 7th and 8th days or caught a bad cold around that time? It is not difficult to imagine other factors that might explain the reduced smoking in addition to the intervention itself.

Nonetheless, the design in Figure 8.10 represents an improvement over descriptive case studies. For one thing, change is associated with a specific intervention. For another, a number of alternative explanations

Figure 8.10

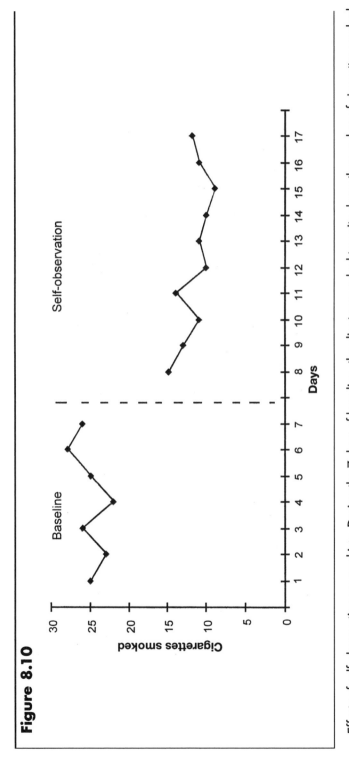

Effects of self-observation on smoking. During the 7 days of baseline, the client was asked to write down the number of cigarettes smoked each day just before he went to sleep (self-report). Beginning with Day 8, the client was asked to record each cigarette smoked at the time he smoked it (self-observation). The implementation of self-observation is associated with a rather dramatic decrease in cigarettes smoked.

for the change can be dismissed. If we elaborate the design a bit, still higher quality outcomes are possible. In Figure 8.11, for instance, an additional phase appears in which self-observation is discontinued; smoking returns almost to baseline levels in the third phase of the evaluation.

Whereas Figure 8.10 depicts what is known as an A–B design, Figure 8.11 illustrates an A–B–A design involving the use of an additional baseline phase. This particular version of the A–B–A involves introducing self-observation following baseline and removing it after 10 days, thereby returning to baseline conditions. This arrangement often is referred to as a withdrawal design (because the intervention is withdrawn). The A–B–A design is more convincing because threats to internal validity are further controlled. For example, because the data return toward baseline levels when the intervention is withdrawn, it is less likely that some history effect coinciding with self-observation actually caused the reduction.

A further refinement is accomplished by reintroducing the intervention in the A–B–A–B design portrayed in Figure 8.12. Reinstating the intervention on Day 24 is associated with a second dramatic drop in smoking. In effect, this step replicates the initial A–B portion of the design. Repeated changes in behavior with the introduction and withdrawal of the independent variable strengthen the conclusion that the changes are the result of that variable.

Replicability

Replicability is an important characteristic of practice evaluation, just as it is in science. Repeated, replicable changes in the dependent variable as the independent variable is introduced and withdrawn are more convincing than a single such change.

One of the difficulties with A–B, A–B–A, and A–B–A–B designs is obtaining baseline data. It is often imperative to begin treatment immediately, foregoing the opportunity to obtain true preintervention baseline data. Figure 8.13 illustrates a design that can be useful in situations such as these; it presents hypothetical data showing the impact of therapist interpretations on self-disclosure in psychotherapy clients. The data illustrate the fact that useful evaluations can be undertaken even when true baseline data cannot be obtained in advance of treatment. They also show how different therapeutic tactics can be tried with a client and their effectiveness determined in a single treatment session.

Figure 8.11

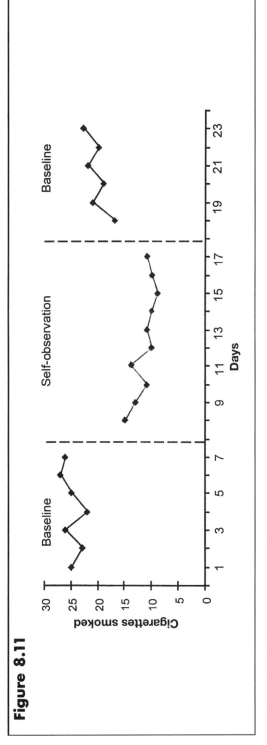

Effects of self-observation on smoking in an A–B–A-type single-case experiment.

Figure 8.12

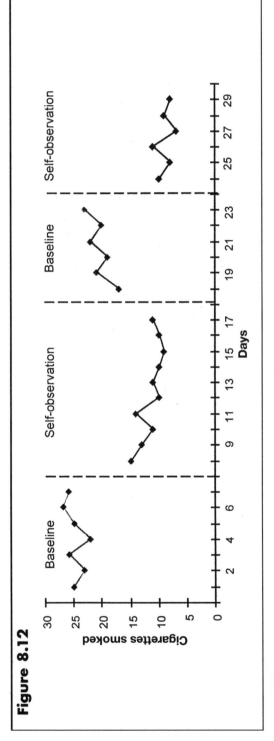

Effects of self-observation on smoking in an A–B–A–B-type single-case experiment.

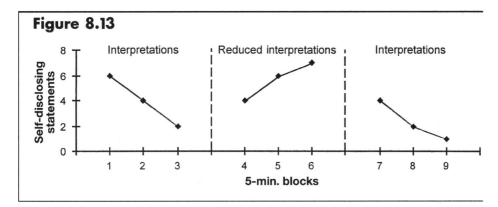

Figure 8.13

Effects of interpretations on self-disclosure. In this B–A–B-type design, the therapist interprets the client's comments during the initial phase and keeps track of the number of self-disclosing statements the client makes. The entire evaluation occurs in a single therapy session, in which conditions are changed after three successive 5-minute blocks. It can be seen that self-disclosing appears to decrease during the first phase, increases when the therapist does less interpreting in the second phase, and decreases again when the therapist reinstates more interpreting in Phase 3.

The figure shows that interpretations can have a dampening effect on self-disclosure with this client; presumably, the therapist in the above example will minimize interpretations in the future to facilitate client self-disclosure.

Multiple-Baseline Designs

The single-case experimental designs described so far rely on systematically introducing and withdrawing (or otherwise changing) the independent variable. In some cases this feat is hard or even impossible to accomplish. Consider the psychologist who develops a series of videotapes illustrating correct ways to use relaxation exercises. The plan is to have clients view the tapes while carrying out the exercises at home. The psychologist wants to evaluate the impact of the tapes using single-case experimental methodology but cannot see how the information on the tapes can be withdrawn once a client is exposed to it. Figure 8.14 illustrates a design that can be useful in such circumstances, known as a *multiple-baseline design*. In such cases, the intervention is implemented in a time-staggered fashion across two or more series of data points. These series, or baselines, can be achieved in different ways. In the figure, they represent steps in the relaxation program completed correctly by three clients before (baseline) and after watching the videotapes (intervention). The critical feature of the design is the varied

Figure 8.14

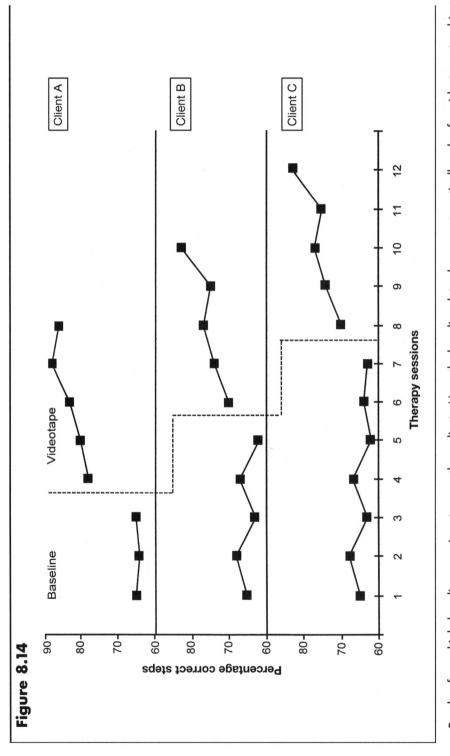

Results of a multiple-baseline experiment across three clients. Here, the baseline data change systematically only after videotapes teaching steps in a relaxation program are introduced. Because the clients are exposed to the tapes at different times, it is unlikely that an environmental variable produced the gains in accuracy rather than the tapes themselves.

lengths of the baselines for the different clients. The figure shows that baseline data change systematically only after videotapes are introduced. Because the clients are exposed to the tapes at different times, it cannot be argued plausibly that some coincidentally occurring environmental variable produced the gains in accuracy rather than the tapes themselves. In other words, staggering the timing of the intervention enhances the internal validity of the design. Replicating the intervention across two additional clients also enhances the believability of the effect.

Multiple-baseline or combined-series designs require two elements (Hayes et al., 1999): (a) more than one data series, preferably at least three, and (b) introduction of the independent variable in a temporally staggered fashion (i.e., after baseline phases of different lengths). A number of ways exist to obtain more than one data series. The data can come from multiple clients, as in the preceding example, or they can occur in the same client. Within a single client, data can be obtained from several different unrelated behaviors, or they can be obtained from the same behavior at different times of the day, under different stimulus conditions, or in different settings.

A hypothetical example of a multiple-baseline analysis carried out across multiple settings for the same behavior of a single client involves an 8-year-old boy taken by his parents to a child psychologist because "he never seems to mind." The psychologist and parents develop a program that rewards the boy for starting to comply with requests within 5 seconds. Every time he does so, he gets a star on a 3×5 card he carries, with stars exchangeable at the end of the day for certain rewards or privileges. The psychologist wants the parents to see the value of reward programs because parents are more likely to try the approach with other behavior if they are convinced they work. To demonstrate the effectiveness of their work with their son, the psychologist suggests to the parents an evaluative design involving the successive introduction of the reward program in different settings. The parents report that several of the boy's teachers also have trouble getting him to respond to their requests in a timely fashion. The psychologist consults with the teachers and obtains their cooperation in the evaluation. The teachers agree to collect data in their classes and to implement the program there as well.

Thus, the parents and the boy's math and social studies teachers all begin recording each request they make and noting whether the boy responds within 5 seconds throughout the day at home and during math and social studies classes at school. Because the number of re-

Figure 8.15

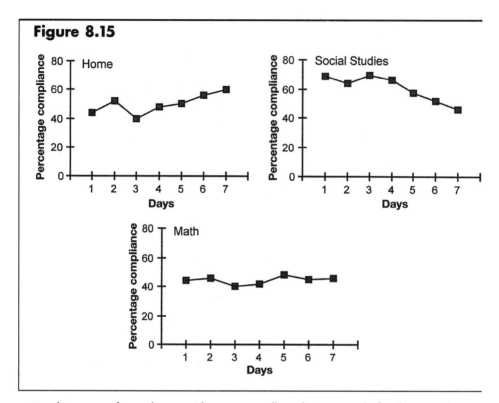

Baseline rates of compliance with requests collected concurrently for the same boy in three different settings. Data from the social studies and math classes are stable; the social studies data appear to be most stable, however, because they are trending in a direction opposite to what is expected.

quests varied across settings and across days within settings, compliance was graphed as the percentage of requests to which the child responded in the allotted time (see Figure 8.15). After 7 days it can be seen that the percentage of compliance was similar in the three different settings. At home and in social studies class, there appear to be trends in the data, however. At home, it looks as though the boy's compliance is actually improving, whereas in social studies it appears to be getting worse. There are no apparent trends in the math-class data.

Stability

The psychologist examines each graph to determine whether it is stable enough to warrant starting the reward program. *Stability* is defined as a condition of the data that allows us to estimate the effects of extraneous influences with sufficient accuracy that the effects of the independent variable can be demonstrated over and above such influences (Barlow,

Hayes, & Nelson, 1984). Stability is a characteristic of any data series, and it is especially important in evaluating the adequacy of baselines. Stable baselines are necessary before changing phases in order to maximize the power of single-case experimental designs. To determine whether a series is stable, attention is paid to three aspects of the data: (a) level, (b) variability, and (c) trend. These characteristics are examined in the context of the effects the intervention is likely to produce. In other words, the practitioner makes an educated guess as to the kind of impact to expect from the intervention. Is it designed to increase or decrease behavior? Is it expected to have a large, immediate impact or a smaller, more gradual impact?

With respect to *level*, the most important concern is whether there is sufficient room for the intervention to show an effect. Usually this is not a problem, because the behavior would be targeted for change only if it were occurring at unsatisfactorily high or low levels in the first place. It occasionally happens that problems are less serious than originally thought, however, a situation that becomes evident when objective data are collected. In those cases, the baseline figures are either surprisingly high for an acceptable behavior or low for an unacceptable one. As a result, interventions supposed to increase or decrease behaviors, respectively, will have a hard time showing any impact because ceiling and floor effects can be operating. Fortunately, this is not a problem for the data in Figure 8.15; adequate room exists for the intervention to produce improvements in compliance in all three settings.

Concerning *variability*, an easy rule to remember is to minimize it within a phase, wherever possible. If within-phase variation is minimal relative to between-phase differences, the impact of an intervention is easier to evaluate. Look at the data in Figure 8.16. Does it look like the treatment is having an effect? The percentage of compliance appears somewhat higher in the treatment phase than in baseline. Mean compliance during baseline is 34.3%, compared with 54.2% in the treatment phase, a substantial increase. Unfortunately, the differences are obscured by the high degree of variability within both phases. Now consider the data in Figure 8.17. Does it look like this treatment is effective? Because the variability in both baseline and treatment phases is so much lower than in Figure 8.16, the treatment appears more clearly effective in Figure 8.17. Yet the means of the two phases are virtually identical to those in Figure 8.16 (i.e., 34.3% and 54.7%, respectively).

Finally, with respect to *trend*, the optimum condition might be a series whose trend is in a direction opposite to that expected when the

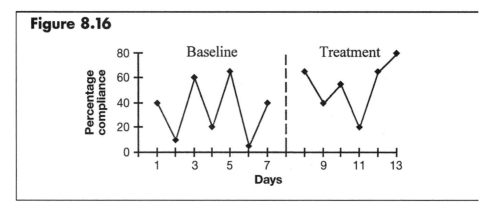

Figure 8.16

Comparison of baseline and treatment compliance data using highly variable data. The differences are obscured by the high degree of variability within both phases, thwarting interpretation.

treatment was implemented. Next best would be a *stationary series* (i.e., one that shows no trend at all). Figure 8.15 clarifies this point: Note that the series showing compliance at home reveals a slight upward trend, whereas that in social studies is heading downward. At the same time, compliance in math class appears to be unchanging across days. Because the psychologist expects the reward program to increase compliance, the social studies data are seen as the most stable, given the definition of stability we are using. The math data also are stable, but the data at home are not, because they are already going in the same direction expected of the reward program. When baseline data are

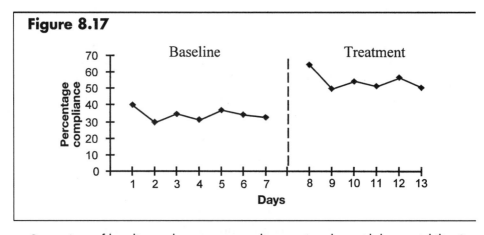

Figure 8.17

Comparison of baseline and treatment compliance using data with low variability. Because the variability in both phases is relatively low, comparison of the two conditions is possible. Treatment clearly appears to be effective.

trending in the direction anticipated to result from an intervention, it is often wise to leave well enough alone, because the problem may be taking care of itself. This is an oversimplification, of course; whether to intervene also might be gauged by the speed of change noted during baseline. Even though the trend may be in a favorable direction, change might be slower than desirable. When such a condition exists, often it may be wise to wait and see whether the series reverses or becomes stationary.

If waiting is not an option, whether to go ahead in the face of a positive baseline trend depends on the expected impact of the intervention. If intervention is likely to accelerate the trend appreciably, the baseline might provide a stable enough background to evaluate its effects. Figure 8.18 depicts such a situation. The trend in compliance during the baseline phase is steady and rather gradual. The trend accelerates considerably with the introduction of treatment, however. In other words, the treatment is associated with enough change in both trend and level to permit optimism about its effectiveness. True, it looks as though simply waiting eventually would have resulted in levels of improvement comparable to those reached with the treatment. This outcome takes longer, however. Furthermore, it assumes that the trend evident during baseline will continue.

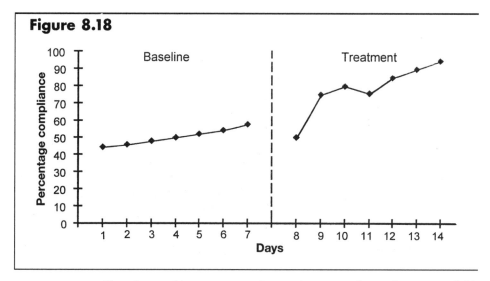

Figure 8.18

Comparison of baseline and treatment compliance data using data reflecting trend differences. The trend in compliance during the baseline phase is steady and rather gradual. The trend accelerates considerably with the introduction of treatment, however. The treatment is associated with enough change in both trend and level of compliance to permit optimism about its effectiveness.

To summarize, the careful practice evaluator examines baseline data continually to determine when they become stable. Stability is essentially a data context in which the effects of extraneous factors are sufficiently clear to permit assessing the impact of one's independent variable at its anticipated strength.

Let us return to the discussion of multiple-baseline designs started earlier. The data in Figure 8.15 represent baselines of the same behavior for the same boy collected concurrently in three different settings. Now that we know the importance of stability and ways to determine it, we can reexamine the three graphs in the figure. It is reasonable to conclude that data in at least two of the graphs are stable—those from social studies and math classes. Of these, social studies data appear more stable because they are trending in a direction opposite to what is expected when the reward program is introduced. On that basis, the psychologist decides to intervene first in the social studies class. A practical factor also supports this decision in that the child's behavior is becoming worse in this context. Meanwhile, baseline data continues to be kept in the home or math class settings, with no changes in the way in which compliance is managed. After a period of time, the intervention is associated with systematic change in the social studies class, and it is introduced into one of the remaining settings. Again, which of these settings to choose depends on the relative stabilities of their baselines. The most stable series is selected next. When change is associated with the intervention in the second setting, it is finally introduced to the third. The results might be something like those seen in Figure 8.19.

The multiple-baseline design can be a powerful way of suggesting causal relationships between independent and dependent variables in practice evaluation. Its strength relies substantially on the replicability inherent in the design. Whereas it is relatively easy to propose alternative explanations for changes in simple A–B designs, repeating baseline-to-treatment changes several times, as in multiple-baseline designs, makes alternative explanations less plausible. This is especially so when baselines are of different lengths, are stable, and change only after the intervention is introduced. Of course, it helps if the change is substantial and immediate, but this is not necessary for the multiple-baseline design to prove its superiority over simple A–B or even A–B–A arrangements.

The single-case experimental designs described in this chapter are examples of arrangements useful to practice evaluators who want to show causal relationships between their interventions and important

Figure 8.19

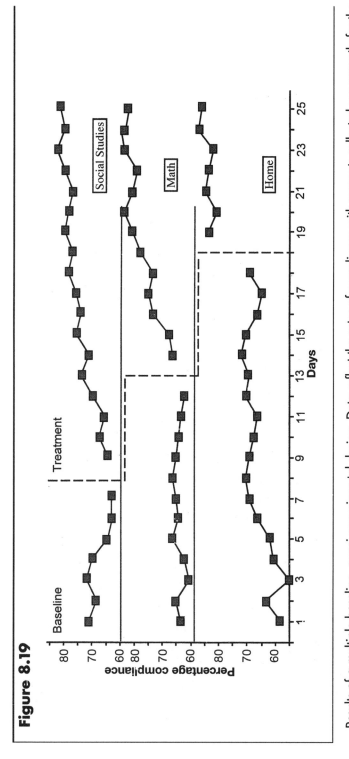

Results of a multiple-baseline, quasi-experimental design. Data reflect the rates of compliance with requests collected concurrently for the same boy in three different classes.

client behavior. They illustrate the possibility of developing evaluative information of relatively high quality from practice settings in which conducting true experimental studies is impractical. These examples merely represent a few of the dozens of single-case experimental designs available to practitioners. More complex designs are described in detail in Hayes et al. (1999) and Poling and Grossett (1986).

Generalizability

The single-case experimental design has an important place in the armamentarium of knowledgeable practice evaluators. It is not enough to conduct an experiment on a single case and conclude that an intervention is effective, however. The practitioner seeks generalizable information; he or she wants to have some confidence that a procedure found beneficial in one instance will apply to other clients as well. The amount of confidence that is warranted is directly proportional to the number of times the intervention has been shown to be effective. Thus, the practitioner repeats the evaluation on as many clients as practical over some period of time and compares the results. The extent to which natural variation has occurred in client characteristics and in the conditions surrounding the implementation of the procedures establishes the findings' robustness and generalizability.

For example, clients seeing a family therapist for help with relationship issues might be treated with a particular novel approach. The clients vary in terms of the severity of the communication problems they experience. Over time, the clinician may accumulate 20 or 30 couples for whom the novel procedure has been evaluated using a single-case experimental design. Assuming that the findings of each evaluation have been positive, the practitioner has confidence in the general applicability of the approach across couples who vary in initial severity. Furthermore, the practitioner can calculate the amount of change from baseline to treatment for each couple and correlate it with initial severity levels. This analysis can show the extent to which the procedure's appropriateness depends on how serious a couple's problems are in the first place. A high correlation would indicate that the procedure is most useful for those with the most severe problems; no correlation supports the use of the procedure with all clients, regardless of initial problem severity. In addition, the practitioner who accumulates objective effectiveness data over numerous cases can look for relationships between degree of effectiveness and other variables from the client domain illustrated in Figure 6.1. Does it appear more effective with younger than older couples? With better educated couples? With newly married couples?

Answers to questions such as these begin to position the practitioner to be able to answer the ultimate practice evaluation question: What intervention, applied by whom, to which clients, in what ways, produces what effects, for what problems, in what time period; and how does it do it (Kiesler, 1971; Paul, 1969)? The basic single-case experimental designs presented here are not sufficient to answer this question, nor is it likely that one practitioner will ever have the time and other resources to carry out enough evaluations to answer the question. Speedier evolution of clinical practice can be promoted by collaborative efforts of multiple practitioners. Such practice research networks are being developed in psychiatry and are encouraged by psychologists as well (e.g., Barlow, 1996). The formation of cooperating networks of practitioners who agree to use objective measures and to pool their data can provide an intriguing interface between science and practice and do a great deal to eliminate artificial differences between these two types of endeavor.

Summary

This chapter has been about arranging the data from objective measures described in chapter 7 to answer practice evaluation questions of various levels of complexity. The chapter describes general design strategies, including descriptive, relational, and experimental approaches, and outlines the relevance of each strategy for answering specific evaluative questions as well as the strategies' advantages and disadvantages. Both between- and within-case designs are covered. The next chapter, the last of the three "tools" chapters, describes how to analyze the data gleaned from the research designs described so far.

Supplemental Reading

Cook, T. D., & Campbell, D. T. (1979). *Quasi-experimentation: Design and analysis issues for field settings.* Chicago: Rand McNally.

Hayes, S. C., Barlow, D. H., & Nelson-Gray, R. O. (1999). *The scientist practitioner: Research and accountability in the age of managed care* (2nd ed.). Boston: Allyn & Bacon.

Kazdin, A. E. (1998). *Research design in clinical psychology* (3rd ed.). Boston: Allyn & Bacon.

Pedhazur, E. J., & Schmelkin, L. P. (1991). *Measurement, design, and analysis: An integrated approach.* Hillsdale, NJ: Erlbaum.

Analysis Tools for Evaluating Outcomes

Some circumstantial evidence is very strong, as when you find a trout in the milk. (Henry David Thoreau; cited in Suen & Ary, 1989, p. 157)

C hapters 7 and 8 described two of the essential tools in practice evaluation: measurement and design. Recall that the goal of evaluation is to establish relationships between variables as a means of answering certain questions about the effectiveness of the practice. When a relationship is demonstrated, the strength of the relationship must be evaluated. Is it strong enough to be considered reliable? Would the relationship be found again if the evaluation were repeated? Practice evaluators also want to know whether the relationship is large enough to be practically useful. Can the change in the problem be considered clinically significant? Statistical and clinical significance are not the same; it is quite possible for a relationship to show the first and not the second.

This chapter deals with the strength of relationships between variables documented in practice evaluations. It focuses primarily on relationships between independent and dependent variables as demonstrated in designs of the experimental and quasi-experimental variety. The strength of relationships found in correlational evaluations is interpreted from product–moment correlation coefficients.

Statistical Analysis

Most students of undergraduate statistics know that the differences resulting from experimental studies of relationships in the behavioral sciences are not considered demonstrated until they are shown to be statistically significant. In other words, changes in the dependent variable thought to be produced by the independent variable have to be analyzed using an appropriate statistical test. If the changes are too large to be the result of chance alone, they are considered to be "real" differences; they are deemed reliable and are expected to be found again if the study is repeated. If the changes in the dependent variable are too small to be statistically significant, they are said to be the result of chance variation (i.e., unreliable differences not likely to be repeated).

Statistics thus provide tools for assessing whether a relationship exists. In the practice world, new approaches to intervening with problems are announced constantly, whether the problems are speech dysfluencies, motor deficiencies, psychological–emotional difficulties, or organizational inefficiencies. More often than not, evidence of the intervention's effectiveness is limited. Indeed, the evidence often consists merely of testimonials of people exposed to the approach or people hired by the purveyors of the approach to trumpet its benefits in the media. Such evidence should be treated with skepticism. The testimony of satisfied customers or compensated pitch men is just one way of evaluating the worth of an idea or the effectiveness of a particular treatment. Empirical evidence, collected in well-designed evaluations and shown to be statistically reliable, is another. As Kazdin (1992) observed, statistical criteria are not perfect, but they do afford a measure of consistency when determining whether a relationship is believable.

In experimental designs of the two-group, true-experiment variety, groups are compared after exposure to the independent variable. Initially equivalent, the groups are now different, and the issue becomes the confidence one can have that the difference is the result of the manipulation of the independent variable. Various statistical tests return a value resulting from comparing groups. For instance, a common test of differences between two groups, the t test, produces a t of a certain value. When the value is entered into a table of the t distribution, along with the number of subjects involved, the probability that the value is the result of chance can be determined. Similarly, when multiple groups are compared using the analysis of variance, an F value is returned. A table of the F distribution can be consulted to determine whether that particular value, given the number of participants and groups involved, is greater than could be expected by chance.

Errors in Inference and Statistical Power

Establishing the statistical significance of the results of group comparisons allows us to infer something about the larger population from which the sample is drawn. If we have sampled wisely, the results of the evaluation can be generalized to the larger population with some confidence. In designing the evaluation, efforts should be made to ensure that a relationship will be found if one truly exists.

Two common errors can be made in interpreting the results of an evaluation. *Type I errors* occur when a difference is inferred that has not been shown. In other words, the evaluator concludes that a relationship exists between the independent and dependent variables when, in fact, the relationship is no more than would have occurred by chance alone. Another way of saying it is that a Type I error results when the *null hypothesis* (i.e., there is no relationship) is rejected by mistake. The probability of making such an error is the alpha level, or confidence level, chosen for the evaluation. It is conventional to set alpha at .05 or .01. If alpha is set at .05, the likelihood of concluding that a relationship exists when one really does not is 5 times in 100. In another example, if the F ratio returned from an analysis of variance is reported to be $F = 4.78$, $p < .01$, the chance of making a Type I error is less than 1 in 100.

Type II errors occur when a relationship exists between the independent and dependent variables but the evaluation fails to detect it. In other words, the null hypothesis should be rejected, but it is not. The index of this type of error is known as the *beta level* of the study. It follows, therefore, that the probability of concluding that a relationship exists when it actually does (i.e., the probability of not making a Type II error) is $1 - \beta$. This last term is also known as the power of a study.

As noted by Rosnow and Rosenthal (1999), considerations of power help in planning a study and interpreting its results. In setting up an evaluation to explore relationships among variables, it is important to do whatever can be done to give the relationship a chance to be shown. If it is there, we want to know it. If we arrange an evaluation with too little power, we might mistakenly conclude that no relationship exists. This would be a waste of valuable resources and delay improvements in the practice that might be made if the results were positive. Therefore, we want to design the evaluation to avoid Type II errors. To do this, we want to make sure we have enough power built into the design of the evaluation.

According to Rosnow and Rosenthal (1999), three variables are involved in determining the power or sensitivity of a study: (a) alpha, (b) sample size, and (c) effect size. The first variable to consider is the size of the effect (relationship) we expect to find. By *effect* we mean the difference between the means of the groups in an experimental design, or the size of the correlation coefficient in a relational design. If the relationship is likely to be large, it is easier to show than if it is small, and the resources needed for the evaluation are correspondingly fewer. If we expect to uncover large effects, fewer participants will be needed. How do we know how large an effect to expect? This interesting question has different answers, depending on whether practical or scientific questions are being pursued in the study. This book approaches effect size from the practical perspective. In general, to be practically useful, effect sizes must be larger than those needed to be scientifically useful. Science can advance even when relationships between variables are small, as long as they are dependable, and future research can elaborate on those relationships. The practitioner, however, wants effects large enough to make a meaningful difference in the lives of clients he or she serves.

To know how large an effect to plan for, the evaluator has several choices. One source of relevant information is the literature on similar evaluations. If it is known that a particular procedure typically produces differences between treated and untreated clients of a specific magnitude, the evaluator might use that difference to set an effect size. To illustrate, a psychologist might have an interest in evaluating a new type of treatment for people with obsessive–compulsive disorder (OCD). Evaluations of other approaches for this disorder have reported differences between treated and untreated client groups. Suppose the psychologist plans to use a t test to compare a group treated using the new approach with an untreated control group. We can estimate the effect size the psychologist might obtain using the t others have reported along with the sizes of the groups compared. Thus,

$$d = \frac{2t}{\sqrt{df}} \tag{9.1}$$

where d is the difference between the independent means of two groups divided by the standard deviation of the population, t represents the results of a t test comparing the means of the two groups, and df is the degrees of freedom associated with the comparison ($df = n_1 + n_2 - 2$). Let us assume that previous studies have produced mean differences of approximately 20 points on a commonly used OCD scale, with standard deviations of 8.5 using groups of 30 people each. If we know the t from such studies to be approximately 2.35, we can solve for d. Thus,

$$d = \frac{2(2.35)}{\sqrt{58}}$$ (9.2)
$$= .62.$$

This is considered a medium effect (see Cohen, 1988). Assuming we are satisfied with an alpha level of .05 and are using a two-tailed test of significance, we can enter the result into a table provided by Cohen to find the number of participants needed for the evaluation. Before doing so, however, we must decide the power, or sensitivity, we want our study to achieve. Remember that power is an index of the likelihood the evaluation will find a relationship between variables if one actually exists. If we set it at .60, the sample size suggested is 40 per group. If we want correspondingly more power, we need correspondingly larger sample sizes, given the medium effect size we expect to find. For example, to increase power to .80 requires increasing sample sizes to 65 per group.

In the example above, an experimental design was used. Relational designs also can be subjected to power analysis. To illustrate, for a "medium" correlation (effect size) of .30, a design with a power of .60 requires 55 participants, assuming an alpha of .05 and two-tailed test. Increasing the power to .80 increases the requisite sample size to 85.

Clinical Significance

Conventional statistical tools document the reliability of relationships found in evaluation studies. They do not tell us whether the relationships are of much use, however. As suggested above, it is quite possible for treatments to produce effects that are statistically significant and replicable but not useful. That is, a group of participants receiving the treatment can show a mean that is reliably different from a group not receiving the treatment but still not be recovered clinically. Effect sizes are some improvement over conventional p values, but they still do not provide the practitioner with the information needed to judge the effectiveness of interventions with individual clients.

A major step toward a more useful statistic was introduced with the concept of *clinical significance* (Jacobson, Follette, & Revenstorf, 1984; Jacobson & Truax, 1991; Jacobson, Roberts, Berns, & McGlinchey,

1999). Essentially, clinically significant change occurs when a client's behavior reliably becomes more like a member of a normal than of a dysfunctional population after undergoing some form of treatment. To determine this, a cutoff point must be established on the outcome measure of interest (Kendall, Marrs-Garcia, Nath, & Sheldrick, 1999). To illustrate, people undergoing psychological treatment for emotional problems might complete an evaluation instrument periodically to monitor their progress. One such measure, the OQ-45.2 (Ogles, Lambert, & Masters, 1996), includes items tapping symptom distress, interpersonal relations, and social role effectiveness. Mean scores for normal and psychiatric samples have been found to be 45.2 and 83.1, respectively, with respective standard deviations of 18.6 and 22.2. As a client improves, moving from the patient mean toward the normal mean, he or she eventually should reach the *clinical cutoff point*, which is the point beyond which the client can be said to be more like people without psychiatric problems than like people with them. The formula for establishing this point, by Jacobson and Revenstorf (1988), is as follows:

$$C = \frac{S_0 M_1 + S_1 M_0}{S_0 + S_1} \tag{9.3}$$

where S_0 is the standard deviation of the normative sample, S_1 is the standard deviation of the dysfunctional population, M_0 is the mean of normative sample, and M_1 is the mean of dysfunctional population. For the OQ-45.2, the cutoff has been set at 63.

In addition to having a score more like that of normal than of dysfunctional people after treatment, the client must show change toward the normal population score that is large enough to be reliable. Just as differences between groups need to be reliable when applying conventional statistical criteria involving p values, differences in scores before and after treatment by individual clients also must be reliable. Clinically reliable change can be established for any outcome measure according to the following formula:

$$RC = \frac{X_2 - X_1}{S_{diff.}} \tag{9.4}$$

where X_2 = posttest score, X_1 = pretest score, and

$$S_{diff} = \sqrt{2(S_{e_{meas}})^2} \tag{9.5}$$

Figure 9.1

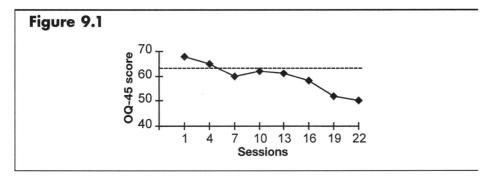

Progress of a hypothetical client in a psychological treatment. The dashed line is the OQ-45.2 cutoff.

where $S_{e_{meas}}$ is the standard error of measurement, found by

$$S_{e_{meas}} = \sigma\sqrt{1 - R} \qquad (9.6)$$

where σ is the standard deviation of the scores on the measure, and R is the reliability of the measure.

RC can be viewed as a standard score. Scores greater than 1.96 reflect change that would have been expected solely as a result of chance only 5 times in 100. For the OQ-45.2, the amount of change needed before it can be said to be clinically significant is 14 points. When the cutoff point and RC are considered together, it can be seen that a client might move from above the cutoff and into the normal range and not have made clinically significant change. An example of this can be seen in Figure 9.1. Here a depressed client's progress on the OQ-45.2 is monitored every third session. It can be seen that the client drops below the cutoff by the 7th session and remains below it thereafter. At the 7th session, the client has gone from an initial score of 68 to 60. Although this change is encouraging, it is not until the 19th session that the change is great enough to be considered reliable. Ending treatment after the 7th session would have been premature because the 8-point change was not large enough to be stable. Indeed, the upturn after the 7th session shows that the client's improvement was not yet sufficient to remain consistently in the nonclinical range.

Relationship Between Statistical Significance and Clinical Significance

The availability of an objective method for establishing clinically significant change provides another criterion to use in evaluating the effectiveness of a particular intervention. The outcomes evaluator can now ask how many clients treated with a certain procedure showed enough change to be considered clinically improved, supplementing the customary statistical criterion involving *p* values. It is interesting to compare the two approaches when evaluating the same outcome data. Jacobson and Truax (1991) provided an example of such a comparison using data from Jacobson et al. (1989), in which two different types of marital therapy were compared. They concluded that the addition of clinical significance measures supplements, rather than contradicts, the information available from conventional inferential statistical approaches. They add, however, that the clinical significance measures produced information that "led to more modest conclusions regarding the efficacy of the treatment in question" (p. 17). In analyses of earlier data from other marital therapy outcome studies (Jacobson et al., 1984) and from treatments of agoraphobia (Jacobson, Wilson, & Tupper, 1988), Jacobson et al. (1989) found that although treated participants did better than control groups, a disappointingly small percentage could be called truly recovered.

Others (e.g., Barkley, Guevremont, Anastopoulos, & Fletcher, 1992; Kazdin, Bass, Siegel, & Thomas, 1989; Kazdin, Esveldt-Dawson, French, & Unis, 1987; Robinson, Berman, & Neimeyer, 1990) have reached similar conclusions. Kazdin et al. (1987) compared cognitive–behavioral problem-solving skills training (PSST), a nondirective approach, and a non-specific-factors control group in treating children's antisocial behavior. Statistical differences at posttreatment favored the PSST approach on the primary dependent measures, which were the Total Behavior Problem and Social Competence scores of the Achenbach Child Behavior Checklist (Achenbach, 1991). Kazdin et al. (1987) then explored the clinical impact of the treatment, using cutoff scores suggested by Achenbach and Edelbrock (1983). Only 3 of the 17 PSST children (17.6%) for whom there were posttreatment data fell within the "normal" range (i.e., below the cutoff score) on the Total Behavior Problem Scale. A somewhat better showing was found for social competence, with 8 of the 13 children (61.5%) scoring in the normal range.

The use of measures of clinical significance is relatively new, and it is not without controversy (Hsu, 1999; Speer & Greenbaum, 1995). It is too soon to determine conclusively how they compare with traditional measures of statistical significance. Early evidence from studies such as these suggest that they are more conservative, however. In other words, it looks as though it is easier to show that an intervention produces an effect when the criterion is a *p* value resulting from a statistical comparison of two or more groups than when the criterion is one of being more like normally functioning people than like dysfunctional people. This situation presents interesting issues for the practice evaluator. The studies described above were conducted under relatively controlled conditions by university researchers, and the results obtained can be considered about as good as can be expected for the particular interventions. What are likely to be the results of such interventions under the messier conditions of applied settings? Would any of Kazdin et al.'s (1987) children reach clinically significant levels of change in the rough-and-tumble real world of clinical psychology? In other words, do the results of efficacy studies such as these hold up in effectiveness studies? (See chapter 11.)

Criteria of Effective Performance

The analyses of clinical significance just discussed assume that normal functioning is the relevant criterion to use in evaluating effectiveness. Other benchmarks can be used as well; Howard, Martinovich, Lutz, Brill, and Grissom (1996) identified five: (a) clinical improvement, (b) behavior that no longer meets the criteria for a particular diagnosis, (c) improvement that is as much as can be expected for a particular client, (d) sufficient improvement that retreatment for the same difficulty is not likely to be needed in the next 6 months, and (e) improvement that produces normal functioning.

To these benchmarks can be added the criterion of effective performance. Not too many years ago, it was considered normal to have a serum cholesterol level of 233. We now know this to be too high for optimum cardiovascular health. Thus, judging dietary and exercise programs to be effective if they move clients' cholesterol below 233 is no longer appropriate; a more stringent criterion (i.e., below 200) is likely to be used. In another example, judging the mobility of a person with physical disabilities to be inadequate because he or she does not walk independently between two points within a normal amount of time seems overly restrictive. A more reasonable criterion might be based on the speed necessary to cross between two points to achieve some practical outcome (e.g., to avoid being hit when crossing a street).

Finally, suppose a teacher is using a phonetic approach to teach first-grade children to read. A task analysis of the subskills needed to read words shows consonant sounds and vowel sounds to be important, both in isolation and in combination. Before combinations (e.g., "de," "tu") are taught, however, some skill with the sounds in isolation (e.g., "d," "u") is needed. What criterion should be used to determine whether a child has this latter skill? Should we assume readiness for combinations when the child reaches "normal" proficiency with sounds in isolation? If so, we move the child to the next level when performance reaches normal. However, normal can represent a wide range of performance, depending on how it is defined. It would not be unusual to consider one standard deviation on either side of the mean to represent normal performance, for example. Suppose the typical first-grader reads consonant sounds in isolation at a rate of 45.6 correct per minute, with a standard deviation of 6.3 per minute. A child could be considered normal with a rate of 39.3 (45.6 − 6.3). This seems to be a much different level of proficiency from a child with a rate of 51.9 (45.6 + 6.3), yet both are in the normal range. Is either performance adequate? What if we moved both children on to combinations and kept track of the time it took them to reach a predetermined level of mastery on this new skill? Who would get there faster and with fewer errors?

A different criterion could be used to determine adequate performance. Rather than the average performance of first graders on each of the skills, we might find out the skill level needed to master the next subskill in the fastest time and with the fewest errors. This could be done by moving children through the subskills after a certain amount of training regardless of their performance. The preceding skill levels of children mastering the next skill could be examined to see who learns the skill the fastest. In other words, speed of mastery of later skills would be compared with competence on earlier ones. The level of earlier competence associated with the fastest subsequent mastery then could be set as the criterion of effective performance for the earlier skill. Children would stay on a skill until their proficiency reached this criterion rather than until it approximated normal. Other ways of determining effectiveness criteria exist, of course. For example, competent readers can be identified and their rates on each of the subskills determined.

Clarifying the meaning of scores on dependent measures by comparing them with criteria of effective performance is a measurement tradition known as *criterion-referenced assessment* (Glaser, 1963; Livingston, 1977). Space does not permit exploration of the similarities and differences between this approach and clinical significance, except to note that the former uses criteria other than normal performance, which is an inherent aspect of the latter. Many examples of criterion-referenced assessment can be found in everyday life, including licensing examinations for driving a car or flying a plane.

Whether one chooses to use statistical significance, normal functioning, effective performance, or some other criterion when evaluating a practice depends on a number of factors, including the purpose of the evaluation, its intended audience, and the availability of alternative criteria. Statistical significance is likely to remain the most widely used measure, although certainly there are times when a criterion of normal functioning is appropriate, and times when criteria representing some minimal level of competent performance are preferable. Still another tradition involves the use of visual analysis to determine effectiveness, a topic I explore next.

Visual Analysis

As described in chapter 8, the practice evaluator often has an interest in determining the effectiveness of interventions applied in individual cases. It is appropriate in such circumstances to use single-case experimental designs and to represent the results of the evaluation in the form of graphs. Most often, the graphs show changes in a series of data points collected over time. The information contained in time-series graphs can be more useful than that presented in bar graphs or tables, especially because it shows variations in behavior with systematic introductions and withdrawals of an intervention, days of the week, particular times of the day, setting differences, and so on. Figure 9.2 is an example of such a graph. Heeding a few suggestions can lead to effective use of visual analysis.

Select Chart Types to Match the Evaluation Question

Graphic representations are most useful when they are carefully constructed. (For an introduction to the basics of graph construction, see Henry, 1994; and Tufte, 1992.) Begin with deciding exactly what information the graph is to convey. Most important, organize the figure in such a way that the evaluative question gets answered. This step is facilitated when the relationship between variables implied in the question is shown clearly in the figure. The data in Figure 9.2 are from an experimental analysis of the relationship between self-observation and smoking. We can infer that the question must have been "Does self-

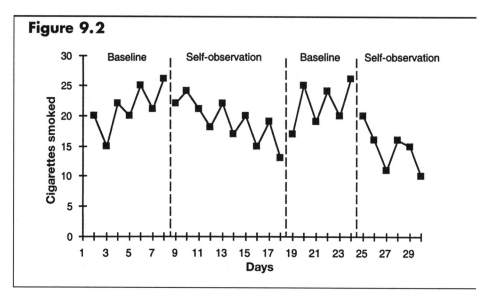

Figure 9.2

Effects of self-observation on smoking.

observation of cigarettes smoked result in less smoking?" Now consider the data presented in Figure 9.3. What question is suggested by this arrangement? Unlike the causal relationship between self-observation and smoking represented in Figure 9.2, the data in Figure 9.3 show a correlational relationship, suggesting a question such as "Is there a correlation between self-observation and cigarettes smoked?" Finally, consider the data in Figure 9.4. The evaluative question was supposed to be, "What is the comparative effectiveness of self-observation, homework, and talk-oriented therapy in the treatment of smoking?" The or-

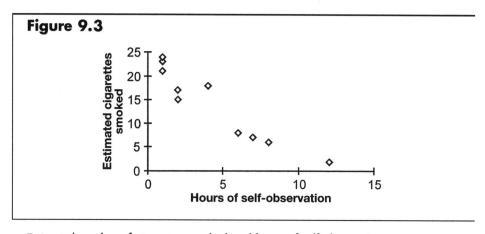

Figure 9.3

Estimated number of cigarettes smoked and hours of self-observation.

Figure 9.4

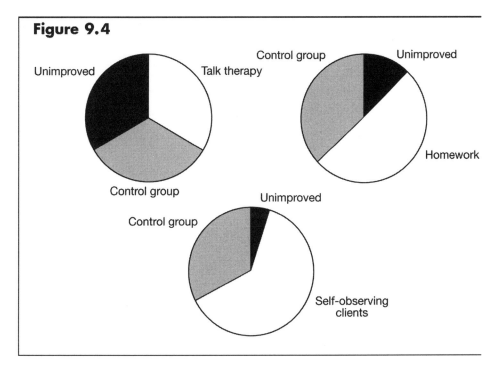

Hypothetical ineffective visual display comparing treatments to reduce smoking.

ganization of the figure obscures the primary interest of the evaluators, however. The use of separate pie charts for each treatment group, comparing it against an untreated control group, implies more interest in the absolute effectiveness of the individual treatments than in comparing them with one another. For comparative purposes, the arrangement in Figure 9.5 is clearer, and the presentation in Figure 9.6 is clearer yet. It can be improved by rearranging the conditions, putting the highest bar first, the second highest next, and so on. It is clear which of the figures communicates the intent of the evaluation design most effectively.

Follow Graphing Conventions

After deciding the best arrangement and type of graph to use, follow common conventions in constructing the graph. Several sources that describe these conventions include the *Publication Manual of the American Psychological Association* (APA, 1994), the *Journal of Applied Behavior Analysis* (Bailey, 1998), Johnston and Pennypacker (1993), Parsonson and Baer (1978), and Tufte (1992). These conventions can be quite de-

Figure 9.5

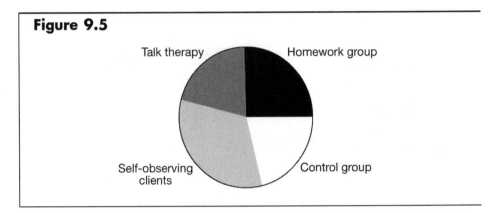

Comparison of treatments to reduce smoking in a single pie chart.

tailed, and they cannot be covered thoroughly here. Because the time-series format like that illustrated in Figure 9.2 is frequently used by practice evaluators examining change over time, the following sections describe a few of the more common conventions used with this format. The recommendations are from the *Journal of Applied Behavior Analysis.*

Axes and Labels

Labels for the different phases of the design should be descriptive, placed at the top of the figure, and centered in the phase. Vertical dashed lines separate the phases of the design, and points between phases are not connected across these lines. The horizontal axis represents the independent variable (or some unit of time in the case of time-series analyses). The vertical axis represents scores on the depen-

Figure 9.6

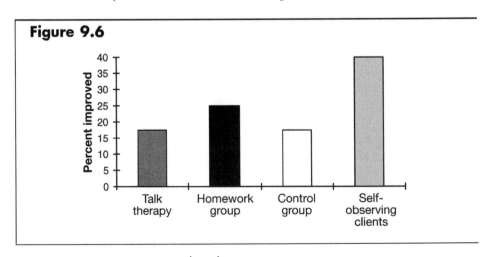

Comparing treatments using a bar chart.

dent measure. The horizontal axis ends with the last session number or date of data collection. All information is kept within the boundaries of the figure created by the axes, except for axis labels, data labels, phase labels, and the figure caption. For clarity, keep the number of lines on a graph to five or fewer. When using more than one line, label each and draw an arrow from the label to its corresponding line. Different data point symbols and line patterns can also be used to distinguish lines better.

What about the units on the axes? Should they be continuous, or are discontinuities permissible? What scale of measurement is appropriate? Where should the axes cross? Answers to these questions depend on the clarity of the graphs. If a particular approach leads to clearer interpretation, other things being equal, it is acceptable to use it. It is important to avoid creating graphs that mislead, however. This can happen inadvertently or through deliberate manipulation of some aspect of the graph. To illustrate, consider the data presented in Figure 9.7; they represent the benefits of a new diet for weight lifters. The new diet is associated with a 5-pound mean difference in pounds bench pressed by the lifters. The left panel of the figure highlights this difference, making it appear more important than it does in the right panel. Is this appropriate, or is it an example of the old saying "Figures don't lie, but liars figure"? The answer depends on the importance of the 5-pound difference. Suppose the difference between the weight lifted by champion weight lifters and people coming in second is typically less than 5 pounds. In such a context, a 5-pound difference would be quite important. Or suppose until now, differences between diets in terms of

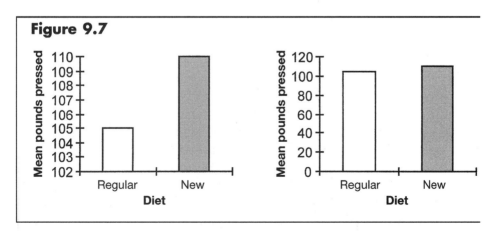

Figure 9.7

A comparison of graphic presentations with different scales on the vertical axis.

mean have hovered around 2 to 4 pounds. Again, a 5-pound difference would seem substantial. If the winning margin or differences between treatments were typically much larger than 5 pounds, however, the left panel would be inappropriate because it emphasizes a small, unimportant effect.

As to where the axes should cross, there is no ironclad rule. The range of values on the vertical axis usually can be satisfactorily represented by starting just below the lowest value on the dependent measure and extending to just above the highest value. It generally is not necessary to begin at zero. The data presented in the left panel of Figure 9.7 show this type of scale. Of course, the caveats concerning misrepresentation still apply.

Although no ironclad rules exist for the horizontal axis, either, take care to represent the variability in the dependent variable in an optimal way. Maximizing systematic variability (e.g., differences between phases) provides the clearest picture of the relationship between the independent and dependent variables. Johnston and Pennypacker (1993) likened the horizontal axis to a microscope, with different units similar to different lenses. The smaller the unit chosen, the more fine grained the analysis can be. It is useful to consider the time unit that is most meaningful to the evaluation you are conducting, however. To illustrate, the daily cash register receipts of cashiers in retail establishments are normally examined to determine whether they reconcile with the amounts shown by the register. Suppose a program is undertaken at a large supermarket chain to train cashiers to be more accurate. Suppose further that the program consists of a series of classes and experiences that take place over a 4-week period. It would make sense to represent the data from such a program in terms of daily discrepancies. A graph showing mean discrepancies in monetary values over days seems more appropriate than one showing these discrepancies on an hourly or weekly basis.

Whatever the time unit chosen, it is preferable to show changes in the data continuously over the entire period of the evaluation. That is, equal units on the horizontal axis should represent equal amounts of time. In addition, it is a good idea to present data in terms of real calendar time. For example, the data in the top panel of Figure 9.8 are presented in terms of days, whereas those in the bottom panel are presented in real calendar time. The program involved having a client track the use of positive comments to others during the day for a 7-day baseline period. The client's mean for that period was 5.0 per day. Treat-

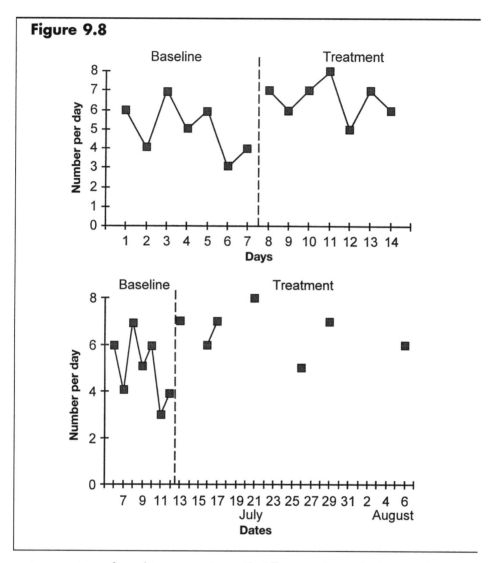

Figure 9.8

A comparison of graphic presentations with different scales on the horizontal axis.

ment involved instructing the client to beat the baseline average each day for another 7-day period. It appears from the top panel as though a slight increase in praising ensued. Indeed, the mean for the treatment phase rose to 6.6 per day. It also appears from the top panel that the client was conscientious in implementing the program, doing so consistently during the 7 days following baseline. The bottom panel is more informative, however, and gives a somewhat different picture. It is clear when the data are plotted in real calendar time just how inconsistent the client's use of the procedure was. Furthermore, although the data are the same and thus produce a mean of 6.6 per day, it is not so clear that treatment is associated with an increase. The astute practice evaluator might use the real-time presentation to goad the client into using the procedure on a more consistent basis.

Clearly, there are no inviolate rules for presenting data in graphic form. The most important recommendation is to consider the audience for the information and the type of impact you want the data to have. Then, present them in a way that facilitates your message without misleading the reader in any way.

Keep It Simple

An important consideration in preparing graphic displays is simplicity. As Morrison (1996) noted, a good rule is to "maximize the data-to-ink ratio" (p. II.C.9). He provided an excellent example of a violation of this rule in a graph similar to Figure 9.9. The figure displays much confusing, redundant information. In contrast, Figure 9.10 displays the same information in a way that is much simpler and, therefore, easier to interpret. Youngstrom (1999) recently provided a similar comparison, observing that using software charting programs (e.g., Excel) without modifying their default settings can violate the data-to-ink ratio rule.

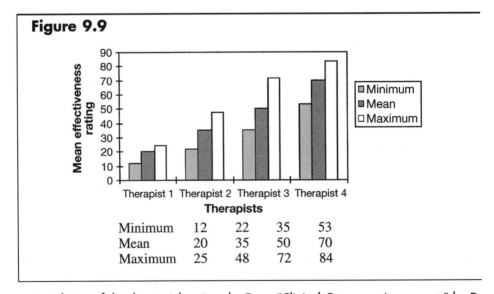

Figure 9.9

	Therapist 1	Therapist 2	Therapist 3	Therapist 4
Minimum	12	22	35	53
Mean	20	35	50	70
Maximum	25	48	72	84

A violation of the data-to-ink ratio rule. From "Clinical Outcomes Assessment," by D. Morrison, in C. E. Stout, G. A. Theis, and J. M. Other (Eds.), *The Complete Guide to Managed Behavioral Healthcare* (pp. II.C-1–10), 1996, New York: Wiley. Copyright 1996 by Wiley. Adapted with permission of John Wiley & Sons, Inc.

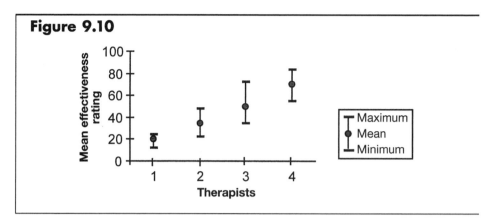

Graph maximizing the data-to-ink ratio. From "Clinical Outcomes Assessment," by D. Morrison, in C. E. Stout, G. A. Theis, and J. M. Other (Eds.), *The Complete Guide to Managed Behavioral Healthcare* (pp. II.C-1–10), 1996, New York: Wiley. Copyright 1996 by Wiley. Reprinted with permission of John Wiley & Sons, Inc.

Interpreting Visual Displays

Confronted with results such as those in Figure 9.2, the practice evaluator has to determine whether and how they can be useful. Several criteria are available for this purpose. The first is likely to be experimental (see Risley, 1970). Applying this criterion, the question is whether there appears to be a systematic relationship between the independent and dependent variables. From a cursory visual analysis of Figure 9.2, it seems clear that smoking varies systematically with the introduction and removal of self-monitoring. This interpretation is most likely the result of the substantial differences in the level of smoking from phase to phase. Now, consider the data in Figure 9.11. Again, a cursory visual analysis reveals systematic differences in smoking across phases. This time, however, concluding that a relationship exists between self-observation and smoking is most likely the result of attending to changes in the amount of variation in smoking from one phase to the next. It appears that self-observation is associated with more day-to-day consistency in reported smoking than occurs in baseline conditions. Finally, consider the data presented in Figure 9.12. Once again systematic variation is evident across phases. Now, however, the most noteworthy feature of the between-phase differences is the change in slope, or trend. Smoking appears to be increasing across the 7 days of the first baseline period. With the introduction of self-observation, the trend changes to a downward one, then it turns upward once again with the

Figure 9.11

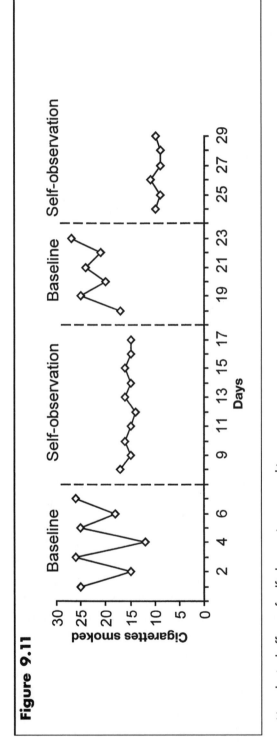

Hypothetical effects of self-observation on smoking.

Figure 9.12

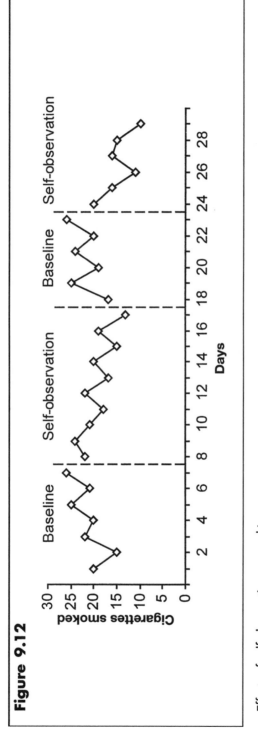

Effects of self-observation on smoking.

return to baseline conditions. Finally, reintroduction of self-observation is associated with another decreasing trend.

Combining Visual and Statistical Analyses

The issue of statistical versus visual analysis is a complex one, and much has been written about it. Fortunately, as the earlier discussion of clinical significance made clear, the practice evaluator does not have to choose between them. Indeed, the combination of the two approaches sometimes can lead to optimum results. As is now clear, comparisons can be made both visually and statistically. Our first reaction might be that it is superfluous to use both. It appears rather obvious from the data in Figures 9.2, 9.11, and 9.12 that self-observation works. Clearly, fewer cigarettes are smoked when self-observing than when not. Why bother with further analyses?

This question is reasonable, and the answer to it is in some dispute. One view is that an experimental effect cannot always be determined reliably from visual analyses (see DeProspero & Cohen, 1979; Gottman & Glass, 1978; Jones, Vaught, & Weinrott, 1977). As Jones et al. (1977) noted, conclusions from visual analyses often are not supported by statistical analyses. Conversely, statistical analysis can find results that are not apparent to the naked eye. Finally, Jones et al. showed that statistical analysis can "discover" relationships in the data that were not apparent or even looked for visually.

In addition to an experimental criterion of usefulness, however, the practice evaluator might want to use a therapeutic or clinical criterion, as described earlier in this chapter. It has been argued that this is a superior yardstick when building a technology of behavior change. According to Baer (1977), if a clinical "problem has been solved, you can *see* that; if you must test for statistical significance, you do not have a solution" (p. 171, italics in original). The practice evaluator, concerned with the development of the most effective services, is not likely to be much interested in "small effects detectable by sensitive statistical procedures but undetectable by mere inspection of graphs" (Gottman & Glass, 1978, p. 199). The scientist is interested in reliable effects of any size, however, because even the smallest might confirm a theoretical position or be enhanced by future increases in experimental control or other procedural improvements.

Both descriptive and inferential uses of statistics have a place in supplementing visual analysis. Descriptive statistics are less controversial and are found more often in practice evaluations than are inferential statistics. The discussion of the data in Figure 9.8 presented earlier, for instance, referred to the mean of the baseline and intervention phases. It was helpful to have a summary measure of each of these phases. Other descriptive statistics (e.g., median, mode) can summarize the level of behavior seen during a phase, and still others can summarize variability and trends (Ottenbacher, 1992). An example of the latter can be traced to Shewhart's (1931) use of bands around the mean of a series of data points to monitor quality control in manufacturing plants. The bands were set at two standard deviations on either side of the mean. Data points outside these bands became exceptions that were examined more closely. Indeed, this is a common statistic in the repertoire of stock market traders, who use breaks above or below trading channels (bands) around a stock's moving average as evidence that a change in the stock's fortunes is at hand.

It would seem a rather straightforward undertaking, therefore, to compute an average for a series of data points and its corresponding standard deviation. Bands corresponding to, say, two standard deviations on either side of the series mean could be extended from the baseline into the subsequent intervention phase and the data points in this phase examined. If they are within the band, the intervention can be said to be ineffective. When a certain number of successive points appear outside the bands, the level of the series can be said to have changed in important ways.

Unfortunately, the simplicity of this strategy is misleading because it relies on the assumption that points in the series are independent of one another. When points in a series are not independent of one another, the data are said to be *autocorrelated*. In other words, data later in the series can be predicted from data earlier in the series. This situation is problematic when applying common inferential statistical tests to the data because autocorrelation affects alpha levels and, therefore, the probability of Type I errors. In other words, the results of comparing baseline and intervention data using a t test or analysis of variance would be significantly in error. In situations such as these, more sophisticated statistical procedures known as "time-series analysis" have been recommended (see Jones, Vaught, & Weinrott, 1977).

Of course, the need for statistics unaffected by autocorrelation assumes practice evaluators' data series usually are, indeed, autocorrelated. Although some analysts have presented evidence of extensive autocorrelation, others have argued that it is of limited concern. On the one hand, Glass, Willson, and Gottman (1975) studied 95 different time series, finding autocorrelation in all but 16. Likewise, Jones et al. (1977) reported finding extensive autocorrelation in 24 studies published in the *Journal of Applied Behavior Analysis*. On the other hand, Huitema (1985) noted that analyses showing serial dependency or autocorrelation are based on the wrong scores. According to him, it is the residuals that must be independent in order to meet the assumptions of standard inferential statistics. The studies showing autocorrelation have used raw scores, however. When reanalyzed using residuals, Huitema found the series originally analyzed by Jones et al. (1977) not to be serially dependent. His conclusions have been challenged (see Suen & Ary, 1987), and the debate continues. Interested readers are encouraged to familiarize themselves with current arguments before using inferential statistics to evaluate differences between phases in time-series data.

Returning to the use of descriptive statistics for a moment, the practice evaluator can benefit from recent applications attempting to describe and predict the course of treatment in individual cases. Examples from education involve quantifying the amount of trend in a nonstationary series. To illustrate, look once more at the data presented in Figure 9.8. In the baseline phase, it appears that the frequency of praises or compliments is decreasing over time. Whether there really is a decrease can be evaluated more clearly with the use of a trend line of some sort. An easy one to use has been described by White and Haring (1980) as the *split middle line of progress* (also known as the "celeration line"), which results from finding the middle date and the middle rate of the data in two halves of a phase and connecting them with a line. An illustration of how this is done is provided in Figure 9.13. The hypothetical data represent change over days in the number of positive thoughts experienced by a client complaining of depression. For the baseline period, the client was instructed merely to record each pleasant thought he had during the day. The baseline data are divided into first and second halves at Day 4. The middle date of the first half is Day 2; that for the second half, Day 6. The rates for the first three days are 6, 4, and 7. Thus the middle rate for the first half is 6. Likewise, the rates for the three days of the second half are 6, 3, and 4, with the middle being 4. By connecting the middle date and middle rate of the first half of the baseline (i.e., 6) and the middle date and middle rate of the second half (i.e., 4), a trend line or "split middle line of pro-

Figure 9.13

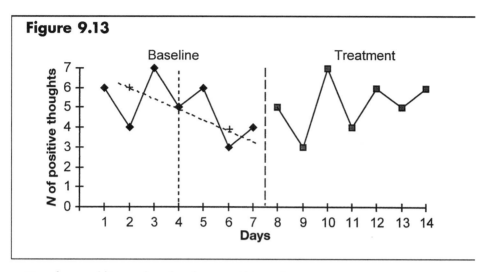

Use of a trend line to describe change within a phase.

gress" is produced. This line, superimposed on the baseline data in Figure 9.13, clarifies that the trend is downward. The practitioner could show the client that he is less optimistic over the baseline period and propose an intervention that can reverse this trend. The practitioner suggests that the client engage in at least one activity he finds enjoyable over the next week and that he continue to record positive thoughts.

When the client returns the following week, his data can be charted, as shown in the treatment phase of Figure 9.13. It appears from the data that the intervention resulted in a change in the frequency of positive thoughts. We can improve the clarity of the presentation by superimposing another trend line through the data in the intervention phase (Figure 9.14). The declining trend evident in the baseline phase is eliminated in the treatment phase. Indeed, rather than continuing to decrease, the client's positive thoughts show an increase over days.

It is of interest to examine the level of change brought about with the introduction of treatment. Differences in level are addressed by measures of central tendency, such as the mean and median. We can calculate the mean of each phase and represent it by a line drawn through the phase at that point. Doing this for the data in Figures 9.13 and 9.14 produces the chart in Figure 9.15. Lines representing performance levels (mean scores on measures of performance) within phases can help illustrate the impact of treatments. In Figure 9.15 it becomes clear that although the client is showing an increase in positive thoughts, the level of positivity is practically the same as during the

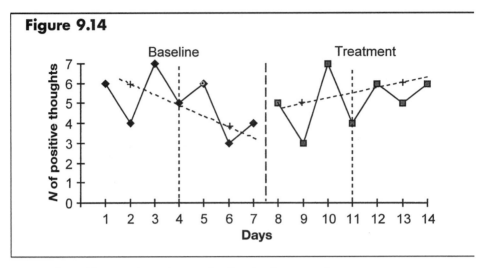

Figure 9.14

Use of trend lines to show changes in direction between phases.

baseline phase (M = 5.0 and 5.1 for baseline and treatment phases, respectively).

Figure 9.16 presents another example of the use of visual indicators of central tendency. Here, the impact of self-observation is small, and it can be obscured quite easily by the within-phase variability in the data. The addition of the mean lines in the figure helps show the effectiveness of the intervention more clearly.

More complex analyses involving both visual and statistical components are starting to be used to evaluate clinical practice. In the ex-

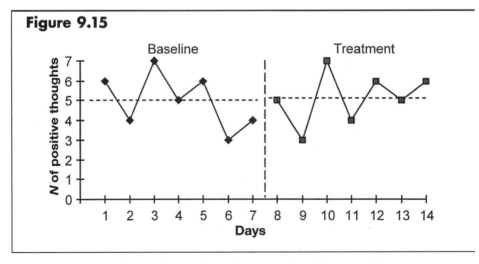

Figure 9.15

Hypothetical use of mean lines to show changes in level between phases.

Figure 9.16

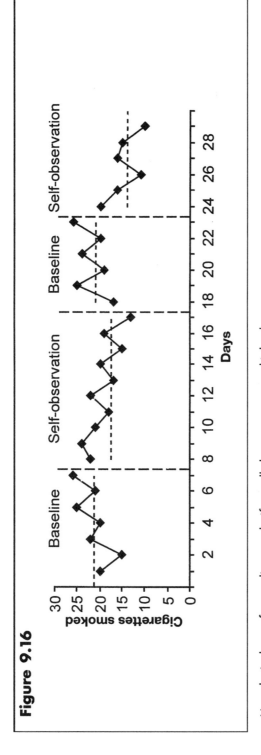

Hypothetical use of mean lines to clarify small changes across multiple phases.

amples above, we show trend lines computed from baseline data that are available already. Other procedures permit the prediction of the likely outcome of an intervention even before we collect baseline data. Howard et al. (1996) recently described how assessment information collected from individual outpatient psychotherapy clients at the start of treatment could be used to predict improvement over the course of that treatment. Using hierarchical linear modeling (about which more is said in the next chapter), Howard et al. illustrated how the expected course of improvement for an individual client is predictable. Such information as the severity of the problem; how long it has been a problem; and a measure of current well-being, symptoms, and level of functioning is entered into a formula developed from the analysis of hundreds of similar cases. The hypothetical or predicted course of improvement can be compared with the client's actual change in treatment. Boundaries can be constructed around a curve representing expected improvement. Actual progress falling above or below the bounds in early sessions can alert involved stakeholders to high probabilities of success or failure, respectively. Better than expected progress would indicate the need for continued treatment because a good fit appears to exist between the treatment approach and the client. Worse than expected progress would be a signal that change is needed because a mismatch apparently exists between the treatment and the client.

Howard et al. (1996) studied treatment trajectories for approximately 200 therapy cases and found that a single assessment below the failure boundary soon after the 8th session predicted poor outcomes after Session 20. Only a third of the clients scoring below the boundary showed "reliable improvement after Session 20." At the same time, two thirds of those scoring above the failure boundary showed reliable improvement. A similar approach using progress trajectories with individual clients is described by Kadera, Lambert, and Andrews (1996).

The tactics suggested above are a way to predict probable outcome and to determine effectiveness on a moment-by-moment basis. Thus, it is possible to make changes to improve outcomes for individual clients as soon as it is apparent how their actual progress compares with the progress expected for them. This type of evidence is of immense value to the practitioner and the client because it can help prevent client–therapist mismatches as well as wasted time and other resources. The combination of visual and statistical forms of analysis thereby provides substantial predictive and descriptive power and increases the sophistication of practice evaluation substantially. Currently, effectiveness is evaluated almost entirely after the fact, as exemplified in the hypothetical data in Figures 9.10 to 9.16. That is, data from a course of treatment are analyzed to determine whether the client is benefiting from ongoing treatment or has benefited from treatment already completed. With the advent of procedures such as Howard et al.'s, effectiveness can be estimated before the fact as well.

If this seems like an unusual suggestion, consider its implications. Suppose three psychologists offer services to restore people with severe depression to effective functioning, each using a different treatment approach. Suppose all three psychologists are on the panel of a managed care organization (MCO) that collects data permitting the type of prediction that Howard et al. (1996) discussed. Depressed clients with particular characteristics therefore are predicted to improve differentially, depending on which psychologist they see. Ideally, some clients will be predicted to improve more rapidly with particular therapists. In other words, client–therapist matching will make a difference. If so, careful assessment of clients requiring services needs to precede their assignment to therapists to maximize therapeutic outcome. The MCO uses profiles to evaluate the effectiveness of panel members, but this information usually is historical because it is based on the experience of the organization with individual service providers. When it becomes possible to evaluate providers in advance, the potential purchasers of a service (whether individual clients or MCOs) should be able to inquire whether evidence-based (i.e., effective) interventions are provided by someone who also has the training, experience, and other characteristics known to relate to the treatment the client needs. They are likely to seek services from providers who are known to be effective.

Criteria of Functional Effectiveness

Before leaving the topic of analyzing the results of practice evaluations, a final comment is in order concerning the appropriate criteria to use. The ultimate purpose of evaluation is to convince someone of something. If practitioners want to show that services are beneficial, they must first ask who their audience is. Is it the client receiving services, significant others of the client, the practitioner him- or herself, payers of the services provided, or professional colleagues? Once the audience is known, the evaluation can be designed to have maximum impact. The question then becomes "What type of information is going to have the greatest impact on the target audience?" If clients are the primary audience, testimonials from similar clients can be quite influential. If payers are the audience, more objective data on levels of improvement and costs to reach those levels are likely to carry weight. If colleagues are the audience, objective data on recognized outcome measures, along with analyses showing the reliability of the findings, are going to be important.

Another way of saying this is that practice evaluation occurs for a reason. It has a function (i.e., to produce some type of effect). That effect involves changes in someone's behavior. If those changes are ones sought by the evaluator, the practice is said to be effective. The use of functional effectiveness as a criterion is pragmatic; it is in the spirit of practice evaluation, generally, and it keeps us grounded in reality. If consumers of the practice evaluation data respond as though the practice is effective, for all practical (functional) purposes, it is effective.

Evaluating the Evaluation

A subtle but important distinction should not be overlooked in this discussion of criteria of effective practice. The whole evaluative process is undertaken to determine whether the practice is accomplishing its owner's goals and permitting the realization of the owner's personal vision. Thus, the evaluation itself can be more or less effective, depending on whether it produces information useful in reaching that determination. In other words, regardless of whether the data are positive, they must permit a clear judgment of the practice's effectiveness. If they do, the evaluation itself can be said to be successful. An important reason for undertaking evaluations is to improve the quality of the services provided, to be sure. A more fundamental purpose, however, is to determine whether a vision is being realized. These purposes are related to one another, and they are not the same. Services might be quite effective from the standpoint of benefit to clients yet not serve to advance the practitioner's personal vision.

The effective practice evaluation permits the evaluator to determine whether a vision is being realized. It is the provider's vision that is most relevant here, so provider behavior is the source of criteria for determining evaluation effectiveness. An evaluation is successful if it leads to changes that advance the provider's vision. This is a straightforwardly practical (or functional) approach to establishing the worth of an evaluative effort, of course, and other criteria also can be used. The point is merely that practice evaluation is undertaken for a reason, and evaluating evaluation needs to be considered in that light.

Summary

This chapter, the last of three chapters on the tools of outcomes evaluation, presents the analytic tools needed to determine the reliability and usefulness of relationships between variables examined in an evaluation. Two major analytic traditions are presented: statistical and visual. The approach described in this chapter applies equally well to all practice components, although each component might require different criteria for determining the impact of an intervention. For instance, returning the administrative services component of the practice to "normal" would probably not be a useful criterion. Criteria involving effective performance and functional impact would apply, however.

The previous chapters presented the purpose of practice evaluation and suggested the types of questions to ask. They also discussed and classified the variables implied in the relationships contained in evaluation questions, described different ways of operationalizing those variables, and outlined criteria for assessing their quality. The chapters provided strategies for organizing the data to highlight the relationships between variables and analytic strategies for showing the reliability of the relationships. The next chapter discusses more advanced analytic strategies.

Supplemental Reading

Carr, J. E., & Burkholder, E. O. (1998). Creating single-subject design graphs with Microsoft Excel. *Journal of Applied Behavior Analysis, 31*, 245–251.

Farrell, A. D. (1999). Statistical methods in clinical research. In P. C. Kendall, J. N. Butcher, & G. N. Holmbeck (Eds.). *Handbook of research methods in clinical psychology* (2nd ed., pp. 72–106). New York: Wiley.

Kendall, P. C. (Ed.). (1999). Clinical significance [Special section]. *Journal of Consulting and Clinical Psychology, 67*, 283–339.

Tufte, E. (1992). *The visual display of quantitative information.* Cheshire, CT: Graphics Press.

10 Advanced Outcomes Evaluation

A recurring theme throughout this book is that smart professionals are constantly evaluating. This chapter combines many of the ideas presented earlier to produce comprehensive and sophisticated approaches to practice evaluation. The purpose of the chapter is to present tactics that can take the seasoned independent practitioner to new levels in terms of the quality and specificity of evaluative questions to explore. It is likely to be useful to psychologists who have been in practice for a number of years and who have amassed both significant experience and sufficient data to enable use of more complex analyses. At the same time, the information in this chapter can be of immediate use to evaluators working for large organizations, who manage great amounts of data and must answer questions involving service effectiveness for hundreds of clients on an ongoing basis.

Chapters 7, 8, and 9 presented basic measurement, design, and analysis concepts that permit most evaluation questions to be pursued quite adequately. When we exceed the limits of the basic notions, however, more advanced methodology can be helpful. This chapter introduces some of the more advanced ideas in measurement, design, and analysis. The treatment is admittedly introductory, and the reader may want to consult more complete discussions to use the methodology most effectively. Entire books exist on some of the topics covered in just a few pages in this chapter. In keeping with the organization of chapters 7 through 9, advanced measurement concepts are treated first, followed by advanced design and, finally, advanced analysis procedures.

Advanced Measurement Concepts

The basic underpinnings of measurement involve operationalizing the variables implied in evaluation questions and their related hypotheses (see chapter 7). The main ways of doing this include interviews, self-reports, rating-by-others, self-monitoring, and direct observation. As emphasized earlier, multiple data sources are important for at least two reasons. First, representational validity requires the convergence of different ways of assessing a phenomenon so that scores on a measure are the result of something more than factors inherent in the measure itself. Second, the multiple stakeholders in human services have their own perspectives, which are not completely overlapping; a complete understanding of the effectiveness of the practice requires information unique to each point of view.

Multitrait–Multimethod Matrices

Representational validity reflects the fidelity with which a measure portrays a particular phenomenon. Key to this type of evidence when assessing constructs are convergent and discriminant validity (Campbell & Fiske, 1959; Fiske & Campbell, 1992). To show the first requires assessing more than one construct using more than one method. To show the second requires finding that constructs not supposed to be highly related to the construct of interest are, indeed, independent of it. A large number of correlations can result when two or more constructs are assessed in two or more ways. The multitrait–multimethod (MTMM), matrix originally proposed by Campbell and Fiske (1959), can facilitate organizing and analyzing the extensive information contained in those correlations. Table 10.1 illustrates the correlations that result when we assess three behaviors—eye contact, trembling, and time spent listening to music—in three different ways (self-report, self-observation, and direct observation). Knowing the organization of the MTMM matrix can help analyze the information.

Looking at Table 10.1, several patterns are apparent. First, the values on the validity diagonal are significant and large enough to encourage further study. Second, when all the behaviors are assessed using the same method, correlations among the behaviors (as in the hetero-behavior–monomethod triangles) are consistently higher than when they are assessed using different methods (i.e., in the heterobehavior–heteromethod triangles). Third, the pattern of correlations evident

Table 10.1

Hypothetical Multitrait–Multimethod Matrix of Behaviors Assessed by Different Methods

	Self-report Eye contact	Self-report Trembling	Self-report Listen to music	Self-observation Eye contact	Self-observation Trembling	Self-observation Listen to music	Direct observation Eye contact	Direct observation Trembling	Direct observation Listen to music
Self-report									
Eye contact									
Trembling	-0.56								
Listening to music	0.23	0.12							
Self-observation									
Eye contact	0.67	0.28	0.07						
Trembling	-0.32	0.73	0.06	-0.62					
Listening to music	0.10	0.09	0.84	0.21	0.18				
Direct observation									
Eye contact	0.55	0.15	0.10	0.64	0.17	0.12			
Trembling	0.15	0.48	0.06	-0.38	0.75	0.09	-0.66		
Listening to music	0.08	0.10	0.63	0.13	0.11	0.80	0.19	0.22	

Note. The heterobehavior–monomethod triangles of the MTMM matrix include the correlations between variables that result from using the same method to assess each of them. These appear within a solid border. The heterobehavior–heteromethod triangles (dashed border) represent correlations between two behaviors that result from using different methods to assess each of them. The values in italics and underlined represent convergent validity; these appear on the validity diagonal (Campbell & Fiske, 1959) and are statistically significant. Finally, information as to the reliability of the measures can appear on the major diagonal, although for ease of exposition, reliability values are not included in this table.

among the behaviors in the heterobehavior–monomethod triangles is the same in the heterobehavior–heteromethod triangles, providing evidence of convergent validity. This result assures us that something over and above the measures themselves is contributing to the scores on all three measures. In other words, the behaviors of interest are substantial enough that one can assess them in multiple ways.

The correlations in Table 10.1 also provide evidence of discriminant validity: Although trembling and eye contact correlate (albeit negatively), neither correlates highly with time spent listening to music. For theoretical reasons we expect them to be independent of this behavior, and they are. The practice evaluator can take heart from analyses such as these. By showing that the measures correlate with behaviors we expect them to correlate with and not with behaviors from which we expect them to be distinguishable, MTMM matrices provide evidence of representational validity for the measures.

Campbell and Fiske's (1959) original presentation of the MTMM matrix relied on visual analyses to determine the relative contributions of trait and method to scores being correlated. In the years since, different statistical approaches to the process have appeared, including confirmatory factor analysis (e.g., Cole, Gondoli, & Peeke, 1998; Floyd & Widaman, 1995) and the progressive use of several statistical approaches (Bagozzi, 1993). Space does not permit their detailed treatment here; interested readers can consult those sources as well as Ozer and Reise (1994), who recommended continuing the tradition of visual analysis.

Multiple Measurement Models

Sophisticated practice evaluators concern themselves with the nature of the measurement models underlying the variables included in their analyses. Bollen and Lennox (1991) made a clear distinction between models that assume traits are causal, or determinative, of behavior and models assuming that behavior defines constructs. The two models have clearly different implications in terms of classical psychometric concepts; for example, it is becoming increasingly clear that the reliability concepts introduced in chapter 7 have different degrees of relevance depending on the fundamental nature of the variable in question.

Effect-Indicator Model

To illustrate, consider a construct such as "gender chauvinism." Assume that it is characterized by a collection of attitudes and other behaviors having to do with making decisions on the basis of gender when gender is clearly irrelevant. Gender chauvinism can be viewed as a trait that develops early in people and is relatively stable over the course of their lives. Assessing it can take the form of a number of descriptive statements relevant to the concept that are arranged in the form of a scale, along with instructions to choose from a limited range of response alternatives (e.g., yes–no, true–false, 0 to 4 rating). Bollen and Lennox (1991) referred to items comprising a scale as *indicators* to signify their connection to the underlying trait. When responses to the indicators (i.e., scale items) are assumed to result from the underlying trait, the measurement model is said to be an *effect-indicator* model. This name reflects the fact that responses to the indicators are the effects of the underlying trait.

Causal Indicator Model

Alternatively, consider a concept such as timeliness on the part of clients. Although it is possible to view timeliness as a traitlike construct that develops early in life and is relatively unchanging, it can be more parsimonious to view it as an index of the extent to which a person keeps commitments related to time. Timeliness might be indexed by tracking the percentage of appointments arrived at on time, the mean minutes late, the percentage of homework assignments completed on schedule, the payment of bills on time, and so forth; a person's score on timeliness would be a composite of scores on items of this type. Note that these indicators are not assumed to be the result of an underlying trait, as in the case of chauvinism. In other words, the person's behavior relevant to time use is not thought to be the result of some trait of "punctuality." Rather, the reverse is true (i.e., the score on a measure of timeliness is determined by the items making up the index themselves). When the indicators (scale items) are the sole basis for the underlying index, the measurement model is said to be a *causal indicator* model. This term reflects the fact that the items (or indicators) cause the index to be what it is and that no underlying construct exists apart from the indicators.

Bollen and Lennox (1991) included the possibility of mixed-measurement models underlying certain scales. In these, some of the indicators appear to be effects of a latent trait, whereas others appear to be more causal. For example, on the Center for Epidemiological Studies Depression Scale (Radloff, 1977), items such as "I felt depressed" appear to be the effect of depression, whereas items like "I felt lonely" are more causal. That is, loneliness might be seen as causing depression rather than being the result of it. A person feeling lonely is not interacting with others; this leads to feelings of depression.

The implications of this analysis are important. For effect-indicator measurement models, each item is assumed to be equivalently determined by the latent trait. Items are interchangeable, therefore, and a measure of their interchangeability is their internal consistency as reflected by the coefficient alpha. When the underlying measurement model is of the effect-indicator type, the scale is expected to show high internal consistency. When the underlying model is causal, however, no such expectation exists: The score on a measure is a composite of the individual items, which are not viewed as interchangeable. With causal models there is no requirement that items correlate highly with one another. Indeed, each contributes in unique ways to the total score (i.e., defining the construct). Altering items changes the meaning of the composite score and, therefore, the construct being measured. Astute practice evaluators know the model underlying each measure to be used and apply the appropriate psychometric criteria (e.g., accuracy, reliability, and validity) when determining the quality of the measure. Unfortunately, it is rare for authors to specify the nature of the model underlying their measures, making it difficult to determine exactly which psychometric criteria are relevant.

Advanced Design Concepts

The three design traditions in human services program evaluation include descriptive, relational, and experimental approaches. Experiments most often provide the highest quality information; when carried out properly, they are the only type of approach that permits cause–effect conclusions. Earlier (in chapter 5), it was suggested that practice evaluators map out a program of evaluation that uses progressively more elaborate designs. Regardless of the practice component being evaluated, it is useful to begin with a descriptive evaluation. Doing so provides an objective description of the practice and important baseline information against which to evaluate change. Details such as the rate of new referrals, demographic characteristics of clients, types of presenting complaints, costs of service components, and average income per client are helpful to enumerate on an ongoing basis.

As Paul (1966) pointed out, initial questions about effectiveness are likely to be of the "Does it work?" variety. Answers vary in quality depending on the sophistication of the design, which can range from simple case studies without measurement to true experiments involving two or more comparison groups.

Once effectiveness has been determined, comparative questions can be asked. With respect to advertising, for example, mailings targeted to carefully selected zip codes or potential clientele with particular demographic profiles can be evaluated against a baseline of minimal or no advertising. Assuming a carefully designed evaluation, increases in business can be attributed to the advertising campaign. The practitioner wants to know whether this outcome is the best that can be expected or whether other approaches, such as radio spots or advertisements in community newspapers, might lead to even more business.

Comparative Effectiveness Questions

The comparative stage of practice evaluation follows the effectiveness stage and uses designs in which two or more approaches are used either simultaneously or in an alternating sequence that controls for order effects. In the advertising example, newspaper ads and targeted mailings could be initiated at the same time, and new clients could be asked how they heard about the service. To avoid the contaminating effects of some clients being exposed to both types of advertising, it is important to implement the advertising in geographically separated areas; randomly assigning clients in each area to one of the two forms of advertising should lead to equivalent groups. Of course, the practitioner might want to know how well the approaches work both independently and in combination with one another. In such a case, geographic areas can be assigned randomly to three experimental conditions: targeted mailings, newspaper ads, and a combination of both.

When using comparative designs, we assume that we know the individual effectiveness of the procedures we are comparing—this is also true for comparisons involving combinations of individual procedures. The evaluative question we are asking is not whether they work, but whether one is more effective than the others. If evidence of the individual effectiveness of the interventions is available, the evaluation can proceed with the comparison of three conditions. If evidence is lacking as to the independent effectiveness of any of the procedures, a no-treatment control condition can be added. Thus, we would randomly

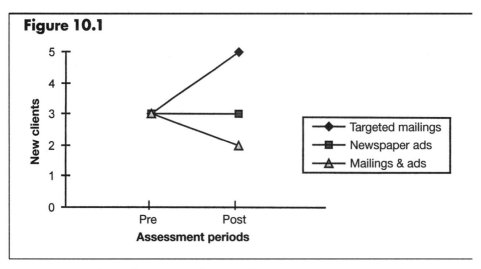

Figure 10.1

Comparison of the effectiveness of three different advertising strategies for generating new clients.

assign geographic areas to receive (a) targeted mailings, (b) newspaper ads, (c) both, or (d) no advertising at all. Comparing the results of a, b, and c with d establishes their individual effectiveness.

If we did not include the control condition, results such as those in Figure 10.1 would be difficult to interpret. It looks as though targeted mailings increased the number of new clients, that newspaper ads had no effect, and that the combination actually reduced the number. But what would have happened if the evaluators had done no advertising at all? Suppose geographic areas not exposed to any advertising were included as an untreated control condition, as shown in Figure 10.2? Now it looks as though two of the strategies produce worse results than no advertising at all. By adding the control group, it becomes apparent that the number of new clients would have increased even without any advertising. The fact that two of the strategies are associated with fewer new clients than would have been expected without any advertising at all suggests that they actually are detrimental. Additionally, the original expectations for targeted mailings shown in Figure 10.1 have to be tempered when the control condition is included. Although superior to the other approaches, targeted mailings still are only slightly better than doing nothing. When the expenses of advertising are calculated, doing nothing might be the most cost-effective alternative.

Figures 10.1 and 10.2 illustrate that controls are needed if earlier evaluations have not shown the independent effectiveness of one or

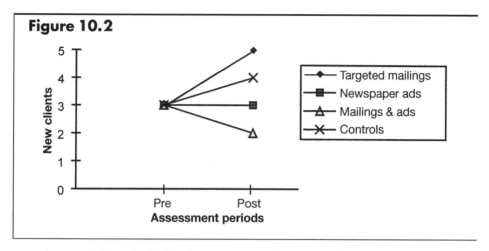

Figure 10.2

Evaluation of the individual and comparative effectiveness of three different advertising strategies for generating new clients.

more of the strategies we are comparing. These circumstances require the comparative evaluation to serve double duty: It must provide information about whether one of the strategies is effective in the first place as well as about how the different approaches compare. Again, a control group is not necessary when we know from extensive previous work that the different strategies are effective in their own right. If we know already that all three approaches compared in Figure 10.1 are effective individually, that design is sufficient.

Effective-Ingredient Questions

The comparative stage of practice evaluation gives way to a stage in which a relatively coarse, multidimensional intervention is decomposed to find out why it works. In those designs, an intervention has passed the comparative effectiveness test and is now at the effective-ingredient stage, where the evaluative question becomes "Why does it work?"

In between-case types of evaluative design, the best approaches to "why" questions involve factorial arrangements in which multiple independent variables are examined both alone and together. To illustrate a simple form of a factorial design, consider the psychological therapy for treating anxiety described earlier. The treatment has a number of factors that might be responsible for its effects. For one thing, it involves active efforts to educate the clients about the nature of anxiety. For another, the client is asked to do relaxation exercises every other day and to record the amount of time they take. Finally, the client is given graduated-exposure exercises as homework. Suppose the psychologist wants to know how much the relaxation and graduated-exposure components each contribute to the effectiveness of the intervention. Suppose further that the therapist wants to know whether exposure has to be gradual or the full feared stimuli can be presented immediately. Finally, imagine the psychologist wonders whether type of exposure depends on whether the client is relaxed.

The evaluative questions thus become (a) "Does training in relaxation contribute more to treatment success than exposing clients to feared stimuli?" (b) "Does gradually exposing clients result in more treatment success than exposing them to feared stimuli at maximum strength right from the first (i.e., flooding)?" and (c) "Do the effects of gradual versus immediate exposure vary depending on whether the client receives relaxation training?" The psychologist formulates the following three hypotheses: (a) Clients who receive relaxation training improve more than clients who are exposed to feared stimuli without relaxation training, (b) clients who receive gradual exposure improve more than clients receiving immediate exposure, and (c) clients who receive gradual exposure along with relaxation training show the most improvement.

A study to test the hypotheses is diagrammed in Table 10.2. The data are analyzed using analysis of variance (ANOVA) statistical procedures. If the means in the first row (combined using statistical techniques) are statistically lower than those in the second, the first of our hypotheses is supported. The second hypothesis is examined by comparing the apparently lower means in the first column of the table with those in the second column (again, statistically combining the entries in each column). If the column 1 means are statistically lower than those in column 2, the second hypothesis is supported. Finally, com-

Table 10.2

Hypothetical Mean Anxiety Scores of Clients Treated With Exposure

Relaxation training	Type of exposure	
	Graduated	Immediate
Present	48.4[a]	83.5[b]
Absent	72.7[c]	92.8[d]

Note. Superscripted letters denote cell reference.

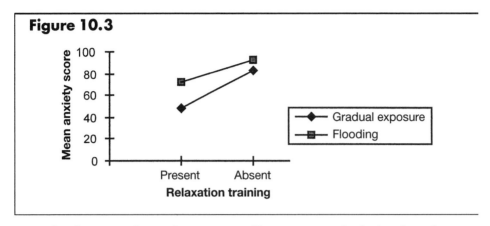

Figure 10.3

Results of a 2 × 2 design showing main effects on anxiety for both independent variables and an interaction between them.

paring the data in cell "a" with those in all other cells tests the third hypothesis, that the most improvement occurs in clients receiving gradual exposure and relaxation training. Assuming that its apparently lowest value is statistically reliable, the third hypothesis is supported. In ANOVA terminology, these results reflect main effects for both independent variables as well as an interaction between them.

Figure 10.3 graphically presents the data in Table 10.2 and shows that clients who receive relaxation training show lower levels of anxiety than do those not receiving such training. Assuming that this difference is statistically reliable, in ANOVA terms we say that a main effect exists for relaxation training. It results from comparing the mean of the two groups who get training with the mean of the two groups who do not. Thus, the data support the first hypothesis. With respect to exposure, the figure shows that exposing clients to feared stimuli gradually is associated with lower anxiety than exposing them to such stimuli immediately. We can see this by comparing the mean of the two flooding groups' points with the mean of the two points representing the gradual exposure groups. Again, assuming this difference is statistically reliable, we say there is a main effect for type of exposure. Thus, the data support the second hypothesis. Finally, it appears the most benefit comes from training clients in relaxation and exposing them to feared stimuli gradually. Another way of saying this is that the effects of type of exposure are potentiated by relaxation. In ANOVA terms, there is an interaction between the two independent variables. The effects of one of them are qualified by the other. This is apparent from looking at the lines for the two exposure types in Figure 10.3. It can be seen that they are closer together when no relaxation training occurs, and that they spread apart somewhat when clients receive this training. If the effects of relaxation training are the same for both types of exposure, the lines are perfectly parallel. The lowest point in Figure 10.3 is for clients gradually exposed to feared stimuli who also receive relaxation training; these results support the third hypothesis. When a significant interaction effect exists, it is a signal that the effects of one independent variable depend on the other. In such situations, there is likely to be little interest in the main effects per se. In fact, it is inappropriate to interpret them without considering the implications of the interaction.

The beauty of factorial designs is their ability to answer effective-ingredient questions in practice evaluation. The example in Figure 10.3 is the simplest of factorial designs, yet it clearly produces quite a bit of useful information. It should be noted that the data in the figure represent but one of eight outcomes possible from a 2 × 2 factorial (Ray, 1993). It shows main effects for both independent variables and an interaction between them. Figure 10.4 illustrates a different outcome for the same evaluation. The data show no main effects or interactions, indicating that it does not matter whether clients receive training or not. Moreover, the total absence of effects for relaxation training is clear, regardless of the type of exposure the clients receive. Assuming the data turn out more like those in Figure 10.3 than in 10.4, the practitioner learns something about the importance of several of the components of this particular psychological therapy. It seems clear that the best approach for treating anxiety is to train clients to relax and to expose them to feared stimuli gradually.

Note that although the 2 × 2 design represented in Figures 10.3

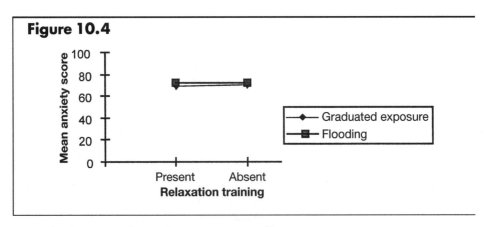

Figure 10.4

Results of a 2 × 2 design showing no main effects or interactions.

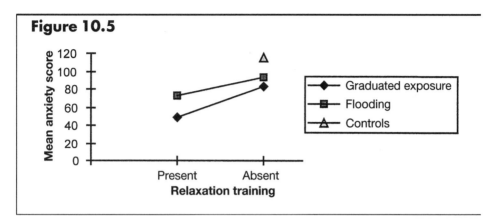

Figure 10.5

Results of a 2 × 2 design with untreated controls.

and 10.4 provides a lot of useful information, there are some conclusions it does not permit. For it to be useful in answering "why" questions at this stage of practice evaluation, we must assume that more fundamental questions have been answered. More specifically, we must know the psychological treatment we are dismantling is effective in the aggregate. In other words, it has been tested against no-treatment controls and been found to be superior. If this has not previously been shown, we can include such a control group in the present design.

Suppose we do this and observe the results in Figure 10.5. The diagram shows a 2 × 2 factorial design with untreated controls added as a fifth group. Again, assuming the results are statistically reliable, we can say relaxation produces some improvement; that exposure does, too; and that the best results appear to be obtained in people given relaxation training and graduated exposure to feared stimuli.

Between-case designs such as the 2 × 2 factorial with untreated controls in Figure 10.5 are complex and require resources that can exceed those of many practices. To be specific, the psychologist would have to assign clients at random to five different groups to carry out this analysis. Although the exact number of clients needed in each group cannot be determined precisely without conducting a power analysis, it is likely that at least 15 would be required. Optimally, 75 clients with the same problem would be assigned at random to the five groups, with treatment applied concurrently to four of them. This arrangement might not be feasible given the number of clients seen and the variety of problems treated in a typical practice. Of course, designs of this complexity and greater can be undertaken more easily in the evaluations typical of the largest MCOs.

Figure 10.6

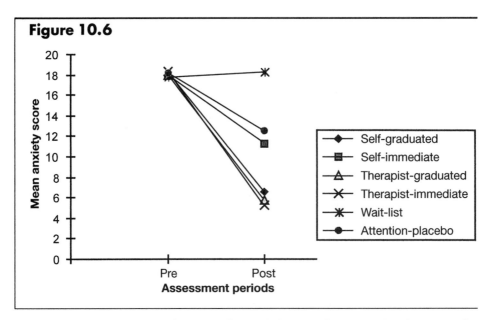

Pretest and posttest results of a 2 × 2 factorial design with untreated and non-specific-treatment (i.e., attention-placebo) controls. All treatment groups have lower anxiety on the posttest, whereas the untreated, wait-list controls do not change. Self-guided exposure appears to be as effective as therapist-guided exposure as long as contact with the feared stimulus is gradual rather than immediate. When the therapist is involved, gradual and immediate forms of contact are equally effective. The last two findings reflect an interaction effect: The effects of speed of exposure depend on whether the client or the therapist guides the exposure. Finally, when self-guided exposure is used, there is improvement in anxiety, but if exposure is immediate, self-guided exposure is no more effective than providing clients with the nonspecific factors associated with most forms of therapy (in this case, attention-placebo treatment).

Before leaving the topic of multifactorial designs, it is worth considering an elegant approach that includes pre- and posttreatment assessment along with untreated and nonspecific-treatment control groups. Adding these embellishments can result in the data shown in Figure 10.6. The addition of control groups along with pre- and posttreatment assessment provides much more information about the effectiveness of an intervention. If we assess participants before treating them, we can determine whether they change and by how much. Another benefit is that we can establish whether randomization produces equivalent groups. Finally, we can evaluate the effects of the independent variables alone and in interaction more thoroughly because they can be compared with the untreated and nonspecific-treatment control conditions.

In summary, a multifactorial design that includes untreated and nonspecific-treatment controls assessed before and after intervention is an especially efficient use of practice evaluation resources. All three major questions (i.e., Does it work? Does it work as well as or better than another treatment? Why does it work?) can be answered in a single evaluation. The design maximizes client as well as therapist time and produces extensive data.

Unfortunately, designs of such elegance are difficult to implement in the typical practice. First, because of their complexity, they require relatively large numbers of participants. The simple 2×2 design described above involved six different groups. Assuming 10 people per group, a pool of 60 people, all experiencing problems with anxiety, would be required to start the study. The precise number of participants needed can be determined through power analysis (see chapter 9); interested readers are advised to consult Cohen (1988) or Kraemer and Thiemann (1987) for more details.

Within-case designs can provide a reasonable alternative for practice evaluators who have limited resources for evaluation (see chapter 8). More complex within-case designs, such as those discussed by Hayes, Barlow, and Nelson-Gray (1999), can examine effective-ingredient types of evaluation questions also. To illustrate, suppose an organizational consultant is asked to help a major software company improve the performance of its technical support staff. The company is getting too many complaints that customers are on hold for long periods before their calls are answered. Because the company is high tech, it has plenty of data available on the average time customers have to wait for a technician to answer their calls. Moreover, data on each technician are available. The company is considering hiring more technicians and adding telephone lines. Before taking these steps, however, it decides to bring in a consultant to determine whether the present system can be improved.

The consultant suggests providing two simple forms of feedback at the end of each day's shift. One type involves a count of the number of calls handled by the technician during the shift. The second type of feedback is the mean time (in minutes) per call handled. Using separate A–B–A evaluation designs, the consultant determines that the number of calls handled increases when technicians are provided either type of feedback. In other words, both are effective ways of improving performance. The consultant now turns to the comparative effectiveness of the two approaches. One way to design the analysis would be to alternate the two types of feedback in an A–B–A–C–A design and compare the data from B and C phases. Assume that feedback on number of calls handled is implemented in the B phase, and feedback on the average length of calls handled is implemented in the C phase. A higher level of total calls handled in one phase or the other would support the superiority of the corresponding feedback type. Unfortunately, this design includes an important confound in the form of the order in which the interventions are introduced. Suppose technician performance is higher in the C phase. How do we know this is not the effect of first receiving feedback in the B phase? As Hayes et al. (1999) pointed out, this confound can be managed by adding additional participants who receive the interventions in the reverse order. Thus, the comparison becomes both within and between series (e.g., A–B–A–C–A vs. A–C–A–B–A). If one intervention is more effective than the other regardless of whether it occurs first or second, its effectiveness cannot be argued to be the result of its order in the sequence.

Another within-case design for answering comparative questions involves alternating interventions in a random or nearly random order. The alternating treatments design (Barlow & Hayes, 1979) involves rapidly changing the conditions and examining the effects on the dependent variable over time. In effect, two (or more) series are compared, each representing the data obtained when a particular intervention is in place. In the example above, hourly frequencies of technical support calls handled are observed under alternating conditions in which the technician is given feedback each hour on either the number of calls handled or the mean length of calls handled. (Of course, the example is for the purposes of illustration; such small time increments may not be appropriate for this particular evaluation situation.) The data resulting from this evaluation might approximate those presented in Figure 10.7, which shows that providing feedback about the number of calls handled is associated with handling more calls than is feedback about how long the technician spends on each one.

An advantage of the alternating-treatments design (ATD) is that order effects are unlikely because of the rapidly alternating treatments. A potential disadvantage of the ATD is multiple-treatment interference, a phenomenon reflecting the fact that a treatment behaves differently when used at the same time or close to another treatment than when used alone (Hayes et al., 1999). In other words, the rapid alternation of the two types of feedback in the present example creates a somewhat artificial context. Does their joint use result in differences in their effectiveness, and if so, in what ways?

Figure 10.7

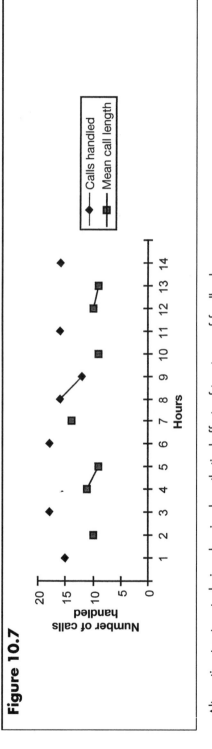

Alternating treatments design showing hypothetical effects of two types of feedback.

This brings up another relevant question concerning the present example. What is the effectiveness of the two types of feedback if given concurrently? Interventions cannot always be combined, of course, but in the present case it is reasonable to expect that feedback about both number and length of calls handled could easily be given to technicians at the same time. Assuming it is already known that both interventions are individually effective, a within-series design of the A(B + C)A can be used.

Within-case evaluative designs thus can be used to answer comparative questions. It is not necessary to have large numbers of clients who can be assigned randomly to multiple treatment conditions, as in the factorial designs described earlier. What about effective-ingredient questions though? Is it possible to use within-case strategies to decompose complex interventions and examine what it is about them that makes them work? Suppose the organizational consultant in the above illustration had initially proposed an intervention in which technicians received both types of feedback and incentive awards for exceeding their previous level of performance. To determine whether the intervention "package" works and to discover its critical ingredients, a within-series design of A(B + C + D)A can be supplemented with additional phases. For example, A(B + C + D)A–B–A(A + B + C)A–C–A(A + B + D)A–D–A addresses both "whether" and "why" questions. The complete intervention is compared repeatedly with contiguous phases in which it is absent. Moreover, each of its major components is compared with similar treatment absent (baseline) conditions. The possibility of order effects is a concern and can be checked by using additional technicians exposed to other treatment orders, such as A(B + C + D)A–C–A(A + B + C)A–D–A(A + B + D)A–B–A). Many other examples of within-case designs have been described in the literature (see Hayes et al., 1999; and Franklin, Allison, & Gorman, 1997).

In summary, practice evaluators can use advanced experimental designs from both between- and within-case traditions to move systematically through a sequence of designs that provide progressively more specific information about a given treatment. Starting with general effectiveness questions of the "does it work?" variety, evaluators can use arrangements from either tradition, depending on the particular evaluative question and the available resources. Promising interventions shown to work at this stage can be advanced to the comparative stage, where more complex designs are needed. Again, both between- and within-case approaches are appropriate alternatives. Finally, interventions shown both to work and to work better than other interventions are moved on to the effective-ingredient, or decomposition, stage to address questions of why they work.

Conceptual Errors and Biases

When implementing any of the experimental designs discussed in this and previous chapters, it is important to avoid research errors. Again, Underwood's (1957) definition of a research error is "a discrepancy between what *is* concluded and what can be concluded" from the conduct of a particular study (p. 89). When the internal validity of a study has been compromised, a lethal error has occurred, and nothing definitive can be said about the effects of the independent variable on the dependent one. Additional errors and biases astute evaluators work to avoid include ignoring base rates, ignoring sample size, and failing to appreciate regression toward the mean.

Ignoring base rates is what Tversky and Kahneman (1974) referred to as insensitivity to the prior probability of an outcome. They provide the following example of reading a personality description of someone and predicting the likelihood that person has a particular occupation:

> Steve is a rather introverted individual, shy, and withdrawn. He is neat and orderly and has a passion for detail. He is little interested in people or in the concrete realities of everyday life. He is always willing to help others. Which of the following is most likely to be Steve's occupation?
>
> - airline pilot
> - farmer
> - salesman
> - librarian
> - physician

Even though the relative number of farmers is quite a bit larger than that of librarians, people commonly ignore this base-rate difference and choose librarian. Tversky and Kahneman suggested this is because of a common reliance on the *representativeness heuristic*—a tendency to view the probability of a particular outcome in terms of the degree to which it represents something familiar. In the example, the probability of Steve's being a librarian is judged in terms of how closely his description matches the stereotype of librarians.

Kahneman and Tversky (1971) explicitly manipulated base rates and showed that participants' judgments were unaffected. In the study, participants were given brief personality descriptions of several people.

In one condition, the people were said to be sampled from a larger population of engineers and lawyers in which the proportions were 70% and 30%, respectively. In another condition, the proportions were reversed. In both conditions, participants were asked to read the descriptions and assess the likelihood of their belonging to an engineer or a lawyer. Unexpectedly, participants gave nearly identical probability judgments for both conditions. Apparently they made their guesses on the basis of the match between the personality descriptions and common stereotypes of lawyers and engineers, virtually ignoring base-rate probabilities. In other words, when the description was "representative" of the stereotype, it controlled participants' judgments more strongly than did base-rate information. Tversky and Kahneman observed that participants matched objective probabilities when they were not provided personality descriptions, being required merely to judge whether an unknown person was an engineer or a lawyer; they relied on base rates only in the absence of any other information. Bar-Hillel (1980) suggested the *principle of relevance,* which might explain the base-rate problem. Briefly, she argued that highly relevant information renders information of low relevance irrelevant. In the Kahneman and Tversky study, the highly relevant personality descriptions of lawyers and engineers rendered the base-rate information irrelevant.

Another interesting judgment error appears to arise from a belief in the *law of small numbers:* In this belief, a sample that is more representative of a judge's experience is believed to be more likely than one that is dissimilar. For example, if a study has shown that a particular result occurs at a $p < .05$ with a sample of 20 participants, even statistically sophisticated judges state that a sample of 10 participants is highly likely to replicate the result (Tversky & Kahneman, 1971). In another demonstration, the same authors asked participants to make up distributions of the mean height of men for samples of 10, 100, and 1,000 drawn from a larger population in which the mean height was 170 cm. The variance of the population heights was not provided. Participants' distributions were the same across sample size, even though sampling theory holds that the variance and sample size are inversely related. Put another way, the probability of obtaining an average height, say greater than 6 ft, was judged the same regardless of the size of the sample. According to Tversky and Kahneman, this error occurs because participants judge the likelihood of a sample result in terms of its correspondence with their experience. Thus, the probability of a mean height of a certain magnitude is evaluated by examining how well it represents the mean height in the population of men. If representativeness is controlling judgments, the likelihood of a particular outcome will be independent of the size of the sample.

Advanced Correlational Designs

Chapter 8 described basic approaches to showing relationships among variables and introduced the subject of multiple regression analysis. Chapter 9 discussed the controversial issue of provider profiling in the context of predicting success in treatment based on information about a particular therapist. Both chapters described the use of correlational procedures to make important practical decisions. Practitioners want to know what variables are related to client satisfaction so that the practice can be organized to maximize it. Third-party payers want to know the likelihood that a given client will be treated successfully by a specific practitioner. The goals of both types of stakeholders can be achieved by using sophisticated multivariate statistical procedures, several of which are briefly described in the sections that follow. The techniques are not treated in detail, and interested readers are encouraged to consult the cited references for more information.

Returning to the prediction of client satisfaction described in chapter 8, recall that specific ways of measuring the variables selected from the temporal, setting, intervenor, and intervention domains were developed. A multiple regression equation can be derived that would include each variable with its appropriate weight and produce the most accurate prediction of satisfaction. It is typical in practice evaluation for an approach like this to be completely empirical and wholly uninformed by theoretical concepts. The practical issue of finding out which variables are related to satisfaction so they can be manipulated to enhance the satisfaction of future clients is what drives the practice evaluation.

Model Building

Much research in the behavioral sciences has had a similarly empirical character, sometimes appearing to be a blind search for statistically significant relationships among variables for which convenient data are available. A shift in the nature of correlational research has occurred, however, with a priori theory guiding the selection of variables and suggesting the types of relationships expected among them. This

Figure 10.8

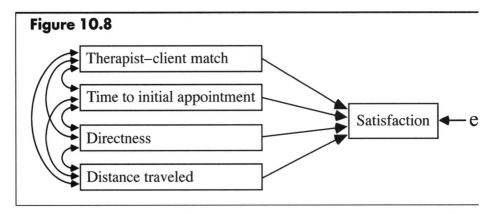

A single-stage model for predicting client satisfaction using four independent variables. *e* = other variables affecting satisfaction not correlated with the four variables of interest here.

change has been facilitated by the development of powerful analytic concepts and procedures, such as path analysis (Pedhazur, 1982), causal modeling (Nunnally & Bernstein, 1994), and hierarchical linear modeling (Bryk & Raudenbush, 1992).

To illustrate the use of some of these concepts, recall the example in chapter 8 in which the evaluator is informed by a particular ecological theory of how a practice should be run. Figure 10.8 depicts the theoretical relationship among the variables being examined. The model makes it clear that the evaluator acknowledges correlations among each of the four independent variables and views their impact on satisfaction as direct. The double-arrowhead lines connecting these variables reflect their intercorrelations. In the model, all four are treated as exogenous; that is, they are viewed as resulting from causes "outside the model" (Pedhazur, 1982, p. 178). The model in Figure 10.8 is a "single-stage model" (or a single-equation model) because satisfaction, the dependent variable, is treated as being affected by the independent variables, which themselves are intercorrelated. One multiple regression equation can be developed to test this model, and each of the independent variables is expected to have a significant weight, or influence, in the equation.

The relationships among the exogenous variables are set outside the present analysis and are not the focus of the evaluation. In other words, they are treated as given. As Pedhazur and Schmelkin (1991) noted, the possibility of the effects of one of the independent variables being mediated through others (e.g., the possibility that distance traveled is negatively correlated with satisfaction only as distance is positively correlated with time to initial appointment) is not discernible in single-stage models. Furthermore, the *e* variable in Figure 10.8 reflects other variables external to the model affecting satisfaction that are not correlated with time, directness, distance, and match, the independent variables. It is important to identify their lack of relationship when setting up the model; failing to do so constitutes a *specification error.* Such errors can result in "biased estimates of the effects of the independent variables in the model" (Pedhazur & Schmelkin, 1991, p. 310).

What if the evaluator had a more complex understanding of the relationships among the variables in Figure 10.8? Suppose the ecological theory guiding the practice did call for the effects of some of the independent variables to be moderated through others. For instance, let us suppose that time to first appointment has a direct effect on satisfaction and that its impact also is moderated through the therapist–client match. Likewise, the directness of the treatment (i.e., its perceived relevance to the client's problem) can be viewed as directly affecting satisfaction as well as being moderated through the therapist–client match. Finally, distance traveled to the practice's office is hypothesized to affect satisfaction directly. A model representing these relationships is diagrammed in Figure 10.9. In this model, three of the original independent variables are still viewed as exogenous and as having direct effects on satisfaction. Two of them (time and directness) also affect satisfaction as moderated through the therapist–client match, which is now considered an endogenous variable. (An *endogenous variable* is "one

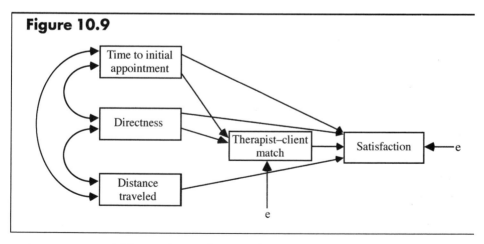

Figure 10.9

A two-stage model for predicting client satisfaction using endogenous and exogenous variables. e = other variables affecting satisfaction not correlated with the four variables of interest here.

whose variation is to be explained by exogenous and other endogenous variables in the causal model"; Pedhazur, 1982, p. 178.) The model in Figure 10.9 is a two-stage model because there are two dependent (endogenous) variables (match and satisfaction). Two multiple regression analyses are developed to test this model, one for each of the endogenous variables. (Note that the theoretical notions being advanced here are hypothetical and intended solely for purposes of illustrating the application of causal modeling in practice evaluation.)

It is likely that a number of factors affect the variables of interest to practice evaluators. The practitioner's understanding of the relationships among these factors constitutes his or her theory of the practice. The example used here involves a hypothetical "ecological" theory of a practice; it is general and meant to provide understanding for and guide decisions related to the operation of the practice as a whole. Although appealing, such a grand theory may be unrealistic in many situations—or at least premature—because the idea of having a theory to guide something as concrete and applied as a personal service is rather novel itself. It is probably more realistic for practitioners to have more narrowly proscribed, "minitheories," representing their understanding of specific variables important to their services, such as the satisfaction variable mentioned here.

The two-stage model for predicting satisfaction in Figure 10.8 can be elaborated rather easily. The addition of other independent variables would lead to new direct or indirect relationships involving exogenous or endogenous variables. Corresponding equations showing the endogenous variables regressed on their respective independent variables signify additional stages of the model. Without difficulty, three-, four-, and higher stage models can be specified, depending on the extent to which the underlying theory has been elaborated. The stability of models with more than a few independent variables is difficult to achieve, however. For the purposes of practice evaluation, it is probably best to limit explanatory models to four or fewer independent variables.

The Mediator–Moderator Distinction

In the discussion of complex correlational analyses a distinction often is made between mediator variables, such as therapist–client match (Figure 10.9), and moderator variables (Holmbeck, 1997). When single-stage models involving zero-order relationships between independent and dependent variables are specified, a third variable—a *moderator*—

sometimes can affect the relationship. To illustrate, consider the correlation between stress and depression. As Cole and Turner (1993) observed, it is generally assumed that stress is not sufficient to lead to depression in any direct sense. Rather, it is assumed to have its effects through other (moderator) variables (see Figure 10.10). In Beck's (1963) theory of depression, for instance, certain depressogenic people are likely to make cognitive errors about or distort events they experience (e.g., overgeneralization, personalization). These cognitions interact with the experienced events, leading to depressed affect.

The impact of the predictor variable (negative life event) on the outcome variable (depression) is qualified in terms of the moderator variable (cognitions). In ANOVA terminology, an interaction exists between the independent variables of negative event and cognitions concerning their effects on the dependent variable, depression. Thus, a moderator variable is a "qualitative (e.g., sex, race, class) or quantitative (e.g., level of reward) variable that affects the direction and/or strength of the relations between an independent or predictor variable and a dependent or criterion variable" (Baron & Kenny, 1986, p. 1174). Figure 10.10 shows that moderator variables are comparable to predictor variables in that both are exogenous, or independent variables.

Now, consider the relationship between life events and emotion. In the moderator model in Figure 10.10, both negative events and cog-

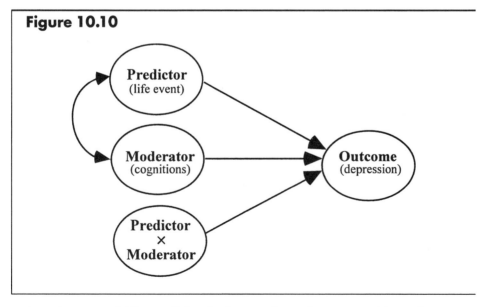

Figure 10.10

A moderator model for predicting the impact of negative events on depression.

nitions directly affect depression. Their interaction is of interest in testing a moderational hypothesis. Alternatively, one might explain negative life events as affecting depression because they are *mediated* through some other variable (e.g., cognitive activity). In such a view, a negative event does not lead directly to feelings of depression. Rather, it has its effect through the inferences one makes about the event (Dryden & Ellis, 1988; see Figure 10.11). The activating event, per se, does not result in a particular emotion. Instead, it is the activating event mediated through the cognitive activity of the person experiencing it that leads to the emotion. Depending on the interpretation of the event, different emotions are experienced. Thus, if one decides that the event is awful and should not have happened, it is likely that depression will follow; if one concludes that the event is just unfortunate, the emotion is not as severe or pathological as depression.

Mediators are third variables through which an independent variable of interest acts on a dependent variable. When such a third variable accounts for the relationship between the independent and dependent variables, it is said to be a mediator. Baron and Kenny (1986) provided three conditions that must be met for a variable to have this status:

1. Changes in an independent variable account for changes in the variable presumed to be a mediator (Path 1 in Figure 10.11).
2. The dependent variable and the presumed mediator are correlated (Path 2 in Figure 10.11).
3. When relationships between the independent variable and the presumed mediator (Path 1) and between the mediator and the dependent variable (Path 2) are controlled, there is no longer

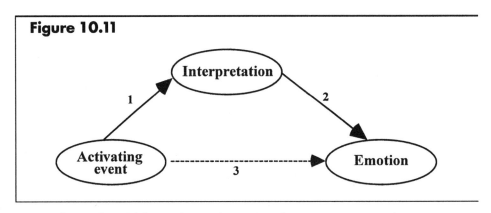

Figure 10.11

A mediational model for predicting the impact of negative events on depression.

a relationship between the independent and dependent variables (Path 3 in Figure 10.11).

Baron and Kenny (1986) referred to Path 3 in terms of a continuum, with the strongest evidence of a single mediating variable provided when this path is reduced to zero. Path 3 is sometimes shown as a dashed line to indicate a "partial mediational model" (e.g., Cole & Turner, 1993, p. 272).

As the above illustrations make clear, it is important to distinguish the character of the explanatory variables in one's theory relating them. The same constructs are used quite differently to predict depression in the models (see Figures 10.10 and 10.11). Designating the intended status of variables carefully can help clarify competing theoretical explanations of phenomena. Mediational versus moderational interpretations then can be tested, for example, with support emerging for one theoretical view over another. Clarity in mediator–moderator designations can facilitate the reconciliation of apparently inconsistent theoretical positions as well. As Baron and Kenny (1986) noted, there may be occasions when disagreements about mediators can be cleared up by viewing some of them as moderators.

It is also useful to recognize that variables can serve as moderators in early stages of practice evaluation and lead to mediator-type explanations later. The reverse is also a possibility. Finally, complex path analyses explaining some phenomena can include both types of variable.

Advanced Analysis Concepts

Chapter 7 discussed the definition of variables in measurable terms and some elementary concepts concerning the construction of measures. The importance of assessing the psychometric characteristics of newly developed measures was covered under the rubrics of reliability and validity. With respect to the first of these, several types of reliability were discussed, especially the concepts of temporal and internal consistency. Variables of interest to practice evaluators are likely to comprise multiple indicators; it is important to specify whether they are effect-type indicators or causal ones (Bollen & Lennox, 1991). Effect indicators are sometimes referred to as reflective indicators, or "reflectors" (e.g., Costner, 1969), referring to the fact that they reflect or result from an underlying latent variable. An example of the model underlying such reasoning is presented in Figure 10.12.

Figure 10.12

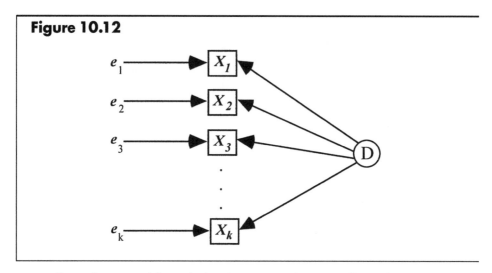

An effect-indicator model, in which indicators are shown as effects of a latent variable. The indicators (X_1, X_2, X_3, ... X_k) are treated as determined by or resulting from the latent variable D. e = other factors uniquely influencing specific indicators.

Assume that a practice evaluator is interested in assessing the severity of the problems for which clients seek assistance. Assume further that problem severity is assessed using a measure with multiple indicators. (If using self-report or rating-by-other measures, the term for indicator would be "item.") The practitioner might envision a model similar to that in Figure 10.12, in which responses to items are determined by the severity of the problem the client experiences. Let us imagine further that the practitioner has a "generic" measure of problem severity, which applies regardless of the type of problem presented. Such a measure might contain items such as those in Table 10.3. Classical measurement theory in the social sciences assumes that items in measures such as this are equally determined by the underlying variable. In other words, the items are interchangeable indicators of the construct being measured. A related assumption is that the measure is unidimensional (i.e., tapping a single latent variable; DeVellis, 1991). To the extent that homogeneity, or unidimensionality, is present, interpretations of scores on the measure are easier. A score of 5, for example, can be considered the equivalent of any score of 5 obtained on the measure, without regard to the particular items used in producing it.

Chapter 7 described several ways of assessing the internal consistency or homogeneity of measures, the most important of which is Cronbach's coefficient alpha. A sufficiently large alpha is some assurance of item equivalence within a measure; it is not designed to explain or

Table 10.3

Examples of Generic Items in Scales Assessing the Effects of Psychological Problems

Item	Never	Seldom	Usually
1. Because of my problem, I have difficulty sleeping at night.	0	1	2
2. My problem causes me to lose interest in eating at times.	0	1	2
3. I get preoccupied with my problem and forget what I am doing.	0	1	2
4. Other people are lucky they don't have a problem like this.	0	1	2
5. There are times when I feel like just being alone so I can deal with my problem.	0	1	2
6. I am concerned that people will think poorly of me for having this problem.	0	1	2
7. My interest in sex has decreased since I've been dealing with this problem.	0	1	2
8. I don't see how I can continue to function unless this problem is resolved.	0	1	2

Note. Substitute a specific disorder (e.g., depression, drinking) for "problem" in these items to see how they are used in some scales.

represent the structure of a set of indicators, however. To understand the organization of indicators relevant to an underlying variable and to test the assumption that they are equally determined by it, factor analysis commonly is used. Two general approaches to factor analysis are exploratory and confirmatory.

Exploratory Factor Analysis

Suppose an evaluator were interested in how the 8 items in Table 10.3 hang together or covary. A table of intercorrelations of all the items could be produced and examined for patterns of relationships. With $k = 8$ items, there are $28[k(k - 1)/2]$ correlations to explore. Looking for patterns in a large matrix of correlations can be a daunting task, and most measures in the human services contain more than 8 items. Fortunately, factor analysis exists to facilitate the process and to make it more systematic. If the evaluator wonders whether all the items are related to a single underlying problem, a factor analysis can be performed to examine this. If the results yield a single factor on which all 8 items "load" (correlate), the scale is interpreted as unidimensional. If several factors emerge, the scale must be seen as multidimensional. This poses problems for the evaluator with a single-factor view of the scale. In any event, the evaluator uses factor analysis to search for (i.e., explore) the dimensions underlying responses to indicators in the scale.

Exploratory factor analysis (EFA) also is used to reduce the number of variables needed to explain a phenomenon. The interest here is in combining a large set of indicators into a smaller number that sufficiently account for most of the reliable information in the larger set. Continuing with the above example, imagine that the evaluator interested in a global measure of problem severity has been giving clients an 80-item scale for several years. Clients take a long time to complete the 80-item measure, and the practitioner decides to explore ways of reducing its size. Intercorrelations among the items are factor analyzed, and the resulting structure is examined. The emergence of a single large factor supports unidimensionality. More important for the present purpose though, is the possibility of narrowing attention to the items loading it most highly. These might yield a shorter measure that contains most of the reliable information carried in the original set of 80 items.

Floyd and Widaman (1995) pointed out some fundamental differences in the two approaches to EFA. They argue that different types of analytic procedure should be used with each. When the dimensions underlying a set of indicators are being explored, *common factor analysis* is used. When data reduction is the goal, *principal components analysis* (PCA) is used. The procedural differences in these approaches are beyond the scope of this book, but it is important to appreciate their different conceptual bases. In common factor analysis, an effect-indicator measurement model is assumed. Covariation among the indicators is explained by the factors, which, in turn, are seen as determinants of the indicators. With PCA, economy is stressed; no assumption of underlying variables causing responses to the indicators is necessary in such uses. In fact, because the resulting factors are actually the optimally weighted sums of the indicators themselves, they can be viewed as caused by the indicators. The use of PCA thus assumes a causal-indicator measurement model (Floyd & Widaman, 1995). As Cliff (1987) noted, the relative merits of PCA and common factors approaches have been argued vigorously in the literature, with studies showing how they can produce similar or different results depending on the circumstances in which they are used. Nunnally and Bernstein (1994) observed that similar results emerge when the number of variables is 20 or more, for example. The complex arguments surrounding this controversy are beyond the scope of this book; it is enough to agree with Pedhazur and Schmelkin (1991) that PCA is a data reduction technique stressing economy. Common factors methods seek to explain common variance in a correlation matrix. The goals of the two approaches are different, and their underlying measurement models differ as well.

Strictly speaking, EFA is undertaken when the investigator does not have any a priori assumptions about the underlying structure of a measure. It is most useful in developing scales designed to get at some dimension or construct of interest. In scale development it is customary to assume unidimensionality. That is, a homogeneous measure is usually the goal of the investigator. Thus, a large set of items is generated, all of which are thought to relate to the construct of interest. These are administered to a large number of people, and relationships among the items are examined via factor analysis. If a single factor emerges and most of the items load on it, the analysis supports the assumption of unidimensionality, and the developer can proceed to refine the scale, eliminating items with low loadings or other unsuitable properties.

If multiple factors emerge, the developer faces challenging decisions. Depending on the relative sizes of the factors, they can be retained or discarded with various levels of difficulty. A large factor accompanied by several small ones is a structure that can encourage the developer to continue pursuing a unidimensional measure. A structure consisting of multiple factors of approximately equal size can be more problematic. It cannot be easily dismissed as a perturbation of the item pool that can be handled by retaining some items, discarding those that do not load a common factor, searching for new items that will load a common factor, and repeating the analysis. When multiple substantial factors emerge from an EFA of a set of indicators thought to reflect a single construct, the investigator is faced with redefining the construct, developing better indicators, or both.

If the revised definition leads to the conclusion that a multidimensional construct is more theoretically satisfying than a unidimensional one, the developer has some choices in how to proceed. Logically, each of the dimensions can be seen as a construct in its own right, requiring its own measure. The developer can construct items appropriate to each, administer them, and explore their interrelationships through factor analysis. The process is repeated for each dimension. Again, the assumption is that a unidimensional structure will emerge. Alternatively, items specific to each dimension can be generated and administered simultaneously to a large group of people. Interrelationships among the items can be examined using cross-structure analysis (Pedhazur & Schmelkin, 1991). In specifying a multidimensional structure for a set of items, however, the investigator engages in a priori hypothesis formulation. As such, the analysis moves from exploratory to confirmatory, even though the theoretical basis for the multidimensionality assumption might be quite informal or tentative.

Confirmatory Factor Analysis

When theorizing about the organization of a data set takes place, the theory can be tested via subsequent analyses. Theorizing may concern the number of constructs underlying relationships among observed variables. It also may be concerned with estimating the characteristics of the relationships among factors (e.g., factor loadings and correlations between factors). Suppose a measure of client satisfaction has been used to evaluate the satisfaction of the inpatients of a large health maintenance organization (HMO). Factor analysis reveals four dimensions of satisfaction: perceived competence of the medical practitioners, ease of access to services, concern and politeness of staff, and pleasantness of the physical surroundings. The principals of a large outpatient group practice decide they want to try the measure with their patients. After some period of use, they decide to examine the nature of satisfaction with their outpatient clients. They expect the same four dimensions to emerge when they analyze their data. In effect, they hypothesize that the same factor structure characterizes the satisfaction construct in their outpatients as in the HMO inpatients. CFA is undertaken to test this hypothesis. In this example, theory is minimal to nonexistent; nonetheless, the factor structure resulting from the outpatient analysis can be compared with that of the inpatients to confirm that the two satisfaction constructs are comparable.

More complex theoretical notions can be advanced and tested through CFA, of course. An evaluator might hypothesize that general client satisfaction has a number of component variables and therefore develop a pool of items to represent each of the variables. Clients then respond to the items, and the results are correlated and factor analyzed. Examining the factors confirms or disconfirms the structure, thereby supporting or failing to support the evaluator's theoretical understanding of the satisfaction construct. More advanced theorizing can lead to hypotheses of causal relationships among variables, as depicted in Figure 10.9.

Using CFA to test hypotheses involving indicators in a scale can pose challenges, however (Floyd & Widaman, 1995). The difficulty occurs at the first stage in the process. The evaluator must start by specifying a model to be tested. Prior exploratory analyses can be of great assistance here, especially if used to develop and perform initial refinements on a measure. Nonetheless, it is difficult to confirm factor structures suggested by these analyses when using measures of typical length (e.g., 15–30 items) because of problems specifying all of the correlated error terms likely among the items. Perhaps for this reason, CFA is relatively less frequently used at the level of individual scale development and refinement. Kishton and Widaman (1994) proposed an item-parceling procedure for these circumstances, which essentially involves creating subsets (parcels) of items and specifying which subsets are expected to load which factors in the model.

Practice evaluators concerned with developing client satisfaction measures specific to their own practices might use the parceling approach. For example, as suggested in the earlier example involving HMO inpatients, satisfaction can be conceptualized as multidimensional. Perhaps it includes perceptions of provider competence, comfort felt with the office design and furniture, ease of access, politeness of office staff, and time spent waiting. Measures for each of the five dimensions can be developed and refined using exploratory factor analysis. The five variables then can be entered into a model predicting client satisfaction such as that shown in Figure 10.13, which depicts a two-stage model with a single moderating variable (i.e., time spent waiting).

Each of the independent variables in Figure 10.13 might comprise multiple (say, five) indicators, resulting in an overall scale length of 25 items. The design represents a causal model and assumes different indicators for each of the independent variables. Such models have been referred to by various names in the literature, including path analysis, analysis of covariance structures, and structural equation modeling. Computer programs (e.g., EQS, Bentler, 1989; LISREL, Jöreskog & Sörbom, 1989) have greatly facilitated their use and evaluation and have become so popular that they are often used in place of the term *causal modeling* (Pedhazur & Schmelkin, 1991). The model in Figure 10.13 can

Figure 10.13

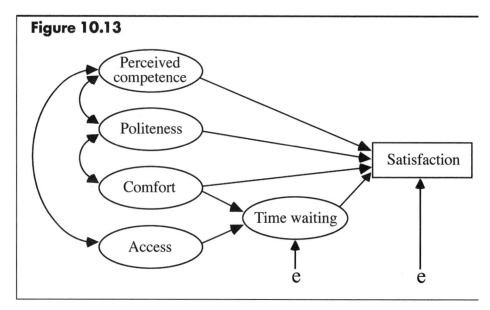

A two-stage model for predicting client satisfaction with one endogenous and four exogenous variables. e = other factors uniquely influencing specific indicators.

be subjected to analysis using LISREL or EQS to test its fit to data generated with the satisfaction measure. Details of such analyses are omitted here, although interested readers are referred to excellent presentations of structural equation modeling in Marcoulides and Hershberger (1997), Nunnally and Bernstein (1994), and Pedhazur and Schmelkin (1991).

Hierarchical Linear Modeling

Chapter 9 discussed issues of client change and differential provider effectiveness with clients presenting the same problems. Again, stakeholders in the provision of behavioral health services, especially the payers, are keenly interested in identifying which providers are most effective with which types of client. Data in Table 4.3 illustrated quite clearly the enormous cost differences incurred by providers who vary in the amount of change they produce per session of therapy.

Managed care organizations (MCOs) track the costs incurred by different providers; they maintain profiles on each provider to identify variation in the quality of services provided. Ultimately, of course, the company seeks to eliminate this variability so as to ensure uniformly high-quality, cost-effective services among practitioners. This common goal in commercial enterprises is characterized by concepts such as statistical process control (Shewhart, 1931; Wheeler & Chambers, 1992), continuous quality improvement (Juran, Seder, & Gryna, 1962), and total quality management (Deming, 1986). To achieve this goal, data must be kept on the types of client seen and the relative effectiveness of services provided by different practitioners. When enough data are accumulated, it is possible to match clients with providers to generate the most favorable service outcomes. In statistical terms, a regression equation is developed for each provider such that overall effectiveness with a given client can be predicted. Clients are assessed on multiple characteristics shown to be related to clinical change. Their scores on these variables are plugged into the equations for service providers on the MCO's provider panel, and they are assigned to the provider for whom the equation predicts the best possible outcome.

Realistically, we are a long way from routine use of client and provider profiling in this fashion. A major difficulty is the large amount of data required by conventional statistical approaches to developing the multiple regression equations that would allow this type of matching. Most practitioners see clients with a variety of problems. It would take many years to accumulate enough clients who have a given diagnosis to enable the construction of a reliable regression equation that would allow success to be predicted in individual cases. Fortunately, the problem of predicting outcomes for small numbers is confronted in many practical contexts, which has stimulated the development of innovative statistical procedures for handling it. One such innovation is hierarchical linear modeling (HLM).

Also referred to as "multilevel linear modeling," "random coefficient regression modeling," and "covariance component modeling," among other terms (Bryk & Raudenbush, 1992), HLM takes advantage of the relatively common organization of data in multilevel, hierarchical ways. For example, consider a large bank with many branch offices. The branches might be distributed across a number of cities within a state or region. If management consultants are interested in evaluating the effects of cross-functional teams on worker productivity and turnover, units in the analysis can include workers, branches, cities, and states. Workers can be considered to be units nested within branches; branches nested within cities, and cities nested within states. If observations of productivity and turnover are taken repeatedly over time, curves (or line graphs) for individual workers (branches, cities) can be generated. Variations in the implementation of cross-functional team concepts then can be examined for their association with changes in productivity and turnover across time.

In the case of individual service providers, comparisons of their effectiveness with different types of clients also can be be understood in terms of hierarchically organized data. Suppose that multiple providers make up the panel of a particular MCO and that each provider sees clients with a variety of diagnoses or problems. Ideally, a prediction equation would be developed for each provider. Doing so would allow individual client scores on relevant variables to be entered into the equation and success estimated for the client with each potential provider. Put another way, a provider who is seeking authorization to provide services for a particular client would forward relevant assessment information about the client. The MCO would apply its regression equation to the data and determine the likely outcomes of this particular provider–client match. (The client's wishes might be one of the assessment variables). Assuming the predicted outcomes are within the boundaries acceptable to the company, services will be authorized. If they are not, the company might suggest another of its panel members or another type of service altogether (e.g., psychotherapy rather than medication).

HLM can be used to develop the relevant equations for predicting outcomes in this situation. Data from individual practitioners are likely to be too few to permit appropriate analysis using traditional multiple regression analysis. With HLM, however, data can be pooled across panelists and used to provide separate equations for each. Using multiple observations of different clients treated by multiple providers, a hierarchical data set such as that in Figure 10.14 can be arranged. Levels 1 through 3 of the hierarchy are represented by observations (assessment occasions), clients, and providers, respectively. At Level 1, repeated observations allow for an improvement curve to be developed (i.e., modeled) for each client. As Bryk and Raudenbush (1992) observed, the frequency and timing of observations need not be the same for each client. The authors provided formulae for models at each of the stages and examples from studies of student growth in academic subjects. To illustrate, a linear model Level 1 equation is

$$Y_{ti} = \pi_{0i} + \pi_{1i}a_{ti} + e_{ti},$$

where Y_{ti} is the observed status of the ith individual at time t. We assume this can be predicted from knowledge of the person's initial status, π_{0i}; plus the person's expected improvement rate, π_{1i}; and the session, a_{ti}, represented by time t. Errors, e_{ti}, are expected to be independent and normally distributed with a common variance.

In a similar fashion, equations can be developed to model the second and third levels of the hierarchy. In addition, predictor variables can be entered in the equations, allowing for individual differences to be tested. For example, the client's age and duration of the problem might be added to a Level 2 model and tested for contributions to predictive accuracy. Likewise, therapist variables can be added to a Level 3 model to assess their contribution.

The use of HLM can move us progressively toward the goal of selecting the most appropriate intervention for clients seeking services. At first glance, it appears that such a methodology would be of greatest interest to large organizations of service providers with many clients. MCOs are especially interested in predicting the type of service configuration most likely to provide adequate care for patients with particular problems, which is why they maintain data on individual providers and are beginning to produce profiles (albeit crude ones at this point) such as those depicted in Figure 4.4. As mentioned previously, however, given the large numbers of clients needed, we are a long way from being able to model the effectiveness of individual providers with any accuracy.

Nonetheless, the logic and calculation procedures of HLM can be instructive to individual practitioners and to large organizations. For example, in the data set represented in Figure 10.14, "treatment" can replace "provider" at Level 3. The diligent practitioner can accumulate data for dozens of clients seen over the years and treated in different ways. Eventually, the practitioner can develop equations to predict the success of the treatments with clients presenting with particular characteristics. Whether the equations are ever produced, the goal of doing so can be of considerable help in stimulating the practitioner to collect

Figure 10.14

Provider_1 $\quad$ Provider_2 ...... Provider_N

Client_1 $\quad$ Client_2 ... Client_N

o_1 $\quad$ o_2 ... o_N

A three-level hierarchically organized data set. Each *N* provider treats *N* clients, who are assessed on *N* occasions (o). When enough clients have been treated, equations that combine client and provider characteristics are developed and used to predict client change.

and organize data systematically enough to facilitate other practice evaluation efforts and overall practice accountability. Preparation and planning are general benefits of practice evaluation, and their value is especially evident in reviewing literature related to one's practice, a topic to which we now turn.

Meta-Analysis

Learning about some aspect of a field of scientific or practical endeavor involves examining literature published on that topic. However, it can be cumbersome to synthesize information if extensive published work exists on the subject. Perhaps more important, it can be difficult to do so objectively. Reviewers are likely to approach the task with preconceived ideas that bias their approach in significant ways, which can lead to ignoring, deemphasizing, or even misinterpreting relevant research. Fortunately, recent years have seen the emergence of a methodology for conducting reviews, *meta-analysis*, which objectifies the process. In doing so, it reduces (but does not eliminate) the likelihood of some of these problems.

Meta-analysis is essentially an analysis of analyses. It involves statistical procedures for aggregating the results obtained from a number of studies to provide more reliable estimates of the magnitude of any effects reported. In a meta-analysis, the unit of analysis is the study. Studies in an area of interest are viewed as a population that can be studied and characterized much as any other population. Depending on the particular meta-analytic approach taken, studies can be aggregated without regard to differences in their features, or designated characteristics of each study can be quantified, coded, and placed into a data matrix. The data set then can be analyzed to determine which features are related to treatment effects.

Meta-analyses increasingly are appearing in published literature reviews, and some have become well known and frequently cited (e.g., Smith & Glass, 1977). In one example, Eagly and Carli (1981) reviewed studies of gender differences in persuasiveness and tendencies to conform; they found that sex of the author predicted the magnitude of the effects found. Male authors reported women to be more easily influenced (compared with men) than did female authors.

In addition to the benefits of their greater objectivity, meta-analyses can assist practice evaluators in another important way. Many evaluative studies suffer from small sample sizes, which can lead to low-power designs with high probabilities of Type II errors (see chapter 9). In a meta-analysis, the results of a number of small but otherwise carefully conducted studies can be aggregated. In the combined studies, effects may reach a level of significance that was not evident when the studies were looked at individually. Of course, it can be difficult to obtain small, no-effect studies to include in a meta-analysis, given the general bias toward publishing only significant results. Determined evaluators need diligence in pursuing the "fugitive literature" to find as much of the research in an area as possible. Good suggestions for doing this can be found in White's (1994) chapter on literature retrieval.

Practice evaluators can take advantage of meta-analysis in aggregating the results of their own efforts as well. Suppose data are kept routinely on the effectiveness of a particular treatment for different types of problem. These data involve the use of numerous outcome measures. After applying the treatment for a period of time, the practitioner examines whether the treatment works for clients complaining of depression. Results are in the right direction, but they fall short of statistical significance, given the small number of clients treated. The practitioner also tries the procedure with people experiencing panic attacks and with couples seeking improved relationships, again obtaining similar "promising but not significant" results. By combining the results of all the small evaluations, the practitioner can use meta-analysis to establish whether the treatment is effective. The increased power afforded by the larger N of the combined studies is more likely to reveal a statistically significant outcome.

It is important to consider the bases for including studies in a meta-analysis. In the present example, studies evaluating the impact of a single form of treatment on multiple problem types were lumped together. The results of the analysis indicate whether the treatment works in general, although they mask the possibility that it works with some types of problem and not with others. Moreover, if the treatment actually makes matters worse, negative effect sizes can offset positive ones, thereby reducing average effect sizes and increasing the likelihood of a Type II error for the meta-analysis itself. In practice evaluative uses of meta-analysis, as in this example, the evaluator's interest can be in the general effectiveness of the treatment, especially if the treatment is relatively generic itself (e.g., self-monitoring, homework, bibliotherapy). It is best to use generic outcome measures in these cases, such as Howard's Mental Health Index (Sperry, Brill, Howard, & Grissom, 1996; see chapter 4).

When meta-analysis is used to pursue scientific questions, it is not desirable to lump together studies using different outcome measures without first demonstrating some covariation among them. Otherwise, one could aggregate studies for which the outcome involved one particular construct with those involving another. There may be no theoretical basis for assuming the interchangeability of the constructs. The practitioner might like to know the extent to which self-monitoring is related to improvement of problems, whether the client is being treated for depression, decreased range of motion, or stuttering. The bases for including studies in meta-analyses have been argued in the literature, and interested readers are encouraged to examine excellent articles on the subject by Bangert-Drowns (1986) and Wortman (1983).

An appealing aspect of meta-analysis is its relative computational simplicity. One need not have a PhD in statistics, nor even extensive formal statistical training, to conduct one. Indeed, Rosenthal (1995) remarked that the computations involved in most meta-analyses are so trivial that he has never felt the need to use a software program to do them. To be sure, such programs exist (e.g., Meta-analysis; Biostat, 1998), and they are correspondingly simple to run. Numerous good sources can be consulted for the specifics of conducting meta-analyses (e.g., Cooper, 1998; Rosenthal, 1991, 1995).

When conducting a meta-analysis, the reviewer essentially obtains all the empirical literature available on the topic of interest, including studies varying in design, participants, setting, dependent measures, strength of independent variables, and numerous other characteristics. Remember, the intent is to document relationships among variables, and these relationships can come in many forms. Correlations, ANOVAs, t tests, and other statistics are likely to have been used for this purpose. Simple counts of the number of studies confirming a particular outcome, those disconfirming it, and those with nonsignificant results can be produced. This is the typical "box score analysis" (Light & Smith, 1971) of narrative reviewers; it is not the essence of meta-analysis, which goes beyond merely noting whether the results support a particular hypothesis. For instance, the reviewer might note also the various p values reported in the studies; these can be transformed to z scores (Rosenthal, 1978), permitting an estimation of the probability of the relationship. This particular approach to meta-analysis has been referred to as the "combined probability method" because it "defines the probability that the pooled subjects would be distributed among treatments as they are in the collected studies" (Bangert-Drowns, 1986, p. 394).

As Green and Hall (1984) noted, counts such as these establish whether a statistically significant relationship exists between variables across studies, but they say nothing about its size. It is common for meta-analytic reviewers to report effect sizes, however. The most frequent way of doing this is to divide the mean difference of two groups being compared by their pooled standard deviation. In the case of experimental and control group comparisons, the difference between the means of the groups is divided by the standard deviation of the control group (Bangert-Drowns, 1986). This results in a statistic known as Cohen's d (Cohen, 1977), which is readily seen as the standardized mean difference between the groups. If correlations are reported, they can be used directly as measures of effect size.

The reviewer records effect sizes for each study, computing them when not provided, and proceeds with conventional statistical analyses. In other words, after compiling a list of all relevant studies and recording their effect sizes, the reviewer examines whatever relationships are of interest. The situation is analytically comparable to any other study, except that the unit of analysis in meta-analysis is the study itself, rather than the individual study participant.

To illustrate the process, if a practice evaluator is interested in whether having clients complete homework leads to superior treatment outcomes, he or she can examine differences between clients given and not given homework who are treated in a certain way. Clients receiving other types of treatment also can be assigned to homework and no-homework groups, and differences in their outcomes noted. Over some period of time, the practitioner accumulates a number of comparisons of groups given different forms of treatment, some of which have done homework and some of which have not. For any given treatment, the difference in outcomes for the homework and no-homework groups might be in the right direction (i.e., favor homework), but not be large enough to be statistically significant. When Cohen's d has been calculated for each of these comparisons, its average can be reported and easily interpreted. In so doing, the evaluator may find homework to be quite beneficial, whereas previous individual studies had lacked the power to show it.

Glass and Kliegl (1983), for example, examined the effects of 17 different types of psychotherapy and found the average of the effect-size measures for each type to be .85 (ranging from .14 to 2.38). Thus, two distributions of a measure of mental health drawn from people who receive psychotherapy and those who do not have means separated by .85 standard deviations. In other words, the median for the people receiving psychotherapy is above 80% of the area of the curve representing the control group. Said another way, the person getting psychotherapy is, on average, better off when completing it than 80% of the people who do not. This is easily determined by treating d as z and looking up its value in a table of the normal curve found in the back of most elementary statistics texts.

Green and Hall (1984) summarized the advantages of meta-analysis as follows:

- It encourages the reviewer to organize her or his thinking ahead of time, formulating specific questions the review is to answer.
- It objectifies the review process, providing some protection against preestablished biases of the reviewer that can lead to overlooking or underweighting relevant literature.
- It permits significant relationships to emerge that were heretofore masked by the low power of small-N studies.
- It permits the testing of some hypotheses that can be examined only when the study is the unit of analysis, such as when research team or research site is the independent variable of interest.
- It allows documentation of moderator or interaction effects. The reviewer can ask whether there is an effect and also whether the magnitude of the effect varies with important aspects of the study, such as the strength of its independent variables, the gender of the investigator, and the nature of its design, among others.
- It can treat large amounts of data efficiently, something that is beyond the capacity of most individual reviewers—multiple variables and their interactions can be as easily analyzed in 300 studies as they can in 20, once they have been coded.

Before leaving the topic of meta-analysis, it is worth noting that it has been applied in several ways. As described by Bangert-Drowns (1986), the applications can be arrayed on a continuum representing the extent to which outcome variation among studies in an area is quantified. At one end of the continuum are traditional narrative reviews. In the middle, the rather liberal approach recommended by Glass and Kliegl (1983) might be placed. At the other end are so-called secondary analyses, which are reanalyses of published data using different bases for aggregation. The cluster analysis suggested by Light and Smith (1971) is an example of a secondary analysis. The liberal approach taken by Glass has been criticized on a number of grounds and defended to various extents (see Bangert-Drowns, 1986). Nonetheless, the reviewer contemplating using meta-analysis is advised to take a position somewhat to the "right" of Glass. Such a stance involves some minimum standard of methodological adequacy for a study to be included and care not to lump together studies with different dependent variables.

Missing Data

Practice evaluations involve collecting various types of information from many different people. The information varies in complexity, and people vary in the consistency with which they provide it. Moreover, procedural inconsistencies can lead to data omissions of one type or another. In the earlier example (Figure 10.8) involving the prediction of client satisfaction on the basis of time to initial appointment, directness of treatment, distance traveled, and therapist–client match, $N = 60$ clients would generate a 5×60-element data matrix with 300 pieces of information. It would not be surprising for some of those cells to be empty. How should one handle missing data?

This is a problem that practice evaluators and research scientists confront on a daily basis, and no universally agreed-on "best solution" exists for it. Statistical analysis software programs treat missing data in different ways. Most common is to delete cases with incomplete data on a listwise or pairwise basis. In the first, all data for a particular case are disregarded in analyses. Thus, if complete data were unavailable for 2 of 60 clients, correlations between our four predictors and satisfaction would be based on 58 clients. In the second (pairwise deletion), client data are disregarded for any pair of variables of which one has missing information. Thus, if "distance traveled" scores were missing for 2 of the 60 clients, correlations involving this variable and others would be based on 58 rather than 60 clients. The client's data still would be included in analyses that do not involve "distance traveled," however.

As Farrell (1999b) noted, listwise deletion is the default setting in many software programs. It has the virtue of all statistics being calculated on the same number of participants. At the same time, entirely excluding participants with only one missing data point can result in a greatly reduced sample size. Moreover, if the data are missing for some systematic (i.e., nonrandom) reason, results of the analysis might be biased (Farrell, 1999b). Although pairwise deletion appears attractive because only the client's missing data are excluded, it has its own problems. For instance, it is difficult to determine the size of one's sample when analyses are based on different data subsets. In addition, patterns of correlations or covariances can result that are not possible mathematically (Farrell, 1999b).

Rather than deleting client data from analyses when we encounter missing values, we can use replacement procedures. For example, blank cells in a data matrix can be filled with the mean of the existing data for a variable. This can be a satisfactory solution when large Ns are involved and relatively few cells are empty. With small Ns, many empty cells, or both, mean substitution can lead to unrepresentatively small variance estimates and biased estimates of population means if data are not missing at random.

Additional strategies, such as unweighted means estimation (Winer, Michels, & Brown, 1991), regression equations to estimate replacement values (Farrell, 1999b), and expectation maximization (Little & Schenker, 1995) are available for dealing with missing values. Each has advantages and disadvantages. Space does not permit elaborating on them here, and in the final analysis, the best approach is to collect information carefully and completely, minimizing data loss before the analysis stage of the evaluation cycle (Farrell, 1999b).

Summary

This chapter builds on the basic concepts of measurement, design, and analysis introduced in chapters 7 through 9 to cover more advanced approaches to these topics. With respect to design, advanced experimental designs involve moving beyond simple "does it work?" questions to comparative ones and eventually, mechanism of effect questions. Between-case designs involving analysis of variance statistics are particularly well suited to showing the separate and joint effects of different independent variables. Complex factorial designs can be effective ways of studying specific factors, although they often require large numbers of participants and other resources the average practitioner might not have available. Within-case designs are useful alternatives in these cases. Among these are A–B–A–C–A and alternating treatments designs that permit comparative evaluations, and A(B + C + D)A–B–A(A + B +

C)A–C–A(A + B + D)A–D–A designs that begin to address interactions. Other approaches include path analysis, analysis of covariance structures or structural equation modeling, factor analysis, and hierarchical linear modeling. The practitioner who has absorbed the information presented thus far is equipped with the intellectual and methodological tools that help to answer most evaluative questions. The practical applications of some of these tools are illustrated in the next chapter.

Supplemental Reading

Bollen, K., & Lennox, R. (1991). Conventional wisdom on measurement: A structural equation perspective. *Psychological Bulletin, 110,* 305–314.

Bryk, A. S., & Raudenbush, S. W. (1992). *Hierarchical linear models.* Thousand Oaks, CA: Sage.

Campbell, D. T., & Fiske, D. (1959). Convergent and discriminant validation by the multitrait-multimethod matrix. *Psychological Bulletin, 56,* 81–105.

Hoyle, R. H. (1995). *Structural equation modeling: Concepts, issues, and applications.* Thousand Oaks, CA: Sage.

Examples of Outcomes Evaluations

This chapter offers examples of evaluations of the direct services component of several practices. The studies summarized in the sections that follow illustrate ways in which skilled providers study the effectiveness of their services; the disorders include deviant sexual behavior, couple distress, panic disorder, depression, and chronic headaches. The practice evaluation cycle described in chapter 3 provides the framework for describing the studies, and the chapter ends by recommending a set of criteria for practice evaluation reports.

Effectiveness of a Treatment for Sex Offenders

One of the best documented examples of psychological service delivery is the work of Maletzky (1980, 1991, 1993, 1997). Using behavior therapy to treat maladaptive sexual behavior, Maletzky reported outcomes with hundreds of men. In an article on pedophilia and exhibitionism, he compared the effectiveness of treatment provided men who either sought help on their own or were referred by the court (Maletzky, 1980).

In this case, the evaluative question was, "Is there a difference in outcomes between self-referred and court-referred men treated for maladaptive sexual approach behavior?" Maletzky (1980) did not advance specific hypotheses, although implicit is the notion that the type of referral affects the treatment outcome. The independent variable in the evaluation is referral type, and the dependent variable is treatment outcome. Maletzky described his 100 clients as comprising 38 homosexual male pedophiles and 62 exhibitionists. Dividing these into court- and self-referred subgroups resulted in a total of four groups receiving treatment. Mean ages of the groups were comparable, at 32.1 for the pedophiles and 34.4 years for the exhibitionists; the age range was 17–65. The mean years of education completed also were comparable, at 10.5 for the pedophiles and 11.3 for the exhibitionists. Among the pedophile clients, approximately 31% of the self-referred (M = 15) and 42% of the court-referred (M = 23) group were married, whereas approximately 65% of both self-referred (M = 30) and court-referred (M = 32) exhibitionist groups were married.

Maletzky (1980) defined the two values on his independent variable as follows:

- *Self-referred:* "patient entered therapy of his own accord without coercion from a legal source" (p. 308).
- *Court referred:* "patient entered therapy under coercion from a legal source" (p. 308), which included as a condition of probation (62%); as a condition of parole (7%); neither of these, but released by the court provided they sought treatment (9%); and men whose attorneys advised them into treatment prior to their court hearing (22%).

Maletzky defined his dependent variables in terms of the following measures:

- overt maladaptive behavior, weekly self-reported frequencies
- covert maladaptive behavior, weekly self-reported frequencies
- penile plethysmograph records, before and after treatment and at 6-, 12-, 18-, 24-, and 30-month follow-up
- legal records during and after treatment
- collateral contacts ratings of client's progress and how well the client followed the program
- treatment session attendance. (pp. 309–310)

Treatment consisted of weekly covert sensitization sessions for 24 weeks, with booster sessions every 3 months for 3 years. Maletzky described several adjunctive techniques carried out supplemental to covert sensitization. He did not include data showing the integrity of the treatment approach, a reasonable omission given that the treatment itself was not being evaluated.

Maletzky (1980) found no effects for his independent variable, indicating that the treatment was equally effective whether a patient came to treatment of his own volition or was remanded by authorities. All subgroups showed statistically significant improvement, although they did not differ from one another on the self-report measures. A "percentage improved" measure also showed comparable percentages improved in each group. Essentially the same results were reported for the plethysmographic measure. Correlations between self-report and plethysmographic data at 6- and 36-month follow-ups revealed relatively high values ($r = .72–.89$ at 6 months, $.65–.85$ at 36 months). Again, there were no differences among groups. Collateral data also showed no differences among groups at either 6- or 36-month follow-ups. Attendance data showed more sessions missed by self- than court-referred clients (67% vs. 33%), although this difference was not statistically significant. Reviewing legal records over the 36-month follow-up period produced no group differences in illegal behavior. Only 8 of the 100 men had charges filed against them during this time, a number likely to be too small to show statistical significance. Maletzky concluded that treatment techniques effective with self-referred clients can be effective with court-referred clients as well.

Evaluating the effectiveness of community treatment for sex offenders, Maletzky (1993) reviewed records of 4,381 pedophiles, looking for factors associated with treatment success. Pedophiles with fewer victims were more likely to experience successful treatment, as were those who were familiar with and living with the victim. Force, failure to admit some responsibility for the offense, and unstable histories of employment and relationships with others were negatively associated with success. It is interesting to note that frequency and duration of sex offenses did not predict response to treatment. It is common in psychological interventions to find more seriously impaired clients less responsive to treatment (e.g., Elkin et al., 1995), although the reverse relationship, in which more seriously impaired clients are more responsive to treatment than less impaired ones, is also documented (e.g., Ruma, Burke, & Thompson, 1996).

Maletzky's (1980, 1993) work is a good example of practice evaluation by a provider specializing in treating a particular type of problem who has accumulated data on a sizable number of clients. What about the psychologist with a more general practice, who sees too few clients with any given disorder but nevertheless wishes to evaluate treatment effectiveness? As pointed out earlier in this book, satisfactory design and analysis options exist for evaluating effectiveness with individuals or with small groups of clients. For example, Paul, Marx, and Orsillo (1999) evaluated the effects of acceptance-based psychotherapy (see Hayes,

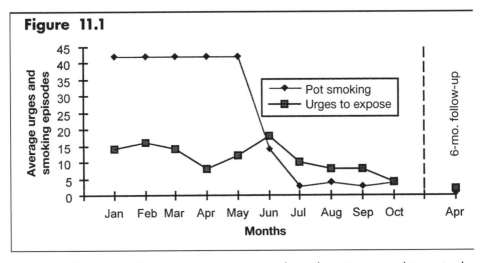

Figure 11.1

Average frequency of urges to expose (per month) and marijuana-smoking episodes (per week) in a 20-year-old man being treated for exhibitionism. From "Acceptance-Based Psychotherapy in the Treatment of an Adjudicated Exhibitionist: A Case Example," by R. H. Paul, B. P. Marx, and S. M. Orsillo, 1999, *Behavior Therapy, 30,* p. 158. Copyright 1999 by the Association for Advancement of Behavior Therapy. Reprinted with permission.

Strosahl, & Wilson, 1999) with a 20-year-old man arrested for exhibitionism. They provided documentation of the client's progress over 10 months of treatment (Figure 11.1). The client self-monitored two variables hypothesized to relate to the probability of exhibiting himself: (a) urges to expose and (b) frequency of smoking marijuana. As the figure shows, from January to June both variables remained stable, suggesting relatively minimal treatment impact.

At this point, treatment was changed somewhat to introduce principles of functional analytic psychotherapy (FAP; Kohlenberg & Tsai, 1991). As Paul et al. noted, FAP focuses on the experience of the client's problematic behaviors as they occur in the therapy session itself. The therapist accepts these behaviors and reinforces any attempt by the client to replace these behaviors with goal-focused behavior. Paul et al. found that with the introduction of aspects of FAP, the client reported substantially reducing his marijuana usage; several months later, urges to expose himself decreased as well. In keeping with Rosen and Proctor's (1981) notion of ultimate and instrumental therapy goals (see chapter 2), both behaviors monitored in Figure 11.1 represent progress toward the instrumental goal of eliminating the clients' exhibitionism. Additional instrumental goals involved reducing the client's depression and anxiety, as measured by the Beck Depression Inventory (BDI) and

Beck Anxiety Inventory, respectively. Pretreatment scores of 22 on both measures decreased to 8 by the end of treatment and to 2 and 1, respectively, at the 6-month follow-up. The authors reported no data on the ultimate goal of reducing actual exposures to zero.

Although their evaluation was not an experimental test of the benefits of acceptance-based psychological therapies, Paul et al. (1999) provided a good example of the use of multiple objective measures with an individual case to demonstrate treatment effectiveness. It is not difficult to see how the advantages of adding elements of FAP to ongoing acceptance-based therapy might be evaluated experimentally in a multiple-baseline design across several clients receiving treatment for the same problem.

Psychological Therapy for Panic Disorder

Much research on anxiety disorders and depression illustrates a common approach to showing whether and how well treatments work. This section describes efficacy studies on both disorders that involved randomized controlled trials (RCTs). Because the efficacious treatment evaluated in the RCT may not be effective in the practitioner's office, this section also includes descriptions of effectiveness studies, which examine whether the positive outcomes of the efficacy studies generalize to routine clinical practice.

Efficacy Studies

In a series of carefully conducted studies, Barlow and colleagues developed and demonstrated the efficacy of a behavioral treatment for anxiety attacks and panic (Barlow, Craske, Cerny, & Klosko, 1989; Barlow & Craske, 1989, 1994). Panic disorder is a difficulty experienced by approximately 1.5% to 3.5% of the population, according to Markowitz, Weissman, Ouellete, Lish, and Klerman (1989). Associated problems that people with panic disorder experience can include impaired interpersonal relationships, work difficulties, increased substance abuse, suicide attempts, and greater use of behavioral and physical health treatment resources.

Barlow et al.'s (1989) approach (now popularized as "mastery of your anxiety and panic," or MAP) involves individual treatment sessions in which clients learn anxiety management techniques and practice them in actual anxiety-experiencing situations between sessions. Clients learn progressive muscle relaxation using the procedures of Bernstein and Borkovec (1973), which they practice twice a day. The approach includes cognitive restructuring, in which clients learn to reevaluate "beliefs and appraisals about environmental and internal physiological cues" (Barlow et al., 1989, p. 266). Ten-item hierarchies of progressively more anxiety-eliciting situations are developed for each client; items include visualizing anxiety-producing situations, spinning, and over-breathing. By exposing clients to internal anxiety-associated physiological cues, they can apply new cognitive coping skills in anxiety-producing situations and reduce the likelihood that a panic attack will ensue.

In a controlled study of 56 clients meeting *Diagnostic and Statistical Manual of Mental Disorders, Third Edition Revised* (American Psychiatric Association, 1987) criteria for panic disorder experiencing no or only mild agoraphobic avoidance, Barlow et al. (1989) explored the efficacy of the MAP approach, progressive relaxation, and a combination of MAP and relaxation. The evaluative questions were "Do MAP, progressive relaxation, and MAP plus relaxation work?" and "What are their comparative efficacies?" No specific hypotheses were advanced. Variables in the study included the three types of treatment, anxiety, panic, depression, somatic symptoms, daily functioning, pleasantness, and medication use. Clients were between ages 18 and 65 ($M = 35.5$ years) and predominantly female (70%). In addition to meeting diagnostic criteria for panic disorder, the clients had to be free of substance abuse or dependence and have no major depression, psychosis, or organic brain disorder. Clients had been experiencing panic attacks for a mean of 7 years.

Assessment procedures were extensive and included rating-by-other, self-report, and self-monitoring measures. The Anxiety Disorders Interview Schedule–Revised (ADIS-R; DiNardo, O'Brien, Barlow, Waddell, & Blanchard, 1983; see chapter 7) provided the diagnosis; it was supplemented by interviewer ratings of the severity of the client's disorder. Interviewers also rated anxiety and depression using the Hamilton Anxiety Rating Scale (Hamilton, 1959) and the Hamilton Rating Scale for Depression (HRSD; Hamilton, 1960), respectively. Participants completed self-report measures including the Beck Depression Inventory, the State–Trait Anxiety Inventory–Trait Form (Spielberger, 1983), the Cognitive–Somatic Anxiety Questionnaire (Schwartz, Davidson, & Goleman, 1978), the Fear Questionnaire (Marks & Mathews, 1979), and the Psychosomatic Rating Scale (Cox, Freundlich, & Meyer, 1975). Clients reported daily life functioning using the Subjective Symptom Scale, which asks for ratings on an 8-point scale of the extent to which anxiety interferes with functioning in five areas. Self-monitoring data were obtained by asking the clients to rate anxiety, depression, and pleasantness four times each day using the same 8-point scale. In addition, the number and intensity of anxiety and panic attacks were monitored along with the amount of daily medication used.

Several of these instruments were combined to create two composite measures: "treatment responder" and "end state functioning." Clients were considered responders to treatment if they showed a 20% improvement in scores on at least three of four measures: interviewer's severity rating, Fear Questionnaire, number of panic attacks per week, and Subjective Symptom Scale. Clients were considered to have high end state functioning if they had three of the following indicators:

- a score of 2 or lower on the interviewer's severity rating
- a score of 2 or lower on the client's self-rating of severity
- zero panic attacks per week
- a score of 2 or lower for mean anxiety self-monitored
- a score of 10 or lower on the Subjective Symptom Scale.

The evaluation design was a simple pre–post comparison of the three treatment groups and a wait-list control group. Clients were randomly assigned to groups, with treatment provided by a total of 10 therapists closely following treatment manuals describing each approach. Integrity checks, which involved audiotaping each session, were performed on a randomly selected subset of treatment sessions. Therapists listened to the sessions selected for checking and rated the subject therapist on several dimensions. In addition, the rater judged which of the treatment groups the session represented and whether the session was from the introductory, rehearsal, or application phase of treatment. The therapy was correctly identified in all 35 sessions sampled. The correct phase of treatment was identified in 31 of the 35 tapes.

Results showed that all three treatments produced benefits and that the changes were significantly greater than changes in the wait-list control condition, thus answering the question of whether the treatments worked. Significantly more clients dropped out of the relaxation group (33%) than either the control (6%) or MAP groups (6%), although the rate was not significantly different from the dropout rate for the combined treatment (17%). Dropouts were less severely disordered than clients remaining to completion and were more likely to have taken some form of medication for their condition prior to participating in the study.

Positive responding was comparable across the three groups (83% for relaxation, 58% for MAP, 62% for combined treatments) and was significantly more likely than for clients in the control group (17%). High end state functioning was achieved for 0%, 50%, 46%, and 46% of the control, relaxation, MAP, and combined-group clients, respectively. The proportion of clients in each treatment group that reached high end state functioning was significantly different when individually compared with the control group, but the difference was not significant between treatment groups. The proportion of clients in each group showing zero panic attacks after treatment differed significantly, at 36%, 60%, 85%, and 87% for the control, relaxation, MAP, and combined-group clients, respectively. Of the possible pairs being compared, only MAP–control and combined group–control comparisons were statistically significant. Follow-up data at 6 months showed no significant changes from posttreatment levels, indicating that the gains were retained.

Barlow's work, like Maletzky's, is remarkable for the thoroughness of its documentation. Not only do extensive data describe the pre- and posttreatment status of clients, but treatment manuals describe interventions in detail, and treatment integrity was monitored throughout in the studies. The many measures of treatment efficacy include four of the five major assessment methods (interview, self-report, rating-by-other, and self-monitoring). Moreover, change measures, such as percentage responding, percentage reaching high end state functioning, and percentage remaining panic free, are more clinically meaningful than relying exclusively on differences in group means. At this time, the MAP approach appears to be the treatment of choice when treating clients complaining of anxiety and panic.

Effectiveness Studies

Wade, Treat, and Stuart (1998) examined the transportability of Barlow's empirically supported approach to a community mental health center. Using studies by Barlow et al. (1989) and Telch et al. (1993) as benchmarks, Wade et al. compared the results obtained for 110 clients receiving MAP treatment for the standard 15 sessions in a community setting. Exclusion criteria were relaxed: Adult participants were accepted for treatment regardless of age, comorbid diagnoses, history or prior treatment, medical condition, use of medications, personality dysfunction, presence of agoraphobia, or frequency or severity of panic attacks. As in the Barlow et al. study, however, clients were excluded who were actively psychotic, dependent on alcohol or drugs, or experiencing a behavioral disorder brought on by a medical condition. All clients had to meet *DSM-III-R* criteria for panic disorder with or without agoraphobia; diagnoses resulted from interviews using a modified version of the ADIS–R. As in Barlow et al. and Telch et al., most of the participants were female (70.9%). Their mean age of 31.1 years made them slightly younger than Barlow et al.'s or Telch et al.'s clients and somewhat less experienced with panic, having a mean of 5.9 years since their first panic attack. At least mild levels of agoraphobia were experienced by most (79.4%) of Wade et al.'s clients, with 46.7% meeting criteria for moderate or severe agoraphobia.

With minor exceptions, Wade et al. (1998) used the same measures as those of Barlow et al. (1989). Clients were exposed to MAP treatment in group (82.7%), individual (11.8%), or combined group and individual formats (5.5%). All individual sessions conducted by less experienced therapists were audiotaped and the clinic director used these as a basis for supervision. Supplementing this approach to ensuring treatment integrity were written outlines of the material to be covered in each session.

Results from Wade et al.'s (1998) clients were remarkably similar to those reported by Barlow et al. (1989) and Telch et al. (1993). The dropout rate was 26.4%; dropouts were defined as those who failed to attend at least 8 of the first 11 sessions. Dropouts tended to be younger and less well educated than completers and generally reported more depressive symptoms and more antidepressant medication use at intake. They also were significantly more likely to have one or more comorbid *DSM-III-R* Axis I diagnoses. Completers reported a longer history of panic attacks and agoraphobia than did dropouts.

The clinical significance of treatment gains was determined by calculating the percentage of clients in the normal range on four measures before and after treatment: freedom from panic altogether, anticipatory anxiety, avoidance, and depression. The latter three showed similar results in the Wade et al. and Telch et al. studies. Wade et al.'s finding that 87.2% of their clients were free of panic after treatment is comparable to Barlow et al.'s 84.6% and Telch et al.'s 85.3%. Thus, the results of the more tightly administered RCTs of Barlow et al. and Telch et al. appear to generalize to an applied setting, supporting the conclusion that the MAP approach to treating anxiety and panic is both effi-cacious and effective.

Whereas these studies address the questions of whether MAP works and how it compares with alternatives, more recent work deals with MAP's effective ingredients. In a case study exploring what provokes panic, Hofmann, Bufka, and Barlow (1999) reported the treatment of a 30-year-old woman diagnosed with panic disorder with agoraphobia and anxiety disorder not otherwise specified. To elicit moderate amounts of anxiety and physical sensations, the researchers instructed the client to breathe through a narrow cocktail straw. She was taught to do this during the 6th treatment session and asked to practice three times a day between the 6th and 7th sessions. In addition, she was in-structed to record both her level of anxiety and the intensity of the bodily sensations experienced during the process. Ratings were made on an 8-point scale, where 8 represented extreme sensation. The impact of the provocation procedures is shown in Figure 11.2. After 6/1, anx-iety, the though variable, began to drop, whereas the intensity of phys-ical sensations remained relatively unchanged over time, even though progressively more provocative procedures were used. Additional mea-sures of treatment effectiveness included the Anxiety Sensitivity Index (ASI; Peterson & Reiss, 1987), a scale assessing the extent to which common physical symptoms (e.g., rapid heart rate, shortness of breath) are frightening, and ADIS-R, used to document initial and continuing diagnostic status. The client's ASI score declined from 34 to 22, and her posttreatment diagnosis was panic disorder with agoraphobia in par-tial remission. Thus, the client benefited from treatment but did not completely accomplish her ultimate goals. Hofmann et al. (1999) re-ported that she still had panic attacks, although "less panic-related fear and avoidance" (p. 313), and that she avoided driving but not any of her other fear-provoking situations.

The data in Figure 11.3 are from a second case reported by Hof-mann et al. (1999). They represent progress over 11 months of treat-ment in anxiety and intensity of sensations for a 25-year-old woman with the same diagnoses as the previous case. Her initial panic-provocation procedures involved (a) running in place for 1 minute and (b) holding her breath for 30 seconds. The two exercises were to be practiced after Sessions 6 and 7, essentially providing an intervention after five or six baseline sessions. The client reported comparatively high levels of anx-iety and intensity of bodily sensations for the first 6 treatment days, after which anxiety began to drop. Intensity of bodily sensations remained

Figure 11.2

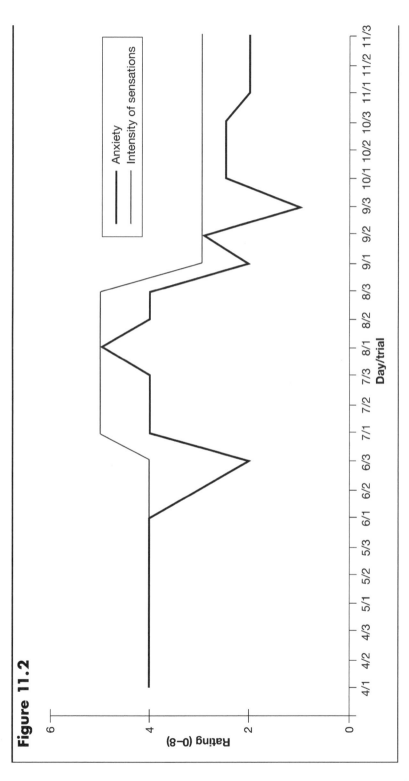

Changes in anxiety and intensity of physical sensations in a client over time with the practice of panic-provoking exercises: breathing through a thin straw, spinning in a chair, and hyperventilating. The figure shows blocks of 3 days 1 month apart (e.g., 4/1–4/3, 5/1–5/3). Moderate levels of anxiety and intensity of bodily sensations are consistently reported for the first 7 days (4/1–6/1). Anxiety begins to drop after this point, and therapy proceeds to additional provocation procedures (e.g., spinning in a chair and hyperventilating) in her hierarchy. The intensity of physical sensations remains relatively unchanged over time, even though progressively more provocative procedures are used. The figure presents a realistic example of a client who benefits from treatment but does not completely accomplish her ultimate goals. From "Panic Provocation Procedures in the Treatment of Panic Disorder: Early Perspectives and Case Studies," by S. G. Hofmann, L. F. Bufka, and D. H. Barlow, 1999, *Behavior Therapy, 30*, p. 312. Copyright 1999 by the Association for Advancement of Behavior Therapy. Reprinted with permission.

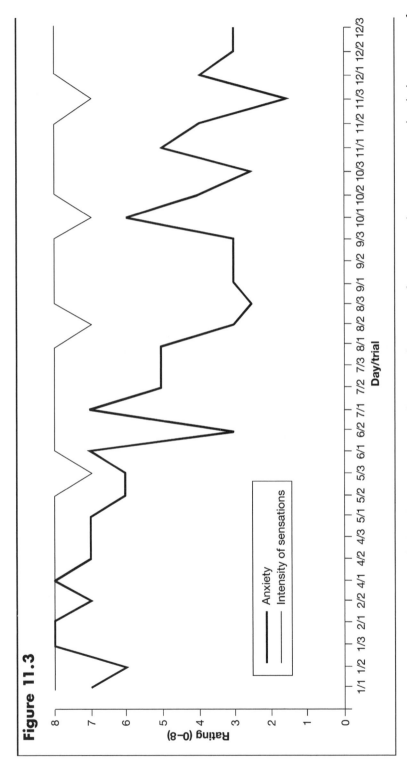

Figure 11.3

Changes in anxiety and intensity of physical sensations in a client over the course of an 11-month treatment period with the practice of panic-provoking exercises: Running in place, holding her breath, and spinning in a chair. From "Panic Provocation Procedures in the Treatment of Panic Disorder: Early Perspectives and Case Studies," by S. G. Hofmann, L. F. Bufka, and D. H. Barlow, 1999, *Behavior Therapy, 30,* p. 314. Copyright 1999 by the Association for Advancement of Behavior Therapy. Reprinted with permission.

high, although the client's pretreatment ASI score of 25 dropped to 10 following treatment, reflecting mild sensitivity to bodily reactions accompanying anxiety. She was diagnosed as "in partial remission" for "both anxiety disorder diagnoses," which were described as "no longer clinically significant" (p. 313).

The cases illustrated in Figures 11.2 and 11.3 provide examples of the use of single-case evaluations to explore "why does it work?" or "critical ingredients" evaluative questions. Although the relative contribution of panic provocation components cannot be determined from these cases, the importance of including them in the treatment package is supported (Hofmann et al., 1999). Moreover, the case studies show clearly that complex, resource-intensive, multifactorial designs involving many cases are not necessary for determining the critical components of multidimensional treatment procedures.

Evaluation of Psychological Therapy for Depression

Perhaps the most extensively studied psychological difficulty is depression. Research on treatments for alleviating it has been among the best supported and, not surprisingly, among the best designed. The existence of clearly written manuals describing ways of treating depression (e.g., Beck, Rush, Shaw, & Emery, 1979; Klerman, Weissman, Rounsaville, & Chevron, 1984) contribute to research on the subject.

Efficacy Studies

The largest and best known of a number of excellent efficacy studies appearing in the literature in recent years is the Treatment of Depression Collaborative Research Program (TDCRP; Elkin et al., 1989), which was carried out with the support of the National Institute of Mental Health (NIMH).

The researchers asked two major evaluative questions: (a) whether cognitive therapy and interpersonal therapy reduce symptoms associated with depression (compared with a minimal treatment condition and an alternative approach already known to be effective) and (b) whether the treatment modes differ in their efficacy. No specific hypotheses guided the study. The treatments included cognitive therapy (CT), as described by Beck et al. (1979); interpersonal psychotherapy (IPT), as described by Klerman et al. (1984); and imipramine hydrochloride (Tofranil). IPT assumes depression to result from problems in interpersonal relationships. Therapy occurs in individual sessions over a relatively brief 12- to 16-week period. Imipramine, a tricyclic antidepressant medication, was the drug of choice for depression treatment at the time of the study.

Participants consisted of 250 clients randomly assigned to conditions at one of three study sites throughout the country. To be included, participants had to meet research diagnostic criteria (Spitzer, Endicott, & Robins, 1978) for a major depressive disorder. In addition, they had to score 14 or higher on the HRSD. Clients were predominantly female (70%) and White (89%), and their ages ranged from 21 to 60 ($M = 35$ years), and 40% were married or cohabiting. The current depressive episode, on which the diagnosis was based, had to have lasted for at least the 2 weeks prior to beginning treatment. People were excluded from participating if they had a current substance abuse problem or serious medical problem, were experiencing a bipolar or panic disorder, or were receiving other treatment for depression. The stability of the pretreatment diagnosis was ensured by requiring participants to meet diagnostic criteria twice—first at prescreening and again 1 to 2 weeks later.

An extensive battery of assessment instruments was administered to document the client's status before treatment, during treatment, at treatment termination, and over a follow-up period. These included the HRSD, the BDI, the Dysfunctional Attitude Scale (A. N. Weissman, 1979), the Social Adjustment Scale (M. M. Weissman & Paykel, 1974), a global rating of adjustment, and the Endogenous scale from the Schedule for Affective Disorder and Schizophrenia–Change Version (Endicott, Cohen, Nee, Fleiss, & Sarantakos, 1981). Thus, interview, self-report, and rating-by-other measures were included.

The use of three different sites allowed a multitreatment, multisite, repeated-measures design with random assignment of participants to four conditions at each location. Treatment conditions included CT, IPT, imipramine, and placebo. The last two also involved a clinical management component to supervise the client's medication and provide "support, encouragement, and direct advice if necessary" (Watkins et al., 1993, p. 859). The placebo condition allowed a check on the adequacy of imipramine treatment and served as a control for the two psychotherapies. Twenty-eight therapists, all trained in the specific therapies, were carefully selected. Further mastery-based training after selection helped ensure competence in treatment implementation. Different therapists conducted each of the treatments. The same psychiatrists implemented both imipramine and placebo treatments in a double-blind fashion, however. As mentioned earlier, therapists followed treatment manuals specifically describing how to implement the approach. Treatment integrity was assessed using the Collaborative Study Psychotherapy Rating Scale (Hollon, Waskow, Evans, & Lowery, 1984). Ratings of audiotapes of the sessions distinguished the treatments, and the tapes were correctly identified as representing a particular treatment 95% of the time.

Treatment was carried out over a period of 16 weeks. The actual number of therapy sessions ranged from 16 to 20. The dropout rate ranged from 23% (IPT) to 40% (placebo), with *dropout* defined as leaving treatment with "less than 15 weeks and/or 12 sessions of treatment" (Elkin et al., 1989, p. 974), although differences across the conditions were not statistically significant. Assessments occurred before the start of treatment, at a mean of 4.2, 8.2, and 12.2 weeks during treatment, at termination, and at follow-up intervals of 6, 12, and 18 months. Results were analyzed using 3 (site) $\times$ 4 (treatment conditions) repeated-measures analyses of covariance (ANCOVAs) for each of the individual measures, with marital status being the single covariate. Marital status was statistically controlled for because it was found to be positively related to improvement and to differ across the groups, with fewer married participants in the CT condition.

The data analysis was extensive and is beyond the scope of this book. To summarize, clients receiving CT and IPT showed substantial improvements over the course of treatment, as did the medication-treated clients. Moreover, the effects of the different treatments were similar at termination (Watkins et al., 1993). Although statistically significant improvements supported the efficacy of the treatments, the clinical significance of the changes was somewhat disappointing. Fewer than half of the clients obtained scores in the "recovered" range on the BDI at termination, and all active treatments produced similar recovery data. At the 18-month follow-up assessment, few clients remained recovered (recurrence rates ranging from 33% to 50% across treatments), and no differences in recurrence were found across the treatment conditions (Shea et al., 1992). Other accumulating evidence supports the benefits of CT in preventing relapse, however, and there is some reason to expect its superiority to medications (Gorman, 1994).

The finding of at least comparable benefits for the psychological therapies and medication is of no small consequence. At the time of the NIMH study, antidepressant medication was widely regarded as the treatment of choice among behavioral health professionals, especially physicians. Perhaps not surprisingly, many researchers have taken another look at the NIMH data, not always agreeing with the original conclusions. In a reanalysis of the original data, Klein and Ross (1993) found pharmacotherapy to be more effective than the psychological therapies for the most severely depressed clients, a finding echoed by Elkin et al. (1995). Jacobson and Hollon (1996) called attention to site effects with some of the analyses, noting that Elkin et al. (1989) commented that CT had worked well with the most severe clients at one of the sites, producing improvements similar to those with imipramine. According to Jacobson and Hollon, differences across sites may have resulted from "allegiance" effects and differential competence of the therapists. They noted the reliable research finding of better effects for treatments implemented by people with sympathetic theoretical orientations.

Several studies have directly addressed the question of the relative superiority of pharmacotherapy versus cognitive therapy (e.g., Blackburn, Bishop, Glen, Whalley, & Christie, 1981; Hollon et al., 1992; Murphy, Simons, Wetzel, & Lustman, 1984; Rush, Beck, Kovacs, & Hollon, 1977). Hollon et al. (1992) examined the separate and joint effects of CT and imipramine for treating depression. Their evaluative question apparently was, "Can the results of earlier studies showing the superiority of cognitive therapy to imipramine be replicated when pharmacotherapy is adequately operationalized?" No hypothesis was stated explicitly.

Hollon et al. (1992) looked for correlations between type of treatment and depressive symptoms. They examined 107 depressed clients seeking treatment for depression at psychiatric facilities in a major Midwest city. To be included in the study, clients had to meet Research Diagnostic Criteria for major depressive disorder, score 20 or higher on the BDI, and score 14 or higher on the HRSD. Exclusion criteria included psychosis; bipolar disorder; organic brain syndrome; and generalized anxiety, panic, phobic, or obsessive–compulsive disorder if it was primary (i.e., more problematic than the depressive disorder). People with antisocial personality disorder, somatization disorder, diagnoses of alcoholism or drug abuse within the previous year, or who were actively suicidal were excluded, as were those who had medical conditions contraindicating imipramine use or a history of nonresponse to imipramine within the past 3 months. Finally, people with an IQ of less than 80 were excluded. In addition, clients had to pass a screening process that included an interview incorporating administration of the Schedule for Affective Disorders and Schizophrenia–Lifetime Version (SADS-L; Endicott & Spitzer, 1978) as well as numerous self-report instruments. Video-tapes of the interviews were reviewed, and the consistency of the diag-nosis was checked. High agreement between original diagnoses and those given by the reliability checkers (96%) was found. Only the clients meeting the RDC criteria both times were included in the study.

In addition to the BDI and HRSD, patients were assessed using the Raskin Depression Scale (RDS; Raskin, Schulterbrandt, Reatig, & McKeon, 1970), the Global Assessment Scale of the *DSM-III-R*, and the MMPI. The Depression scale of the MMPI was combined with the BDI, HRSD, and RDS to form a composite self-report measure of depression.

Of the participants ultimately assigned to treatment, 80% were fe-male. Participant age ranged from 18 to 62 (M = 32.6), and 32% were married or cohabiting. Forty-eight percent had at least some college coursework, with 20% not completing high school. Mean IQ was high average (M = 112.2) for this lower middle socioeconomic status sample. The evaluation was a multigroup, repeated-measures arrangement in which clients were initially assessed and then randomly assigned to one of four conditions: CT, pharmacotherapy without continuation, phar-macotherapy with continuation, or combined CT and pharmacother-apy. Additional assessments occurred after 6 weeks and at termination of treatment at 12 weeks. CT clients received a maximum of 20 individ-ual sessions over the 12-week study period. Therapists were four expe-rienced clinicians who were trained in CT by three of the study's au-thors. No mention is made of the use of a treatment manual, but at least two of the authors were trained in Beck's laboratory. Listening to audiotapes of sessions and rating them with scales specifically developed for this purpose served to assess treatment integrity. The measures showed clear differences between the CT and imipramine sessions and no differences between the CT-only and CT-plus-imipramine sessions, indicating satisfactory levels of treatment integrity.

The pharmacotherapy treatments (imipramine only or in combi-nation with CT) included weekly sessions like those of the NIMH col-laborative study. Medication management was discussed, and clinical management was administered in which supportive counseling, limited advice giving, and discussion of life functioning occurred. Separate 50-minute sessions were conducted for clients also receiving CT sessions specifically focusing on CT. Board-certified psychiatrists provided all pharmacotherapy. Imipramine dosages were adjusted individually to en-sure that all clients reached adequate clinical responsiveness and were monitored by checking blood levels throughout the study.

Results were presented in terms of all clients initially assigned to treatment and those who completed their respective treatment. A relatively high attrition rate (40%) occurred across treatment groups; noncompleters were defined as people failing to finish all 12 weeks of protocol treatment. Whether analyzed for all participants or completers only, all three treatments produced significant reductions in depressive symptomatology. Interestingly, more than 90% of the improvement occurred by the end of 6 weeks for the CT and pharmacotherapy groups. The combined group was the only group that continued to show gains from the 6-week point to the end of treatment. As for differences between CT-only and imipramine-only treatments, none was found at any assessment point, whether looking at completers only or all participants. Using more clinically relevant recovery criteria based on BDI and HRSD scores, approximately 60% of completing participants were classified as recovered on posttreatment measures; this finding did not differ across conditions. Finally, when treatments were compared in terms of the participants' initial severity of depression, results failed to support the superiority of CT or imipramine. Likewise, no differences were found in the two modes' efficacy with severely depressed clients. The authors concluded that CT and imipramine were comparably effective. Moreover, this equivalence prevailed regardless of initial severity level. Combining the treatments did not result in superior effects.

Effectiveness Studies

Do the benefits found in carefully conducted RCTs like the ones described in the previous section apply in the "real world?" Recall that Wade et al. (1998) demonstrated that an efficacious treatment for anxiety and panic generalizes to a clinical context. Similarly, Persons et al. (1999) compared the outcomes of clients treated with CT in a private practice with those obtained in RCT studies. Patients ($N = 45$) were treated for depression using either cognitive therapy alone ($n = 27$) or CT plus pharmacotherapy ($n = 18$). The overall evaluative question was "Do results of RCTs generalize to routine clinical practice?" The researchers' hypothesis was that they do, and they compared outcomes from their private practice clients with those of the TDCRP (Elkin et al., 1989, 1995; Shea et al., 1992; Watkins et al., 1993) and the RCT carried out by Hollon et al. (1992).

Persons et al.'s (1999) clients were adults seeking treatment for depression who scored 14 or higher on the BDI. Persons assigned psychiatric diagnoses to clients using *DSM-III-R* criteria after several initial sessions. As a group, the private practice clients were more heterogeneous than those of the RCTs. All the RCT clients met criteria for major depression, but only 71% of Persons et al.'s clients did so. Additional diagnoses for their clients included bipolar disorder (7%) and panic disorder (18%); moreover, 20% of the private practice clients had substance abuse problems (none of the RCT clients did), and 16% had major medical difficulties. Demographically, the two samples were similar. The mean age of Persons et al.'s clients was 32 years, 60% were female, and 87% were white; 11% had had previous psychiatric hospitalizations. Education levels were somewhat higher in Persons et al.'s clients (56% had completed college vs. 40% in the RCT). Mean pretreatment BDI scores were significantly lower ($M = 22.4$) for Persons's clients than for RCT clients ($M = 26.8$). Many of Persons et al.'s clients received concurrent treatment (22.2%), whereas none of the RCT clients did.

Persons used a case-formulation approach (Persons, 1989) and individual, weekly, 50-minute sessions. The approach was generally cognitive–behavioral, but the standardized order of implementation prescribed by Beck et al. (1979) was not followed. Instead, treatment was individually tailored for each client. Although sessions generally focused on depression, other clinical problems took priority in some sessions. Clients in the CT-plus-pharmacotherapy treatment received the latter from physicians in the community. The mean number of therapy sessions was 34.8 (compared with a maximum of 20 sessions for RCT clients).

Results were presented for all clients treated, completers and dropouts. Looking first at the CT-only group, Persons et al. (1999) reported significantly lower pretreatment mean BDI scores ($M = 21.7$) than reported by either the NIMH collaborative study (Elkin et al., 1989; $M = 27.0$) or by Hollon et al. (1992; $M = 30.1$). Posttreatment means (11.7 for Persons et al.'s, 13.4 for Elkin et al.'s, and 13.3 for Hollon et al.'s) are comparable across the studies, however, suggesting that treated clients reached comparable levels of depression whether participating in the more tightly proscribed treatment of the RCT studies or the more flexible treatment of clinical practice. Essentially the same results were reported for clients receiving CT-plus-pharmacological intervention. RCT clients were significantly lower than Persons' on pretreatment BDI scores ($M = 23.6$ vs. 32.0), but again, there were no differences between private practice and RCT clients on posttreatment scores (M = 12.0 vs. 12.9).

Using a more clinically meaningful outcome—the percentage of clients with posttreatment BDI scores in the nonclinical range—44% of the private practice group receiving only CT reached this level. This outcome compares closely with the 49% and 44% for the NIMH and Hollon et al. RCTs, respectively. Similar results were obtained for the clients receiving both CT and pharmacotherapy. Persons et al. concluded that their results provide useful effectiveness data to supplement the efficacy data from the RCTs. They suggested that studies such as theirs can serve a "linking" or bridging function between laboratory and applied contexts. Finding comparable results in the two settings should help answer clinicians' questions concerning the applicability of outcomes generated in the relative sterility of RCT studies.

The Wade et al. (1998) and Persons et al. (1999) studies are important because they demonstrate the generalizability of outcome data produced in well-controlled studies. These RCTs have attempted to show that carefully specified, reliably implemented treatments for anxiety disorders and depression can produce substantial benefit. The results of the efficacy and effectiveness studies provide a powerful demonstration of empirical support for anyone interested in arguing the worth of psychological therapy.

All the studies mentioned thus far involve a large number of clients. The independent practitioner wishing to evaluate treatments for depression and having few resources can benefit from exemplary work by C. Jensen (1994). Jensen used a combination of CT and IPT to treat depression in female clients of a community mental health center. C. Jensen took advantage of the fact that the waiting period for services at the clinic was approximately 10 weeks. Randomly assigning clients to waiting periods of 3, 4, or 5 weeks allowed the use of a multiple-baseline design to evaluate the effectiveness of the CT-plus-IPT combination. Figure 11.4 shows C. Jensen's results. C. Jensen's data add to the effectiveness literature supporting psychological therapy for depression. Furthermore, they provide useful information on the effects of combining two therapies known to be effective in their own right. It is of interest to know whether the combination works better than either CT or IPT by itself, and the present data do not enlighten us on this issue. Nonetheless, C. Jensen provided another example useful to practitioners wanting to examine treatment effectiveness within the limits of the resources typically available to them.

Figure 11.4

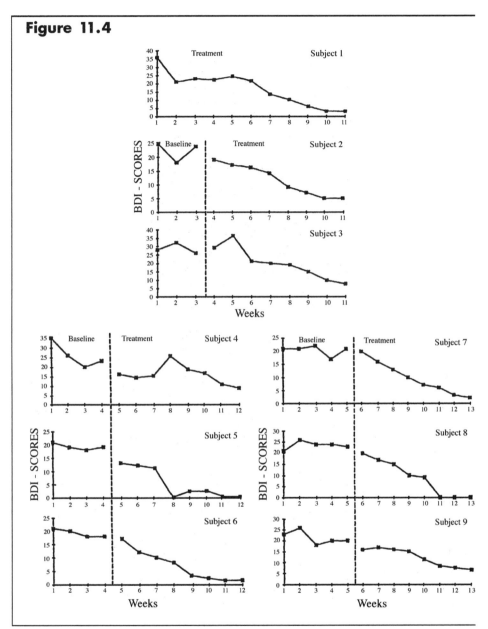

Results are from C. Jensen (1994). The data show changes in depression over 8 weeks of treatment. The data for the 9 clients treated are organized by increasing length of baseline, from no weeks (Subject 1) to 5 weeks (Subjects 7, 8, and 9). Comparing the baseline BDI scores, all of which are in the clinical range, with those at the end of treatment, all of which are now in the nonclinical range, shows the effectiveness of the approach. In addition, BDI scores are relatively stationary during baseline and show decreasing trends after treatment is introduced. From "Psychosocial Treatment of Depression in Women: Nine Single-Subject Evaluations," by C. Jensen, 1994, *Research on Social Work Practice, 4,* 277–279. Copyright 1994 by Sage. Reprinted with permission.

Empirical Support for Psychological Therapy for Couples' Distress

Controlled laboratory studies have shown psychological therapy to be helpful in treating dysfunctional relationships in couples (e.g., Baucom & Hoffman, 1986; Cordova & Jacobson, 1993; Pinsof & Wynne, 1995; Shadish, Ragsdale, Glaser, & Montgomery, 1995). Jacobson (Cordova & Jacobson, 1993) more recently referred to the field as integrative behavioral couple therapy (IBCT), known first as behavioral marital therapy (BMT) and then as behavioral couple therapy (BCT). Changes over the years reflect the observation that the approach developed for traditional heterosexual married couples is applicable to gay and lesbian couples as well. Furthermore, to be applicable to a higher percentage of couples, tactics directed at goals other than change, the nearly exclusive focus of earlier versions, were integrated into the approach. Although about two-thirds of couples can be helped with BCT, a significant minority do not appear to benefit from its focus on compromise and change. Recognizing that those couples might benefit from an approach focusing less on change and more on accepting the relationship for what it is and finding ways to live effectively within it, Jacobson, Christensen, and colleagues (Cordova & Jacobson, 1993; Cordova, Jacobson, & Christensen, 1998; Phelps & Jacobson, 1998) have been developing IBCT.

Efficacy Studies

A representative study of the efficacy of a behavioral approach to couples' distress is that of Hahlweg, Revenstorf, and Schindler (1984), who pursued the evaluative question of whether BMT leads to changes in communication and problem-solving skill. No specific hypotheses were advanced. The variables examined in the study were treatment (BMT), communication, and problem solving. Participants were middle-class German couples recruited through public service radio announcements (70%) or referred from behavioral health agencies or professionals in the community (30%). Inclusion criteria required a primary complaint of distress in the relationship other than a sexual dysfunction. Mean duration of distress was 3.9 years. Fifty-seven percent of the couples reported that they quarreled two to three times per week; 28% were satisfied with their sexual relationship. Mean age of the participants was 33.5. The mean duration of the marriages or cohabitation was 8.1 years, and 79% of the couples had at least one child.

Measures included separate interviews with each member of the couple and direct observations of the couples' problem-solving interactions from videotapes. The observations and interviews were conducted before and after treatment. Various communicative acts were scored from the videotapes, including verbal ("direct expression," "acceptance and agreement," "critique," "refusal,") and nonverbal ("positive," "neutral," "negative") categories.

The study design was a three-group, pretreatment–posttreatment comparison, with random assignment of couples to BMT or wait-list control conditions. The third group was a nondistressed couples comparison recruited through notices in a health facility and word of mouth. The nondistressed group consisted of 12 couples. The three groups did not differ statistically on any of the demographic variables. Quarreling and sexual dissatisfaction were higher in the couples assigned to BMT and wait-list groups, however. Of the 50 couples randomly assigned to treatment or wait-list groups, 29 and 14, respectively, were finally included in analyses. Technical difficulties with videotaping procedures eliminated the others. BMT couples participated in 15 weekly "conjoint or conjoint-group" (members of the couple participated together; Hahlweg et al., 1984, p. 555) sessions following pretesting. Wait-list couples remained untreated for a period of 3 to 4 months after the initial assessment.

Results were analyzed in a variety of ways and are summarized briefly here. Efficacy was determined primarily from posttest comparisons of BMT and wait-list groups on the directly observed verbal and nonverbal communicative acts using ANCOVA with the pretreatment score as the covariate. Significant differences favoring BMT couples were obtained on six of the eight categories compared. Only the "neutral (verbal) information" and "neutral (nonverbal)" categories failed to show differences. In addition, the clinical significance of the results was determined by comparing the posttest means of the BMT couples with those of the nondistressed group. The means of the two groups were comparable for all verbal categories, showing that treatment brought distressed couples to within normal ranges on measures of verbal communication. Despite high percentage increases in nonverbal communicative acts, however, the BMT couples did not reach the level of the nondistressed group on these behaviors.

Hahlweg et al. (1984) concluded that BMT was successful in "increasing the partner's self-disclosure, mutual understanding, and the generation of specific and positive problem solutions, while decreasing blaming, criticizing, and sidetracking" (p. 563) in conversations with each other. They also discussed the comparability of their findings with those of the BMT literature more generally. Notably, their results, which were based on directly observed interactions, were more positive than is typically the case with results that are based on self-report measures. The authors suggested that their results might be related to the fact that direct observation measures specifically assess the communicative behaviors actually focused on in therapy. Self-report measures may tap more global characteristics of the relationship that take longer to change. If so, these measures may be inferior to direct observations for monitoring ongoing progress in treatment.

Effectiveness Studies

In an interesting study, Jacobson et al. (1989) examined the generalizability of benefits of tightly controlled laboratory studies of BMT such as those of Hahlweg et al. (1984). Their aim was similar to that of the Wade et al. (1998) and Persons et al. (1996) studies in that they wanted to know what happens to the impact of efficacious treatments when moved from the laboratory to the clinical context. Unlike Wade et al. and Persons et al., however, Jacobson et al. compared efficacy with effectiveness in the same study.

Their evaluative question was essentially, "What happens when a structured, research-based approach to couple therapy is compared with a more flexible, individually tailored approach?" No hypothesis was stated. The variables related in the study included type of treatment and clinical outcome. Participants were 30 couples who sought marital therapy at a university psychology clinic. Apparently the only exclusion criterion was "significant physical violence" (p. 174) occurring in the relationship during the year immediately preceding treatment. The age of the couples ranged from 27 to 64, with a mean of 41, and the husbands and wives had means of 15.8 and 14.8 years of education, respectively. The couples had been married for a range of 6 months to 38 years, with a mean duration of 11.4 years.

Measures included the Marital Satisfaction Inventory (MSI; Snyder, 1981), the Dyadic Adjustment Scale (DAS; Spanier, 1976), and the direct-observation coding system used in Hahlweg et al. (1984). The MSI is a 280-item multidimensional self-report measure of marital functioning that yields scores on 11 different dimensions. One of these, global distress (GDS), assesses overall marital satisfaction. Additional scales scored for this study include affective communication, problem-solving communication, sexual functioning, financial conflict, and leisure activities and time together. The DAS is a self-report measure of marital adjustment. As with the MSI, it is completed separately by each spouse. Hahlweg et al.'s direct-observation measure was scored for the same variables mentioned above (e.g., direct expression, acceptance and agreement).

The evaluation design was a two-group, pretest–posttest arrangement with random assignment of couples to either (a) structured, inflexibly sequenced, researchlike treatment or (b) more fluid, individually tailored, clinical-like treatment. Assignment to treatment conditions occurred after pretesting. Structured treatment consisted of 20 sessions proceeding in a sequence that was invariant across couples. Treatment was modularized by designating specific sessions to cover particular topics, which included (a) behavior exchange [increase positives between spouses], (b) companionship enhancement [increase quality of shared leisure activities], (c) communication training [receptive listening and expressive communication skills], (d) problem-solving training [conflict resolution skills], (e) sexual enrichment [communicating about, initiating and refusing, dysfunctions], and (f) generalization and maintenance [preparation to continue the process after treatment]. Flexible treatment covered the same three initial sessions as the structured approach, but then became tailored to the requirements of the individual couples. Clinical teams developed treatment plans in supervision groups that also served to monitor their implementation. Supervision time was kept equal across both types of treatment. Twelve therapists were carefully trained to provide both types of treatment, with all seeing at least one couple in each condition. Flexible treatment was constrained only in that it had to fall within one of the six treatment modules described above (see a–f). Sequencing and time spent on each module were allowed to vary, as was the total number of treatment sessions for a couple.

Sessions were audiotaped as a check on the integrity of both forms of treatment and to ensure that they differed from one another. Trained viewers rated tapes on 11 items related to the different treatment modules. In addition, a check on the success with which the two groups distinguished themselves in terms of structure or flexibility also was conducted by comparing the content discussed on the tapes for three of the sessions. This content was prescribed in the structured form, but it was allowed to vary in the flexible version of treatment. Finally, therapists and spouses also filled out forms at the end of each session that asked what the therapists did in the session. Items on the forms also asked about the content of the modules presumably in the sessions. Comparisons of data from the two types of therapy showed significant differences in the content dealt with in the same session number, evidence that therapists were structured or flexible as they were supposed to be. In addition, the total number of sessions differed for the two approaches, as expected. For couples completing structured treatment, all were seen for 20 sessions, whereas flexibly treated couples ranged from 8 to 53 sessions, with an average of 22.

Assessments at posttreatment and 6 months later showed significantly increased marital satisfaction for couples in both conditions and no differences between them. Results were similar for the other self-report measures and for the direct-observation measure. That is, both approaches produced similar benefits. Results were maintained when assessed with the DAS at 6 months following treatment, although both groups showed significant decreases in satisfaction compared with immediate posttreatment scores. Using the measure of clinical significance described in chapter 9 (see Equation 9.3, p. 228), Jacobson et al. compared treatment approaches in terms of the percentage of couples recovered after therapy. With the DAS, 64% of couples in the structured condition and 63% of those in the flexible condition improved. Both conditions produced the same percentage of couples actually recovered (50%). Similar results were obtained with the GDS. A nonsignificant trend was found for flexibly treated couples to maintain gains better on the follow-up assessment.

The authors concluded that theirs was a conservative test of the benefits of individually tailored marital treatment because of the high degree of overlap in content of the structured and flexible approaches. They do not discuss the implications of their findings for their generalizability to the clinical setting.

Empirical Support for Psychological Therapy for Chronic Headache

A final example of an empirically supported psychological therapy comes from the treatment of headaches. Both psychological and pharmacological approaches to treating this problem can produce benefits (Gauthier, Ivers, & Carrier, 1996); moreover, as with depression and anxiety disorders, both efficacy and effectiveness literature are available.

Efficacy Studies

In one of the largest studies on the subject, Blanchard et al. (1985) reported the effects of relaxation treatment and two types of biofeedback on headaches. They asked, "What are the individual and combined effects of relaxation training and biofeedback on headaches?" No specific hypotheses were stipulated. The investigators looked for correlations between the type of treatment and headache symptoms. Participants were 250 people diagnosed with migraine headaches, tension headaches, or a combination of both. Criteria for the diagnoses were clearly defined and conformed to those of the Ad Hoc Committee on Classification of Headache (1962) and the information provided by Diamond and Dalessio (1978). Two independent diagnoses were made for each participant, the agreement of which was 80% or better. About one half of the clients were self-referred in response to publicity about treatment availability; the rest were referred by professionals or previously treated clients. The sample consisted of 94 people diagnosed with tension headaches, 72 diagnosed with migraines, and 84 diagnosed with both. Participants were predominantly female (74%) and ranged in age from 18 to 68 (M = 38.6 years); the group had suffered from problem headaches for a mean of 17.1 years.

Measures included a headache diary, in which participants rated their degree of headache four times each day (from none to intense). A mean daily headache rating was generated from a headache index created from the diary. In addition, researchers used the BDI, the State–Trait Anxiety Inventory, the Psychosomatic Symptom Checklist (Cox, Freundlich, & Meyer, 1975), the Rathus Assertiveness Scale (Rathus, 1973), the Social Readjustment Scale (Holmes & Rahe, 1967), and the MMPI.

The evaluation involved a between-groups comparison of improvement shown on the headache index. Using procedures outlined by Bernstein and Borkovec (1973), researchers examined relaxation training in 10 individual sessions over an 8-week period. Between sessions, clients were expected to practice at least 20 minutes each day. Tension headache sufferers for whom relaxation training was not successful (n = 32) received EMG biofeedback training, which involved 12 sessions of standardized training in which clients received auditory feedback to assist them in controlling tension in the frontal portion of their foreheads. Vascular headache sufferers (n = 39 across the migraine and combined migraine–tension group) for whom relaxation training was not successful received thermal feedback, which involved 12 sessions in which clients were trained to increase the temperature in their hands using visual and auditory feedback. In addition, they were provided a home thermal biofeedback device and asked to practice warming their hands daily, along with continuing their relaxation practice.

Results are presented in terms of headache index data calculated by comparing 4 weeks of baseline (i.e., pretreatment) data with 4 weeks of either posttreatment ($n = 140$) or last 2 weeks of treatment plus 2 weeks posttreatment ($n = 110$) data. Participants were classified as improved, slightly improved, or unimproved based on index rating reductions of 50% or more, 25 to 49%, and less than 25% respectively. The researchers present rather detailed findings by type of headache and treatment. A summary of the results shows that 35% of participants receiving only relaxation training improved. Of those receiving relaxation combined with biofeedback, 50% improved. Among the vascular headache sufferers, 23.8% of those receiving only relaxation training improved. When thermal feedback was added to relaxation, 52.2% of the participants could be classified as improved, showing a clear superiority for the combined approach to this type of problem. Among the tension headache sufferers, 56.5% showed improvement when the relaxation-only group was combined with relaxation-only failures who subsequently received biofeedback training. The groups were combined to have a group comparable with the vascular headache sufferers that also got relaxation and biofeedback. Blanchard et al. reported long-term maintenance of benefits to be high, noting that at least 83% of clients rated as improved at the end of treatment remained so 1 year later. The authors discussed more clinically meaningful improvement measures, such as "free of headaches entirely," but this is an unrealistic criterion considering its apparently low occurrence in the general population.

Blanchard et al. concluded that their improvement rates are probably conservative in that their clients all were treated according to rigidly prescribed protocols. Clients treated in clinical contexts should experience better outcomes because their therapists have the flexibility to vary the approach and to deal with other issues of importance to the client. Note that the presumably greater effectiveness of more flexible clinical approaches does not appear in the studies of Persons et al. (1999) and Jacobson et al. (1989). Furthermore, Blanchard et al. noted that the headache index appears to be conservative, on the basis of other findings that it underestimates change assessed by global ratings of improvement given by clients after treatment. They report that global ratings show about 35% more improvement than the headache index does.

More recently, Sartory, Müller, Metsch, and Pothmann (1998) compared psychological and pharmacological approaches with headache treatment. Their evaluative question was, "What are the comparative benefits of pharmacological and psychological therapies used to treat migraine headaches in children?" No specific hypotheses were presented. The variables were type of treatment and headache symptoms. Participants were 43 children (17 females and 26 males) ranging in age from 8 to 16 ($M = 11.3$ years) who had experienced migraine headaches for a mean of 4.6 years. They were recruited from a pediatric hospital and the general community. Inclusion criteria included a specific diagnosis consistent with International Headache Society (1988) guidelines, with a duration of at least 6 months, and at least two attacks within the previous month. Exclusion criteria included developmental or neurological disorders and headaches secondary to another condition.

Measures included a headache diary, from which frequency, duration, and intensity data were obtained. The researchers used 4-week baseline and posttreatment periods, as did Blanchard et al. (1985). In addition, they tracked use of analgesic medication and obtained mood ratings. Blood-volume pulse amplitude—measuring blood flow—was also obtained for children in the psychological treatment groups.

Treatment was of two major types: medication (metoprolol), and psychological (stress management, relaxation training, biofeedback). Medication was administered orally in a single daily dose. Children attended weekly sessions at the clinic for renewal of the prescription. Psychological treatment consisted of 10 individual hour-long sessions over a 6-week period, during which children received stress management training. In addition, half the children received biofeedback training and half received training in progressive relaxation. Biofeedback consisted of monitoring blood flow in the temporal artery of the more involved side of the head and feeding it back through a visual display consisting of a vertical beam whose width varied with the amount of blood flow in the artery. The child was instructed to narrow the beam and was praised for doing this successfully. Homework assignments were given between treatment sessions. Progressive relaxation consisted of tense-and-release training, moving through different parts of the body for five sessions. Cued relaxation then was introduced and followed by differential relaxation while standing and walking. Homework assignments were given between treatment sessions.

The researchers reported results for several measures, including the percentage of children who improved by at least 50% on a headache index that combined intensity and frequency of headaches. The data showed that 80%, 53.3%, and 41.7% of the children in the relaxation, biofeedback, and metoprolol groups improved, respectively. The treatments combined showed a "marginally significant" ($p < .06$) pretest–posttest change on a multivariate analysis of variance on frequency, duration, intensity, and analgesics taken. Blood-volume pulse amplitude was not significantly affected by treatment type, although there was a slight trend toward increased constriction by the biofeedback group. The authors concluded that stress management combined with relaxation training was significantly more effective than pharmacotherapy. Biofeedback results were not significantly different from results of the other two treatments.

Effectiveness Studies

In a study of the effectiveness of headache control procedures applied in clinical contexts, Allen and Shriver (1998) involved the parents of children with migraines. They examined the benefits of extending treatment into the home setting by having parents follow guidelines. Children ages 7 to 18 ($N = 27$) were randomly assigned to groups receiving biofeedback alone or biofeedback in combination with parents trained in pain management guidelines. Whereas both groups improved significantly on headache measures, children whose parents were given pain management guidelines showed significantly greater reductions in number of headaches and remained free of them at a higher percentage. Moreover, clinically significant improvements were greater for this group.

Griffiths and Martin (1996) showed the generalized effectiveness of a cognitive–behavioral approach to treating headaches in children. They randomly assigned 42 chronic headache sufferers ages 10–12 years to one of three treatments: clinic based, home based, or wait-list control. Clinic-treated children received an eight-session program, whereas those receiving home-based services received the first three sessions in the clinic and then worked at home with the assistance of treatment manuals. Headache diaries served as the principal assessment method, although medication use also was monitored along with anxiety, self-efficacy, coping, and depression. The authors reported both treatment approaches to be effective in reducing headaches, whereas the wait-list control children remained unchanged. They discussed their findings in terms of the greater cost effectiveness of the home-based approach.

Efficacy, Effectiveness, and Relationships Between the Studies

Distinguishing between efficacy studies (i.e., those conducted in laboratory contexts as RCTs) and effectiveness studies (i.e., those run in more normal clinical surroundings as less well-controlled efforts) is becoming the convention in psychology, and it is widely discussed in the literature (e.g., Clarke, 1995; Hoagwood, Hibbs, Brent, & Jensen, 1995; Jacobson & Christensen, 1996; Seligman, 1995). What is the relationship, if any, between the two types of evaluation? On the one hand, efficacy and effectiveness literature can be viewed as independent bodies of knowledge, minimally informing one another. Researchers can explore theoretically interesting relationships in well-controlled laboratory studies, communicate their findings to other researchers, and not worry much about real-world applications. At the same time, practitioners can pursue the development of clinically effective interventions without much concern for theoretical bases and in circumstances that do not permit high levels of experimental control. They can talk to one another about their findings, forward effectiveness information on to third-party payers, and not worry about verifying results in more tightly controlled studies. On the other hand, efficacy and effectiveness literatures can be viewed as interdependent and complementary. In this regard, asymmetrical or symmetrical perspectives are possible.

Asymmetrical Relationships

From an asymmetrical perspective, theory-based treatments found to be efficacious in the laboratory are transported to applied environments, where concern arises about how they are applied. The expectation is that a faithful replication occurs in the clinical setting. Findings of limited generalization are taken seriously, and explanations are framed in terms of variables not controlled or variables representing differences between research and clinical contexts.

Systematic desensitization, one of the best studied psychological therapies ever invented, offers a good example. Originally developed out of laboratory work on the origins of emotional responses in animals, Wolpe (1958) later described its application to phobic behavior in humans. Many RCTs have examined its efficacy in the years since (e.g., Paul, 1966; Trent & Fournet, 1987). Other examples come from Skinner's (1938) early research on the operant behavior of animals. His work led to applied behavior analysis, with the clear and direct application of laboratory principles of behavior to human problems (e.g., Fuller, 1949; Lindsley, 1960). More recently, basic research on the principles underlying stimulus equivalence has been shown to have implications for applied problems (Dougher, 1998; Hayes & Hayes, 1992).

Asymmetry also can work in the other direction. That is, researchers can scrutinize more closely the procedures generated in the field, described in case reports, and found in well-documented case studies. A good example of this is the discovery of eye movement desensitization reprocessing (EMDR; Shapiro, 1989). Shapiro initially described the procedure and presented data on its effectiveness in a clinical setting in which clients experienced emotional reactions to traumatic memories. Similar successes were reported by other clinicians (e.g., Marquis, 1991; Wolpe & Abrams, 1991). Researchers then began exploring the efficacy of EMDR in controlled laboratory studies (e.g., J. A. Jensen, 1994; Muris et al., 1998; Wilson, Becker, & Tinker, 1995). CT has traveled a similar trajectory. First developed by Beck (1961) out of his clinical observations and later formulated as a system of psychotherapy (Beck, 1976), the approach has been among the most extensively studied clinical interventions ever subjected to RCTs, as the studies described in this chapter demonstrate.

Symmetrical Relationships

From a symmetrical perspective, the work of basic researchers and applied scientists is complementary. Phenomena first observed and replicated in the laboratory are explored in applied contexts, and vice versa, often by the same investigators. Studies from this perspective include those of Hayes, Kohlenberg, and Hayes (1991) on the functions of language. Thoughts can derive functional control over other types of behavior because of their participation in equivalence classes, for example (Hayes, 1989). Thus, to understand how to change behavior, one might study variables controlling the formation and change of equivalence classes, which might be done best in the controlled conditions of a laboratory. The impetus for doing so, however, might come from observations of emotional responding in a clinical context. Findings in the laboratory can be examined for effectiveness in the clinic by the same researchers. They can then return to the laboratory to refine and explore further any lessons learned.

Not all observers see relationships between laboratory and applied settings as important, whether symmetrical or asymmetrical. Poling, Picker, Grossett, Hall-Johnson, and Holbrook (1981) documented a disconnection between the work of experimental and applied behavior analysts, for example, and asked whether anyone actually cared. Howard (1998) recently noted that in psychology, "little treatment development is actually based on established psychological principles" (p. 716). He is optimistic that this is changing, however, saying that the stage is now set for greater mutual influence and that the distinctions between applied and basic research are blurring. Some of the work on stimulus equivalence seems to be of this blurred type.

Silberschatz (Persons & Silberschatz, 1998) questioned the value of RCTs, such as those above, saying that the psychotherapy of experienced clinicians does not lend itself to RCT methodology. In this regard, he echoed Seligman (1995), who claimed that "the efficacy study is the wrong method for empirically validating psychotherapy as it is actually done, because it omits too many crucial elements of what is done in the field" (p. 966). He recommended surveying people actually going through therapy to see whether it is working for them. One can agree with Hollon (1996) that causal agency cannot be determined from satisfaction surveys. For this, there probably is no substitute for the RCT.

Testing efficacious procedures in applied contexts is a powerful strategy, whether the relationship between the laboratory and the real world is symmetrical or asymmetrical. Examples of both types of study are presented in this chapter to make a point about the nature of the efficacy–effectiveness connection. Efficacy and effectiveness can be seen as evaluative tactics on a continuum, representing the confidence one can have that the tactics demonstrate causal agency. At one extreme is the study that is so tightly controlled that Underwood's (1957) one basic principle of research design is followed (i.e., "the effects of the independent variables can be evaluated unambiguously"; p. 86). Carefully conducted RCTs are at this end of the continuum. At the other extreme are effectiveness studies of the type recommended by Seligman. In those studies, so many competing explanations exist for relationships between treatment and outcome variables that there is no hope of unambiguously interpreting the effects of treatment variables. It is reasonable to assume that more systematic information about a procedure's benefits comes from starting with effectiveness designs closer to the RCT end of the continuum.

One can envision a program of research that advances systematically along the efficacy–effectiveness continuum. Starting with tightly controlled RCTs, studies can loosen their controls gradually. Just moving to an applied context might be the first step because it shows the resilience of the procedure in a situation that is inherently less well controlled in a number of important aspects. Moving along the efficacy–effectiveness continuum can be seen as a sort of controlled loosening in which a good deal of overlap occurs in the early stages and diminishes as gradual variation occurs in independent and dependent variables, including client characteristics.

Minimal Criteria for Practice Evaluations and Effectiveness Studies

The recommendations in Exhibit 11.1 come as no surprise to the reader persevering to this point in the book. The exhibit summarizes obser-

Exhibit 11.1

Suggested Minimal Criteria for Practice Evaluations

- Ask an answerable evaluative question that specifies a relationship between variables.
- Ground the question in theory.
- State specific directional hypotheses.
- Identify the population represented by participants.
- Use high-quality measures known in the field, supplemented by local-purpose measures.
- Use multiple-assessment methods.
- Repeat assessments multiple times.
- Include integrity checks on the independent variable.
- Document change at different levels.
- Choose the evaluative design carefully, attending to both internal and external validity.
- Analyze data in ways appropriate to the question and the audience for the evaluation.
- State results clearly.
- Formulate and articulate conclusions consistent with the question and the results.
- Give the implications of your findings.

vations made throughout this book, beginning with the outcomes evaluation model. That model (see Figure 3.1) recommends beginning with an evaluative question, which should be answerable and should specify at least a general relationship between two or more variables. In the service provision world, these are some aspect of the practice and some outcomes that are expected to result from that aspect. Note that evaluative questions can and should be addressed to multiple components of a practice, not merely to direct services.

The evaluative questions should be elaborated into a specific hypothesis. A good evaluator makes clear what is expected at the outset and states those expectations in terms of directional relationships between variables that are examined in defined samples of participants. Directional hypotheses are essential to efficient practice evaluations. The variables related in the hypotheses must be measurable and specific. This can be determined by examining their specificity. Vaguely worded or general variables often imply unwarranted uniformity, leading to the lack of a clear understanding of what is being evaluated or what is found (Kiesler, 1971). The "Does medicine work?" question illustrates the problem. Further clarity is provided when the population (e.g., clients receiving services from ABC Management Consultants, residents of a small Midwestern town) in whom the relationship is to be studied is specified. By doing so, the evaluator alerts other professionals to the potential applicability of any findings to their situation.

Measures should be identified and carefully described. This goes for independent and dependent variables. High-quality evaluation includes integrity checks on the independent variable or procedure, permitting confidence that the procedure was implemented as described. More than one type of assessment method (e.g., interview, self-report, and direct observation) should be used, in keeping with the value of evaluating a practice from the multiple viewpoints of different stakeholders concerned with its outcome. As the effectiveness studies above illustrate, evaluation results are easiest to interpret when they are based on the same measures used in the efficacy studies preceding them. It is a good idea to include measures that are standard in the field for this reason. They can be supplemented with measures idiosyncratic to your situation and probably should be. This allows local conditions to be documented as well.

Especially important in evaluations of direct services are measures of different levels of change. Minimally, high-quality assessment of the attainment of ultimate goals (Rosen & Proctor, 1981) is needed. Where they exist, these should include measures well known in the professional community and used by others for similar evaluations. If a measure is developed specifically for a given practice situation, its adequacy in terms of criteria discussed in chapter 7 must be reported. In addition, measures addressing instrumental goals should be included. These should assess variables determined by theory to be relevant to accomplishing the ultimate outcomes. By including them the practitioner gains information as to whether change in certain mediating variables is actually needed for outcomes to be achieved. This information can be valuable in refining services and maintaining continuous quality improvement. Finally, measures of intermediate goals are informative and can lead to early changes in procedure if they indicate less-than-adequate implementation. Failing to keep appointments or to bring in homework are examples. Assessment of intermediate goal attainment can be useful, although it is not as critical as assessing instrumental goals. Whether intermediate goals are being met usually can be inferred from measures of progress on instrumental ones.

The evaluative design should be considered carefully, with attention to internal validity. One should not assume automatically that controlled arrangements cannot be implemented in service settings; even if multiple-group, between-case designs are not possible, few situations do not lend themselves to controlled, within-case evaluations of the type discussed in chapters 8 and 10. Whatever arrangement is used, however, it is important that it include repeated measurement—before treatment and at its termination. Ideally, it would include ongoing assessment of instrumental and intermediate goal attainment.

Plan an analysis that is appropriate to the evaluation question and the audience you are trying to reach. Consider the need for complicated statistics and the relatively more straightforward visual presentation of your findings. If you are a program evaluator in a large managed care organization, for example, population statistics are important. Your design needs to address the relevance of findings to an entire population served (or potentially served) by the organization. Small, statistically significant changes that might not reach clinical significance can be of considerable importance when multiplied over many lives.

In this regard, state your results in such a way that the answer to your evaluation question is obvious. Start by addressing your hypotheses and noting whether they are supported. Be aware of the assumptions of statistics used, and describe the probable impact of any methodological problems in your design and data. Be sure to provide data on the practical implications of your findings. This can be done in terms of measures of clinical significance as discussed in chapter 9 or as in the effectiveness studies above, which show percentages of treated clients who moved into "improved" or "normal" ranges on measures of ultimate goals. It also can be done by showing the social validity (Wolf, 1978) of the changes you produce. Do significant others in the client's environment think the change is useful?

Next, state the conclusions of your evaluation. Do this in a way that parallels your evaluative question and hypotheses. If you evaluated the effect of switching from monthly billing to time-of-service collections, for example, start your conclusions section with a clear statement of what you found. It may seem obvious, but evaluators too often get caught up in explaining some secondary finding or excusing some methodological difficulty before getting around to saying what was found. If you tested several hypotheses, present data bearing on them in the order in which you presented them in the introduction to your study. Keep your conclusions within the boundaries set by the nature of your design, analyses, and results. If you plan and carry out statistical tests, for example, you should set alpha levels ahead of time and evaluate findings against them. Avoid saying that results were "marginally significant" or "showed a trend toward significance" if they do not surpass your alpha levels. In this way, you sidestep the common error of interpreting nonsignificant results as though they were significant.

Finally, say something about the implications of your findings. It is acceptable to be a bit speculative here, so exercise your imagination a little. Let your audience in on just how your data might be useful to them. Pay particular attention to how future evaluations can be carried out more effectively. Let people know what you would do differently a second time around, and say why. Others have not thought as much about work in this area as you have. They do not think of implications that seem obvious to you.

Summary

This chapter presents examples of practice evaluations from several different problem areas. It focuses on data from direct services components because comprehensive practice evaluations, as described in the model presented in chapter 3, are not available. The ideal strategy outlined in this chapter involves a program of evaluation that advances along a continuum of controlled loosening of structure and increasing variation in independent and dependent variables as well as people served.

Supplemental Reading

Jacobson, N. S., Dobson, K. S., Truax, P. A., Addis, M. E., Koerner, K., Gollan, J. K., Gortner, E., & Prince, S. E. (1996). A component analysis of cognitive behavioral treatment for depression. *Journal of Consulting and Clinical Psychology, 64,* 295–304.

Nathan, P. E., & Gorman, J. M. (Eds.). (1998). *A guide to treatments that work.* New York: Oxford Press.

Nishith, P., Hearst, D. E., Mueser, K. T., & Foa, E. B. (1995). PTSD and major depression: Methodological and treatment considerations in a single case design. *Behavior Therapy, 26,* 319–335.

12 Ethical Issues in Outcomes Evaluation

O utcomes evaluation involves practitioners' examining what they do and how effectively they do it. If their "evaluating" behavior conforms with established principles of right and wrong, of what society deems as "good, right, and virtuous" (Neilson, Knott, & Carhart, 1950, p. 1592), we say it is moral or ethical. The subject of this chapter is the ethics of practice evaluation—the study of what is moral in evaluation. A system of moral principles would constitute a set of practice evaluation ethics. At present, no agreed-on set of such principles exists. Nor is it the purpose of this chapter to develop one. Instead, the intent is to challenge the reader to consider some of the important issues and moral dilemmas confronting practitioners when they seek information about their effectiveness.

The chapter starts by describing why people might behave unethically. It goes on to discuss ethical behavior in research involving human participants and explains why ethical principles that apply to human participants in research do not always apply to practice evaluation because the goals of the two enterprises are fundamentally different. The chapter then focuses on ethical concerns of special relevance to the evaluation of human services. Issues of particular concern when evaluation is done for sponsoring organizations or agencies are outlined. Finally, the chapter provides recommendations for the ethical conduct of practice evaluation.

Reasons for Unethical Research Practices

Lessons from the history of social sciences and medical research provide numerous reasons why skirting the bounds of ethical practice can tempt investigators. The most obvious reason is the avoidance of extra effort. Knowing and following a set of ethical strictures adds to the time and work necessary to conduct research. Moreover, ethical research requires more resources. For example, more participants might have to be screened if full disclosure of the details of a study in advance makes it harder to recruit participants, adding to the researcher's time and effort. If procedures are likely to have strong effects on participants, it might be necessary to have emergency measures available. Arranging appropriate professional backups in the event that a participant experiences unexpected emotional or physical reactions adds to research costs. Concern about such reactions can lead to restricting participation to people who are less likely to have them, increasing recruitment costs as the pool of available participants shrinks proportionately.

Garnering resources can be an additional incentive for cutting ethical corners in human participant research. Obtaining funding from government and private agencies is more likely when one has a track record of successfully conducted studies. The likelihood of being asked to sit on committees, editorial boards, and grant-review panels increases as one's record of published research grows. Doing significant research quickly and getting it published can be facilitated by overlooking ethical strictures normally imposed on behavioral science research. Although less common in the social and behavioral sciences than in medicine and biology, financial rewards for successful researchers can contribute to unethical practice as well. University-based investigators frequently pay their own summer salaries and portions of their academic-year salaries from research grant funds, for example.

Ethical Behavior in Research Involving Human Participants

To guard against some of the errors of previous researchers and protect against important incentives for behaving unethically, various organizations, agencies, and regulatory bodies have promulgated principles of ethical conduct for research involving human participants. The federal government considers such research to be any systematic study involving people for the purpose of producing generalizable knowledge (Sieber, 1992). This is a potentially quite inclusive definition, depending on what is meant by some of its terms. For example, "for the purpose of producing generalizable knowledge" implies that the intent of the investigator is critical. If it is to produce generalizable knowledge, research is involved; if not, the activity is something else. In other words two elements are critical: (a) the production of knowledge and (b) the intent for that knowledge to be generalizable. These criteria appear to eliminate administrative data-gathering activities of the customer satisfaction or student-evaluation-of-professor sort because they have a fairly circumscribed local purpose, not a broadly general one. Sieber (1992) discussed what comes under the heading of human research and is reviewed by institutional review boards (IRBs). She dismissed "administrative data gathering that has no scientific purpose" and "classroom demonstrations of research, done solely for pedagogical purposes" (p. 10). In her definition of human research, Sieber introduced the requirement that covered activities be scientific, allowing for the possibility that not all research with humans is scientific.

In chapter 1, I describe science as the behavior of people producing laws that explain the nature of particular phenomena; in other words, science is the production of generalizable information about phenomena by showing relationships among variables relevant to those phenomena. This might be a somewhat more useful definition than the federal government's (see Sieber, 1992) because it avoids divining the investigator's purpose, and it remedies the problem of how to categorize projects that start out as routinely administrative and become scientific. If broadly generalizable new information is necessary for a work to be called "scientific," it is unlikely that the same activity can be both routinely administrative and scientific. More about this is said later when differences between research and practice evaluation are encountered.

Ethical Principles of Research Involving Human Participants

In the United States, the National Commission for the Protection of Human Subjects in Biomedical and Behavioral Research has called attention to three ethical principles and six associated norms governing the conduct of scientific research (National Commission, 1978). Sieber (1992) listed the principles as follows:

1. *Beneficence:* maximizing good outcomes for science, humanity, and the individual research participants while avoiding or minimizing unnecessary risk, harm, or wrong.
2. *Respect:* protecting the autonomy of (autonomous) persons, with courtesy and respect for individuals as persons, including those who are not autonomous (e.g., infants, people with mental retardation, people with senility).

3. *Justice:* ensuring reasonable, nonexploitative, and carefully considered procedures and their fair administration; fair distribution of costs and benefits among persons and groups (i.e., those who bear the risks of research should be those who benefit from it).

The six norms are

1. that the research design be valid
2. that the researcher be competent
3. that risks and benefits be identified
4. that participants be selected who are appropriate for the overall purposes of the study
5. that voluntary informed consent be obtained
6. that participants be informed concerning whether they will be compensated for any harm that befalls them during the conduct of the study. (Seiber, 1992)

Organizations representing professional researchers (e.g., the American Educational Research Association, the American Evaluation Association) have published ethical principles of practice and research. For example, the code of ethics of the American Association for Public Opinion Research includes 10 principles and a set of standards covering minimal disclosure when disseminating research results. The American Psychological Association's (1992) ethical principles contain standards that generally apply to research activities occurring in the practice of psychology. These have been abstracted and included in Appendix B. Although they are specific to psychologists, a cursory glance shows their relevance to other professions as well. Principles 6.06 through 6.19 are specific to research with humans.

Informed Consent

Included in the APA's standards and consistent with the norms of the National Commission (1978) is the requirement that researchers obtain the voluntary informed consent of participants. *Voluntary* means that the person agrees to participate freely, without coercion, threats, or undue inducement. *Informed* means that the participant has been given information in writing concerning

- the purposes of the research
- the expected duration of the participant's involvement
- the procedures to be followed

- any foreseeable risks or discomforts the participant might experience
- any benefits that might accrue to the participant or others
- alternative procedures or courses of treatment, including non-participation in the research
- how confidentiality or anonymity is preserved and any limits to both
- whether compensation or treatment for unforeseen harms is available
- whom to contact for answers to questions about the research and about rights participants have and whom to contact in case harm is experienced
- the fact that participation is voluntary, with no penalty or loss of benefits for refusing
- the participant's right to terminate involvement at any time
- the participant's right to receive a copy of the signed consent form.

Additional elements of informed consent may be included, depending on whether the research is medical or behavioral and social. For example, participants have a right to know whether a pharmaceutical company is funding research on the effects of a particular drug.

Psychologists have studied whether the use of consent procedures leads to different outcomes in research involving human subjects. Singer (1978) provided one group of survey respondents with a consent statement to sign that contained detailed information about the research. Another group, randomly selected, was not given this information. No significant differences were found in survey completions or the quality of responses that were attributable to the consent process. More recently, Singer, Von Thurn, and Miller (1995) published a meta-analysis of empirical survey research on the effect of ensuring confidentiality for research participants. They found that when confidentiality was guaranteed the quality of responses was somewhat higher when surveyors asked about highly sensitive issues. Otherwise, guarantees of confidentiality appear to have little effect on whether people agree to participate or how they respond when they do.

Loftus and Fries (1979) noted that people are highly suggestible and that fully informing them can lead them to believe they have experienced things that have not occurred. They describe the use of placebo medications in drug studies, noting that participants in one such study, after receiving informed consent and experiencing the placebo, reported unlikely physiological reactions. They concluded that inform-ing participants of possible adverse reactions has the potential to pro-duce these reactions, given the well-documented effects of suggestion. In the extreme, Loftus and Fries warned that heart attacks can be brought on by the informed consent process—the stress of the process can lead to coronary spasms and, ultimately, the attack itself. If explicit suggestions in informed consent procedures lead to such stress, the implications of conscientiously providing complete information can be serious.

Deception

Lying to participants or deceiving them has a long history in social sciences research and is used extensively (Adair, Dushenko, & Lindsay, 1985). Providing less than full and complete disclosure of the nature of a study during the informed consent process is one end of a continuum of deceit that all participants in research unavoidably experience. The other end consists of deliberate attempts to mislead people into think-ing the study is about something other than what it is. Although the literature treats deception as a discrete concept that either occurs or does not occur in a particular project, it seems more intellectually hon-est to admit that deception occurs in varying degrees in all studies. The issue is more about whether deception occurs in amounts no greater than necessary for the research to be conducted effectively. Nonethe-less, because a deliberate attempt to mislead participants is commonly what is meant by deception, our discussion focuses on this end of the deception continuum.

Suppose that you are interested in studying the sexual behavior of men visiting prostitutes. To get the most accurate information possible, it is necessary to use direct observation. If you inform prostitutes' cus-tomers ahead of time that you will be observing their behavior from a closet, will the behavior of the customers or prostitutes be affected? If knowledge of being observed alters their behavior in unknown ways, the external validity of the study's findings are compromised because the behavior of the participants cannot be said to characterize the usual behavior of prostitutes and their customers when unobserved. Similarly, imagine you are interested in studying the activities of members of a therapy group. If you are open about your intentions and seek permis-sion of group members to attend their meetings for this purpose, how can you be sure that they will behave normally when you are there?

Walster (1965), in a study of the effects of self-esteem on heterosocial attraction, gave personality tests to a group of female participants. She then provided contrived reports to some of the women stating that they were not very creative and lacked imagination. This information was designed to lower the self-esteem of the participant. A male confederate of the experimenter posing as another participant in the study struck up conversations with the women and expressed interest in them. The women's attraction to the male was assessed; it was expected to differ depending on whether their own self-esteem had been enhanced or lowered by the earlier manipulation. After the experiment the women were debriefed, told of the male's true purpose, and informed that he was not especially interested in them. Could the women have experienced psychological harm as a result of the experience? Although we do not know for sure, on the face of it, the answer seems to be yes.

Walster, Bersheid, Abrahams, and Aronson (1967) addressed the effectiveness of debriefing procedures in a subsequent study. After giving personality tests to participants, the researchers provided false feedback, telling some participants that they had excellent social skills and others that their skills were poor. After a debriefing, the participants were assessed once more to determine whether the debriefing had been effective. The participants given positive feedback continued to rate themselves more highly than those given negative feedback. Debriefing therefore may not be a completely effective antidote to the effects of deception.

These examples of the use of deception are just a few of the hundreds available in the social science literature (Adair et al., 1985). Indeed, until recently its use was so common it appears to have affected the behavior of average bystanders to the detriment of others. For example, when a student was shot on the campus of the University of Washington in 1973, many of the bystanders were reported not to have helped because they thought the shooting was part of some social science research and had been staged (Warwick, 1982). The use of deceptive tactics is still prevalent, despite the existence of IRBs and other safeguards of human research participants (Sieber, Iannuzzo, & Rodriquez, 1995).

Given the documented negative effects of deception, is there any justification for continuing to permit it in social sciences research? Covert observational research may not be as ethically discomfiting as deliberately deceptive research for most researchers. Indeed, observation of public behavior in which the participants cannot be individually identified is not even required to be submitted to IRBs for approval unless it places participants at risk for civil or criminal liability or deals with illegal behavior, drug use, alcohol use, or explicit sexual behavior. Nonetheless, some researchers believe even covert observational research to be unethical and think it should be prohibited. The American Anthropological Association code of ethics condemns it, pointing to its impracticality and undesirability (see Neuman, 1997).

Sieber (1992) identified four justifications for the use of deception:

1. to achieve stimulus control or random assignment of participants.
2. to study responses to low-frequency events.
3. to obtain valid data without serious risk to participants. For example, in research on conflict, one may use confederates who will not escalate the conflict beyond the level needed for the purposes of the research.
4. to obtain information that would otherwise be unobtainable because of participants' defensiveness, embarrassment, shame, or fear of reprisal (p. 64).

Sieber's justifications are methodological; an alternative approach would be to determine whether the same research objective can be obtained with less deception. Sieber (1992) also identified three alternatives to obviously deceptive research. The first is to use simulated situations in which the participant is asked to play a role. For example, in Zimbardo's (1972, 1973) prison study, college student participants were instructed to act as though they were prisoners or guards. Having the prisoners picked up ("arrested") with Palo Alto police vehicles and booked at the jail enhanced the realism of the scenarios.

The second alternative is to use participant observation, in which members of a group serve as data takers. Research with families (e.g., Jacob, Tennenbaum, Bargiel, & Seilhamer, 1995) is a good example. Parents can be asked to keep track of certain behaviors of children or of each other, or even of themselves. Presumably the parents' data are less susceptible to the reactive effects of being observed than are the data of nonparticipant observers sent in by researchers. Sieber's third alternative involves asking participants to consent to the researchers' withholding some of the details until after the study is completed. In other words, they waive their right to be informed. One of the withheld details can be the fact that they are deceived.

Practice evaluators often find themselves confronted with some level of deception in attempts to obtain information about the effects of their interventions. Participant observers can certainly be used in working with families, but parents' objectivity can be less than optimal, necessitating other ways of collecting data. Clever alternatives to participant observation have included the use of tape recorders in various locations around the house. Jacob, Tennenbaum, Seilhamer, Bargiel, and Sharon (1994) examined the reactivity of direct observation of family interactions by recording the dinner conversations of families under conditions varying in levels of obtrusiveness. In one condition, a tape recorder was placed in the dining area of the home, and the family was instructed to activate it immediately at the start of the evening meal. This was thought to be the most obtrusive form of observation, the one likely to be associated with the most reactivity. In a less obtrusive condition, tape recorders placed in suitcaselike containers were located around the home, with one remaining in the dining area. Families were led to believe that the recorders would be activated by timers at random times throughout the day. In reality, the only active tape recorder was in the dining area. It was programmed to be active for the same hour each day. Despite rather extensive analyses, Jacob et al. could find little reactivity. On concluding their study, they thoroughly debriefed families about the deception and explained why it was necessary. In addition, families were permitted to listen to the tapes and delete any objectionable material. The researchers reported that none of the families exercised this option.

Other examples of deception in the pursuit of accurate evaluative data include telling clients in advance that "naturalistic" assessment procedures "might" be used and obtaining their consent. Sieber (1992) referred to this as "consent to deception" (p. 67). For example, clients undergoing training in assertion might be telephoned by a research assistant posing as a salesperson or recruiter of volunteers and exposed to a series of progressively more demanding requests. The purpose is to see whether the client's likelihood of refusing increases as treatment progresses. In a laboratory study of the effects of role-playing, Higgins, Frisch, and Smith (1983) used a confederate who engaged study participants in conversation while waiting for the start of an experiment. The confederate asked to borrow class notes from the participant. The requests were designed to be progressively more unreasonable. Participants informed in advance that the confederate was not a real participant and that their assertiveness was being assessed behaved more assertively than other participants (i.e., they were more likely to refuse the most unreasonable requests).

The implications of such research are clear. It appears that informing clients about the purposes of assessment can result in changes in the target behavior. Of course, it might result in less target behavior if the behavior is negative. The use of deception in such cases is ethically defensible if clients are forewarned and fully debriefed following treatment termination. After all, ethical practice requires evaluating its effectiveness, and the intent of the practitioner is to collect data of the highest quality in order to evaluate that effectiveness.

Another alternative to deception involves using different assessment methods. In evaluating family interaction, for example, one can ask family members to report how they relate to one another rather than going into the home to observe it directly. Unfortunately, self-report measures are affected by their own reactivity, and it is well known that respondents "present" themselves in ways that can differ substantially from reality. An interesting example comes from research on schoolyard bullying by Pepler and associates (Craig & Pepler, 1997; Pepler & Craig, 1995; Pepler, Craig, Ziegler, & Charach, 1994). They used covert videotaping and wireless microphones to study aggressive behavior in school-age children. They also surveyed bullying using self-report measures with the children. Their measures revealed the behavior to occur equally among boys and girls, although boys were statistically more likely to admit it on the surveys. Resorting to less privacy-invading assessment methods to avoid ethical issues with covert observation therefore may not be a satisfactory substitute. Perhaps the best compromise is the "consent to concealment" option suggested by Sieber (1992). For school-age children, informed consent comes from a parent or guardian.

Debriefing

Telling a person the purposes of research and its true nature after he or she has taken part in it is referred to as *debriefing*. Debriefing also includes, at a minimum, telling the person how his or her reactions are typical. The purpose of debriefing is to minimize any harm that might accrue to people from involvement in the particular research. According to Kazdin (1998), debriefing should occur "if there is any deception in the experiment or if crucial information is withheld" (p. 420). Given the argument that all research involves some level of deception, this would require debriefing in every case. The ethical standards of the APA suspend this requirement in cases where "scientific or humane values justify delaying or withholding this information" (APA, 1992, p. 1609). Effective debriefing returns the participant to at least the same level of psychological functioning as before the study began.

The importance of debriefing might be proportional to the risk of harm resulting from taking part in the study. For example, if participants are told as part of a study that they are unimaginative (Walster, 1965) or that they might have "tendencies toward mental illness or an early grave" (Kazdin, 1998, p. 421), it is important that they are disabused of this as quickly and effectively as possible after the study ends. Indeed, it may be a good practice to follow up several times over some period after the study to be sure there are no lingering effects. This form of distributed, or multicontact, debriefing is particularly important when clinical participants are involved in research study, especially if there is any possibility their condition will get worse during their course of involvement.

The purpose of debriefing is to minimize harm that might result from taking part in research. Kazdin (1980) alerted us to times when debriefing can bring its own harms, however. He gives an excellent personal example involving data collection for his master's thesis. The study examined whether self-perceived competence is related to altruism (Kazdin & Bryan, 1971). Contrived performance feedback (e.g., that their performance was "fair" or that it was "very good") was given to participants after they completed various experimental tasks. They were then asked to donate blood to a civic blood drive. Participants given feedback that they were "very good" (i.e., competent) were more likely to donate. One of the women participants became upset, crying hysterically when told her performance had been competent; she reported later that she had a long history of criticism and that no one ever told her she did things well. She was reassured to find she could do something competently. Kazdin reported that she then asked for reassurance that the report of her performance was accurate. Because the reports had been assigned randomly, independent of actual performance on the tasks, there was no way he could assure her of their accuracy. He decided to continue the deception and told her that the reports were accurate and that her "design was original and very well done" (p. 392; her experimental task was to produce an aesthetic design). This seems to be an instance where humane values justified withholding accurate information about the study.

Other examples of problems actually created by the debriefing process itself include the jading of public perceptions, as illustrated by the University of Washington shooting mentioned above. Telling participants that they have been deceived can lead to a general distrust of social sciences research and reluctance to believe even the debrief. As Kazdin (1980) noted, participants can become so distrustful that they think the debriefing is actually a continuation of the study itself. The potential difficulties posed by debriefing cannot be avoided by avoiding the process, however. What if participants in helping or altruism studies were among those who did not stop to help the "victim?" If they were not subsequently told about the nature of the study, they might form the impression that they are not particularly helpful or caring people. Telling them it was only a study might possibly mitigate such an impression. Korchin and Cowan (1982) distinguished between deceptive debriefing and inflicted insight, noting that deceptive research arrangements often present a dilemma of choosing between them. In *deceptive debriefing,* incomplete disclosure is used to protect participants from the harmful effects that full disclosure might bring, as in the example of Kazdin's master's thesis. In *inflicted insight,* participants' flaws are highlighted for them by giving them insights they did not seek; indeed, until the research occurred they may have been successful at minimizing these flaws. Clearly, debriefing study participants is a complex process that requires careful thought and execution. If the goal is to leave participants no worse off than when they entered the research, care is required. As Kazdin suggested, the debriefing process itself should be evaluated.

Some researchers (e.g., Baumrind, 1985; Ortmann & Hertwig, 1997) have argued that the way to avoid dilemmas associated with debriefing requirements is to stop doing research that involves deception, however benign. That approach effectively would mean abandoning nearly all research, however, because so much of it involves some element of deception. A more proactive stance is to conduct research on the debriefing process itself. Variables of interest include the contents of the debrief, whether the participants' reactions were normalized for them, whether the debrief is distributed (consists of multiple contacts with the debriefer) or single contact, the timing (e.g., immediate vs. delayed) of the debrief, characteristics of the person conducting the debrief, and the interaction between these variables and characteristics of the participant. For example, gender- or race-matched debriefer–participant pairings might produce different effects than mismatched pairings. Fortunately, examples of research on debriefing already are beginning to appear in the literature (e.g., Soliday & Stanton, 1995; K. M. Taylor & Shepperd, 1996).

Privacy, Anonymity, and Confidentiality

Research involving humans inevitably invades their privacy. Sieber (1992) provided an excellent discussion of privacy in terms of personal boundaries. Crossing those boundaries can involve more than obtaining sensitive, private information from someone. Sieber noted that privacy also is invaded when a person is exposed to things that he or she normally avoids. For example, presenting pornographic material to someone who normally takes pains not to come into contact with it is invading the person's privacy. Depriving people of information to which they would normally have access also can be considered an invasion of privacy, especially when it prevents them from making fully informed decisions. In addition, actions that lead to reduced personal autonomy can be considered invasions of privacy, as when a manager finds out from a researcher studying company morale that a particular employee is considering quitting and decides to beat him to it by firing him first. From Sieber's analysis, a test of privacy invasion would seem to involve asking the following question: To what extent has a person revealed information she or he normally would not have, obtained information generally avoided, been deprived of information required to make important decisions, or experienced reduced personal autonomy? Note that it is not a question of whether a person's privacy is invaded by involvement in research. The issue is rather how much it has been, because all research crosses boundaries in one or more of these ways.

When the boundary crossed involves information not normally shared, issues of anonymity and confidentiality become important. Sometimes privacy is invaded without prior consent, as in well-known observations of the sexual behavior of gay men in public restrooms (Humphreys, 1975) or of men urinating in public restrooms (Middlemist, Knowles, & Matter, 1976). Other examples include tapping telephone lines and eavesdropping on conversations in restaurants or on public transportation. Geller, Russ, and Altomari (1986) observed alcohol drinking of 243 patrons of drinking establishments in a small college town without their knowledge. Likewise, Gaul, Craighead, and Mahoney (1975) and Hill and McCutcheon (1975) observed the eating habits of people who were obese. One can legitimately argue that some of these examples cross the line from ethical to unethical, especially those in which the people observed might reasonably have presumed that they were acting privately (e.g., urinating or having sex in public restrooms). The ethical researcher should respect the privacy rights of participants, invading them only to the extent necessary for the research to be accomplished and doing so with safeguards to protect the identity of the people from whom information is obtained.

Anonymity generally is accorded research participants in one of two ways. First, at the point of data collection, participants can be asked not to reveal their names. Second, if names are required initially to facilitate the coordination of data from multiple measures, they can be replaced later with unique identification codes. The list of names can then be destroyed or kept by the researcher under lock and key. There are limits to the assurance of anonymity, of course. For instance, in longitudinal research it is necessary to keep track of people so that they can be contacted at repeated intervals. Moreover, some publicly available information is not anonymous, such as the amount paid for real estate or, in certain cities, the size of one's house.

Confidentiality means that the researcher does not divulge information obtained from participants to others without permission. If the information is released, it is done anonymously (i.e., without names attached to it) and in an aggregated form so that identifying a specific person's data would not be possible. When information obtained in case studies is revealed, elaborate care is taken to ensure that it cannot be linked to the individual or organization providing it, usually by changing key identifying details, such as the city in which the person or organization is located. Any information not necessary for understanding the research can be changed to protect the participants' identity.

Researchers can provide anonymity or confidentiality, or both. Of the two, anonymity appears to offer the greatest protection to participants because even if information is divulged, it cannot be linked specifically to individual participants. In some research, participants are not assured anonymity, but information obtained from them is kept confidential. This arrangement frequently occurs in public health research (e.g., HIV testing) and occurs when the researcher has a continuing need to be able to identify participants' specific data or when participants want to be credited in some way for involvement or to be notified of the results. In many cases, however, there is no need to match names with specific data. Case studies are good examples of studies that provide anonymity but not confidentiality. The best protection for individual privacy comes from instituting procedures to ensure both anonymity and confidentiality.

In reality, there is only so much privacy protection researchers can offer participants. When it comes to researcher–participant relationships, communication is not "privileged," as in other professional relationships (e.g., those between clients and their therapist or lawyer), and attorneys and legislatures can subpoena records. However, some courts have ruled in favor of investigators who refuse to comply, holding that communications with participants are similar to those between informants and journalists and therefore are deserving of protection (Culliton, 1976). Nevertheless, failure to turn over subpoenaed documents because of adherence to higher moral or ethical principles can run afoul of the law and result in time spent in jail. Neuman (1997) cited the case of a doctoral student in sociology at Washington State University who spent 16 weeks in jail for refusing to reveal confidential information obtained from research participants.

Recent federal legislation permits researchers to refuse to disclose confidential information concerning research participants. Apparently the researcher cannot be compelled to provide the names of people involved in a study as long as the researcher has obtained a certificate of confidentiality from the U.S. Department of Health and Human Services (DHHS; see the Public Health Service Act, 1970). Certificates can be obtained for investigations in which the research objectives cannot be achieved without assuring confidentiality, and they protect data even for studies receiving no financial support from the government. Additional information is available from the Office for Protection from Research Risks, National Institutes of Health in Bethesda, MD.

In cases where law and ethics collide, the investigator has to determine the reasonable course to take. For instance, when a participant discloses in the conduct of a study that he or she is likely to commit an act of bodily harm to someone, the researcher may have a duty to warn the potential victim. Psychotherapy practitioners have no option in such situations because the law requires the warning (*Tarasoff v. Board of Regents of the University of California,* 1976). Moreover, the ethical standards of the APA require that psychologists disclose confidential information without the consent of the client "to protect the client or others from harm" (APA, 1992, p. 1606). The duty to warn emerged from a tragic case in which a psychotherapy client confessed to his therapist his intention to murder his girlfriend. Although the therapist wanted to warn the victim, his supervisor intervened, warning of the client's right to confidentiality. When the client carried through on his threat, the victim's family sued the University of California, resulting in the well-known *Tarasoff* decision. Although the *Tarasoff* decision is specific to therapist–client communications, its logic clearly applies to researcher–participant communications as well. Recent research in areas such as domestic violence, AIDS, and child sexual abuse has generated additional concerns about the duty to warn and the limits of confidentiality between research investigators and their participants (C. C. Peterson & Siddle, 1995). The issues are complex and should be fully understood before embarking on research involving guarantees of confidentiality to participants.

Minimizing Harm

The principle of beneficence of the National Commission (1978) requires that unnecessary risk, harm, or wrong to participants be minimized in conducting research. Among the most important harms are legal, physical, and psychological damage.

Legal Harm

Suppose a study asks people their opinions about certain forms of illegal behavior and whether they have ever engaged in specific illegal behaviors themselves. Or suppose a researcher interested in cults joins one to become a participant observer. In the course of involvement in cult activities, the researcher becomes aware of sexual behavior between adult members and some of the children. Divulging this information to authorities puts the research participants at harm of legal reprisal. Finally, suppose in the course of a field study of the behavior of subway riders an investigator observes a robbery. The robber is a participant (albeit unwittingly) in the study, and identifying him to the police definitely involves legal harm.

These examples involve different levels of responsibility by the researcher. What has been promised potential participants as a condition of their involvement? In surveys of people about illegal behavior, it is likely that potential volunteers are told explicitly that their responses will be kept confidential. As noted earlier, coding schemes that make it impossible for anyone to identify who gave a particular response protect participants as well as researchers (from possible subpoenas) in this type of research. The would-be cultist who observes child sexual abuse is on shakier grounds, however. Child abuse must be reported in all 50 states, by researchers as well as by other professionals whose communications with clients are normally privileged. Investigators contemplating research where activities requiring mandatory reporting, such as child abuse, might come to light should inform potential participants of legal requirements to report such information to authorities. Finally, observing a robbery on a subway presents almost no moral or ethical conflicts for investigators, because observations of activities in public places are not governed by confidentiality requirements (although one would want to maintain anonymity of the participants). Lest you think this a straightforward example, however, in which reporting and serving as a witness would be an easy choice, consider the principle of beneficence again. Does stepping up as a witness maximize good outcomes for science and humanity? Suppose the victim was not hurt and the amount stolen was $25. Would this warrant reporting when possible negative societal reaction to researcher snooping might lead to tightened regulations on social sciences research?

Physical Harm

Physical harms that might potentially befall those involved in research also must be minimized. To illustrate, research on psychologists' treatment of panic might involve panic provocation procedures (e.g., Hofmann, Bufka, & Barlow, 1999), which could exacerbate cardiac problems. The use of some novel apparatus might involve the risk of malfunction, with potential injury to the user or those nearby. Zimbardo (1972, 1973) terminated his prison experiments early when he became concerned that the "guards" might inflict physical harm on the "inmates." The researcher has a duty to inform participants of the possibility of physical harm and then to watch carefully to protect them from it, including premature termination of the study if danger is imminent.

Psychological Harm

Psychological or emotional harm can be the most difficult to protect against. Hence, researchers need special sensitivities here. Embarrassment, anxiety, confusion, and discomfort are some of the psychological reactions people involved in social sciences research might experience. Ethical and moral strictures require investigators to minimize these unpleasant reactions to the extent consistent with conducting scientifically valid research. Being aware of the possibility of such reactions is an important first step in minimizing them. For example, suppose you were interested in the development of altruism in children. You decide to study bystander intervention among children on elementary school playgrounds. You arrange a series of staged events, including a child spending the entire recess sitting by herself staring into space, two children arguing loudly with each other, a child throwing litter on the ground, two children physically fighting, and a child lying on the ground moaning. You note reactions of bystander children to each of these events and later give a "debriefing" presentation at a meeting of the entire student body in the school's auditorium. Some children in the audience remember observing the scenes on the playground and doing nothing about them. What if they felt guilty at the time, and now feel even worse as they are reminded of their earlier inaction? The sensitive researcher takes steps to mitigate such reactions. Consulting with peers and others already familiar with the research topic of interest can help sensitize the researcher to potential harms. Informed consent, together with careful debriefings that are evaluated for effectiveness, are essential to reducing psychological and emotional harm to research participants.

Protection of Human Participants Through IRBs

Because of concerns over abuses, the U.S. government requires universities and other organizations receiving DHHS funding to develop procedures to provide for the review of all research involving human participants, whether the research receives direct DHHS funding or not. Federal regulations (Federal Policy for the Protection of Human Subjects, 1981) require universities and research organizations to establish IRBs, which are committees of five or more people to review proposals for research involving human participants. Research is reviewed regardless of whether it receives funds from extramural sources. Investigators contemplating research are advised to familiarize themselves with the IRB process at their institution in advance of planning their study. The person serving as the IRB administrator is the best source of relevant information and knows about such important matters as the format for the research protocol to be submitted and the deadlines and meeting dates of the board. A comprehensive discussion of IRBs and the protections they afford research participants is beyond the scope of this book. Readers desiring more information are encouraged to consult Sieber (1992) and the bimonthly journal *IRB: A Review of Human Subjects Research*.

Do Principles of Research Ethics Apply to Outcomes Evaluation?

Up until now, this chapter has emphasized ethics in research projects. Because this is a book about practice evaluation, however, you might be wondering how much of this discussion is relevant. To answer this, consider Barlow, Hayes, and Nelson's (1984) distinctions between treatment research and treatment evaluation. Treatment and research can be placed on a continuum of information-gathering activities; at one extreme is pure treatment; at the other, pure research. Pure treatment aims to improve client outcomes and has no interest in advancing science; pure research aims to further science and has no interest in improving client outcomes. Treatment evaluation, while having a secondary interest in advancing science, focuses primarily on improving client outcomes. Although treatment research has a secondary interest in improving client outcomes, it focuses primarily on advancing science.

This taxonomy can help clarify whether the data-gathering activities of the practitioner put clients at risk for any reason. For example, if treatment research is underway, client interests may be secondary to advancing scientific knowledge. In such situations, there may be some reduction in likely benefits to participating clients compared with situations in which their welfare is paramount. If treatment evaluation is underway, however, client interests are primary. A possible substitute term, *scientific treatment research,* might clarify that the aim is to produce new knowledge that is broadly generalizable.

A useful addition to Barlow et al.'s (1984) taxonomy might be an objective that represents practice evaluation. The purpose of such an objective is neither science nor the client, but the adequacy of the practice itself. Of course, there is a strong secondary interest in client welfare, but only insofar as its variation is necessary to show practice effectiveness. Indeed, the practice cannot be 100% effective with all clients and learn anything about the variables responsible for this enviable state of affairs. It must be less than 100% effective with some clients in order to produce necessary variation. Thus, an interest in practice evaluation puts the service provider on the horns of a dilemma. On the one hand, a primary interest in understanding practice effectiveness requires some variation in it, meaning less than optimal outcomes for some clients. On the other hand, forsaking practice evaluation in the short run to focus primarily on helping clients is not in their benefit in the long run. In fact, this book contends that ethical service provision requires evaluation. The point is not that a principal interest in evaluation leads practice evaluators deliberately to be less than 100% effective in order to create the needed variation. Rather, the client's welfare is simply not their primary focus. In such cases, the client can be seen as at risk for less than optimal service, just as they are in scientific treatment research. One might argue that procedures for protecting clients' rights in these situations are as important as they are for protecting human participants in research. Perhaps in the future professional organizations will institute a type of peer review process for purely evaluative pursuits. Meanwhile, it may be enough to note that no practice is ever likely to be 100% effective and thus unevaluable. Moreover, service providers have strong interests in helping their clients, often to their own disadvantage. It is unlikely that many clients experience harm as a result of overzealous practice evaluation efforts.

Ethical Concerns of Special Relevance to Practice Evaluation

This chapter has pointed out differences between research and practice evaluation and noted that their ethics differ somewhat as well. For example, it is not necessary to submit plans for practice evaluations to an IRB before implementing them because their goal is not to produce generalizable scientific knowledge. Are some ethical principles both specific to practice evaluation and different from those governing research and service provision? Major professional organizations (e.g., APA) provide ethical standards for practice and for research, but they do not appear to have considered the need for separate standards for practice evaluation itself. As we discuss below, organizations of professionals devoted specifically to evaluation provide ethical guidelines for their members.

Requirement for Practice Evaluation

Of initial interest is whether ethical standards of psychologists require the evaluation of one's practice. Barlow et al. (1984) asked whether we have "an ethical obligation to promote treatment evaluation" (p. 285) and provide good reasons for it. Without actually answering the question, they wondered whether a provider can ever know whether a client is making progress "without repeated, systematic measurement" (p. 285). In addition, they questioned whether a client can be truly informed of the nature of an intervention if it has not been carefully specified somewhere. As noted in chapter 1, the APA ethical standards do not require evaluation, but they are not completely silent on the issue either. Standard 1.06 requires psychologists to "rely on scientifically and professionally derived knowledge when making scientific or professional judgments or when engaging in scholarly or professional endeavors" (APA, 1992, p. 1600). This standard appears to mean that routine practice decisions, such as when to make changes in treatment, when to terminate it, or whether to implement it in the first place, must be based on objective evidence. Examples of such evidence are provided in the time-series designs described in chapters 8 and 10. In those arrangements, data are collected in an ongoing fashion throughout the course of treatment and are used to make the types of professional decisions referred to in the standard. If a practitioner routinely collects data, practice evaluation is taking place, whether explicitly or not. Thus, although ethical standards may not explicitly require evaluation, they appear to come close to doing so, at least in the case of psychological practice.

Ethical Guidelines Specific to Practice Evaluation

With respect to guidelines specifically covering practice evaluation, the American Evaluation Association (AEA) outlined five principles governing its members:

1. systematic inquiry (that evaluation represents systematic and data-based inquiries)
2. competence (that evaluations be undertaken by people prepared and able to conduct them effectively)
3. integrity/honesty (that evaluation should be carried out in ways that assure the integrity and honesty of the process)
4. respect for people (that evaluators respect the stakeholders with whom they interact, including their dignity, safety, and self-worth)
5. responsibilities for general and public welfare (that evaluation is conducted in a larger social and temporal context and that evaluators should include diverse perspectives and work to understand and make allowances for the broadest effects of their work).

Shadish, Newman, Scheirer, and Wye (1995) elaborated extensively on these principles.

A set of ethical statements more specific to evaluation activities of human services providers appears in Bloom, Fischer, and Orme (1995; also see Exhibit 12.1). Although Bloom et al.'s excellent recommendations are for single-case designs using time-series data, they can be applied to practice evaluation in general. According to Bloom et al., evaluation is an intrinsic part of service provision and ethical guidelines governing the professional conduct of the practitioner apply. They have developed a Client Bill of Rights that includes the client having the "right to know what the problem is," the right to know what services cost, and so on.

Another organization of human services professionals, the Association for Advancement of Behavior Therapy (AABT), published a list of eight ethical issues for its members (AABT, 1977). The issues are phrased as questions, and those of special relevance to practice evaluators are presented in Exhibit 12.2. It is noteworthy that AABT includes evaluation as a necessary element of ethical practice. Although it is not specifically stated, it appears to assume that the competence requirement in treatment (see Exhibit 12.2, Item H) extends to competence in practice evaluation. This issue is comparable to the AEA requirement that evaluations be carried out by people competent to conduct them.

Barlow et al. (1984) called attention to three general concerns that are not addressed in typical professional practice ethics statements. First, they warned against doing research in the guise of practice evaluation. When the objective is clearly to advance the aims of science, the participants are entitled to protection. These requirements cannot be avoided by hiding a research agenda under a practice cloak. Second, Barlow et al. note that presenting practice evaluations to professional audiences generates special risks for the confidentiality of clients. Clients must be informed of these risks, give their consent, and be afforded special precautions to preserve their anonymity. Third, accountable, high-quality monitoring practices require additional resources in terms of time and money as well as inconvenience to the client, who must collect data, bring them to sessions, and respond to the provider's reactions to them. Bloom et al.'s (1995) eighth statement goes directly to the need to balance the costs of evaluative efforts against their benefits (see Exhibit 12.1). As Barlow et al. (1984) observed, "if quality intervention requires more work, then saving a client this effort may be penny-wise and pound-foolish" (p. 288). In addition to these three gen-

Exhibit 12.1

Ethical Statements Concerning Practice Evaluation

1. *Provide demonstrable help:* In keeping with the service-providing context of practice evaluation, providing assistance to the client is foremost. It is not sufficient to assert that this happens, however. It must be shown with objective information.
2. *Demonstrate that no harm is done:* Show by objective means that neither the client nor others are made worse as a result of the evaluative process. Avoiding significant harm, either to the client or to others, takes precedence over helping the client.
3. *Provide clients with informed consent:* Involve clients in discussions about the details of the evaluative aspects of the services they receive in advance of beginning the services, obtaining their input and agreement.
4. *Respect the client's right to self-determination:* Seek the client's input concerning service goals and the means of measuring progress toward them.
5. *Minimize intrusion in the intervention by the evaluation process:* Use unobtrusive measurement when possible, and permit intervention to take precedence whenever a conflict occurs.
6. *Terminate evaluation if harm occurs:* If the client is discomfited by the evaluation process, whether physically, psychologically, or socially, use procedures that do not have such effects.
7. *Protect the client's right to confidentiality:* This varies depending on the nature of the service being provided. As discussed above, except in cases where danger to others carries a duty to warn, client-therapist communications are privileged. In providing organizational consulting activities, such a privilege does not exist. Clients should be informed of the limits of confidentiality and of the potential that evaluative data can be subpoenaed.
8. *Balance the costs and benefits of evaluation:* Obtaining objective data in an ongoing fashion carries costs in terms of client time, energy, and so on. These costs should be weighed against the benefits of evaluating, and evaluation should continue only if the result is favorable.
9. *Conduct evaluations that respect the client's individuality:* Consider differences in race, ethnicity, socioeconomic status, and gender when designing and implementing evaluations. Be sensitive to different perceptions of data-gathering procedures, and make sure they do not get used in ways that can harm the client.
10. *Be aware of the value implications of professional actions:* Evaluation is not theory bound. It can assess the implications of the theory, however, and thus provide evidence for the usefulness of implied values.

Note. From *Evaluating Practice: Guidelines for the Accountable Professional* (2nd ed.), by M. Bloom, J. Fischer, and J. G. Orme, 1995, pp. 632–636, Boston: Allyn & Bacon. Copyright 1995 by authors. Adapted with permission.

Exhibit 12.2

Selected Ethical Concerns for Evaluators from the Association for Advancement of Behavior Therapy

Concern A. Have the goals of treatment been given adequate consideration, and are they written?

Concern E. Has the adequacy of treatment been evaluated, and has that evaluation included quantitative measures of the problem and its progress over the course of treatment?

Concern H. Is the therapist qualified to provide treatment?

Note. From "Ethical Issues for Human Services," by the Association for Advancement of Behavior Therapy, 1977, *Behavior Therapy, 8*, pp. 763–764. Copyright 1977 by Harcourt/Academic Press. Adapted with permission.

eral concerns are ethical issues related to assessment, design, data ownership, and evaluation sponsorship.

Assessment-Related Issues

Concerning assessment and progress monitoring, the highest quality data are likely to come from more direct assessment methods, the most direct of which involve observing the client's behavior or products of that behavior. Even when the client has been informed of these methods, participated in their selection, and given consent, privacy rights remain an issue. Would less obtrusive methods (or no methods at all) be used if practice evaluation were not occurring?

Design-Related Issues

Design issues specific to practice evaluation also merit consideration; they are best illustrated in procedures used to provide control or baseline conditions against which to examine treatment effects. With designs of the multigroup, between-case variety, clients often are randomly assigned to a control group that receives minimal treatment or none at all. In treatment outcome studies, a common practice involves assigning people to a wait-list control condition in which treatment is delayed but eventually provided. With designs of the within-case, time-series variety, repeated assessment occurs during a baseline period before receiving treatment. What are the ethics of withholding treatment (control group) or delaying it (baseline) so that its effectiveness can be determined? A client's condition might deteriorate while waiting, or the delay could increase the discomfort that is leading the client to seek treatment (Kazdin, 1998). But if it is true that withholding usually occurs in the context of evaluating an unproven treatment in the first place, is treatment really being withheld? What are the ethics of applying an unproven approach?

One solution to the problem of obtaining control (i.e., no-treatment) data to compare with treatment data involves using a within-case time series design of the B–A–B variety (see chapter 8). Kazdin (1998) recommended using between-case, multiple-groups designs in which treatment is withheld or delayed only in "situations in which subjects are willing to wait and are unlikely to suffer deleterious consequences" (p. 432). He suggested that volunteer clients in a community clinic are more appropriately assigned to no-treatment or wait-list control groups than are clients contacting places such as crisis centers.

Data Ownership

When research is conducted using human participants, questions can arise as to the ownership of any data that result. Information is obtained from people, taken away and analyzed, and used in reports. What are the ethics covering the use of this information? What if it is used for profit? What if it is used against a participant in some way, either directly or indirectly? Discussions of privacy and confidentiality already have touched on the first of these. What about indirect uses, though, such as taking a person's responses to an opinion survey out of context and using them to support the views of an organization whose politics the person abhors? Is this ethically acceptable, even if anonymity is ensured by aggregating the person's responses with those of others?

Can the information obtained from clients in the course of practice evaluations be sold to marketing companies or others to use for their own purposes? Neuman (1997) recognized the existence of an information industry whose business involves obtaining, analyzing, packaging, and selling data about us to anyone willing to pay for it. Information about voting preferences, buying habits, and leisure activities is regularly collected for commercial and other purposes. Thieves can be tracked by monitoring their use of stolen credit cards. The supermarket "club cards" we are encouraged to use each time we buy groceries allow easy cataloging of our spending habits. Do insurance companies obtain this information to determine how much alcohol we buy, whether we smoke, or how often we use patent medicines? Clearly, information has value and can be viewed as private property that is bought and sold. Neuman suggested that it is a form of intellectual property much like copyrights, software, or patents. Like these things, it continues to have "relevance for its original owner after it is exchanged" (p. 468), unlike most types of physical property. Should we agree with Neuman that informed-consent procedures include a clause stating that if information about us is subsequently sold we get a share of any profit?

Practice evaluators are more likely to be concerned with how client data are used by other stakeholders than whether they can be sold for profit. Increasingly, managed care organizations (MCOs) require detailed information as a condition for reimbursement for or advance authorization of services. What is done with this information? How much are practitioners told about how client data are treated so that they can inform clients and receive their consent to collect and forward these data? Chapter 6 discusses practice management software options for practitioners as a way of organizing and storing large amounts of client data, some of which involve forwarding information electronically to be maintained in large information systems owned and operated by the software publisher. Who else besides the subscribing practitioner has access to this information? What security precautions are taken by the publisher to safeguard the client's privacy? What legal and other remedies does the client have if security is breached? Would participating service providers and their clients even be informed if this happened? Practitioners must take these considerations into account when gathering data and do whatever they can to safeguard their clients' privacy interests.

Sponsored Program Evaluations

Like research in the biomedical and physical sciences, much social and behavioral sciences research is funded by grants or contracts from government or other sources. These sponsors expect to exercise various amounts of influence over the conduct of the research and the disposition of its findings. Sponsors seek to influence research components such as the variables studied, the nature of the design or methodology, the dissemination of findings, and whether to reveal the sponsor's identity. No doubt researchers would prefer that the sponsors take a hands-off approach; in the "real world," however, it is reasonable to expect some sponsor involvement in the research.

On a large scale, for example, the federal government plays a substantial role in determining what is studied. When an epidemic (e.g., AIDS) threatens public health, research aimed at controlling it is likely to receive high priority by the National Institutes of Health, and funding is earmarked for work in this area. Moreover, if the immediate concern is with stopping its spread, research aimed at changing human behavior is likely to receive higher priority than research into the origins of the disease. A large pharmaceutical company might spend millions of dollars underwriting research to reverse male-pattern baldness and require the researchers to agree not to disclose the chemical composition of any treatment they discover. A large tobacco company might sponsor research on the attitudes of teenagers toward smoking. Fearing that participants will be scared off or bias their responses, the company hides its connection with the research and requires the investigators to sign statements that they will not reveal its sponsorship either. Sponsors also suppress research results. Neuman (1997), for example, reported that in a study on the effects of state-sponsored gambling underwritten by the Wisconsin Lottery Commission, findings on negative social effects were removed by the commission prior to the release of the report along with "recommendations to create social services to help compulsive gamblers" (p. 457). All of these intrusions place limits on scientific investigators. They pose ethical dilemmas of various difficulty that will affect each researcher differently.

One might ask what sponsor-imposed limits have to do with the ethics of practice evaluation—after all, the average service provider funds evaluation activities out of practice resources and is not beholden to outside sponsors. Unfortunately, this is a naive view of practice evaluation politics. Similar constraints exist in practice evaluation and in externally sponsored scientific research. For example, consider a service provider who decides to study the effectiveness of a particular treatment. The practice evaluation question concerns whether the treatment is useful for clients with different diagnoses. Pulling the records of all clients receiving the treatment over a period of time and sorting them by diagnosis is possible because the practitioner has kept track of this information and stored it in retrievable ways—but the information was available in the first place because MCOs routinely requested it as a condition for providing reimbursement.

Sponsor intrusions and potential ethical compromises are even more likely for practitioners employed directly by health maintenance organizations (HMOs). Practice evaluations by HMO employees can be considered works for hire that are owned by the company. Release of findings is likely to be carefully controlled, especially if they are unflattering, and the choice of subject matter and method of study are apt to be scrutinized closely, with evaluators reigned in if they wander into controversial areas. *Newsweek* suggested ways in which MCOs study patient satisfaction so as to maximize favorable outcomes (Spragins, 1997). For example, by presenting survey data on all of its participants together, MCOs obscure the fact that some patrons are sicker than others are and use services more extensively. The healthy participant who makes one or two visits a year might be quite satisfied. People with chronic medical conditions who make more frequent use of services might have substantially different views, however.

Other procedures that can increase the likelihood of positive outcomes include designing one's own form (rather than using a nationally standardized one that allows comparisons with other practices), surveying participants by calling them on the telephone at dinnertime when they are likely to be brief (and positive), and lumping together responses of "satisfied," "somewhat satisfied," and "very satisfied" into a broad category called "satisfied." Evaluators employed by the organizations they are evaluating have to take special care to preserve their objectivity. Belonging to evaluation societies and sharing concerns with others in similar positions can help. In addition, communicating openly with upper management about what are and are not acceptable evaluation practices in the professional community can minimize attempts to compromise one's own ethical standards.

Recommendations

The extensive discussion of ethical issues in this chapter is daunting and can lead the novice evaluator to wonder whether another line of work might be more fitting. The purpose of the chapter is not to scare readers, however, but to inform them comprehensively of some of the challenges facing conscientious evaluators. The most important lessons are summarized in the form of recommendations and presented in Exhibit 12.3. If evaluators study these carefully and follow them consistently, they will be on solid ethical footing. The practice evaluator can begin to ensure ethical behavior by consulting the guidelines of professional organizations such as the APA. These can be supplemented with evaluation-specific guidelines, such as those of the AEA, Bloom et al. (1995), and the items in Exhibit 12.3.

Exhibit 12.3

Recommendations Concerning Ethical Practice Evaluation

- Remember that ethical responsibility rests with you.
- Know and follow the ethical principles of professional organizations in your discipline.
- Know the difference between practice evaluation and research.
- Avoid conducting research in the guise of practice evaluation.
- Obtain and maintain a high level of skill at practice evaluation.
- Obtain fully informed consent from people providing evaluative information.
- Explain any limits to the confidentiality of information you obtain.
- Avoid deception whenever possible, and always debrief participants when it is used.
- Discuss practice evaluation activities with other professionals on a regular basis.
- Consider joining a practice evaluation organization or starting a special interest group on evaluation within your primary professional association.
- Compose a set of evaluation guidelines and policies for your practice.
- Involve others, including clients, in the design of your practice evaluation studies.
- Maintain respect for the dignity, safety, and self-worth of participants.
- Restrict interpretations of findings to the limits imposed by the study's design.

Summary

To be sure, important differences exist between research and outcomes evaluation. The distinction is not trivial because misclassified evaluation as research invokes a panoply of protections and procedural oversights that can be cumbersome and discouraging to people merely interested in whether their practice works. Misclassifying research as evaluation can deprive participants of the procedural safeguards that are essential to research activities in which participant welfare is secondary to advancing scientific knowledge.

Outcomes evaluation can serve as a bridge between research and practice. The openness characterizing research and the secretiveness characterizing practice are major distinctions keeping these enterprises apart, despite important similarities in the ways they conceptualize and solve problems. The necessarily greater openness of practice evaluation, together with its use of scientific methodology, can go a long way toward blurring some of the differences.

Ethical concerns of special relevance to practice evaluators include the question of whether ethical practice requires its evaluation. If decisions in the context of providing services are to be based on objective evidence, as the APA appears to require, it would seem that ethical practitioners should evaluate their practice routinely. The conscientious reader might be concerned that no reasonable practice evaluation could ever avoid all the pitfalls described in this chapter and still follow most of the recommendations presented here. A quick review of the examples of extensive practice evaluations in chapter 11 should be a useful antidote for such concerns.

Supplemental Reading

Bersoff, D. M., & Bersoff, D. N. (1999). Ethical perspectives in clinical research. In P. C. Kendall, J. N. Butcher, & G. N. Holmbeck (Eds.), *Handbook of research methods in clinical psychology* (2nd ed., pp. 31–53). New York: Wiley.

Miller, D. J., & Hersen, M. (Eds.). (1992). *Research fraud in the behavioral and biomedical sciences*. New York: Wiley.

Rosenthal, R. (1994). Science and ethics in conducting, analyzing, and reporting psychological research. *Psychological Science, 5,* 127–133.

Sieber, J. E. (1992). *Planning ethically responsible research.* Thousand Oaks, CA: Sage.

13 Telling Others About Your Findings

E ach repetition of the evaluation research cycle (see Figure 3.1) advances our knowledge of an area. In science, the goal of advancing knowledge is a cumulative process, with each new study standing on the shoulders of preceding ones. The reaction of other scientists to our findings can result in improvements in conceptualizations, methodology, and data analysis. To advance scientific knowledge, it is crucial to communicate results to others. If no one is told about the findings of a study, no increase in our understanding of a phenomenon occurs. Therefore, whatever activity the researcher has engaged in cannot properly be termed "science" because it does not add to the collective knowledge base. In other words, without dissemination there is no science. The importance of communicating the results of research activities is evident.

Does communicating the results of evaluative studies have the same importance as communicating the results of scientific research? The answer is *yes* and *no*. Evaluating practice effectiveness is likely to have more circumscribed implications. Its purpose is limited to improving services. It is not designed to produce generalizable information to advance our understanding of a phenomenon. In this sense, disseminating results is not a defining characteristic of outcomes evaluation. Given the goal of continual service improvement, however, sharing the results of evaluations with others can evoke responses that can lead to changes and improvements. Of course, it is possible for the solo practitioner to conduct a study and improve his or her approach on the basis of its findings without consulting with colleagues. Communicating outcomes of evaluative studies to others and considering their reactions is likely to result in even more improvement, however, because of the potentially greater value of multiple perspectives.

A simple example of a practitioner who wonders whether mailed reminders lead to fewer missed appointments illustrates this point. Suppose the practitioner randomly assigns clients to receive such notices or not and tallies appointment data over the next 6 months. The practitioner finds no difference in the rate of appointments missed by the two groups and concludes that reminders are a waste of time. He or she presents the results to members of a local professional organization, who voice several responses. One person notes that studies have shown more promising results for telephoned reminders. Someone else describes research showing the importance of timing the mailings and wonders whether the presenter mailed them too far in advance of the appointment. On the basis of these reactions, the practitioner decides to study the matter further, this time varying the time and type of reminder. It is easy to see how the feedback received from communicating the results of the initial evaluation to others can lead to changes, reformulated evaluative questions, and another study to answer them. Information obtained from practice evaluations thus can lead to cumulative improvements in practice knowledge, just as information obtained from research in the hard sciences benefits those endeavors.

It is fair to say that scientific and practice evaluation enterprises differ. The importance of communicating results may be greater for the scientific community, given its goal of increasing our knowledge of the way the world works. Scientists are taught to value open, clear, and objective description of their procedures to others, but practitioners have more self-interest at heart when conducting evaluations of their effectiveness. If they discover more effective ways of doing something, is it in their best interests to tell others about it? Getting and keeping a competitive advantage can be important to a practitioner's survival. Thus, an incentive toward secrecy exists in the world of practice that is uncharacteristic of science. That is not to say scientists are not covetous of their findings and never seek to hide them from others who might be pursuing similar breakthroughs. At some point, however, they have to make them available to the scientific community, so that they can receive credit for them. The credit received is generally proportional to the extent to which the findings advance our knowledge.

The remainder of the chapter assumes that you are sufficiently convinced of the benefits of dissemination to learn more about it. Although most of the literature on disseminating one's research is oriented toward researchers in the sciences, much of it applies to practice evaluation as well.

Deciding to Present

Do you have something to say that will interest other people? Will telling others about your evaluation efforts make a meaningful contribution? If you did your homework in designing and conducting your evaluation in the first place, the answer to both questions is likely to be yes. In other words, before you initiate an evaluation project, you should review the relevant literature to find out what others have already discovered. To avoid "reinventing the wheel," your evaluation should differ from others in significant ways, such as different measures, design, or analysis. When you build on previous work, you are more likely to extend it in novel ways. Communicating how you have done this to others makes a useful contribution, and they are likely to want to hear about it.

Deciding What to Present

Take the time to consider carefully exactly what you want to tell others about your evaluation results. Start by asking yourself why you want to share the results in the first place. You could have many reasons, including wanting suggestions for improving future evaluations, impressing peers that your practice seeks continual improvement, and stimulating discussion of more effective ways to implement services. Once you know why you are sharing your results, you can decide who your audience should be. For example, if you would like immediate input from peers concerning how to improve your results with a particular type of treatment, you might make an oral presentation at the monthly meeting of your local professional society. Or, if you want to use positive evaluation results to increase your customer base, you might decide to write a story for the local newspaper.

The most readily disseminated information is likely to concern the effectiveness of the direct service components of the practice, especially if your results are positive. The practitioner is well served by publicizing successes of studies asking the Does it work? question. As well, outcomes showing the relative effectiveness of different types of intervention are likely to be worth communicating. That is, the results of studies involving questions such as "Does it work better than . . ." or "How does it compare with . . .?" generally are likely to find a ready audience of interested professionals. Disseminating evaluation results of other practice components (e.g., administrative, staff training) can also produce dividends. For example, sharing the relative effectiveness of different practice-building strategies can result in useful feedback from peers. If one presents this information at meetings of a marketing association, even more valuable reactions are likely. Of course, as with presenting the outcomes of scientific research studies, it is best to emphasize positive findings. It is not a good idea to showcase practice failure; there can be many reasons why positive outcomes are not forthcoming.

After deciding what to present, who your audience is, and what the general format of your presentation should be (e.g., conference presentation or journal article), it is time to focus your content more precisely. This process involves identifying and retaining the essence of your evaluation and its findings while discarding much interesting detail that can interfere with clear communication. How does this distillation begin? A good place to start is with the limits set by those in charge of the particular dissemination outlet (e.g., conference, journal, newspaper) you plan to use. Different outlets have different formats and length limitations for you to follow. Journals rarely state specific page limits, but one can glean a reasonable estimate of their requirements by examining current issues. Counting the page lengths of a random selection of articles can give you an idea of the editor's expectations. Requests for papers from professional conferences are likely to have stricter length requirements, stating that explicitly in the "call for papers."

Staying within the length limits usually means saying less than you would like to say. A good way to determine what to eliminate when writing an oral or written presentation of material is to ask yourself the questions in Exhibit 13.1. The goal is to provide just the right amount of information for someone to be able to replicate what you did. When space limitations are tight, however, you might not be able to provide that kind of detail; in such cases, an addendum or appendix with the additional information is sometimes acceptable, or you can include a footnote explaining how readers can contact you or your associates for the details.

It is usually the case that with enough care, practice, and revisions, clear and repeatable descriptions emerge. Often, these require consid-

---

Exhibit 13.1

Questions Useful in Reducing the Length of Oral or Written Presentations

- What was done?
- Why it was done?
- What was found?
- What are its implications?

---

erably fewer words than originally anticipated. Arriving at this happy state is easier if you mercilessly analyze each sentence and ask whether every word is necessary. More help is available from grammar-checking computer software, which analyzes prose passages and makes suggestions for improvement. Another helpful approach is to ask a colleague to read the presentation and suggest material that can be eliminated. As Fiske and Fogg (1990) observed, "one can only do so much alone. One needs to get a number of colleagues to help by reading one's paper as carefully and critically as possible" (p. 597). We are likely to have much more affinity for material we slaved to produce in the first place; disinterested others can wield the editorial knife with much more ease and effectiveness.

Effectively organizing the material also helps to distill the essence of outcomes evaluation. Good organization supports reduced length by promoting clarity. By listing the sequence of steps involved in conceptualizing, designing, carrying out, and analyzing your practice evaluation project, you need fewer words to explain the process. Good organization eliminates the need to repeat material and can communicate the logic of the project. Some publications' author guidelines require a particular type of organization; you should follow those guidelines carefully. Start with an outline, and use standard outlining conventions. Limiting yourself to no more than three levels of headings helps to keep your work tightly focused.

Deciding Where to Present

Typically, service providers have the option of disseminating information from outcomes evaluations in two major venues: professional conferences and print media. It is common to use one of these and not the other, although the best approach is likely to involve both. A third venue, electronic media (i.e., the Internet), is rapidly becoming an important means of sharing professional information as well. If you plan to publish a particular set of findings, it is advisable to present them at a conference first; colleagues attending the presentation can provide useful suggestions for improving the presentation before you submit it for publication. Another approach is to ask for comments from participants in various listservs, chat rooms, and other forums on the Internet.

Conference Presentations

Professional organizations typically send out calls for presentations well in advance of their next convention. These "calls" describe the types of submission that are suitable and the format that all submissions should follow. Common presentation types include invited addresses; individual presentations based on papers, which are grouped into sessions according to topic; presentations at a symposium; comments on a narrow topic as a member of a panel discussion or roundtable discussion; and poster sessions. Regardless of format, it is common for organizations to require contributors to submit an abstract or summary of what they plan to present at the conference. If the organization publishes its conference proceedings in print or on CD-ROM, it is likely to have rather strict formatting requirements. For example, it might require the presenter to complete a form that in addition to blanks for the name, address, and so forth, contains a paragraph-size rectangle, within which the abstract must fit using a specific typeface (e.g., Times Roman 12).

Poster sessions are visual presentations of research projects; they also can be thought of as short versions of long papers. Authors are assigned to a specific display board and a time for displaying the poster, during which the author is expected to be available to answer questions and discuss his or her research. Because poster sessions emphasize charts and other visual aids, it is common for authors to bring copies of the paper on which the poster is based and distribute them during the session.

Presenters might or might not prepare written materials or distribute a formal paper to accompany oral presentations. A written version is more likely for invited addresses, which are occasionally published later in a journal of the organization. It is less likely when one gives a talk as part of a paper session or symposium, and rare for comments delivered as a participant in a panel or roundtable discussion. Practice evaluators who submit abstracts of papers for conference presentations should incorporate reactions to the oral presentation into the paper and submit the revision for publication as soon as possible following the conference.

Publications

Various types of publication are available for evaluators to use as outlets for the results of their work, including newsletters of professional organizations, peer-reviewed journals, books, and the popular press. Your goals determine which of these to use. If the primary goal is to get information about your findings into the hands of the general public, the popular press is the best outlet. If the goal is to communicate the general nature of the work to other professionals in a rapid fashion, association newsletters can be a good choice. Assuming they accept this type of submission, newsletters are likely to have less of a backlog of articles to publish. In addition, it is likely that more members will read something in a newsletter than in a professional journal because they are published more frequently and in briefer, more easily digested formats. Newsletter articles can be peer reviewed, but they may not receive the same level of critical scrutiny as most journal submissions. The latter are the outlet to choose if you plan to include much specific detail.

Peer-reviewed journals subject submitted papers to close scrutiny through a process taking several months at best. If accepted, editors frequently request revisions and may or may not send the revised version out for further review. It is common for journal editors to ask reviewers to assign papers to one of several decision categories: accept as is, accept with revisions, revise and resubmit, or reject. The good news is that outright rejection is only one of four options. The bad news is that rejection is the option most often used by some highly selective journals. Nonetheless, if you take care to select the most appropriate outlet for your work and prepare it according to that outlet's guidelines, your chances of avoiding rejection can improve greatly. Clearly, the process is arduous, and one has to take it seriously. Moreover, if the editor ultimately accepts the paper, it may be some time before it appears in print, depending on the backlog of the particular journal. The rewards for successfully transcending the hurdles, however, are significant in terms of influencing others in the field and obtaining recognition for one's own work, largely because journals serve an archival function. Most journals are on the shelves of libraries in various places throughout the world and on microfilm or in electronic format at many others. Perhaps more important, many journal articles are abstracted and included in widely available databases. Thus, investigators interested in your area of research are able to access your article easily.

Books are an especially good means of dissemination when someone has collected data for some time and has rather extensive findings to report (e.g., Hart & Risley, 1995). Because space limitations are not as stringent in books as in professional journals, books provide the opportunity to describe more of the details of the particular evaluation. Moreover, appendices provide a place to present more extensive data, including the raw data themselves. Books can be a valuable archive of information that others can access and analyze in other ways.

You can elect to publish and distribute a book by way of the commercial process, or you can publish it independently. The latter approach, sometimes known as "vanity publishing," is not highly regarded in professional circles, especially among academicians. The relatively low regard of this form of dissemination stems mainly from its avoidance of the peer review process. Anyone with the money and resources can publish a book and assert practically anything in it, regardless of whether the assertions have any empirical support. Although it is true that books published commercially are not subjected to the same level of peer scrutiny as articles in professional journals, they do get some review before appearing in print. Editors read and evaluate a book prospectus, and they often ask noted professionals in the field to review and offer comments as well. When the first draft of a book is complete, it often is sent to reviewers for commentary before being revised and eventually published. Those steps are less likely for vanity press books, unless the author himself or herself takes the initiative to obtain peer feedback.

Disseminating information in the popular press is another way to disseminate your results. Although it occurs outside the peer review process, mass media provide a speedy way to communicate with a large number of readers. Alerting the public to a potentially effective (or ineffective) procedure can give hope in some cases and prevent wasted time in others. In addition, articles describing your outcomes in local newspapers can help build a clientele, provided the description is positive. Professional organizations often have guidelines governing ethical ways of presenting information to the popular press.

Be aware that publication in a newspaper or other popular outlet —indeed, any publication that has a wide distribution—can preclude subsequent publication in a professional journal because of the long-standing prohibition against duplicate publication. To illustrate, the American Psychological Association (APA) has a policy against submitting papers to APA journals "describing work that has been published in whole or in substantial part elsewhere" (APA, 1994, p. 296). This prohibition is intended, in part, to prevent distortions in the cumulative knowledge we have in an area. Multiple publication of the same material can make it appear as though we have more information about a phenomenon than we do. Researchers generally accept the "publish first, popularize second" strategy for getting word to the general public about scientific findings that can affect their quality of life.

Giving Effective Oral Presentations

Assuming you decide to present your findings first and publish them later, how can you do this? Apprehension about speaking before groups is common (Pollard & Henderson, 1988) and has been studied extensively in the behavioral sciences under such labels as "speech anxiety," "communication apprehension," "speech phobia," "evaluation anxiety," and "presentation anxiety." Giving effective talks is important enough and apprehension about it so widespread that most colleges and universities have classes in public speaking. Some even require such classes in the undergraduate curriculum.

Elements of Effective Presentations

We can discuss the elements of effective presentations in terms of the three major behavior content areas described in chapter 7. Polished public speakers have effective cognitive, motor, and physiological skills relevant to oral communication. Let us look more closely at those skills.

Cognitive Skills

If we have to give a talk, we are likely to appraise the situation immediately and make statements to ourselves about it that range from "This should be easy" or "It will be fun" to "Why did I ever agree to do this?" or "I'm never good at getting up before groups." This private speech, or self-talk, essentially falls into positive or negative categories. Positive self-talk usually accompanies looking forward to the task and approaching it willingly. Negative self-talk usually accompanies dreading the task and avoiding it. *Cognitive ecology* is the process of "cleaning up" your thoughts—getting rid of negative ones, which are accompanied by avoidance, and replacing them with positive ones, which are accompanied by approach (Mahoney & Mahoney, 1976). *Cognitive ecological strategies* can help with this task (Cone & Foster, 1993). For example, eliminating negative self-talk is easier if you first decide to view the presentation as a challenge rather than a threat. Challenges focus our attention and energy; we look closely at what we have to do and are careful not to overlook anything. Threatening situations, in contrast, lead to escape and avoidance; we turn away from the threat, look for ways to avoid or escape it, and attend to it only as much as necessary to keep it at a distance.

Positive self-talk can be categorized as approach behavior because it generally involves focusing on the task, preparing effectively, and being physically ready to give the talk when the time arrives. "I will enjoy interacting with the audience" and "I will take deep breaths and enunciate clearly" are examples of cognitive behavior associated with approaching or engaging more fully in the task. The disadvantages of saying negative things to one's self largely stem from their association with escape and avoidance. "I will probably make a fool of myself," and "I'll lose my train of thought" are the type of cognitive behavior associated with turning away from or avoiding the task; statements such as these can interfere with effective presentations because they distract one's focus from the task at hand, turning it to irrelevant self-evaluative concerns instead.

Negative emotions often are associated with irrational thinking of the "I have to do this perfectly" or "This will be awful" variety. Ellis long has argued the hazards of irrational thinking and suggested strategies for dealing with it (Ellis & Harper, 1961). For example, where is it written that a presentation has to be perfect? The impossibility of giving the completely defect-free talk is evident with a few moments of thinking. All that is really expected is a competent presentation, not a perfect one. Planning in advance for the inevitable mistake and realizing that you will make some mistakes (as every fallible human being will) can go a long way toward minimizing anxiety and the negative self-talk that goes with it.

Motor Skills

What do you see when you look at polished speakers? Are they hanging onto the podium as if their life depends on it? Does their face have a look of dread, fear, or boredom? Do they speak in a monotone, with frequent "ums" and "ers," and pause to clear their throats? Do they sway back and forth while looking mostly over the heads of the audience? Do they read their presentation? Do they use audiovisual materials and handouts? Do they speak loudly enough so that everyone can hear them? Do they use gestures effectively? Do they keep one hand in their pocket, jingling spare change? Do they go past their allotted time?

Skilled presenters do some of these things and avoid others. We base our impression of their effectiveness largely on the motor behavior we observe in the course of the presentation. The items in Exhibit 13.2 represent most of the behaviors effective presenters show. Notice that the items are framed in positive terms (i.e., what skilled presenters actually do), rather than in negative ones (i.e., ineffective behaviors they avoid). The exhibit can be helpful to people wanting specific information about how to be effective and how to measure their progress while practicing to improve. Note that the checklist is not a formal assessment instrument and has no psychometric information available for it. It is interesting to know that effective presenters pace their talks smoothly. But how do they learn to *do* that? Entire college classes teach the mechanics of public speaking, and we cannot go into them further here. Interested readers are referred to the resource list at the end of this chapter.

Physiological Skills

In addition to their effective cognitive and motor behavior, skilled presenters manage their physiological arousal as well. Most of us notice some increase in autonomic behavior, such as heart rate, breathing, sweating, and muscular tension, in our face, neck, and other parts of our body when we face tasks that we find personally threatening. As we become more accustomed to the activity and better at it, we experience a lessening of this autonomic arousal. This reduction results from learning how to manage the physiological aspects of the task, just as we have learned effective ways of handling its cognitive and motor components. Whether our increased effectiveness with physiological behavior is the result of specific instruction or a by-product of increased cognitive and motor skill, it is essential to maximally fluent performance.

Among the approaches that can lead to effective management of

Exhibit 13.2

Checklist of Effective Presentation Skills

Instructions: Use this checklist to assess your behavior during or immediately after an oral presentation. You may complete it yourself while watching a videotape of the talk, or you may ask someone else to complete it as you give a presentation. Note that the response options are yes and no. If the behavior occurred during the talk, answer yes. If it did not occur, answer no. You can add the marks in the "yes" column to determine a total score if you wish. This checklist provides an estimate of the overall effectiveness of the motor components of your public speaking repertoire. You can use it to monitor change as you work at improving your skill. The checklist's primary purpose, however, is diagnostic. Look at the items marked no and work to convert them to yes.

Item	Yes	No	
1.	____	____	Spoke with several members of the audience before beginning the presentation
2.	____	____	Thanked the audience for being there
3.	____	____	Smiled at the audience early in the presentation
4.	____	____	Stated the purpose and organization of the talk at the beginning
5.	____	____	Stated preference for questions during talk or saved to the end
6.	____	____	Made eye contact with at least three audience members during the talk
7.	____	____	Kept face and front toward the audience throughout the presentation
8.	____	____	Used audiovisual equipment effectively
9.	____	____	Used humor
10.	____	____	Varied loudness and pitch of voice
11.	____	____	Spoke loudly enough for all to hear
12.	____	____	Used gesture effectively
13.	____	____	Kept within the stated time limits
14.	____	____	Used supporting material (e.g., anecdotes, jokes, quotations, statistics, analogies)
15.	____	____	Varied facial expression to keep pace with changes in content of the talk
16.	____	____	Dressed appropriately for the occasion
17.	____	____	Allowed time for questions at the end
18.	____	____	Repeated questions before answering them
19.	____	____	Paused to think about each question asked
20.	____	____	Kept answers to questions concise (i.e., less than 30 seconds)
21.	____	____	Paced the presentation effectively
22.	____	____	Spoke in a clear, confident voice
23.	____	____	Moved comfortably around the platform or front of room.

Comments: _____

physiological responses are biofeedback, progressive relaxation, meditation, yoga, the martial arts, self-hypnosis, and imagery training. For example, a noticeable characteristic of effective oral presenters is that their breathing is controlled and regular. Moreover, they often stand with their weight centered evenly on the balls of both feet. Their face, especially their forehead is free of obvious tension lines, and they move in a smooth and apparently relaxed way. As was true for the motor behavior above, increased skill with physiological responses can come from learning how to perform them more effectively. Again, this is not the place to offer the details of such training, but teaching yourself the basics of progressive relaxation or enrolling in a yoga class is a good place to start. Biofeedback training also can be useful. References for learning more about effective physiological responding include Bernstein and Borkovec (1973), Houghton (1996), Poppen (1988), and Snaith (1998).

The Importance of Preparation

When I first entered the army many years ago, an old drill sergeant was fond of reminding young recruits of the importance of preparation. "Always remember the 5 Ps," he said; "prior planning prevents poor performance." This is good advice when preparing an oral presentation. Start with the audience: Who are they? What are three to five pieces of information that you want them to remember?

Some expert presenters begin their planning with the last step in their preparation. In *backward chaining*, they start by imagining that they are looking out into the audience at the start of their talk. They get a good visual sense of who is in the audience, what the room looks like, and the physical arrangements of the podium or speaking area. When this is clearly in view, they work backward step-by-step, identifying all the things they need to do leading up to the talk, including arriving early enough to set up and greet people as they arrive. Then they determine the amount of time they have before the talk is to occur, and they schedule the steps they need to complete by certain points. They then begin carrying out the identified tasks. If they do these one after the other on the schedule they have prepared, the talk will be ready for delivery at the appointed time. Most important, they keep their own anxiety or arousal under control by knowing they are ready.

Other presenters confine their preparation to shorter periods of time just before they are to give the talk. Pressure-motivated presenters sometimes view planning too far in advance as interfering with spontaneity. They are likely to put much work into last-minute preparation and are therefore apt to include fewer details. Note that they still plan their presentations; they merely take a different approach to their planning.

A good strategy for novice presenters is to write the talk before delivering it. Be careful here, though. A well-written talk is a good beginning, but it does not sound as good as it reads. Do not plan to stand up and read the written version. Use it to prepare notecards and overheads that can cue your actual delivery. Power Point slides can be useful here.

The organization of research articles in professional journals provides a good model for presenting the results of your practice evaluation. Start with a description of the context: Describe your outcomes, the services provided, the clientele, the locations, and the staff. A carefully worded description should lead to the evaluative question you asked and the hypotheses you developed to help answer it. Next, describe your evaluation design, measures used, data collection procedures, analysis, and results. Last, discuss the implications of your findings and mention how your practice changed as a result of your findings. After the presentation, you can take questions and comments from the audience.

After writing your presentation or preparing a detailed outline, think about the audiovisual aids you can use to heighten its impact. Carefully anticipating their use is second only to the importance of planning the presentation. Choosing the right aids and using them competently are aspects of presenting that speakers often take for granted, but it is important to get training in both. When composing your visual aids, remember that they should assist understanding, not take away from your presentation. Make sure that your slides or overheads support the goal of your presentation. Prepare them to be attractive, appropriate in number (i.e., they should convey only the essential information), large enough (or loud enough) to see or hear from the back of the room, and accurate. Also be strategic about where to place the aids in the course of your presentation. When using audiovisual equipment, you should find out who will provide the equipment and how soon it will be available before the talk. Give yourself plenty of time to load your materials and make sure you know how to use the machine. You also should have a backup plan for the problems that often occur with audiovisual equipment; you may want to consider whether to use written handouts as well.

Some presenters like to include in their handouts copies of each slide or overhead transparency, an approach greatly facilitated by using Power Point. This approach reduces the audience's need to take notes, thereby giving you more of their attention, and also gives you a "Plan B" should the equipment fail. It is a good idea to use the all-or-none rule in this regard: If you include any of your slides or transparencies in the handouts, include them all. It is annoying to listeners to follow along with their own copies only to find that some slides have been omitted. In addition, organize and sequence the handouts so they are in the order you plan to use them in your presentation. Give the handouts to the audience at the start of the talk rather than at the end.

Rehearsal is probably the most important element of preparing to give an oral presentation. Rehearsal is useful for everyone, particularly the novice presenter. Dress rehearsals are an excellent technique. If possible, run through the talk ahead of time in the room where you will give it, at the same time of day, and with all the equipment and handouts you plan to use. Wear the clothes (including the shoes) you expect to have on when you give the formal talk. This process exposes you to most of the stimuli you will experience when delivering the talk, allowing you to become comfortable with them and minimizing any surprises (e.g., feeling faint at 5 p.m. because it has been a long time since lunch). If full dress rehearsal in the actual delivery setting is not possible, find a room like it. It can be helpful to have someone listen to your rehearsal and provide feedback. Their reactions during and after the presentation can be quite instructive. It is also a good idea to record your presentation, using videotaping when you can. If videotaping is not feasible, audiotaping is essential. When you replay the tape, you notice various aspects of your voice, mannerisms, use of audiovisual equipment, eye contact, and demeanor that you can change to enhance the talk.

An important and often overlooked aspect of preparation is anticipating the type of question you will get. With a little thought, you can identify several categories of question, such as the following:

- context of the evaluation (e.g., "Do you have any clients from other countries?" "What is the typical socioeconomic status of your clients?")
- procedure (e.g., "Why didn't you use the 'XYZ' measure to assess outcomes?")

- results (e.g., "What was the justification for using a two-tailed test of significance?")
- implications (e.g., "How is this relevant in an era of increased penetration by managed care?" "Do you think psychological assistants with minimal supervision could use this technique effectively?").

Preparing general responses to categories of questions in advance of the talk can lead to more effective answers when you present.

Dealing with questions often is the most anxiety-producing part of the process for novice presenters. It is helpful to (a) anticipate the questions you are most likely to get and (b) remember that questions are useful in their own right. Concerning the latter, questions can be great sources of information in that they let you know how well you are getting across your message. In addition, they tell you something about your audience, allowing you to modify your approach accordingly. (When several students in an advanced statistics course ask what a mean is during the first class, you know you have to alter your understanding of "advanced.")

Of course, it is always possible that the audience will include one or two tough customers who seem to be there just to challenge or even embarrass you. Experienced presenters respond to hecklers using techniques in a particular sequence; pausing after any question to compose a thoughtful reply is always a good tactic, especially with hecklers. Next, you can paraphrase and restate the question and ask the heckler if that is what he or she meant. It can also be useful to ask for elaboration (e.g., "I'm not sure I understand the question, would you be so kind as to elaborate for me?"). Doing so can produce information about the attacker that might include something you have in common; voicing this agreement can be an effective way of defusing the situation (e.g., "I agree wholeheartedly with your point about X. I'm not sure we have had the same experience with it, however."). Remember to keep all responses within 30 seconds and provide no more than two answers to a given question. Move on to other questions with "I'll be glad to discuss that further with you afterward." Being brief avoids losing other members of the audience, who are looking to you for leadership in this situation.

Finally, be sure to prepare your cognitive, motor, and physiological behavior just before beginning your talk. Some presenters like to meditate the half-hour ahead of time. Others go through relaxation exercises. You can combine these approaches to managing arousal with visualization exercises in which you form a picture of yourself successfully presenting your ideas to an appreciative audience. Notice how confident you sound and how self-assured you look as you move in front of your listeners. Notice that you are saying positive things to yourself, such as "This is going to be fun" or "I'm going to give them some information they will find very useful." When you get up to speak, have a glass of water nearby. Take several deep breaths that you hold for a 3- or 4-count before exhaling. Look into the audience and notice several smiling, attentive people. Concentrate on them as you begin your talk. When you finish, remember the questions and comments you receive. Write them down as soon as possible so that you can use them to prepare your presentation to submit for publication.

Understanding the Peer-Review Process

When you are submitting your findings for publication, it is helpful to know how papers get reviewed and how they are accepted or rejected. Knowing the factors that influence editorial decisions and some of the research on the peer review process can be useful as well. This section covers these issues and includes specific suggestions for improving the odds that your paper will be accepted. The discussion focuses on journal submissions rather than newsletters of professional organizations because journals tend to have similar processes, whereas newsletters can be much more idiosyncratic.

Professional journals are usually of two types: (a) official publications of professional organizations and (b) proprietary publications of commercial publishing houses. Both types have an editor (or editor-in-chief) who presides over the intellectual operations of the journal, which include soliciting and receiving manuscripts; overseeing their review; accepting or rejecting them; giving feedback to authors; receiving and reviewing revised manuscripts; and identifying topical issues, themes, or directions of the field about which to invite and publish a special issue or series of papers. Editorial assistants are responsible for the administrative duties involved in logging in, numbering, and filing submissions as well as mailing them to reviewers identified by the editor. The assistant often is responsible for following up with reviewers, reminding them of deadlines, and sending thank-you letters along with copies of other reviewers' comments and the editorial decision letter.

The editor selects a board to assist in the intellectual aspects of the journal's operations. Members of the editorial board usually are experts in the field who have published numerous articles themselves. They generally serve limited terms, renewable at the pleasure of the editor. Editors serve limited terms, the lengths of which are set by the professional organization or by agreement with the publisher, in the case of proprietary journals. Often an organization has a publications board or publications committee that sets policies for its various publications, including the process of selecting journal editors, the length of their terms, and whether and how much compensation they are to receive. The terms of editors typically are shorter for organizationally sponsored journals, with 3- or 6-year periods being common. Editors of proprietary journals are more likely to sit for indefinite terms that commonly exceed 3 to 5 years.

When the editor receives a manuscript, he or she examines it to determine whether it is appropriate for the journal. If appropriate, the editor then identifies two or more reviewers and sends the paper to them, together with a request that they review it and provide comments and a recommendation as to the paper's publishability. Usually the editor includes guidelines to the reviewer as to format and tone for the review, along with a deadline for returning the review. By agreeing to examine a paper, the reviewer accepts an important responsibility. Determining the worthiness of someone else's description of their work can be daunting. Communicating the impression of that worthiness is particularly challenging. It takes skill to know whether the work is of high quality, whether the report is adequate, and whether a contribution is being made to the field. Moreover, providing commentary to authors in such a way that they benefit requires consummate skill. If they use the information to do further work in the area that is of higher caliber, the reviewer has succeeded. If they become discouraged or angry and do no further work, the reviewer has failed.

The editor receives the independent comments of the reviewers, studies them, conducts his or her own review, forms an opinion as to publishability, and prepares written comments to the authors. It is not necessary for the editor to agree with the reviewers. Nor is it necessary for reviewers to agree with one another. Indeed, much literature shows that disagreement is common. For example, Fiske and Fogg (1990) examined convergence between the comments made by reviewers of papers submitted to APA journals. They reported that "in the typical case, two reviews of the same paper had no critical point in common . . . reviewers . . . wrote about different topics, each making points that were appropriate and accurate" (p. 591). Thus, the wise editor uses multiple reviewers who are likely to attend to different aspects of the paper under consideration. Incidentally, reviewers appear to pay the greatest attention to interpretations and conclusions, followed by conceptual, pre-execution issues. Fiske and Fogg found that 16.1% and 15.2% of the weaknesses noted by reviewers were in these areas, respectively. Gott-fredson (1978) reported greater agreement between reviewers and editors on items leading to rejection of manuscripts than on ones leading to their acceptance.

It is possible for reviewers to focus on different issues within a paper and still agree on its publishability. Unfortunately, Fiske and Fogg (1990) found differences here as well, noting that "recommendations about editorial decisions showed hardly any agreement" (p. 591). Theirs is one of many studies addressing the reliability of the reviewing process and variables influencing it. The generally low agreement between reviewers has led to charges of carelessness and bias in the editorial process. Some have wondered whether unknown authors are at a disadvantage and whether institutional prestige plays a part in decisions (e.g., Bradley, 1981; Mahoney, 1982). Others have suggested that editors minimize such biases by instituting blind reviews, which eliminate any means of identifying authors from papers before sending them out for review (Ceci & Peters, 1984; Peters & Ceci, 1982). Some journals now permit authors to elect to have their papers reviewed blindly.

In a controversial study, Peters and Ceci (1982) resubmitted articles to journals that had already published them some time earlier. Before doing so, they changed the author's name and institutional affiliation from one of high prestige to a fictitious one. Eight of the 12 previously published articles were rejected on the second submission on the basis of methodological deficiencies. The study catalyzed extensive interest in and controversy over the issue of blind reviews. Kupfersmid (1988) summarized research in the area noting that even when papers are deliberately "blinded," reviewers can identify the author about 25% of the time anyway. This can occur through the use of methodology that the author is known to use frequently, a high frequency of self-citations, and other means. He also noted the lack of research consensus concerning whether an author's identity, status, or institutional prestige plays a part in a paper's acceptance.

Given the generally agreed-on low reliability of the reviewing process and the failure to find conclusive evidence of specific biasing factors, what is the best course of action for practitioners who want to publish evaluation results? A reasonable tactic might be to borrow from findings in the literature on interpersonal attraction (e.g., Byrne, 1997; Dryer & Horowitz, 1997). People who are similar are attracted to one another. It is probably accurate to assume that the successful contributor is more similar than dissimilar to the editors and reviewers of professional journals. If you have concerns that you are different from these "peers" in important ways, it might be in your best interests to request blind reviews of your submissions. You can prepare them with all identifying items removed and ask the editor to honor your request. This approach is noncontroversial in most cases. Remember though, it is not known whether blinding efforts make any difference. We do know, however, that taking care to prepare your paper to conform to the format requirements of the journal you have selected and proofreading it to eliminate errors and awkward writing can enhance acceptance.

Preparing Manuscripts for Submission to Journals

Getting a paper ready for submission requires attention to structural matters and content. Structural matters are the easiest to deal with as long as you organize yourself well and attend carefully to detail.

Structure of a Journal Article

Maximize your chances for acceptance by selecting the best possible journal for your study and preparing your submission to match that journal's style requirements. A good way to choose a journal is to look for ones that publish papers similar to yours. Most major libraries have lists giving the names of journals in their collections, and some of these lists are available on the Internet (e.g., http://www.carl.org). From the list you can identify publications that sound promising. Obtaining copies of recent issues of those journals can confirm whether they publish work like yours. Journals commonly include information for those wishing to submit articles somewhere in each issue; this information can be as brief as "authors should submit four copies of manuscripts prepared according to the *Publication Manual of the American Psychological Association*" or as long as several pages.

Even though formats vary across journals and you must conform to the requirements of the journal to which you are submitting, there are common elements. In the social and behavioral sciences, many jour-

---

Exhibit 13.3

Titling a Journal Article: Recommendations From the *Publication Manual of the APA*

A good title should do the following:

- Summarize the main idea of the paper
- State the main topic
- Identify the variables or theoretical issues being studied and the relationships between them
- Be fully explanatory when standing alone
- Compress easily to a running head used in the published version
- Avoid abbreviations
- Avoid redundancies and words serving no useful purpose
- Be approximately 10–12 words long.

---

nals follow APA style. Papers in this style use a four-part structure in which manuscripts first introduce the context for the study, then follow with a method section, in which they describe how the study was conducted. Next is the results section, in which findings are presented. Finally, the discussion section gives the author's interpretation of the findings and their implications. Additional components include the cover page, abstract, references, figures, tables, and appendices. Examples of submission format for manuscripts appear in the APA publication manual along with marginal notations highlighting many of the important APA formatting conventions. Consult the complete publication manual for additional requirements.

Title

Remember that the first thing someone sees is the title of an article. As with many first meetings, initial impressions are important, and it is critical to give careful consideration to composing a title. Exhibit 13.3 presents recommendations adapted from the APA publication manual for composing titles. Composing a title to meet those requirements can appear overwhelming. How will you ever write an entire paper if this many considerations apply to the title alone? Practice can help, of course, as can attending to some of the following recommendations. First, consider the following title:

> A Study of the Effects of Free-Weight Training on Depression Assessed by the BDI in College Males Who Are Moderately Depressed

How does it conform to the recommendations in Exhibit 13.3? It certainly summarizes the main idea and identifies the variables related (free-weight training and depression) in the study. Furthermore, it appears to be fully explanatory. In addition, one can easily abstract a running head (e.g., "Effects of Free-Weight Training on Depression") from it. Notwithstanding these attributes, however, there are several problems with this title. For one, the title uses an abbreviation for the Beck Depression Inventory. In addition, it includes redundant words (e.g., "A Study of . . .") and methodological details (i.e., the type of participant and their clinical status), which are not necessary in titles. This excess material causes the title to be twice the recommended length. Consider the following revision:

Free-Weight Training Reduces Depression

Does this revision meet the criteria set forth in Exhibit 13.3? This title gets the "brief is beautiful" award. Moreover, it can serve as its own running head, although a briefer running head (e.g., "Free-Weight Training and Depression") could be used as well. Note also that the title does something not mentioned in the APA recommendations: It states the findings concerning the relationship between the variables being studied. Stating findings is generally a good idea, although it is rare to see it in print (for unknown reasons). Experimental and correlational studies can have titles that state findings. For example, "Smoking Is Negatively Correlated With Sexual Potency" is a concise title meeting the criteria in Exhibit 13.3. Titles that begin with "The Effect of " or "Associations Between" leave us wondering what the effect or associations really are. Why not state the findings in the title and avoid the mystery? Results specifying titles also tend to be shorter. To illustrate, the APA publications manual (1994, p. 7) cites the following as a good title:

Effect of Transformed Letters on Reading Speed

Eliminating the mystery can result in the following:

Transformed Letters Increase Reading Speed

Of course, if several transformations exist, some increasing and some decreasing reading speed, it is necessary to alter the title accordingly. This might lead to some increase in length, although probably not beyond the recommended 10 to 12 words. Furthermore, the increased information communicated is likely to be well worth a few extra words.

Abstract

The next important component of a published article is its abstract. Indeed, the APA publication manual suggests that the abstract can be the "most important paragraph in your article" (p. 8). Abstracts are important for two reasons: First, the abstract is likely to be entered into numerous databases and could be the only contact people have with the article. Second, along with the title, the abstract is part of the first impression readers form of the paper. If you write the abstract well, you can interest readers in the rest of the article. If you write it poorly, you discourage further interest.

The carefully crafted abstract of an evaluation study includes the following:

- the variables being related
- the participants, including descriptive characteristics (e.g., age, gender, and number)
- methodological detail, including measures used; apparatus; and names, dosage levels, and means of administering drugs
- results, including statistical significance levels
- conclusions, implications, and applications of findings.

You should compress all of the above information into 100–120 words. As the publication manual notes, "the abstract needs to be dense with information but also readable, well organized, brief, and self-contained" (p. 8). The last criterion is especially important for readers who never see anything beyond the abstract. It should stand on its own in terms of conveying the essence of the study, meaning that you should explain abbreviations the first time you use them, write out the names of tests and drugs, and define unique terms.

Introduction

The initial component of the full paper is the introduction. By describing relevant literature, it provides the context for the study. Good introductions acknowledge the work of others that led up to your own. Show the reader how your study is the logical outgrowth of previous work. Retain brevity by citing only the most directly pertinent literature, avoiding interesting but peripheral work. At the same time, provide enough information that readers who are not specialists in the area can understand what you have done and why. The last paragraph of the introduction should include your statement of the problem, which can be in the form of an evaluative question; you also can state specific hypotheses at this point. Remember to make clear the variables you are manipulating and the relationships you expect to find between them. The bases for your hypotheses should be clear after reading the last paragraph of the introduction. Finally, be sure to describe the design you used to test the hypotheses. Do not begin this section with a sub-head that says "Introduction," and keep the length to five or fewer double-spaced, typewritten pages.

Method

Following the introduction, the method section describes how you conducted the study. It is important to be thorough in this section. A test of completeness is whether you have included sufficient detail for someone reading the paper to replicate your procedures precisely. Several subsections make up the method section. The first of these, *participants*, describes the people who provided the data. Remember, the goal of research and evaluation is to discover generalizable knowledge. To know whether results apply to people not included in your particular study, a reader must have sufficient information about your participants. At a minumum, include numbers, age, sex, ethnicity, and socioeconomic status levels. When using clinical samples, describe their diagnoses and severity levels. If you used a demographic characteristic or diagnosis as a variable in the study, describe it carefully and include its operational definition (e.g., socioeconomic status level "as measured by the Hollingshead and Redlich [1958] method" or "mild depression as defined by scores between 9 and 22 on the Beck Depression Inventory"). As the APA publication manual points out, careful description of participants facilitates later meta-analyses, even if the characteristics were not major variables in your study. Incidentally, the possibility of meta-analysis is an important reason for describing other methodological details completely as well. It also is helpful to explain why you chose the particular sample of participants. Did it represent a subset of a larger population, say, all clients served in a practice? Did you select them randomly from this population?

After describing participants, present any apparatus used in data collection. If the equipment was unique—that is, designed specifically for the study—provide a detailed description, perhaps even including schematic drawings or blueprints. If you used assessment instruments, describe them and identify their source. Clarify their relevance to the constructs being related in the study if it is not obvious. Describe the psychometric characteristics of the measures that are relevant to your study. For instance, if you are reporting on a pretest–posttest comparison, the temporal stability (test–retest reliability) of your measures is important. If relevant psychometric information is lacking, you need to collect it as part of your study. If you used a direct-observation measure, for example, inform readers of the procedures used to check its reliability. The fact that reports show it to be reliable in previous studies does not mean it is similarly reliable in yours. Check the agreement between independent observers (see chapter 7) and report it in this part of the method section. Some investigators include this information in the results section, but this is a misplacement unless the study is about the reliability of a particular measure. When using a measure as part of the methodology to study variables, include psychometric information in the method section. This information can come from others or from analyses you complete in the course of your investigation.

A procedures subsection often follows the description of apparatus or measures. It describes how you went about collecting the data using the devices. In the procedures subsection, one might find such sentences as "Participants were met with individually 1 week before starting treatment. They received the BDI, HS, and STAI-T in counterbalanced order following a Latin square design," or "the first author and his assistant observed each family at home. Family members were observed interacting during the hour just before dinner. They were asked to remain in one of two adjoining rooms, to keep the television turned off, and to make no telephone calls." Specific sentences throughout the procedures subsection permit subsequent investigators to duplicate the steps you followed.

Results

The results section describes the study's findings. It summarizes your data and your analyses. Begin this section with a general statement of the primary findings. Follow with the data that support your findings, and include any tables and figures that are central to understanding your results. Be descriptive at this point. Remember that interpretation belongs in the discussion section. Work from major to minor findings, and present supporting data in the same order. A good rule is to keep to the same order used when presenting hypotheses in the final paragraph of the introduction. If your first hypothesis was that specifically targeted marketing strategies are more effective than general ones, present data relevant to this hypothesis first. Follow it with less central information showing the association between the effect of marketing and client characteristics (e.g., age, income, distance lived from the practice). Take pains to avoid the robotlike listing of findings in the order they appear on the printout of your statistical software program (Kazdin, 1995).

The tables and figures should drive home your major findings. They take considerable space and are expensive to typeset, so use them sparingly. There is no need to use a figure for a simple finding that you can communicate easily in the text itself, and the same is true for tables; both supplement information included in the text. Tables and figures should always be referred to in the text. A frequent error is to present tables or figures without calling the reader's attention to them. Be sure to tell the reader where to look in a table or figure for data supporting a particular outcome being described. For instance, "the first two columns of Table 3 show the data for abused and nonabused children."

It is hard to imagine results without statistics. When presenting them, follow the APA publication manual's recommendations carefully. Among these are to name the specific test being used, state the obtained values with the test, and include the degrees of freedom, significance (probability) level, and the direction of any effect. Include descriptive statistics along with inferential statistics. Means, medians, and associated measures of variability are minimum requirements here. Remember, most readers are familiar with statistics, so you do not need to explain basic concepts. If you have used a rare or esoteric statistical test, however, do take time to provide a rationale and explain its use. Because statistical significance is rarely the most important outcome criterion in outcomes evaluations, it is also a good idea to present information on clinical significance or on the magnitude of any effects observed (see chapter 9).

After presenting your results in an orderly manner, it is time to discuss them, identify their implications, and draw some conclusions. Begin the last section—the discussion section—with a statement of how the findings support your hypotheses, keeping to the order used in the results section. Next, show how your findings fit with the literature cited in the introduction and how they modify and extend this literature. Identify any shortcomings and ambiguities in your study, and note how they affect your conclusions. Suggest ways in which investigators can avoid those problems in the future studies that seem logical, given your findings. The discussion section is often a place of tension between what the author wants to say about the relationships being studied and what the procedures and data permit the author to say (Kazdin, 1995). Stick close to the data here, and avoid the trap of discussing an "almost significant" finding as though a relationship really exists. Also, avoid overgeneralizing to variables and participants not included in your evaluation. Discussion sections are usually brief (2–4 manuscript pages), in part to discourage wild speculation.

Writing a Journal Article

The structure of the article is a good guide for its content. If you know what each of the major sections is supposed to convey, you have a good idea of what their contents should be. Remembering the basic rules of composition, spelling, and organization can be the most challenging aspect of writing like a professional, however. If you have forgotten some of these rules, you can review the basics in books specifically designed for that purpose (e.g., Corbett & Finkle, 1994). Humility can be helpful here as well. Remember that even the best writers' papers are copyedited before publication, and this occurs after numerous rewrites of earlier versions. It said that Sir Isaac Newton "made at least eight drafts of the *Scholium Generale* for the second edition [of *Principia Mathematica*]" (Koyré, 1965, p. 262).

Beyond the basic rules of grammar and APA format, several useful sources address important considerations in preparing a manuscript for submission to a professional journal. A particularly helpful book is by Sternberg (1993). Among the best known articles on the topic is Maher's (1978) guide for assessing research articles. Although written for reports of research in clinical psychology, his "guide" can be useful as a checklist to apply to any paper presenting the results of empirical studies in the behavioral sciences. Indeed, it can provide a review of the basic design, measurement, analysis, and ethical concepts covered in this book. If you know what Maher is asking with each of his questions and can answer them with respect to a randomly selected journal article, you have an excellent grasp of outcomes evaluation methodology. His paper covers each of the major sections of journal articles described in this chapter and is presented in its entirety in Appendix A.

Other excellent papers on the topic of writing papers include those by Bem (1995), Kazdin (1995), Maxwell and Cole (1995), and Rosenthal (1995). Kazdin covered writing that specifically deals with assessment instruments and their evaluation. His introductory section is more general, however, and applies to all types of reports of empirical studies. Moreover, because all empirical investigations involve the use of measures, his comments about assessment instruments and their presentation have general applicability to practice evaluation as well. Bem discusses ways to prepare effective literature reviews. Writing specifically for people considering submitting papers to *Psychological Bulletin,* his suggestions also generally apply to anyone writing research papers for publication, especially given that all papers have to include some review of the literature in their introductions. Because a broad range of readers consults papers appearing in *Psychological Bulletin,* papers have to be written in a manner that is accessible to people who have "no expertise in statistics, meta-analysis, or experimental design" (p. 172). Writers interested in excellent suggestions for improving their clarity would be wise to consult Bem's article.

In the event you undertake a meta-analysis and are preparing a paper on your results, Rosenthal's (1995) article tells you how to do it. Rosenthal took readers through the four major sections of journal articles, showing how they would be different if presenting a meta-analysis. The major differences are in the method and results sections, and he describes them in useful detail. He made it clear that one can conduct meta-analyses in a variety of ways and encouraged the use of designs that are "simple, basic, and intuitive" (p. 190) and the preparation of reports having the same qualities. Cooper (1998) provided an even more extensive treatment of how to carry out and present the results of literature reviews.

Maxwell and Cole (1995) offered guidance in preparing methodological papers, which usually cover design, measurement, and statistics. Even if you do not see yourself writing a paper on some methodological aspect of practice or outcomes evaluation and have no interest in what Maxwell and Cole have to say, consider that their purpose is to provide tips for both writing and reading methodological papers. They note that papers on statistics often are difficult to understand not merely because they present complex concepts but also because of the "tacit assumption that the rules of good writing cease to apply when writing about statistics" (p. 193). They offer excellent suggestions for presenting methodology more clearly as well as a hierarchical approach for reading methodological papers. In this approach, the reader avoids an initial "word for word from the beginning" tactic and instead skims the entire paper to develop a broad understanding at the outset. The reader can focus on careful reading of the introduction and conclusion on the second pass, continuing to skim the rationale leading to the latter. On the third reading, the reader can attack the author's arguments more intensely. Just as writers have to write and rewrite many times, the reader can expect several "rereads." Maxwell and Cole end their paper with a list of 15 specific suggestions, many of which apply to writing generally.

Reviewing the basic rules of grammar, knowing APA format, and following the suggestions in these papers enhance the chances that your submission will meet with a favorable review. In addition, if you incorporated feedback from presentations of your outcomes evaluation to one or more audiences before submitting it, you have a greater chance of success. Concerns expressed by such audiences are likely to mirror those of editors, so it is good to deal with them ahead of time.

Preparing Grant Proposals

If your work occurs in an agency or organized health-care delivery system, someone might ask you to respond to a request from a funding agency for grant or contract proposals (i.e., "request for proposals" [RFPs]). Preparing and submitting RFPs involves many of the same structural and content issues discussed above. Most funding agencies have broadly defined formats they expect applicants to follow, and many include specific forms to facilitate the process. Not much room exists for creative writing in the parts of the proposal dealing with budget, staffing, equal opportunity assurances, and other administrative matters. Most proposals require a narrative section, however, in which you provide a description of what you want to do and how you use the support. This section generally parallels the structure of the four parts of empirical journal articles described above, so the suggestions for writing papers can help with writing grant proposals. Some excellent resources devoted specifically to writing successful grant applications are available (e.g., Holtz, 1979; Krathwohl, 1977; Locke, Spirduso, & Silverman, 1987).

In addition, on the basis of his own experience reviewing grants for a major federal agency, Oetting (1986) identified 10 mistakes that can be lethal in proposal writing (see Exhibit 13.4). Although the warnings are for research grant applications, some also apply to grants submitted to fund services. Oetting warned that the most important of all

---

Exhibit 13.4

Ten Mistakes to Avoid When Submitting a Research Grant

1. Writing a research grant when the primary purpose is to fund treatment
2. Proposing research that is not in the investigator's areas of strength
3. Leaving out important details, assuming reviewers recognize you as an expert who (of course) knows the nitty-gritty of doing the research correctly
4. Ignoring feedback from previous submission(s) of the proposal, resubmitting essentially the same one
5. Planning to develop an assessment instrument without showing awareness of the highly complex nature of this activity
6. Tacking a topic area of interest to the funding source onto a proposal that has little to do with the topic in order to get funding for the researcher's real interest
7. Proposing research to solve a problem that really does not exist
8. Making excuses for known flaws in the study, such as why a control group cannot be included
9. Using assessment instruments not appropriate for the study
10. Not submitting a grant application in the first place.

Note. From "Ten Fatal Mistakes in Grant Writing," by E. R. Oetting, *Professional Psychology: Research and Practice, 17,* 1986, pp. 570–573. Copyright 1986 by the American Psychological Association. Reprinted with permission.

the errors is the 10th: not applying for funding if you need it. There are thousands of funding sources, both in and out of the government, and many directories of philanthropic organizations and foundations include descriptions of the types of activity they support.

Criticism and Commentary: The Castor Oil of Adult Professionals

This chapter is about baring the soul of your work to other people. Doing so opens many opportunities, and among the most useful are also the most dreaded. Others see your work and evaluate it. Of course, we disseminate our findings to get the responses of others in the first place because their reactions generate improvements in our future work. Criticism is good. It shows us how others see our work. It gives us information we can use to get better. It can also be hard to take.

What are some constructive ways of dealing with criticism? An easy way is to prepare for it. Typically, we upset ourselves less when we know what to expect. In the publishing world, rejection is common. According to Eichorn and VandenBos (1985), APA journals accept no more than 2% of the initial submissions they receive. This is a daunting figure. Knowing it prepares us to expect our initial attempt to be rebuffed. There is comfort in knowing we have company—lots of it. Even greater comfort can come from realizing that our chances improve considerably with a revised manuscript. Eichorn and VandenBos reported the probability of acceptance for revisions to be 20% to 40%, depending on the journal. This figure lowers the overall rejection rate for APA journals from the initial 98% to 75%. The question is, How can you be among the fortunate 25%?

If you take the suggestions of this chapter seriously, you will be a long way toward achieving success in publishing your paper. If you react constructively to the high likelihood of initial rejection, you improve your chances even more. In addition to being prepared for the likelihood that your first attempts will not be rewarded, several other tactics can keep you in the game. *Reframing* the commentary from criticism to "useful ideas for improvement" is an important first step. Remember, the job of the reviewer is to help you make the paper and the work it is reporting better; expect there to be more criticisms than accolades in the review. Reminding yourself that the rejection is strictly business, nothing personal, can help you deal with criticisms constructively. Reviewers direct their comments at your work or its expression, not at you as a human being. When you get a review, read it quickly and put it away. Come back to it after several days and look at each point more closely. Decide which ones make the most sense, and prioritize your changes. Was the reviewer simply confused by the way you described something, or did you make a mistake that you cannot remedy at this point? No research or evaluation is perfect. If you have merely confused the reader, revising usually leads to clarification. If you have made an error, the issue becomes whether you can acknowledge it and still show how the results can be useful.

Plan to complete a revision and resubmit your paper within 60 days. An even shorter time period is better. The point is to maintain the momentum, keep your eyes on the prize, and not rest until the paper is accepted. When you have gone through the submit–reject–revise–resubmit sequence with several different papers—some of which ultimately will be accepted—you will feel more confident in the process. You also are more likely to see your evaluation efforts through the complete program evaluation cycle. When this happens, you have received an extensive amount of commentary and are in an excellent position to formulate your next research or evaluative question and continue the evolution of your investigative program.

Summary

Scientific research occurs when human activity increases the cumulative knowledge we have about a phenomenon. For knowledge to grow, we must communicate the results of our work to others. Thus, without dissemination, scientific research has not occurred. For a practitioner to improve the quality of his or her practice on a continual basis, his or her evaluative effort needs to improve as well. Doing so requires reactions from others. If we do not disseminate our findings, we do not get this feedback. From the standpoint of continual quality improvement, submissions to professional journals are the best outlet because of the greater rigor of their peer review process. Rejection is common for all types of written submissions, especially those to professional journals, where initial acceptance rates can be as low as 2%. Dealing effectively with rejection is important, and ways of doing so include preparing for it, reframing it, and responding to it in a timely and constructive manner. Keeping up your momentum helps you see research and outcome evaluation efforts through the entire cycle, from the initial question to dissemination and to formulating the next question and starting the cycle again.

Supplemental Reading

American Psychological Association. (1994). *Publication manual of the American Psychological Association* (4th ed.). Washington, DC: Author.

Bem, D. J. (1995). Writing a review article for *Psychological Bulletin. Psychological Bulletin, 118,* 172–177.

Galvan, J. L. (1999). *Writing literature reviews: A guide for students of the social and behavioral sciences.* Los Angeles, CA: Pyrczak.

Hoff, R. (1992). *I can see you naked.* Kansas City, MO: Andrews & McMeel.

Kazdin, A. E. (1995). Preparing and evaluating research reports. *Psychological Assessment, 7,* 228–237.

Kupfersmid, J. (1988). Improving what is published: A model in search of an editor. *American Psychologist, 43,* 635–642.

Leech, T. (1992). *How to prepare, stage, and deliver winning presentations.* New York: AMACOM.

Locke, L. F., Spirduso, W. W., & Silverman, S. J. (1987). *Proposals that work: A guide for planning dissertations and grant proposals* (2nd ed.). Newbury Park, CA: Sage.

Maxwell, S. E., & Cole, D. A. (1995). Tips for writing (and reading) methodological articles. *Psychological Bulletin, 118,* 193–198.

Rosenthal, R. (1995). Writing meta-analytic reviews. *Psychological Bulletin, 118,* 183–192.

Sternberg, R. J. (1993). *The psychologist's companion* (3rd ed.). New York: Cambridge University Press.

Woodall, M. K. (1993). *How to think on your feet.* New York: Warner Books.

Resources

Toastmasters International: speaking opportunities for members in supportive and organized group sessions; 800/993-7732, http://www.toastmasters.org.

The Executive Speechwriter Newsletter: timely suggestions for writing more effective speeches; c/o Joe Taylor Ford, Ed., Emerson Falls, St. Johnsbury, VT 05819, 802/748-4472, 802/748-1939 (fax), 800/748-4472, http://www.wordsink.com.

Handilinks: http://www.handilinks.com for a list of directories in the United States and around the world.

The Commerce Business Daily: current information on funding initiatives of the U.S. government.

Appendix A: A Reader's, Writer's, and Reviewer's Guide to Assessing Research Reports in Clinical Psychology

Brendan A. Maher
Harvard University

The Editors of the *Journal of Consulting and Clinical Psychology* who served between 1974 and 1978 have seen some 3,500 manuscripts in the area of consulting and clinical psychology. Working with this number of manuscripts has made it possible to formulate a set of general guidelines that may be helpful in the assessment of research reports. Originally developed by and for journal reviewers, the guidelines are necessarily skeletal and summary and omit many methodological concerns. They do, however, address the methodological concerns that have proved to be significant in a substantial number of cases. In response to a number of requests, the guidelines are being made available here.

Topic Content

1. Is the article appropriate to this journal? Does it fall within the boundaries mandated in the masthead description?

Style

1. Does the manuscript conform to APA style in its major aspects?

Introduction

1. Is the introduction as brief as possible given the topic of the article?
2. Are all of the citations correct and necessary, or is there padding? Are important citations missing? Has the author been careful to cite prior reports contrary to the current hypothesis?
3. Is there an explicit hypothesis?
4. Has the *origin* of the hypothesis been made explicit?
5. Was the hypothesis *correctly* derived from the theory that has been cited? Are other, contrary hypotheses compatible with the same theory?
6. Is there an explicit rationale for the selection of measures, and was it derived logically from the hypothesis?

Method

1. Is the method so described that replication is possible without further information?
2. Subjects: Were they sampled randomly from the population to which the results will be generalized?
3. Under what circumstances was informed consent obtained?
4. Are there probable biases in sampling (e.g., volunteers, high refusal rates, institution population atypical for the country at large, etc.)?
5. What was the "set" given to subjects? Was there deception? Was there control for experimenter influence and expectancy effects?
6. How were subjects debriefed?
7. Were subjects (patients) led to believe that they were receiving "treatment"?
8. Were there special variables affecting the subjects, such as medication, fatigue, and threat that were not part of the experimental manipulation? In clinical samples, was "organicity" measured and/or eliminated?
9. Controls: Were there appropriate control groups? What was being controlled for?
10. When more than one measure was used, was the order counterbalanced? If so, were order effects actually analyzed statistically?

11. Was there a control task(s) to confirm specificity of results?

12. Measures: For both dependent and independent variable measures —was validity and reliability established and reported? When a measure is tailor-made for a study, this is very important. When validities and reliabilities are already available in the literature, it is less important.

13. Is there adequate description of tasks, materials, apparatus, and so forth?

14. Is there discriminant validity of the measures?

15. Are distributions of scores on measures typical of scores that have been reported for similar samples in previous literature?

16. Are measures free from biases such as
    a. Social desirability?
    b. Yeasaying and naysaying?
    c. Correlations with general responsivity?
    d. Verbal ability, intelligence?

17. If measures are scored by observers using categories or codes, what is the interrater reliability?

18. Was administration and scoring of the measures done blind?

19. If short versions, foreign-language translations, and so forth, of common measures are used, has the validity and reliability of these been established?

20. In correlational designs, do the two measures have theoretical and/ or methodological independence?

Representative Design

1. When the stimulus is a human (e.g., in clinical judgments of clients of differing race, sex, etc.), is there a *sample* of stimuli (e.g., more than one client of each race or each sex)?

2. When only one stimulus or a few human stimuli were used, was an adequate explanation of the failure to sample given?

Statistics

1. Were the statistics used with appropriate assumptions fulfilled by the data (e.g., normalcy of distributions for parametric techniques)? Where necessary, have scores been transformed appropriately?

2. Were tests of significance properly used and reported? For example, did the author use the *p* value of a correlation to justify conclusions when the actual size of the correlation suggests little common variance between two measures?
3. Have statistical significance levels been accompanied by an analysis of practical significance levels?
4. Has the author considered the effects of a limited range of scores, and so forth, in using correlations?
5. Is the basic statistical strategy that of a "fishing expedition"; that is, if many comparisons are made, were the obtained significance levels predicted in advance? Consider the number of significance levels as a function of the total number of comparisons made.

Factor Analytic Statistics

1. Have the correlation and factor matrices been made available to the reviewers and to the readers through the National Auxiliary Publications Service or other methods?
2. Is it stated what was used for communalities and is the choice appropriate? Ones in the diagonals are especially undesirable when items are correlated as the variables.
3. Is the method of termination of factor extraction stated, and is it appropriate in this case?
4. Is the method of factor rotation stated, and is it appropriate in this case?
5. If items are used as variables, what are the proportions of yes and no responses for each variable?
6. Is the sample size given, and is it adequate?
7. Are there evidences of distortion in the final solution, such as singlet factors, excessively high communalities, obliqueness when an orthogonal solution is used, linearly dependent variables, or too many complex variables?
8. Are artificial factors evident because of inclusion of variables in the analysis that are alternate forms of each other?

Figures and Tables

1. Are the figures and tables (a) necessary and (b) self-explanatory? Large tables of nonsignificant differences, for example, should be

eliminated if the few obtained significances can be reported in a sentence or two in the text. Could several tables be combined into a smaller number?

2. Are the axes of figures identified clearly?
3. Do graphs correspond logically to the textual argument of the article? (e.g., if the text states that a certain technique leads to an *increment* of mental health and the accompanying graph shows a *decline* in symptoms, the point is not as clear to the reader as it would be if the text or the graph were amended to achieve visual and verbal congruence.)

Discussion and Conclusion

1. Is the discussion properly confined to the findings or is it digressive, including new post hoc speculations?
2. Has the author explicitly considered and discussed viable alternative explanations of the findings?
3. Have nonsignificant trends in the data been promoted to "findings"?
4. Are the limits of the generalizations possible from the data made clear? Has the author identified his/her own methodological difficulties in the study?
5. Has the author "accepted" the null hypothesis?
6. Has the author considered the possible methodological bases for discrepancies between the results reported and other findings in the literature?

Appendix B: Selected Ethical Standards Relevant to the Conduct of Research in Psychology

1.14 Avoiding Harm

Psychologists take reasonable steps to avoid harming their patients or clients, research participants, students, and others with whom they work, and to minimize harm where it is foreseeable and unavoidable.

1.16 Misuse of Psychologists' Work

(a) Psychologists do not participate in activities in which it appears likely that their skills or data will be misused by others, unless corrective mechanisms are available.

(b) If psychologists learn of misuse or misrepresentation of their work, they take reasonable steps to correct or minimize the misuse or misrepresentation.

1.19 Exploitative Relationships

(a) Psychologists do not exploit persons over whom they have supervisory, evaluative, or other authority such as students, supervisees, employees, research participants, and clients or patients.

From *Ethical Principles of Psychologists and Code of Conduct* (American Psychological Association, 1992).

(b) Psychologists do not engage in sexual relationships with students or supervisees in training over whom the psychologist has evaluative or direct authority, because such relationships are so likely to impair judgment or be exploitative.

1.22 Delegation to and Supervision of Subordinates

(a) Psychologists delegate to their employees, supervisees, and research assistants only those responsibilities that such persons can reasonably be expected to perform competently, on the basis of their education, training, or experience, either independently or with the level of supervision being provided.

(b) Psychologists provide proper training and supervision to their employees or supervisees and take reasonable steps to see that such persons perform services responsibly, competently, and ethically.

(c) If institutional policies, procedures, or practices prevent fulfillment of this obligation, psychologists attempt to modify their role or to correct the situation to the extent feasible.

1.23 Documentation of Professional and Scientific Work

(a) Psychologists appropriately document their professional and scientific work in order to facilitate provision of services later by them or by other professionals, to ensure accountability, and to meet other requirements of institutions or the law.

(b) When psychologists have reason to believe that records of their professional services will be used in legal proceedings involving recipients of or participants in their work, they have a responsibility to create and maintain documentation in the kind of detail and quality that would be consistent with reasonable scrutiny in an adjudicative forum. (See also Standard 7.01, Professionalism, under Forensic Activities.)

1.25 Fees and Financial Arrangements

(a) As early as is feasible in a professional or scientific relationship, the psychologist and the patient, client, or other appropriate recipient of psychological services reach an agreement specifying the compensation and the billing arrangements.

(b) Psychologists do not exploit recipients of services or payors with respect to fees.

(c) Psychologists' fee practices are consistent with law.

(d) Psychologists do not misrepresent their fees.

(e) If limitations to services can be anticipated because of limitations in financing, this is discussed with the patient, client, or other appropriate recipient of services as early as is feasible.

(f) If the patient, client, or other recipient of services does not pay for services as agreed, and if the psychologist wishes to use collection agencies or legal measures to collect the fees, the psychologist first informs the person that such measures will be taken and provides that person an opportunity to make prompt payment.

3.03 Avoidance of False or Deceptive Statements

(a) Psychologists do not make public statements that are false, deceptive, misleading, or fraudulent, either because of what they state, convey, or suggest or because of what they omit, concerning their research, practice, or other work activities or those of persons or organizations with which they are affiliated. As examples (and not in limitation) of this standard, psychologists do not make false or deceptive statements concerning (1) their training, experience, or competence; (2) their academic degrees; (3) their credentials; (4) their institutional or association affiliations; (5) their services; (6) the scientific or clinical basis for, or results or degree of success of, their services; (7) their fees; or (8) their publications or research findings. (See also Standards 6.15, Deception in Research, and 6.18, Providing Participants With Information About the Study.)

(b) Psychologists claim as credentials for their psychological work, only degrees that (1) were earned from a regionally accredited educational institution or (2) were the basis for psychology licensure by the state in which they practice.

5.01 Discussing the Limits of Confidentiality

(a) Psychologists discuss with persons and organizations with whom they establish a scientific or professional relationship (including, to the extent feasible, minors and their legal representatives) (1) the relevant limitations on confidentiality, including limitations where applicable in group, marital, and family therapy or in organizational consulting, and (2) the foreseeable uses of the information generated through their services.

(b) Unless it is not feasible or is contraindicated, the discussion of confidentiality occurs at the outset of the relationship and thereafter as new circumstances may warrant.

(c) Permission for electronic recording of interviews is secured from clients and patients.

5.02 Maintaining Confidentiality

Psychologists have a primary obligation and take reasonable precautions to respect the confidentiality rights of those with whom they work or consult, recognizing that confidentiality may be established by law, institutional rules, or professional or scientific relationships. (See also Standard 6.26, Professional Reviewers.)

5.03 Minimizing Intrusions on Privacy

(a) In order to minimize intrusions on privacy, psychologists include in written and oral reports, consultations, and the like, only information germane to the purpose for which the communication is made.

(b) Psychologists discuss confidential information obtained in clinical or consulting relationships, or evaluative data concerning patients, individual or organizational clients, students, research participants, supervisees, and employees, only for appropriate scientific or professional purposes and only with persons clearly concerned with such matters.

5.04 Maintenance of Records

Psychologists maintain appropriate confidentiality in creating, storing, accessing, transferring, and disposing of records under their control, whether these are written, automated, or in any other medium. Psychologists maintain and dispose of records in accordance with law and in a manner that permits compliance with the requirements of this Ethics Code.

5.07 Confidential Information in Databases

(a) If confidential information concerning recipients of psychological services is to be entered into databases or systems of records available to persons whose access has not been consented to by the recipient, then psychologists use coding or other techniques to avoid the inclusion of personal identifiers.

(b) If a research protocol approved by an institutional review board or similar body requires the inclusion of personal identifiers, such identifiers are deleted before the information is made accessible to persons other than those of whom the subject was advised.

(c) If such deletion is not feasible, then before psychologists transfer such data to others or review such data collected by others, they take reasonable steps to determine that appropriate consent of personally identifiable individuals has been obtained.

5.08 Use of Confidential Information for Didactic or Other Purposes

(a) Psychologists do not disclose in their writings, lectures, or other public media, confidential, personally identifiable information concerning their patients, individual or organizational clients, students, research participants, or other recipients of their services that they obtained during the course of their work, unless the person or organization has consented in writing or unless there is other ethical or legal authorization for doing so.

(b) Ordinarily, in such scientific and professional presentations, psychologists disguise confidential information concerning such persons or organizations so that they are not individually identifiable to others and so that discussions do not cause harm to subjects who might identify themselves.

5.09 Preserving Records and Data

A psychologist makes plans in advance so that confidentiality of records and data is protected in the event of the psychologist's death, incapacity, or withdrawal from the position or practice.

5.10 Ownership of Records and Data

Recognizing that ownership of records and data is governed by legal principles, psychologists take reasonable and lawful steps so that records and data remain available to the extent needed to serve the best interests of patients, individual or organizational clients, research participants, or appropriate others.

6.06 Planning Research

(a) Psychologists design, conduct, and report research in accordance with recognized standards of scientific competence and ethical research.

(b) Psychologists plan their research so as to minimize the possibility that results will be misleading.

(c) In planning research, psychologists consider its ethical acceptability under the Ethics Code. If an ethical issue is unclear, psychologists seek to resolve the issue through consultation with institutional review boards, animal care and use committees, peer consultations, or other proper mechanisms.

(d) Psychologists take reasonable steps to implement appropriate protections for the rights and welfare of human participants, other persons affected by the research, and the welfare of animal subjects.

6.07 Responsibility

(a) Psychologists conduct research competently and with due concern for the dignity and welfare of the participants.

(b) Psychologists are responsble for the ethical conduct of research conducted by them or by others under their supervision or control.

(c) Researchers and assistants are permitted to perform only those tasks for which they are appropriately trained and prepared.

(d) As part of the process of development and implementation of research projects, psychologists consult those with expertise concerning any special population under investigation or most likely to be affected.

6.08 Compliance With Law and Standards

Psychologists plan and conduct research in a manner consistent with federal and state law and regulations, as well as professional standards governing the conduct of research, and particularly those standards governing research with human participants and animal subjects.

6.09 Institutional Approval

Psychologists obtain from host institutions or organizations appropriate approval prior to conducting research, and they provide accurate information about their research proposals. They conduct the research in accordance with the approved research protocol.

6.10 Research Responsibilities

Prior to conducting research (except research involving only anonymous surveys, naturalistic observations, or similar research), psychologists enter into an agreement with the participants that clarifies the nature of the research and the responsibilities of each party.

6.11 Informed Consent to Research

(a) Psychologists use language that is reasonably understandable to research participants in obtaining their appropriate informed consent (except as provided in Standard 6.12, Dispensing With Informed Consent). Such informed consent is appropriately documented.

(b) Using language that is reasonably understandable to participants, psychologists inform participants of the nature of the research; they inform participants that they are free to participate or to decline to participate or to withdraw from the research; they explain the foreseeable consequences of declining or withdrawing; they inform participants of significant factors that may be expected to influence their willingness to participate (such as risks, discomfort, adverse effects, or limitations on confidentiality, except as provided in Standard 6.15, Deception in Research); and they explain other aspects about which the prospective participants inquire.

(c) When psychologists conduct research with individuals such as students or subordinates, psychologists take special care to protect the prospective participants from adverse consequences of declining or withdrawing from participation.

(d) When research participation is a course requirement or opportunity for extra credit, the prospective participant is given the choice of equitable alternative activities.

(e) For persons who are legally incapable of giving informed consent, psychologists nevertheless (1) provide an appropriate explanation, (2) obtain the participant's assent, and (3) obtain appropriate permission from a legally authorized person, if such substitute consent is permitted by law.

6.12 Dispensing With Informed Consent

Before determining that planned research (such as research involving only anonymous questionnaires, naturalistic observations, or certain kinds of archival research) does not require the informed consent of research participants, psychologists consider applicable regulations and institutional review board requirements, and they consult with colleagues as appropriate.

6.13 Informed Consent in Research Filming or Recording

Psychologists obtain informed consent from research participants prior to filming or recording them in any form, unless the research involves simply naturalistic observations in public places and it is not anticipated that the recording will be used in a manner that could cause personal identification or harm.

6.14 Offering Inducements for Research Participants

(a) In offering professional services as an inducement to obtain research participants, psychologists make clear the nature of the services, as well as the risks, obligations, and limitations.

(b) Psychologists do not offer excessive or inappropriate financial or other inducements to obtain research participants, particularly when it might tend to coerce participation.

6.15 Deception in Research

(a) Psychologists do not conduct a study involving deception unless they have determined that the use of deceptive techniques is justified by the study's prospective scientific, educational, or applied value and that equally effective alternative procedures that do not use deception are not feasible.

(b) Psychologists never deceive research participants about significant aspects that would affect their willingness to participate, such as physical risks, discomfort, or unpleasant emotional experiences.

(c) Any other deception that is an integral feature of the design and conduct of an experiment must be explained to participants as early as is feasible, preferably at the conclusion of their participation, but no later than at the conclusion of the research. (See also Standard 6.18, Providing Participants With Information About the Study.)

6.16 Sharing and Utilizing Data

Psychologists inform research participants of their anticipated sharing or further use of personally identifiable research data and of the possibility of unanticipated future uses.

6.17 Minimizing Invasiveness

In conducting research, psychologists interfere with the participants or milieu from which data are collected only in a manner that is warranted by an appropriate research design and that is consistent with psychologists' roles as scientific investigators.

6.18 Providing Participants With Information About the Study

(a) Psychologists provide a prompt opportunity for participants to obtain appropriate information about the nature, results, and conclusions of the research, and psychologists attempt to correct any misconceptions that participants may have.

(b) If scientific or humane values justify delaying or withholding this information, psychologists take reasonable measures to reduce the risk of harm.

6.19 Honoring Commitments

Psychologists take reasonable measures to honor all commitments they have made to research participants.

6.21 Reporting of Results

(a) Psychologists do not fabricate data or falsify results in their publications.

(b) If psychologists discover significant errors in their published data, they take reasonable steps to correct such errors in a correction, retraction, erratum, or other appropriate publication means.

6.22 Plagiarism

Psychologists do not present substantial portions or elements of another's work or data as their own, even if the other work or data source is cited occasionally.

6.23 Publication Credit

(a) Psychologists take responsibility and credit, including authorship credit, only for work they have actually performed or to which they have contributed.

(b) Principal authorship and other publication credits accurately reflect the relative scientific or professional contributions of the individuals involved, regardless of their relative status. Mere possession of an institutional position, such as Department Chair, does not justify authorship credit. Minor contributions to the research or to the writing for publications are appropriately acknowledged, such as in footnotes or in an introductory statement.

(c) A student is usually listed as principal author on any multiple-authored article that is substantially based on the student's dissertation or thesis.

6.24 Duplicate Publication of Data

Psychologists do not publish, as original data, data that have been previously published. This does not preclude republishing data when they are accompanied by proper acknowledgment.

6.25 Sharing Data

After research results are published, psychologists do not withhold the data on which their conclusions are based from other competent professionals who seek to verify the substantive claims through reanalysis and who intend to use such data only for that purpose, provided that the confidentiality of the participants can be protected and unless legal rights concerning proprietary data preclude their release.

6.26 Professional Reviewers

Psychologists who review material submitted for publication, grant, or other research proposal review respect the confidentiality of and the proprietary rights in such information of those who submitted it.

References

Achenbach, T. M. (1991). *Manual for the Child Behavior Checklist/4-18 and 1991 Profile.* Burlington: University of Vermont, Department of Psychiatry.

Achenbach, T. M., & Edelbrock, C. (1983). *Manual for the Child Behavior Checklist and Revised Child Behavior Profile.* Burlington: University of Vermont, Department of Psychiatry.

Ad Hoc Committee on the Classification of Headache. (1962). Classification of headache. *Journal of the American Medical Association, 179,* 717–718.

Adair, J. G., Dushenko, T. W., & Lindsay, R. C. L. (1985). Ethical regulations and their impact on research practice. *American Psychologist, 40,* 59–72.

Aiken, L. R. (1996). *Personality assessment: Methods and practices* (2nd ed.). Seattle, WA: Hogrefe & Huber.

Albrecht, K. (1994). *The northbound train: Finding the purpose, setting the direction, shaping the destiny of your organization.* New York: AMACOM.

Allen, K. D., & Shriver, M. D. (1998). Role of parent-mediated pain behavior management strategies in biofeedback treatment of childhood migraines. *Behavior Therapy, 29,* 477–490.

Allport, G. W. (1937). *Personality: A psychological interpretation.* New York: Holt.

Allport, G. W. (1962). The general and the unique in psychological science. *Journal of Personality, 34,* 405–422.

American Psychiatric Association. (1952). *Diagnostic and statistical manual of mental disorders.* Washington, DC: Author.

American Psychiatric Association. (1987). *Diagnostic and statistical manual of mental disorders* (3rd ed. rev.). Washington, DC: Author.

American Psychological Association. (1992). Ethical principles of psychologists and code of conduct. *American Psychologist, 47,* 1597–1611.

American Psychological Association. (1994). *Publication manual of the American Psychological Association* (4th ed.). Washington, DC: Author.

Anderson, B. L., Kiecolt-Glaser, J. K., & Glaser, R. (1994). A biobehavioral model of cancer stress and disease course. *American Psychologist, 49,* 389–404.

Ashbaugh, R., & Peck, S. M. (1998). Treatment of sleep problems in a toddler: A replication of the faded bedtime with response cost procedure. *Journal of Applied Behavior Analysis, 31,* 127–129.

Association for Advancement of Behavior Therapy. (1977). Ethical issues for human services. *Behavior Therapy, 8,* 763–764.

Atkeson, B. M., Calhoun, K. S., Resick, P. A., & Ellis, E. M. (1982). Victims of rape:

Repeated assessment of depressive symptoms. *Journal of Consulting and Clinical Psychology, 50,* 96–102.

Attkisson, C. C., & Zwick, R. (1982). The Client Satisfaction Questionnaire. Psychometric properties and correlations with service utilization. *Evaluation and Program Planning, 5,* 233–237.

Azrin, N. H., & Powell, J. (1969). Behavioral engineering: The use of response priming to improve self-medication. *Journal of Applied Behavior Analysis, 2,* 39–42.

Baer, D. M. (1977). "Perhaps it would be better not to know everything." *Journal of Applied Behavior Analysis, 10,* 167–172.

Baer, D. M., Wolf, M. M., & Risley, T. R. (1968). Some current dimensions of applied behavior analysis. *Journal of Applied Behavior Analysis, 1,* 91–97.

Bagozzi, R. P. (1993). An examination of the psychometric properties of measures of negative affect in the PANAS-X scales. *Journal of Personality and Social Psychology, 65,* 836–851.

Bailey, J. S. (1988). Manuscript preparation checklist. *Journal of Applied Behavior Analysis, 21,* 119–120.

Baker, B. L., & Brightman, A. J. (1997). *Steps to independence* (3rd ed.). Baltimore: Brookes.

Bangert-Drowns, R. L. (1986). Review of developments in meta-analytic method. *Psychological Bulletin, 99,* 388–399.

Bar-Hillel, M. (1980). The base rate fallacy in probability judgments. *Acta Psychologica, 44,* 211–233.

Barkley, R. A. (1998). Attention-deficit/hyperactivity disorder. In E. J. Mash & R. A. Barkley (Eds.), *Treatment of childhood disorders* (2nd ed., pp. 55–110). New York: Guilford Press.

Barkley, R. A., Guevremont, D. C., Anastopoulos, A. D., & Fletcher, K. E. (1992). A comparison of three family therapy programs for treating family conflicts in adolescents with attention deficit hyperactivity disorder. *Journal of Consulting and Clinical Psychology, 60,* 450–462.

Barlow, D. H. (1988). *Anxiety and its disorders: The nature and treatment of anxiety and panic.* New York: Guilford Press.

Barlow, D. H. (1996). Health care policy, psychotherapy research, and the future of psychotherapy. *American Psychologist, 51,* 1050–1058.

Barlow, D. H., & Craske, M. G. (1989). *Mastery of your anxiety and panic.* Albany, NY: Greywind.

Barlow, D. H., & Craske, M. G. (1994). *Mastery of your anxiety and panic II.* Albany, NY: Greywind.

Barlow, D. H., Craske, M. G., Cerny, J. A., & Klosko, J. S. (1989). Behavioral treatment of panic disorder. *Behavior Therapy, 20,* 261–282.

Barlow, D. H., & Hayes, S. C. (1979). Alternating treatments design: One strategy for comparing the effects of two treatments in a single subject. *Journal of Applied Behavior Analysis, 12,* 199–210.

Barlow, D. H., Hayes, S. C., & Nelson, R. O. (1984). *The scientist practitioner: Research and accountability in clinical and educational settings.* New York: Pergamon.

Baron, R. M., & Kenny, D. A. (1986). The moderator–mediator variable distinction in social psychological research: Conceptual, strategic, and statistical considerations. *Journal of Personality and Social Psychology, 51,* 1173–1182.

Barrios, B. A. (1993). Direct observation. In T. H. Ollendick & M. Hersen (Eds.), *Handbook of child and adolescent assessment* (pp. 140–164). Boston: Allyn & Bacon.

Baruffol, E., Gisle, L., & Corten, P. (1995). Life satisfaction as a mediator between distressing events and neurotic impairment in a general population. *Acta Psychiatrica Scandinavica, 92,* 56–62.

Baucom, D. H., & Hoffman, J. A. (1986). The effectiveness of marital therapy: Current status and application to the clinical setting. In N. S. Jacobson & A. S. Gurman (Eds.), *Clinical Handbook of marital therapy* (pp. 597–620). New York: Guilford Press.

Baumrind, D. (1985). Research using intentional deception: Ethical issues revisited. *American Psychologist, 40,* 165–174.

Beck, A. T. (1961). A systematic investigation of depression. *Comprehensive Psychiatry, 2,* 163–170.

Beck, A. T. (1963). Thinking and depression. *Archives of General Psychiatry, 9,* 324–333.

Beck, A. T. (1976). *Cognitive therapy and the emotional disorders.* New York: International Universities Press.

Beck, A. T. (1983). Cognitive theory of depression: New perspectives. In P. J. Clayton & J. E. Barrett (Eds.), *Treatment of depression: Old controversies and new approaches* (pp. 265–284). New York: Raven Press.

Beck, A. T. (1988). Cognitive approaches to panic disorder: Theory and therapy. In S. Rachman & J. D. Maser (Eds.), *Panic: Psychological perspectives* (pp. 91–109). Hillsdale, NJ: Erlbaum.

Beck, A. T., Rush, A. J., Shaw, B. F., & Emery, G. (1979). *Cognitive therapy of depression.* New York: Guilford Press.

Beck, A. T., Ward, C. H., Mendelsohn, M., Mock, J., & Erbaugh, J. (1961). An inventory for measuring depression. *Archives of General Psychiatry, 4,* 561–571.

Beck, J. S. (1995). *Cognitive therapy: Basics and beyond.* New York: Guilford Press.

Beed, W. T., & Stimson, R. J. (Eds.). (1985). *Survey interviewing: Theory and techniques.* London: Allen & Unwin.

Bem, D. J. (1995). Writing a review article for *Psychological Bulletin. Psychological Bulletin, 118,* 172–177.

Bentler, P. M. (1989). *EQS structural equations program manual.* Los Angeles, CA: GMDP Statistical Software.

Berk, R. A. (1979). Generalizability of behavioral observations: A clarification of interobserver agreement and interobserver reliability. *American Journal of Mental Deficiency, 83,* 460–472.

Berman, W. H. (1998). Psychology in managed health care: Introduction. *Clinical Psychology: Science and Practice, 5,* 51–52.

Berman, W. H., Hurt, S. W., & Heiss, G. E. (1996). Outcomes assessment and management in managed behavioral healthcare. In C. E. Stout, G. A. Theis, & J. M. Oher (Eds.), *The complete guide to managed behavioral healthcare* (pp. II-D.1–II.D.10). New York: Wiley.

Berman, W. H., Rosen, C. S., Hurt, S. W., & Kolarz, C. M. (1998). Toto, we're not in Kansas anymore: Measuring and using outcomes in behavioral health care. *Clinical Psychology: Science and Practice, 5,* 115–133.

Bernstein, D. A., & Borkovec, T. D. (1973). *Progressive relaxation training.* Champaign, IL: Research Press.

Bernstein, I. N., Bohrnstedt, G. W., & Borgatta, E. F. (1975). External validity and evaluation research: A codification of problems. *Sociological Methods and Research, 4,* 101–128.

Best, J. A., & Steffy, R. A. (1971). Smoking modification procedures tailored to subject characteristics. *Behavior Therapy, 2,* 177–191.

Beutler, L. E., & Hamblin, D. L. (1986). Individualized outcome measures of internal change: Methodological considerations. *Journal of Consulting and Clinical Psychology, 54,* 48–53.

Biglan, A., & Hayes, S. C. (1996). Should the behavioral sciences become more pragmatic? The case for functional contextualism in research on human behavior. *Applied and Preventive Psychology, 5,* 47–57.

Biostat. (1998). *Comprehensive meta-analysis* [Computer program]. Teaneck, NJ: Author.

Blackburn, I. M., Bishop, S., Glen, A. I. M., Whalley, L. J., & Christie, J. E. (1981). The efficacy of cognitive therapy for depression: A treatment trial using cognitive therapy and pharmacotherapy, each alone and in combination. *British Journal of Psychiatry, 139,* 181–189.

Blanchard, E. B., Andrasik, F., Evans, D. D., Neff, D. F., Appelbaum, K. A., & Rodichok, L. D. (1985). Behavioral treatment of 250 chronic headache patients: A clinical replication series. *Behavior Therapy, 16,* 308–332.

Bloom, M., Fischer, J., & Orme, J. G. (1995). *Evaluating practice: Guidelines for the accountable professional* (2nd ed.). Boston: Allyn & Bacon.

Bollen, K., & Lennox, R. (1991). Conventional wisdom on measurement: A structural equation perspective. *Psychological Bulletin, 110,* 305–314.

Bracht, G. H., & Glass, G. V. (1968). The external validity of experiments. *American Educational Research Journal, 5,* 437–474.

Bradburn, N. M., & Sudman, S. (1982). *Asking questions: A practical guide to questionnaire design.* San Francisco: Jossey-Bass.

Bradley, J. V. (1981). Pernicious publication practices. *Bulletin of the Psychonomic Society, 18,* 31–34.

Bromley, D. B. (1986). *The case-study method in psychology and related disciplines.* New York: Wiley.

Bryk, A. S., & Raudenbush, S. W. (1992). *Hierarchical linear models.* Thousand Oaks, CA: Sage.

Byrne, D. (1997). An overview (and underview) of research and theory within the attraction paradigm. *Journal of Social and Personal Relationships, 14,* 417–431.

Campbell, D. T. (1960). Recommendations for APA test standards regarding construct, trait, and discriminant validity. *American Psychologist, 15,* 546–553.

Campbell, D. T., & Fiske, D. (1959). Convergent and discriminant validation by the multitrait-multimethod matrix. *Psychological Bulletin, 56,* 81–105.

Cannell, C. F., & Kahn, R. L. (1985). Interviewing. In G. Lindzey & E. Aronson (Eds.), *The handbook of social psychology* (3rd ed., Vol. 2, pp. 526–595). New York: Random House.

Carr, E. G., Levin, L., McConnachie, G., Carlson, J. I., Kemp, D. C., & Smith, C. E. (1994). *Communication-based intervention for problem behavior. A user's guide for producing positive change.* Baltimore: Brookes.

Carr, J. E., & Burkholder, E. O. (1998). Creating single-subject design graphs with Microsoft Excel. *Journal of Applied Behavior Analysis, 31,* 245–251.

Ceci, S., & Peters, D. (1984). How blind is blind review? *American Psychologist, 39,* 1491–1494.

Chapman, L. J., & Chapman, J. P. (1967). The genesis of popular but erroneous psychodiagnostic observations. *Journal of Abnormal Psychology, 72,* 193–204.

Chapman, L. J., & Chapman, J. P. (1969). Illusory correlations as an obstacle to the use of valid psychodiagnostic signs. *Journal of Abnormal Psychology, 74,* 271–280.

Clarke, G. N. (1995). Improving the transition from basic efficacy research to effectiveness studies: Methodological issues and procedures. *Journal of Consulting and Clinical Psychology, 63,* 718–725.

Clement, P. W. (1996). Evaluation in private practice. *Clinical Psychology: Science and Practice, 3,* 146–159.

Clement, P. W. (1999). *Outcomes and incomes: How to evaluate, improve, and market your psychotherapy practice by measuring outcomes.* New York: Guilford Press.

Cliff, N. (1987). *Analyzing multivariate data.* San Diego: Harcourt Brace Jovanovich.

Cobb, S., & Romfo, C. (1991). *The Stephen Cobb user's guide to FileMaker.* New York: McGraw-Hill.

Cochran, W. G. (1977). *Sampling techniques* (3rd ed.). New York: Wiley.

Cohen, J. (1960). A coefficient of agreement for nominal scales. *Educational and Psychological Measurement, 20,* 37–46.

Cohen, J. (1977). *Statistical power analysis for the behavioral sciences.* Hillsdale, NJ: Erlbaum.

Cohen, J. (1983). The cost of dichotomization. *Applied Psychological Measurement, 7,* 249–253.

Cohen, J. (1988). *Statistical power analysis for the behavioral sciences* (2nd ed.). Hillsdale, NJ: Erlbaum.

Coie, J. D., Dodge, K. A., & Coppotelli, H. (1982). Dimensions and types of status: A cross-age perspective. *Developmental Psychology, 18,* 557–570.

Cole, D. A., Gondoli, D. M., & Peeke, L. G. (1998). Structure and validity of parent and teacher perceptions of children's competence: A multitrait–multimethod–multigroup investigation. *Psychological Assessment, 10,* 241–249.

Cole, D. A., & Turner, J. E., Jr. (1993). Models of cognitive mediation and moderation in child depression. *Journal of Abnormal Psychology, 102,* 271–281.

Cone, J. D. (1977). The relevance of reliability and validity for behavioral assessment. *Behavior Therapy, 8,* 411–426.

Cone, J. D. (1978). The behavioral assessment grid (BAG): A conceptual framework and a taxonomy. *Behavior Therapy, 9,* 882–888.

Cone, J. D. (1995). Assessment practice standards. In S. C. Hayes, V. M. Follette, R. M. Dawes, & K. E. Grady (Eds.), *Scientific standards of psychological practice: Issues and recommendations* (pp. 201–224). Reno, NV: Context Press.

Cone, J. D., DeLawyer, D. D., & Wolfe, V. (1985). Assessing parent participation: The Parent/Family Involvement Index. *Exceptional Children, 51,* 417–424.

Cone, J. D., & Foster, S. L. (1993). *Dissertations and theses from start to finish.* Washington, DC: American Psychological Association.

Cone, J. D., Nyberg, T., & Watson, M. E. (1983). *Staff–pupil interaction recording system (SPIRS).* Unpublished manuscript, West Virginia University, Morgantown.

Cone, J. D., Sweitzer, M., Casper-Beliveau, S., Rausch, D., & Sousa, L. (1995, November). *Training parents to teach self-help skills increases child misbehavior and raises parents' stress.* Poster session presented at the annual meeting of the Association for Advancement of Behavior Therapy, Washington, DC.

Conners, C. K. (1990). *The Conners Rating Scales.* North Tonawanda, NY: Multi-Health Systems.

Cook, T. D., & Campbell, D. T. (1979). *Quasi-experimentation: Design and analysis issues for field settings.* Chicago: Rand McNally.

Cook, T. D., & Wittmann, W. W. (1998). Lessons learned about evaluation in the USA and some possible implications for Europe. *European Journal of Psychological Assessment, 14,* 97–115.

Cooper, H. (1998). *Synthesizing research: A guide for literature reviews* (3rd ed.). Newbury Park, CA: Sage.

Corbett, E. P. J., & Finkle, S. L. (1994). *The little English handbook.* Glenview, IL: HarperCollins.

Cordes, A. K. (1994). The reliability of observational data: I. Theories and methods for speech–language pathology. *Journal of Speech and Hearing Research, 37,* 264–278.

Cordova, J. V., & Jacobson, N. S. (1993). Couple distress. In D. H. Barlow (Ed.), *Clinical handbook of psychological disorders: A step-by-step treatment manual* (2nd ed., pp. 481–512). New York: Guilford Press.

Cordova, J. V., Jacobson, N. S., & Christensen, A. (1998). Acceptance versus change interventions in behavioral couple therapy: Impact on couples' in-session communication. *Journal of Marriage and Family Counseling, 24,* 437–455.

Costner, H. L. (1969). Theory, deduction, and rules of correspondence. *American Journal of Sociology, 75,* 245–263.

Cox, D. J., Freundlich, A., & Meyer, R. G. (1975). Differential effectiveness of electromyographic feedback, verbal relaxation instructions, and medication placebo with tension headaches. *Journal of Consulting and Clinical Psychology, 43,* 892–898.

Craig, W. M., & Pepler, D. J. (1997). Observations of bullying and victimization in the school yard. *Canadian Journal of School Psychology, 13,* 41–59.

Cronbach, L. J. (1970). *Essentials of psychological testing* (3rd ed.). New York: Harper & Row.

Cronbach, L. J., Gleser, G. C., Nanda, H., & Rajaratnam, N. (1972). *The dependability of behavioral measurements: Theory of generalizability for scores and profiles.* New York: Wiley.

Cronbach, L. J., & Meehl, P. E. (1955). Construct validity in psychological tests. *Psychological Bulletin, 52,* 281–302.

Csikszentmihalyi, M., & Larson, R. (1987). Validity and reliability of the experience-sampling method. *Journal of Nervous and Mental Disease, 175,* 526–536.

Culliton, B. J. (1976). Confidentiality: Court declares researcher can protect sources. *Science,* 193, 467–469.

Davidson, G. C., & Lazarus, A. A. (1995). The dialectics of science and practice. In S. C. Hayes, V. M. Follette, R. M. Dawes, & K. E. Grady (Eds.), *Scientific standards of psychological practice: Issues and recommendations* (pp. 95–120). Reno, NV: Context Press.

Deming, W. E. (1986). *Out of the crisis.* Cambridge: Massachusetts Institute of Technology, Center for Advanced Engineering Study.

Denison, D. R., & Mishra, A. K. (1995). Toward a theory of organizational culture and effectiveness. *Organization Science, 6,* 204–223.

Deprospero, A., & Cohen, S. (1979). Inconsistent visual analysis of intrasubject data. *Journal of Applied Behavior Analysis, 12,* 573–579.

Derogatis, L. R. (1983). *Description and bibliography for the SCL-90-R and other instruments of the psychopathology rating scale series.* Baltimore: Johns Hopkins University School of Medicine.

DeVellis, R. F. (1991). *Scale development: Theory and applications.* Newbury Park, CA: Sage.

Diamond, S., & Dalessio, D. J. (1978). *The practicing physician's approach to headache* (2nd ed.). Baltimore: Williams & Wilkins.

DiNardo, P. A., Barlow, D. H., Cerny, J. A., Vermilya, B. B., Vermilya, J. A., Himaldi, W. G., & Waddell, M. T. (1986). *Anxiety Disorders Interview Schedule–Revised* (ADIS-R). Unpublished manuscript, State University of New York, Albany.

DiNardo, P. A., O'Brien, G. T., Barlow, D. H., Waddell, M. T., & Blanchard, E. B. (1983). Reliability of *DSM-III* anxiety disorder categories using a new structured interview. *Archives of General Psychiatry, 40,* 1070–1074.

Dougher, M. J. (1998). Stimulus equivalence and the untrained acquisition of stimulus functions. *Behavior Therapy, 29,* 577–591.

Dryden, W., & Ellis, A. (1988). Rational emotive therapy. In K. S. Dobson (Ed.), *Handbook of cognitive–behavioral therapies* (pp. 214–272). New York: Guilford Press.

Dryer, D. C., & Horowitz, L. M. (1997). When do opposites attract? Interpersonal complementarity versus similarity. *Journal of Personality and Social Psychology, 72,* 592–603.

DuBois, P. H. (1970). *A history of psychological testing.* Boston: Allyn & Bacon.

Dupuy, H. J. (1977). *A current validational study of the NCHS general well-being schedule* (DHEW Pub. No. HRA 78–1347). Hyattsville, MD: U.S. Department of Health, Education, and Welfare, National Center for Health Statistics.

Eagly, A. H., & Carli, L. L. (1981). Sex of researchers and sex-typed communications as determinants of sex differences in influenceability: A meta-analysis of social influence studies. *Psychological Bulletin, 90,* 1–20.

Edwards, A. L. (1957). *The social desirability variable in personality assessment and research.* New York: Dryden.

Edwards, A. L. (1990). Construct validity and social desirability. *American Psychologist, 45,* 287–289.

Eichorn, D. H., & VandenBos, G. R. (1985). Dissemination of scientific and professional knowledge: Journal publication within the APA. *American Psychologist, 40,* 1309–1316.

Eifert, G. H., Schulte, D., Zvolensky, M. J., Lejuez, C. W., & Lau, A. W. (1997). Manualized behavior therapy: Merits and challenges. *Behavior Therapy, 28,* 499–509.

Eisen, S. V., Grob, M. C., & Klein, A. A. (1986). BASIS: The development of a self-report measure for psychiatric inpatient evaluation. *Psychiatric Hospital, 17,* 165–171.

Elkin, I., Gibbons, R. D., Shea, M. T., Sotsky, S. M., Watkins, J. T., Pilkonis, P. A., & Hedeker, D. (1995). Initial severity and differential treatment outcome in the National Institute of Mental Health Treatment of Depression Collaborative Research Program. *Journal of Consulting and Clinical Psychology, 63,* 841–847.

Elkin, I., Shea, M. T., Watkins, J. T., Imber, S. D., Sotsky, S. M., Collins, J. F., Glass, D. R., Pilkonis, P. A., Leber, W. R., Docherty, J. P., Fiester, S. J., & Parloff, M. B. (1989). National Institute of Mental Health treatment of depression collaborative research program: General effectiveness of treatments. *Archives of General Psychiatry, 46,* 971–982.

Ellis, A. (1957). Outcome of employing three techniques of psychotherapy. *Journal of Clinical Psychology, 13,* 344–350.

Ellis, A., & Harper, R. A. (1961). *A guide to rational living.* Englewood Cliffs, NJ: Prentice-Hall.

Endicott, J., Cohen, J., Nee, J., Fleiss, J. L., & Sarantakos, S. (1981). Hamilton Depression Rating Scale: Extracted from regular and change versions of the Schedule for Affective Disorders and Schizophrenia. *Archives of General Psychiatry, 38,* 98–103.

Endicott, J., & Spitzer, R. L. (1978). A diagnostic interview: The Schedule for Affective Disorders and Schizophrenia. *Archives of General Psychiatry, 35,* 837–844.

Endicott, J., Spitzer, R. L., Fleiss, J. L., & Cohen, J. (1976). The Global Assessment Scale: A procedure for measuring overall severity of psychiatric disturbance. *Archives of General Psychiatry, 33,* 766–771.

Epstein, S., & O'Brien, E. J. (1985). The person–situation debate in historical and current perspective. *Psychological Bulletin, 98,* 513–537.

Erdman, H. P., Klein, M. H., & Greist, J. H. (1985). Direct patient computer interviewing. *Journal of Consulting and Clinical Psychology, 53,* 760–773.

Eugster, S. L., & Wampold, B. E. (1996). Systematic effects of participant role on evaluation of the psychotherapy session. *Journal of Consulting and Clinical Psychology, 64,* 1020–1028.

Eyberg, S. M., & Ross, A. W. (1978). Assessment of child behavior problems: The validation of a new inventory. *Journal of Clinical Child Psychology, 8,* 113–116.

Eysenck, S. B. G., & Eysenck, H. J. (1963). An experimental investigation of desirability response set in a personality questionnaire. *Life Sciences, 5,* 343–355.

Fairburn, C. G., Marcus, M. D., & Wilson, G. T. (1993). Cognitive behaviour therapy for binge eating and bulimia nervosa: A comprehensive treatment manual. In C. G. Fairburn & G. T. Wilson (Eds.), *Binge eating: Nature, assessment, and treatment* (pp. 361–404). New York: Guilford Press.

Farrell, A. D. (1999a). Evaluation of the computerized assessment system for psychotherapy evaluation and research (CASPER) as a measure of treatment effectiveness in an outpatient training clinic. *Psychological Assessment, 11,* 345–358.

Farrell, A. D. (1999b). Statistical methods in clinical research. In P. C. Kendall, J. N. Butcher, & G. N. Holmbeck (Eds.), *Handbook of research methods in clinical psychology* (2nd ed., pp. 72–106). New York: Wiley.

Farrell, A. D., Camplair, P. S., & McCullough, L. (1987). Identification of target complaints by computer interview: Evaluation of the computerized assessment system for psychotherapy evaluation and research. *Journal of Consulting and Clinical Psychology, 55,* 691–700.

Farrell, A. D., & McCullough-Vaillant, L. (1996). Computerized assessment system for psychotherapy evaluation and research (CASPER): Development and current status. In M. J. Miller, K. W. Hammond, & M. M. Hile (Eds.), *Mental health computing* (pp. 34–53). New York: Springer.

Favell, J. E., Realon, R. E., & Sutton, K. A. (1996). Measuring and increasing the happiness of people with profound mental retardation and physical handicaps. *Behavioral Intervention, 11,* 47–58.

Federal Policy for the Protection of Human Subjects. (1981). 45 C.F.R. § 46.

Fensterheim, H., & Raw, S. D. (1996). Psychotherapy research is not psychotherapy practice. *Clinical Psychology: Science and Practice, 3,* 168–171.

Ferrans, C. E., & Powers, M. J. (1992). Psychometric assessment of the Quality of Life Index. *Research in Nursing and Health, 15,* 29–38.

Fiedler, F. E. (1967). *A theory of leadership effectiveness.* New York: McGraw-Hill.

Fischer, J., & Corcoran, K. (1994). *Measures for clinical practice: A sourcebook* (2nd ed.). New York: Macmillan.

Fiske, D., & Campbell, D. T. (1992). Citations do not solve problems. *Psychological Bulletin, 112,* 393–395.

Fiske, D., & Fogg, L. (1990). But the reviewers are making different criticisms of my paper! *American Psychologist, 45,* 591–598.

Fixsen, D. L., Phillips, E. L., Wolf, M. M. (1972). Achievement Place: The reliability of self-reporting and peer-reporting and their effects on behavior. *Journal of Applied Behavior Analysis, 5,* 19–30.

Floyd, F. J., & Widaman, K. F. (1995). Factor analysis in the development and refinement of clinical assessment instruments. *Psychological Assessment, 7,* 286–299.

Follette, W. C. (1995). Correcting methodological weaknesses in the knowledge base used to derive practice standards. In S. C. Hayes, V. M. Follette, R. M. Dawes, & K. E. Grady (Eds.), *Scientific standards of psychological practice: Issues and recommendations* (pp. 229–247). Reno, NV: Context Press.

Foster, S. L., & Cone, J. D. (1986). Design and use of direct observation systems. In A. Ciminero, K. S. Calhoun, & H. E. Adams (Eds.), *Handbook of behavioral assessment* (2nd ed., pp. 253–324). New York: Wiley.

Foster, S. L., & Mash, E. J. (1999). Assessing social validity in clinical treatment research: Issues and procedures. *Journal of Consulting and Clinical Psychology, 67,* 308–319.

Fowler, D. R., Finkelstein, A., Penk, W., Bell, W., & Itzig, B. (1987). An automated problem-rating interview: The DPRI. In J. Butcher (Ed.), *Computerized psychological assessment: A practitioner's guide* (pp. 87–107). New York: Basic Books.

Frank, J. D. (1961). *Persuasion and healing.* Baltimore: Johns Hopkins University Press.

Frankfort-Nachmias, C., & Nachmias, D. (1992). *Research methods in the social sciences* (4th ed.). New York: St. Martin's Press.

Franklin, R. D., Allison, D. B., & Gorman, B. S. (1997). *Design and analysis of single-case research.* Mahwah, NJ: Erlbaum.

Freud, S. (1957). Mourning and melancholia. In J. Strachey (Ed. & Trans.), *The standard edition of the complete psychological works of Sigmund Freud* (Vol. 14, pp. 243–258). London: Hogarth. (Original work published 1917)

Frisch, M. B. (1998). Quality of life therapy and assessment in health care. *Clinical Psychology: Science and Practice, 5,* 19–40.

Frisch, M. B., Cornell, J., Villanueva, M., & Retzlaff, P. J. (1992). Clinical validation of the Quality of Life Inventory: A measure of life satisfaction for use in treatment planning and outcome assessment. *Psychological Assessment, 4,* 92–101.

Froyd, J. E., Lambert, M. J., & Froyd, J. D. (1996). A review of practices of psychotherapy outcome measurement. *Journal of Mental Health, 5,* 11–15.

Fuller, P. R. (1949). Operant conditioning of a vegetative human organism. *American Journal of Psychology, 62,* 587–590.

Gaul, D. G., Craighead, W. E., & Mahoney, M. J. (1975). Relationship between eating rates and obesity. *Journal of Consulting and Clinical Psychology, 43,* 123–125.

Gauthier, J. G., Ivers, H., & Carrier, S. (1996). Nonpharmacological approaches in the management of recurrent headache disorders and their comparison and combination with pharmacotherapy. *Clinical Psychology Review, 16,* 543–571.

Geller, E. S., Russ, N. W., & Altomari, M. G. (1986). Naturalistic observations of beer drinking among college students. *Journal of Applied Behavior Analysis, 19,* 391–396.

Gladis, M. M., Gosch, E. A., Dishuk, N. M., & Crits-Christoph, P. (1999). Quality of life: Expanding the scope of clinical significance. *Journal of Consulting and Clinical Psychology, 67,* 320–331.

Glaser, R. (1963). Instructional technology and the measurement of learning outcomes. *American Psychologist, 18,* 519–521.

Glass, G. V., & Kliegl, R. M. (1983). An apology for research integration in the study of psychotherapy. *Journal of Consulting and Clinical Psychology, 51,* 28–41.

Glass, G. V., Willson, V. L., & Gottman, J. M. (1975). *Design and analysis of time-series experiments.* Boulder: Colorado Associated University Press.

Goldman, B. A., Mitchell, D. F., & Egelson, P. E. (Eds.). (1997). *Directory of unpublished experimental mental measures.* Washington, DC: American Psychological Association.

Goodman, L. A., & Kruskal, W. H. (1954). Measure of association for cross classification. *Journal of the American Statistical Association, 49,* 732–764.

Gorden, R. L. (1975). *Interviewing: Strategy, techniques, and tactics* (rev. ed.). Homewood, IL: Dorsey Press.

Gorman, J. M. (1994). New and experimental pharmacological treatments for panic disorder. In B. E. Wolfe & J. D. Maser (Eds.), *Treatment of panic disorder: A consensus development conference* (pp. 83–90). Washington, DC: American Psychiatric Press.

Gottfredson, S. (1978). Evaluating psychological research reports: Dimensions, reliability, and correlates of quality judgments. *American Psychologist, 33,* 920–933.

Gottman, J. M., & Glass, G. V. (1978). Analysis of interrupted time-series experiments. In T. R. Kratochwill (Ed.), *Single-subject research: Strategies for evaluating change* (pp. 197–235). New York: Academic Press.

Gottman, J. M., & Leiblum, S. R. (1974). *How to do psychotherapy and how to evaluate it.* New York: Holt, Rinehart, & Winston.

Green, B. F., & Hall, J. A. (1984). Quantitative methods for literature reviews. *Annual Review of Psychology, 35,* 37–53.

Green, C. W., & Reid, D. H. (1996). Defining, validating, and increasing indices of happiness among people with profound multiple disabilities. *Journal of Applied Behavior Analysis, 29,* 67–78.

Greenberg, L. S. (1986). Change process research. *Journal of Consulting and Clinical Psychology, 54,* 4–9.

Greenwald, A. G. (1997). Validity concerns and usefulness of student ratings of instruction. *American Psychologist, 52,* 1182–1186.

Griffiths, J. D., & Martin, P. R. (1996). Clinical- versus home-based treatment formats for children with chronic headache. *British Journal of Health Psychology, 1,* 151–166.

Gutek, B. A. (1978). Strategies for studying client satisfaction. *Journal of Social Issues, 34,* 44–56.

Hahlweg, K., Revenstorf, K., & Schindler, L. (1984). Effects of behavioral marital therapy on couples, communication and problem-solving skills. *Journal of Consulting and Clinical Psychology, 52,* 553–566.

Hamilton, M. (1959). The assessment of anxiety states by rating. *British Journal of Medical Psychology, 32,* 50–55.

Hamilton, M. (1960). A rating scale for depression. *Journal of Neurology, Neurosurgery, and Psychiatry, 23,* 56–62.

Hammen, C. L. (1980). Depression in college students: Beyond the Beck Depression Inventory. *Journal of Consulting and Clinical Psychology, 48,* 126–128.

Haring, N. G. (1977). Measurement and evaluation procedures for programming with the severely and profoundly handicapped. In E. Sontag, J. Smith, & N. Certo (Eds.), *Educational programming for the severely and profoundly handicapped* (pp. 189–202). Reston, VA: Council for Exceptional Children.

Hart, B., & Risley, T. R. (1995). *Meaningful differences in the everday experience of young American children.* Baltimore: Brookes.

Hartmann, D. P., & Wood, D. D. (1990). Observational methods. In A. S. Bellack, M. Hersen, & A. E. Kazdin (Eds.), *International handbook of behavior modification and therapy* (2nd ed., pp. 109–138). New York: Plenum Press.

Hawkins, R. P. (1979). The functions of assessment: Implications for selection and development of devices for assessing repertoires in clinical, educational, and other settings. *Journal of Applied Behavior Analysis, 12,* 501–516.

Hawkins, R. P., Mathews, J. R., & Hamdan, L. (1999). *Measuring behavioral health outcomes: A practical guide.* New York: Kluwer Academic/Plenum Press.

Hay, L. R., Hay, W. M., & Angle, H. V. (1977). The reactivity of self recording: A case report of a drug abuser. *Behavior Therapy, 8,* 1004–1007.

Hayes, S. C. (1989). A contextual approach to therapeutic change. In N. S. Jacobson (Ed.), *Psychotherapists in clinical practice: Cognitive and behavioral perspectives* (pp. 327–387). New York: Guilford Press.

Hayes, S. C., Barlow, D. H., & Nelson-Gray, R. O. (1999). *The scientist practitioner: Research and accountability in the age of managed care* (2nd ed.). Boston: Allyn & Bacon.

Hayes, S. C., & Cavior, N. (1977). Multiple tracking and the reactivity of self-monitoring: I. Negative behaviors. *Behavior Therapy, 8,* 819–831.

Hayes, S. C., & Hayes, L. J. (1992). Verbal relations and the evolution of behavior analysis. *American Psychologist, 47,* 1383–1395.

Hayes, S. C., Kohlenberg, B. S., & Hayes, L. J. (1991). The transfer of general and specific consequential functions through simple and conditional equivalence relations. *Journal of the Experimental Analysis of Behavior, 56,* 119–137.

Hayes, S. C., Strosahl, K., & Wilson, K. (1999). *Acceptance and commitment therapy: Understanding and treating human suffering.* New York: Guilford Press.

Haynes, S. N., & Horn, W. F. (1982). Reactivity in behavioral observation: A review. *Behavioral Assessment, 4,* 369–385.

Haynes, S. N., Richard, D. C. S., & Kubany, E. S. (1995). Content validity in psychological assessment: A functional approach to concepts and methods. *Journal of Consulting and Clinical Psychology, 7,* 238–247.

Hays, W. L. (1963). *Statistics for psychologists.* New York: Holt, Rinehart, & Winston.

Henry, G. T. (1994). *Graphing data.* Thousand Oaks, CA: Sage.

Hersen, M., & Turner, S. M. (Eds.). (1994). *Diagnostic interviewing* (2nd ed.). New York: Plenum Press.

Higgins, R. L., Frisch, M. B., & Smith, D. (1983). A comparison of role-played and natural responses to identical circumstances. *Behavior Therapy, 14,* 158–169.

Hill, S. W., & McCutcheon, N. B. (1975). Eating responses of obese and non-obese humans during dinner meals. *Psychosomatic Medicine, 37,* 395.

Hoagwood, K., Hibbs, E., Brent, D., Jensen, P. (1995). Introduction to the special section: Efficacy and effectiveness in studies of child and adolescent psychotherapy. *Journal of Consulting and Clinical Psychology, 63,* 683–687.

Hobbs, W. R. (1983). *Your time and your life.* Chicago: Nightingale-Conant.

Hofmann, S. G., Bufka, L. F., & Barlow, D. H. (1999). Panic provocation procedures in the treatment of panic disorder: Early perspectives and case studies. *Behavior Therapy, 30,* 305–317.

Hollingshead, A. B., & Redlich, F. C. (1958). *Social class and mental illness.* New York: Wiley.

Hollon, S. D. (1996). The efficacy and effectiveness of psychotherapy relative to medications. *American Psychologist, 51,* 1025–1030.

Hollon, S. D., DeRubeis, R. J., Evans, M. D., Wiemer, J. J., Garvey, J. G., Grove, W. M., & Tuason, V. B. (1992). Cognitive therapy and pharmacotherapy for depression: Singly and in combination. *Archives of General Psychiatry, 49,* 774–781.

Hollon, S. D., & Kendall, P. C. (1980). Cognitive self-statements in depression: Development of an automatic thoughts questionnaire. *Cognitive Therapy and Research, 9,* 443–453.

Hollon, S. D., Waskow, I. E., Evans, M., & Lowery, H. A. (1984, May). *System for rating therapies for depression.* Paper presented at the meeting of the American Psychiatric Association, Los Angeles, CA.

Holmbeck, G. N. (1997). Toward terminological, conceptual, and statistical clarity in the study of mediators and moderators: Examples from the child–clinical and pediatric psychology literatures. *Journal of Consulting and Clinical Psychology, 65,* 599–610.

Holmes, T. H., & Rahe, R. H. (1967). The social readjustment scale. *Journal of Psychosomatic Research, 11,* 213–218.

Holt, R. R. (1988). Judgment, inference, and reasoning in clinical perspective. In D. C. Turk & P. Salovey (Eds.), *Reasoning, inference, and judgment in clinical psychology* (pp. 233–250). New York: Free Press.

Holtz, H. (1979). *Government contracts, proposalmanship and winning strategies.* New York: Plenum Press.

Houghton, D. M. (1996). Autogenic training: A self-hypnosis technique to achieve physiological change in a stress management programme. *Contemporary Hypnosis, 13,* 39–43.

Howard, K. I. (1996, November). *Patient profiling: Quantifying progress.* Seminar presented at the annual meeting of the Association for the Advancement of Behavior Therapy, New York.

Howard, K. I. (1998). Some relationships between basic and applied research. *Behavior Therapy, 29,* 717–719.

Howard, K. I., Brill, P. L., Lueger, R. J., & O'Mahoney, M. T. (1995). *Integra outpatient tracking system.* Philadelphia: Compass Information Services.

Howard, K. I., Kopta, S. M., Krause, M. S., & Orlinsky, D. E. (1986). The dose-effect relationship in psychotherapy. *American Psychologist, 41,* 159–164.

Howard, K. I., Lueger, R. J., Maling, M. S., & Martinovich, Z. (1993). A phase model of psychotherapy outcome: Causal mediation of change. *Journal of Consulting and Clinical Psychology, 61,* 678–685.

Howard, K. I., Martinovich, Z., Lutz, W., Brill, P. L., & Grissom, G. R. (1996). *Patient profiling: An application of random coefficient regression models to depicting the course of outpatient psychotherapy.* Unpublished manuscript, Northwestern University, Evanston, IL.

Howard, K. I., Moras, K., Brill, P. L., Martinovich, Z., & Lutz, W. (1996). Evaluation of psychotherapy: Efficacy, effectiveness, and patient progress. *American Psychologist, 51,* 1059–1064.

Hsu, L. M. (1999). Caveats concerning comparisons of change rates obtained with five methods of identifying significant client changes: Comment on Speer and Greenbaum (1995). *Journal of Consulting and Clinical Psychology, 67,* 594–598.

Huitema, B. E. (1985). Autocorrelation in applied behavior analysis: A myth. *Behavioral Assessment, 7,* 107–118.

Humphreys, L. (1975). *Tearoom trade: Impersonal sex in public places* (enlarged ed.). New York: Aldine.

Iglehart, J. K. (1996). The National Committee on Quality Assurance. *New England Journal of Medicine, 335,* 995–999.

International Headache Society. (1988). Classification and diagnostic criteria for headache disorders, cranial neuralgias and facial pain. *Cephalalgia, 8,* 19–25.

Jacob, T., Tennenbaum, D., Bargiel, K., & Seilhamer, R. A. (1995). Family interaction in the home: Development of a new coding system. *Behavior Modification, 19,* 147–169.

Jacob, T., Tennenbaum, D., Seilhamer, R. A., Bargiel, K., & Sharon, T. (1994). Reactivity effects during naturalistic observation of distressed and nondistressed families. *Journal of Family Psychology, 8,* 354–363.

Jacobson, N. S., & Christensen, A. (1996). Studying the effectiveness of psychotherapy: How well can clinical trials do the job? *American Psychologist, 51,* 1031–1039.

Jacobson, N. S., Follette, W. C., & Revenstorf, D. (1984). Psychotherapy outcome research: Methods for reporting variability and evaluating clinical significance. *Behavior Therapy, 15,* 336–352.

Jacobson, N. S., & Hollon, S. D. (1996). Cognitive–behavior therapy versus pharmacotherapy: Now that the jury's returned its verdict, it's time to present the rest of the evidence. *Journal of Consulting and Clinical Psychology, 64,* 74–80.

Jacobson, N. S., & Revenstorf, D. (1988). Statistics for assessing the clinical significance of psychotherapy techniques: Issues, problems, and new developments. *Behavioral Assessment, 10,* 133–145.

Jacobson, N. S., Roberts, L. J., Berns, S. B., & McGlinchey, J. B. (1999). Methods for defining and determining clinical significance of treatment effects: Description, application, and alternatives. *Journal of Consulting and Clinical Psychology, 67,* 300–307.

Jacobson, N. S., Schmaling, K. B., Holtzworth-Munroe, A., Katt, J. L., Wood, L. F., & Follette, V. M. (1989). Research-structured vs clinically flexible versions of social-learning-based marital therapy. *Behaviour Research and Therapy, 27,* 173–180.

Jacobson, N. S., & Truax, P. (1991). Clinical significance: A statistical approach to defining meaningful change in psychotherapy research. *Journal of Consulting and Clinical Psychology, 59,* 12–19.

Jacobson, N. S., Wilson, L., & Tupper, C. (1988). The clinical significance of treatment gains resulting from exposure-based interventions for agoraphobia: A reanalysis of outcome data. *Behavior Therapy, 19,* 539–552.

Jensen, C. (1994). Psychosocial treatment of depression in women: Nine single-subject evaluations. *Research on Social Work Practice, 4,* 267–282.

Jensen, J. A. (1994). An investigation of eye movement desensitization and reprocessing (EMD/R) as a treatment for posttraumatic stress disorder (PTSD) symptoms of Vietnam combat veterans. *Behavior Therapy, 25,* 311–325.

Johnston, J. M., & Pennypacker, H. S. (1993). *Strategies and tactics of behavioral research* (2nd ed.). Hillsdale, NJ: Erlbaum.

Jones, R. R., Vaught, R. S., & Weinrott, M. (1977). Time-series analysis in operant research. *Journal of Applied Behavior Analysis, 10,* 151–166.

Jöreskog, K. G., & Sörbom, D. (1989). *LISREL: Analysis of linear structural relationships by the method of maximum likelihood* (Version 7). Mooresville, IN: Scientific Software.

Juran, J. M., Seder, L. A., & Gryna, F. M. (1962). *Quality control handbook.* New York: McGraw-Hill.

Kadera, S. W., Lambert, M. J., & Andrews, A. A. (1996). How much therapy is really enough? A session-by-session analysis of the psychotherapy dose–effect relationship. *Journal of Psychotherapy Practice and Research, 5,* 132–151.

Kahneman, D., & Tversky, A. (1973). Availability: A heuristic for judging frequency and probability. *Cognitive Psychology, 5,* 207–232.

Kane, M. T. (1992). An argument-based approach to validity. *Psychological Bulletin, 112,* 527–535.

Kaplan, R. M., & Saccuzzo, D. P. (1997). *Psychological testing: Principles, applications, and issues* (4th ed.). Pacific Grove, CA: Brooks/Cole.

Kaufman, A. S., & Kaufman, N. L. (1983). *K-ABC: Kaufman Assessment Battery for Children.* Circle Pines, MN: American Guidance Service.

Kazdin, A. E. (1977). Assessing the clinical or applied significance of behavior change through social validation. *Behavior Modification, 1,* 427–452.

Kazdin, A. E. (1980). *Research design in clinical psychology.* New York: Harper & Row.

Kazdin, A. E. (1992). *Research design in clinical psychology* (2nd ed.). Boston: Allyn & Bacon.

Kazdin, A. E. (1993). Evaluation in clinical practice: Clinically sensitive and systematic methods of treatment delivery. *Behavior Therapy, 24,* 11–45.

Kazdin, A. E. (1995). Preparing and evaluating research reports. *Psychological Assessment, 7,* 228–237.

Kazdin, A. E. (1998). *Research design in clinical psychology* (3rd ed.). Boston: Allyn & Bacon.

Kazdin, A. E., Bass, D., Siegel, T., & Thomas, C. (1989). Cognitive–behavioral therapy and relationship therapy in the treatment of children referred for antisocial behavior. *Journal of Consulting and Clinical Psychology, 57,* 522–535.

Kazdin, A. E., & Bryan, J. H. (1971). Competence and volunteering. *Journal of Experimental Social Psychology, 7,* 87–97.

Kazdin, A. E., Esveldt-Dawson, K., French, N. H., & Unis, A. S. (1987). Effects of parent management training and problem-solving skills training combined in the treatment of antisocial child behavior. *Journal of the American Academy of Child and Adolescent Psychiatry, 26,* 416–424.

Keith, K. D., & Schalock, R. L. (1992). The Quality of Life Questionnaire. *The Behavior Therapist, 15,* 106–107.

Kelley, T. L. (1927). *Interpretation of educational measurements.* Yonkers-on-Hudson, NY: World Book.

Kelly, G. A. (1955). *The psychology of personal constructs* (Vol. 1). New York: Norton.

Kelly, M. B. (1977). A review of the observational data-collection and reliability procedures reported in *The Journal of Applied Behavior Analysis. Journal of Applied Behavior Analysis, 10,* 97–101.

Kendall, P. C., Marrs-Garcia, A., Nath, S. R., & Sheldrick, R. C. (1999). Normative comparisons for the evaluation of clinical significance. *Journal of Consulting and Clinical Psychology, 67,* 285–299.

Kendall, P. C., & Wilcox, L. E. (1979). Self-control in children: Development of a rating scale. *Journal of Consulting and Clinical Psychology, 47,* 1020–1029.

Kent, R. N., & Foster, S. L. (1977). Direct observational procedures: Methodological issues in applied settings. In A. R. Ciminero, K. S. Calhoun, & H. E. Adams (Eds.), *Handbook of behavioral assessment* (pp. 279–328). New York: Wiley.

Kerlinger, F. N. (1986). *Foundations of behavioral research* (3rd ed.). New York: Holt, Rinehart & Winston.

Kidder, L. H., & Judd, C. M. (1986). *Research methods in social relations* (5th ed.). New York: Holt.

Kiesler, D. J. (1971). Experimental designs in psychotherapy research. In A. E. Bergin & S. L. Garfield (Eds.), *Handbook of psychotherapy and behavior change: An empirical analysis* (pp. 36–74). New York: Wiley.

Kinsey, A. C., Pomeroy, W. B., Martin, C. E., & Gebhard, P. H. (1953). *Sexual behavior in the human female.* Philadelphia: Saunders.

Kirk, R. E. (1982). *Experimental design: Procedures for the behavioral sciences* (2nd ed.). Belmont, CA: Brooks/Cole.

Kishton, J. M., & Widaman, K. F. (1994). Unidimensional versus domain representative parceling of questionnaire items: An empirical example. *Educational and Psychological Measurement, 54,* 757–765.

Klein, D. F., & Ross, D. C. (1993). Reanalysis of the National Institute of Mental Health Treatment of Depression Collaborative Research Program general effectiveness report. *Neuropsychopharmacology, 8,* 241–251.

Klerman, G. L., Weissman, M. M., Rounsaville, B. J., & Chevron, E. S. (1984). *Interpersonal psychotherapy of depression.* New York: Basic Books.

Kohlenberg, R. J., & Tsai, M. (1991). *Functional analytic psychotherapy: Creating intense and curative therapeutic relationships.* New York: Plenum Press.

Korchin, S. J., & Cowan, P. A. (1982). Ethical perspectives in clinical research. In P. C. Kendall & J. N. Butcher (Eds.), *Handbook of research methods in clinical psychology* (pp. 59–94). New York: Wiley.

Korotitsch, W. J., & Nelson-Gray, R. O. (1999). An overview of self-monitoring research in assessment and treatment. *Psychological Assessment, 11,* 415–425.

Kouzes, J. M., & Posner, B. Z. (1987). *The leadership challenge: How to keep getting extraordinary things done in organizations.* San Francisco: Jossey-Bass.

Kouzes, J. M., & Posner, B. Z. (1995). *The leadership challenge: How to keep getting extraordinary things done in organizations* (2nd ed.). San Francisco: Jossey-Bass.

Koyré, A. (1965). *Newtonian studies.* Cambridge, MA: Harvard University Press.

Kraemer, H. C., & Thiemann, S. (1987). *How many subjects? Statistical power analysis in research.* Newbury Park, CA: Sage.

Krasner, L. (1962). The therapist as a social reinforcement machine. In H. H. Strupp & L. Luborsky (Eds.), *Research in psychotherapy* (Vol. 2, pp. 61–94). Washington, DC: American Psychological Association.

Krathwohl, D. R. (1977). *How to prepare a research proposal: Suggestions for those seeking funds for behavioral science research* (2nd ed.). Syracuse, NY: Syracuse University, School of Education.

Kubany, E. S., & Slodgett, B. B. (1973). Coding procedure for teachers. *Journal of Applied Behavior Analysis, 6,* 339–344.

Kupfersmid, J. (1988). Improving what is published: A model in search of an editor. *American Psychologist, 43,* 635–642.

Lambert, M. J. (1994). Use of psychological tests for outcome assessment. In M. E. Maruish (Ed.), *The use of psychological testing for treatment planning and outcome assessment* (pp. 75–97). Hillsdale, NJ: Erlbaum.

Lambert, M. J., & Brown, J. (1996). Data-based management for tracking outcome in private practice. *Clinical Psychology: Science and Practice, 3,* 172–178.

Lang, P. J. (1971). The application of psychophysiological methods to the study of psychotherapy and behavior modification. In A. E. Bergin & S. L. Garfield (Eds.), *Handbook of psychotherapy and behavior change: An empirical analysis* (pp. 75–125). New York: Wiley.

Larson, R. (1989). Beeping children and adolescents: A method for studying time use and daily experience. *Journal of Youth and Adolescence, 18,* 511–530.

Last, C. G., Hansen, C., & Franco, N. (1998). Cognitive–behavioral treatment of school phobia. *Journal of the American Academy of Child & Adolescent Psychiatry, 37,* 404–411.

Lawrence, E., Heyman, R. E., & O'Leary, K. D. (1995). Correspondence between telephone and written assessments of physical violence in marriage. *Behavior Therapy, 26,* 671–680.

Lawshe, C. H. (1975). A quantitative approach to content validity. *Personnel Psychology, 28,* 563–575.

Lebow, J. (1982). Consumer satisfaction with mental health treatment. *Psychological Bulletin, 91,* 244–259.

Levinson, D. J. (1962). The psychotherapist's contribution to the patient's treatment career. In H. H. Strupp & L. Luborsky (Eds.), *Research in psychotherapy* (Vol. 2, pp. 13–24). Washington, DC: American Psychological Association.

Levy, R. L. (1977). Relationship of an overt commitment to task compliance in behavior therapy. *Journal of Behavior Therapy and Experimental Psychiatry, 8,* 25–29.

Lewinsohn, P. M., & Hoberman, H. (1982). Depression. In A. S. Bellack, M. Hersen, & A. E. Kazdin (Eds.), *International handbook of behavior modification and therapy* (pp. 397–431). New York: Plenum Press.

Light, R. J., & Smith, P. V. (1971). Accumulating evidence: Procedure for resolving contradictions among different research studies. *Harvard Educational Review, 41,* 429–471.

Lindsley, O. R. (1960). Characteristics of the behavior of chronic psychotics as revealed by free-operant conditioning methods. *Diseases of the Nervous System, 21,* 66–78.

Little, R. J. A., & Schenker, N. (1995). Missing data. In G. H. Arminger, C. C. Clogg, & M. E. Sobel (Eds.), *Handbook of statistical modeling for the social and behavioral sciences* (pp. 39–75). New York: Plenum Press.

Livingston, S. A. (1977). Psychometric techniques for criterion-referenced testing and behavioral assessment. In J. D. Cone & R. P. Hawkins (Eds.), *Behavioral assessment: New directions for clinical psychology* (pp. 308–329). New York: Brunner/Mazel.

Locke, L. F., Spirduso, W. W., & Silverman, S. J. (1987). *Proposals that work: A guide for planning dissertations and grant proposals* (2nd ed.). Newbury Park, CA: Sage.

Loftus, E. F., & Fries, J. F. (1979). Informed consent may be hazardous to your health. *Science, 204,* 11.

Lucas, G. M., Chaisson, R. E., & Moore, R. D. (1999). Highly active antiretroviral therapy in a large urban clinic: Risk factors for virologic failure and adverse drug reactions. *Annals of Internal Medicine, 131*(2), 81–87.

Maher, B. A. (1978). A reader's, writer's, and reviewer's guide to assessing research reports in clinical psychology. *Journal of Consulting and Clinical Psychology, 46,* 835–838.

Mahoney, M. J. (1977). Some applied issues in self-monitoring. In J. D. Cone & R. P. Hawkins (Eds.), *Behavioral assessment: New directions in clinical psychology* (pp. 241–254). New York: Brunner/Mazel.

Mahoney, M. J. (1982). Publications, politics and scientific progress. *Behavioral and Brain Sciences, 5,* 220–221.

Mahoney, M. J., & Mahoney, B. K. (1976). *Permanent weight control.* New York: Norton.

Malatesta, V. J. (1995). Case formulation enhances treatment effectiveness. *The Behavior Therapist, 18,* 201–203.

Maletzky, B. M. (1980). Self-referred versus court-referred sexually deviant patients. *Behavior Therapy, 11,* 306–314.

Maletzky, B. M. (1991). *Treating the sexual offender.* Newbury Park, CA: Sage.

Maletzky, B. M. (1993). Factors associated with success and failure in the behavioral and cognitive treatment of sexual offenders. *Annals of Sex Research, 6,* 241–258.

Maletzky, B. M. (1997). Exhibitionism: Assessment and treatment. In D. R. Laws & W. R. O'Donohue (Eds.), *Sexual deviance: Theory, assessment, and treatment* (pp. 40–74). New York: Guilford Press.

Marcoulides, G. A., & Hershberger, S. L. (1997). *Multivariate statistical methods: A first course.* Hillsdale, NJ: Erlbaum.

Markowitz, J., Weissman, M., Ouellete, R., Lish, J., & Klerman, G. L. (1989). Quality of life in panic disorder. *Archives of General Psychiatry, 46,* 984–992.

Marks, I. M., & Mathews, A. M. (1979). Brief standard self-rating for phobic patients. *Behaviour Research and Therapy, 17,* 263–267.

Marquis, J. N. (1991). A report on seventy-eight cases treated by eye movement desensitization. *Journal of Behavior Therapy and Experimental Psychiatry, 22,* 187–192.

Maruish, M. E. (Ed.). (1994). *The use of psychological testing for treatment planning and outcome assessment.* Hillsdale, NJ: Erlbaum.

Maxwell, S. E., & Cole, D. A. (1995). Tips for writing (and reading) methodological articles. *Psychological Bulletin, 118,* 193–198.

McCord, J. (1978). A thirty-year follow-up of treatment effects. *American Psychologist, 33,* 284–289.

McDill, E. L., McDill, M. S., & Sprehe, J. T. (1969). *Strategies for success in compensatory education: An appraisal of evaluation research.* Baltimore: Johns Hopkins University Press.

McFall, R. M. (1970). Effects of self-monitoring on normal smoking behavior. *Journal of Consulting and Clinical Psychology, 35,* 135–142.

McFall, R. M. (1991). Manifesto for a science of clinical psychology. *The Clinical Psychologist, 44*, 75–88.

McFall, R. M. (1995). Models of training and standards of care. In S. C. Hayes, V. M. Follette, R. M. Dawes, & K. E. Grady (Eds.), *Scientific standards of psychological practice: Issues and recommendations* (pp. 125–137). Reno, NV: Context Press.

Meehl, P. E. (1960). The cognitive activity of the clinician. *American Psychologist, 15*, 19–27.

Mental health: Does therapy help? (1995, November). *Consumer Reports, 60*(11), 734–739.

Mental Health Corporations of America. (1995). *Customer satisfaction measurement system for behavioral health care organizations.* Pensacola, FL: Author.

Messick, S. (1983). Assessment of children. In P. H. Mussen (Ed.), *Handbook of child psychology* (4th ed., pp. 477–526). New York: Wiley.

Middlemist, D., Knowles, E. S., & Matter, C. F. (1976). Personal space invasions in the lavatory: Suggestive evidence for arousal. *Journal of Personality and Social Psychology, 33*, 541–546.

Mischel, W. (1968). *Personality and assessment.* New York: Wiley.

Mook, D. G. (1983). In defense of external invalidity. *American Psychologist, 38*, 379–387.

Morrisey, G. L. (1992). *Creating your future.* San Francisco: Berrett-Koehler.

Morrison, D. (1996). Clinical outcomes assessment. In C. E. Stout, G. A. Theis, & J. M. Oher (Eds.), *The complete guide to managed behavioral healthcare* (pp. II.C.1–II.C.10). New York: Wiley.

Muris, P., Merckelbach, H., Holdrinet, I., & Sijsenaar, M. (1998). Treating phobic children: Effects of EMDR versus exposure. *Journal of Consulting and Clinical Psychology, 66*, 193–198.

Murphy, G. E., Simons, A. D., Wetzel, R. D. S., & Lustman, P. (1984). Cognitive therapy and pharmacotherapy, singly and together in the treatment of depression. *Archives of General Psychiatry, 41*, 33–41.

National Commission for the Protection of Human Subjects of Biomedical and Behavioral Research. (1978). *The Belmont report: Ethical principles and guidelines for the protection of human subjects research* (DHEW Pub. No. OS 78-0012). Washington, DC: U.S. Government Printing Office.

Neilson, W. A., Knott, T. A., & Carhart, P. W. (Eds.). (1950). *Webster's new international dictionary of the English language* (2nd ed.). Springfield, MA: Merriam.

Nelson, R. O. (1977). Methodological issues in assessment via self-monitoring. In J. D. Cone & R. P. Hawkins (Eds.), *Behavioral assessment: New directions in clinical psychology* (pp. 217–254). New York: Brunner/Mazel.

Nelson, R. O. (1981). Realistic dependent measures for clinical use. *Journal of Consulting and Clinical Psychology, 49*, 168–182.

Neuman, W. L. (1997). *Social research methods: Qualitative and quantitative approaches* (3rd ed.). Boston: Allyn & Bacon.

Newman, M. G., Kenardy, J., Herman, S., & Taylor, C. B. (1997). Comparison of palmtop-computer-assisted brief cognitive–behavioral treatment to cognitive–behavioral treatment for panic disorder. *Journal of Consulting and Clinical Psychology, 65*, 178–183.

Nunnally, N. C., & Bernstein, I. H. (1994). *Psychometric theory* (3rd ed.). New York: McGraw-Hill.

O'Brien, W. H., & Haynes, S. N. (1995). Functional analysis. In G. Buela-Casal (Ed.), *Handbook of psychological assessment* (pp. 493–524). Madrid, Spain: Sigma.

Oetting, E. R. (1986). Ten fatal mistakes in grant writing. *Professional Psychology: Research and Practice, 17,* 570–573.

Ogles, B. M., Lambert, M. J., & Masters, K. S. (1996). *Assessing outcome in clinical practice.* Boston: Allyn & Bacon.

Orne, M. T. (1962). On the social psychology of the psychological experiment: With particular reference to demand characteristics and their implications. *American Psychologist, 17,* 776–783.

Ortmann, A., & Hertwig, R. (1997). Is deception acceptable? *American Psychologist, 52,* 746–747.

Ottenbacher, K. J. (1992). Analysis of data in idiographic research. *American Journal of Physical Medicine & Rehabilitation, 71*(4), 202–208.

Ozer, D. J., & Reise, S. P. (1994). Personality assessment. *Annual Review of Psychology, 45,* 357–388.

Parsons, H. M. (1974). What happened at Hawthorne? *Science, 183,* 922–932.

Parsonson, B. S., & Baer, D. M. (1978). The analysis and presentation of graphic data. In T. R. Kratochwill (Ed.), *Single subject research: Strategies for evaluating change* (pp. 101–165). New York: Academic Press.

Pasewark, R., Fitzgerald, B., Thornton, L., & Sawyer, R. (1973). Icons in the attic: Research activities of clinical psychologists. *Professional Psychology, 4,* 341–346.

Patterson, D. Y., & Berman, W. H. (1991). Organizational and service delivery issues in managed mental health services. In C. S. Austed & W. H. Berman (Eds.), *Psychotherapy in managed health care: The optimal use of time and resources* (pp. 19–32). Washington, DC: American Psychological Association.

Paul, G. L. (1966). *Insight vs. desensitization in psychotherapy: An experiment in anxiety reduction.* Stanford, CA: Stanford University Press.

Paul, G. L. (1969). Behavior modification research: Design and tactics. In C. Franks (Ed.), *Behavior therapy: Appraisal and status* (pp. 29–62). New York: McGraw-Hill.

Paul, R. H., Marx, B. P., & Orsillo, S. M. (1999). Acceptance-based psychotherapy in the treatment of an adjudicated exhibitionist: A case example. *Behavior Therapy, 30,* 149–162.

Paulhus, D. L. (1984). Two-component model of social desirability responding. *Journal of Personality and Social Psychology, 46,* 598–609.

Pavot, W., & Diener, E. (1993). Review of the Satisfaction With Life Scale. *Psychological Assessment, 5,* 164–172.

Pedhazur, E. J. (1982). *Multiple regression in behavioral research: Explanation and prediction* (2nd ed.). New York: Holt, Rinehart, & Winston.

Pedhazur, E. J., & Schmelkin, L. P. (1991). *Measurement, design, and analysis: An integrated approach.* Hillsdale, NJ: Erlbaum.

Pepler, D. J., & Craig, W. M. (1995). A peek behind the fence: Naturalistic observations of aggressive children with remote audiovisual recording. *Developmental Psychology, 31,* 548–553.

Pepler, D. J., Craig, W. M., Ziegler, S., & Charach, A. (1994). An evaluation of an antibullying intervention in Toronto schools. *Canadian Journal of Community Mental Health, 13,* 95–110.

Perri, M. G., Martin, A. D., Leermakers, E. A., Sears, S. F., & Notelovitz, M. (1997). Effects of group- versus home-based exercise in the treatment of obesity. *Journal of Consulting and Clinical Psychology, 65,* 278–285.

Persons, J. B. (1989). *Cognitive therapy in practice: A case formulation approach.* New York: Norton.

Persons, J. B. (1991). Psychotherapy outcome studies do not accurately represent current models of psychotherapy: A proposed remedy. *American Psychologist, 46,* 99–106.

Persons, J. B., Bostrom, A., & Bertagnolli, A. (1999). Results of randomized controlled trials of cognitive therapy for depression generalize to private practice. *Cognitive Therapy and Research, 23,* 535–548.

Persons, J. B., Mooney, K. A., & Padesky, C. A. (1995). Interrater reliability of cognitive–behavioral case formulations. *Cognitive Therapy and Research, 19,* 21–34.

Persons, J. B., & Silberschatz, G. (1998). Are results of randomized controlled trials useful to psychotherapists? *Journal of Consulting and Clinical Psychology, 66,* 126–135.

Peters, D., & Ceci, S. (1982). Peer-review practices of psychological journals: The fate of published articles, submitted again. *Behavioral and Brain Sciences, 5,* 187–195.

Peterson, C. C., & Siddle, D. A. T. (1995). Confidentiality issues in psychological research. *Australian Psychologist, 30,* 187–190.

Peterson, R. A., & Reiss, S. (1987). *Test manual for the Anxiety Sensitivity Index.* Orland Park, IL: International Diagnostic Systems.

Phelps, M. A., & Jacobson, N. S. (1998). Integrative couple therapy: Balancing change and acceptance. *Crisis Intervention and Time-Limited Treatment, 4,* 49–66.

Phillips, K. A., & Rosenblatt, A. (1992). Speaking in tongues: Integrating economics and psychology into health and mental health services outcomes research. *Medical Care Review, 49*(2), 191–231.

Pinsof, W. M., & Wynne, L. C. (1995). The efficacy of marital and family therapy: An empirical overview, conclusions, and recommendations. *Journal of Marital and Family Therapy, 21,* 585–613.

Poling, A., & Grossett, D. (1986). Basic research designs in applied behavior analysis. In A. Poling & R. W. Fuqua (Eds.), *Research methods in applied behavior analysis: Issues and advances* (pp. 7–28). New York: Plenum Press.

Poling, A., Picker, M., Grossett, D., Hall-Johnson, E., & Holbrook, M. (1981). The schism between experimental and applied behavior analysis: Is it real and who cares? *The Behavior Analyst, 4,* 93–102.

Pollard, C. A., & Henderson, J. G. (1988). Four types of social phobia in a community sample. *Journal of Nervous and Mental Disease, 176,* 440–445.

Poppen, R. (1988). *Behavioral relaxation training and assessment.* Elmsford, NY: Pergamon Press.

Public Health Service Act, amended 1970, 42 U.S.C. 242a, 301d.

Radloff, L. S. (1977). The CES-D scale: A self-report depression scale for research in the general population. *Applied Psychological Measurement, 3,* 385–401.

Raskin, A., Schulterbrandt, J. G., Reatig, N., & McKeon, J. J. (1970). Differential response to chloropromazine, imipramine, and placebo. *Archives of General Psychiatry, 23,* 164–173.

Rathus, S. A. (1973). A 30-item schedule for assessing assertive behavior. *Behavior Therapy, 4,* 398–406.

Ray, W. J. (1993). *Methods: Toward a science of behavior and experience* (4th ed.). Pacific Grove, CA: Brooks/Cole.

Riggs, D. S., & Foa, E. B. (1993). Obsessive compulsive disorder. In D. H. Barlow (Ed.), *Clinical handbook of psychological disorders* (2nd ed., pp. 189–239). New York: Guilford Press.

Risley, T. R. (1970). Behavior modification: An experimental–therapeutic endeavor. In L. A. Hamerlynck, P. O. Davidson, & L. E. Acker (Eds.), *Behavior modification and ideal mental health services* (pp. 103–127). Calgary, Alberta, Canada: University of Alberta Press.

Robinson, L. A., Berman, J. S., & Neimeyer, R. A. (1990). Psychotherapy for the treatment of depression: A comprehensive review of controlled outcome research. *Psychological Bulletin, 108,* 30–49.

Roethlisberger, F. J. (1977). *The elusive phenomena: An autobiographical account of my work in the field of organized behavior at the Harvard Business School.* Cambridge, MA: Harvard University Press.

Rogers, R. (Ed.). (1997). *Clinical assessment of malingering and deception* (2nd ed.). New York: Guilford Press.

Rogosa, D. R. (1980). A critique of cross-lagged correlation. *Psychological Bulletin, 88,* 245–258.

Romanczyk, R. G., Kent, R. N., & Diament, C. (1973). Measuring the reliability of observational data: A reactive process. *Journal of Applied Behavior Analysis, 6,* 175–184.

Rosen, A., & Proctor, E. K. (1981). Distinctions between treatment outcomes and their implications for treatment evaluation. *Journal of Consulting and Clinical Psychology, 49,* 418–425.

Rosenthal, R. (1966). *Experimenter effects in behavioral research.* New York: Appleton-Century-Crofts.

Rosenthal, R. (1976). *Experimenter effects in behavioral research* (enlarged ed.). New York: Irvington.

Rosenthal, R. (1978). Combining the results of independent studies. *Psychological Bulletin, 85,* 185–193.

Rosenthal, R. (1991). *Meta-analytic procedures for social research.* Newbury Park, CA: Sage.

Rosenthal, R. (1995). Writing meta-analytic reviews. *Psychological Bulletin, 118,* 183–192.

Rosenthal, R., & Rosnow, R. L. (1975). *The volunteer subject.* New York: Wiley.

Rosenthal, R., & Rosnow, R. L. (1984). *Essentials of behavioral research: Methods and data analysis.* New York: McGraw-Hill.

Rosnow, R. L., & Rosenthal, R. (1999). *Beginning behavioral research: A conceptual primer* (3rd ed.). Upper Saddle River, NJ: Prentice-Hall.

Ruma, P. R., Burke, R. V., & Thompson, R. W. (1996). Group parent training: Is it effective for children of all ages? *Behavior Therapy, 27,* 159–169.

Rush, A. J., Beck, A. T., Kovacs, J. M., & Hollon, S. D. (1977). Comparative efficacy of cognitive therapy and pharmacotherapy in outpatient depressives. *Cognitive Therapy and Research, 1,* 17–37.

Ruta, D. A., Garratt, A. M., Leng, M., Russell, I. T., & MacDonald, L. M. (1994). A new approach to the measurement of quality of life: The Patient-Generated Index. *Medical Care, 32,* 1109–1126.

Sartory, G., Müller, B., Metsch, J., & Pothmann, R. (1998). A comparison of psychological and pharmacological treatment of pediatric headache. *Behaviour Research and Therapy, 36,* 1155–1170.

Schacht, T. E. (1991). Formulation-based psychotherapy research: Some further considerations. *American Psychologist, 46,* 1346–1347.

Schwartz, G. E., Davidson, R. J., & Goleman, D. J. (1978). Patterning of cognitive and somatic processing in self-regulation of anxiety: Effects of meditation versus exercise. *Psychosomatic Medicine, 40,* 321–328.

Schwartz, S. (1991). Clinical decision making. In P. R. Martin (Ed.), *Handbook of behavior therapy and psychological science: An integrative approach* (pp. 196–215). New York: Pergamon Press.

Scriven, M. (1967). The methodology of evaluation. In R. M. Tyler, R. M. Gagné, & M.

Scriven (Eds.), *Perspectives of curriculum evaluation* (pp. 39–83). Chicago: Rand McNally.

Sechrest, L., & Figueredo, A. J. (1993). Program evaluation. *Annual Review of Psychology, 44,* 645–674.

Sechrest, L., McKnight, P., & McKnight, K. (1996). Calibration of measures of psychotherapy outcome studies. *American Psychologist, 51,* 1065–1071.

Sederer, L. I., & Dickey, B. (1996). *Outcomes assessment in clinical practice.* Baltimore: Williams & Wilkins.

Seligman, M. E. P. (1995). The effectiveness of psychotherapy: The *Consumer Reports* study. *American Psychologist, 50,* 965–974.

Seligman, M. E. P. (1996). Science as an ally of practice. *American Psychologist, 51,* 1072–1079.

Shadish, W. R., Newman, D. L., Scheirer, M. A., & Wye, C. (Eds.). (1995). *Guiding principles for evaluators: New directions for program evaluation* (No. 66). San Francisco: Jossey-Bass.

Shadish, W. R., Ragsdale, K., Glaser, R. R., & Montgomery, L. M. (1995). The efficacy and effectiveness of marital and family therapy: A perspective from meta-analysis. *Journal of Marital and Family Therapy, 21,* 345–360.

Shapiro, A. K., & Morris, L. A. (1978). The placebo effect in medical and psychological therapies. In S. L. Garfield & A. E. Bergin (Eds.), *Handbook of psychotherapy and behavior change* (2nd ed., pp. 369–410). New York: Wiley.

Shapiro, F. (1989). Eye movement desensitization: A new treatment for post-traumatic stress disorder. *Journal of Behavior Therapy and Experimental Psychiatry, 20,* 211–217.

Shapiro, M. B. (1961). A method of measuring psychological changes specific to the individual psychiatric patient. *British Journal of Medical Psychology, 34,* 151–155.

Shapiro, M. B. (1966). The single case in clinical–psychological research. *Journal of General Psychology, 74,* 3–23.

Sharpe, J. P., & Gilbert, D. G. (1998). Effects of repeated administration of the Beck Depression Inventory and other measures of negative mood states. *Personality and Individual Differences, 24,* 457–463.

Shaughnessy, J. J., & Zechmeister, E. B. (1990). *Research methods in psychology* (2nd ed.). New York: McGraw-Hill.

Shea, M. T., Elkin, I., Imber, S. D., Sotsky, S. M., Watkins, J. T., Collins, J. F., Pilkonis, P. A., Beckham, E., Glass, D. R., Dolan, R. G., & Parloff, M. B. (1992). Course of depressive symptoms over follow-up: Findings from the National Institute of Mental Health Treatment of Depression Collaborative Research Program. *Archives of General Psychiatry, 49,* 782–787.

Shewhart, W. A. (1931). *Economic control of quality of manufactured product.* New York: Van Nostrand.

Shiffman, S., Hufford, M., Hickcox, M., Paty, J. A., Gnys, M., & Kassel, J. D. (1997). Remember that? A comparison of real-time versus retrospective recall of smoking lapses. *Journal of Consulting and Clinical Psychology, 65,* 292–300.

Shontz, F. C. (1965). *Research methods in personality.* New York: Appleton-Century-Crofts.

Shulman, J. M. (1998, August). *Surviving managed care: Hands-on practice building, outcomes, and marketing strategies.* Workshop presented at the meeting of the American Psychological Association, San Francisco, CA.

Sieber, J. E. (1992). *Planning ethically responsible research.* Thousand Oaks, CA: Sage.

Sieber, J. E., Iannuzzo, R., & Rodriquez, B. (1995). Deception methods in psychology: Have they changed in 23 years? *Ethics and Behavior, 5,* 67–85.

Singer, E. (1978). Informed consent: Consequences for response rate and response quality in social survey. *American Sociological Review, 43,* 144–162.

Singer, E., Von Thurn, D. R., & Miller, E. R. (1995). Confidentiality assurances and response: A quantitative review of the experimental literature. *Public Opinion Quarterly, 59,* 66–77.

Skinner, B. F. (1938). *The behavior of organisms.* New York: Appleton-Century-Crofts.

Skinner, B. F. (1945). The operational analysis of psychological terms. *Psychological Review, 52,* 270–277.

Skinner, B. F. (1953). *Science and human behavior.* New York: Macmillan.

Smith, M. L., & Glass, G. V. (1977). Meta-analysis of psychotherapy outcome studies. *American Psychologist, 32,* 752–760.

Snaith, P. (1998). Meditation and psychotherapy. *British Journal of Psychiatry, 173,* 193–195.

Snyder, D. K. (1981). *The Marital Satisfaction Inventory manual.* Los Angeles, CA: Western Psychological Services.

Snyder, M., & Swann, W. B., Jr. (1978). Hypothesis-testing processes in social interaction. *Journal of Personality and Social Psychology, 36,* 1202–1212.

Soliday, E., & Stanton, A. L. (1995). Deceived versus nondeceived participants' perceptions of scientific and applied psychology. *Ethics and Behavior, 5,* 87–104.

Spanier, G. B. (1976). Measuring dyadic adjustment: New scales for assessing the quality of marriage and similar dyads. *Journal of Marriage and the Family, 38,* 15–28.

Spanier, G. B., & Filsinger, E. E. (1983). The Dyadic Adjustment Scale. In E. E. Filsinger (Ed.), *Marriage and family assessment: A sourcebook for family therapy* (pp. 155–168). Beverly Hills, CA: Sage.

Speer, D. C. (1992). Clinically significant change: Jacobson and Truax (1991) revisited. *Journal of Consulting and Clinical Psychology, 60,* 402–408.

Speer, D. C., & Greenbaum, P. E. (1995). Five methods of computing significant client change and improvement rates: Support for an individual growth curve approach. *Journal of Consulting and Clinical Psychology, 63,* 1044–1048.

Sperry, L., Brill, P. L., Howard, K. I., & Grissom, G. R. (1996). *Treatment outcomes in psychotherapy and psychiatric interventions.* New York: Brunner/Mazel.

Spielberger, C. D. (1983). *State–Trait Anxiety Inventory, Form Y manual.* Palo Alto, CA: Consulting Psychologists Press.

Spitzer, R. L., Endicott, J., & Robins, E. (1978). Research Diagnostic Criteria: Rationale and reliability. *Archives of General Psychiatry, 35,* 773–782.

Spitzer, R. L., Williams, J. B. W., Gibbon, M., & First, M. B. (1992). The Structured Clinical Interview for *DSM-III-R* (SCID). *Archives of General Psychiatry, 49,* 624–629.

Spragins, E. E. (1997, May 5). The numbers racket: An HMO's approval rating may not say much about its quality. *Newsweek, 129*(18), 77.

Sternberg, R. J. (1993). *The psychologist's companion* (3rd ed.). New York: Cambridge University Press.

Strupp, H. H., Horowitz, L. M., & Lambert, M. J. (Eds.). (1997). *Measuring patient changes in mood, anxiety, and personality disorders: Toward a core battery.* Washington, DC: American Psychological Association.

Suen, H. K., & Ary, D. (1987). Autocorrelation in applied behavior analysis: Myth or reality? *Behavioral Assessment, 9,* 125–130.

Suen, H. K., & Ary, D. (1989). *Analyzing quantitative behavioral observation data.* Hillsdale, NJ: Erlbaum.

Tarasoff v. Regents of the University of California, 551 P.2d 334 (Cal. 1976).

Taylor, C. B., Fried, L., & Kenardy, J. (1990). The use of a real-time computer diary for data acquisition and processing. *Behaviour Research and Therapy, 21,* 93–97.

Taylor, K. M., & Shepperd, J. A. (1996). Probing suspicion among participants in deception research. *American Psychologist, 51,* 886–887.

Telch, M. J., Lucas, J. A., Schmidt, N. B., Hanna, H. H., Jaimez, T. L., & Lucas, R. A. (1993). Group cognitive–behavioral treatment of panic disorder. *Behaviour Research and Therapy, 31,* 279–287.

Timmreck, C. W., & Bracken, D. W. (1997). Multisource feedback: A study of its use in decision making. *Employment Relations Today, 24,* 21–27.

Trent, R. M., & Fournet, G. P. (1987). The effects of hypnotherapeutic restructuring, systematic desensitization, and expectancy control on mathematics anxiety, attitude, and performance in females and males. *Educational and Psychological Research, 7,* 137–150.

Tufte, E. (1992). *The visual display of quantitative information.* Cheshire, CT: Graphics Press.

Turk, D. C., & Salovey, P. (Eds.). (1988). *Reasoning, inference, and judgment in clinical psychology.* New York: Free Press.

Turkat, I. D., & Maisto, S. A. (1985). Personality disorders: Application of the experimental method to the formulation and modification of personality disorders. In D. H. Barlow (Ed.), *Clinical handbook of psychological disorders* (pp. 502–570). New York: Guilford Press.

Tversky, A., & Kahneman, D. (1971). Belief in the "law of small numbers." *Psychological Bulletin, 76,* 105–110.

Tversky, A., & Kahneman, D. (1974). Judgment under uncertainty: Heuristics and biases. *Science, 185,* 1124–1131.

Ulrich, L., & Trumbo, D. (1965). The selection interview since 1949. *Psychological Bulletin, 63,* 100–116.

Underwood, B. J. (1957). *Psychological research.* New York: Appleton-Century-Crofts.

Wadden, T. A., Vogt, R. A., Andersen, R. E., Bartlett, S. J., Foster, G. D., Kuehnel, R. H., Weinstock, R., Buckenmeyer, P., Berkowitz, R. I., & Steen, S. N. (1997). Exercise in the treatment of obesity: Effects of four interventions on body composition, resting energy expenditure, appetite, and mood. *Journal of Consulting and Clinical Psychology, 65,* 269–277.

Wade, W. A., Treat, T. A., & Stuart, G. L. (1998). Transporting an empirically supported treatment for panic disorder to a service clinic setting: A benchmarking strategy. *Journal of Consulting and Clinical Psychology, 66,* 231–239.

Wahler, R. G., & Fox, J. J. (1980). Solitary toy play and time out: A family treatment package for children with aggressive and oppositional behavior. *Journal of Applied Behavior Analysis, 13,* 23–29.

Wallander, J. L., Conger, A. J., & Conger, J. C. (1985). Development and evaluation of a behaviorally referenced rating system for heterosocial skills. *Behavioral Assessment, 7,* 137–153.

Walster, E. (1965). The effect of self-esteem on romantic liking. *Journal of Experimental Social Psychology, 1,* 194–197.

Walster, E., Bersheid, E., Abrahams, D., & Aronson, V. (1967). Effectiveness of debriefing following deception experiments. *Journal of Personality and Social Psychology, 6,* 371–380.

Ware, J. E., Jr. (1986). The assessment of health status. In L. H. Aiken & D. Mechanic (Eds.), *Application of social science to clinical medicine and health policy* (9th ed., pp. 204–228). New Brunswick, NJ: Rutgers University Press.

Ware, J. E., Jr., & Sherbourne, C. D. (1992). The MOS 36-Item Short-Form Health Survey (SF-36). I. Conceptual framework and item selection. *Medical Care, 30,* 473–483.

Warwick, D. P. (1982). Types of harm in social science research. In T. L. Beauchamp, R. Faden, R. J. Wallace, & L. Walters (Eds.), *Ethical issues in social science research* (pp. 101–123). Baltimore: Johns Hopkins University Press.

Watkins, J. T., Leber, W. R., Imber, S. D., Collins, J. F., Elkin, I., Pilkonis, P. A., Sotsky, S. M., Shea, M. T., & Glass, D. R. (1993). Temporal course of change in depression. *Journal of Consulting and Clinical Psychology, 61,* 858–864.

Watson, D., & Tellegen, A. (1985). Toward a consensual structure of mood. *Psychological Bulletin, 98,* 219–235.

Webb, E. J., Campbell, D. T., Schwartz, R. D., Sechrest, L., & Grove, J. B. (1981). *Nonreactive measures in the social sciences* (2nd ed.). Boston: Houghton Mifflin.

Weick, K. E. (1985). Systematic observational methods. In G. Lindzey & E. Aronson (Eds.), *The handbook of social psychology* (3rd ed., Vol. 1, pp. 567–634). Menlo Park, CA: Addison-Wesley.

Weimer, W. B. (1976). *Psychology and the conceptual foundations of science.* Hillsdale, NJ: Erlbaum.

Weissman, A. N. (1979). *The Dysfunctional Attitude Scale: A validation study.* Unpublished doctoral dissertation, University of Pennsylvania.

Weissman, M. M., & Paykel, E. S. (1974). *The depressed woman: A study of social relationships.* Chicago: University of Chicago Press.

Wheeler, D. J., & Chambers, D. S. (1992). *Understanding statistical process control* (2nd ed.). Knoxville, TN: SPC Press.

White, H. D. (1994). Scientific communication and literature retrieval. In H. Cooper & L. V. Hedges (Eds.), *Handbook of research synthesis* (pp. 41–55). New York: Russell Sage Foundation.

White, O. R., & Haring, N. G. (1980) *Exceptional teaching.* Columbus, OH: Merrill.

Wilson, G. T. (1996). Manual-based treatments: The clinical application of research findings. *Behavior Research and Therapy, 34,* 295–314.

Wilson, G. T. (1997). Treatment manuals in clinical practice. *Behaviour Research and Therapy, 35,* 205–210.

Wilson, S. A., Becker, L. A., & Tinker, R. H. (1995). Eye movement desensitization and reprocessing (EMDR) for psychologically traumatized individuals. *Journal of Consulting and Clinical Psychology, 63,* 928–937.

Windelband, W. (1921). *An introduction to philosophy* (J. McCabe, Trans.). London: Unwin.

Winer, B. J., Michels, K. M., & Brown, D. R. (1991). *Statistical principles in experimental design* (3rd ed.). New York: McGraw-Hill.

Wolf, M. M. (1978). Social validity: The case for subjective measurement or how applied behavior analysis is finding its heart. *Journal of Applied Behavior Analysis, 11,* 203–214.

Wolpe, J. (1958). *Psychotherapy by reciprocal inhibition.* Stanford, CA: Stanford University Press.

Wolpe, J., & Abrams, J. (1991). Post-traumatic stress disorder overcome by eye movement desensitization: A case report. *Journal of Behavior Therapy and Experimental Psychiatry, 22,* 39–43.

Wortman, P. M. (1983). Evaluation research: A methodological perspective. *Annual Review of Psychology, 34,* 246–256.

Yeaton, W. H., & Sechrest, L. (1981). Critical dimensions in the choice and maintenance of successful treatments: Strength, integrity, and effectiveness. *Journal of Consulting and Clinical Psychology, 49,* 156–167.

Yenney, S. L., & American Psychological Association Practice Directorate. (1994). *Business strategies for a caring profession.* Washington, DC: Author.

Youngstrom, E. A. (1999, November). *Data dashboards: Information displays that help drive treatment and organizations.* Paper presented at the meeting of the Association for Advancement of Behavior Therapy, Toronto, Ontario, Canada.

Zimbardo, P. G. (1972). Pathology of imprisonment. *Society, 9,* 4–6.

Zimbardo, P. G. (1973). On the ethics of intervention in human psychological research. *Cognition, 2,* 243–256.

Zinbarg, R. E. (1998). Concordance and synchrony in measures of anxiety and panic reconsidered: A hierarchical model of anxiety and panic. *Behavior Therapy, 29,* 301–323.

Author Index

Numbers in italics refer to listings in reference sections.

Subject Index

About the Author

John D. Cone, PhD, a professor of clinical psychology at United States International University (San Diego, CA), earned his BA in psychology from Stanford University and his MS and PhD from the University of Washington. He has taught at the University of Puget Sound, West Virginia University, and the University of Hawaii. He is a Fellow of both the American Psychological Association and the American Psychological Society. His research interests include the development of idiographic assessment methodology; childhood sexual abuse, and the development, implementation, and evaluation of large-scale delivery systems, especially for people with developmental disabilities. His publications include *Dissertations and Theses From Start to Finish: Psychology and Related Fields* (with Sharon L. Foster; American Psychological Association, 1993). A frequent organizational consultant, he is past editor of *Behavioral Assessment* and currently teaches courses in behavior therapy, research design, assessment methodology, dissertation planning, and parent–child interventions. When not professionally active, John spends his time jogging, windsurfing, and sailing the waters of the blue Pacific.

monition that she would never sleep with a man who was talked about the way those cops were talked about in her old neighborhood had become the touchstone of their marriage. He knew that, in the end, she would never stand in his way. He would be able to get her to agree to it, if he decided to go forward with the undercover role. But would it be worth it?

And how would he deal with the likely eventuality that his new role would almost certainly result in some of his fellow officers being locked up? If it came to that, McCarthy had always believed that he would know how to deal with it, with the scorn and the accusations that he was a traitor to the badge. But would he?

On the way home the next morning, he almost missed the exit for Sloatsburg. By then it was daylight and he was facing a searing sun. It was an exit that he had always turned onto by reflex, by automatic pilot, thousands of times before. Not this time, though. Was that a forewarning of what his life would be like?

After the night's events, after the adrenaline had finally shut down, after the race was over for a day, he would finally have to face Millie. And tell her.

He was always preoccupied, always trying to plan two steps ahead, more focused on who he was supposed to be in his investigations than on who he really was. Now, if he accepted their proposition, it would only get worse.

As far as the consequences were concerned, McCarthy knew practically nothing about the dangers, both physical and emotional, that long-term undercovers faced, because at that point, in the early 1970s, the NYPD had no experience at all in running such operations. Frank Serpico had been a one-in-a-million aberration, a dedicated idealist who had brought the department and the city along on his personal mission, kicking and screaming all the way.

McCarthy knew that he was no Serpico. He didn't want to be one.

* * *

His wife was still in bed when he finally got home. She was almost awake. He started talking, carefully explaining what had happened, reconstructing the cryptic conversation between him and the inspector.

By the time he was finished, Millie was wide awake, her head still in the center of the pillow, her dark, thick hair spread out on either side like the most luxuriant fan that he had ever seen. She had remained quiet, breathing steadily, her chest rising and falling under a thin sheet. Whenever she concentrated like this, her eyes appeared not even to blink. Millie's tense motionlessness alone spoke to him.

The last part of it that he brought up was the children, Christine and little Billy. Somewhere down the line, they might be faced with a kid in the schoolyard who taunted them about their father—either that he was a bad cop or a snitch.

"I don't know if any kid can handle that," he said without turning to look at her.

"You can't do it," she said finally, firmly. "Nothing's worth that."

McCarthy raised himself to an elbow and faced her. "If you aren't going to be there on this, then I don't want it either."

Time passed. Too much time. "Yes you do," she answered. "You want it more than you ever wanted anything. It's in your voice. This is what you dreamed about. This would mean really being a cop." She practically pounced on him; he thought she was going to hit him. "Don't lie to me, Bill. Or to yourself."

He wanted to just let it go now. The inspector was right.

Then it was Millie's turn. "This is the way that it's going to be," she said. "I will have to push our baby's carriage around the block, and have people look at me, and point at me and the baby after we leave, wave their fingers, and say what they say about policemen who take money. And I will never be able to tell them that it was all an act. The women will stop talking when I come near them; they'll just get that look. Because, deep down, they want me to know that *they* know. Nothing else will ever make them feel so good.

"That's what you're asking me to do."

Then, he kissed her and asked, "Will you be there with me? I have to know now."

She reached over, took his hand, kissed it, then, ever so gently, she took his face in her hands and touched her lips to his.

He immediately pulled the sheet off, got out of bed, sat next to the night table and picked up the telephone receiver. Then he carefully unfolded the piece of paper that the inspector had given him.

Millie sighed, rolled away from him and placed the pillow over her head. But the pillow could not drown out the sound of her husband's voice.

"Yes." That was all Bill McCarthy said. Then, he placed the receiver back on its cradle, walked away from the bed, away from Millie, and left their bedroom.

THIRTEEN

A Prison isn't a place as much as sounds and feelings—
cold, clanging. When they close that gate behind you, it
locks in place. Send a cop to prison, regardless of the
crime or length of time, and it's always the death
sentence.

MOTHER'S MAXIM

On the surface, very little changed at first for McCarthy after
he agreed to assume his undercover role for the first deputy
commissioner.

Suspicion and wariness had become the new guiding principles of the NYPD after Knapp. What started out as a healthy
sort of paranoia, inspired by the movement to reform, quickly
collapsed into a form of psychosis.

"If the gambling module phone rang, and if a guy on the Pimp
Team happened to answer that phone, the captain would yell.
Nobody knew what anyone else was doing. Nobody was supposed to know because you had to worry about people selling
out what you were investigating.

"The department spent an inordinate amount of time then
devising what they called integrity tests. These tests involved
cops following other cops, attempting to catch them in compromising situations. They were like spot checks against corruption, but almost immediately, that got out of control. Half

the cases we worked on then weren't really cases at all, but elaborate integrity tests. And you never knew if *you* were the real target or somebody else.

"The police department always wanted you to do something wrong. The other guys you worked with always wanted you to do something—not really wrong—just a little wrong, so that then, they could do wrong too, and know that you were in no position to turn them in.

"There wasn't even a reasonable standard of integrity. It was a gross standard of integrity. The standard of integrity that I required for myself was a schizophrenic, psychotic standard. But it made me free to target whomever I wanted.

"In the 'integrity tests' that the NYPD was constantly experimenting with, they actually staged an event, like a bribe, and then monitored it to see if you would behave in an appropriate manner.

"Once, I was called to assign two people to go to a certain bar at twelve o'clock on a particular day to see if there was any prostitution action going on in there, a very famous bar in Manhattan.

"I asked the captain who gave me the order whom he wanted the integrity test on.

"'What are you talking about?' he said.

"'Isn't this an integrity test?' I was furious, because now I was sure it had become an integrity test on *me*.

"He denied it again. 'It's just a bar on the East Side and I want to see if there's any prostitution action going on.'

"'Listen,' I told him, 'since you're not willing to take me into your confidence, then I have no obligation to you. I'm gonna go out there, assign two people and tell them it's an integrity test, and then on Wednesday everybody gets stars on their report cards.'

"Finally, the captain said, 'Now, wait a second....'

"What had happened was that the Internal Affairs Division had called him and directed him to do an integrity test on two people—to assign them as they are normally assigned, through the sergeant.

[109]

"Then he admitted it. 'How do you know it's an integrity test?'

"I said, 'Because in my whole life, nobody ever told me to send two men three days from now anywhere.' They'd normally tell you to send the guy right away.

"'All right, it's an integrity test,' he said weakly, 'Give me two names.'

"I gave him my two best men.

"'Why would you do a test on your two best men?' he asked.

"'Why? Because they're the only two I'd ever trust. The rest of them I *don't* trust, already. You only test the ones you trust.'

"He just looked at me like I had explained the mystery of the universe to him.

"I was sure that a bribe attempt would be made on the cops at the bar by a spook from Internal Affairs.

"I decided to play along—except, I made it my business to drop by the bar myself, unannounced, just to make sure that my people weren't going to be set up. I had one man outside as a backup.

"I go in, sit off to the side and wait to see what happens. My detectives were already in there. They didn't see me.

"At the bar there are a few people, tough guys, winos, businessmen, a typical New York crowd. There's also this hooker I happen to know, Maria—a gorgeous Italian woman, about thirty-five years old, who once upon a time had been the queen of the Manhattan wiseguys. She had suffered some tough breaks over the years, but in that faint bar light, she still looked good. I hadn't seen her in a long, long time.

"She jumps up from the bar as soon as she sees me and runs into the kitchen. Next thing I know, the pimp who owns the place tells me that Maria has to see me right away in the back. He sounds excited, points toward the kitchen.

"I go in and there's this Maria, in the corner, crying, bawling her eyes out. I was sort of surprised she even remembered me.

"All of a sudden, she raises her head, gives me one of those looks, and grabs me, hugs me, almost knocks me down. Then she reaches around and pulls her shirt off. No bra, no anything.

Just two of the biggest breasts I ever saw. She hugged me some more. Smashes her tits right against my chest.

"I couldn't just act like, 'Oh, get away from me, you're a whore.' So, I put my arms around her, tried to calm her down.

"Now I *really* think it's a setup. All the pimps who had been paying off the cops were mad as hell at me. I figured this was their way of getting rid of me.

"They were going to take a picture of me with her, naked, give it to my enemies in the police department and get me transferred, or fired or arrested; get a morals charge on me.

"By that point, I was looking around for the cameras. It's either blackmail or an integrity test. I go down, regardless. But, if it's a test, where the hell are the Internal Affairs cops?

"Maria starts telling me her story. As she does, she spins around and shows me this stab wound on her back, an ugly scar. That was why she had taken her shirt off.

"'The guy who did this to me is sitting out there at the bar,' she says. 'I know he's gonna do it again. He'll kill me, you have to help me.'

"Now I'm confused. Is this a test or the real thing?

"I check the bar. My two cops are in the booth, and now there's a very obvious plant from Internal Affairs with them. He's beating their ears, attempting to bribe them.

"I'm not concerned about those two. I know my detectives aren't going to go for it. They'll report it to me and that will be the end of it.

"But what about Maria? 'Stay put,' I warn her.

"As soon as my cops leave, I take the guy at the bar and spread him, search him, the whole cop routine. I take a bowie knife off him and call for a wagon. As soon as it comes, I send him on his way.

"Then, I go back to see if Maria is okay. But she's gone.

"Was it attempted blackmail or an integrity test? To this day, I'm still not sure. But that was the NYPD in the witch-hunt days.

"Looking back on it, the approach that was made to me that night on Centre Street could very well have been an integrity

[111]

test too. I didn't even consider that then. I was too much in love with the idea of going undercover.

"All this integrity testing was something in addition to the real cases, the legitimate police work, like running wiretaps and taking out pimps and dealing with all the leads that called for further investigation as a result of what was intercepted on the wiretaps.

"You could never be sure of all the influences at work, real or imagined. You never knew, for example, which powerful person, inside or outside of the department, you might inadvertently be scaring by listening to the taps. You never knew how badly you could be hurt by the things you were finding out.

"And you didn't know all the devious ways that you were being obstructed, administratively, at the top levels of command in the police department, by the decisions that were made about 'go' or 'no go' on a certain case.

"That intrigue and interference even worked its way down to whether you could obtain a certain warrant or not. I used to cringe sometimes when I requested a warrant because I never could be sure who might not want that warrant served. Nor did I know the lengths to which they would go to stop me.

"We had a new police commissioner, Patrick Murphy. He was John Lindsay's man and we figured him for an egghead, an academic. The only weapon he ever used in his whole life was a typewriter. But his mandate was clear: He was there to force the whole hierarchy of the police department, practically an entire generation of commanders, the guys who had come up right after World War Two, to either get out or be demoted.

"That's what it was really all about. A purge. That was Lindsay's answer to corruption. Murphy was his hammer.

"Practically the whole Thirteenth Division, for instance, which was a Brooklyn unit, was locked up. There were cops in handcuffs all over the city."

* * *

Bob Leuci, whom most people came to know as the Prince of the City, typified the kind of cop who ran afoul of the integrity tests in the early 1970s. He was one of the best casebreakers in the SIU, the Special Investigating Unit of the Narcotics Division.

Targets included the men and women who were the pioneers in such dope connections as the Colombian and the East Asian. The French Connection to Marseilles had already become a celebrated case. They took over from there.

Pad money and temptation were all around the celebrity cops in the vaunted SIU. Some of them succumbed. Bob Leuci had his own problems at that point, his own dark corners. With ruthless efficiency, the prosecutors attempting to prove the existence of systematic corruption in the SIU used Leuci to make cases against lawyers, bail-bondsmen, organized crime figures, and, ultimately, against his own partners.

"By the start of 1973, I was working for the division commander, in the tower of power, One Police Plaza, on the twelfth floor, Central Investigation Section. *Permanent cadre,* the supersleuths, the cops' cops. Years later, I would return to command the Vice headquarter unit.

"What you actually did there was surveillance on members of your own division or special jobs for the commissioner.

"They still had me out in the field, of course, attempting to attract attention. I was literally waiting for the first nibble, the first good payoff reach.

"Bob Leuci, in the SIU, was down on the eleventh floor. We had a parallel existence. I was doing in Vice what he was doing in Narcotics. Trying to make the biggest cases we could.

"SIU had always been a bunch of renegades—the sort of undisciplined, free-lance detectives who had never been answerable to anybody. I was one of the new sergeants who had been put in place to try to control cops like that.

"Leuci was never a guy I trusted, not like a David Durk or a

Saint Paul. He convinced the world that he was an honest cop who had committed one indiscretion, had experienced guilt pangs about it, and had then gone to the government to make a deal to square things. I was always skeptical. But, then again, at least I was being consistent. I rarely got along with other cops. To me, Leuci was a meat eater like the rest of them and he sold out his partners.

"I always had very mixed feelings about what Leuci had done. What made it worse was that, technically, I was about to go into the same business as Leuci. I kept agonizing over whether I had made the right decision. The idea of working undercover against pimps or anybody else who tried to bribe cops was great. But if another cop somehow got caught up in all that, and I had to work on him too, well, that gave me no satisfaction at all.

"The most obscene part about the whole *Prince of the City* saga was that in the end, the prosecutors decided to give some captain, instead of some ordinary cop, the deal to cooperate—to become a state's witness, based on Leuci's testimony. It looked to me like the brass were taking care of their own once again.

"I call them the Legion of the Melting Shields. They consist of the top cops at One Police Plaza who, when they experience any degree of political pressure, for any reason, fold. Their tin badges start to leak down their legs. Instead of using the leather shield cases to carry their badges that the rest of us have, the exclusive members of the Legion need asbestos cases.

"I just hoped that, as I got in deeper and deeper with my new role as an undercover, that no one from their Legion would ever be in a position to decide my fate.

"Nobody really believed that the city wanted to do anything to clean up the corruption. They had been forced into it, publicly dragged through the streets. Experienced, mature people at headquarters never trusted Lindsay or Murphy or their motives. It was a time, however, when a cop could actually do an honest job and no one would dare try to stop him."

* * *

The changes that were seismically ripping apart the NYPD were no less alarming to another interested group—the Five Families.

Every time Carlo Gambino consulted his Richter scale he saw another twelve register. Big Paul Castellano was the underboss. John Gotti was still biding his time, attempting to develop the personal loyalties and the power base that would one day allow him to make his move.

All Five Families shared the same concern. They needed corrupt cops to remain in business. The prospect of real reform was threatening. The last thing they could tolerate was the police suddenly changing the rules in the Life.

However, many of the very people in power—in law enforcement —whom they used to call would no longer answer their phones.

There was only one solution. The Families would have to begin finding and recruiting some new cops, some new people who were willing to listen to reason. All they had to do was find them and pay them. Enough.

FOURTEEN

As soon as people suspect that a cop is *Taking Money*, people will line up to hit on him like a bakery, like people taking numbers after the twelve-fifteen mass on Sunday.

M O T H E R ' S   M A X I M

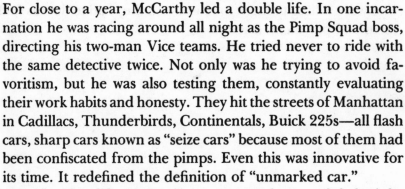

For close to a year, McCarthy led a double life. In one incarnation he was racing around all night as the Pimp Squad boss, directing his two-man Vice teams. He tried never to ride with the same detective twice. Not only was he trying to avoid favoritism, but he was also testing them, constantly evaluating their work habits and honesty. They hit the streets of Manhattan in Cadillacs, Thunderbirds, Continentals, Buick 225s—all flash cars, sharp cars known as "seize cars" because most of them had been confiscated from the pimps. Even this was innovative for its time. It redefined the definition of "unmarked car."

In his other life, McCarthy was attempting to subtly let it be known that he might, indeed, be open for the "reach."

"All the time, I was planting seeds in people, dropping them in conversations about things I wanted to do and about how much money I would need to do them.

"My own life-style changed, too. I guess I became the *Super Fly* version of a cop—drinking scotch and running around all night. And feeling guilty as hell about it when I would go home to Millie. It was the biggest con job I ever pulled—all working from my base in the Pimp Squad. I conned most of the cops and all the bad guys into believing that I had begun to turn into the kind of cop who becomes so immersed in the Life that he can no longer keep his balance, no longer distance himself from it."

Living out his bluff, McCarthy began to socialize with the kind of rogue policemen he had once taken pains to avoid. It was one thing to spend all day chasing the bad guys; it was something entirely different to spend all night carousing in their bars and clubs, attempting to score with their women and reveling in the kind of borderline behavior that usually landed normal people in handcuffs, sitting in the back of a paddy wagon.

The handful of cops who did know about McCarthy's new role came to see in him still another dimension—that of the diabolically clever undercover operative. His playacting was uncanny.

"No one ever challenged me. No one had the guts to challenge me. If I told people in the Life, through my actions, that I was corrupt, then I had to be corrupt. That went for the other cops, too. They had no trouble accepting that. Figuring out the motives behind the actions of honest cops gave them far more trouble."

Throughout this period, the team was still dealing with pimps and prostitutes on a regular basis, discovering anew that the things they had learned at the academy and the guidelines in the *NYPD Patrol Guide* would never apply in the Life.

Every after-hours bar in New York "paid." That was the expression. The cash either had to go to some Mafia Family or its associates or to the cops—or frequently, to both. Every vice enterprise had to "belong" to somebody, the hookers as well as the real waste. That was the only way to guarantee protection. Money made it happen every time. Forget about the sex or the dope or the gambling—they were just the commodities.

"A 'goulash house' was a place that would have drinks and gambling and women. That was the old Mafia term for the after-hours clubs. Some of those places were as elaborate as casinos. Very heavy people inside. All made guys. Wiseguys. Capos and up. And gorgeous whores in low-cut dresses wearing the fanciest jewelry that money could buy.

"If you have wiseguys, you are automatically going to have good times and good-looking women. That's the sweetest part of the Life. Take the typical wiseguy's girlfriend, for instance.

"She's a broad who can give you a blow-job while she's still chewing gum. To them, that's a true Italian princess. She could go under a table and give head while you eat spaghetti. A bimbo.

"She's got big tits; has to have great tits. That's a job description. Her name's Maria. She's wearing tight pants. And she's got all this teased hair that if you touched it, it would stick to your hand. She's just another whore, but a whore with a Madonna complex. And she likes to be around power. That's how these girls get off. They're into subservience. They pamper their man because he gives them all these favors—he's their god. Whores with a contract."

Eventually, McCarthy got his men all thinking the same way with each prostitute or pimp or john they arrested: Every time you rolled somebody's finger for a print, you enjoyed the opportunity of a lifetime. That print could tell you whether there's a warrant outstanding, a detainer, or even a traffic ticket. Some of the biggest cases were solved through breaks that came about in just that way. McCarthy's unit was developing valuable intelligence from the ground up. From the pavement on Seventh Avenue.

"Every night you had to be out there. In the middle of it. Living it. Gathering intelligence, collecting IOUs, proving yourself, over and over. You had to be out in the Life. We were the Pimp Squad, the pimp police. They knew us, we knew them.

"They would all talk to me because they thought I already knew everything they were telling me. When we would go through the big, thick books that contained mug shots, it was like we were going through a family album, just reminiscing. That's how close I got to it.

"The pimps and the girls in the Life were never 'informing' on anyone, because they didn't think they were telling me anything I hadn't guessed. Plenty of times one of them would approach me because they thought they might learn something from me. They were all afraid of each other, suspicious, worried. They were all threatened by each other, convinced that every one of their friends was working undercover for the cops. And we did everything we could to foster that belief.

"I was also locking up pimps. If a whore took a beating and wanted to sign papers on 'her man,' I would have her make a tape-recorded phone call to the pimp, tell him, 'Honey, I'm gonna give you all my money; I loves you and I wanta come back.' If he would agree to it that would be incriminating, and that was excellent evidence. That's how you did it—playing them off against each other.

"The notion that pimps are *real* men—and that's what a prostitute would say—just means that the pimp can't be pussy-whipped. Every other guy she meets pays for her pussy; that's her only source of income, of power over the johns. But the pimp doesn't *have* to pay. Therefore, she really has no hold over him. Ergo, the pimp must be some kind of superman.

"That sounds simplistic, but most of the women I met in the Life were looking for very uncomplicated answers. What they never understood was that many of the pimps are asexual. The reason they can refuse the woman is not because they have so much sexual facility or the willpower not to perform; it's just lack of libido.

"I would go out every night trying to jump pimps. We used to stop them, haul them out of their pimp-mobiles, bang them up against the door or spread-eagle them over the hood, and demand some ID. We would never accept their driver's license as identification. We had to see their social security card. The reason for that was we could then take that SS number and find out if the guy had filed income taxes or not. You cannot, in the United States of America, find out if a person has filed taxes unless you have his social security number. That was how we finally got some of them.

"Following the pimps took us to the after-hours clubs.

"An after-hours club is where you go to blow your coke. And dance, be seen, flaunt your gold chain and your fancy woman.

"That's the high society of the Life. Being able to show up at and spend your money in one of these pimp clubs or after-hours bars was what you worked for.

"This was the night life—but the underground night life, the secret Vice clubs. It might not even start until three in the morning, four. The pimps would come in with their bottom lady, their top earner, and treat her to booze and coke as a reward. She would carry his coke and his gun for him, in return, and take the collar, if the cops happened to come in. He wouldn't be holding anything. Two hours later, he'd spring her from the lockup.

"There was no point to making all that money from sex for pay if you couldn't spend it. These aren't the kind of people who are going to go to Dun & Bradstreet for investment advice; they aren't sophisticated enough to start investing in offshore banks. That came much later with the Colombian cartels.

"Then you would see people jet-streaming on coke. Flying. You will never see anybody doing coke sitting down, not for long anyway. They're all speeding around, jumping, dancing. Just jabbering away. On coke your feet never touch the ground.

"In one part of the room, a guy will be hitting on a girl; over on the other side, a pimp might be trying to 'cap' a whore, or recruit her for his stable; talking sugar-shit to her. Just constant activity. Not connected, but not entirely unassociated, either.

"The most notorious pimps, the flashiest ones, were known as the 'gentlemen of leisure,' the Super Flies. For all their garishness, they did seem to have a little more style, finesse, then.

"You would see them wearing gold coke spoons, diamond-studded, around their necks. Everybody, men and women, had at least one extremely long fingernail, for scooping up the powder. I've seen them throw down hundred-dollar bills and be able to squeeze the corners so they would pop open when they snorted.

"The people who ran the after-hours clubs were always in the legitimate bars, trying to invite and encourage people to come to their clubs later and spend money.

"But these were people who were already in the Life. How would you do it? Tell them you got a new cassette player? Come on. No, you'd have to tell them that you had good coke. And, as a matter of fact, the manager might be bringing in samples of coke right there, just like a Fuller Brush salesman, trying to sell his stock.

"Square people think that prostitution means a woman who spends her life on her back with her legs spread. But that's just what they do during their working hours. That's not the Life.

"Cocaine is the Life. It's crack if you're only clearing fifteen dollars for a blow-job. As you can afford to, you trade up. Conditions change; there will always be a different drug of choice. Next it will probably be ice—that's a derivative of methamphetamine. In those days, though, it was coke. The people who did it figured they were okay; it wasn't like they were taking heroin. Heroin was what they called *real dope*. Coke had star-status. It was celebrity dope. They were doing a thousand dollars a night up their noses. That was the reason they lived, the whole point of their lives.

"The clubs were dominated by the black pimps. But not owned by them, never owned by them. Ownership was strictly organized crime.

"I was in plenty of those places and I actually saw salad bowls full of cocaine, maybe a hundred thousand dollars worth of coke sitting out in a bowl on the table, like you would put out a bowl of potato chips on a coffee table for a party. A kilo out on the table.

"Anybody in the club was invited over to take a dip. Half the time, in the beginning, it was so brazen, so accepted that if you went to those places you had to do coke, that they didn't even care if you were a cop—you were still welcome to a friendly snort.

"Even if a cop went out *not* intending to get into trouble, he couldn't always help it.

"From the dealer's side, the major contractors for the big loads were all Italian or Chinese. The Colombians were just getting into it. Asians are taking over the actual importation now, but then, on the street level, the Five Families were the only game in town. All the dealers used coke then, from the little guy to the big guy—from a scratched arm to a five-hundred-dollar suit.

"There were so many things going on simultaneously at so many different levels. Nothing happened by itself. Besides pretending to be corrupt, and attempting to attract attention that way, I still had to do my normal Vice routine, like busting places for gambling or pedos. If you wanted to, if they allowed you to, you could have gone out into Manhattan every night, cast your Vice net, and reeled in some pervert like Peter Big. This was New York. It was all out there.

"However, there was never a time in Vice when you were not touched by political considerations.

"For example, you would suddenly be called away from all the organized crime or pimp intelligence that your team might be working on to respond to somebody's personal request.

"That always seemed to happen with pedos. A report would land on your desk that the gay child of some prominent person may have gotten himself in big trouble by dropping his load where he shouldn't have, or by trying to buy pussy or dope from the wrong people.

"These kids would walk on the wild side, over and over, and

never expect to have to pay for it. But the Life has a way of evening things out. Invariably, some kid from an Ivy League school would spend the night with some male prostitute or transvestite, get fucked in more ways than one, and now he's in the hospital, bleeding from the ass, and his father or mother or the family priest wants revenge.

"They make a phone call to the right person. Pressure is applied. It could be political or religious or low-level blackmail or something as innocent as just wanting to do somebody you may see at the next cocktail party a favor.

"The cops—*always* the Vice squad, which means my guys— are called in. We don't even get the whole story until later. But we're the soldiers. We have to go out and mug somebody. That's how the system works. That's why there is so much delay, why things take so long to get to court. The police can never operate freely in an ideal world, they are constantly being menaced by some mysterious authority figure who is biased to make sure that an investigation comes out one way or the other.

"And those were simply the typical working conditions of Vice.

"At the same time, I'm doing this Jekyll and Hyde undercover routine, waiting for some fruitful contact to be made. And, it seems to be happening. Slowly. I'm beginning to hear whispers about all these people on Park Avenue who want to bribe me to lay off their whorehouses. Cops from all over Manhattan were coming up to me, envious as hell, telling me about all the money I could make, wishing to hell they were me.

"Talk about balls in the air."

FIFTEEN

The *Feds* are not cops. They only make arrests by appointment and that appointment is the result of some meeting where there were yellow legal pads and Cross pens and magistrates and attorneys and everybody felt very safe. They are fancy restaurant cops. They do nothing summarily, and if you don't do anything summarily, like jumping out of a car and grabbing a guy who's raping a woman, then you aren't a real cop.

M O T H E R ' S   M A X I M

Some of those balls that McCarthy was attempting to juggle were represented by the contacts he was making on the street.

By that time, he was concentrating his efforts on the Upper East Side, the traditional power neighborhood in New York. There, vice was a refined, variegated experience. Pleasure, especially the illicit kind, seemed to hold a unique appeal for people who, to McCarthy's way of thinking, should have known better. He would never be able to place himself inside the head of the dissipate.

There was one case in particular that had always intrigued—and infuriated—him. It had begun as a Vice job. Then, the FBI had stepped in, citing jurisdictional prerogative. The animosities and competition among the different levels of law enforcement had ruined more than one investigation. When it came to brokering these turf wars, the cops usually lost.

"The heir to one of the oldest family fortunes in New York had allegedly been kidnapped by two people from Ireland. The trail was cold. An arrest had been made, too. Kidnapping seemed like a pretty mundane job for the feds. Except for one thing. The case had all sorts of holes in it. And the cops knew all about it.

"This was a very celebrated Upper East Side family. The FBI had recovered the young heir under mysterious circumstances. But they refused to provide us with any details. My beef was that it had been a Vice job all along and I had always wanted in. But, no go.

"The kidnap victim was homosexual, a well-known pedophile. He eventually married and fathered a child and became a socialite. But on the street, in the Life, the real players knew how kinky his tastes were and how deep his pockets were.

"We never believed the kidnapping story, we always thought that he had been the victim of an extortion plot. That was where the two Irishmen fitted in. But there was never anything we could hold the heir on. We couldn't *prove* that he had made a false police report. The feds didn't even want to consider it.

"I knew about a very vicious gang that only shook down pedos. As marks, they liked to prey on rich guys, or out-of-towners who used credit cards. That was the gang's MO.

"William McKinney, who had been a police impersonator for over thirty years, was the leader of this gang. You run into them in law enforcement. They are people who pretend to be police officers in order to force innocent or not-so-innocent victims to pay them bribes to avoid being arrested. It's rare for one of them to stay in business very long. You hear about them pretty quickly. But this McKinney was a real exception to that rule.

He'd made a profession out of it—and a damn good living, too. His particular scam was to make false arrests on sex charges, then offer to let the mark buy his way out.

"He had been arrested thirty-five times and had to be the most exceptional police impersonator I ever met. He would only pick marks who didn't have soled shoes. They had to be wearing new shoes, expensive shoes. That was a quirk he had. I think he believed that it would lead him to a better class of victims.

"After one of his accomplices would set up the victim, McKinney used to break into the hotel room—during the sex act, if he could time it right—and make his 'arrest.'

"McKinney actually had the balls to bring the victims down to the Manhattan district attorney's office while everybody was out at lunch, usually between one P.M. and two P.M.

"He'd take them into one of the interviewing rooms, pretending to be a detective, and extort money from them right there in the Manhattan district attorney's office.

"A variation would be for McKinney to pick up his 'prisoner' from another member of the gang and then take him to a real police station to be booked. That was brazen.

"McKinney parked outside the station, left the mark in the back of the car. He would pick a police station that had a low windowsill so the occupants of the car could see him go up to the desk, speak to the sergeant there—while he would really be asking for directions—and come back out. The real cops had no idea they were being used too.

"He'd get the desk sergeant to write the directions down—it all seemed innocent enough—then he'd go back out to the car and show the slip of paper to the victim.

"McKinney told them that the paper, which he never let them read, of course, was a 'booking slip.' As far as the victim was concerned, McKinney had to be the real thing. He'd just come out of a police station with a piece of paper in his hand. At that point, they would go somewhere else and, after cajoling and crying and coaxing, McKinney would allow the victim to bribe him out of the arrest.

[126]

"He became such a convincing impersonator that McKinney could go into any station house in New York, walk behind the desk, sign the blotter, call himself 'Inspector McKinney,' and there probably would not be a cop in the place who would challenge him. He knew the system, and the jargon down so well that he could even pull it off on cops. A cop would not believe that McKinney wasn't a boss. He even looked the part—white hair, heavyset, a real Irish bulldog.

"McKinney forged his own search warrants, his own arrest warrants. He typed them up on stolen police department forms. He could write or talk in any legal terms; he had all the blank affidavits and could manufacture his own court documents. He could come to your door with a piece of paper signed by a judge; you'd look at it and swear it was authentic.

"During the course of their operations this gang had also extorted money from an United States Army general, who eventually committed suicide. But not before he paid fifty thousand dollars.

"Every Vice cop in New York knew about William McKinney. He was another Peter Big, another huge embarrassment.

"In an unrelated case we chanced to lock up a skinny, fourteen-year-old blond hustler—a chicken; the pedos are the chicken hawks. He flipped and began to cooperate.

"This kid tells me that his lover is a pedophile king named 'John Wayne' and that he had been used as the pedo bait in some famous kidnapping case, which was really a shakedown, after all.

"As soon as he told us that, I knew that he had to be talking about the same case that had been bugging Vice for years.

"This kid's name was Larry Waters. He was mad at McKinney over a beating he had taken from him, so it was get-even time.

"There are certain bars in New York where people who want to buy children for the purpose of sexual exploitation go. It's an underground network.

"Larry Waters would wait to be picked up at a place on the East Side. This was the same bar that the 'kidnap' victim had frequented years back. A typical meat rack. The male whores just lounged around waiting until a pedo came in and started feeling them up. When one of them hit on Waters they thought they were just getting a date; they didn't realize they were getting McKinney, too.

"To try and trap McKinney, we took a room in a hotel in midtown and planted a detective there who was supposed to be a rich pedo. The plan was for Larry Waters to single him out to McKinney as a potential mark.

"But I didn't have much faith in Waters. So I secretly introduced into the plot a 'disgruntled' Irish policeman who had been laid off by the city. They only worked with other Irishmen. Another quirk.

"There actually had been layoffs at that time in New York, so it was a solid cover. I had this cop befriend Larry Waters, who believed he was really a laid-off cop who wanted to do a little hooking or pimping on the side. Waters bought the story because so many cops really do moonlight that way. And get away with it.

"Waters introduced this undercover guy to McKinney and he was invited to join the gang. They loved the idea of having a real cop to work with. So now, I have somebody on the inside. And I've had Waters from the beginning. I was double-banging Waters. He figured he was double-crossing *me* and McKinney. That's how these people were. They couldn't walk across Fifth Avenue unless they lied about it.

"Larry Waters then returns to the extortion gang and says, 'I got a date with an out-of-towner who's got a lot of money. We're supposed to meet at the Holiday Inn on Fifty-seventh Street.' This out-of-towner is actually another one of my men.

"The plan was for Waters to come into the suite and within fifteen minutes he would go to bed with the guy. Then, immediately, McKinney would break into the room and 'arrest' the pedophile.

"If the mark resisted or didn't offer to buy his way out, there would be violence. They would always beat up the mark a little bit. Just to seem like real cops.

"At the appointed hour, we are in two adjoining rooms, waiting for McKinney to show. We had the room wired like it was in stereo. There was even a videotape camera going. I brought in a tech guy to hide it in the bathroom and do all the recording. He's in there with his headset on. This was going down like a documentary. I was so careful.

"The connecting door had been taken off the hinges so that we could pop it and surprise them.

"My undercover cop is set. If he feels that he is in danger, and he wants us to come into the room, for any reason—it didn't matter if we had the case made or we didn't have the case—his only obligation is to give us the *code word* and drop to the floor, preferably behind the bed. I didn't want to have to worry about shooting him. The code word was *slick*.

"Nine o'clock, Waters comes into the room. Right on time.

"In the adjoining room, there's me, a Vice detective, Pete Madison, and our captain, Larry Hepburn. Hepburn wanted in on this one, too. As time went by, Captain Hepburn would become a major influence in my career; back then, though, we were still feeling each other out.

"Pete Madison is positioned on a chair, facing the adjoining doors. Our door is already open, so it's just their door that we have to go through. I'm ready to go.

"We sat there in silence. Waiting. Madison is carrying a double-barrel shotgun, breathing heavy. He's my artillery.

"As far as we're concerned, this is a go.

"At some point within the next fifteen minutes, they're going to break into the room. My cop is in there in his underwear; we're wearing bulletproof vests; this is it.

"Almost as soon as Larry Waters arrives in the room, he drops his pants, jumps up on the bed, and pretends to start screwing my detective to make it look good for McKinney and his gang.

"By this time, we're all breathing pretty heavy. I can actually hear my watch going *tick, tick, tick.*

"Madison is really tuned up. He puts two rifle rounds in the shotgun, clicks and the barrel back into the stock and closes up the thing.

I look over at Hepburn to see what he's doing, he's behind me on the edge of the bed. I can hear *him* breathing, too. This is wraparound tension.

"And all of a sudden the shotgun goes BA-BA-BA-BOOM! I hit the floor and Hepburn jumps up from the bed like he's on a trampoline and Pete Madison has been knocked over backward; he's somersaulted over his chair from the recoil of the cannon he's just shot off.

"That BOOM was the loudest thing I ever heard in my life. Not just a gunshot, but an explosion. I was right next to Madison. The gunpowder clogged my nostrils. If it were helium, it would have lifted me off the bed.

"It looked like Hiroshima—the cloud of gunpowder rose right up; it was only a seven-foot ceiling and it spread out like a mushroom cloud.

"I look over and there's a hole in the door as big as a basketball. The tech guy comes running out and rips his earphones off.

"It was only at that point, after all that delayed, benumbed reaction, that I realized that *we* had fired the shotgun. Madison had discharged it by accident. That was one of the single scariest things that ever happened to me as a cop. That thing was like an elephant gun. We couldn't have done any more damage with a rocket-launcher.

"I open the door to the room where Waters and the detective were. But I don't see anybody. I'm sure that we've killed Waters and the undercover man and maybe the people in the next room, too.

"The slug had exited the room and had traveled out across the hall through the front door of the room we were in. It took out shrapnel from the first door and drove it through the second door. One solid deep-bore slug. A cannonball. That's what we used. No birdshot. Our big guns fired solid projectiles. It was devastating.

"Never, ever again would I allow anyone to even touch a shotgun, except me. Had we fired that gun inside, against the interior wall, it would have taken everybody out in the next six rooms.

"It wasn't until then that I see Larry Waters' head coming up real slowly next to the bed. My cop is *under* the bed. He isn't taking any chances. Miraculously, neither one was hit.

"Now I have to check next door. See if we killed anybody. I run downstairs, get the key off the manager. I threaten the manager that if he comes upstairs, I'll arrest him, I'll throw him in Rikers for the rest of his life. We had never warned him that we were cops in the first place. Understandably, the guy was going nuts.

"The people downstairs in the lobby heard it; they felt it. The manager is convinced that we're a gang of terrorists. He absolutely does not believe that we could be cops, not the way I'm acting.

"Thank God, the room next door was unoccupied. Because the rifle was pointed down, it hit the floor, tore up the carpet, and ran along the floor of that room. It shredded the carpet, hit and ricocheted off three walls and the slug was lying in the middle of the floor.

"Now, McKinney still hasn't come yet. But he *better* show up because I now have to write up a report proving that at least I arrested *somebody*, because we have accidentally discharged a shotgun in a hotel suite in midtown Manhattan. That will take explaining.

"I tell Waters, 'Get back to McKinney and bring him here at eleven o'clock. Tell him your mark got cold feet and you had to talk him into it again. But tell him he *has* to show because your man has been flashing big bucks.'

"In the meantime, I go back to the station to start the report. You have to notify about ten thousand people that this happened. The duty captain interviewed me. He swore I had to be drunk. He smelled my breath. He wanted to come back to the hotel with me. I ranted and raved. I'm telling the captain in charge, 'You can't go over to the hotel and fuck up my case.' In the end, he decides not to. He doesn't want to get his name mixed up with this.

"I used my gun a lot, but I never liked guns. Experiences like that one helped confirm my aversion to firearms. I never shot anybody. It was just a very effective prop. I was always afraid of guns. I wasn't afraid to wrestle with people, but I was always afraid they were going to get my gun and shoot me with it.

"I have a saying—good guys carry them in their holsters, bad guys carry them in their hands. If you gotta go for it, it's too late. Any cop who has to go for his gun is asking to die.

"I never went anywhere without my gun. I had two—a service revolver, a Smith and Wesson .38; and a snub-nose .38—that was my off-duty gun. I still have the guns, but I haven't looked at them since I left the job. They're hidden in my house.

"Some cops are patent leather police. They're the guys who touch their holster and get a hard-on. They're into leather. They have matching belts, buckles, and holsters and speed loaders and quick-draw and dry fire. Most of them are maniacs. Probably they shouldn't even be armed.

"After what happened in the Holiday Inn, I wasn't sure that *we* should be armed.

"I go back to the hotel. I only have about a half hour. I vacuum the rug. I vacuum the hallway floor and I get two red napkins and stuff them in the holes in the door. I had to hope that the bad guys didn't notice the holes in the door.

"Eleven o'clock comes. Bingo. Waters shows up, goes into the room, my detective is in his underwear, his fly is open; he's standing there scratching his crotch.

"In walks McKinney and a second guy, a masher. The next thing you know, we hear the night table go over; they hit my detective, knock him over the bed, slap him around till he's bleeding; then the lamp goes, all this furniture is crashing. He was a tough kid. Before it all started we had gone over the potential peril and he had said to me, 'Mother, if I have to take a beating, I can handle it.'

"Then, as we're listening, they negotiate a price, tell him how much it's gonna cost him to get out of this arrest. Then he says, as loud as he could, without screaming, 'Okay, *slick*.'

"That's our signal. We break down the door.

"The big guy with McKinney says, 'Fuck him, let's kill him. It's a setup.' And he goes for a gun. Madison and the undercover kid jump McKinney.

"I drop my shoulder, I hit the big guy. I just kept my shoulder down and drove him into the bathroom and banged him against the sink, cracked his back. But he keeps on coming—he's about six-six, 260 pounds. He runs right over me, charges out of the bathroom.

"He took me down hard. I didn't see it coming. But I still have him by his leg and he drags me out into the hallway, stomping on my shoulder and my neck.

"I finally get to my feet and who comes in to help me but Captain Hepburn. We'd forgotten all about him and left him back in the other room. Hepburn starts punching in this narrow, dim hotel hallway. That's great, except that he's punching the hell out of the back of my neck trying to reach around and get to the other guy.

"After I take a mauling, we finally get him handcuffed. And he starts screaming, 'Don't handcuff me, don't handcuff me, I'm psychotic. I can't be handcuffed.'

"The tape is still running. Everybody's doing the right thing. Then Captain Hepburn says something like Clint Eastwood would say, trying to sound tough, like, 'I'll knock your lights out.' The only thing I had to defend at the trial on that whole proceeding was, 'Who was that voice on the tape threatening to beat the guy up after he was handcuffed?' Hepburn had watched too many movies.

"The next day, coincidence of coincidence, we find out that the big guy who practically tore my head off, the muscle for McKinney, just happened to be a fed himself—a special agent for ATF—Alcohol, Tobacco and Firearms. He moonlighted as a legbreaker for McKinney.

"That was just one of the reasons why I never liked working with the feds."

SIXTEEN

Manhattan Vice is doors with little windows. And knocks on those doors and people peeking out and letting you in. It's lookouts and bouncers and whores. And booze. And cocaine. It's like a costume ball. Except everybody is Count Dracula.

MOTHER'S MAXIM

The night that Sinbad first began—December 3, 1973—Bill McCarthy was parked in a rubbish-strewn alley, on the east side of Third Avenue, midtown, peeing into a Clorox bottle. He was on a surveillance. So much for the storied glamor of detective work, of Manhattan Vice.

He was sharing his space that evening with two mangy dogs, several cats, a family of long-tailed rats, and several winos and vent-men who appeared to be in various stages of semiconsciousness.

From time to time, McCarthy would twist into a squat and very carefully aim a stream of pee into the wide-mouthed opening of the Clorox bottle, which he'd looted from Millie's laundry, then he'd toss out the contents through the side window of the car. He tried hard not to spill any on his hands.

Stationed there like a movie cop, with black binoculars taped to a black dashboard, he was spying, watching a bar from a prone position on the cold floor of his brown, 1972 Matador station wagon, a car that he was convinced no self-respecting thief would ever try to boost.

He had to use his own car on this surveillance—he was squashed underneath the dashboard—because all the regular Vice cars were up on blocks. New York was just then taking its first hit of bankruptcy. That turned-out-pockets high would become addictive. The cops, being on the front lines of municipal indigence, felt it first. Of course.

McCarthy had been planted inside the Matador for a total of eleven hours; his back hurt, his neck ached, his torso was twisted. Thermoses of bad coffee had already turned both his stomach lining and his kidneys into screaming casualties.

He was headed into the twelfth hour—real darkness now—and still no sign of the drug buy that was supposed to be going down. More than anything else he wanted to get his hands on the junkie informer who had set this whole thing up and make him die a painfully slow death.

The joint he was watching, Adam's Rib, was one of the suspected pimp bars that his team had targeted as a likely payoff spot for cops on the take. Making cases like that was the lifeblood of Vice.

In an unrelated piece of what, at the time, seemed to be good luck, an informant had also snitched to them about this big drug buy that was supposed to take place that very night at the club. McCarthy's Vice team would work it from their end, initially, then turn it over to Narcotics if the tip was good. A double-bang case like that always looked good in the old personnel jacket.

But eleven hours was a long time to wait. For anything.

McCarthy figured he'd make it an even twelve. He'd just hit the Clorox bottle again, so he knew his bladder would be good for a while. Then he'd bag it and head home to Sloatsburg.

These plans were taking shape in his mind as he stuck his head up from the floor and happened to see a white male, alone, move in close and disappear behind his station wagon.

This could be the beginning of the buy.

Suddenly, McCarthy was back at the top of his game. He listened and looked and waited: the three most important things that any detective must do.

[135]

Apparently, they didn't even realize that he was in the car. He was ecstatic. Even New York grows quiet eventually, and this was one of those moments. The windows were rolled down despite the cold, and he thought he could hear himself and the guy outside breathing. It was that still.

The man who had disappeared behind the Matador walked briskly; he was skinny, puny almost, his spongy white skin set off by a dark turtleneck sweater. Topping it all was a balding head and a meticulously trimmed beard, the kind you had to check in the mirror half a dozen times a day to make sure that not a single stray hair had curled out of place. Actually, he looked sort of normal except for the nervous way he kept checking over his shoulder. McCarthy didn't recognize him. But so what? Half of New York was into buying either dope or sex. Join the club. He didn't particularly care whom he locked up.

A minute or two later, a huge black man, big enough to be a draft choice of the Giants or Jets, with rippling, body-by-Nautilus muscles, his flesh glistening in the moonlit night, came trotting along, leading two dogs on one leash, Great Danes. The dogs literally had their noses in the air and pranced like the kind of nasty, pampered mutts who were used to microwaved bones.

McCarthy had no idea what to expect next nor could he guess who was about to buy what from whom.

But, from behind his car, he could hear the sound of a belt buckle being opened, then the distinct unzipping of zippers. In his mind's eye, he could visualize pants coming down and being dropped. His experienced ears even picked up the muffled sound of skin scraping on the ground. Then he heard the telltale moans of sex.

What the hell was going on?

Fascinated, McCarthy still kept himself carefully concealed, but snaked his way over the car interior, to the cargo area in the back, to see just what was going on.

At that moment, one of the dogs started howling. And she wasn't baying at the moon.

Both men were crouched behind his car, still unaware he was

inside, using it to balance themselves, while they had sex with the dogs, screwing them doggie-style, from behind, as the animals weaved from side to side on those long, unsteady legs. All four of them—two dogs and two humans, as near as McCarthy could tell—kept rhythmically pumping out brief, urgent balloons of condensed breath in the gnawing cold. The pulsing regularity of sex was made starkly visible.

Then the two men dropped the leash and the black guy and the white guy started humping each other; the big black guy bent the little white man over at the waist and quickly took charge, lifting and positioning him like a doll. In the space of about ten minutes, they changed positions and variations about five times. By then, the rear of the Matador was vibrating so much that McCarthy actually started bouncing around inside.

As soon as they were finished, the big black man put himself back in his pants, zipped his zipper, and marched away again, still leading the two enormous, now whimpering dogs. Next, McCarthy watched as the little white guy made his exit, passing his car a second time; he had his handkerchief up to his face and he was wiping white splashes of semen off his perfectly trimmed beard.

Throughout the entire strange tableau, not a single word had been exchanged between the two men. It had been eerily anonymous sex; the only sounds that had been made came from the dogs or from the zippers and buckles.

McCarthy's first instinct had been to jump out and arrest them. But that still would have left him wondering which crime, exactly, had been committed, unless you counted cruelty to animals. And he wasn't about to get the dogs to sign papers on either one of them. It just wasn't worth it. The drug deal might still be going down somewhere. At least he could hope.

It wasn't by accident that those two had found each other. Their whole point was the chance of being discovered. Compulsive behavior. McCarthy had seen it before. That was the most electric aspect of the whole thing—that risk of being found out. There were equal elements of amusement and disgust in his reaction. Vice was getting to him, all right; was it ever. He didn't need a police counselor to tell him that.

Before the twelfth hour had become the thirteenth, McCarthy straightened up in the Matador and called it off.

As he drove home he kept thinking about the typical—at least for Vice—New York street scene that had just unfolded. Bestiality off-Broadway. God, did he love New York. The only thing he wanted to do was take a hot shower and stay in there forever. He didn't even plan to wake Millie.

One week later, following his orders, Harold Schiffer and John Scarpa, two of McCarthy's best cops, were parked outside a different after-hours club on East Fourteenth Street, hoping to witness the same alleged drug buy that he had had under surveillance, or better yet, the same corrupt behavior by cops that had brought Vice to the land of the pimp bars in the first place.

At a few minutes before 2:00 A.M. they watched as a car pulled into the intersection at Second Avenue. It was a pimpmobile. No mistaking that. Long and loud and tacky. There was even a layer of cheap fur on the swept-back roof where the padded vinyl had originally been installed. Lincoln Con-tin-ental. So fine.

Within seconds, the door opened, the pimp emerged, a massive black Super Fly in a purple felony hat, wearing a long fur coat and two stunning women on each arm.

McCarthy had passed on the description of the two men who had humped the dogs behind his car, hoping that one of them still might somehow be involved in the narcotics traffic in the neighborhood. There was no question that the black pimp matched the description of the dog-walker.

As the two cops watched, the pimp began to sniff at the damp night air just the way his two Great Danes had a week before. Then, walking like a circus act, arms in arms, unsteady, reeling, they all began moving together. The women showed plenty of nylon ass and stretched garter belts under their short skirts; they were carrying enough cleavage to hide a crate of melons. Then the five of them turned the corner at Fourteenth Street.

[138]

This was the night Life. In all its lewd, almost theatrical glory.

Schiffer, dressed like Sam Spade, saw them knock on the door of the club, gain entrance, and appear to head upstairs.

It looked interesting enough to be enticing. He was a nosy cop to begin with and it had been a slow night. Schiffer's natural restlessness and curiosity had already won out.

"Let's check it out," he said to Scarpa, a cautious, thoughtful Italian from Queens who had probably never once lost his lunch money at school.

Scarpa followed his nature and was skeptical: "They ain't gonna let us in there."

Schiffer listened, as he always did, but he refused to hear.

"You don't know if they will or they won't till you ring the frigging bell and the door opens and the guy looks at us."

Scarpa still thought he was crazy. And maybe he was. There had to be some reason why he got along so well with McCarthy.

"Nobody's gonna even know why we're up there," Schiffer told him, as he opened the door and climbed out. "Don't worry about it, Johnny."

The two cops quickly crossed the street and soon were right behind the pimp and his swishing stable. Schiffer knocked and the door opened, just a crack.

From the darkness inside, two small, watery rodent eyes stared out at the tall, sinister-looking detective. These were the moments that Harold Schiffer lived for. Not *being* a cop as much as *playing* a cop.

Immediately, he could see that the doorman was an old, wrinkled Jewish guy that he knew from somewhere. What Schiffer couldn't discern from the man's make-them-work-for-it non-reaction was whether he knew him from being a *cop* or from the synagogue or the garment district or who-knew-where. With Schiffer, perhaps the leading Zionist in the NYPD, it could have been anyplace in New York.

"So, how're you doing?" he said to the old man. "I know you from somewhere, don't I?"

The doorman took a second long look and said something in Yiddish that Schiffer missed. Then, without saying another word or hesitating, he opened the door wide enough to let the two men in.

Escorting them, he found seats for both detectives at the upstairs bar. It wasn't much of a bar. Just six or seven stools and a bartop that needed wiping.

Schiffer glanced over at one of the large, seedy booths in the rear of the club and caught a snapshot image of the pimp they'd seen outside fondling one of the girls who had been on his arm. He had his hand inside the front of her dress, cupping a large nipple and breast.

The place looked "dirty" as only experienced cops could assess. Several of the biggest pimps in New York were there—Schiffer and Scarpa both recognized them—along with some of the highest-priced whores in Manhattan. They were all off-duty now. This was their downtime and there wasn't enough money in the whole world to get laid just now. Everybody needed a break.

There was cocaine everywhere; the city's black and white underworlds were mixing freely. Women were lazily dancing with other women and the pimps were quietly talking shop. At practically every booth, heads kept tilting back in the abrupt, spastic jerk that always followed a hit. Coke was still daring then, new; it was the Super Fly high.

Schiffer also saw another face he recognized—Barry Stein, a pretentious hustler and a very ambitious hood. Stein affected a businessman's clothes and mannerisms, but underneath the thousand-dollar suits Schiffer imagined a character composed of pus and larval droppings.

Stein noticed them, gave both cops a quick once-over, but made no move beyond that. If he smelled the musty scent of the NYPD on their baggy suits, he did a good job of not showing it.

This club—which seemed to be Stein's, the way he walked around giving orders to the barmaids—was almost unknown to the rest of Vice, outside of McCarthy's own team. And they weren't even sure what it was. But that mystery was clearing up now—it was an R-and-R retreat, sort of like an old-fashioned opium den, safely removed from the combat zone on Seventh Avenue or Times Square. Here, you took a toot and let down your hair. Everybody's batteries came out for a recharge.

A place like this could prove to be too valuable to bust prematurely. They had a perfect excuse to make a move, to pull out the handcuffs because of the coke, but they were there, they hoped, to gather intelligence, to try to stay mildly undercover in order to build up to bigger and better things. Narcotics could always make the pinch for the odd kilo later on. That wasn't necessarily doing it by the book, but that was the way good Vice cops always operated.

Schiffer and Scarpa both ordered drinks. They realized in that wordless sense of knowing that passes between two police partners that they had stumbled onto something very big here—but they had no way of knowing how big.

Schiffer had to diplomatically turn down a complimentary round from the old cocker doorman who was now beginning to act friendly, mostly in Yiddish. That made Schiffer sure that he *didn't* know him from being a cop. The detective checked his watch. Almost 3:30 A.M., approaching last call. And the place was still going strong.

To prove a liquor code violation the bartender would have to actually accept U.S. currency in exchange for a drink. They were witnessing that. Plus the cocaine. Within their first five minutes there, they had gathered more than enough for a warrant. Without ever realizing it, Schiffer and Scarpa had launched Sinbad. The day would come, later, when Bill McCarthy was ready to kiss them for it.

But all that was long before they snatched Tony Vitaliano.

Just before they were ready to leave, one of the whores—a good-looking girl with straight black hair and no underwear as far as they could see—asked Schiffer to dance. Just before she'd made her move, Barry Stein had stopped by her booth and whispered something to her.

Once she had Schiffer on his feet, on the floor, with his arms around her shoulders and her arms encircling his ass, she began what amounted to an informal frisk, beginning with her knee planted firmly and provocatively between his legs. Then, to keep his hands safely occupied, she lowered them to her breasts.

As they moved, very slowly, languidly almost, she began rubbing him up and down, from his ankle to his thigh. She was feeling around for a gun.

He could have told her he wasn't wearing one. He wasn't that stupid. But she had clearly been given orders to find out for herself. Very deftly, very quickly, she continued to pat down the small of his back, both armpits, and finally his groin—where she discovered a monumental erection, but no .38 detective special, no weapon.

As soon as the song ended, she kissed him and excused herself, heading for the ladies' room. Barry Stein immediately got up and followed her.

That's when Schiffer and Scarpa decided to exit too.

Out on the street, Scarpa asked, "What was that all about? The whore?"

"Just checking," he said. "I imagine Stein asked her to see if I was a cop, if I was holding a piece."

"You weren't. Neither was I."

Schiffer smiled wickedly. "Which means that now, he just isn't sure. Are we or aren't we? And if we are, what the fuck were we doing there tonight if we didn't lock anybody up?"

SEVENTEEN

A good *Boss* in the police department will tell you what he wants you to do and if it turns out bad, he will remember that he told you to do it.
A boss who will never hurt you is a boss who doesn't make decisions. A boss who is a real gentleman will take care of you when you get drunk. Because he's a gentleman. But, when you want him to be your advocate, to go to bat for you, to bang on the table for you, he won't be there, because he's too much of a gentleman. If it doesn't work out, you're all alone.

MOTHER'S MAXIM

McCarthy was poking skeptically at a tuna and American cheese on whole wheat, nursing a warm Pepsi and just finishing up an article about the Knicks in the *Daily News,* when Schiffer and Scarpa stopped by his desk to tell him what had happened with Barry Stein and the pimp bar on Fourteenth Street. By then, a gray, snowy dawn was breaking over the silver obelisks of the New York skyline. The rest of the world was stumbling to a sleepy breakfast, but McCarthy and the Pimp Team in Vice were only just beginning to wind down from the night before.

He listened as he always did, took a small bite, smelled the too-fishy-tasting lump of a sandwich as it stared back at him from the nest of its thick deli wrapping paper, and decided to stick with the Pepsi. The one thing he knew for certain was that his stomach would never recover from being a cop.

"When the broad felt you up," he said to Schiffer, "did she happen to whisper anything in your ear about what pleasures fifty bucks would buy?"

Schiffer smiled uneasily. "Sorry, boss," he answered. "No solicitation."

"So what do we have?"

"Liquor code violations coming out the kazoo..." Schiffer said.

"Which are bullshit, at best..." McCarthy interjected.

"And people taking cocaine like they were drinking coffee."

"Which *isn't* bullshit," he cut in this time.

"So?" the detective asked him.

"So...I think we go for a warrant. But I don't send in you two guys again because we may be able to use you on this later. If we're really lucky, Stein still isn't completely sure that you're cops."

"I like that," Scarpa said, opening his mouth for the first time.

"So do I," McCarthy answered. "I'll go in with Vitaliano. We make a move tomorrow night."

"You go for the coke, right?" Scarpa asked.

"Wrong," McCarthy replied, surprising both of his men. "All we go for is the illegal liquor sales. We go for the bullshit pinch. Then, we see what happens." He looked up from his desk, grinned, and took one last, desperate bite at the tuna and cheese.

Schiffer and Scarpa immediately understood.

What McCarthy didn't have to explain was that he was hoping—gambling, actually—that in the process of serving the warrant, which was technically a glorified misdemeanor, a nothing case, somebody at the bar would panic and begin waving money in his face, or in Vitaliano's, to try and make things square.

That would be a Vice case; the kind that he was looking for. He'd been angling for months to get someone in the Life, preferably a pimp with connections, to hit him with a payoff deal.

That could start a plan in motion that McCarthy had been hatching for months. It was to be the genesis of Sinbad.

The three of them nodded to one another and started to head home. "By the way," McCarthy called after them, "did anybody screw any dogs?"

Early on, McCarthy had realized that he had to let his team know what kind of boss they could expect him to be. That was why he could count on cops like Harold Schiffer and John Scarpa. The very first thing he had done was impress upon them the fact that he was not a gentleman—at least not in the traditional NYPD understanding of that term. He did not tolerate drunks; he refused to cover for anybody.

If they still wanted to work for him, that was fine—but it had to be on McCarthy's terms. Back when he was an ordinary street cop he saw that partners were people you had to make deals with fast. They could be either good or bad. But you had to agree. You had to be of the same mind. Honest *or* dishonest.

That was most important. And for McCarthy they had better be honest. He didn't care if his partner was a big guy or a little guy, a coward or a brave cop, or if he smelled. He just never wanted to have to worry about him being dishonest; he would have nothing to do with that.

When he became a sergeant and took over the Pimp Team in Public Morals, he went to great pains to get that same message across. The rest, he hoped, would take care of itself.

Frustration for any cop was knowing what to do, but not being able to do it. Allowed to do it. Vice was like going through a dark, dangerous forest to get to the good part, to get to the significant arrests. He had to guide them, had to show them how to keep trying to push the rock up the mountain, never stopping for a second, because that's when it would roll back over you. If you wanted it to happen in Vice, you had to *make* it happen.

The police department didn't want to see all of its cops become frustrated, because that meant that there would be too many guys walking around out there with guns. Frustrated, well-armed guys. And that could become very costly, very fast.

They tried to avoid that by allowing the system to subtly teach its cops, even its potentially good cops, to survive by doing nothing. Absolutely nothing. Do fucking nothing—that was the message of government to its law enforcers. Do only what they made you do. Slide by. But there was a fallacy in that. Just about every cop McCarthy had ever met had, at one point or another, joined the police department precisely because he wanted to *do* something. Maybe he only wanted to be corrupt—but damn, he wanted to go out and make even that happen. You could never take that away from cops and expect them not to rebel in their own devious ways.

McCarthy saw his role in Vice as being that of an expediter for his team. He had already formed some very definite opinions on what separated good bosses from bad. If pounding his fist on the desk in a superior officer's office was what it took to make his men respect him—going in and pounding it for them either because they couldn't do it for themselves or because they were afraid to—then he had made his mind up to follow that course. He had never worked for a boss like that, but he had always wanted to. That became his vision, his dream. And even in a place like the Pimp Team in Vice, you had to have a dream.

He much preferred becoming a partner, rather than a boss, to the detectives under him. He saw it as his responsibility as well as an opportunity to show them exactly how he wanted the job done. The team was at its best when he infused it with his holy sense of mission—if that made the chief of detectives a devil, so be it. As long as it allowed McCarthy to emerge as the simulacrum of the mythic leader his Vice cops had been looking for he was willing to ride with it.

The reaction of his team to this approach, to a boss who actually wanted them to be better cops and take chances and run risks, was profound. To McCarthy with his tough brand of idealism this only seemed natural, the way things were supposed to be. But to the cops who worked for him, it had been a revelation. No one had ever come in before and said all this and then tried to make good on it.

In the beginning, it had been tough getting them all to think as a single unit. He started to have his "team" meetings outside the office, away from the big bosses. He picked a place in Chinatown. There was blunt symbolism in that too. Chinatown, with its Tongs (organized crime gangs imported from Mainland China, centuries-old, tribal) and whores and elaborate secret gambling casinos, was the proverbial belly of the beast. Vice cops had to be really hardass honest guys to hang out there and *not* become corrupted. Chinatown to the NYPD was like the ancient seat of all Vice temptation. To McCarthy's mind that made the setting perfect.

They would spend a great deal of time there together, feeling each other out, getting to trust one another, developing the esprit de corps that every unit in the police department wished it had. And since they were in the neighborhood anyway, they also developed more new, valuable intelligence on gambling and prostitution in Chinatown—as much by accident as by design—than all the Pimp Teams before them.

It didn't take them long to determine that most gambling was multilevel in Chinatown, with games like Mah-Jongg upstairs and the secret casinos downstairs—*three* sub-basements down, in some cases, below the noodle factories and fortune cookie bakeries.

Fetching, honey-skinned whores with watery almond eyes—downcast eyes—were delivered on order, like complimentary drinks to a crap table in Las Vegas. Once a girl had become too Americanized, too fluent in English, or simply too burned out and broken down—literally too loose and stretched—from the constant demands of marathon sex, she would be rotated back to Hong Kong or the mainland, back to a peasant brothel where the less demanding local customers didn't consist of high rollers who might drop a hundred grand in one night of looking at snake eyes.

Few of the women lasted past their twentieth birthdays; many

[147]

started at fourteen or fifteen. By eighteen they had usually become the debauched senior citizens of the Chinatown whore trade. A handful might then drift into massage parlor work, which was relatively safe, if a bit like being held captive all day. Others who remained were recruited for the thriving escort services—pussy delivered to your door. That was dangerous as hell, because you never knew who or what would be waiting behind that door. In fact, McCarthy had never met an escort girl—and he knew dozens—who had not, at one time or another, been raped, assaulted, kidnapped for a few hours, or subjected to some combination of all three.

The one thing that the foreign whores would never do was work the streets. Maybe back home, but never in New York. Here, they were as much prized for their passivity and willingness to hang around all night doing absolutely nothing, waiting until a customer happened to remember them, to look up from his card game, as they were for their skills in bed—skills which distinguished many of them as the finest hookers in Manhattan. By contrast, American women were expected to be more aggressive, ready-to-please, sexual initiators who weren't afraid to whisper "Suck you off?" in the ear of a total stranger. Or even scream it through his car window.

Each political faction among the Chinese also had its own gambling parlors. The Communists had the most elaborate setup. They used a place near Catherine Street called the House of the Gold Doors. Except the doors weren't actually gold, only *painted* gold. Underneath they were solid steel. That was the sort of information that would come in very handy to the next cop who tried to take the place with a sledgehammer. And McCarthy himself was frequently the team's sledgeman.

All the while, the Pimp Team was becoming that cohesive unit that McCarthy had aimed for.

About a week after Schiffer and Scarpa had made their observations, the Pimp Team received the go-ahead to serve the warrant on Barry Stein's bar. But there was an added complication. There was a new captain in charge of Vice then—Larry Hepburn. He wanted to see a pimp bar because he'd never been near one in his life and he decided that since he was now the boss of Public Morals, visiting a pimp bar might be a good idea. He saw it as a field trip, as a class trip almost. By then, his reputation as "Flash Gordon"—because of his space cadet tendencies—was already sacred writ in the NYPD.

Hepburn was an odd duck, a ruddy-faced, redheaded eccentric, a sort of absent-minded professor, tweedy and frequently lost in a pungent cloud of pipe or cigar smoke, who had only recently been handed Vice. His predecessor, another prize, had been unable to reconcile his strict New York Catholic upbringing with all the pornography he had to confiscate and look at and with all the half-dressed whores he had to interrogate. On the surface, Hepburn was an improvement, but as far as McCarthy was concerned, he still seemed ill suited to command Vice. Hepburn was a guy who went through life perpetually amazed by what he found. That almost innocent sense of credulity could get a cop sent to jail in the corruption cauldron that was Vice.

The midlevel bosses like McCarthy, who served directly under Hepburn, were struck by his intelligence and honesty—in fact, he had been chosen for the sensitive job precisely because he was straight, and because nontainted bosses were hard to come by in the paranoid era that followed the revelations of the Knapp Commission.

McCarthy groaned when he found out that Hepburn had selected his team for the show-and-tell. But he wasn't surprised. The new captain might have seemed like an eccentric, but he was nobody's fool. Hepburn was a genuine police buff who recognized and admired superior performance, and that was exactly what McCarthy's team had been consistently turning in.

They were scheduled to serve the warrant on the Fourteenth Street bar at approximately 5:00 A.M.—well past the legal closing time. The team had assembled at midnight, reviewed their work for that tour, and then hit the street.

McCarthy and Tony Vitaliano took Captain Hepburn with them and began barhopping. They planned to end up at Barry Stein's place.

Hepburn was excited, like a kid almost. At one point during the evening, when he had disappeared to use the men's room, McCarthy turned to Vitaliano and said, "Can you believe Flash?" Then he began mimicking the captain. "It's like, 'Oh, wow, we're going to the zoo to see the zebras. Take me to see the elephants. Then I wanna see the chimpanzees, and the orangutans. Oh, boy, look at the orangutans. Oh, look at the brown one! Look at all the pimps!'"

"The guy's a buff," Vitaliano said. "The department's full of them. He's a good guy. What do we care? For once we have a quiet night."

Both cops knew that working under "buffs," as they called them, was the story of the NYPD. Commanders, usually, they were highly entertained by the job, almost like groupies. Most had never really been called upon to do anything more than look good, have "command presence," which actually meant they had to look good in a uniform, especially at funerals for slain cops or while marching in parades or turning out for other functions at the Building at One Police Plaza.

Hepburn had come from that environment, that background, and the cops in Vice were watching him skeptically. He would more than make up for his buff status during the crunch time of Sinbad, but that night, in the very beginning, no one could guess that Hepburn would turn out to be a member of the smallest minority in New York—a boss, an officer whom the real cops looked up to.

Everything seemed to be a surprise to Larry Hepburn, including even hunger. Once, he had showed up for an undercover job on a bicycle because his car wouldn't start so he rode to work on his kid's bike instead. The Flash stories were endless.

In every bar they hit that night, Tony Vitaliano could have passed for a blood relative of the Columbo Family. As long as people didn't know him as a cop, they would be convinced that he was a hood. He looked the part. McCarthy and Hepburn stayed in the background while Vitaliano went into his act. He was supposed to be playing the part of a small-time hood out on the town. He milked the role like a farmer with both hands on an udder.

In the kinds of places they were visiting, you always walked in, looked around, and then went right down to the end of the bar and stood there with your back against the wall—but not *too* close, you didn't want to bring home any roaches—and then you watched the front door and the bathroom door. That's where the action would develop: sex and drug deals through the bathroom door—if you saw someone down on her knees, you knew she wasn't making a novena—and stickup guys with guns in their hands through the front door. Just as long as you had those three things covered in the Life—sex, drugs, and guns—you had it all.

Places like that were being robbed all the time, any time, and McCarthy wanted to be situated with no blind sides and only one door that he had to watch. You never, ever sat down. In fact, that was the first instruction he had given to Hepburn that night. Never relax; not here, not in this kind of place. You just never knew who might come walking in, or what sort of piece he might be holding. Any way you could, you tried to take the high ground in a pimp bar.

They spent the first few hours in the first few places checking out the local talent, recognizing some tough guys—a pimp bar was like their clubhouse—and waiting to see if anything happened to fall their way.

By the time they hit the third place, Hepburn was still in a trance and the other two cops were growing impatient. Vitaliano had turned sullen and McCarthy was looking to start a fight. Boxing was like a tonic for him; he didn't much care whether he won or lost, the workout would relax him.

They were in a bar now where the girls were indiscriminately working the crowd, trying to separate the pimps, who wouldn't think of paying, from the johns, who couldn't reach for their wallets fast enough.

There was a tier of blue-padded booths, like overstuffed furniture, just above the crowded floor level, set off by a handsome wrought-iron railing. This was where the girls were making their money—women with vacant looks and preoccupied expressions—giving customers rough hand-jobs under the tables, behind the long, oversized tablecloths that covered the small, round cocktail tables. It was right out in the open, not ten feet from the couples dancing on the floor, urgent sex in the middle of a crowded bar. Classic whoring.

McCarthy timed them. The captain was oblivious until it was pointed out to him. Five minutes, no more. Five minutes of a girl sort of leaning into her john, their shoulders touching, not really in intimacy, just in closeness, as her hands would then quickly disappear into the guy's lap. A minute or two later her wrist and arm would begin pumping furiously between the john's thighs, working him steadily in that knowing, pistonlike rhythm, while she never left her seat in the booth. A few of them used their free hands to sip drinks.

It was as regimented as close-order drills. Exactly five minutes later, or less, one john after another would suddenly bolt back red-faced, squirm around in a little spasm, and jerk his head and upper body as he climaxed, shooting off into one of the small napkins that the whores had thoughtfully provided. Linen napkins. The same linen that would then be circulated back, maybe laundered, maybe not, to be used as napkins when you sat down to dinner.

There were variations from place to place, but it was the typical industry of the bust-out bar. Occasionally, a girl would actually drop under the table for a blow-job, but that was rare. The whores hated that. It was too much work. After seven or eight guys, you were nearly out of commission; your knees would hurt, your tongue would swell up and you'd have trouble swallowing and your jaw would ache so much you could barely open your mouth. Plus, the johns were constantly bucking back and pulling out too fast and coming on your face or hair or clothes. Then you had to add in extra costs for ruined makeup, dry-cleaning bills, and so forth. Blow-jobs were just too damn

[152]

much overhead. At least that was how one of the women in the Life had explained her reasoning to McCarthy. He never forgot that.

He had heard all these complaints and more from many of the women his team arrested. Essentially, they were business-women, depending more on volume than anything else, and, even with the cops, they enjoyed shoptalk. For them, sex had to be fast, anonymous, relatively safe, and above all, cost-effective. Put all those criteria together, and you couldn't beat a friendly hand-job. You could work all night that way, john after john, and never have to worry about anything more se-rious than a sore hand and stiff shoulder. As long as the bar was supplying the tablecovers and the johns, it was a snap. That might not have seemed especially romantic, but the johns were in no position to complain. Not every whore had it that much to her liking; many of them really had to put out, on their backs, but no human body was ever intended to take that kind of abuse night after night. They usually didn't last very long. A year or two or even three, at the most. Then, either the Life or the drugs killed them. Once their looks and bodies went they had to rely on volume alone and that was invariably the quick beginning of a very rapid end. It was cocaine in the beginning, crack later on, as the trade and the traffic on the streets changed. McCarthy had buried his share.

They had been watching many different versions of this activity all night, wherever they went. Hepburn was getting an edu-cation. But the time was racing by and they would soon be due at Stein's bar on Fourteenth Street.

McCarthy was pointing that out to them when, to his absolute amazement and momentary panic, who happened to walk into the bar they were getting ready to leave but Barry Stein himself. It was as if he had leaped right out of McCarthy's thoughts. He'd been a Vice cop for a long time, but nothing that spooky had ever happened before.

The three of them froze. McCarthy knew Stein from mug

shots, but the two of them had never met. Larry Hepburn was a total outsider. However, as Stein quickly took in the crowd and the people leaning against the bar, his eyes immediately settled on Tony Vitaliano and stayed there.

McCarthy instantly reviewed everything he knew about the pimp. He'd just gotten out of Attica prison, done fifteen years; he had to be in his mid-fifties by now; pretty big guy before he went upstate. He had been in on a swindle involving airline tickets and he was the one who got caught. That part could have been a setup; Stein taking a hard fall for somebody bigger. His bar on Fourteenth Street, a bar that he had suddenly started to call his own only a few short months out of Attica, with no visible income, could very well have been his reward for services rendered, for doing somebody else's time in the joint.

The most interesting thing about Barry Stein was his old girlfriend. She was a madam with better mob connections than practically any other woman in New York, at least any other woman McCarthy was aware of.

The word on the street was that the girlfriend had given him up to the cops so she would be free to screw around with one of the premier wiseguys. Stein had had no alternative but to accept that deal uncomplainingly—if he wanted to stay alive, that is.

But she had done more than spread her legs for another hood. She had robbed him, too. And that was a far more serious offense. Years later, long after Sinbad, McCarthy would discover that Stein had also been hatching a plan to have his old girlfriend framed by the police so that he could get five minutes alone in her apartment, just five uninterrupted minutes, with no chance of her or her new boyfriend coming in on him. That would have been his payback for the way she gave him up. It turned out that she had stuffed every venetian blind in the place with his money, in that fat hollow bases at the bottom of the windowsills. Almost a hundred thousand dollars of his stash was missing and that was where he figured it had to be hidden.

The only thing they knew that night, though, was that Barry Stein had somehow gotten the jump on them.

Then, as if on cue, Stein began to make his way through the crowd, toward the cops. He was one brazen son of a bitch.

Hepburn had no way of picking it up, but McCarthy, pretending to cough into his scotch and water—he'd been downing scotch all night and struggling not to give in to the buzz he was developing—asked Tony, in a hoarse whisper, "You two acquainted?"

All Tony had time to do, before Stein was on top of him, was nod a hasty yes.

McCarthy still couldn't believe the timing on it all. But the only thing he could do was lay back and make small talk with one of the better-looking whores as Barry Stein grabbed Tony the V for a huddle down at the other end of the bar.

Stein was sweating. After the briefest sort of preliminaries, he offered to buy Tony a drink and said, "I think there were two guys in my place last week and I think they were cops. I maybe have a problem." Then he described, accurately and in detail, Harold Schiffer and John Scarpa.

Vitaliano listened, said nothing beyond the obligatory grunts and waited for Stein to make a play. He noticed that the pimp's hands were actually shaking. He was sniffing badly, too, as though he had the worst head cold of his life. Coke, Vitaliano thought, as Stein's small hands involuntarily sought out his nostrils every few seconds.

The cop still let the long silence that had suddenly developed between them do his talking.

"So, look, Tony," the pimp finally said, "it would be worth your while."

That was all. Not another syllable. But that was enough.

Tony said, "Wait, I'll have to talk to my boss." Then, he momentarily left Stein and walked over to McCarthy. "We're in." he said. "This guy wants to reach."

The sergeant smiled. Just a little. They couldn't risk giving it away now. They just looked at each other. They knew.

Reach meant pay, payoff, bribe, cough up whatever it would take to make the problem go away.

McCarthy and Vitaliano acted as though they were conferring

for Stein's benefit. But they had rehearsed all this long before.

Then they left Captain Hepburn at the bar, still looking around wide-eyed as though he were on a tour, and the two cops walked outside with Barry Stein.

They talked some more in the cold and wind of Manhattan. Stein skimmed over the surface of the frozen ground as if he were tap-dancing on a bed of nails. Some part of his anatomy, it appeared, always had to be in motion. McCarthy, who had never seen anyone as nervous as Stein, blew into his hands to keep warm. The remaining effects of the scotch were completely gone now—temperature close to zero had taken care of that. Tony was utterly into his role now and was rapidly taking over the conversation. Suddenly, the three of them fell silent as a bus and a car exchanged blasts of their horns.

Stein repeated it again. "Listen, I think I got a problem."

After more fencing he explained that a few nights before two guys who looked like cops had been at his place, for no apparent reason, scoping out the talent and preparing, he was afraid, to either close him down or shake him down. He never mentioned the presence of the drugs. Finally, referring to Scarpa and Schiffer, Stein said, "I could tell, them guys will be back to cause me problems."

McCarthy, as Tony's boss, appeared to agree reluctantly. "Okay, this could be a pain in the ass for me, but we'll look into it."

Now the two cops had done their part. But not as far as the law was concerned. Even though they had just entered into a conspiracy with a convicted felon for the purpose of obstructing justice in exchange for a bribe, they would need more. A lot more. They would need tapes and a log of contacts and the kind of irrefutable evidence that a smart lawyer would be unable to turn into mush in front of a jury. McCarthy was only too familiar with the routine. They hadn't really, technically, said more than ten words about anything in particular. And they had no idea what kind of information or intelligence they could squeeze out of Stein. All that would have to come later. Much later. But this was a start. A great start.

Wrapping his light jacket tighter across his shoulders, the pimp told McCarthy, "Maybe there's something we can work out where I take care of you..."

The cops listened some more. This was what they were waiting for. Stein was incriminating himself more every time he opened his mouth.

"What did you have in mind?" McCarthy asked.

Stein refused to become any more specific than that. "It can be arranged" was all he would commit himself to.

That would have to be good enough. McCarthy then made an excuse to go back into the bar.

He found Hepburn and told him that they would have to leave immediately. Something had come up. At that point, in that bar, he was afraid to tell him any more.

"No way," Hepburn said. "This is fun here. All these pimps. All these whores. Where we going now? Why do we have to leave?"

McCarthy became more insistent.

"Why?" Hepburn pressed him. "Why can't we do the warrant tonight? I need to know. Why not? Tell me."

"I can't go into all that in a fucking bar," McCarthy said. He was getting hot himself, trying to act cool and nonchalant in front of the pimp.

Just then, Stein and Vitaliano walked back in from the cold. McCarthy saw them. Stein was beginning to look at McCarthy and Hepburn like he was now regretting what he had just done. That was the last thing the Vice cop wanted. The whole situation was crazy. Stein had no idea that McCarthy was there with a warrant in his pocket, a warrant that could close Stein down. But now, of course, they had to forget the bullshit liquor violation and really set him up good for attempted bribery and whatever else they could get. If it went right it could turn into an old con man's sting. And there could be no more deserving a mark than sleazy Barry Stein.

Finally, McCarthy half-screamed at Hepburn. "No talking here, Captain, we *gotta* leave now."

"I didn't finish my drink."

[157]

Hepburn was the most dense man McCarthy had ever seen.

"Captain, I said we *gotta* get out and if I have to I will hit you over the head and carry you out of here. Something very big is going down right now. Something I can fill you in on later. You see that guy with Vitaliano?" He pointed to Stein.

Hepburn nodded.

"He's about five seconds from realizing that we are setting him up for the worst fall of his life. I can see it in his eyes. He's about to change his mind. He's the kind of a guy who changes his mind with a gun. *Capisce?*"

Hepburn frowned like he was a little kid being forced to leave somebody's birthday party. "But I told my wife I'm gonna serve a warrant tonight. They'll all be waiting for the details tomorrow."

McCarthy started to physically lift him up from the barstool. At that point, the captain came along peacefully.

The guy definitely wanted to bribe them. That much had been established, they quickly explained to Larry Hepburn outside. But they would need permission to go on what was known as a "control pad," which was the same thing as setting up a sting. A real pad would have been the real thing—bribery. And the old NYPD had been notorious for the number of cops on pads. The okay for an undercover operation like this would have to come down from Internal Affairs.

Anybody could serve a warrant. But if they could go along with Barry Stein for a while, if they could get the narcotics connection in the club, locate the big supplier, see who *his* connection was, then that, as McCarthy pointed out to Hepburn, "could be a fucking marvelous collar."

Right there on the corner they had what amounted to a team meeting and decided to go ahead with it. Hepburn promised to take care of Internal Affairs.

A few minutes later, McCarthy found Stein in the bar. He'd just come out of the bathroom and his nose looked as though he'd been able to make a score while the cops had been outside.

His nervousness had been replaced by an even more annoying overconfidence.

"We got a deal," McCarthy told him. "I just squared it with my man outside."

Stein looked at the Vice cop as though he had just ordered him up from the menu and now he was having second thoughts. "You just bought the deal," the pimp said. "But remember one thing. I just bought *you*."

McCarthy suddenly felt like one of his whores. He also had to fight hard against an overwhelming urge to take the warrant out of his pocket and shove it down Barry Stein's throat. But that would have been too easy. He had far better plans for this chump.

Ignoring the insult, McCarthy continued. "What are we talking about on my end?"

"I want Fourteenth Street left alone. That's a hundred a week. I may need other places left alone. I may need some places hit. I'll let you know."

"A hundred each, right?" McCarthy haggled. This part was especially humiliating, bargaining with this piece of shit. But as long as he was pretending to be a corrupt cop, he had to act like one.

"Each," Stein finally said. "You guys are *worse* than whores."

They didn't bother to shake on it. That was a good thing, too. McCarthy would have broken his arm.

The night had almost ended. And what a helluva night it had been. From where he stood on that windy corner outside this foul pimp bar McCarthy wanted to believe that he could see all the way to Sinbad's conclusion. But that, of course, would have been fooling himself. Still, he could see enough of the future to know that something unforgettable was about to take place, something bigger and probably more dangerous than anything he had ever faced before.

McCarthy looked down toward the slow buildup of traffic on the East Side. The morning didn't get much of a chance to wake up and blink the sleepiness away in New York.

First there were a few sets of headlights, just two pinpoints moving purposefully along the black, silent streets. Then a whole school of them. It was going to be one of those bitterly cold December days in the city that began with a blue tint leaking through the clouds, just before the dawn sky exploded in deep reds and yellows as the sun broke through. The whole thing was almost too pretty to be part of the Vice world. But it was. Even in Vice.

Just then, Tony Vitaliano and Larry Hepburn came out to see if Stein was gone.

"It's okay," he told Tony. "The sleaze left. We're all in on it for a C-note a week."

The two cops laughed. Their acting had been more than convincing. Captain Hepburn looked just a little nervous. This was new to him; he hadn't been a street cop for a very long time.

"Do you know what we just did?" McCarthy said. "We just made that little creep's whole day. As soon as we went in with him, his status in the Life went way the hell up. Now he has a police contact. He's going to go around and tell people all over Manhattan that he has two Vice cops in his pocket."

Tony was beaming. "It's that great," he said; the incongruity of that statement bounced right off him.

"We're bought and paid for now," McCarthy confirmed, thoroughly pleased with their night's work.

Then, as if to punctuate the amazing events of the last couple hours, Tony the V cleared his throat and hawked up a mouthful of spit which he deposited on the exact spot on the pavement where Barry Stein had stood.

"Hey," McCarthy pretended to rebuke him. "Let's show a little respect for our new partner."

"Respect this," Tony answered, suddenly grabbing at his crotch.

This time, even Flash Gordon broke up.

Operation Sinbad had begun.

EIGHTEEN

Some of the most honorable people I ever met were
Crooks.

M O T H E R ' S   M A X I M

■

Following that initial encounter, McCarthy and Vitaliano began
to meet with Stein on Second Avenue and Fourteenth Street
once a week. Stein would walk up to them on the corner and
hand them an envelope with hundred-dollar bills inside. In the
beginning, few words were exchanged. That cash, as well as all
subsequent money accepted by McCarthy or his men as part of
Sinbad, was then turned in to the Public Morals Unit, Headquarters Division, One Police Plaza.

The money was never late; the count was never short. This
went on for three months, from December 1973 until February
1974. McCarthy had decided—and had convinced his bosses—
that the best way for him to establish his identity as a cop who
could be "reached" was to convince people that his Pimp Team
was in the bag as well. Few corrupt cops could accomplish much
for the people paying them as loners anyway. Having a whole
team or squad on the pad, however, was not only cost-effective,
but was also the traditional way of trickling down payoffs in the
NYPD, from commander to individual cop. In this case, from
Sergeant McCarthy to Vitaliano, and thence to the others.

In the beginning their meetings took place out in the open,
always close to passing traffic. This was clearly a precaution on
Stein's part against electronic eavesdropping. Later, after they
had become more comfortable in each other's presence, they

would meet inside the after-hours club. By then, the two cops had become relaxed in their unaccustomed roles and Barry Stein had evidenced such quick trust in McCarthy that he quietly started dropping hints about other possible money-making opportunities into their casual conversation.

The two cops always tried to be together. There were two good reasons for that. First, for mutual protection. Second, one of them would always be in a position to serve as a witness. Someday, they hoped, all of what they were getting would end up in court. The prosecution would need at least one unimpeachable witness.

Another point to consider was the protocol of the underworld. Having Tony along gave McCarthy added weight as a significant contact. The mob mentality demanded that a valet, a coat-holder to the mighty, be present. That was Tony's mission—to act as a straight man. Eventually that playacting would change, as it so often did in undercover operations, and Tony would become the focus of the game.

There were different roles for different people; within a single case as complex as Sinbad, the cops knew that they could be called upon to assume multiple, simultaneous identities, from good cop to bad cop to hood. The trick was in keeping them all separate and in remembering which role went with which phase of the clandestine game.

At every turn, it seemed, Stein or his friends were planning some illegal deal that could bring the police down on them. As long as he was willing to act as a participant, no matter how passive, McCarthy could expect a cut. That was the deal that was tacitly being offered to him.

People like Barry Stein worked full-time at the science of corrupting. A week never went by that didn't include some mention of hot merchandise that was for sale, or some vice racket that needed police protection. McCarthy didn't even have to act that interested. All he had to do was listen.

In most of their conversations, the availability of narcotics came up. It was the coin of the realm in vice, the hard currency of the street. Stein's reasoning was consistent: Since the cops confiscated so much cocaine during raids and arrests, and since their intelligence on the activities of various pushers was the most thorough in New York, it only made sense to turn to "bad" cops like McCarthy as the most reliable sources of drugs.

Stein approached him about it three times. He needed all the cocaine he could get his hands on. McCarthy kept putting him off, arguing that it was all too risky, but he also let him know that he was weakening. That stretched the string out a little further. McCarthy never said that he *couldn't* get it for him. He just acted reluctant.

Once, when they were sitting in the club about three o'clock one afternoon, with the girls just starting to come in, getting ready for the customers that night, Stein leaned over to McCarthy and said, "How do you feel about a stickup?"

"I don't have any feelings," he told him. "That's too dumb to discuss."

The pimp grinned at him as if to say that McCarthy would understand it all after he had finished explaining it. "It's not dangerous if the people we stick up can't complain," Stein said. "That's the beauty of it."

He wanted McCarthy to begin helping him rob drug dealers. He had it worked out that whenever they were together with a group of people—and if that group included one of the dealers he had in mind—he would identify him for the cop by putting his arm around the pusher's shoulders. McCarthy was to take it from there.

Together, they drove to several heavy narcotics spots in Manhattan and the Bronx. They used Stein's car; the pimp drove and McCarthy acted as the muscle for him. He didn't always make it clear that McCarthy was a cop who happened to be in his pocket, but he did make it clear that the tough Irishman was not to be antagonized. Stein knew just where and with whom to apply his ominous threat of intimidation.

Every place they stopped, there would be one or two people whom Stein would put his arm around. They were the ones who held the heavy weight, the big kilo loads. Most of the names and faces were new to McCarthy. It was valuable intelligence.

At that point he didn't know how much of it was current with the Narcotics Squad, but at least he would be able to point a finger at some people about whom the police had previously only had suspicions.

Stein urged McCarthy to use the Pimp Team like a stickup crew and just follow these dealers, learn their patterns. Then confront them and threaten to lock them up, unless they came across with a payoff. He was also very anxious for McCarthy to steal their narcotics so that Stein could resell them.

McCarthy's split would be half. He could distribute his share to the rest of the squad any way he saw fit. Relative to the going rate on the street, that was a handsome offer. Stein genuinely seemed to like the cop and wanted to get even closer to him. McCarthy had given him the idea that he had a great head for business.

Tempting as that plan was from an intelligence point of view, since it would eventually take the police to many of the top dealers in Manhattan, McCarthy still couldn't agree to it. It wasn't NYPD policy. The people he was reporting to, at the first deputy commissioner level, refused even to consider it.

Technically no one, not even an undercover cop, could stick people up—thereby committing a felony—and then give the proceeds, drugs and cash, to someone else, to Barry Stein.

That was where McCarthy had to draw the line. There were imaginative ways to get around it. For example, McCarthy could have introduced other undercover cops to Stein for him to resell the drugs. But there wasn't enough of a budget for that, nor did the people running the show have that sort of risk-taking vision.

This was taking place in 1973–74 and the police were, literally, making up the undercover manual as they went along.

During the course of all this Stein had only one stipulation: He would only finger dealers for McCarthy to rob, providing that he could guarantee they wouldn't be arrested.

That was his curious kind of morality. It was perfectly ethical, from his point of view, to steal from them, extort them, beat them up; that was part of the cost of doing business in the Life.

But Stein would never be party to getting anybody locked up. McCarthy had to swear to this.

Stein maintained his honor. He wouldn't actually cooperate with the *police*, but he saw nothing wrong in cooperating with a corrupt policeman.

For his part, McCarthy had a separate agenda. He had to keep reminding Stein that he wanted to make friends, line up easy payoffs, turn over some fast money. He couldn't take a chance on robbing people.

For a little while, that held the pimp off. But McCarthy also knew that it would start up again. It was only a matter of time.

McCarthy sensed that people like Stein were motivated by common sense. There were certain things that one bad guy would never do for another bad guy. Like take a stupid risk. Eventually, every cop who ever worked undercover came to understand this. The average bad guy knew when and how to say no. Otherwise, he had no one's respect.

In the end, McCarthy and Vitaliano just had to be convincing actors. Offers of sex were even more troublesome than schemes to make money. It was common practice to *insist* that a cop on the take have sex with one of the girls—just to test his credibility. Barry Stein offered one of the hookers to McCarthy after a few meetings.

Faced with that sort of temptation, with that kind of clearcut opportunity to prove oneself to the target of the investigation, most cops will succumb and thereby jeopardize the whole case and other people's lives, or they might fall apart and actually admit that they are undercover. It's never the bad *guys* who find you out, it's the women.

McCarthy handled it in the only way he could. He screamed at Stein, "Go to hell! You think *I* need *you* to get laid? Take your slut and get out of here. Who do you think you are? Do I need you to pimp for me? You think I'm gonna get laid when you want me to get laid? I'm no performing dog."

Stein backed off. The woman was sent on her way. Actually, the decision was easy for McCarthy. Any kind of sex play was an impossibility. He was wearing a wire throughout this period and the device was concealed around his testicles.

During the course of their meetings that winter, Stein introduced McCarthy to a man named Freddy Kane, who claimed to be a part owner of the club on Fourteenth Street, where the Vice cops were supposed to be providing protection.

Suddenly, there was a second player in the game.

Kane, about six feet two, a very dark-skinned black man with a thin build and a hoarse, three-pack-a-day voice, always showed up in sunglasses. McCarthy knew that he was an East Side pimp with an uncommonly fancy stable of hookers. However, his main source of illegal income was gambling. He used marked cards and could play poker all night long.

Kane seemed promising. One of his partners was William Smith, Philadelphia Smith. Smith, a huge, brutally violent pimp, would become player number three. He treated everyone, especially his women, with a sadistic cruelty that bordered on the psychotic. The turnover in his stable was constant; every week he sent a different hooker to the emergency room.

Smith also lived out the stereotype of the Super Fly, sporting capes and what the Vice cops referred to as "felony hats"— wide-brimmed, garish fedoras in the early 1970s (probably baseball caps worn backward today).

Philadelphia Smith was never without a knife or a gun. Or a Bible. Before sitting down with anyone, including McCarthy, who met him one night in Stein's club, Smith had a habit of laying either the gun, a German Luger, or the knife, a big bowie knife with a blade that was fat enough to slice through a ham, on the table in front of him. Then he'd put the Bible next to the weapons.

At that first meeting, Philadelphia Smith came right to the point. He was in the market for police intelligence. Could he deal?

After a long pause, the Vice cop answered, "Can you pay?"

Smith glared at him, reached into his pocket and pulled out what McCarthy guessed was about five thousand dollars in cash. He fanned it out on the table. Barry Stein was practically drooling.

"What that look like?" Philadelphia Smith growled.

"It looks like we're in business," McCarthy said. "What do you need?"

Smith had recently been out partying in Las Vegas, where his car had been riddled with bullets. He had barely escaped. He was scared. The attack had been unprovoked, as far as he knew, and the person or persons behind it remained a mystery. Smith was afraid that it would happen again, on his home turf, in New York. He didn't believe that they—whoever "they" might be—would miss again.

McCarthy had heard nothing about any of this, nor did he have any guess as to why it had happened. Smith, though, was convinced that the cops *had* to know. The cops knew everything, he said.

McCarthy felt like saying, "I only wish . . ." but he just listened.

The big pimp wanted to see the police intelligence file on the incident. McCarthy, for his part, was pretty positive that no such file existed. At least not in New York. He could check with the Nevada cops. That was a longshot too.

McCarthy took it as a challenge. He hated Smith and was already warming to the chance to scam him.

He questioned the pimp about what had happened, carefully extracting information and details that he didn't even realize he was furnishing to the cop.

A few days later, based entirely on what Smith had inadvertently told him, plus a few guesses supported by inventive and uncheckable fabrications, McCarthy wrote a phony report on official NYPD intelligence forms. Vitaliano typed it up. Flawlessly. The two cops improvised as they went along, embellishing, hinting darkly at the presence of "West Coast mob interests" in Las Vegas and concluding with the admonition: "The intended victim, William Smith, appears to be a marked man." By the time they were finished, they were laughing so hard, they could barely look at each other.

The "report" traced the attack to a fictitious pimp in Las Vegas who, being aware of Philadelphia Smith's formidable reputation, decided to launch a preemptive strike against him before he had a chance to move into that wide-open town. The report named no sources whom Smith could call on his own and served the higher purpose of flattering Smith's enormous ego.

A week later, McCarthy delivered the report to Smith. He allowed Barry Stein to see the file, but made sure he had no opportunity to read it. Stein wasn't that stupid.

McCarthy, Stein, and Philadelphia Smith all sat down around a large round table in a back room of the club. McCarthy waited.

After spending about twenty minutes with the report, his face buried in the text, tiny wire-rimmed reading glasses propped on the bridge of his nose, Smith looked up, slowly removed the glasses and said to McCarthy, "They worried about me, right?" He sounded very satisfied with himself.

"Scared enough to try to kill you."

Smith's mind was already on the next order of business. "Now, I got to know who set me up, man." Then he reached for the bowie knife. And the Bible. "An eye for an eye, brother. I am in need of a name."

McCarthy didn't have a clue. He couldn't take a chance on fingering anybody, either, because Smith might attempt to kill that person. Right here and now he could look very good or very bad.

"You set yourself up," the cop said, as Smith turned suddenly skeptical. "Anything that goes down in New York gets pony-expressed out there. People been calling you *the* man here. Some big ears heard that."

Smith thought that over. "I *do* have a reputation," he said.

"There you go." McCarthy felt his stomach sliding back down from his windpipe.

"You done real good," the pimp finally said.

He opened the Bible and folded the intelligence report inside. Neatly.

"I hope you pay real good," McCarthy said.

"There best be more where this came from." Smith handed an envelope to the cop.

McCarthy counted out five thousand dollars. Then he

checked the envelope and nodded to the pimp.

That improbable incident marked him as a crooked cop who could deliver anything for the right price. It cinched his credibility and his place on Stein's pad.

At no point in his entire police career had Bill McCarthy ever felt more a part of, more a player in, the Life than at that very moment.

"It was fun, so much fun. It was like being the head puppeteer. You were pulling people's strings, watching their hands move, their legs jerk around, and the bastards were so dumb they thought they were doing it all by themselves.

"We kept on moving, kept going, convinced that, sooner or later, the head-bangers like Philadelphia Smith and the sleazeballs like Barry Stein would give us somebody really significant.

"And we were going from guy to guy, from Smith to another bagman for Freddy Kane, and then another and another. We were moving right up the line. And I'm doing absolutely nothing, really. Just taking envelopes of money from people and building my reputation as the biggest whore on the NYPD.

"I can tell you that, personally, my dealings with these pimps were doing nothing to enhance my standing among the cops I worked with who *were* straight and who *didn't* know what was going on. It got to the point where I would walk into a room, all conversation would stop and they would walk out one by one. The only cops who were friendly to me were the ones *I* used to do that to.

"By the end of February, I meet Bobby Brody. *This* was the kind of guy I had been looking for. In the pecking order, he was several steps above Barry Stein; actually, he was what Stein hoped to become someday.

"First, he's a white guy, the first one since Stein. These people are not equal opportunity employers. Color does make a big difference. I have now moved up a notch. I'm not dealing with the street hustlers now.

"We figured Brody owned about six bars in Manhattan. All

[169]

hidden interests. He was known as a major corrupter. He'd been paying off cops for twenty-five years that we knew of, but he had never taken a collar.

"Brody was in his fifties, Jewish, a knock-around kind of guy, very good-looking, charming, tough, but far from being a thug. He carried himself like a gentleman. Respectable-looking, good suits, never any foul language; if he showed up someplace, even the hookers disappeared.

"He worked out of a bar that he owned on Lexington Avenue, in midtown Manhattan, called Tattler's. In the old days, a cop was not allowed in that bar. Only bosses. The bosses would show up in there regularly to pick up their payoffs. Visit with Brody, have a drink or two. All very civilized.

"Tattler's had whores in it. Brody just pretended they weren't there. The man was very old school. And they had to be the cleanest-looking hookers you ever saw. You could have taken your mother to that bar. Hell, half the old cops in there taking payoffs were white-haired Knights of Columbus or Holy Name Society men.

"Tattler's was diagonally across the street from another place, The Vogue. Now, The Vogue was a *serious* organized crime bar. Brody was a regular in there, too.

"I told Brody I wanted to make a move, 'across the street.' On The Vogue, be introduced over there and start making my own connections. He knew what I meant. But he told me, 'Billy, you're big, but you're not big enough to go over there. Slow down.'

"He advised me that, as a sergeant, I didn't have enough weight to go into The Vogue and try and shake them down or work with the characters in there. They dealt at a level way over my head. But Brody didn't want to insult me or turn me off, either. He was as diplomatic about it as he could be.

"Brody's son had died right before I met him and he was deeply depressed over that. I found out that he had sealed his son's room in their house and wouldn't let any of his things be touched. There was this horrible emptiness in his life. It was there all the time, the way he looked right through you.

[170]

"To help fill that void, he sort of adopted me. He would never tell me how his son died; that was too private. I surmised it had to do with drugs, but I never brought it up. That was like an open sore.

"He became my coach in the ways of corruption. That was what he knew best, and he wanted to pass it on. I learned more from him than from anybody. But he would never give me any names. I guess because I really wasn't his son, he had to keep that distance between us.

"That was frustrating, the way he could separate business from emotions. He did confide in me that it was actually him, and not Barry Stein, who owned the after-hours club on Fourteenth Street where it had all started. Stein was just the front man, with no real power.

"He let me know that to prove to me how much he was coming to trust me. He also took over the direct payments to me; it had been his money all along. I came right after the gas and electric bills. None of them ever missed a payment. They were the most conscientious people I ever saw.

"At that point, maybe four months into my new undercover role, I was simultaneously being paid by four different people— to provide protection. I suspected that it was all Brody's money. He was quite an organizer. I was beginning to feel like Mr. Fix-It.

"In terms of my police identity, of course, I was still functioning as the head of the Pimp Squad. The difference was now I was behaving like a corrupted cop.

"All the whores knew me, all the pimps, all the bigger fish like Brody. Everybody knew me. All they ever wanted to know was whether they had a problem. I was their insurance policy. That's how they treated me. I would tip them off about anything coming up and square it for them. That was my job.

"After a few more months with Brody, he tells me that he needs cocaine. I recognized this as the exact same pitch that I had been getting from Stein, back at the beginning. That way I knew that it had been coming from Brody all along.

"In a way, it was crushing. I knew how much he had loved

[171]

his son, how much basic decency there was in him. Yet, here he was, ready to forget all about his son, all about everything if he could only score the right coke connection. That made me realize that it was all just a business decision with these guys—and you could not hold your own in the Life, you could not stay in business, without cocaine.

"As an undercover, regardless of how deeply you've gone in, you have to maintain your perspective. You can't get sucked in by the romance, by the good times or the camaraderie—or even the genuine friendships in the Life. Not when you also realize that your value is strictly measured by your usefulness. In this case, by my access to cocaine. I was, in effect, worth my weight in white powder to a man who had been coming to look upon me as a son. That was shattering. But I used it too. I stepped back from that relationship and let it motivate me to perform my job as a cop.

"Maybe, in a strange way, it saved me. Who knows? I was getting to like Bobby Brody an awful lot. I was getting to the point where I *did* want to protect him. I stopped that in its tracks. I focused on what I had to accomplish.

"Brody came at me three times about getting him cocaine. To him, I was a caught cop. He was paying me. He had a problem. His source had dried up. Now, all of a sudden, *I* had a problem too. And he was paying me to fix it.

"Legally, I wanted tape-recorded conversations of his repeated, independent requests for drugs. I would need the tapes to prove that I hadn't entrapped him or supplied him after only one request. By the third request, I was wearing a wire at every meeting with him. He was making my case for me.

"Actually, there wasn't much coke around at that particular time and what was around wasn't any good. It had been stepped on, or diluted, cut too many times. The customers were complaining. Brody was losing business at his clubs and bars. He couldn't compete in the Life. He was afraid that he might be driven right out of business. It was that serious.

"Now, what I dreamed up was this: There was a pedophile

up in the Bronx who was my informant. I knew he used drugs. I decided to pay him a visit.

"I threatened to arrest him if he didn't one, give up his supplier to me and two, tell me the next time he was getting a delivery. I told him that I could take him in at will on a pedo rap. Not exactly true, but close enough.

"By the time I left, I had what I needed. His connection was a pusher in the Bronx, a guy I had run into back when I was hanging out with Barry Stein. The next delivery was a week away. I convinced the pedo that I was going up to the Bronx to rob this supplier and steal his dope.

"I had my cover story. If Brody ever checked, he would turn up the pedo who would explain to him that I was scoring coke by stealing it from his supplier.

"On March 28th, 1974, I finally 'sold' Bobby Brody four ounces of cocaine. It actually came from the police drug pile, from the evidence locker. My bosses okayed it, because they knew that neither Bobby nor the narcotics would ever leave my sight. Not for a moment.

"The special prosecutor in New York then was Maurice Nadjari. He had come in because of the Knapp commission. What I was doing had to be approved at the highest levels and that was Nadjari's office.

"During my first year undercover, I would wear a hidden microphone and tape recorder approximately 250 times. The case number for that wire was #N-72-73. I will never forget it.

"Nadjari's men had secured two adjoining rooms at the Statler Hilton Hotel, at Thirty-third Street and Seventh Avenue. I was in one room with Vitaliano, waiting for Brody; Nadjari's people were in the adjoining suite.

"We were sitting there, red-eyed, with a half-empty bottle of scotch between us, when Brody walked in. It was all for show.

"The cocaine was in a briefcase—in a neat, square package. Brody whistled when he looked at it; all he said was 'Jesus Christ!' He thought I was hell on wheels.

[173]

"I told Brody that I had knocked over some dealer to get it. He looked at me in a way that he never had before. At that moment I knew in my heart that he had already checked; he'd had somebody either follow me up to the pedo's apartment or chase the guy down. Either way, what I was telling him wasn't news. He couldn't hide it. He really *didn't* trust me.

"Then, Brody made a small slit in one of the plastic packages, dipped his little finger in and licked it.

"Brody's tongue swelled up. He said, 'Holy Shit, my mouth! God, what *is* this?' Then, he drank the whole eight ounces of scotch, there on the table. Drained the bottle.

"He turned to me and said, 'Oh, Billy, we're gonna make a lot of money together. We can step on this five times. I can't wait to take this to my chemist. It's unbelievable.'

"I wondered what it must have been like being his son for real. I got the chills.

"Meanwhile, the whole transaction is being recorded. We have a spiked mike and a video—he's on camera. The operation was clinical it ran so cleanly.

"Brody shook hands with me and left the room.

"The minute he stepped outside, special investigators from Nadjari's office pounced on him in the hallway and grabbed the cocaine.

"To make it look really good, they brought him back into our hotel room and began slapping me and Tony around.

"I resisted arrest. Hard. First, they reddened my face; then knocked the wind out of me. Handcuffed me. It was a real collar. I *forced* them to do it that way by acting like a belligerent ass. It was the only way. I made sure that Brody saw me getting knocked around.

"They dragged me out separately from him and Tony. We drove to Nadjari's office, to the fifty-sixth floor of the World Trade Center.

"Brody was brought in a different car. We were placed in separate rooms. The interrogation took hours—under a naked light bulb, just like in the movies.

"After we thought that we had held out long enough to make

[174]

it look good, Tony and I agreed to cut a deal. We'd flip; work off our case by giving them Brody.

"The beauty of it was that the Nadjari people who were with us then, questioning us, really *didn't* know it was an act. That's how tight our security was.

"We did it as another means of establishing our identities— mine and Tony's—as corrupt cops. We even had some of Nadjari's people fooled. Our cover was still tight.

"Brody bought it all. How could he not have?

"After we were released, I remember being on Eighth Avenue and Thirty-third Street. It's about two o'clock in the morning, and I was crying and telling Brody I was gonna commit suicide because my career was over and I had gotten him arrested.

"'Billy, you don't have to do that,' he said, trying to calm me down. 'Don't do that. We can make this right. I got other people I can reach out to. You'll see.'

"He really meant it. When I mentioned suicide, that scared him. *That* told me what must have happened to his boy. No wonder he refused to talk about it.

"Finally, I agreed not to kill myself.

"What you have to understand is that this was a triumph. Maybe bittersweet in a way, but still a victory. Here was Brody, a guy who has been in the Life for twenty-five years, a certified badass, and he had never even been arrested. Now, we had him on a felony. And he didn't even realize that I had done it to him—he was too concerned about losing another son. What a goddamn troubling night that was.

"It was Bang Double Bang. We were pulling off the perfect sting. And I felt like a louse. But, in an awful way, it felt good.

"When I drove back home to Sloatsburg that night, back to Millie and my real world, it suddenly hit me. Here I was living out the adventure of my life. Playing cops and robbers big time.

"Where had it all come from? How had I ever gotten to this amazing event in my life?"

NINETEEN

A Mob Guy could be anything from a fat, roly-poly
Italian papa who eats too much spaghetti to a smooth
businessperson, very con-Ti-nental, the tanned,
Mediterranean type. But all of them spend their entire
lives belching, eating, and taking Maalox.

MOTHER'S MAXIM

McCarthy was standing in a wig shop on Park Avenue South,
fingering a long, curly blond scalp. He held it up, allowed the
rays of sunlight that streamed in through a window behind him
to frame the fake tresses and then, very carefully, he tried
it on.

Tony Vitaliano, impatient, was waiting with him. "Beautiful,
Bill," he said. "You look great in drag. I could take a shot at
you myself. You do it on the first date?"

McCarthy ignored him, then checked out his reflection in the
mirror. Full-face, profile, left, right. He smiled as he brushed
a stray curl away from his temple.

"You're too weird, Bill," the short, dark cop said. "Too fucking weird."

McCarthy removed the hairpiece and put it back on its display
rack. He was already eyeing something red and frizzy.

Just then, the man who had been keeping them waiting
opened his office door and appeared. He didn't greet them but
motioned for both men to follow him. As they watched, a man
named Albert Gold seated himself behind an ornate, antique

desk that seemed long enough to be part of the interstate highway system. His eyes were narrow-set, horizontal, and flat. One eyebrow, the left, arched as though Gold's face had little control over it.

The desk faced Park Avenue. Clearly, this massive boulder of furniture was his buffer as well as his talisman. After taking up his defensive position behind it, Albert Gold finally suggested that his visitors be seated.

It looked as though it would be a long meeting.

Bill McCarthy tried hard to look relaxed.

Gold was thick around the middle, soft in a way not normally associated with the people the two Vice cops usually dealt with. He seemed very anxious to impress upon both of them just how busy a man he was. Gold could say "Hello," and act as though he were granting an audience.

As far as McCarthy was concerned, however, he was just another pimp, albeit an influential one. They sized him up to be a total jerk—but a jerk with some very intriguing connections.

Like most of the men who ran the after-hours clubs and supplied the pimps with cocaine, Gold was an ex-con. His legitimate business was one of the largest wholesale importers of wigs in the United States. He claimed that his products consisted of "90 percent human hair"; the origin of the other 10 percent was left up in the air.

Gold also possessed an IQ over 170 as measured by the New York State Department of Corrections as part of his pre-sentencing catalog. He was a bright, competitive, compulsive gambler. As a whoremaster—one of his lucrative moonlighting sidelines—Gold's reputation was as fastidious as Bobby Brody's. He had never been known to lay a hand on any of the girls. That, apparently, couldn't give him a rush to equal the erotic surge he felt every time he caressed a pair of dice. That's when he would start sweating, loosen his collar, experience an instant elevation in blood pressure, and summon over the nearest casino waitress for a transfusion of a double scotch. In a very matter-of-fact manner, Albert Gold was a total gambling degenerate. His wig business and his whorehouses, in particular, financed his gambling. There was room for very little else in his life.

As a long-time student of his adversaries in Vice, McCarthy had spent considerable time schooling himself in the finer points of Albert Gold. Among pimps, even part-timers several steps removed from the street, Gold was regarded as "serious people." That meant his women serviced clients with unmistakable Mafia ties, among others. Fringe lawyers and businessmen were also plentiful; in fact, just about any OC associate with social-climbing tendencies within the organization tried to get his ticket punched at one of Gold's brothels. They were known as a place where important contacts could be made. As a result, ambitious, dangerous men showed up at his places as regularly as green flies in August.

Gold's was definitely the sort of company that McCarthy wanted to be keeping. Almost alone among the pimps, he could take the investigation to places where no amount of honest police work had ever made a dent before.

One of the brothels supposedly under McCarthy's "protection" at that time was located at at 211 East Fifty-First Street. A pimp with visions of grandeur—Marty Roth—had two connected flats, 2E and 2F, in a luxury apartment building in midtown Manhattan. After renovations, the owners had been able to squeeze seven small bedrooms in there. There was also a living room for meeting, chatting with, and selecting the women, two bathrooms and a tiny kitchen. Five out of the seven bedrooms were usually occupied around the clock. The customers weren't quite up to Sydney Biddle Barrows's standards, but they weren't Times Square, either. It was a kind of middle-management place, catering to rich salesmen, up-and-coming hoods, and prosperous-looking executives from just about every professional field. The women who worked there were just a notch or two below "prime," as Barry Stein would say.

Stein had brokered McCarthy's entering into this arrangement. This confirmed the cop's suspicions that the pimp had been going around, first bragging about, and then selling or "renting" his police contacts—primarily McCarthy.

The Knapp Commission had dried up many of the pads. Crooked cops were almost in a seller's market. Stein was just cashing in—acting just like an agent, getting his 10 or 15 percent, or whatever, based on McCarthy's availability.

"Roth was a young guy, twenty eight years old maybe, not even thirty yet. An entrepreneur. Smartass. A little kid who thought he was too slick to be a wiseguy type. He was gonna make money at anything he tried, you could see that. Deep down, however, he was electrified by the whores. And by the coke. Already he'd become lost in the Life.

"Marty Roth had a secret weapon. He just happened to be Albert Gold's favorite nephew.

"Exactly one week after Stein introduced me to Roth, and after I agreed to see what I could do about keeping Vice away from the house on Fifty-first Street, Roth called me over to the brothel one night and said, How would you like to meet my Uncle Al?

"I practically came in my pants."

"'How do I know you're not wearing a tape recorder? How do I know you're not wired?'

"That was the first thing that Al Gold said to us in his wig shop. Not even how-do-you-do.

"I started to take my shirt off. I decided to get rough with him. I was on my feet, pacing in front of his big desk.

"'What am I here for? Hey, your fucking nephew asked me to come by. I don't invite myself places. I didn't ask to come here. This is bullshit.'

"And I keep taking off my clothes. Tony the V looks at me like I've lost my mind. I just keep stripping—down to my underwear.

[179]

"All of a sudden, Gold begins to act very apologetic. He wants to get down to business now, having thoroughly insulted me. But I'm not exactly dressed for it.

"'You want me to keep going?' I ask him, and I actually begin to step out of my drawers. 'You feel like coming over here and checking my balls for that wire you're so worried about?'

"I really think I embarrassed him. He put his hands up, like he was backing off. I'm still not satisfied, though. So I say to him, 'If you waste my time here today, then you are going to have a bigger problem than you and your nephew think you have.'

"'I'm ready to deal,'" he said almost sheepishly.

"That's when I sat down and started pulling on my pants.

"It turns out this is another setup like Stein and Brody. The kid, Marty Roth, doesn't own a brick, not the house on Fifty-first Street, not any house of prostitution in New York. All the money, all the juice comes from Gold.

"Through the course of the conversation, we make arrangements to protect his prostitution activities at Fifty-first Street. I set up a payment schedule—fifteen percent of the gross for the first two weeks and twenty percent thereafter.

"That was a big bite; we were really coming on like strongarm cops. We had just muscled in and had, in effect, become part owners of a top-of-the-line Manhattan whorehouse. This now would give us access to the girls, too. All I could think about was all the intelligence we would pick up.

"When you buy into a whorehouse, even through a payoff like ours, you are buying human bodies. That is an accepted business practice in the Life. It is the true meaning of white slavery. Any hour of the day or night, if you want to get laid, a whore is there—a dozen whores are there at your disposal. You have the power over them to come in and sample them like a buffet. That's what we had just been offered. If there is any form of human bondage more perverse than that, I haven't run across it.

"By the time we had finished haggling and he had finally agreed to our terms, we were all pretty tired, wrung out.

"But Gold had one more bomb to drop.

" 'There's another house,' he said. 'And I got a problem there. If this other house isn't part of the protection you can provide, then the deal is off. Take it or leave it.'

"I looked over at Tony and he looked back at me. We had no idea about a *second* brothel. We thought we had already worked our way right to the top. He's already giving up the best whorehouse in Manhattan. What more could there be?

" 'You better tell us about it,' I said, not knowing what to expect.

"The problem brothel was hidden in a townhouse on Thirty-first Street. In Murray Hill. That's a very old, once-elegant New York neighborhood. The location seemed, at first, to be a little out of Gold's league.

"Gold, Roth, and a couple other guys were in on the townhouse. The place made a fortune. But they *did* have a problem. That was no exaggeration.

"Their townhouse had been visited by three unknown males who represented Gennaro (Big Jerry) Moretti. Moretti is mob—real mob. He wanted to buy Gold's share of the townhouse. That meant Moretti's crew wanted in. Moretti was with Paul Vario at that time and Vario, of course, was only about one step removed from the Genovese Family. In other words, the Genoveses are moving in.

"Al Gold also had outstanding gambling debts which he owed to Julie Nardi, a 'made guy,' who was big in pornography. Nardi is with the Gambinos, but he's with Moretti, too, at least on the gambling end. So that's double trouble. Nardi can call on the Genoveses or the Gambinos.

"Nardi saw the Murray Hill townhouse as a natural extension of his porno business. Hell, he was ready to move secret cameras right in and maybe begin blackmailing a few of the customers.

"So, as a way of repaying his giant gambling debts, and keeping his legs from being broken, Julie Nardi also tells Gold that he will just take a piece—a big piece—of the townhouse.

"Moretti doesn't know what Nardi is up to. This middles Al Gold, who will be blamed by both of them for selling out to the other guy. Gold really has no place to go on this.

"But wait, there was even *more*.

"Guido Maranzo, another player, had also loaned money to Gold for his gambling. Maranzo wanted to become his 'business associate' too.

"Now there's *three* of them in on it. Each one is a good fellow, a made guy.

"Maranzo, rather than just robbing Gold, moving in on him and maybe scaring away the johns in the process, offered to introduce gambling activities at the townhouse. That way, at least Gold would be able to keep his dignity and pretend that he still ran the place. The townhouse was Gold's best asset and Maranzo did not want to devalue it in any way.

"Maranzo and Jerry Moretti happened to be from warring factions in the same mob—factions who now found themselves fighting for control of the same brothel.

"I said to Gold, 'No wonder you need protection.'

"All he wanted to know was, 'Can you handle it?'

"Can I handle a combination of *three* made guys representing the two largest Mafia families in the world, the Gambinos and the Genoveses, and all fighting over the same whorehouse? Could I do that?

"'No problem,' I said to Al Gold.

"He looked relieved. I certainly wasn't.

"'I knew you could do it,' he told me. 'Bobby Brody said you could pull off anything.'

"Before we left, I could not resist yanking this guy's chain one more time.

"Tony was wearing pimp shoes, with a big, thick heel. Just when Gold believed that I would keep my clothes on, that I was all calmed down over my being insulted about him accusing us of being wired, I reached down and pulled off Tony's shoe.

"Then I threw it up on this handsome desk and said, 'You asshole. The wire was in the shoe all along.'

"I can see that Gold doesn't know how to take this. He desperately wants to believe that I'm joking with him. But he doesn't know me and Tony. He can't be sure. What if we *are* honest undercover cops instead of corrupt fixers?

"He grabbed the shoe and started twisting the heel, but he could not take it apart. He looked up and gave us this nervous, sick laugh. Right? It has to be a joke? Right? He's really sweating.

"I took the shoe back and handed it to Tony. 'Gotcha, Al,' I said. Then we left.

"Actually, I *had* been recording every word of that hour-long conversation. I had the wire where I always kept it—wrapped around my testicles. I had bluffed him when I stripped down to my underwear. Gold never knew. He never would."

As far as McCarthy knew Bobby Brody had never said a word to anybody about getting caught with the cocaine. That was supposed to be their little secret. Hustlers like Brody were forever getting in trouble and running scams behind each other's backs. The way the cop had left it with him, it seemed as though McCarthy was in bigger trouble, anyway. That had been the whole point of the crazy talk about suicide.

To resolve the issue of the cocaine possession, to fix it, to blow out the arrest, McCarthy suggested that they concentrate on getting to a deputy inspector whom he already suspected of being on the take.

Brody liked that; it was the way he always approached problems.

"We were supposed to work on this inspector. Brody wanted me back on the good side of the NYPD. He didn't need a guy who was *too* notorious. What good would he be?

"It so happened that around this time there *was* an inspector who was suspected of protecting another after-hours club at Avenue A and Seventh Street. Other places, too; all black pimp bars. Corrupter bars, as we called them. I passed that information on to my bosses; I assumed they would give it to Nadjari's office.

"But, in the middle of my case, this deputy inspector apparently gets tipped off and has himself suddenly transferred to another borough, out of harm's way. The special prosecutor is left holding the bag. So am I. Our case against him isn't ready yet. Now, it never will be.

"That wasn't part of *my* setup with Brody.

"So now, I know that the cops are playing their own games. We have a leak. Maybe it's in Nadjari's office, maybe it's in the first deputy commissioner's office. I never would find out.

"It really scared me. A lot. This could get me or one of my guys killed. I'm just beginning to appreciate how high up the corruption goes, what total disregard there is for the safety of undercovers.

"We just left it hanging with Brody. There was no resolution in sight."

TWENTY

The *Mafia* is organized crime, but it's not as well organized as people would like you to believe.

MOTHER'S MAXIM

From the outside, the townhouse on East Thirty-first Street, Murray Hill, looked like any one of a hundred similarly sedate, dignified buildings in the immediate neighborhood. The pavement in front of the slightly sagging steps that rose to an impressive door and vestibule was wide and well walked.

Comparable houses were already commanding premium prices in New York. Give the area another decade of creeping gentrification and the value of the property would eventually soar into the million-dollar category.

No one in the local real estate community had even noticed when Al Gold, the big wig importer, and a couple of his friends purchased the townhouse. It was a sound investment and, under the correct circumstances, could even double as a tax shelter.

Everyone, it appeared, was trying to own a piece of midtown Manhattan. Why should the Gold group be any different? They would never lose any money on the place and could always turn around and rent out part of it as office space to a medical group or small law firm or any other kind of business that would benefit from being where the action was in the mid-1970s.

Transforming the townhouse into a splendid, multifloored brothel, complete with a library, drawing room, fireplaces, spacious bedrooms for trysting and authentic Victorian appointments, had been relatively simple. Rehabbing old buildings was all the rage in Murray Hill anyway, so performing extensive renovations to a valuable investment property was not going to attract unwanted attention.

The main risk was in the presence, twenty four hours a day, seven days a week, of rotating shifts of well-dressed, stylishly groomed, drop-dead-gorgeous women.

It got so that you could not pass the townhouse, either on foot or in a car, and *not* see a head-turner. Men out walking their dogs in the neighborhood used to linger there, coaxing their pet to get friendly with one of the trees in front of the townhouse. Delivery men caught on just as quickly. They used to double-park their vans or trucks out front, stall their engines, pretend to be searching for addresses—all because they knew that every few minutes (the wait was never longer than that) one of the sexiest women they were likely to see all day, all week, would either come sauntering out of or into the townhouse.

It became common knowledge in the neighborhood that the townhouse was, indeed, some sort of magnificent brothel. Vivid as the images were that fed people's fantasies about the place, the reality of what was going on inside still exceeded those expectations. The women who worked in the brothel were in the business of giving pleasure, no matter how erotic or fantastic a form it might take. Hookers dressed in French maids' uniforms were on call in one suite, bouncing in apron, garters, and very little else; more sophisticated companions in tennis whites, perhaps, complete with tiny, revealing skirts or snug stewardess uniforms, were available on another level of the townhouse. If one of the customers preferred a girl-next-door type, she was available; rubber fetishes were satisfied; so, too, the desire to be dominated, handcuffed to the bedposts, whatever. It was all for sale. Given the constraints of reason, cost, and safety, every variety of female plaything from imitation high school cheerleader to milkmaid, blond and big-breasted and carrying a pail, was on call.

Al Gold was a merchant who understood the peculiar needs

of the high-end market. He provided the services and the customers paid. The girls started at $150 a session. Fees of $1, 000 a night were not unheard of.

No one approached the door uninvited. Ever. People regarded the establishment as they would a private club. If you belonged there, you knew it and *they* knew it and lengthy introductions were hardly necessary.

There was always a very palpable sense that the townhouse was off-limits to all but a select few. Maybe it was shyness; maybe fear. A natural inclination to avoid confrontation kept normal people away.

There was no doorman, no bouncer; no outward threat. But there didn't have to be. The townhouse, tempting as it was, mysterious, alluring, also bespoke danger. The very first time that he saw the townhouse, Bill McCarthy got the same feeling. This was a menacing, perilous place.

"That May, 1974, Guido Maranzo moved in with gambling and card games, baccarat, poker, dice. And, of course, Maranzo had partners. It was like the mob had come in to pick apart a carcass. For a month everything ran smoothly. I passed the word upstairs and Vice never even looked at the place. Al Gold took that to mean that he was being protected by me. He had no idea that there was nothing to protect him from.

"Then they had a bad falling-out over who was in control of the game. They were really making money at that point.

"In June they shut down all gambling. There were simply too many arguments. That was Maranzo's solution—close it up. Wait for things to calm down.

"Gold became worried then. These were real mob guys. They shot people. He was in over his head and he had no idea what to do about it. A couple weeks later, Maranzo started the gambling up again. Gold conceded that Maranzo was the boss. No argument.

"We decided to go for an application for an eavesdropping warrant at the townhouse. That request brought in the New

York Rackets Bureau and the district attorney's office.

"By now, the investigation had really grown. We had officially named it 'Sinbad,' for 'sin' because of the whoring, and 'bad' because every person involved with this was bad news. Even the feds were trying to horn in—you had us, the special prosecutor, the DA, and the rest of the police department. We weren't aware of it at the time, but the CIA, Immigration, the DEA, and all kinds of people in the U.S. Justice Department were beginning to check in too.

"Everybody on our side wanted a piece of it, not just Nadjari. In the process, a good bit of my cover was blown. It became almost impossible, within the New York law enforcement community, to keep my activities secret any longer. As far as we knew, the bad guys were still buying it, but, in what seemed like overnight, every cop in the city became clued in that Mother was actually on the side of the angels after all.

"That would forever alter any future undercover role that I might be able to play, but at that point the only task I could concentrate on was the one in front of me.

"Every time Al Gold had a conversation with me, I taped him. I was in almost daily contact, at least by telephone.

"The next thing Gold told me was that a loan shark, Pete (Buttons) Bicardi, had come on strong. He was supplying the regulars with money for the big baccarat games.

"I realized I would have to go for a bug on the loan shark, too. Bicardi, the shylock, was being protected or 'spoken for' by Guido Maranzo.

"Bicardi was an imposing, kinky-haired, 250-pound leg-breaker from Brooklyn. He had successfully secured the loan-shark franchise at the townhouse from his bitter rival, Big Jerry Moretti. Moretti's clout was derived from his association with one of the biggest mob bosses in New York at that time, Aniello Dellacroce. Moretti had also originally sent those three strong-arm guys to see Al Gold about buying a piece of the brothel.

"Besides Bicardi, there was another hood at the townhouse—he was actually Bicardi's driver—who, we already knew, had been smuggling illegal aliens in through Canada. The illegals were all from Sicily. They were mobsters-in-training, hit men.

"Bicardi and his driver apparently remembered the old Murder, Incorporated gang and its activities and figured they could make big money with this rent-a-hit-man scheme. The American Mafiosi loved the idea because it gave them another layer of insulation against ever getting caught. Also, the Sicilians were much more dependable than Americans—they didn't do drugs, didn't try to hold the New York Families up for too much money, and you never, ever had to worry about them cooperating with the cops.

"We checked employment records as soon as we got names of the illegals and every single one of them worked in pizza parlors along the East Coast. They were being stashed in the pizza joints as a cover until they were needed. Bicardi was their man—one of their sponsors. He was also willing to lend them money and they loved to gamble.

"And here we were getting limited access to them their first or second month on American soil. In *our* whorehouse, the one we're supposed to be protecting."

Bicardi turned the first floor into a clandestine casino. There were felt-covered card tables; roulette wheels and several enclosures for craps. The baccarat tables were always the most crowded. Next, to protect their growing investment, the Brooklyn hoods set about fortifying the townhouse. A cache of guns was moved in and put at the disposal of their Sicilian allies. Additionally, workmen came in and barred every window from the inside. Bicardi conducted his loan shark business from the secluded third-floor bedroom that had been turned into a library—the room where the wiretap would have to be planted.

The Vice cops were also able to establish that much of Bicardi's money was laundered through an apparently legal water-ice business in Brooklyn. Optimistic plans called for the

[189]

Murray Hill hangout to eventually turn over between twenty-five and fifty thousand dollars a week through prostitution, gambling, and loan-sharking activities.

Al Gold was content to share the profits with his new partners, but Gold himself was sometimes terrified by the rough trade that began moving in. He was running into difficulties keeping girls, too. Some of the new customers were slapping the women around.

Through August of 1974, McCarthy and Vitaliano, working with the special prosecutor's office, were able to develop the most valuable information to date on the new Sicilian Mafia, as well as on the routine mob business that took place at the townhouse.

"At first, Tony and I did not realize what we had here. In hindsight, fifteen years later, we now know that it was the very beginning of the infiltration of the Sicilian Mafia into America.

"Give them a few years and these punks would become a very distinct *second* Mafia, and would come to operate the biggest international drug connection in the world, a hundred times bigger than the French Connection, but back then, who could have guessed that?

"Some of those first Sicilians that we identified in the Murray Hill townhouse turned out to belong to the mob that went on trial for the international Pizza Connection case in New York in 1986–1987.

"We had hit the mother lode. And we didn't even know it. But that's always the way it works in undercover investigations. You're dropping lines in the water, never suspecting what you might pull in.

"The Sicilians would come into the brothel on Thirty-first Street and take over the whole place. They'd come in with their own cigarette vendors, their own cooks, their own food; they came lock, stock, and barrel. Set up a miniature nightclub within the townhouse.

"I used to say to myself—just let these pigs keep eating, because they'll kill themselves. They'll blow up. All they did was eat, eat, eat. The sex had to wait. Getting laid was way back in second place. They even ate before they gambled. You wanted a good way to get killed, all you had to do was interfere with these guys during their meals. We picked up every disgusting sound on the eavesdropping wires. Every belch, every fart. Then, before they went home, they would eat again.

"The girls all had to be out of the place by midnight because that was when the serious gambling began and they didn't want any distractions. Broads were bad luck.

"There was one guy who spoke decent English. His name was Oscar. One night he lost two hundred thousand dollars. I'm listening to this on the other end, dying. This game is bigger than Atlantic City. Oscar doesn't even lose his cool, he's down two hundred G's and he just tells them, very casually, 'I'll have a guy come by in the morning.' That meant that his messenger would have the money. They knew he was good for it.

"The problem I had was that everybody in the place spoke Sicilian. They were all young people, not old people, mostly in their thirties.

"Young American-born hoods don't speak Sicilian. They may know a few words, but they aren't fluent. Of the Five Families in New York, some are more traditionally connected to Italy than others, and those that are connected are dominated by the people who can actually speak Italian. But that's unusual for anybody under the age of sixty or seventy. At least it was until we stumbled on this gang.

"The Sicilians, the real Mafiosi, are very different from American mobsters. They're more traditional, tied to the old country. Worse when it comes to violence and lack of respect for the police, better in areas like gangster skills and loyalty to the clan. And they bring with them this very worldly view that absolutely *anything goes* in the pursuit of cash—that could be murder, drugs, killing innocent bystanders, cutting deals with terrorists or hostile foreign governments. Bad stuff. The thing about them that really hits you is how profoundly un-American they are. As horrible as our OC guys might be, at least we are all working from the same frame of reference. We might be on opposite sides of the street, but we share the same history, the same social values. Not these Sicilians. They come in here, bound by blood, with absolutely no morality beyond greed.

"The American Mafia were like a Boy's Club compared to the Sicilians. Even in the simplest matters. If they were to do their normal rituals, for example, all the tacky *Godfather* stuff, most of which they actually got from the movie, anyway—life does imitate art in the criminal set—they'd have to use index cards, or a TelePrompTer, because somebody would need to tell them what they should do or say next. The Sicilians were spontaneously evil; our hoods had to learn it. That was the difference.

"It became very clear that just bugging my conversations with Al Gold was no longer enough. I would have to intercept the Sicilians, too. That was the next order of business."

TWENTY-ONE

One Police Plaza, the Puzzle Palace, is like whatever's behind the curtain in *The Wizard of Oz*. It's where you have to be if you're a cop.

MOTHER'S MAXIM

"I was practically ready to pack up one night and go home when the telephone rang. It was Al Gold and he wanted to sell me machine guns. I thought we were set on the whorehouse scam and he hits me with this. Machine guns. *That* even I could not resist.

"I learned that Al and his creepy nephew Marty Roth were sitting in Al's wig shop, talking about me, as a matter of fact, about all the business they could count on now that Vice was protecting them, when a fairly potent mob guy we both knew, a burglar, but a made guy, walked in off Park Avenue and dropped a gun on Al's desk. The gun had a silencer screwed on the barrel. He said to Al, 'Find me a buyer.'

"Immediately, he thought of Mother.

"He told the burglar to come back the next day. He kept the gun himself. Figured it might come in handy, with the silencer, especially.

"The burglar walks in the next day carrying this big box, like he just bought something at Sears. Gold paid him for the first gun and asked him if he had anything else to sell.

"'Yeah,' the burglar answers, 'but it's serious stuff. I gotta go heavy on this. Gotta try and make it a one-time thing.'

"Now, Gold figured he must really be into a deal. He looks

at the box. 'So, show me,' Al says, and points to the box.

"The burglar kneels down, takes all this tape and rope off the carton and takes out this gorgeous hunk of U.S. Army ordnance. A combat machine gun. Not a MAC-10 or an Uzi, nothing small like that. *This* is a fucking machine gun. It looks like World War Two in the wig shop. The burglar has been walking around all day in Manhattan with the machine gun, deciding which fence to offer it to.

"Gold explains all this and says to me, 'My man here has connections upstate. He's selling crystal meth to some kids who are in the National Guard. The kids, however, are punks and can't pay. The burglar comes up with a compromise. He'll take it out in trade—back up a truck to the armory when they're walking guard duty there and take away as much stuff as he can load. The machine gun is just a sample.

"Al has the thought that since I'm a cop I must know all sorts of right-wing nuts and gun collectors. I can fence for Al as a subcontractor. That's the deal. A fifty-fifty split. Whatever we can't move, he'll just unload on the Westies—the crazy Irish hit men from the West Side. Those bastards, he says, will buy anything that shoots because whatever *they* don't need, they just send over to their relatives in the Irish Republican Army in Belfast, Northern Ireland. He has this all figured out. From his wig shop to the IRA. Gold, whatever you want to say about him, thought big.

"I told him I would see what I could do.

"Of course, I have to clear all this at One Police Plaza. But how tough a sell can it be? We're about to buy one or more machine guns from a Mafia made man.

"Wrong, again.

"I go in and tell the inspector that Al Gold called me about the machine gun. I want permission to send over one of my men to make the buy.

"'Permission denied.' The jerk says to tell Gold to call it off. 'Give the gun back.' He doesn't want to get involved in anything this big. 'It could blow up in our faces,' he says, clearing his throat.

"Like nothing has ever blown up in *my* face before. I've damn near made a career of it. This guy isn't a cop, he's a professional ass-coverer.

"'BUY THE DAMN GUN,' I shouted back at him.

"This is an inspector in the NYPD and he's too scared to make a decision. I yelled some more. 'You can't tell Gold to give the gun back. How can you give it back to a made guy? We can't let it stay on the street!'

"I just stormed out of his office, slammed the door, figured I had just as much juice as he did—*they* had come to *me* about all this undercover stuff—and just went ahead with it.

"If I had sent over a German shepherd from the police kennel to buy the machine gun, the mob guy would have sold it to the German shepherd, just as long as the dog was introduced by Al. That's how tight I was with these people at that point.

"Instead of the dog I sent over the same young detective, Doug West, whom I had used to trap William McKinney and the ATF agent at the Holiday Inn. This was the cop who had been set up as Larry Waters's mark, his pedo john.

"I set up the buy on a yacht moored at the Twentieth Street pier; Customs had seized it and we were using it like a clubhouse for undercover operations. I hid in a trailer at the foot of the pier and prepared to record the transaction. I was just expecting a one-time deal. By then, Al Gold had stepped out of it. That was understandable. He he had been asked to broker the deal—which he had done. Now, whatever degree of risk existed would be on my end and the burglar's end.

"At that first meeting, Doug West, representing me, purchased three machine guns—two thousand dollars a piece. The burglar and his man brought them to us, wrapped in Christmas paper like presents. Our money had to be stuffed inside Christmas cards.

"Before they shook hands on it, Doug West asked the burglar if he had anything he hadn't shown to Gold.

"The burglar hemmed and hawed and explained that there might be something else, but no more guns. The kids in the National Guard were too scared.

[195]

"'I might be in the market,' Doug told him. 'It all depends on the quality of what you got to offer.'

"The burglar got this weird look on his face and said, 'Oh, I got quality. Don't worry about that.'

"At our next meeting Doug had to go through the Christmas paper routine again. This time, the package he's opening is smaller and much lighter. It *can't* be any kind of weapon.

"It was a violin. One of the six known Stradivarius violins in existence, the burglar swore. This mob guy wasn't just a burglar, he was a *master* burglar. His crew had stolen it from an art gallery somewhere.

"This was another curve they'd thrown at us. We had to get the violin authenticated, but could we risk bringing in an art expert and introducing him into our small undercover circle? *That* had to be a Puzzle Palace decision. Strangely enough, they okayed it without a whimper.

"In the meantime, Doug had set a price—two hundred thousand dollars.

"We had no intention of paying all that out. At the next meeting, we would grab the burglar and the violin, if it turned out to be real.

"Al Gold, of course, had no idea that Doug was a cop. So I was on pretty safe ground. I couldn't necessarily help it if Doug turned out to be undercover, could I? According to the story I had been spinning, that would have put me in as much jeopardy as Gold. That was the same kind of a gamble that I had taken—and won—back with Bobby Brody. I decided it was worth the risk. Besides, I can't emphasize enough that once you are known to be on the street, in the Life, you are expected to be in some kind of trouble just about all the time. That would most certainly apply to a cop like me—who was supposed to be on the take.

"All we had to do was wait for the art expert to come in and verify that the violin really was a Stradivarius. The Puzzle Palace had supposedly checked him out. He worked as a professional art courier, picking up, transporting, and providing security for priceless paintings or statues or jewels, or whatever. One day he'd make a stop in New York, the next night he would surface in London. We assumed that he knew his violins.

"During one of Doug's sit-downs with the burglar, in a very seedy restaurant near the pier, they begin making plans for this art expert to come in on the deal—Doug alibied that he was the big money man and wanted to inspect the Stradivarius personally.

"After a few minutes I hear them talking about Doug's watch. I was in an adjoining booth, drinking a beer and sipping pea soup. Those two were going on and on. And the burglar is saying, 'Thirty-five, thirty-five, thirty-five.'

"It was about four o'clock in the morning, and I could barely stay awake. But they're having this animated discussion.

"Later, I asked Doug, 'What was all that bullshit about your watch? What did he mean, "thirty-five"?'

"Doug, a very handsome, low-key, dedicated cop, gave me one of those looks that told me he was uncomfortable talking about this. I didn't care, though. These were burglars who wouldn't have thought twice about killing a guard or a watchman. They were as brutal as they came. And I figured I had a right to know what the hell my guy was discussing with them. I really liked Doug, but hadn't spent time in a foxhole with him. If I even *suspected* him of double-dealing me, however innocently, his ass was gone, possibly all the way to Attica. When you're running an operation like this, you cannot afford not to get to know people on the job.

"'My watch costs thirty-five hundred dollars,' he said reluctantly. 'It's a Rolex, a *real* Rolex. The guy knew and he was complimenting me on it. I think he's going to ask me to score him one.'

"I let it rest for the moment. I just wanted to wait until I was positive nobody would overhear us.

"That night, right in the middle of all this other stuff that was happening, we had to back up another Vice team that was inside a bar on Forty-third Street, a place called Raffles. It was another one of those pervert bars where they'd stoop down and piss on the ice for mixed drinks.

"We were outside, hiding in my station wagon, hoping that

we wouldn't have to go inside and get in a shootout. I figured this was private enough.

"I was concerned because I really didn't know Doug that well. But I had heard about him. Everybody in the department raved about his cars and clothes and apartment. They were envious.

"I had a nice house too, and pretty decent clothes. I could relate to that up to a point. But Doug was way beyond my league.

"I'm saying to myself, he must have cheap rent or something to afford all that. I like the kid and I don't want to believe he's taking money. But cops don't have thirty-five-hundred-dollar watches. Not even corrupt ones.

"We're out there talking and I'm asking him questions. He tells me where he lives—a place on Central Park with a uniformed doorman out front. The only time I've ever been in places like that I'm serving a warrant on a mob guy or going in with a police dog who sniffs out bombs. It is not a typical cop hangout.

"Here I am a sergeant and he's a detective. I couldn't even pay his goddamn rent. Now I'm really worried about this kid.

"So, I say, 'Doug, I don't mean to insult you but I got a problem with you. There's no way you can pay that rent on your salary. I'm sorry, but I can't work another minute with you unless I have the answer. Because if you're on a pad I have to run your ass out of Vice. And I'm not going to go behind your back. I'm going right up in front of your face. You gotta explain to me how you can afford that on a cop's salary.'

"He says, 'I thought you knew, Mother.'

"'Knew what?'

"'Other income.'

"'Other income? What the hell is that?'

"Then he told me. It turned out that his wife was the heiress to one of the biggest oil delivery companies in New York. That Christmas she bought him a Gucci shield case for his badge to match his Gucci gun belt. He showed it to me.

"That was what I loved about being a Vice cop in New York. Where else could you partner with a cop like Doug West—a kid who was worth about ten thousand times more than the mayor?

[198]

"Here was a guy who could afford to do anything in the whole world and the only thing he cared about was Vice.

"At that moment, I could see a lot of me in Doug. Not the money part, of course, but the personality type. There was this latent part of him that kept drawing him back to the Life. I'll never know if I went into Vice already harboring that secret need or if Vice turned me into this junkie who had to keep coming back to the street, back to the Life to get his danger fix. Either way, the compulsion had taken over the biggest part of me. Maybe that was why I could always spot obsessive behavior in other people. It was like looking into a mirror.

"Doug West was the perfect detective to use on that case. We had pretended that he was an eccentric collector—art and weapons. The fact that Doug happened to be a very wealthy guy who knew his way around the world of privilege was one of the main reasons he had pulled it off so convincingly.

"But that's common in the NYPD, too. Some of the most talented, gifted people on the face of the earth aspire to no higher calling than to become New York City policemen and thus fulfill their fantasies. That was Doug. That was me.

"I worried about the last meeting. I was afraid for Doug. So much could have gone wrong. The violin could have even been a fake. But it wasn't. That arrest went down—right there on the Twentieth Street pier—like some case study you would diagram on the chalkboard at the academy. We left the pier congratulating ourselves.

"Police work is never like that, though. The perverse streak in the universe that refuses to allow you to come away clean was working overtime.

"Exactly two days after we confiscated the Stradivarius, we locked up the burglar and his helpers and sent the art courier on his way, back to London, I think. His body turned up over there with a bullethole behind the right ear. He'd been executed. Professionally.

"That stopped us in our tracks, let me tell you. My control people freaked out—so did Al Gold, for different reasons, of course. We had no way of knowing whether or not our case had led directly to the courier's murder. That was an easy assumption to make, but not necessarily the correct one. He may have died during the course of a robbery, or he may have been mixed up in something that none of us even knew about. I refused to believe that our burglar and his friends had the contacts to get a guy whacked halfway around the world, but I may have been rationalizing. I'll never know.

"Gold reacted just the way a confirmed career criminal always sees things. He was afraid that I had been trapped in the sting and that I was going to go to jail and that I would make a deal for myself and give him up. For weeks after that, he was afraid to call me. Prior to that, I had been hearing from him two, three times a day.

"The one possibility that he never suspected was that I really was honest and that I was the motive force directing the whole operation. He made the same mistake as Bobby Brody. They just could not comprehend a cop being straight if there was no tangible profit in it. That was one edge that I had that I would never lose. They had spent their lives 'reaching' dirty cops and their way of sizing up any situation was inflexible.

"The Puzzle Palace wanted to shut me down, pull me out. Sinbad would be put on hold. Forever.

"I managed to talk them out of that by persuading them that the only thing I really had left to do was to place the bugs in the Murray Hill townhouse. In the end, I guess they weighed the risks and decided that what we were learning about the Sicilian Mafia was worth running out the string a little further.

"I was all for it. But that Stradivarius caper and the tragic way that it ended would haunt me for the rest of my life. The homicide of the art courier remains open to this day. That was one we could never solve."

TWENTY-TWO

If you have good people a *Surveillance* can be like a symphony. It's poetry. It's ballet. It's your pump pumping, your strum strumming. I looked forward to it, especially if the guy we were after moved and if he was good.

MOTHER'S MAXIM

"I installed the bug on the Sicilians in the townhouse myself.

"I had always met with Gold somewhere else, so the staff at the brothel had no idea what I looked like. I was a true silent partner. I just picked a time when I knew Gold wouldn't be around.

"Gus Garen, from NYPD Intelligence, went with me. He was a wire man; probably the best wire man who ever lived. We pretended to be from the phone company.

"First, we had to distort the phone line. That's easy to do from the outside. Then you just wait for them to call up the phone company to complain about the service. You intercept their call, and a few minutes later respond, pretending to be the repairman. Gus even came up with a genuine truck from the phone company.

"When you get a court order for a wire, it has to be for a particular crime and for a particular person. There are a number of technical problems that enter into a bug—like when can you turn it on? You can only turn it on when the subject of the wire is physically in the place. The rules are really tight. And

[201]

you can only open the wire on a conversation to which he is a party. If you record other voices, they must be talking about the same criminal enterprise, or it's no good. If they decide to discuss a different crime, then you have to get the court order amended.

"One of the most difficult things is to be able to identify the various voices when you can't see who they belong to.

"I had two plants—a photo plant, a cop outside, across the street from the townhouse; and a wiretap plant, electronic.

"When the target voice, or person, first entered the house, I had to have a guy follow him as he got out of his car, write down the license plate number, and take his picture as he goes to the door. We recorded his voice as he was greeted inside.

"With the plate number I could find out who the car was registered to, match it up with a picture, and match that with a voice overlay. That's how we gave all the players, the Sicilians, names and numbers. Tedious work. No shortcuts.

"To get the original 'voice exemplar' of Pete Bicardi—so we could match it up later—I had his car stopped in Brooklyn by an ordinary traffic cop who was wearing a wire. And guess what simpleminded Bicardi tried to do? He bribed the cop who stopped him; handed him forty dollars. We got it all on tape. That's another pinch.

"By some crazy coincidence, the day we went in to plant the bug just happened to be the same day they settled the longest telephone company strike in history.

"While I was installing the device, one of the Brooklyn wise-guys walks over to us with the newspaper.

"He's standing right over us; we're on the floor. 'Hey, I hear you got a raise today,' he says. 'How much an hour do you make now? You just got a fucking raise, did you know that?'

"I didn't know a thing. But Gus knew. He used to work for the phone company, so he kept up on it.

"Gus begins, 'A Tech 3 gets $11.22 an hour; a Tech 2 gets...' and he rattles it off. Thank God, we passed the test and the hood walked away. That was close.

"Finally, we installed this ultrasensitive carbon mike on the thick wainscoting that ran along the wall right over the spot where Bicardi sat. We couldn't do it in the casino on the first floor because that was too noisy and we couldn't put the bug in any of the bedrooms because all you ever picked up in there was a whore panting, 'Give it to me, baby, give it to me.'

"There was a room on the third floor, however, that had been enlarged and converted into a library. *That* was for the serious discussions. So the bug went in there. All this required blue-prints and mechanical drawings beforehand. Then, we had to trick the contractor who had made the alterations into telling us what we wanted to know, without alerting him that we were cops. Nobody who bugged the Russians ever went to more trouble.

"Getting the bug in place was only half the battle. Since these people all spoke Sicilian we had to man the listening devices at our end with cops—called interceptors—who were, number one, fluent in the language and, number two, whom we could trust not to tip off the people in the brothel.

"I got thirty names of cops who were fluent in Italian. That's how we started.

"I went back and ran checks on all of them. All the way back to Italy. Who were their relatives? Could anybody be connected?

"Once I decided to even call one of them in for an interview and lay out the task at hand, I would have already given up the investigation. Consequently, I had to be supercautious.

"This was all that my enemies in the department had been waiting for. I'm a hotshot in Vice, I'm Mother, I have my own case going. They wanted to see me take a fall in the worst way.

"I told each prospective interceptor: 'I gotta find out two things. Are you honest and do you speak Italian? But I'm gonna give you your out right now. If you don't wanna work here— and I'm gonna explain to you why you might not want to work here—you tell me that you don't think you speak Italian good enough. I won't know if you do or you don't. But you can walk away now and it won't prejudice your record.

"'Now, I'm gonna tell you why you don't want to work here. If you're a crook, you don't want to work here, because if I find out, I'm gonna stick my gun up your ass and I'm going to fire it six times. And when I'm done, I'm gonna drag you out in the street and run over you with my car, and then I'm gonna piss on your guts and make your children eat 'em. That's if I find out that you're on the take and you're trying to give me up.'

"That first day I interviewed eighteen people and eighteen people told me they didn't think they spoke Italian good enough.

"I went back the next day, interviewed another twenty. Just five could speak Sicilian. I picked one out of the five. He lived in New York, but he *really* lives in Italy. His mother and father didn't speak English; his wife spoke mostly Sicilian. When he went home, he was really going back to Italy.

"This cop also happened to live within one block of Pete Bicardi's house right around the corner from the subject of the investigation. You think anybody in his right mind would have picked him? I took him. I trusted him.

"He spoke every dialect. He could write it, he could read it. The other four guys I settled on understood Sicilian because their grandmothers spoke Sicilian. They were American-Italians. But they didn't compare to this guy. He *lived* Sicilian, Sicilian, Sicilian. When he took his wife to bed at night he felt like he was getting laid back in Italy. Told me that himself.

"The first night Harold Wilson, the assistant DA, came in and went over all the legal, technical stuff—when you could or could not listen in on the wire.

"This was supposed to be a top secret operation. We rented space in a normal Park Avenue office building from a normal landlord. There was no possibility of sending in the troops— all the usual techie people who show up with step-vans and trailers and transformers on wheels. That would have looked like we were invading the neighborhood.

"To make the bug functional on our end, across the street from the brothel, we had to run out over a thousand feet of telephone wire from the carbon mike in the townhouse to the listening post on Park Avenue.

"The only way we could get the line into the plant was to drop it down from the roof, which had an eight-foot overhang, then into the listening post window on the tenth floor where our rented office was located.

"I had to stand out on the tenth-floor ledge and stretch—try and reach the telephone line which was being blown away from the building by the wind. The ledge was no more than twelve inches and I'm afraid of heights.

"Today, with all the improvements that have been made, they could just set up one cop with a tape recorder and a directional mike and stash him ten blocks away. Not back then.

"I'm there that first night with lawyers and people standing around in three-piece suits. They even had trouble opening the window that I was going to have to go out.

"The suits are looking at me. This is my case, this is my wire, that whorehouse across the street is my whorehouse. Out the window I go.

"I sent a man up on the roof to feed a line down to me. It wouldn't reach. All I'm worried about is that some decent citizen down there is going to call the police because he sees me up on the ledge and this other person on the roof and he decides that we are trying to break into the building. That's how you get killed by friendly fire in the police department. I've seen it happen too many times.

"I take two steps and freeze. I'm pressed so hard against the wall that I'm cutting off my oxygen, almost blacking out. The guy on the roof is no help—he's upside down trying to reach the wire down, seeing that I'm in trouble.

"It's my worst fear made real. The wind is pulling at me; I can see the ground, hear the car horns, and my damn feet are just *nailed* there.

"The guy up top is screaming, 'Sarge, Sarge, you can do it, don't fall.'

"I just will my arm to work and I start to reach up for the wire, which loosens my grip and I start to feel myself going, falling. And I am scared.

"At that moment, for the first time in my life, I believe I had

[205]

a vision. I was inching along the ledge, getting closer to the line hanging over the roof and I come right across a window. I looked in that window and I saw my mother. She had died five years ago and I had taken the loss harder than you would expect. The woman had been my friend, my confidante, my mentor.

"She's in that window—her face gauzy, but smiling—and she says to me, 'Billy don't make an ass of yourself. Grab that wire and get back inside.' Which is exactly what I would have expected her to say.

"That was Step One. We hooked the line up to the tape-recorder.

"Step Two was turning my cops into an intelligence-gathering team. Their first night there, my five interceptors walked in all dressed up for an Italian wedding. They never did anything like this before and I was stupid enough that I never told them *not* to look like cops.

"They were so tuned up. This was superspy stuff to them. Talk about motivated kids. They knew they had to stay in there all night because this game goes on all night. But that was fine. I was so proud I really started to *feel* like their Mother.

"The first thing I had to do was 'untrain' them from the academy bullshit. I told them relax; act like this is just a civilian job in a your own neighborhood. Don't let them know you're cops. After that, I went into what are pertinent and nonpertinent conversations. Every moment had to be evaluated.

"The next night, here they come. One guy's got Italian coffee. Another guy's got Italian sausage. Another guy's got lasagna. Another guy comes with ricotta cheese. You could smell the place when you got off the elevator.

"Once those five guys were together, one thing became very apparent to me. I could have saved myself the trouble of all those interviews. The five guys I ended up selecting all had pinkie rings. Honest to God. All the real Sicilians wear pinkie rings—cops or no cops.

"At that time, in this case, I'm working for an asshole deputy inspector who refused to put two interceptor guys in the room together because he wanted to save on paying overtime. And this is just the biggest case in New York. This is the invasion of the American underworld by the Sicilian Mafia.

"But he won't sign the papers.

"I wanted two guys on each shift who didn't know each other. Each cop would think the other was from Internal Affairs, checking up on him, and he would be afraid to lie to us. I couldn't adequately supervise them—I don't speak the language. So how do I know if my own cops are being straight about what the Sicilians are saying?

"I told all this to the deputy inspector. Besides that, you needed two people, because the bathroom was down the hall. If one guy has to leave to take a piss, what're you going to do?

"The inspector comes back at me. 'See if you can get a Porta-Potti.'

"I said, 'I will do better than that. I will get fucking cat litter. My cops can stand in the box and do their business.'

"That was the NYPD mentality. It hasn't changed.

"Once we were installed in our secret office, listening, it was not without its own drama. Or comedy.

"One day I'm out on the street across from the whorehouse, taking down license numbers, and one of my guys comes out and says, 'Sarge, Sarge, you have to come up here right away. There's a guy up here on the tape who just admitted in Sicilian that he killed a guy today and he's about to leave. He's taking an Amtrak train to Washington. He's wearing two guns.'

"My first reaction was to ID him and watch him, but not arrest him, because we can't blow the bug.

"My boss says, 'You can't do that. He's a murderer. Another case will have to be opened.' By now, I'm almost rooting for him to get away with murder. I can't handle any more complications.

"The next day I bring the tape to work. My best interceptor was there. He hadn't been working the night before when all this went down. I say to him, 'Listen to this tape; who did they kill yesterday?'

"He listened about five times, played it over and over, talked

[207]

to some other interceptor in Italian and all of a sudden they both start laughing.

"'I understand how they thought he could have killed somebody,' my cop tells me. 'But he didn't kill anybody.'

"'What? He had two guns. He's leaving on Amtrak.'

"The interceptor explained: 'What he had in the *afternoon*, not on *Amtrak*, was a toothache and the dentist took them out. On the tape he said, "The dentist took them out." But he took out *teeth*, not *people*. There was one syllable difference in the dialect. What he said, literally, was, "I had a pain. He took them out." Not two guns, two teeth.'

"I almost locked up a Sicilian for tooth decay."

TWENTY-THREE

God meant man to sleep at night and you pray for the night to be busy. *The Late Shift* is the toughest thing in police work.

MOTHER'S MAXIM

The Westies were an Irish gang who free-lanced murder for the Italian Mafia. For generations they had occupied the West Side of New York, near Columbus Circle, a couple blocks down from the Hudson River.

By the time that Al Gold had suggested selling the Westies black-market machine guns, they already had thirteen unsolved homicides against them. The Organized Crime Task Force, Detective Bureau, came to Vice for help. They wanted to set up a phony storefront on the West Side in the hope that the gang would approach it for the purposes of extortion.

With McCarthy already insinuated into the Murray Hill brothel, he seemed like the ideal choice to get the clandestine plot off the ground.

The plan called for the Vice team to record everything that happened in the store on film, and maybe, if the cops were lucky, really lucky, some of the Westies might boast about the murders they had committed while the covert camera was running. Most shakedown men made just those sorts of boasts to scare people into paying. The scheme was a longshot, but McCarthy's team was game.

* * *

"There was an inordinate amount of concern because the Westies were so erratic and so violent. How do you protect the undercovers who would be in the store?

"The location was a one-window, one-door variety store, with a counter across the front and a huge back room. Looked just like the mob joint on Mulberry Street. Actually, that store *was* the original headquarters of the Westies. That's why we took it over. Add insult to injury. It was like their clubhouse.

"I knew the Westies. This was Hell's Kitchen, my old neighborhood. These guys would shoot you over a stickball game.

"Four people to work in the store at all times—safety in numbers. And there would always be two 'maintenance men' behind the Dutch door in the back of the store, allegedly working on illegal slot machines that we had set up in there for the express purpose of attracting the attention of the Westies. They would *have* to check out contraband slots in their own backyard.

"Based on past experience, though, I wanted to put more than swinging Dutch doors between my undercovers and the Westies.

"Ballistics was just developing bullet-proof vests for female cops then, trying to get the rigid inserts to conform to breasts. Kevlar had just been discovered as a lightweight alternative to the old-fashioned lead shields. That gave me an idea.

"I went to the firing range and checked out four hunks of Kevlar. Then I went to a tailor on Canal Street and paid him to sew the Kevlar into down-filled vests. Now, the police custom-order vests that way, but that was the first operation that I knew of, ever, where a guy could be wearing a sleeveless vest and have it bullet-proofed and nobody knew it.

"We also built a steel-reinforced counter in front of the existing one. We armor-plated the Dutch doors, too. They were so heavy you couldn't use them, the guys had to climb over them.

"At night I had to sneak in the plates of one-half-inch-thick steel and try not to alert the people living near the store who were friendly with the Westies. The amount of work involved was staggering—finding cops who were carpenters to build it, cops we could trust; changing the walls to install the hidden cameras, microwave transmitters beaming to one of our men across the street; we even took over a room at John Jay College, which is close by, to use as a field command.

"When and if the Westies ever attacked in strength, if the deal went bad—as it easily could—it would be a war.

"The only thing the undercovers would have to do was drop down behind the steel-reinforced counter in the front. The guys in the back room could then open up with a shotgun barrage. That way, they wouldn't have to worry about killing the cops in the front with friendly fire.

"I also remembered what had happened when that shotgun had gone off by accident in the hotel. No question about it—we were getting ready for the Gunfight at the O.K. Corral. The Westies could not be expected to just lay down their guns, they were the kind of wild Irishmen who would take blood for blood.

"Once we had rebuilt the store into a bunker, we put out the word all through the West Side that we were open for business—slots, gambling, any kind of action from fencing stolen goods to hijacking. All the stuff the Westies themselves did.

"We kept the same code word for trouble—*slick*—just for sentimental reasons.

"One week went by, two; we waited. Sooner or later, the Westies would have to show. We were working their side of the avenue in a brazen way. I have to admit that it was beginning to bother me a little that they were staying away, but I couldn't believe that they were on to us.

"One day I'm having trouble with one of the cameras. I call in a tech guy to come and look at it. While the tech guy is in the store, trying to fix it, we find out that they had unintentionally hooked it up wrong when they first put the electronic gear in. Now, the whole undercover operation was transmitting over commercial television, on one of the local UHF frequencies that were available all over the West Side.

They could see everything we were doing in the store. We were prime time—a continuing soap opera. People across the street could watch us while we talked about what we were going to do to the Westies. It was a disaster.

"Now I know why the Westies haven't bothered us. They were probably too busy laughing their asses off. If my undercover operation is on television, I have to shut it down. I jump all over the tech guy who's fixing the camera; he's actually shaking.

"Then, at that very moment, in walks the Department of Finance. They bust us for nonpayment of taxes and begin locking us up. They also grab the tech guy who is carrying his real police ID. Everybody else had a phony ID.

"Finance thinks they've caught a corrupt cop who's working with the Westies—that's who they thought *we* were—and they called a fucking press conference within the hour.

"After all my work, months and months of lugging the steel in, getting the vests, going to the garment center, all the conniving, and then a bunch of accountants from Finance close us down.

"I had to get to the bottom of it. I figured the fix had to be in at the Puzzle Palace. Somebody must have taken a payoff from the real Westies to put us out of business.

"But, as it turned out, it wasn't anything that conspiratorial. What had happened was that the little store next door ratted us out because we had been selling cigarettes cheaper than they were. They called in Finance to get rid of the competition.

"And guess where I got the cigarettes to sell in the first place? From the Department of Finance, up in their warehouse. They had been seized in previous raids as untaxed contraband.

"After that, they *really* started to joke with me about my always refusing to buy cigarettes for people.

"At home, Millie was understandably nervous about the kinds of dangerous, unorthodox assignments I was getting. But I was bullheaded, as usual, and this was what I definitely wanted.

"They started to move me around after that. Sinbad was still in the works; we were intercepting intelligence every week from the Sicilians at Murray Hill and Al Gold had a different scam every week. Our fear was that depending on how much the Westies might have figured out, they could possibly put two and two together and tip off Al Gold about me.

"I wasn't worried, though. I just couldn't see the Westies helping Gold out of the goodness of their hearts. The psychos didn't have hearts.

"The theory was to keep me on the move—but always in touch with Gold and the Murray Hill crew. Don't forget, I was supposed to be available to them night and day, to perform favors and to keep the honest cops away."

There were always more balls, more juggling.

A detective from the 6-2 precinct, Detective Unit, Brooklyn, who had formerly worked in Vice and who knew McCarthy by his reputation in Public Morals, approached him with a worthwhile lead.

The detective had been interviewing an Italian immigrant who was involved with a fraudulent check-writing scheme. This Brooklyn cop figured that immigrant would be a prime candidate to flip and begin working as an informant for Public Morals because he had been a loan-shark victim. That was how he had gotten started writing bad checks.

McCarthy drove out to Brooklyn and interviewed him. He spoke with an almost gelatinous Italian accent; his English was on a par with the Sicilian dialects that McCarthy had been hearing in the tapes at Murray Hill.

He had been arrested for bad checks and he also owed money to nine different loan sharks. The man had no place to go except the police. When McCarthy offered him a deal, he quickly accepted.

* * *

"This poor little Italian was in sad shape. They were all looking to break his legs. He wasn't tough or even particularly polished, just an ordinary person who had gotten in over his head. I had to know if he would be willing to wear a wire. If so, we would make some loan payments for him. He said yes.

"Now, you cannot just give a guy money and send him out to start making payments. The bad guys will say, 'Where is this guy getting the money?' So before he could start making payments, he had to show some kind of legitimate income, a business, a way of making money.

"He had owned a landscaping company. The business had been very successful, but he had lost it all at the track. He loved the ponies.

"I had a detective working for me, Salvatore Montali, born in Italy, raised in Italy, spoke Italian. He was like one of my Sicilian interceptors.

"I made Sal the money man for a phony construction company. The immigrant had two friends. Both were smart, hard workers. One guy was a bricklayer. The other was a carpenter. They only spoke Italian.

"At first, these two partners didn't know anything about the immigrant's involvement with us, and Sal Montali was simply introduced as one of his American cousins. No questions asked. The partners probably figured Sal was mobbed up.

"They started doing construction jobs all over Brooklyn—refacing houses, putting up brick walls, building additions onto houses. This allowed him to start making minimum payments to the different loan sharks and we recorded the conversations.

"In the course of that we start looking at seventeen different OC people. Every one was a 'made man.' Pure Mafia again. And the best part is, half of these people are steady customers at Al Gold's fancy whorehouses. I'm having trouble believing how all this is coming together, how huge Sinbad has become.

"And the business is thriving. Sal becomes the president of the company. Back in Public Morals we're actually making a *profit* off the undercover operation.

"Sal negotiated loans for capos, all in Italian. The mob began to seek him out as this mysterious financial genius. They never thought he was a cop.

"One of the loan sharks our informant had to meet was Frankie Zuffo. He was ugly, mean, bad. He had hands that looked like my thighs. If he slapped you in the face, he could tear your head off.

"When our immigrant informant went back to these people to tell them, 'Listen, I can start paying you fifty dollars a week,' they didn't want fifty dollars a week. They wanted a lot more.

"When he went to meet this Zuffo, I was in the car, backing him up. I took my gun out of my holster and had it between my legs; that's where I always kept it. He was scared and so was I.

"Zuffo tells him he's gonna kill him—fifty dollars a week isn't enough. Our informant stares him down and says, pointing to his shoulder, his head, his leg, 'Listen, you could shoot me here, or here, or here, but if you shoot me, you don't get no money. If you want it, you get fifty dollars. Take it or leave it.'

"That little guy had guts. I'll never forget him. I don't think I would have barked at Zuffo that way.

"Ultimately, we arrested the whole bunch. Took out some of the biggest loan sharks in Brooklyn. But not until after Sinbad."

In one very significant way Operation Sinbad was unique. At no point during that case—which took approximately two years to reach its final, violent conclusion—were the people running the Murray Hill brothel approached by shakedown artists in the employ of New York City. Normally, the authentic criminals had to get in line behind any number of municipal workers, representing a staggering variety of offices and agencies, who ran booming extortion enterprises of their own on the side. Anything could be "fixed," from a license that was out of order to code violations that would be winked at for the right price.

These shakedown schemes that actually originated in City Hall or in one of its satellite offices were a source of real anxiety for undercover operatives like Bill McCarthy. There was no telling how badly an investigation could be jeopardized by avaricious city employees.

"We opened a yogurt shop in Brooklyn, on Bath Avenue, Bensonhurst; this was heavy organized crime country. It was another lend-lease deal. The Brooklyn district attorney needed a couple extra undercovers. He specified a Greek and an Italian. Then he said that he also wouldn't turn down a Jewish officer.

"Now, to understand why the Brooklyn DA was so specific about whom he needed, you must appreciate the way Organized Crime guys think. To them, *all* Italians must either be unpredictable Sicilians who behave erratically or dumb U.S.-born muscle guys. They pigeonhole you. A Greek could legitimately operate a store; the Jew is pegged as the moneyman. These people aren't into ethnic sensitivities. They will settle for the stereotype every time.

"I assign the Brooklyn DA the people he needs from Manhattan Vice. They'll be new faces. Everything should go well.

"The yogurt shop was to run along the lines of the store we built to attract the Westies. Slot machines and gambling in the back room. That makes you a much better victim—there's no way you can run to the police and complain, you already have too much to hide.

"The DA wasn't as much concerned with luring the Brooklyn mob into a shakedown—although he would have taken that in a minute—as he was with waiting there until the undercovers were approached by a neighborhood loan shark he was after, Frankie Torrio, Frankie One Eye or Frank-the-Patch, so named for obvious reasons. He'd lost the eye in a knife fight at the age of fourteen.

"Once we managed to get Frank-the-Patch, the loan shark, on tape offering to do business with us, then the DA would have probable cause to plant a bug in his social club, or headquarters. Conveniently, the social club was only a few blocks down from the place we chose for the yogurt shop.

"I wasn't all that impressed with their plan, but I provided the assistance they requested.

"To make absolutely sure that we would get the Patch to notice us, we rented the store from a realtor who was a known OC agent. He handled no clean properties.

"The day we are moving in, the real estate guy comes by and begins snooping around. Two of my guys are pushing these big old slot machines up a ramp in the back, the machines are covered by a tarp like a painter's drop cloth. I give them the signal to accidently-on-purpose let the tarp fall off. Make it look good.

"Naturally, the real estate man sees this. He gets me by myself. 'You can't do this,' he says. 'You can't bring those slots in here.'

"I give him a look. 'Why, because it's illegal? Don't worry, we'll never get caught and you won't get in any trouble.'

" 'Who cares about that shit?' he answers. 'I'm telling you that you can't use *those* machines because they ain't *my* machines. This is my store, so you have to use my machines. And I take a piece.'

"This is the realtor, on the first day. Like I said, Bath Avenue was real OC country.

"I make a deal with him not to move any more of my slots in. If he gets some for me, I'll use them in the back room. On his terms. I haggled a little. He left satisfied.

"We officially open for business on a Monday. I still can't believe that the real estate guy has a sideline in slot machines. That morning, in walks a guy from the Department of Sanitation. We don't even have any trash yet. We haven't had our first customer yet.

"The very first thing out of his mouth is, 'You don't need to use commercial. I'll have a truck come by first thing every Saturday morning. Just pay the driver.'

"What's he talking about? He's telling me that there will be no need for me to hire a commercial cartage company to take away my trash because, even though it is illegal for the City of New York to do it, he will have a city truck there to pick up my trash. I pay the driver under the table. Another payoff.

"That same afternoon, on the first day, a different truck pulls up. It's a delivery van, not a trash truck. But we haven't ordered anything.

"The driver comes in and says, 'Where do I put the slots?'

"It's like he's making the most routine delivery. The real estate man had sent him.

"On the second day in business a man in a utility company uniform walks in. 'Once a month, I can turn back the meters. Electrical and gas.' *Then* he introduces himself. He was from Con Ed. This illegal service will cost me fifty dollars a month. A bargain.

"Wednesday rolls around. I swear this is true. Three of the ugliest guys I have ever seen in my entire police career walk through the front door. One takes up a position on the door, the other second one comes behind the counter. The spokesman stands in front of me.

"'Who are you with?' Just like that.

"That question is the classic mob introduction. It takes the place of 'How do you do?'

"Then, before I even have a chance to answer, he says, 'My name is Angelo. From now on, you're with me. That will cost you five hundred dollars a week. Anybody bothers you just say you are with me and I am with Carmine-by-the-Bay.'

"He was referring to a major league Gambino Family capo— Carmine is from the Sheepshead Bay area. And if you were under Carmine's protection in Bensonhurst, you were in very good shape.

"But this is all wrong now. Carmine-by-the-Bay is the *wrong* mob guy. We already have a loan-shark indictment ready to drop on Carmine. This would be like sticking two hooks in the same mouth.

"Besides, the Brooklyn DA does not have a hard-on against the Gambinos in this instance, but rather against the Bonanos. He'll do the Gambinos next week. Frank-the-Patch is Bonano. That's who we have to bug.

"But now, with Carmine-by-the-Bay in the picture, we cannot

even approach Frank-the-Patch about getting a loan from him. We can't, in other words, go to the corner, to our neighborhood wiseguys, because Carmine has staked his claim.

"The case is now over. The wrong mob guy is shaking us down. However, we have money and manpower tied up in the yogurt shop and if we pull out too fast that will blow our identities.

"Before he left, Angelo also told us that we would have to begin using Carmine's yogurt exclusively. Now, it wasn't actually *Carmine's* yogurt. It was a big-ticket, brand-name yogurt, but somehow he had moved in on the local distributor. So Carmine-by-the-Bay had a bigger interest in sales volume than the manufacturer did.

"He explained that as part of the protection we were buying from him, we had to use Bonano slot machines in the back room. We better get rid of our slots and the real estate guy's slots. Then, Angelo and his two giant friends left.

"Thursday Angelo calls the store and gives me the name of a person in the Consumer Affairs office at City Hall whose job it is to enforce city code regulations that apply to stores like ours. 'He's good people,' Angelo said. 'You call him if there's a problem with the city. This is a service that we are providing to you free of charge.'

"That was Carmine's reach in City Hall.

"By the time Friday came around, I was ready to call it a week. But the city still wasn't finished.

"Two cops come in and try to sell my undercover people a hot gun. It had been stolen from a National Guard Armory. For all I know, it could have been a gun from the same shipment that Al Gold's burglar had scored. At least this wasn't a machine gun, though. But I can tell you we made it a point to take care of those two cops.

"I left that Friday. We were no closer to Frankie-the-Patch than when we had started. I had to get back to Sinbad.

"Other agencies wanted in, however. So I had to leave some of my people there with the Brooklyn cops. Every time a different law enforcement agency monitors—or joins in on—a case like that, a new log number is assigned to that phase of the investigation. By the time we shut down the yogurt shop there were enough different log numbers to build a log cabin."

The Murray Hill brothel, the primary site of the Sinbad activities, had apparently been allowed to function free of these petty extortions. Not that many people knew about Murray Hill, and the ones that did were intimidated by it.

As far as Al Gold was concerned, though, the reason why Murray Hill had remained unmolested for so long was a cagey Vice cop named Bill McCarthy.

However, in a sudden, brutal turnabout, that profitable status quo would be forever altered.

The very first person Gold contacted about it was McCarthy, his personal pad cop.

TWENTY-FOUR

**In the Life, when an *Insurance Man* comes collecting,
you can either buy his policy or buy the farm. Or, you
can fight back and make him sorry he ever came.
Payback is a bitch.**

MOTHER'S MAXIM

■

AUGUST 1974
THE MURRAY HILL
TOWNHOUSE

Albert Gold sounded frantic. As McCarthy listened, his voice
took on an unaccustomed shrillness, a tone that was close to a
whine. Normally, there was a calculating flatness in Gold's tone.
His emotions, especially as they concerned business, were as
cold as an amphibian's.

McCarthy had taken the call at his desk in One Police Plaza
late on a Friday afternoon. As soon as he picked up the receiver,
the tape began rolling.

There had been trouble at the brothel on Fifty-first Street,
the big adjoining apartments.

The whorehouse had been knocked over by a Brooklyn crew
whom no one seemed to know anything about. Barely able to
stammer out the words, Gold recounted to McCarthy that three
of the gang members had come into the house on a Wednesday,
acting like paying customers, although he had sensed immediately that they seemed more interested in how much cash was

[221]

going through the house than in how compliant the girls appeared to be.

Nervous, Gold had opened his desk drawer, reached inside and taken out a revolver. He laid it across his lap, just in case. But that night nothing happened. The men simply went to bed with some of the girls, paid up and left. No hassles.

Two days later, on a sweltering Friday evening, the same three men returned.

This time they didn't bother pretending to be johns. Instead, they began batting the hookers around, slamming them on the floor, throwing punches. They beat one woman so savagely that they broke seven of her ribs.

They chased away the other customers—but made sure not to harm them—and told the madam who was running it for Al Gold that her "man" would have to begin paying them "insurance" to avoid a repeat performance. They would be back every week, every night, if necessary. Then, on the way out, they left a telephone number in Brooklyn for the "man" to call. It was a classic shakedown. At that moment, Gold explained to McCarthy, his greatest fear was that these extortionists would discover that he was also the major shareholder in the far more profitable Murray Hill townhouse. If they ever got in there, then he would have to face their extortion as well as the anger of the Maranzo Bicardi faction, not to mention the wrath of the Sicilians. Providing security at the whorehouses was Al Gold's job. He knew that Bicardi would hold him to it. So would the Sicilians.

Gold had a desperate message for McCarthy, "You're on my payroll. Start to earn your money."

The Vice cops spent the weekend attempting to find out who had visited Fifty-first Street and why.

"I talked it over with Tony and the rest of the team and we decided that the best course was for us to meet with this gang and represent ourselves as the real owners of the club—claim that Al Gold was just our front man. Then, we would begin making extortion payments just to see where they went.

"As far as we knew there was no immediate way for this shakedown mob to find out that we were cops. Should they discover our identity at any point in the future, we would just pull out as fast as we could. Take the whole crew out if we had to. It was dangerous, but we didn't want to lose our foothold in Murray Hill, either. Besides, it had to look like we were really putting out for Al Gold.

"Actually, we had been hearing unsubstantiated rumors about these stickup men for some time. It was like the rumble of distant drums in the jungle. We knew that a team of cowboys, renegades, were out there, totally out of control, shaking down every Vice joint in Manhattan. At first, we saw this as another opportunity. These shakedown guys *had* to be connected to somebody. We would just run it down. Add to our intelligence. I had the notion that there might be a movement afoot to take over midtown. I could see one of the Mafia Families secretly using these commandos against the others.

"As it happened, that was not the case. However, we were also wrong to think that this gang was just an aberration. They *were* more than extremely dangerous, wild-assed punks who had come riding into Manhattan like Frank and Jesse James. The Five Families did turn out to know about them, but the gang was considered so unpredictable and so gun-happy that nobody was prepared to take them on. Only about once every ten years or so do you see a group like that. Even in New York."

McCarthy's immediate concern was preserving the integrity of Operation Sinbad from interference by these cowboys.

Since Tony Vitaliano could so easily pass for an Italian hood, he was selected to meet with the extortionists as the lead undercover. McCarthy would be the control officer, the primary backup, as well as the overall sergeant/supervisor.

There would be intense pressure on both of them, especially McCarthy. If anything went wrong, it would be his responsibility. His reputation as Mother would face its most severe test.

However, in Vitaliano, he believed that he had the most gifted undercover in New York.

"Tony was a complete detective. Probably the greatest characteristic of a detective is how he ties his tie. That was part of the religion of being a detective. The old-time detective would walk around with his tie open, just hanging over his shirt. That meant he was working full-bore. And that was how Tony dressed. If he had to go out for an interview, the tie would be tied with just the first loop over, but never in a Windsor knot. Windsors were only for a wake or a wedding. Or to testify in court.

"The difference between an ordinary detective and a *good* detective is that the good one can get people to say things, give him information such that after he leaves, they think to themselves, I shouldn't have told him that. And a good detective can do it with finesse. That was Vitaliano.

"All we could do was try and pretend that the danger didn't exist. Deep down, we knew better. But this was the biggest case in anybody's career, the biggest undercover case *ever* in New York, as far as we knew. We used to go all day and all night on nerves and exhilaration. You never saw a group of people who were so into being cops.

"Tony called the phone number that had been left for Al Gold. He sounded calm; I was listening in on an extension.

"Tony grew up with these people. He knew how to talk to them. Right away, they went for it. He agreed to meet with them. It would be three hundred dollars a week. To start.

"This immediately told us that the gang had no idea about Murray Hill, because if they did, they would have asked for much more.

"For the first meeting, we were supposed to go down to Brooklyn, over to a pizza parlor on St. John's Place between Utica and Schenectady avenues. Ask for 'Joe.' That's a mostly black neighborhood now except for the guys who would be there waiting for us. Apparently, they also worked with some black strong-arm men because that corner they picked was black mob all the way. Either they were connected or they were running the risk of poaching. We figured they had to be connected to the black underworld, too. That was almost unheard of then.

"We realized that we would have to go in cold—at least this first time. No backups. Too much of a chance. However, this was a crew that had beaten women unmercifully all over Manhattan; they were killers, too, we guessed. It wouldn't be like storming into Al Gold's wig shop and pulling my pants down and acting bad.

"This was playing for keeps.

"The first time you meet people like this, you must be prepared that they might beat the shit out of you; they're bound to rough you up and threaten you. We went in with our eyes open.

"I was supposed to be Tony's driver. That was my cover. We just reversed our usual roles. Now, I was the schlepp. He wore the wire; the transmitter was in the car. I never expected to have to open my mouth.

"The location where you first meet bad guys is very crucial. It has to be checked. You can find out who was arrested at that spot in the past. They are all creatures of habit.

"We reviewed all we could about past police actions along this part of Utica Avenue. We could not get a make on a single white hood and Al Gold had assured us that these were white guys.

"We were both so hyper that neither one of us got any sleep at all the night before that first meeting. On the way we barely even talked to each other. Tony was like a great thespian concentrating on his role. I was just scared.

"I let him out of the car and he went into the pizza place alone. I hated just abandoning him like that. But I could hear what was going on, of course, because I had the receiver in the car.

"Two countermen were waiting for him. No customers. Just empty tables. 'Either of you guys named Joe?' he asked.

"Nothing for a few minutes. Just an old-fashioned staredown. Finally, one of them wipes his hands on his apron and says, 'Joe ain't in. Try the pool hall across the avenue.'

"Outside, Tony crossed the street, saw the pool hall and went in. One flight up. Any time you're a cop you really hate to see that. It takes you right away from the nearest help. I was the 'help.'

"It's harder to stay outside than to go in. You don't have the same control. In a situation like that, I believed that I could anticipate what they were going to do, and that I could give the right answer before they thought up the next question. But here it was all on Tony.

"Even if it went bad, I was still the boss; I was always responsible. My cop was always off the hook—unless they decided to kill him. That was the risk an undercover took.

"The pool room was nearly empty too. Just one bare light over the table. Three or four hoods, backs to the wall, picked Tony up at the door and eyeballed him crossing the floor.

"There was only one guy playing. Black silk shirt, blue jeans. A really hard face. He's concentrating on a shot, nine ball, side pocket.

"Tony says, 'Is somebody named Joe here?'

"The player punches the cue at the white ball, muffs it badly and then looks up, lifts the cue stick off the tabletop and stares at Tony.

"Then he walks over and says, 'I'm Bobby Gee and you just made me miss my fucking shot.'

"Tony begins to give him some explanation, but this Bobby Gee cuts right through it. 'I got these friends,' he says, 'they did the job on your place and they asked me to act as their intermediary. I have nothing to do with this, understand. They want you to buy an insurance policy. You got a nice business there. No reason to see anything happen to it. These friends of mine are just businessmen like you.'

"And that's how it started.

"At that meeting, much to my surprise, they didn't rough Tony up a bit, because they were more concerned with finding out whom he was with. Up to that point, they were following strict Mafia protocol.

"If I go in there, I can look like a hardass guy, but I could only be a victim or a cop. I'm Irish and I look Irish. He goes in there, they have to be nice to him because he's Italian. They don't know if he's with somebody who's protecting him. They don't know if the place they just hit is already connected with a Family.

"If Tony had really been with somebody, they would have had to just back off. Walk away from it with an apology.

"From that initial conversation, we picked up our first important piece of intelligence on these people. They mentioned Tony Spots. He was a connected guy. They had to be working under his license. He had a journeyman's license in the mob, not like a senior mechanic's. He was a middle-level soldier. Possibly, if he had any, Tony's connections could have outranked his.

"But Tony swore that he had no connections and that he was willing to pay. That was just what they wanted to hear.

"I'm listening outside. I hear Bobby Gee say, 'We're gonna provide you with service. We're gonna protect you.'

"What they don't tell Tony is: We'll protect you from us.

"They go on: 'We're gonna help you. We're gonna be your business consultants; you don't want to operate without us. If you have any problems, you come to us. We'll take care of your problems. Maybe there are some other things we could do together. Maybe we're gonna have some other places and you can help us work there.'

"They even offered to do murders: 'If you're having a beef with somebody, we'll take them out. No problem.'

"After about twenty minutes of this, and after he hands over the money, Tony leaves.

"The lookouts from the pizza parlor are looking me over outside, but they can put up with the fact that he brought one guy with him. That's natural. If Tony was important enough to own a whorehouse, he should be important enough to have a driver like me. Their defenses were down. The second Tony walked outside and put his ass in the car, we got the hell out of Brooklyn."

TWENTY-FIVE

New York has everything. It's got more that's good and more that's bad than any other place in the whole world. It's fast, it's irreverent; it's got tremendous volume, tremendous violence, congestion, hustlers; all kinds of moves, all kinds of speeds.

M O T H E R ' S   M A X I M

"We began to take surveillance photographs all over Manhattan; we became very interested in this group. Followed them. During the next couple of weeks, they hit a few other places and continued to brutalize people. It came to a point, very quickly, where we had a real dilemma.

"I warned Tony to be *very* careful. These punks had already done hard time; they wouldn't hesitate to shoot. The crew had a history of violence that went all the way back to Crazy Joey Gallo and even more sinister current connections that linked it to an associate of the Columbo Family. They were for real.

"They all looked like wiseguys. Four of them were brothers—the Gagliano brothers. All about five-ten, five-nine, average build, between 160 pounds and 180 pounds.

"They needed shaves, had to be cleaned up like streetdogs, gamey dogs. There was something uncivilized about them—like each one had too many hormones, too much animal inside them. They hadn't quite stepped over that evolutionary boundary that made them human. They were always on the verge—of losing control, of violence. And what would take them over

[228]

the edge wasn't always rational. If the Mets lost that night, for example, that could be enough. What makes a volcano finally erupt? It just goes. You could see it in their eyes. Read it in their minds.

"The craziest one of them all was Tommy Mendino, their pal. He had been a cellmate of theirs in Attica.

"He was a paroled killer with murky Hispanic bloodlines and a dark, unsmiling face who had already figured in jobs all over New York as everybody's favorite designated hitter. Mendino fell into that category of psychos who were outside of technique. They didn't need judo or karate or the martial arts or any of that nonsense. All they needed was an excuse to turn bone-crusher, to make a bowling ball out of somebody's face; you couldn't bring down rhinos like that with an elephant gun.

"Years back, at the Blarney Stone bar in Manhattan, I had to fight a tough guy just like that. He was another murderer who seemed ready to flip, to become an informant. But our negotiations had broken down over how much a week the police should be sending his sick mother back in Arkansas as his pay-back for helping them.

"This guy picked me up with one hand—with one hand—along with the barstool I was sitting on. Then he banged me down hard on top of the bar. He happened to have a stomach ulcer at the time and he had been drinking milk for it all night long—milk with scotch. He was bleeding out of his mouth—milk and blood. After I got to know him, he told me that before the ulcer, back when he was feeling better, he could pick up *two* people at once. If this guy liked you, he let you know by butting you in the head.

"I can still see him manhandling me—hands that looked like ham hocks, big gold rings that would fit through a bull's nose, an IQ of room temperature. And the milk and the blood drib-bling out of his mouth. Guys like that are torpedoes; once you point them, there's no calling them back.

"And that's what Tony and I were facing now. I was con-vinced of it. If Sinbad didn't end up getting both of us killed, it wouldn't be their fault.

[229]

"Besides Mendino, a couple other hoods worked with the brothers more or less full-time. But Bobby Gagliano and Tommy Mendino were the bad actors.

"If you saw them, and you knew what you were looking for, you knew they had to be a stickup team. They definitely did not appear to be businessmen. They looked like hitters. You could tell by their expressions. They were all in their early to mid-thirties—just the right age, the right everything. People get smart after thirty five, even hitters. They get a little more wisdom. If you live that long, by then you should have people working for you who can do that. These guys, though, would never be in that position. They were all dead from the neck up, gorillas. They thought they had it all figured out. Violence was the answer to everything.

"And they loved to work over whores; whores almost never fought back. That posture was alien to their line of work. Whores took it lying down—figuratively as well as literally. As soon as a tough guy showed up, they went to their pimp or madam—and there was *always* a pimp, no matter how classy or clean they pretended to be—and the pimp paid off whoever was leaning too hard. The leaners could be cops looking to score an easy note or authentic bad guys. It made absolutely no difference to the leanees. To a whore, a smack in the mouth was a smack in the mouth. And that was how these guys collected their rent, fist first. To a man, they got off on beating up women.

"The guy they reported to—loosely—was Tony Spots, this three-hundred-pound schlump who ate crates of pasta at a sitting. He knew enough to stay insulated.

"It took us about a month to put names with all the faces. Meanwhile, the gang was still in business. And all the time, Gold was calling me or Tony ten times a day, screaming about his townhouse on Thirty-first Street, the big whorehouse, the Murray Hill joint.

"Sooner or later, we knew that the Gaglianos would hear about it and check it out. For punks like them, New York is really a very small town.

"We agonized through three payments. The Gaglianos kept getting more and more friendly with Tony. They made it clear that they wanted him to join them as their bagman and shake down all the other whorehouses. They liked him—he spoke their language and they could see how bright he was. Whether he liked it or not, he was getting drafted.

"Then, Gold gets me by myself one night. He's acting very strangely. For the very first time, Gold seems like he doesn't trust me.

"'What's wrong?' I asked him.

"'They found something in the library that shouldn't have been there.' And he just keeps looking at me; it's my turn to feel uncomfortable.

"Of course, I knew what they had found. In the middle of everything else, with the Gagliano brothers terrorizing everybody on the street, in the Life, they found the bug.

"'What?' I play dumb.

"'Don't fuck with me,' Gold said. 'I pay you guys. Now I think I'm being set up, and I have to *pay* for it?' He is glaring at me red hot.

"'Who set you up? I don't know what you're saying.'

"'They got the townhouse fucking wired. They found it the other day. We were gonna wallpaper in there and had to move the molding. I guess you expected to get paid pretty good to keep quiet about that.'

"I'm thinking on my feet. Gold is so convinced I'm corrupt that he assumes this is just another level of blackmail, another kind of extortion for me to use against him.

"'If you really found what you think you found—if you know what it even looks like—it isn't mine.'

"'The hell it isn't!' He really thinks I'm blackmailing him, scamming him for more money.

"'Is it still there?' I had to know if they moved it, destroy it.

"'It's there,' Gold said. 'Nobody goes in that room anymore. The Sicilians were afraid to touch it. They didn't want to tip anybody off. Told me I have to find out what the crap was going on or they were gonna put me under.'

"This is really the problem. Gold is more frightened of the Sicilians than of anybody. And he has a right to be.

"At least the wire was still in place, for whatever good it would do us now. 'Don't touch it. I'll take care of it,' I told him.

"'No shit—you bet you will.'

"Right there in front of him I made a call; talked to nobody, but pretended I was talking to the office. I asked a few cop questions, then acted like I knew what was up. I hung up and pretended it was all a big secret.

"'What?' Gold said.

"Now it's my turn to be a bastard. 'You dumb asshole,' I said. 'You come in here and accuse me of running a wire into your whorehouse. And you're supposed to be so smart. You think I'm the only cop in New York? You think every cop is as crooked as me?' I had him now.

"'You trying to say something?' Gold was physically backing off, walking across the room from me.

"That wire was put in by a new guy from Gambling— I ain't the only Vice cop, you know. I work whores; he works gambling. That wire—and it really is a cop wire—is his and he's straight. Don't even think about reaching him.

"'You got nowhere to go with him. All you got, you dumb fuck, is me. But I'm a nice guy and I'm gonna square it for you. And it ain't even gonna cost you an extra dollar. But you really owe me now. You tell that to the Sicilians.'

"Gold accepted my lie. Why not? Gold knew all the things he'd done. Plenty of other cops could have known about the casino in the townhouse.

"I saved my ass, but we have now lost that wire for all time. Maybe the townhouse, too. It will only be a matter of time until the Sicilians move on now. Gold will be too hot for anyone to touch. I can see Sinbad dying. It had been a good run, almost a year. That's an eternity in undercover work.

"That very same week, like enough wasn't going on already, the Gaglianos decided to finally visit Thirty-first Street, the Murray Hill townhouse. And the shit, as they say, hit the fan.

"Sure enough, on a Wednesday night, when they usually did

their casing of a place, before they would come back and rob it on a Friday, they showed up at Thirty-first Street.

"As fast as we could ascertain, they still did not know that Fifty-first Street was connected to Thirty-first Street. But we couldn't be sure.

"As luck would have it, one of the girls from Fifty-first Street was sent over to Murray Hill—that *same* Wednesday. It was a step up. She was all excited. When the Gaglianos and Tommy M. came in, she recognized them, knew what was about to go down.

"The hooker tells Gold and he calls us. This guy *really* wants protection now. He would now like for us to blow the Gaglianos away—just to make up for the bug they found. I yell back at him that the bug wasn't my fault. But Gold gets ornery again. He handed his telephone to somebody else, to another pimp whose voice I half-recognized. This guy tells me that he has friends in Brooklyn who will take care of the Gaglianos forever, for a price. Do we want in on the hit? Evidently, they can still use our help.

"Now, my role as a cop on the payroll has just escalated to this discussion about arranging for one or more murders. Never mind the fact that killing the Gaglianos would have been akin to performing a valuable public service. I was still a cop.

"I get him talking and he tells us that all the Manhattan whorehouse owners are about to hire some guns—whoever the hell they are—to protect themselves from our Gaglianos and Tommy Mendino. They are collecting from every house to pool up the money to pay for the contract.

"Next, Al Gold puts out the word that the Murray Hill town-house isn't going to open on the following Friday.

"That was a mistake. The gang would have to know that something was up if that happened. That would have been bad for Tony because he was supposed to meet them the following week.

"We tell Gold that he *has* to open on Friday, even if they do rob him. It's part of our plan to take care of the cowboys for him.

[233]

"All the time, I'm focusing on the Gaglianos like you can't believe. I'm meditating on them. I want to be inside their sick minds. I have to try to take on their identities—outthink them. I'm Mother; that's what I do.

"I can close my eyes and see the brothers and Tommy Mendino, know what they're thinking, feeling:

"We're doing fine with this—this is fun. Getting laid. Shakedowns. This is the Life. What more could we ask for? A steak dinner? This is violent, this is sexual. We go, we case the place. We know that we're coming back to hit it. Even the whores know. You can tell the way they look at us.

"You can't imagine what it's like being there—the thrill of casing the place, the anticipation of coming back and robbing it. This is the race, the excitement, your dick gets hard because the same whore you're going to beat up on Friday night is blowing you right now. That's an explosion of anticipation. That's an orgasm. The foreplay is Wednesday; the orgasm of violence is Friday.

"It's better than a blow-job. We order them around—the whores. Anything we want. Because we've got them scared. It's almost like servitude. It's violent masturbation. You don't participate with them. You're not there to please them or relate to them. Just use them. It's a dog pissing on turf. On the whores. King of the pack. This is the race. The Light. The Vice Marquee.

"We have to put an end to this. But how?

"We didn't want to just surrender our true identities. We might run into the Gagliano crew somewhere down the line. So you don't want to be cops to them. But we have to stop them.

"How can the police department have knowledge of this group and allow them to continue operating? Is Sinbad—no matter how great an undercover operation it is—worth risking the life of every person in New York? They could have killed one of the prostitutes. I always expected that to happen because they thoroughly enjoyed abusing women—sexually and physically. You just couldn't rationalize knowing about this group and not taking them out.

[234]

"That was the conclusion that we all came to.

"Tony would meet them on the following Wednesday, as scheduled. Make the payment.

"From a distance, the rest of the team would follow them back to Brooklyn, just as soon as Tony drove away. We'd put them in where they live, put them to sleep. Make sure they didn't hurt anybody along the way.

"We would come back on Friday because we know they're gonna work Friday. Then we would take them out of the house on Friday, stay with them all day. When they hit Murray Hill that night there would be cops waiting inside, masquerading as regular customers. One of them would be on the door and let the Gaglianos in. They allow the stickup to take place.

"Then, at a prearranged signal, the uniforms would come charging in and arrest everybody. Make it look like a legitimate, routine raid on a whorehouse. It will all seem like one big, nasty coincidence.

"If the Gaglianos and Mendino decided to fight back, they would be outgunned ten to one. And we have our cop witnesses inside who will testify that the Gaglianos robbed the place just before the raid. So we won't have to depend on the testimony of a prostitute who might refuse to talk because she's afraid.

"I wasn't going to be there and Tony wasn't going to be there. So, as far as the Gaglianos are concerned, they don't know how the police got there. They're gonna take a collar. But Tony and I won't blow our covers.

"We just had to sweat out Tony Vitaliano's last scheduled meeting with Bobby Gee."

TWENTY-SIX

For cops, *Fear* is a condition of employment. The first day on the job, you walk out on the street knowing that you might be killed.

MOTHER'S MAXIM

■

2:00 P.M.

HOUSTON STREET

Vitaliano sounded nervous and that could be a problem. Nervous could make him dead. Fast.

McCarthy was listening to the conversation on a remote receiver for a Kel transmitter that was wired to the underside of the dashboard in Tony Vitaliano's flash car. Tony was also recording the deal; there was a tiny Edwards tape recorder stuffed in an empty pack of Camels in his shirt pocket.

But there was something wrong with the way Tony sounded. Just a trace of hesitation. He was coming across as just a little shaky. Actually, more than a little shaky; *very* shaky. And that wasn't like Vitaliano at all.

Vitaliano was sitting in a flash car on Houston Street (he pronounced it *House*-ton, like all real New Yorkers) near the East River Drive and McCarthy was parked a couple of cars in front of him.

The flash car was a biscuit-brown Thunderbird with wire wheels and a roadster roof—any pimp would be proud to drive it, and that was exactly what Vitaliano was pretending to be.

He'd only been there a few moments when one of the bad guys slid into the seat beside him.

As McCarthy knew only too well, the Kel was not the best piece of eavesdropping equipment that money could buy, but it was the best that the NYPD could afford, perpetually strapped as it was to come up with the cash for undercover operations. And the Kel wasn't all that bad. Take away the expected interference from the Manhattan skyline and the Kel could be counted on to do the job.

It was a chilly, early autumn afternoon—one week after McCarthy's seventh wedding anniversary, but he was planning to celebrate it that night. When you were a cop even special dates had to take a backseat to the job. Still, he hoped he could get home a little early.

As he sat in his flash car, nursing a thermos of coffee, listening to Tony the V, he had to settle for being curled up with a shotgun, instead of his wife, Millie.

The big weapon was between his legs—and God, could he think of a few other things that he'd rather have there right about now—doubled-barreled, twelve-gauge, blue steel, as blue as the indigo clouds that were settling in over the murky, calm East River.

All along the sparse riverbank, winter was already leaning hard on the browned-over green spots, drying out the shaggy tufts of wild onion grass, returning the landscape to a mangy no-man's land.

McCarthy didn't talk to his shotgun like some cops did; he wasn't crazy *that* way. He had it there, propped against the steering wheel, just in case. But McCarthy *was* crazy, all right; they all knew that.

Through his rearview mirror, McCarthy could see that Tony still *looked* okay, relaxed and natural. But he kept picking up that little hitch in his voice, and that hitch or whatever the hell it was kept telegraphing a problem.

The shorthand of it was that something was obviously about to go down—something that the cops couldn't see—and Tony the V was reacting to it. Reacting in that he sounded like he was practically having an accident in his pants.

McCarthy knew what the other cops on the team had to be thinking: *One of Mother's children is in trouble.*

Tony was in a very special kind of jeopardy now, the kind that both of them had willingly accepted. If a cop happened to be walking down the block and a guy came out of a liquor store with a gun in his hand and that cop just happened to find himself there, or if he was in the hallway of an apartment building in Harlem, about to break the door down, and he didn't know what was on the other side, that was incidental, accidental danger. Cops couldn't really bitch about that. It came with the job, with the badge. But this was something they had brought on themselves.

On the other side of the street, in the projects on Houston Street near the FDR Drive, McCarthy had his lookouts hiding in a Puerto Rican guy's apartment and his snipers up on the roof. He had a camera crew up there, too. With a telescopic lens they practically could have produced a documentary of Tony handing over his pay off. The bad guys were under the impression that Tony was just as crooked as they were.

But as the skinny second hand on McCarthy's watch kept ticking past the fat twelve, nothing was happening. Not yet. Tony and the other man were feeling out each other, making simpleminded wiseguy small talk, and there wasn't a thing that he could do, except wait. And worry.

The only thing today that had given McCarthy any cause for concern had been the hot dog guy. He had never seen this particular hot dog guy on this particular block of Houston Street before. But today of all days, he had been looking right at him— across the street. That was enough. His antennae went straight up like a warrior ant's.

Then there was the guy on the bench.

Outside the projects on Houston Street a white guy was sitting on a bench. He didn't belong there either.

Put those two things together and McCarthy was glad that he'd brought the shotgun.

So now he knew the bad guys had their own backup in the hot dog truck and on the bench; his team could handle that. He had made the bad guys and that was all that counted.

As he continued to listen on the Kel receiver while Tony the V got even more chummy with his wiseguy friend, McCarthy felt the reassuring weight of the twelve-gauge against his knees. A shotgun would get anybody's attention.

Then he glanced around outside again, through his car window, to make sure that his people were where they should be.

Across the street, the hot dog guy was leaning out of his truck now to hand a wrapped bun and soda to some kid. The man on the bench was pretending to read a newspaper. McCarthy just wanted it to be over.

2 : 1 0 P . M .

Nothing would go wrong.

Just make the payoff and get it over with.

Sinbad was two minutes away from happening, no more.

Just let the suspects think their extortion plan was working. Nothing fancy. Tony could pull that off in his sleep.

But as he checked the rearview mirror again, McCarthy could make out that Tony was looking sharp, very sharp. More composed now. Maybe that hitch in Tony's voice had only been his own overactive imagination. Maybe.

The two of them—Tony and Bobby, the hood who had moved in the front seat beside him—were still talking.

As the conversation came across on the Kel, it now appeared that these punks wanted Tony to go into business with *them*. Bobby was apparently feeling him out on it.

None of this was in the script that McCarthy had imagined. All at once they were hitting Tony with a set of complications that no one on the team had anticipated.

[239]

McCarthy smiled. It seemed like Tony the V had been playing his role *too* well. Now the extortion crew thought he might be better connected than they were.

The words were cryptic, but as McCarthy listened, Bobby kept referring to a "controllership" the crew was about to offer Tony—they wanted Tony to become a kind of bagman for them, not just shelling out protection money for himself, but also collecting from the other whorehouse owners for them.

He immediately saw this as both an opportunity and a danger. They were enticing Tony to go even deeper undercover, but that would really push the chance of Tony's being found out.

Still, there was no good reason to think that the payoff wouldn't go smoothly. No matter what happened, Tony Vitaliano was not going to panic. McCarthy was counting on that.

These guys were slick, give them that; considerably above average; but McCarthy knew that his team was slicker.

This was it. It was coming up fast now.

What should he do? Let Tony play it out or not? Make the payoff and then follow them back to Brooklyn and grab them now?

Once again, he watched through the rearview mirror as Tony appeared to reach into his pocket for the money envelope, but it was taking him an awful long time.

Just then, McCarthy detected an alarming, erratic movement out of the corner of his eye. It looked as though the rapid succession of events was about to make his mind up for him.

Something was going wrong.

Another man, whom none of the backups had spotted, was squeezing into the front seat beside Tony on the other side— they had him between them now.

Where had this second guy come from?

He could hear the wariness in Tony's voice as it came through on the Kel, as he asked about this third party.

Vitaliano: Who's this?
Bobby: That's my man; let him in.

Vitaliano: What's going on?
Bobby: Don't move till I tell you to.

There was a very brief struggle. McCarthy could see Tony reaching for his own gun; from out of nowhere another gun was suddenly being pushed into the cop's temple, and Tony was being forced to surrender his weapon. Then he could make out—at least he thought he could see this—that they were putting some kind of glasses covered with black tape over Tony's eyes.

Bobby: Don't make me use the gun.
Vitaliano: All right.
Bobby: Put your hands where I can see them.
Vitaliano: Where we going?
Bobby: We're going to see the top man; he wants to see you.

Then there was silence.

They were snatching Tony. God only knew why, but the bad guys were kidnapping Tony, kidnapping a cop.
But did they really know that he was a cop?
Then McCarthy heard the words on the Kel receiver that he hoped he would never hear. It was Tony's gravel-pit voice, his cement-syrup delivery.
"No need to pull a gun over this, Bobby...no need to pull a gun over this...."
He said it twice.
That was Tony's prearranged abort signal. As soon as the backup team heard that sentence on the Kel, they were supposed to come charging in like the 7th Cavalry and "recover" Vitaliano because it meant that the deal had disintegrated, there was no turning back and Tony thought that he would be killed.
Then he said it again. He was pleading with his backups to come in and get him the hell out.

[241]

"Bobby, there's no reason to pull your piece on me, we're friends, right?"

McCarthy was halfway out of his seat in the car, ready to blast the shotgun into action when Tony's Thunderbird, driven by the second man who had gotten in beside him, jerked away from the curb on Houston Street, digging ugly black welts into the asphalt as it sped away.

McCarthy looked up at the thickening traffic and felt sick. Sinbad was getting away from him now—hurtling like an out-of-control projectile under its own deadly momentum, a runaway torpedo. Somewhere, somehow, Mother had fucked up.

They were less than a block away from a single-lane entrance to the FDR expressway and that's exactly where the punks who had taken Tony were headed. From there, they could go anywhere in New York, anywhere on the entire East Coast. It connected with every major highway that cut through the city.

McCarthy quickly slid back in his seat behind the wheel, put the shotgun aside and jumped on his own ignition. He knew that his other backup cars would be doing the same thing.

But just before he had a chance to pull up behind the Thunderbird, a second car that belonged to the extortion crew, a crash car, a beat-up yellow Chevy, raced in front of him, cutting off McCarthy and the backups. The kidnappers had obviously been holding this one in reserve.

As Tony's brown T-bird jetted into the merging traffic on FDR, the Chevy crash car stopped dead on the entrance lane, blocking the cops and everything else behind it.

The two guys in that second car kept looking around for a tail.

All the other backups were waiting, helpless, looking to see what McCarthy was going to try next. But it appeared as though they had outwitted him this time. They couldn't even risk using the police radio because they knew from past experience that the extortion gang Tony had been infiltrating kept police band radios in their cars. All they had to do was pick up one transmission and they would know for dead certain that Tony was an undercover cop.

And Tony would be dead.

After months and months of careful, exhausting preparation, Sinbad was coming apart and Tony was in trouble; one of Mother's children was in trouble.

The yellow Chevy waited, blocking the on-ramp through one full minute, two, until they were sure that the T-bird had vanished into the rush-hour traffic.

They looked on helplessly as first the Thunderbird, then the yellow Chevy eased into separate lanes and merged with all the other FDR commuters, not one of whom was even remotely aware of what had just happened.

Tony Vitaliano was gone. For the first time in the history of the New York City Police Department, an on-duty undercover cop had been kidnapped. And it was all Bill McCarthy's fault. He was Mother; he was the control; he was the sergeant in charge. Nothing in McCarthy's long career as a cop had prepared him for this.

In his mind's eye all he could see was the empty space beside Tony Vitaliano's wife and little boy—the space where Tony should have stood.

The worst day of Bill McCarthy's life had just begun.

TWENTY-SEVEN

**When the sirens are going and the lights are on, that's
the *Race*. The car is revving and your body's revving;
your mind is racing; you're thinking about what you're
gonna do and how you're gonna do it when you get
there. And it all happens at once.**

MOTHER'S MAXIM

2:15 P.M.

HOUSTON STREET

McCarthy was praying that at least one of the five backup cars
that had taken off after Tony would be able to bolt ahead of
the rest, and cut off the kidnap car at the next expressway exit.
That was their best shot. But it wouldn't be easy. It would have
to be done inconspicuously—and quickly—because as soon as
the kidnappers realized that they were being tailed, one of their
first impulses might be to kill Tony right there in the front seat,
just for the hell of it, just to eliminate a potential witness. A
tail-car would almost certainly tip them off that Tony was a
cop.

The most maddening thing of all was that, for a time at least,
as long as the interference from traffic and expressway over-
passes didn't prevent it, McCarthy could still pick up the conversation that Tony had been secretly taping on the Kel
transmitter. And what he heard told him that they were definitely looking for a tail—even though they still seemed to be

[244]

buying Tony's cover story. As he listened, they were toying with Tony, making vague threats, trying to sound ominous. And, as anyone in his position would, poor Tony was losing it, losing it badly. He was begging to be let out of the car and those bastards were loving every sadistic minute of it.

It was all a strangely unaccustomed role for McCarthy, a passive role. Like most cops, he was a man of movement, of doing, of getting up and making things happen. But that was beyond his control now. All he could do was curse and agonize and monitor the situation, as it developed, from a distance. Every other active option had suddenly been superseded as the events snatched decision-making away from him.

Still, the rest of his Vice team was waiting for McCarthy to do something, to try something, to order their next move. Oddly, not one of them had emerged from his hiding place or from behind the wheel of his car—the five pursuit vehicles were already lost in the East River Drive traffic and the rest of them were frozen. Part of it was instinctive cop caution—the kidnappers might have left a lookout of their own behind at the intersection where it had all gone down on Houston Street, just in case. But another part of it was pure shock, a kind of momentary paralysis.

2 : 20 P.M.

EAST RIVER DRIVE

The five pursuit cars were still enforcing radio silence to avoid being detected by the kidnappers. The only way they could communicate with each other was through visual sightings and that was practically impossible—the afternoon light was already fading and the volume of traffic was a classic New York crush.

The cop who was having the greatest success sticking with the tail was Bernie Bracken, a veteran Vice cop who was as old country as Irish stew. When Bracken became excited—and his heart was practically retching up out of his throat as he weaved through the cars and trucks and station wagons—you could hardly understand what he was saying for the thickness of his

[245]

County Tyrone brogue. The other cops used to get on the radio and imitate him, hee-hawing like donkeys. Then Bracken would become even more uncontrollable as he got increasingly pissed off and the result was that you could understand him even less. Which was just about where he was now. His favorite comeback was, "I'll kick your fooking arse."

And Bernie Bracken was the only guy McCarthy still had on the trail. He sped along as far as the tollbooth at the Brooklyn Battery tunnel and then had to brake *hard*.

It looked like the whole world was moving in slow motion. Bracken was talking to himself, cursing in a lilting torrent of Gaelic and Brooklynese, "fooking" every car in sight. But he couldn't make the car move any faster.

Tony's Thunderbird was no more than two lengths ahead. One tollbooth lane over. Bracken could make out that he looked okay—except that he seemed to be wearing glasses of some kind, glasses whose lenses were covered by black tape. He sat there stiff, not looking around or from side to side, just like a prisoner.

Bracken kept inching his car up, almost bumping the driver in front of him. He considered jumping out and rushing them, with his own pistol drawn, but that would have really only accomplished one of two things: It would either have gotten Tony killed on the spot or killed on the other side of the bridge, while Bracken stood there, like a chump, as they drove away.

And then, with one abrupt pedal-pull on the ignition, the flash car was gone, through the tollbooth, and Bracken's chance to make any decision had vanished.

Seconds later, Bracken accelerated and didn't even bother to hand the toll taker any money. He left the startled man standing there, threatening to call the cops. But as soon as Bracken pulled out of the toll plaza, he realized that he had lost sight of the Thunderbird. Traffic had thinned out on the other side and the men holding Tony captive had taken advantage of it. There was a sloping rise in the contour of the road, peaking like a pregnant woman's belly.

The excited Irishman looked from left to right, back and

forth. He had to make a quick decision—he could either stay on the highway, continuing up the steep incline, or he could make a right and pull off onto a service road. Going straight would lead to a choice of the Prospect Expressway, or the Belt Parkway.

Bracken almost broke radio silence—he had his hand on the microphone. Then he remembered that this crew had monitored police calls on some of their previous jobs. He decided not to risk it.

Going with his gut, Bernie Bracken wheeled his car straight up the hill. The Prospect Expressway. But his gut was wrong. That's where they lost Vitaliano.

2:25 P.M.

HOUSTON STREET

McCarthy had to get to a telephone to tell somebody what had just happened. There was no page in the *NYPD Patrol Guide*—for what had just transpired, for losing an undercover officer to kidnappers, but he had been a cop long enough to realize that in addition to recovering Tony, there was one more overriding consideration: He had to let the Building One, Police Plaza, know what was going on.

The "building" was One Police Plaza, the imposing fourteen-story brick and concrete citadel in Lower Manhattan that was the hallowed command post for the New York City Police Department.

In McCarthy's world, all energy flowed downward—from the police commissioner's office on the fourteenth floor, under the reinforced steel helicopter landing pad.

The electrical currents that surged forth from that hyper-charged, sputtering, and sizzling nerve center then passed through the nearby offices of the NYPD's four-star chief inspector (now the chief of department) the effective boss of the blue army, then circulated outward through the five super-chiefs: Detectives, Organized Crime Control, Patrol, Inspectional Services, and Personnel.

[247]

From there, the hot charges would be transferred to all seventy-five precincts and five boroughs and thirty thousand assorted cops, quasi cops, cop-fuckers (who differed not at all from star-fuckers), and support minions.

But only the police commissioner could throw the switch that would activate all or part of that complicated circuitry. Cops like McCarthy, mavericks who preferred to free-lance on their own, pursuing private initiatives, were both rare and despised. They actually looked for trouble, and the people who manned the building—desk cops who had not been on the street in decades, paper-pushers in Perry Como sweaters who carried monogrammed coffee mugs from office to office, chatting—had enough problems dealing with all the unsolicited trouble that came walking through the door. A very special ruthlessness was reserved for the troublemakers like McCarthy.

All this was in McCarthy's mind as he drove along Houston Street and searched for a telephone—a telephone that worked. In New York. At dusk. In a lousy neighborhood.

He tried three of them, racing to each one, frantically, from corner to corner, from broken public telephone to broken public telephone.

The first one had no receiver; the second one had a receiver, but someone had ripped off the earpiece. The third one was intact but he couldn't get a dial tone.

He had to drive all the way through the Lower East Side before he finally realized what he should have done all along.

He spied a pizza parlor across the street; a guy in a dirty white shirt and pants and apron was standing in the window, writing down an order.

McCarthy parked his car up on the pavement, left the ignition running, ran into the store and pulled the telephone out of the hands of the terrified pizza man.

He wasn't trying to make friends at that moment and he just didn't care. "Don't argue with me on this," he barked at the pizza man. "I'm a cop, this is an emergency, and if you say one word you're under arrest."

The pizza man looked at McCarthy, immediately surrendered

the telephone, backed away and, as he had been instructed, did not open his mouth. Six or seven customers suddenly got up and left.

McCarthy didn't even know whom he should be talking to at headquarters, in the building, as he dialed an emergency number and babbled what had just happened, pumping, trying to sound calm, coherent, but missing the mark by a mile.

He told them that it had gone bad and that Tony had been kidnapped.

Immediately, the message was passed from a lieutenant to a captain to an inspector, and on to a second inspector, each of whom was stricken by a sense of tremendous personal dread as soon as he heard the bad news. They shared one immediate concern: not for Vitaliano's life, for even as they listened, they were writing him off as a dead man, but for their own careers. Could any of this possibly be blamed on them? Could the simple act of answering the telephone somehow involve them in a loser like this? And everyone who heard it searched desperately for someone else, preferably someone more senior or powerful than they, to dump it on.

They might not have had any idea who Tony was or what Sinbad meant or how high up it went, or what their personal exposure on the damn thing might be; but they did know that this was as bad as it could get. Life and death.

McCarthy had no idea how wild-eyed he looked, how scarily out of control. But as he tried to compose himself, as he handed the telephone back to the pizza man, he could see it in the guy's frightened eyes.

"Thank you," he said in a hollow voice. Then he started to leave.

The pizza man backed away again and just left the telephone receiver dangling by the cord, bouncing off the counter.

Outside, McCarthy pointed his car toward Brooklyn.

McCarthy's first time being scared—really scared—had happened during one of his first fights as a cop. Against a woman.

He could remember being on top of the car, struggling with a woman who was trying to stab him. He was down and she was on top, and as he managed to grab at her knife, he deflected the blade. She was turning it, twisting the shiny pearl handle with everything she had. Then, suddenly, the handle just broke off and hit him on the cheek, drawing blood.

And when he saw a few drops of his own blood running down bright red on his blue uniform shirt—*his blood*—McCarthy realized that she might win. *That bitch might win.*

Up until that moment, he didn't believe that a woman could ever kill him, that anybody could kill him.

He stayed scared for the rest of that day and for the next. And McCarthy never forgot that single, enervating moment—that dramatic glimpse of his own mortality. That was the first time he knew what it meant to be a cop. And as soon as it had happened, he told himself that he didn't want to be one.

McCarthy could imagine how scared his friend must be. He'd seen it, felt it, smelled it like the summer sweat that stays with you all day. It was that special kind of cop's fear that would start out when you went to bed at night and still be there when you woke up the next morning, and just because you had lived through it once didn't mean that it would be any less terrifying the next time.

2:35 P.M.

BROOKLYN

Where was Tony now? This was McCarthy's call, his crime.

Reflex had taken him to Brooklyn. But now he needed more, he needed to think.

It was time to take a chance with the radio. Reluctantly, he reached for it.

He broadcasted one order to the five backup cars: "Go to Brooklyn. You gotta pick them up."

The first thing he had to do was establish his frequency on the Kel receiver. That was just in case other people with that frequency, in other parts of Brooklyn—not his people, of course, but other cops, other units—might be able to pick up the conversation that was going on in Tony's car. By that time, he was way out of range.

Almost as soon as the car had crossed the bridge into Brooklyn, McCarthy was intercepted by Larry Hepburn, the Vice captain.

Hepburn was already on the Brooklyn side of the water when McCarthy pulled up. He was in no mood to be slowed down or lectured. All he could think about as the captain approached was the time, a few months before, when Hepburn had accidentally left a tube of toothpaste in his back pocket, sat down on it, never noticed it, and then walked around for the rest of that day with a fragrant peppermint smear all over his ass.

"Any word yet?" Hepburn asked. He wasn't formal or threatening and didn't seem about to pull any of the bullshit that most commanders could be expected to invoke at a time like this. McCarthy was relieved. Flash Gordon's crimson, mournful face and square features were set in a concerned frown that had suddenly been drained of its tint, like a color key that had malfunctioned somewhere deep inside. Beyond that, it was impossible to read him, just like always. It was the inscrutability of the gifted. There was already an unlighted pipe in his hand.

"The Building's in on it now," Hepburn said. "They have all the help on the way that they can send."

McCarthy, imagining the mad rush that would now be under way at One Police Plaza to get out from under any responsibility that might filter down over Tony, somehow doubted that. But he kept his mouth shut. For a change.

"This whole thing started back when you took me to that after-hours club," Hepburn said forthrightly, referring to the night, many months before, when McCarthy's team had made the first important connection that would eventually allow them to setup Operation Sinbad. All for Hepburn's benefit. "I feel responsible."

McCarthy hadn't heard admissions like that very often. Especially from a superior officer. Hepburn was a ferocious handball player, a tremendous competitor whom he had admired on the court. He was now seeing that toughness outside the gym for the very first time.

"You don't feel as bad as I do," McCarthy told him. "This is my play; my mistake."

At this point, they were no longer playing detective. McCarthy was no expert on kidnapping. Neither was Hepburn. But at least he was right there with them. Armed.

"I'm going to defer to you on this one," Hepburn said. "Sinbad's been your baby. You make the moves. Do whatever you have to do. I'm going over to the Seven-one precinct, get it set up, lay in some phone lines. It's not that far from Gagliano's house."

At least Flash knew his way around Brooklyn, McCarthy thought.

"You meet me over there," Hepburn said. "I can imagine where you're headed."

TWENTY-EIGHT

You went out on the street every day and every day the *Danger* would be there like a whore, waiting, tempting. But you knew you couldn't get enough of it, no matter what your brain said. And the crazy part was, it didn't mean a damn thing.

MOTHER'S MAXIM

■

2:45 P.M.

FLATBUSH

The Gaglianos lived on a street of dilapidated attached houses, row houses, in the worst neighborhood in Flatbush, not far from Brighton Beach. Tiny, weed-rotted gardens in the front, rusted car bodies out back; kids with bad attitudes on the corners. Their street was canopied by the kind of old, half-sick Dutch elms that wearily dipped their leaves right down alongside the curbs.

As soon as McCarthy parked, he realized that he had gotten there ahead of the cops from Brooklyn South, Public Morals, who he hoped were on their way. He knew that Hepburn probably was right—the Building would have to be turning up the heat on this one by now. A cop-killing would be bad enough, but sooner or later, damage control would have to click on to minimize the embarrassment. New York City, sentimental slob of the Western World, despite its callous exterior, absolutely hated to lose a young cop with a pretty wife and a

[253]

little kid. The NYPD was not unmindful of this fact.

On his way over, McCarthy had noticed an unusually high level of helicopter traffic that seemed to be headed out from Manhattan. They were already flying search patterns for Tony's Thunderbird.

He'd visited the Gaglianos' street before, on a couple nights he'd practically tucked them into bed after he'd followed them home. But he had never been inside, had never made a move against them because the thinking behind Sinbad had called for a cat-and-mouse game of waiting out the Gaglianos and gambling that they would lead to bigger and better rodents. That had never worked out quite the way it was supposed to because the brothers and Tommy Mendino had proven to be far too violent, far too vicious, to be allowed to run loose all over the city. Actually, that had largely been the reasoning behind McCarthy's plan to take them down back on Houston Street.

There was still no sign of the brothers as he crossed the street.

Mama Gagliano was past eighty years old, a snapping turtle of a woman in a floral-print housedress. She looked at least one hundred. Her hair was the color of a soiled mattress and her expression was dominated by two small, plucking eyes. The way she flew across the room at McCarthy he could see how her sons had turned out to be the upstanding citizens and stickup psychos that they were.

She was mad and she had a right to be. McCarthy had gotten into her living room by shouldering the front door with one enormous *crash* and then pounding away until he had splintered the doorjamb. That was police work the old-fashioned way: headfirst.

She only spoke Italian and the only phrases that McCarthy could pick up were the sort of multisyllabic, ripely flowing curses that you most often heard thundering down from the upper decks at Giants games that had gotten out of hand. He had to remind himself to stay as calm as possible and refrain from dropping the old bitch on the spot.

While she was yelling at him, he kept screaming, "Tony,

Tony," as he ran through the house. They went on like that for several minutes, he in the lead, she following, trooping from room to room, upstairs and downstairs, cursing each other.

He didn't think for a moment that they had Tony anywhere in the house—or that anybody was there, either, for that matter—but he didn't know what else to do. So he kept it up: "Tony, Tony."

Finally, Mama Gagliano got tired. Slobbering and spitting at him, she retreated upstairs and he just left her alone. That didn't make him feel any better. Scaring eighty-year-old grandmothers half to death wasn't his favorite part of the job. But neither was losing cops.

Her absence gave him a clear shot at the house and he took advantage of it. There would be time to pore over clues later; now all he wanted to do was soak up the feeling of the Gaglianos that permeated the place. Maybe then he would be able to think like they did.

The interior of the house looked a lot more like an animal den than like an air-light in Brooklyn. Not much furniture and an almost empty kitchen.

Apparently, they spent most of their time in the basement—and quite a place it was. They had it set up like a bunker, with boarded-over ground-floor windows and what appeared to be a junkyard for weapons. There were cannibalized parts of rifles and pistols all over the place, firing mechanisms and greasy stocks, dozens of assorted sizes and shapes of guns bows and quivers of steel-tipped arrows and, incongruously, jars and jars of pennies, mayonnaise jars full of pennies. They were great savers, the brothers.

The basement was like their clubhouse. Only instead of baseball cards, they collected weapons. The only thing of any real value that he saw was a list of the whorehouses they had hit for shakedowns and a yellowed copy of *Screw* with the massage parlors and escort services they evidently intended to hit circled in red. Unfortunately, there wasn't anything there that he didn't already know or at least suspect. No indication at all of where they might be holding Tony.

[255]

McCarthy knew that the first thing he had to do was put people on the house—and keep the old lady off the telephone. That's when he remembered about her. Abruptly, he stopped what he was doing and ran back upstairs.

Brooklyn South, Public Morals, had never been friends of McCarthy's. They were archrivals. They boosted pinches and manpower from each other. Forget about professional courtesy—even in an emergency, he could not anticipate how they would respond. Maybe he would get lucky and they really would put out for him, or maybe not. It was like rolling the dice. But he did know, to his regret, that at crunch-time, all that "brother officer" crap usually didn't amount to squat. If the occasion of Tony Vitaliano's being snatched represented an opportunity for someone in blue, someone who hated McCarthy, to stick it to him, they would. That was the NYPD.

However, McCarthy did have one high card that wasn't showing that day. By coincidence, he had one of the most dependable cops he had ever met. John Gorman, a member of his Vice team, at Brooklyn South, Public Morals that day, assisting them on an unrelated case. They would be afraid to try any funny business in front of Gorman, who was known to put other cops on their backsides without too much provocation.

Gorman would also be able to tell all the Brooklyn cops what Tony looked like, because McCarthy was afraid that if there was a shootout Tony would get it first.

He had called Gorman from the Gaglianos' house—Gorman already knew what had happened—and had stayed there until Gorman showed up with a small army of Brooklyn cops. He left them sitting on the place, spread out all around the neighborhood.

There were still three or four more places to check, about ten blocks apart. On the way over, he kept crisscrossing the narrow, dirty streets of Flatbush, searching for Tony's Thunderbird. But the only thing he saw was more helicopters. That had to be the building kicking in. After all that, he decided the best thing he could do would be to head over to the 7-1 and find Larry Hepburn.

Nobody had picked up any transmission from Tony's car, but the wheels were beginning to grind. McCarthy had no way of knowing its full dimension, but a massive recovery plan was already in the works. Hepburn had understated it eloquently when he told him that "the Building's in on it now."

Methodically, with the quasi-military sense of blunt purpose so typical of the New York Police Department, seven thousand cops were being committed to the search for Tony Vitaliano, even as Bill McCarthy was struggling not to give up hope.

With the possible exception of the almost year-long dragnet for the son of Sam serial killer, in which every cop in the city of New York had, at least theoretically and temporarily, been assigned to the case, this was to become the biggest, most intense manhunt ever in New York criminal history. From time to time, the Big Apple press would elevate other glitzy or heartrending cases to a celebrity status, but in terms of a real investment of manpower, equipment, both in the air and on the ground, and especially in terms of departmental focus and concentration, the Vitaliano snatch-and-grab would prove to be the grand-daddy. Despite McCarthy's initial skepticism, the NYPD would end up pulling out all the stops and adopting a virtual scorched-earth strategy to retrieve one of their own and to make the people who had grabbed him pay for it.

Those helicopters that kept buzzing Brooklyn were manned by cops with receivers that were homed in on the hardware in Vitaliano's car and on his person. They were trying to pick up any ghost of a reception off his transmitter. Or spot the car. Or both. Many of the cops they sent up in the skies over New York vomited all over themselves, or all over the pilots, because the Perry Como sweaters in the build-ing who were frantically trying to make the best out of a hor-rid situation had just pulled guys out of sector cars and off the streets. None of them had received as much as five sec-

[257]

onds of training to go up in a helicopter and most of those guys were terrified of heights.

But it didn't matter. One Police Plaza was on fire. Even though McCarthy and the other cops in Brooklyn could not see it, the whole building was lighting up. It started slowly, like a serpentine fuse that was just beginning to hiss, then it picked up speed and finally exploded in a cacophony of action and reaction and war-status activity. And the final dark resolution of the ill-fated Operation Sinbad was under way.

Functioning in a parallel dimension, again far removed from the men in the field, from the real cops, an eruption of another nature was also taking place. It was a fire storm of press activity in the city rooms of newspapers, in the soundless studios of isolated radio personalities, and on the stiflingly hot sound stages of New York television. A full-bore media event was in the making.

A COP HAD BEEN KIDNAPPED!

IN NEW YORK.

IN TIME FOR THE SIX O'CLOCK NEWS.

The reporters, at least enough of them, had police band radios too, scanners. Just like the bad guys.

They were conversant enough with police codes and jargon, not to mention being friendly with half the people who worked at One Police Plaza, to know that *something* was up.

Quickly, they had it confirmed. A cop had been kidnapped; but they had no idea who or why or what the circumstances were. The lid on the details was the tightest that any of the reporters had ever encountered. There was something ominous about it all. But by then, even the cops were violating their own broadcast frequencies, talking about it among themselves. Sooner or later, the reporters knew that they would find out. They called around and warned their rewrite desks and assignment editors and news directors to stand by. Something big, something dramatic, was coming their way, rumbling like a runaway coal car.

But what? Where?

If it bleeds it leads—that was the philosophy directing them all.

For their part, the cops weren't worrying anymore about the Gaglianos or anybody else overhearing them. They were beyond all that now.

3:15 P.M.

7-1 PRECINCT, EMPIRE BOULEVARD, BROOKLYN

The 7-1 precinct was the only secure building that was reasonably close to the Gagliano's house in Flatbush. The 7-1 was an "A" house, a shit-hole, in the parlance of cops like McCarthy, an action station house where the police arrested real criminals for real crimes almost all the time. There were worse places, to be sure, certainly in Harlem or Bed-Sty, but the 7-1 was bad enough.

McCarthy parked on the pavement outside; all the normal parking places had already been taken. That, in itself, was unusual. It meant there were people inside, presumably doing things. It told McCarthy that Flash Gordon had already accomplished something besides sitting around and wringing his hands.

The borough commander of Brooklyn at that time had a reputation for being a hardcase professional cop. He was big, tall, and mean. McCarthy expected the worst from him. He was the kind of a boss who was so deeply into the macho cop mythology that unless your balls clanged when you walked past him, he looked down on you.

Naturally, he was the first person McCarthy ran into.

The borough commander stopped him halfway up the staircase to the detectives' room upstairs. He practically pinned him against the slime-green wall, chest to chest. McCarthy let out a deep breath.

"Who's in charge of you," he snapped to McCarthy. It had to take something very big, very troublesome, to pull him out

[259]

from behind his desk and down to a shit-hole like the 7-1. And McCarthy was acutely aware of the fact that he was the sole cause of the borough commander's sudden discomfort.

McCarthy told him Captain Hepburn, who was upstairs, he guessed.

The borough commander, in uniform by choice, bulky as a blue armored personnel carrier, brushed past him. The man's patent leather police shoes were the size of pontoons.

McCarthy followed him up.

He located Flash Gordon, seated at a borrowed desk, his ear plugged into a phone receiver. There was a white fog of pipe and cigar smoke eerily ringing his head like some haunting aura. Flash was smoking both. Ash had collected on the tops of his hands, on his clothes and all around the desk where he leaned his elbows. He never looked up from his business as the borough commander bore down on him. He could have been Sherlock Holmes, not of 221B Baker Street, but of the Bronx.

"Captain, I don't know what you're doing," the borough commander said. "I don't know anything about your case, but you got my desk. You got any thing you need. I'll do whatever you tell me to do."

And then he left. It was the damnedest thing that McCarthy had ever seen.

Flash Gordon had bluffed him.

"What have we got?" the captain asked.

"Gorman's sitting on the house. Nothing there, though. Just guns in the cellar."

Hepburn frowned when he heard that.

There were thirty-seven locations where the six people definitely associated with the gang had been arrested on previous occasions. Most of them were in Brooklyn.

The best plan would have been to send a couple of detectives to every one of the thirty-seven locations. Any address that had ever appeared on a "yellow sheet," an arrest record, should have been covered.

McCarthy started to spill this out to Hepburn. Somebody

would have to go get the thirty-seven addresses. And phone numbers.

"I got them." Hepburn cut him off. "The phone numbers, too. And I'm placing calls to the cops we want to cover each spot."

"How the hell did you do that?" McCarthy asked.

Flash did what horses do when they paw the ground nervously. Except he was still seated at his borrowed desk. "Well, see...I can do this thing...with numbers. Like a trick."

"Do you mean you memorized them all? You don't even have to write them down?" McCarthy was openly in awe.

"Yeah, it's like that. But I don't remember them, exactly. I just...ah...I *see* them."

"You're talking like seventy, a hundred numbers; thirty-seven locations, Captain."

"Ninety-seven combinations, I think, give or take."

"Ninety-seven..." McCarthy slowly repeated.

He stared at the desk in front of Flash. Not so much as a scrap of paper. Instant recall. Like an idiot savant outcumputing a computer. The genius of Larry Hepburn was coming through.

No one in Vice had known this about him. Hepburn was sitting there, in the eye of the Vitaliano nightmare, handling about twelve different things at once. Not missing a beat. Flash was on. Going ninety miles an hour. And the crazy part was, Flash didn't even realize he was doing it.

McCarthy put out his hands in a gesture of backing off. He wasn't about to screw around with a genius at work.

This was going to be another waiting time and he hated that. But the best place for him was right here, where they had slammed together a command post of sorts, where he could get any information they received from any one of the teams that was fanning out all over Brooklyn, tearing it apart, he imagined.

Then, McCarthy took in his first full look at the room and all the activity therein. There were cops everywhere, in and out of uniform, most on the telephones, a few tracing locations and intersections on a big board that was covered by a map of Brooklyn, placing pushpins where they belonged. Nearly everybody was sweating in shoulder holsters and wrinkled ties pulled down from their necks. The whole place stinking of sweat and dyspeptic dispositions. As he glanced from cop to cop, from mask of concentration to mask of concentration, there seemed to be a palpable chemical synthesis taking place, a chain reaction of fused elemental matter as every brain in the room set itself to the business at hand.

Hepburn read him. "Catch your breath," he said. "Drink some coffee. The first good lead we get you can go out again. There's a time to race around and there's a time to sit." The Captain pushed a steaming mug in his direction. "So sit."

And McCarthy sat and thought about how it had all started, about how the whole damn thing had begun, how his whole police career, how Sinbad, had come to this—to waiting in a smelly, smoke-filled, windowless hellhole of a room in the 7-1 in Brooklyn, wondering if he had somehow managed to get his best friend killed.

As he took the mug of coffee from Hepburn, his muscles relaxed for the first time in hours. He tried lifting the hot liquid to his lips, but as he did so, he spilled two, three, four drops and then an ugly splash of the strong, dark coffee. McCarthy couldn't make his hands stop shaking.

TWENTY-NINE

Cops have a saying: "Jacks are better for openers," As in blackjacks. *Brutality* doesn't have much meaning for cops. But there are informal rules. You should stop kicking a man once he's no longer in a position to hurt you. But I'm not saying cops always observe that rule.

MOTHER'S MAXIM

4:00 P.M.

7-1 PRECINCT, EMPIRE BOULEVARD, BROOKLYN

Some of the longest hours of Bill McCarthy's life were spent that afternoon in the makeshift command post on the second floor of the Empire Boulevard police station.

He and Captain Hepburn worked ceaselessly to coordinate the recovery efforts. Someone had to be in a position to direct the efforts of those 7,500 policemen who had been mobilized, plus the helicopters and radio cars and off-duty cops who had joined in on their own.

That task fell to them and they worked at it as they had never before worked at anything in their police careers.

At that point, almost everything was riding on the success of the teams that Hepburn had assigned to search the thirty-seven previous locations where members of the Gagliano-Mendino crew, or their associates, had been arrested.

Every available member of McCarthy's Vice team hit the streets of Brooklyn, too, backing up the rescuers or searching themselves.

Calls were constantly coming in to both McCarthy and Larry Hepburn—all of them merely reports to update the futility of the mission thus far. None of the Gaglianos had surfaced.

The long afternoon was quickly running into dusk and nightfall. Even the aerial coverage provided by the police helicopters would soon become almost useless.

Time had already run out on the perilous Operation Sinbad. Now it seemed to be running out on Tony Vitaliano as well.

McCarthy and Hepburn were too busy even to talk to each other, fielding calls and questions from anxious cops. But there was nothing to say, anyway.

At one point, Hepburn pushed his chair away from his desk, stuffed the bowl of his pipe full of tobacco and, striking a wooden match against the sole of his shoe, puffed it into life. He looked over at McCarthy and considered reassuring him again that it wasn't his fault—it wasn't anybody's fault—but he decided not to. There would be plenty of time for that later, provided that later did come.

McCarthy attempted to keep his mind clear. At least the task at hand was consuming; it didn't permit much time to dwell on his searing sense of guilt and responsibility.

Messages had come in that Millie had tried several times to call him from home; but McCarthy hadn't taken her calls. He'd just directed one of his men to assure her that he was safe, that no harm had come to him.

He could face admitting to the woman he loved that his inability to get to Tony in time may have already cost him his life. Millie would understand in the wise, forbearing way that she had. That wasn't the problem. Ever facing himself again in the mirror would be the problem.

It appeared that time was passing with a surreal slowness in their command post; actually, the opposite was true. By the time the tightness in McCarthy's own body forced him to get up and stretch and work out the slowly building tension, it was already past five o'clock.

Once he was on his feet, he made up his mind not to sit down again. There was now nothing left for him to do at Empire Boulevard. Somebody else could help the captain work the phones. The rescue teams were in motion, Hepburn had settled into his usual cerebral control.

McCarthy was going back on the street. He knew that no matter what he was not coming in again until he had either found Tony or the Gaglianos. He had to put an end to it that night.

Just out of habit, he had carried his shotgun into the station with him. Very deliberately, McCarthy picked it up.

Hepburn had just taken a call. There was no need to interrupt him. With the big gun swung carefully against his shoulder, McCarthy motioned to his friend that he was leaving. Hepburn half-rose out of his chair, his ear still plugged into the phone receiver.

"Stay there," McCarthy said, waving him off. "I can't wait around here any longer. Later."

But something McCarthy was unaware of was happening. Hepburn put a firm grip on his sergeant's forearm. Flash wasn't letting go.

That stopped McCarthy.

"They just grabbed three of them," Hepburn was barely able to shout out. He couldn't suppress the excitement in his voice; where his cheeks had been ashen, they now washed crimson. "This is John Gorman on the phone. He was getting ready to tell me that the Brooklyn cops spotted them driving around, when they showed up at their house. They must have stopped back to pick something up after you left.

"Gorman was waiting for them. He needs you right away."

McCarthy never even heard that last part. He was already on his way.

* * *

"Three of the Gaglianos are in custody. But no sign of Tony or crazy Tommy Mendino, who would have most likely done the job if they decided to kill Tony.

"*Where was Tony now?* That was still our top priority.

"They show up at their house and the cops jump them. John Gorman lays out one guy over the hood of his car and puts a cocked gun right in his ear. And that was how they took down the Gaglianos. That picture made the front page of every newspaper in New York.

"From three Gaglianos, they get five guns. They started questioning them before I arrived on the scene, but learned nothing. Not a word.

"I walked into the house right after that and I saw one of the brothers sitting there on the floor, squirming. Upstairs, I heard their old lady wailing away again. I'd been through that before.

"The first thing I asked was, 'Has he been tossed? Has he been searched.' They said, 'Yeah, outside. He's clean.'

"I said, 'Pull his pants down. Toss him again.'

"He had a gun down there right next to his balls. Even though he had been handcuffed with about a hundred cops looking on, this guy was still armed. They had never searched his balls; they almost never do.

"He'd been squirming around on the floor, trying to get to the gun. It was a derringer. He would have shot a cop right in that house had he gotten the chance. I know he would have.

"Now I have another concern in the back of my mind. There are dozens of Tony's friends there and they are looking for and tasting blood.

"I *know* that as soon as I leave these cops are going to start to beat the crap out of the Gaglianos. They *will* jack them up. That is a given. I'm actually a little surprised that nobody has pounded on them yet. That's probably because, as the immediate supervisor of Sinbad, I outrank everybody at the crime scene, at least for the moment. That's SOP. They must just be waiting for me to leave.

"If they figure Tony's dead—which I know they do—they

will just give it to them worse. I'm a cop; I know this. I have seen situations like this all my life. This won't merely be a case of police brutality, this will damn near be assassination.

"And, should that happen, the case against this crew will be thrown out the window somewhere along the line by some bleeding heart judge, and, quite possibly, Tony will have died in vain—if he is, in fact, a goner. Deep down, I think he is too.

"I just laid it on the line with those cops. I had to let them know I knew where they were coming from.

"Tony was my friend, this was my fuckup. I was the one who let them kidnap him. Mother was at fault all the way: If anybody was gonna beat the shit out of them, it was gonna be me. I had first call. And I was *not* gonna beat the shit out of them because I was not gonna lose this case. I was not gonna jeopardize it.

"If, at that moment, in that house, I thought that I could have saved Tony's life by beating up one of the Gaglianos, beating him to make him talk, I would have done that. Gladly. But I knew that these punks would just take the beating and still not talk. There would have been no point to it.

"I never beat up people. Never. I never saw police brutality because I wouldn't tolerate it. When three or four cops are locking one guy up and they all take a shot—that's brutality. But that day I would have broken my own rule.

"I screamed at them: 'Don't anybody touch these mother-fuckers. I'll kick *your* ass if you touch them.' I yelled this out to about thirty detectives there. 'This is my case, my partner. If anybody's touching them it's me, and if anybody takes that pleasure away from me, I'll take care of them, too. I'm telling you right now, *don't* touch them.'

"I wasn't going to touch anybody. But I had to make the cops believe that I would.

"Then, once that scene was secure, I talked to each one of the prisoners individually. I took them in a separate room, alone. No other cops.

"I said to each one: 'I know you don't know nothing about this. I know you don't know nothing about kidnapping a cop. I *know* that; but I happen to be that cop's best friend.

[267]

"'I know you don't know nothing, but hypothetically speaking, if you were me, if *your* friend had been snatched, would you worry? If you were just speculating about this, would you worry about your friend?'

"I was letting them understand that whatever they said to me now I could not come back and produce in court. This was man to man.

"Two of them said, 'Bullshit.' Nothing else. Just, 'Bullshit.'

"The third one said, 'No, I wouldn't worry about it.'

"Not one other word. We could have beaten on those guys all night long and it would not have made any difference. Other than the fact that we would have felt a whole lot better.

"What I find out next is that I have a call coming in to their house from Larry Hepburn.

"'They just located Tony's car,' he said. Then he gave me an address near Neptune Avenue, Brighton Beach.

"I take off, just run right out the door. Leave somebody holding the telephone. I'm on my way.

"But before I can even get there, less than two minutes after I get behind the wheel of my car, I hear an emergency bulletin on the radio—*Tony Vitaliano has been recovered alive.*"

THIRTY

A Police Car **is a death trap. Whatever year they**
bought it, it was the low bid. It's been driven twenty-
four hours a day by people who don't care, by cops. A
police car can kill you.

MOTHER'S MAXIM

TONY VITALIANO:

"We went in cautious that day, September 24th, 1974, very
cautious. We were prepared for it to go either way: Take them
down that afternoon or play it out and let them go back to
Brooklyn.

"The first five minutes went great. Bobby was friendly, like
always. Then we started to talk. I sensed that something had
changed; he was looking at me differently, too.

"The problem was the Murray Hill townhouse on Thirty-first
Street. I had never mentioned that place to them, never indi-
cated that I had a piece of it. But I figured that they must know
more than they were letting on. I came right out and asked
them why they had hit that place the week before. I made it
clear that it was *my* house.

"'You guys are hanging me, fucking hanging me,' were my
exact words. 'I'm your friend, but now you done damage to
me, not the other guys.'

"I was merely trying to further establish my credibility as a
pimp, as a whorehouse owner. They knew all about my interest
in Fifty-first Street. I brought up the Murray Hill brothel on

Thirty-first Street on purpose. I acted mad.

"Bobby answered: 'Babe, these people are lookin' to help you. Not hurt you.' That was his stock answer.

"He was still insisting that he was just the middleman on the shakedowns. 'If you would have told us the Murray Hill joint was yours, had leveled with us from the get-go, in other words, there would have been no beef. They would have put a red flag on Thirty-first Street, waked up their people to it. They would have gone right over it. But how did they know it was *your* joint? It could have belonged to some nincompoop.'

"I had betrayed whatever relationship I had with them. That was the message he was so intent on giving me.

"Right there I knew I was in deep trouble because I could see instantly that Bobby Gee was lying to me. They had *already* figured out that I had a piece of the Murray Hill townhouse, along with Bill, through Al Gold. They *knew* that going in— before they even robbed the place. I could see that this was really a ruse. They were toying with me, trying to see how much more information they could extract from me.

"If it was information about any additional whorehouses that I had been holding out about, that was one thing. That would have gotten me a beating for sure. But if they were probing to see if I was a cop, then that would be my death sentence. I wasn't sure which it was.

"All this had been a *test* of my loyalty to them and I had failed. I failed because, in their minds, I had been holding out about Murray Hill from the start, about Thirty-first Street.

"Bobby wanted an explanation.

"'I didn't think you guys could find out about Murray Hill, or hit it,' I told him. 'I was just tryin' to save myself paying protection on the both places.' He did not like that answer.

"Bobby then said, 'This is a powerhouse we work for, Babe. These people can find any-fuckin'-thing out. Ain't nobody gonna stop them. Unless an operation of whores is hooked up with somebody right, they are gonna take that house. You understand what I'm sayin', Tony? They don't care who they got to step on. It's theirs; they want it. They take it. Now, the problem is that we thought you wanted to be a nice fellow about the whole thing, a good fellow—not hold out on nobody. But Tony, you messed up bad about Murray Hill.'

"That was my crime; I was already guilty in their eyes. My sentence would be delivered forthwith.

"'As far as I am concerned,' Bobby told me, 'you are all right.'

"'I hope you convey this to your friends,' I said. 'I'm always one to do the right thing, ain't I?'

"Bobby looked hard at me. 'Until now,' he said, very coldly.

"At that point, Bobby Gee grabbed me around my neck with his left arm in a choke hold, and the other guy squeezed in. They reached down to the right side of my waistband and grabbed for my revolver. Then they pointed the gun at me. I didn't resist after that. Bobby said, 'Put your hands where I can see them.'

"I can only imagine what's happening outside. I assume that Bill is now aware of the fact that this has gone badly. But I have no idea what the team's immediate reaction will be.

"Of course, I want them to come in and get me the hell out of there, but I can't afford for them to come in too quickly, because I will definitely get the first bullet. As bad off as I am, I can still feel for Bill. He has to be going through all the fucking tortures of hell out there, what with his heart telling him to go one way and his head telling him to go the other.

"They put these glasses on me—taped with electrical tape. They were cheap five-and-dime sunglasses. I kept saying, 'No need to pull a gun on me'—I must have said it seven times— as the signal to Bill and the other backups to make their play. Quickly.

"But nothing happened after I said it. Then, to myself, I changed it to 'Oh, *shit*! This wasn't supposed to happen.'

"From the time Bobby Gee let the other guy in the car to the time they drove up the ramp onto the river drive, it was no more than a minute, a minute and a half.

"Bill had no chance at all to come in then. I know that Bill has always blamed himself for what happened, but with sixty, ninety seconds, at best, you just have to be realistic. Bill might be Mother, but he isn't Jesus Christ.

"As it was, they even faked me out because I thought they were going to stay off the drive, but at the last minute, they swerved sharply back onto FDR. No way our guys could have followed them with all the traffic we had that afternoon.

"During that trip they kept asking me about other addresses in Manhattan, other places they intended to hit. Just testing to see if I was connected there, too.

"I thought they would kill me then, there's great places to dump a body off the Brooklyn Battery Tunnel. I kept asking them if they were going to kill me. I believed in my heart I was going to be executed.

"Bobby said, 'We're going to see the top man. He wants to see you. Come along nicely, no problems.'

"I'm wired up now, remember. No sign of the backups. I'm blindfolded. And I knew that at some point I was going to be searched. That would be it. I said several Our Fathers and Acts of Contrition.

"Then Bobby said, 'You have a right to be scared, Tony, really you do. You thought you was so sharp.'

"'I'm so scared I gotta piss,' I told him. That would be the only chance to get rid of the Edwards tape recorder. In a toilet or in the bushes somewhere. I had to risk it.

"'Hold it in.' And he laughed at me.

"'I gotta go; I'll go in the car.'

"'That's the name of the game, Babe. Surprise, surprise, surprise. Thank God, we had that.'

"I know that I started to lose it at that point, lose control altogether, because I was sure that my fellow officers would never be able to recover me now. Not in time. Oh, I knew they would come after me, and I figured there would be a bloody shootout. Bill wouldn't rest until he had taken out whoever had killed me. But by then, what good would it do me?

"I pleaded with them. I asked them to at least get me a drink before they killed me.

[272]

"'Short ride, hold on, Babe' was all that Bobby would say.

"This was a real dilemma. They were prepared to kill me for holding out on them—*not even for being an undercover cop. Let them discover that I was a cop and that would be it, for sure.*

"But almost the second I thought that, it came up.

"'You have any company back there, Tony? You know, bulls? Cops?' He pointed the gun right at me again. 'Don't you lie to us, Tony.'

"'Bobby, you think *I'm* a cop? Is that what this is?'

"'Relax.' But Bobby wasn't relaxed either.

"'I don't have no way of knowin', Bobby. If cops was back there, they weren't *with* me. Maybe they were after me. That could be it. I'm a badass. Don't kill me now, Bobby.'

"'We're taking a ride to see the man, that's all.'

"Even with the tape covering the lens, I could still see out of the glasses because they kept slipping down on my nose. A car pulled up next to us and I could see the face of the driver—it was Bobby's brother. This was their crash car.

"My sense of direction never failed, oddly enough. I guess I was just so familiar with the streets in that part of New York that all I needed to do was to *feel* them. For example, they thought that they had really pulled something over on me by driving into Brooklyn, instead of veering off FDR Drive and taking the Prospect Expressway, the Belt Parkway. But with the taped glasses on, I knew where I was at practically all times.

"At another point, much later, we turned left on Neptune and I made out a sign that read *Brighton*. This was another section in Brooklyn. Not that far from Coney Island. It was always cold and wet and windy around there.

"Almost right after that, we pulled up in front of a wood frame house with a large fat man standing outside in a white shirt and pants. I found out later that he was Tony Spots, their main man, their mob connection.

"We went down the block once, made a U-turn and came back to the house. Another guy was there then.

"The big man stopped the car at the curb. Bobby ordered me out. Spots says, 'Jerkoff, take the shades off.'

[273]

"They grabbed the glasses off my face and pushed me up the steps. We went in through a kitchen, where a pretty girl was sitting on a stool, playing with something on the oven. She looked kind of surprised to see us, but not so startled that this was something she had never seen before. She just kept quiet and stuck her face in the pot on the stove.

"Spots was obviously in charge. 'Go alongside him, two on a side,' he ordered. Then four of them took me to another room.

"I started begging them about being allowed to go to the bathroom again, screaming that I was going to piss on their floor. The girl must have heard that. She nosed in.

"'Hold it in,' Bobby told me. 'It's good for you anyway, holding back a piss like that. What you need is control. I do it all the time. It puts muscles on your dick. It'll make you a better fucker—hold that semen way back. It fittens up the muscles, man. Piss, cut it off; piss, cut it off.' Then he turns to the girl and gives her this little tap on her behind. It was one of the crudest gestures I ever saw, like, this-butt-is-my-property. 'Ain't that right, Baby?'

"The girl turned red, but ignored him and said something about nobody better piss on her kitchen floor, because she is not gonna use her mop to mop up no piss. And she sounded just as tough as the Gaglianos.

"I had this flash of my wife's face then, of our little boy. I asked myself: What kind of animals have I fallen in with?

"I said, 'If you guys are gonna kill me, I gotta see a priest, you gotta send me to church. Give me a cigarette, at least.'

"That didn't make a dent.

"'You search him?' Spots wanted to know.

"'Yeah, he had a piece on him,' Bobby answered.

"Spots was very surprised I had a gun. 'Why'd you bring a piece with you? You take a piece to the meet, why?'

"'I always carry,' I said. 'Ask Bobby.'

"He nodded and said to both of us, 'Relax, relax, you guys.'

"'This is it, Bobby,' I started again. 'The pee. It's comin' now. Sorry.' And I turned to the woman there and gave her the most helpless look that I could manage.

"She started screaming again. 'Get him the hell out of here. Now! You pigs!'

"At least that got them moving. They gave me a shove in the direction of the bathroom. A guy I had never seen before followed me in. I started to lean over the toilet bowl, moaning, like I'm gonna throw up. Then I'm fooling with my fly like I can't get it open. He starts to give me a hard time—but doesn't leave me alone for a second. I was actually trying to gross him out, get him to leave in disgust.

"Then—and I swear this *had* to be the answer to the prayers I had said out in the car—they called him away, back into the room with the rest of them.

"That was all the time I needed. I pulled off the Edwards, looked around real fast to see where I could stash it and all I saw was soap in the bathtub dish. I figured none of these guys are gonna take a bath now, so I just stuck it under the soap.

"As soon as I had stood up away from the tub, and straightened my clothes a little, he came back in and said, 'Strip.'

"That's why they had called him out. Spots wanted me strip-searched. I just beat them to it.

"Tommy Mendino hadn't been around since the snatch. He and I had both gotten out of the car at the same time, but he hadn't come inside the house with me.

"Now, he shows up again. Spots actually deferred to him, asked him if they had been tailed. Did he see any cops?

"Tommy is a stone-cold killer. Just being in the room with him makes it that much more dangerous for me.

"Spots was suspicious because I had no identification of any kind on me and nothing for the car, either. All I had was the gun.

"That was a mistake because all bad guys always carried some phony ID cards just in case the police stopped them for a traffic violation. It was my first nonauthentic bad guy move. Spots had to be suddenly wondering why I'm not even afraid of a routine police search like they are. Particularly since I'm carrying a gun.

"The answer is obvious. But is it obvious to *him*?

"'The car belongs to one of the whores,' I said. 'She loaned

[275]

it to me. She's got all the owner's cards and insurance shit.'

"That seemed to make sense to them. Bobby started in again about the other places they intended to hit again. Just like in the car. Were any of them mine? Were they connected to any of the Five Families that I knew of? This was a standard intelligence debriefing. Who else had a piece of Murray Hill?

"Spots, however, was still very disturbed about the car. They called the plate number in to somebody—to see if it was listed as a police undercover vehicle. The guy on the phone turned away and whispered, 'No hit.' The plate was clean.

"'Search the car again,' Spots ordered. 'Keep it up till you find something.'

"I figure I've just bought myself—and the backup teams out there, Bill—some time. The car would take a while for them to go over thoroughly. I wasn't too concerned about that either. I should have been.

"We sat at a wooden table and started to go over whorehouse addresses in a black book they had taken from one of their robberies. I had no idea what they were showing me, none. The addresses were not known vice locations. They figured I had to know, though. I was in the business too. I guessed that maybe these were the apartments of individual hookers who just serviced a handful of clients on their own. That's what I told them. I guess it was the wrong thing.

"All of a sudden, Bobby snapped out. 'NO BULLSHIT NOW!' he yelled.

"I was humiliating him in front of Spots. I was either giving them wrong answers to questions they already knew the answers to—and assumed I *had* to know, too—or I was just sounding stupid.

"Bobby cuffed me in the head with the flat of his gun. God, did that hurt. It made me momentarily deaf on the left side and sent this sharp pain through the back of my skull. I saw stars and planets and a rainbow. He drew a lot of blood and I nearly passed out.

"Then I made up a story that the book belonged to a madam who had been holding out on me, too. I was just trying to hide my other places from them again. They looked at one another like that could be plausible. A good lie they would accept, not the truth.

"Tommy Mendino came in from the living room then and pointed his gun at my head, cocked: 'TALK!'

"The lids of my eyes were caked with blood and I could just about make out his face. I saw these two black eyes with absolutely nothing alive behind them.

"Spots calmed him down, and Bobby, too. But they acted afraid of him, which made me very afraid.

"Then Spots started to play with me. He pulled out two hundred dollars, slammed it on the countertop and said, 'How much is your life worth to you? How much?'

"Mendino pointed his gun at me again and said, 'Call Al Gold. That cunt is his partner. See if Gold pays the ransom.'

"Then, *I* got it. This *was* a real kidnapping. Up to that point, they had no idea that I was a cop. I had been worrying about that for nothing. They did believe, truly, that I was some fringe Mafia guy like them and that *somebody* would pay to get me back.

"Meantime, people are coming and going. They never stay put. The woman, who I think was Bobby's girlfriend, walked around like nothing unusual was going on, like there were just a bunch of Bobby's friends there watching a ballgame. It was weird, let me tell you.

"They whacked me a couple more times for no particular reason; just being tough guys, showing me they were in control.

"The whole side of my face had blown up by then and my one eye was completely closed. By that point, I guess I presented no threat to anyone, I was so banged up. They all started to loosen up a little. It was still tense, but not like before.

"They put a fifth of scotch in front of me and we all started to drink. I drank the most. This went on for better than a half hour. I was getting drunk, fast. But at least I was alive.

"Two of the brothers came back in from the car after they

finished the search. No problem there, I thought. I was wrong.

"They shoved a piece of paper in front of Spots, smiled, and said, 'This is all we found. Under the mat in the front seat.'

"I'm thinking: *Mat? What mat? What paper? What could they have possibly found?*

"Spots looked the paper over and then pushed it right into my teeth. I stared at it through my one eye that still worked.

"It was an official 'Property of NYPD' motor pool inspection slip.

"Somebody had left it—a 'tire card'—under the floor mat in the front seat. A 'tire card' is a police department form which identifies the tires on the car as belonging to the New York City Police Department.

"Some asshole at the Puzzle Palace must have made them go through the unmarked flash cars like they did with ordinary police blue-and-whites, just to check to see if we had ripped off the good tires and put bad ones back on. It was the kind of all-too-typical bureaucratic bullshit that could get undercovers killed.

"The tire card was right there—like putting a fucking NYPD decal on the door of my T-bird.

"I had just been using the flash car that day to pull up and pay them off and go away. We weren't expecting a full-blown search.

"It got real quiet then. The girl left. Everybody in the house checked his gun. I reached for another drink and they slapped it away, across the room. I got punched again.

"Mendino put his gun up to my head. 'I'm going to kill you, cop,' he said calmly.

"Bobby went nuts. Totally nuts. Total disbelief. He lunged at me, got one hand around my throat, and started to choke me, but Spots pulled him off.

"He sent them out to the car to look some more. It was quiet for a few minutes. I was sitting there, thinking about my son, my wife, my mother; I was going over my whole life, preparing myself to die.

"When the two Gaglianos came back for the third time, they

had found some wires in the ceiling of the T-bird and a lot of other electronic paraphernalia under the dashboard that really was obvious to the experienced eye. My car had been equipped like one huge listening post and now they knew it.

"Then it was like, 'Well, yeah, I *am* a cop. But I'm taking money from these whorehouses and I am a *crooked* cop and I shake down people. I'm just like you guys. We can work this out.'

"I had to admit everything, the whole story. I knew that if they called Al Gold, he would have confirmed that I was working with Bill McCarthy and that we were rogue cops on his pad.

"Spots listened and concentrated. 'We were looking to make some money from you,' he said. 'But if you're a cop, that's no good. You got no money.'

"'Al Gold will still pay,' I said.

"Spots just made a face like I was being ridiculous. But I thought they half-bought that explanation and half-didn't buy it. They were weighing the next move.

"They didn't know what to do with me. Bobby Gee kept talking about Frank Serpico, whom I knew, of course. Way before he was even famous. They were afraid that I had to be another Serpico. They were paranoid that I might be under-cover instead of corrupt. If they only knew.

"They produced a tape recorder from somewhere in the house and made me repeat the rogue cop story again.

"'That's for my lawyers,' Spots said. 'That's for entrapment. If they try to hit us with that.'

"Twenty more minutes went by and they broke up into small groups. Every so often, Tommy or Bobby would bang my head again. I couldn't see much at all by that point because the blood had clotted over my hair and eyes. I don't even remember what they were talking about. I imagine I had become semiconscious. I do recall that even sitting down and in pain, I had this strange sensation of floating. Something inside was attempting to very gently, but firmly, detach me from my predicament. Today, after what I've read and learned, I look back on that as something approximating what they call a near-death experience. Whatever it was, I came to feel a deep sense of resignation and tranquillity.

"The thing I feared most was being left alone with Mendino. I knew by his eyes what he wanted to do.

"Of course, that's exactly what happened. Everybody walked out of the room except me and Tommy. I made my mind up that I would get it then. I tried to make my peace with God.

"A telephone call had been made, and it seemed like all they were waiting for was a call back. Maybe they needed to clear the decision to kill me with somebody higher up. I was trying to make sense of it.

"Then the telephone rang. I never saw who answered it.

"Finally, Spots came back into the room where I was. He walked over, yanked up my head by the hair and said, 'So you're really a cop.'

"I think he must have called somebody in the police department to check on me and whoever it was—to this day we have no idea—gave me up; the whole thing. After that call Spots knew all about Operation Sinbad. They had penetrated our top level of security.

"Spots just wanted to make sure that I knew that he knew and then he turned his back on me.

"Before he left, I heard him instructing Bobby that they had to make sure they left separately—except for Tommy and Bobby. Spots told those two, 'You wait here and take care of the cop.'

"That was it—my death sentence.

"I was positive that as soon as Spots left the house, it would all be over. He would have never let anything happen to me while he was there, because he didn't want to take the heat. On their own, though, they could do what they wanted. And Tommy and Bobby wanted to kill me.

"In about a minute, they pulled me to my feet again and they dragged me across the floor, to the door.

"What I found out much, much later, was that the Edwards in the bathroom soap dish *had never stopped recording*. Any time they went in there to talk out of earshot of me, their conversation was recorded. They never did think to check the bathroom or look in that soap dish.

"The very last thing the Edwards ever picked up was Tony Spots's voice, loud and clear, saying: *'Kill the cop, but make sure nobody finds him.'*

"Then the front door opened. The cold air brought me to a little bit and Bobby started to push me down their steps.

"Tommy Mendino's voice sounded far away as he said, 'You're going for another ride.'

"My head was down. I didn't want to look at them. I was concentrating on my mental image of my wife. This would be my last ride."

THIRTY-ONE

**No one ever recovers from being a *Victim*. They are
sad, pathetic, rattled, ruined. They will never be the
same again. Including cops.**

MOTHER'S MAXIM

■

7:00 P.M.

**ONE POLICE PLAZA,
TWELFTH FLOOR
TONY VITALIANO:**

"As soon as I felt that cold, wet air on my face, just as they're
shoving me down the steps, BOOM! the Brooklyn Homicide
cops hit them like a wave. More cops than I had ever seen in
my life. Cops everywhere. Guns, shotguns, rifles, riot gear;
mounted police galloping down the street in a cavalry charge
formation. I could hear the helicopters closing in, descending
and landing. The wind from their rotor blades almost blew me
over. I felt just like I was in a war.

"Then somebody was lifting me up. I had hands and arms
under me all the way around. I was being carried like a baby.

"Tommy and Bobby disappeared under this mountain of
bodies, tackling them, laying them out. I thought that everybody
had been killed right there. Bobby went for his gun. I knew
that. Tommy, too. But it was all over.

"It was finished. I was still alive. I shouldn't have been. I
should have been killed a dozen times, even back in the car, in
the beginning.

[282]

"All I was aware of at that second was that, somehow, Mother had made them recover me."

BILL McCARTHY:

"Vitaliano had been rescued, semiconscious, but alive. Bobby Gagliano and Tommy Mendino were captured while dragging him out of Bobby's girlfriend's house. They were taking him to the place where the undercover cop was to be executed.

"They could not go for their guns quickly enough and Brooklyn Homicide was all over them.

"*Tony's* in shock. He's less than three miles away. He's unconscious—and he's drunk. *Drunk?* That's what I'm hearing. But he's okay. They're checking him over at Coney Island Hospital. A real pit.

"I wanted to go to the hospital to see Tony; I wanted that more than anything, but I couldn't go. There were other responsibilities—all mine—and I still had at least one person to apprehend.

"I figured that the one major player connected to the Gaglianos was this Tony Spots, so he had to have the answers.

"At the hospital, Tony had mentioned his name, too, to the Brooklyn Homicide detectives. They called me immediately with that information. We have five of the six people involved in the kidnapping in custody. Tony Spots is number six. We have to get him.

"Somebody had been sent to Tony's house to be with his wife and little son. The police chaplain was there, too. The Building was doing all the right stuff by that point, but I wanted to be there too. Instead, I had to report to the Building myself. Get this squared away.

"Tony Spots wasn't a big mob guy. He was just a mob guy. A Gambino soldier. He was just a very greedy earner. The sort of person the Gaglianos would gravitate to.

"He's the big fish. He's the catch. He ties us into the official Mafia on this case. But how do we get him? We don't know. He's hiding. He's gone. He's like the wind.

"We know there are twenty gambling places, mostly old

neighborhood social clubs, that are linked to Spots.

"Those were the places where we sent out shotguns teams. Six teams of six detectives, with six sergeants, all wearing flak-jackets, heavy bullet-proof vests, and armed with shotguns, *empty* shotguns.

"I made up the list of places to visit. All six teams had to go into each club racking up the shotguns, screaming, 'We want Spots! If Spots don't surrender, your place is going to be destroyed!' And every place got six visits—all from different cops.

"I contrived that hysterical, angry police response. I wanted them to believe that the cops were out of control over this.

"The word went out that night that there would be no peace in Brooklyn until Spots was surrendered to us.

"As soon as they would enter a place—by that I mean break down the door; we figured we had this one won and we were feeling pretty good—they started racking up the shotguns.

"That is a sound that you never forget once you hear it. You look at those two barrels and figure they will blow you through a wall.

"The cops only had one thing to say: Give up Tony Spots.

"At location after location in Brooklyn, it was the same. It was like the cops had gone mad. *That's* what we wanted them to believe.

"There was a sergeant, a black, Puerto Rican guy, very black, very close friend of mine. His name was Paul Enrique, now retired. Paul was only about five-nine, 135 pounds. But he had this old bullet-proof vest; it must have weighed 80 pounds. It went all the way down to his knees. When he wore it he looked like a knight in armor—the Black Knight.

"I remember saying to Hepburn that night, 'Can you imagine seeing this guy going in the door of an Italian social club in Brooklyn, racking up the shotguns?'

"Paul Enrique was my hard-charger that night. Paul took on Brooklyn all by himself. Can you imagine sitting in a social club, playing poker? You feel perfectly safe because you know you're the Mafia, nobody can touch you. But all of a sudden, the door

[284]

comes crashing down and these gladiators break in with shotguns, and there's Paul Enrique like the Black Knight, yelling at you in Spanish.

"If you tried to do something like that today, the cops wouldn't even know how to do it. You had experienced cops then. Good cops. The kids today—they just don't know.

"They don't know how to control without actual violence. But there was *no* violence that night; just the *threat* of total destruction. That was real police work.

"And we also had license that night. No one was going to entertain a civilian complaint against us. Just the cops against Brooklyn. May the best man win.

"I couldn't leave headquarters. This night is going on forever. The police commissioner is there; the district attorney is there; four or five assistant district attorneys are there writing warrants.

"A few hours before, none of these people were even available. They didn't even want to know what was happening. But now it's safe. This is a win.

"Every boss in New York City wanted a piece of me. Some of them were prepared to ream me out; others had decided that this had been a heroic rescue and they wanted in on the happy ending.

"All that would have to wait. I had better things to do.

"I now have all sorts of obligations to inform the police department. I am getting calls from ten thousand people. There are now all kinds of chiefs wanting to talk to me as the immediate supervisor. Plus, people in the public information division have to have something to tell the press. They all want an interview.

"They tell me that the governor is on the phone. He can smell how well this is turning out.

"The police commissioner wants to know about the case and the mayor and, of course, the first deputy commissioner wants to know—Sinbad started in his office with my undercover assignment—and they're all asking me.

"At this point there is an information hysteria. It's a combi-

[285]

nation of natural curiosity and of people in authority who need information to communicate to other people. This is the Puzzle Palace taking over.

"In the meantime, I get a surprise call from Tony Spots's lawyer.

"I said to him, 'You better get your client to surrender, because if he goes out on the street he might get killed because there's a whole army of angry cops out there. You better have him surrender right away; every hour it's getting worse.'

"The lawyer, he doesn't know anything. Naturally. This is part of the game. He says, 'I don't know where my client is. I don't know if I can find him. I don't know what his problem is. He didn't do anything.' And I'm guessing that as he's saying this, Spots is probably right next to him.

"I pushed it. 'Yo, be a friend,' I told him. 'Have him surrender. We want him. Alive. He's considered armed and dangerous. There could be a confrontation. He could get killed. By accident. Protect your client from getting "accidented."'

"The next call from the lawyer came in at two o'clock in the morning. 'You can come out and pick him up,' was all that he said.

"Spots had surrendered himself to the police in Nassau County. He didn't have the guts to surrender to the New York City Police Department.

"It was only then that I started to come down a little.

"I just wanted to be with Millie. I still hadn't apologized to her for missing our belated, once-postponed anniversary dinner. Tony's kidnapping had gotten in our way.

"I was really ashamed of myself for not having called her sooner. Now she would be seeing it all on television, instead of hearing it from me.

"Still, I was celebrating—celebrating in my mind and heart. Tony was back. I knew he was in shock, and the whole side of his head was swollen. And I'm just beginning to find out how badly he'd been beaten during all those hours of his captivity, but he *was* alive.

"But once again, I would have to make Millie wait. It was

important for me to get to the hospital. I owed that much to Tony.

"Coney Island Hospital was like a slaughterhouse in those days—old, blood-splattered hallways, depressing. It was awful to see him in there. And he looked bad. Like he was *very* lucky to be alive.

"I still can't recall all of it—I know I got there, probably, by then, it was the next day. I was just numb. I couldn't even talk to him. We just hugged each other.

"Then I said, 'You bum, all you had to do was wait. *I* was the one who had to get you back.'

"He was hurt, in pain, but he smiled, pushed himself up a little on his shoulder and said, 'Never again, Mother, not even for you.'

"I think I might have cried after that."

THIRTY-TWO

**Most of the *Lawyers* that cops deal with hang out in the
lobby of the criminal courts building. Polyester suits
and gravy stains on their ties. They steal your money
and then plead you. They have about as much social
conscience as a strain of AIDS virus. Lawyers are
ghouls who make their money off your grief.**

M O T H E R ' S   M A X I M

Sinbad's impact on Bill McCarthy was profound. Nothing would
ever be the same again. Nearly losing Tony Vitaliano had frightened the entire team.

Before, there was a sense of invulnerability about them. They
went out, did their jobs, and believed that nothing tragic could
ever happen. They existed in a world of shocking unreality of
reckless risks and rash impetuosity. But Sinbad had proven just
how fragile that precarious code of manhood could be. Their
new feelings of mortality united Mother's team with an eerie
sense of just how close to the precipice they had ventured.

Sinbad had made him reevaluate the whole concept of undercover work. Accordingly, McCarthy began to rewrite the
department's operational procedures; often, he was spelling
them out—at least as far as undercovers went—for the very
first time.

Other units in the NYPD soon picked up on his concern.
From his restlessness emerged a well-considered policy and pro-

tocol for covert action. It was adopted piecemeal at first, then department-wide.

Despite his unorthodox methods, McCarthy was developing an unlikely reputation as "command material." In the beginning, that was no more than amusing to him; later, however, it became an opportunity that he would have to come to terms with.

In the protracted criminal trial that followed Vitaliano's abduction, the defense attempted to portray Mother's shaken team as out-of-control, kamikaze cops—police mavericks who were every bit as dangerous as the felons they pursued.

As the sergeant in charge, Mother took most of the heat.

"I was cross-examined for nine hours by five defense attorneys. Vitaliano was on the stand for almost six days. The first thing they tried to nail me on was our reluctance, throughout the case, to return to the pool hall on Saint John's Place to make all the subsequent payoffs. Why had I insisted on meeting the Gaglianos in Manhattan?

"It was hard to see the point they were getting at. This seemed so totally unrelated to the kidnapping.

"But as soon as I realized that there were four black jurors, I caught on. They were trying to backhandedly portray me as a crazy, racist cop.

"They said I wouldn't go back to that part of Brooklyn to make the subsequent payoffs because I didn't like black people and I refused to travel to a black neighborhood in Brooklyn, if I could help it.

"'Isn't it true that you don't like black people?'

"They asked that question a hundred different ways. I could see by the faces of the four black jurors that a seed of doubt about my character was definitely taking root.

"This was absurd, considering the other issues at stake in Sinbad, but these defense lawyers didn't care.

"I was a racist. That was their defense. Nobody black was even remotely connected to the case. I was still a racist.

"During that cross-examination, my daily activity reports—DARs—also came up.

"Now, I was supposed to be a corrupt cop throughout Sinbad. I had all my expenses in order. As part of my undercover role I was drinking half a bottle of scotch every night. I was supposed to be a crook. A bad guy. I gotta be doing something wrong. You can't go in those after-hours clubs and pimp bars singing *Kyrie, Eleison*.

"You have to be a mover, so I'm smoking and I'm drinking. Gambling. I was making dirty money. I had to buy, buy, buy. Drinks all around. Every night. So on my DAR, I had expenses of forty and fifty dollars for drinks. 'Food and drink for cover,' it was called. The defense had full disclosure of my DARs.

"One of the lawyers tried to make use of his interpretation of the 'Food and drink for cover' by asking me, *'Do you still have your drinking problem, Sergeant?'*

"'I wasn't aware that I had one,' I said.

"He throws up nine months of activity reports and says that I spent all this money on drinks, so I had to be an alcoholic. The DARs are his proof. So now he's trying to tell the jury I'm a drunk as well as a racist. And we haven't even gotten to the kidnapping yet.

"I remember thinking to myself: This son of a bitch, I should have gotten my family in here. My wife is Puerto Rican, one-third black, actually. My kids have to get the sickle-cell anemia test. My kids are part black. Puerto Ricans are descended from black blood and Indian blood. One of Millie's aunts is called 'Negrita,' which means 'little black lady.' Millie's grandfather *was* a black man. There's black blood in every drop of blood in my children's veins.

"Now, I'm sitting there mindful of all this, wishing that I could somehow communicate it all to the jury, and he's trying to crucify me. But you have to answer the questions.

"His bias is that I am an Irish-Catholic-pig-racist-head-breaker-cop. Billy Lace Curtain.

"I resented what they were trying to do. I hated them for that. But there wasn't a thing I could do about it.

"All the defense lawyers were mob lawyers and these were some of their favorite tactics. One of them was a partner of the guy who had just successfully defended the BLA, the Black Liberation Army. And he was excellent.

"Mob lawyers are always on; they're never off. They're always looking to suck up to you; they'll bullshit you; they're flag-wavers; they're patriots; they're anything that works; they're always trying to buy you lunch; always sweet-talking you and then, once your defenses are down, they will lunge right for the jugular vein.

"They'd shoot your first-born; they'd kill your kids. And they don't realize they're trapped. When they become a mob lawyer, they're a mob lawyer for life. You ain't allowed out. You can't decide that you're no longer gonna retain this client. *He* retains *you*. You're in. And you're in for life.

"They're just part of the mob; no different from criminals. They're the mouthpiece and they hide behind reasonable doubt.

"Their whole drill is to create a smoke screen, like they were attempting to do in Sinbad. If it's apparent that their clients are guilty, then brand the cop, the accuser, as a racist. Confuse the issue. Better yet, obscure it altogether.

"All they need to do is create that reasonable doubt in the mind of a jury. Or fear. Either way, they get paid and they don't especially care. Whatever they have to do, they do it.

"This rejection of conventional moral choices allows them to live very well, make a lot of money. A few of them are actually star-struck by Mafia types. They like to get down and wear the pinkie rings on their own little fingers. In that way, they are identical to the star-fucker whores who like to hang out with the big Mafia types. You can see them in any high-class bar in Manhattan.

"A mob lawyer is manicured—white, clear nail polish on his nails. Razor haircut. Reeks of cologne. A hint of gold—maybe a neck chain, a wrist chain, a Rolex watch, and thin, thin shoes, expensive leather.

"Most of the prosecutors we had on our side were young,

[291]

inexperienced, didn't know a thing. They were either afraid of the competition or overly impressed with themselves; some of them were very idealistic but as soon as they'd get smart, and get their ticket punched for their two or three years of public service, they'd get out and become defense attorneys too.

"There were all kinds of meetings throughout this entire case. I can't say that I saw our side, the prosecutors, at their best. They didn't like cops, either. Probably didn't believe us.

"Aside from the racist innuendoes, one of the big problems that the prosecution had was that there were about 250 tape-recorded conversations that had been made during Sinbad. All of that was part of the case. Just a mountain of work.

"They had real difficulty mastering all that evidence.

"At one point during the trial, one of the defense lawyers asked me, *'Sergeant, when you were with these prostitutes, when you were being corrupted and taking money from these prostitutes; when you were drinking, when you had your alcoholic problem; how much money did you get paid, Sergeant?'*

"'I don't know,' I told him.

"*'You mean to tell me that you were in charge of the case and you don't know how many bribes, how much money you received from those whores? Those pimps?'*

"I said, 'No, I have no idea.'

"*'Sergeant, you tell me you were in charge and you don't even know how many times you were bribed by those whores?'*

"'No.'

"*'Why, Sergeant?'*

"I said, 'Counselor, my obligation to truth is to remember as vividly and as accurately as I can until such time as I have made a competent police report. Then I allow the report to remember for me, so, if you would like, I can do the statistical search of my accurate police reports, and provide you the number of incidents and the actual amounts, if you'd like.

"'All I have to refer to are my accurate police reports. I have no obligation to remember after I have accurately documented the event.'

[292]

"He laughed in my face, then turned to the jury and tried to get them laughing at me, too.

"It went on like that for the whole day that I was on the stand. And these guys were pissed. They were outraged. All they wanted to do was run rings by me.

"Then they brought up the fact that during one day of Sinbad, one day during the course of a case that had gone on for parts of two years, I had not been to work. I had either been off sick or on another undercover assignment.

"A call had come in for me that day, and Tony had taken it. Tony wrote up a report on it. He followed procedure to the letter. It was very important information. Very, very important information.

"But I wasn't there to countersign Tony's report of the call. It just happened. An oversight.

"The lieutenant who was there had signed the report in my place. So, in this entire case there was that one piece of paper that I hadn't signed personally.

"The defense spent the entire day, during cross-examination, trying to trap me with this thing. Why didn't I sign the paper? Why? Why wasn't I on top of the case? Was I some lazy, half-drunk sergeant who hated black people, who never reported to work, and who failed to countersign the papers he was supposed to sign?

"It was fun, though. I loved it. I loved being cross-examined. I loved dueling with the best.

"I guess I convinced them after all. We got our convictions."

As a result of Operation Sinbad, six people connected with the stickup and extortion crew that kidnapped Tony Vitaliano were sentenced to prison terms ranging from seven and a half to fifteen years.

Additionally, sixteen people were either arrested or indicted on an array of Vice charges that developed from the investigation centered on the Murray Hill townhouse.

[293]

The amount of raw intelligence that Sinbad provided was staggering. Much of it was used by investigators and prosecutors who would later score a number of spectacularly successful victories against all five New York crime Families in the years to come. Also extremely significant were the leads that grew out of Sinbad's early warnings concerning the existence of the Sicilian Mafia on American soil. That harrowing story of international drug smuggling and assorted other crimes would not be resolved until the prolonged series of investigations and trials known collectively as the Pizza Connection case.

However, not everything connected with Sinbad lent itself to such satisfying resolution. No corrupt cops were arrested. Several, however, were transferred or forced to accept early retirements.

Bill McCarthy remained convinced that the electronic "bug" that was so mysteriously detected at the Murray Hill townhouse was the result of a leak. But he was never able to pinpoint the fellow cop who had sold him out.

McCarthy left the Pimp Squad, Public Morals, the Organized Crime Control Bureau, on December 12, 1976. That was a sad day. It marked the end of Mother's Pimp Team.

Years later, he would return as a lieutenant to command Vice. But of course, it would never be the same.

After the Knapp Commission, to encourage the police to avoid corruption, and to reward good arrests in the bribery area, the NYPD created the Integrity Review Board.

"When a guy made a big bribery arrest—Sinbad was the textbook example—he would be sent before the Integrity Review Board to be promoted to detective or transferred to a more desirable assignment.

"I was 'rewarded' by being transferred to the Detective Bureau. I didn't particularly want to go to the Detective Bureau. It was a coveted assignment, but I was already 'permanent cadre' in the OCCB, the Organized Crime Control Bureau. That was actually a better job—the old five-borough concept. The real reward would have been letting me the hell alone.

"For me, it was take your reward or else. Mainly, their secret agenda was to rotate me *out* of Vice because they didn't want you to stay there too long or you really would get too friendly with the bad guys.

"Then, a guy could go ten years without the gold shield, the detective's badge. He might make hundreds of collars, do all the overtime, work on his own time, perform brilliantly as a plainclothes cop, but when he was evaluated, if he wanted to stay in Vice, he had to be in the top quarter even to be considered for permanent cadre or for the gold shield.

"Today, with equal opportunity, and racial and promotional quotas, if you're breathing and you have two years in an investigative assignment, you usually get the shield whether you deserve it or not.

"That, more than any other single thing, has probably destroyed the professional caliber—and certainly the morale—of the NYPD.

"Going to the Detective Bureau meant catching cases. Everything that came in. You caught it. You got all the paperwork, all the missing persons, robberies, commercial robberies, assaults, homicides; it was really a lot of clerical work. There was tremendous pressure to maintain a high clearance rate.

"It had been much better to work at the Organized Crime Control Bureau. That was like a ticket to have fun. But the Detective Bureau was my reward and I had to accept it.

"What was Tony's reward? They promoted him to sergeant—after calling him out of his hospital bed to take the civil service exam—and allowed him to stay as a boss in the OCCB.

"Tony was really messed up from the experience of the kidnapping, from being pistol-whipped so savagely. He developed a twitch in his face, which was the physical scar, but he was even more battered by the psychological after effects.

"Before, Tony had been a happy-go-lucky kind of a good guy type detective. He joked about everything. Yet it changed him so much—it changed all of us so much—that seven or eight years after the incident, Tony still couldn't talk about it. Before, he was always cheery, upbeat, talking fast.

"After Sinbad, his nerves were shot. That's the only way I can put it.

"Years later, after they came to appreciate the significance of a hostage incident like this, they interviewed Tony, tried to get a sense of what it was like to be held captive under such life-threatening circumstances.

"Eventually, Tony's experience—his insights—helped the NYPD put together one of the finest 'hostage negotiation' units in the world. But it had been a tough way to go about getting on-the-job training.

"Back when it happened they just told him to take a couple sick days and didn't even rotate him out of routine duty. No counseling, no follow-up, no nothing. I was worried. I was afraid that he might go out on the street and try to shoot somebody, just as a result of poststress syndrome. He had gone through hell. They were aware of that postcombat as a result of soldiers coming home from Vietnam, but I guess they figured it didn't count with cops.

"They only replaced you if you dropped. Nobody had any concern or sentimentality. But now, sixteen years later, they give long talks about police stress management. None of that existed then. They wouldn't have cared, anyway. There was a different notion of what made a good cop then, it was a different time, a much wilder time.

"If you weren't useful to them, you were gone. They'd get somebody else. That's all. The command structure of the NYPD just kept rolling along. Individual cops like me and Tony would always come and go; the Building was forever."

THIRTY-THREE

You can arrest all the pimps, seize all the drugs, close down all the gambling, scare all the johns, drive all the pornography underground and chase away all the hookers and when you're all finished, the *Life* will still be there, just the same as before. All the cops do is keep score.

MOTHER'S MAXIM

In every way, Operation Sinbad had changed Bill McCarthy's life. Initially, the personal sacrifice seemed unbearable. There were times when he had to question whether the job, especially Vice, was worth it. Had he been dedicated or merely foolish?

His always-neglected off-duty life came in for a sober re-evaluation. Millie and the children were growing further and further away from him. No matter how hard he tried to leave Vice, to leave the Life behind him when he went home to Sloatsburg, he never quite managed to do it.

Even when he was at home, he wasn't always *there*. Bleak moods and a deepening sense of desperation left him withdrawn. In his mind, he kept playing out Sinbad again and again. He could see what was happening to himself and his family. At the very least, McCarthy needed some radical change from Vice, from the stress and surreality of staying undercover too long.

There was a genuine crisis at home, too. His father, an invalid by then, had moved in with them and the family was running out of living space as well as patience. McCarthy's once excusable neglect of the home-front in favor of a single-minded devotion to his career was putting the whole family in jeopardy.

Something had to give. He would have to find a larger house, and one probably much further away from the city to be able to afford it. That would mean an even longer commute and that many more hours stolen from Millie and the children.

During his years in Vice, McCarthy had earned his master's degree at John Jay and was already embarking on the long road toward a doctorate. That would require a tremendous investment of his time too.

McCarthy had always moonlighted—driving a cab teaching pickup courses at John Jay, anything to supplement what the City of New York paid its warriors. Now, the prospect of establishing a second career, not just part-time work, took on some urgency.

Medicine had always fascinated him, so he had begun a course of study that would get him a nurse's degree—psychiatric care—and later, he hoped, a well-paying position in hospital administration. That would be a radical departure from police work, but he was becoming alarmed, almost despondent, about all that he had already sacrificed.

Despite its seductive pull on an ambitious cop, there was a limit to how long anyone could survive in the Life. Eventually, even Bill McCarthy had to accept that.

"I could only survive running undercovers for so long. It was dangerous work; I knew that I was spending too much time away from my family and I was already serving my second tour in the Life. I could not expect to stay hot—or lucky—forever.

"I had almost convinced myself that either a fantastic opportunity would have to open up within the department, where I would have total administrative control and the semblance of a normal schedule, or I would take my master's degree and my nurse's certification and put in for an early pension.

"I was directionless, but if leaving the police force was what it would take to keep my marriage going and let me begin acting like a father again, then I was willing to put in my papers.

"I was just coming off three years in the Puzzle Palace as the commanding officer of the Public Morals Headquarters Unit. This was 1984.

"I'd been through the Son of Sam murders with the Bronx Detective Homicide Task Force, I'd pulled desk duty in the 2-0 precinct, and Sinbad had been over for almost ten years, but I was still living it every day.

"I was just about to start a new undercover role with a trucking company in the garment center. I had made the preliminary contacts with a millionaire designer we had our eye on.

"For the first time I was beginning to ask myself if I really *wanted* to go underground again. Unless your response to that is instantly affirmative, more reflex than reasoning, then you shouldn't do it.

"I never wanted to become one of those cops who needed the department *more* than it needed him. I was probably lying to myself about that, but I had to hold on to something. That something had always been Millie and the children, even during the worst undercover days.

"Now, I was determined to make a decision based on what was best for them instead of what I wanted.

"Very few of the people who worked with me ever understood the police department or their place in it. I did. I had very, very few romantic notions. My run in Vice had come to an end. It came down to either getting out of the Life while I still could or allowing it to consume me. I just wouldn't do that to the people I loved.

"Cops make a big show about *Family*. But it's almost never sincere. You trot out the wife and kids when it's convenient or politic to do so. Cops are basically selfish. I always hated that about myself.

"But it was sad, though, just like the end of the world. I really didn't know if I could face not being a cop."

AFTERWORD

**You never have to worry about a *Big Bomb*. The big
ones you never even feel. It's the *Little Bombs* you
worry about. They will take an arm or a leg or an eye,
but leave the rest of you.**

M O T H E R ' S   M A X I M

■

N Y P D   B O M B   S Q U A D
H E A D Q U A R T E R S
1 0 T H   A N D   B L E E C K E R   S T R E E T S
G R E E N W I C H   V I L L A G E
A P R I L   1 9 8 4

The chief of detectives had only been in his new job for three
weeks when he buzzed in Bill McCarthy. His office in the Puzzle
Palace had that unpacked look; as though the occupant were
still a little uneasy about hanging up the pictures of his wife
and kiddies. But the new chief had a decision to make, about
the Bomb Squad and about Bill McCarthy.

"Why do you even want the Bomb Squad?" he asked as
McCarthy sat down.

"Six months ago, I didn't want it," McCarthy admitted. And
he told him what his career in Vice had meant, what Sinbad
had meant.

Then the chief of detectives repeated his question. "Why do
you want the Bomb Squad *now*?"

"*You* come highly recommended," McCarthy said. A classic Motherism.

"What? Are you some wiseass Vice cop?"

They both knew that McCarthy was.

"Listen," McCarthy told him, "the word about you is that you're a good boss. Do you think I'd be here for an interview, after everything I've been through in this department, if your reputation wasn't way up there? They're still very happy with me where I am. I can stay in Vice till it kills me."

"Which it will," the chief said. "Probably sooner than later." Then he laughed. "But wait a minute, who's interviewing who here?"

"Look, Chief, if you want someone to say black is white, you got the wrong guy. If you want somebody to be a hero, you got the wrong guy. If you want a mule, I'm a good mule. All I will say in my behalf is this: If I had worked for you before, you'd want me to work for you again."

The chief of detectives gave McCarthy a glassy fisheye. Every boss at One Police Plaza seemed to be issued that particular look along with his room assignment. "Jesus Christ, you're spunky."

Nobody had called Bill McCarthy "spunky" in twenty years. That expression took him all the way back to the playgrounds at Rockaway, back to the endless summers of basketball.

"Chief, this is what you get, no more, no less."

He had McCarthy's folder open on the desk in front of him. He was rated the number one lieutenant in the Organized Crime Control Bureau. He had earned that rank every year for the last thirteen years, wherever he had served.

"I think that will be enough," the chief of detectives said after long moments of reflection.

"Enough what? You want me to leave?" McCarthy was a little puzzled.

"No, I want you to stay," the chief said. "I think we might still need you for a long, long time."

On April 24, 1984, Bill McCarthy was assigned to the Bomb

Squad, New York City Police Department, as the commanding officer.

McCarthy had gotten his wish. One last meaningful opportunity had opened up inside the NYPD. The hours would be more regular, the paranoia of undercover work could be left behind forever and, most important, McCarthy would be able to remain a policeman just a little while longer.

"The first time I had been approached about becoming the commander of the Bomb Squad was by the chief of the Arson Explosion Division. I said no.

"I was still decompressing from Vice at that point. And I did need a change—my marriage and my entire family needed a change. But I refused even to consider a transfer to a unit as radically different from what I had known as the Bomb Squad. I think I was still trying to prove something to myself after Sinbad.

"But considering who was asking me, it was a difficult offer to turn down. The person telling me to take the job was Kenneth Gussman, now *Inspector* Gussman. If I had an older, better friend, I never met him.

"The second time he asked me—the position as Bomb Squad Commander was still vacant—Gussman pressed me on it.

" 'I'll go for the interview,' I finally said.

"This was high-level NYPD politics; there was no kidding myself about that. The Bomb Squad was one of the premier assignments in the entire city. I was a little scared. Was I just going to be camouflage as part of the selection process? Had the stiff with the political juice already been preselected? Or was this a legitimate shot? In other words, had the deal already been cut by the long knives at the Puzzle Palace?

"Gussman didn't hold back. 'I don't believe that any person has been selected yet,' he said. 'This one is too important; this one is life and death on one of those bomb sites.'

" 'Nobody's sending me out for cigarettes, you mean?'

"He remembered our special lifelong code. 'No cigarettes,' Gussman said.

"I knew that the Bomb Squad was isolated from the rest of the police department. It didn't care about the rest of the world. It was an inbred, notoriously dangerous place to work. They were still using the same manual from the World's Fair days, back in the 1960s. The most technologically complex unit in the NYPD would have to be dragged into the twentieth, into a world of terrorism and mass murder.

"It was a private fiefdom. Even the police commissioner and the mayor backed off from the Bomb Squad Commander. In the trenches, when a hot package was being gingerly handled, his word was better than God's. No NYPD boss exercised as much personal power, as much raw command prerogative. In action, the Bomb Squad Commander's orders were *never* countermanded. There was just too much danger, too much at stake.

"The Bomb Squad Commander didn't just sit down with other cops, he went to power meetings called by every federal agency, by the mayor, by the governor, by the White House; every foreign embassy in New York needed him for security; every bomb cop in the world took his cue from New York.

"As much as I had loved Vice, this was looking pretty damn promising. I was already angling to achieve a distinction in the department known as 'a lieutenant with the money,' a detective commander—still a lieutenant—who earned captain's pay or better, while enjoying considerably more authority than the normal captain. That's an anomaly, but in the NYPD anything is possible, even an archaic but cherished tradition like lieutenant-with-the-money. As the boss of the Bomb Squad, I would have a clear shot at it. Eventually, even that did come, too, in 1986, after I had been at the Bomb Squad for two years.

"Depending on your personality and your tolerance for pressure, the Bomb Squad could either be Siberia or paradise. I was crazy enough to buy the paradise angle.

"Something as simple as Fourth of July fireworks was a paramount—if bizarre—part of the job. That was also part of my indoctrination. Fireworks were and are, of course, illegal. That's because they are so unstable and so extremely dangerous in the hands of anybody but experts. Civilians hardly ever get blown up by bombs, but they lose hands and eyes to fireworks every summer.

"There's a huge black market in New York, especially in Chinatown, for underground fireworks. Cops are among the worst abusers. They figure they are immune to getting in trouble for supplying all their friends in the neighborhood with fireworks—after all, the guy is a cop.

"The Bomb Squad does—or should—police this black market. Only one problem. Traditionally, the Bomb Squad was the best place to boost contraband fireworks—and I'm not talking about Joe Patrolman, I'm talking about calls from Gracie Mansion, from the mayor's office, or even from the state capitol in Albany, telling the Bomb Squad Commander where he should *deliver* the fireworks. It was usually to so-and-so's annual picnic or Fourth of July party.

"Were these people in for some surprises. If I had refused to buy cigarettes for Kenny Gussman way back when, I was sure as hell going to refuse to act as delivery boy for the politicians.

"I knew going in that traditions like that—illegal as they might be—would die hard. But, die they would.

"My mind was made up. Fireworks was the perfect target of opportunity for me. If I could fight and win this pure insider's battle, as the new kid on the block, testing my will and reputation for maniacal integrity against all the major players in the city, then I was sure that I would also win the life-and-death decisions later on—the ones that would affect the safety of every man in the Bomb Squad.

"I went in looking for a fight. Hoping for one. And whenever it came, I knew I would survive it, because I had survived the Life."

* * *

[304]

For the next three years and four months, until he retired as a lieutenant-with-the-money, detective commander, New York City Police Bomb Squad, Bill McCarthy would divide his time between the Bomb Squad headquarters at Tenth and Bleecker and the bomb disposal range—City Island at Rodman's Neck.

On that barren, windswept peninsula, bordered on three sides by some of the coldest water in the North Atlantic, with the police pistol range in the foreground and Pelham Parkway climbing on steel girders in the distance, the men and women of the NYPD Bomb Squad go about their perilous ritual of deactivating, disposing, and investigating bombs or explosive devices of any description.

The moment you drive through the gate and begin passing the Quonset huts, the kennels for the explosives-sniffing police dogs, the classroom buildings and the nine firing ranges on the left, a parking lot on the right, you realize that you have entered a very separate existence.

For incoming bombs, hauled at maddeningly slow speed on fat, armored wagons that look like parade floats save for the distinctive NYPD decals, the destination is always the sand bunkers. There, the actual nerve-wracking technical work of taking a bomb apart, piece by piece, fuse by fuse, mechanism by mechanism, is carried out. It is a grim ceremony, a thorny rite of passage for every cop who has ever worked on the Bomb Squad.

Occasionally, cops die here. They firmly believe that the devices they have brought back to the range can be rendered safe enough to dismantle—and they are wrong. One of McCarthy's predecessors was seriously injured under just such circumstances, his face literally blown off.

Some of the most memorable, tension-charged explosives incidents in the history of New York City would occur during McCarthy's Bomb Squad tour.

"For as long as I can remember, the Bomb Squad headquarters has been located on Tenth Street, between Bleecker and Hudson. That's the Village. Millie lived right around the corner on Charles Street when I first met her.

"It's one of the truly magical neighborhoods in New York. On a buttery spring day, With the late breeze picking up and the old trees beginning to turn green, you can stroll along that block and forget that Manhattan Vice ever existed.

"My first day on the job there, my state of mind reflected those feelings. Of course, there were questioning looks, doubtful glances, the old bomb vets grumbling. But I was used to that. In Vice, back on Centre Street, the same thing had happened and I had been able to overcome it. I was confident—I was more than confident, I was like a kid on Christmas morning. I knew I was going to *love* running a proud outfit like this where tradition was more important than anywhere else in the NYPD.

"I was at my new desk for exactly fifteen minutes when they put my first call through. I thought it was Millie. I hoped it would be Millie. It wasn't.

"'Good morning, Lieutenant,' the strange voice said. 'This is Detective Richard Pastorella.'

"Richie Pastorella had been a bomb expert—until one blew up in his face. Now he was blind, partially deaf, and he had lost the use of one hand. And he was suing the police department for millions.

"I was the new boss and Richie was still such a great cop that he felt it was his duty to let me know the score. Just in case the Puzzle Palace had given me a snow job, he intended to set me straight about the level of risk, the competence—or lack thereof—of my people, and the appalling neglect of any and all safety procedures that had built up over time.

"Richie was preparing me for the worst.

"I thanked him for it. Ever since we had nearly lost Tony Vitaliano, I had become Vice's fanatical, pain-in-the-butt Mother about caution, protection for undercovers, and contingency planning. Compared to the imminent threat of death in the Bomb Squad—every day, on every call—Vice had been almost tame.

"Richie wanted me to remember him, wanted me to be aware

of what had happened to him because of the existence of a sloppy, unprofessional disregard for the safety of the brave men and women who had to go out there and take the damn things apart.

"He just wanted to make sure that I wasn't some One Police Plaza medal-maggot parade cop, the kind of cop who would be willing to deliver fireworks to all the politicians. That was something else he warned me about.

"But I wasn't that kind of cop and never had been. Not in Vice, not in the Bomb Squad.

"I promised Richie Pastorella during that first phone call that I would prove myself to him.

"Then he said, 'Mother'—which was the very first time that any cop connected with the Bomb Squad had called me that; I didn't even know for sure if they knew about the name—'Mother, that's just what I wanted to hear. Coming from you, I would not have expected anything less.'

"All at once, this strange new office, these skeptical people, this overwhelming challenge—it all felt like home to me. Thanks to Richie Pastorella."

Bill McCarthy would finally retire from the NYPD on July 1, 1987. One of his last and most memorable official duties while with the Bomb Squad squad was to to provide all bomb and explosives security for the Statue of Liberty celebration during the summer of 1986. Among the people he was protecting then was the President of the United States.

"I felt like I was exiting at the right time. In a blaze of glory, so to speak. I couldn't help but contrast that triumphant departure with one of my first-ever bomb runs.

"It happened at Saint Patrick's Cathedral, at Christmastime.

"An explosive device had been left on the main altar. The call came in and was relayed to me on the street.

"That night the city, glowing and twinkling with Christmas

lights and traffic and all the maddening, irresistible energy of New York, had never looked better to me.

"I think I felt like every other cop I've known who was willing to be honest with himself—I felt like the city *belonged* to me. I was a New York *cop*, it was the best thing a man could ever be.

"I had beaten the slow-moving Bomb wagon there by several minutes. A nervous young priest greeted me on the pavement. The Traffic Division already had barricades set up; the pavements had been cleared. It was just me and the priest.

"We walked up the main aisle together. He was shaking, but I felt this eerie calm.

"Halfway up there, just far enough for him to show me where the device was hidden, I sent him back. But he hesitated, felt that he had to stick with me. Maybe he was preparing to administer the last rites. I'll never know.

"As soon as he was gone, I just stopped dead and *listened*. The stillness was haunting; the arch of the ceiling seemed to vault as high up as the stars outside.

"I was alone with God and the bomb.

"Then I saw him. The bomber.

"He was just an ordinary-looking guy, except for one thing. He was holding the detonator button down on the switch, a deadman's switch. If he moved his finger, we both would die. Instantly.

"I got as far as the altar rail and realized that I could not catch my breath. I could not keep pace with my own heartbeats.

"The bomber stood there like an altar boy—waiting for the sacraments.

"I thought that I could actually hear the bomb *ticking*.

"I looked at the face of every statue in that church, at every plaster feature, every painted eye. I knew they were looking back at me wondering what I was going to do.

"All I could hear was the *ticking*.

"I was *Mother;* what would I do?

"Then, I thought of my own mother again. How she had prayed so hard for me to become a priest and how I had disappointed her so deeply. I wanted to tell her that at least I had

[308]

made it to the main altar at Saint Pat's, at least I had made it that far.

"Then, this feeling of tranquillity came over me and I actually relaxed. I looked up at that guy, at that bomber, and knew—*knew*—that everything was going to be fine. He wasn't going to press that button and he wasn't going to kill us.

"'Don't move,' I told him, calmly, almost gently. 'I'm coming up there and we're walking out of here together. You, me, and the thing in your hand.'

"Then I began to slowly walk toward him. I had my hands out in front of me so that he could see that I wasn't going to hurt him.

"And if I happened to be wrong this time, if my bluff finally failed me, at least I *was* on the main altar at Saint Pat's. Doing my job. Being a New York cop.

"This had to be an express bus to heaven. The Big Guy had to be up there waiting for me."

ABOUT THE AUTHORS

BILL McCARTHY retired from the New York City Police Department as a detective commander in July 1987. His last assignment was as the commanding officer of the Bomb Squad. He is currently an associate director of training at John Jay College of Criminal Justice, and a doctoral candidate in criminal justice at the City University of New York. He is also president and founder of Threat Research, Incorporated, an international security consulting firm.

MIKE MALLOWE is a senior editor at *Philadelphia Magazine* and a frequent contributor to many national magazines. His last book was a novel about organized crime, *The Meat Man*.